D1733751

Handbook of Tests and Measurements for Black Populations

Volume 1

Handbook of Tests and Measurements for Black Populations

Volume 1

Reginald L. Jones, Editor
Hampton University

1996
Cobb & Henry Publishers, Hampton, VA

For information, contact:

Cobb & Henry Publishers
1 Sutton Place
Hampton, VA 23666
Telephone: (804) 827-7213
Fax: (804) 827-1060

Cover design by Mark van Bronkhorst and cover preparation by Matthew Bodie, Digital Prepress. Printed in the United States of America.

Library of Congress Cataloging-in-Publication Data

Handbook of tests and measurements for black populations/Reginald L.
    Jones, editor
        p.   cm.
    Includes bibliographical references and indexes.
    ISBN 0-943539-07-2 (v. 1). --ISBN 0-943539-08-0 (v.2)
    1. Psychological tests. 2. Psychometrics. 3. Afro-Americans-
-Psychological testing. I. Jones, Reginald Lanier, 1931-
BF176.H37 1996
150' .28' 7--dc20   96-3834
                                                                CIP

Contents

Part III. Children: Cognitive Approaches and Measures

Part IV. Children: Self-Esteem Measures

Part V. Children: Race-Related Tests and Measures

Part VI. Measures for Adolescents and Young Adults

Part VII. Language Assessment and Attitude Measures

Part VIII. Measures of Parental Attitudes and Values

Part IX. Measures of Family Structure and Dynamics

Contents Volume 2

Preface

Contributors

Part I. Introduction and Overview

1. **Handbook of Tests and Measurements for Black Populations:**
Introduction and Overview
Reginald L. Jones

Part II. World-View Measures

2. **Belief System Analysis Scale and Belief and Behavior Awareness**
Scale Development: Measuring an Optimal Afrocentric World-View
Linda James Myers, Derek Montgomery, Mark Fine,
and Roy Reese

3. **A Comparison of African and European Groups Utilizing a World-**
View Opinionnaire
Richard C. Kelsey and Robert M. Ransom

Preface

Many psychological practitioners, scholars and the lay public have long been critical of the use of psychological tests administered to African Americans. In response to their concerns, a number of alternative instruments have been developed, but unfortunately these instruments are widely scattered and have been unavailable to all but the most persistent sleuths. This *Handbook* assembles and describes a diverse sampling of psychological tests and measures developed for use with African Americans. Identifying the measures has been a challenge. I drew upon the knowledge of individuals known to be active in test construction, canvassed the psychological and education literature, and networked at conferences and professional meetings. At practically every turn I found individuals who had developed measures themselves or who were familiar with others who had done so—as masters theses or doctoral dissertations, as a part of research studies, or as key components of programs of research. It thus appears that many scholars and practitioners are developing instruments for the assessment of African American populations. Many of these unpublished tests and measures are presented in the *Handbook*.

More than one hundred instruments and approaches are represented in the *Handbook's* eighty-six chapters. Implicit in all chapters is the view that tests and measures must be developed that have African American history, characteristics, experiences, behaviors, and needs as their foundation. This is not to deny that the underlying constructs or that some of the measures themselves may have utility for other populations. Indeed, many of the tests and measures presented herein represent measures of well-known constructs such as self-esteem, stress, coping, etc., that have been developed and standardized on Whites. In the *Handbook,* these constructs are conceptualized from an African American frame of reference and use items and content that are appropriate for African Americans. Other measures in the *Handbook* are specifically unique to African Americans. These include such measures as perceived racism, coping with racism, African American acculturation, African American identity development, Black personality, and African self-consciousness, to name a few.

The tests and measures included in the *Handbook* are in various stages of development. As is true for most extant psychological tests and measures, none has been comprehensively validated. Except for the review chapters, all *Handbook* authors were required to provide information on their instrument's rationale and construction as well as data on reliability, validity and plans for future studies. Realizing the nascent nature of tests and measures included in the *Handbook*, it is important to encourage researchers and other potential users of the measures to become apprised of future studies that might be undertaken and to network with *Handbook* contributors. To facilitate such communication, information on how *Handbook* authors can be contacted is provided at the end of each chapter.

In reviewing materials for final preparation of the *Handbook*, I encountered correspondence indicating I had asked some contributors to submit their manuscripts to me more than a decade ago. Conceptualization of the volumes and communication with some authors began even earlier. The work you have before you, therefore, is the outcome of more than a decade of effort and activity.

I attribute the idea of the *Handbook* to the final sentence in an article by Robert L. Williams, "Abuses and Misuses in Testing Black Children," that was published in the first edition of *Black Psychology* (Jones, 1972). Williams concluded, "Black professionals must be about the business of developing appropriate measuring instruments and Black educational models for Black children" (p. 90). Williams' recommendation is as appropriate today as it was more than twenty years ago. His admonition lay dormant during my two-year stint (1972-74) as Professor and Director of the University Testing Center at Haille Sellassie I University in Ethiopia where I developed tests and selection procedures for university students and public and private sector personnel in Ethiopia, and as I completed two subsequent editions of *Black Psychology* (Jones, 1980, 1991). I am certain his views influenced *Psychoeducational Assessment of Minority Group Children: A Casebook*, a volume I edited in 1988 that presents alternative procedures for assessing children of several ethnic groups, including African Americans, Native Americans, Hispanics, and Asians.

In some respects, the delay in publication (from the early 1980's to 1996) has been fortuitous since authors who submitted their manuscripts fully a decade ago have updated their work with new validation and reliability studies (and in some instances fully revised measures). In addition, I was able to add some twenty-five measures (the latest in April, 1995) that were not available when the *Handbook* was first conceptualized. Over the years, there has been a noticeable growth in the sophistication of authors— those who submitted the early work as well as recent contributors. As the reader will see, the measures presented herein have impressive foundations in theory, and have utilized appropriate psychometric methods in instrument construction and validation. A solid foundation has thus been laid for utilization and further development of the measures. Providing culturally-specific measures which practitioners, researchers, and scholars can use and build upon is a primary purpose of the *Handbook*.

The tests and measures included herein speak for themselves, but it is important to highlight, if only briefly, some of the issues that have contributed to the perceived need to develop tests and measures for African Americans. Included in the introductory chapter, Chapter 1, entitled "Handbook of Tests and Measurements for Black Populations: Introduction and Overview," is discussion of issues such as test bias, culture-fair, culture-free, and culture-specific tests; limitations of comparative studies; standards for test development; information on guidelines for authors who contributed their work; and caveats and information on use of the *Handbook*.

I am grateful to many individuals for their assistance in the completion of the *Handbook*. Margaret Brewton and Elmire Robinson at the University of California, Berkeley, provided invaluable assistance in word processing and other aspects of manuscript preparation as did, especially, Carol Brooks and Lakisha Lyttle, and also Jacqueline Sanders, Pamela Reilly, Hazel Whitaker, Elise Vestal, Jennifer McGugins, Shaina Pomerantz, and Raqiyah Mays at Hampton University. I am also indebted to Jerome Taylor of the University of Pittsburgh and Harold Dent of Hampton University for their suggestions for improving Chapter 1, and to my close personal friend, Aubrey Escoffery, formerly Chair, Department of Psychology, Norfolk State University, for his assistance in reviewing the final manuscript. Robert L. Newton, Jr. was a key assistant at Hampton University. I am especially indebted to Robert for the care and dedication he gave in guiding the manuscript to completion, including word processing, communicating with authors, and proofreading, to name a few. All of us, editor and authors alike, express our sincere gratitude to Robert for his dedicated and highly competent work.

To ensure accuracy, all contributors reviewed their typeset chapters–some more than once. We have attempted to provide the most accurate work possible and hope that few, if any, errors remain. We will be grateful to you, the reader, for calling our attention to errors that need our further attention.

As always, I am indebted to my wife, Michele, for enduring the long journey to completion of the *Handbook*. She has been an active prod when I tired of the work and an understanding spouse when work on the volumes seemed to overwhelm other parts of our life. She has been steadfast in support of me and this work. Michele, I thank you deeply, sincerely, and with love.

Reginald L. Jones
Hampton, Virginia

References

Jones, R. L. (Ed.). (1972). *Black psychology*. New York: Harper & Row.

Jones, R. L. (Ed.). (1980). *Black psychology* (2nd ed.). New York: Harper & Row.

Jones, R. L. (Ed.). (1988). *Psychoeducational assessment of minority group children: A casebook*. Berkeley, CA: Cobb & Henry.

Jones, R. L. (Ed.). (1991). *Black psychology* (3rd ed.). Berkeley, CA: Cobb & Henry.

Contributors

Walter R. Allen, Ph.D.
Professor, Department of Sociology, University of California, Los Angeles (UCLA), and Associate Director, Robert Wood Johnson Clinical Scholars Program, UCLA, School of Medicine, Los Angeles, California

James A. Banks, Ph.D.
Professor and Director, Center for Multicultural Education, University of Washington, Seattle, Washington

Eileen Bartolomucci, Ph.D.
Licensed Psychologist, Inter Care H.M.O., Instructor, Department of Psychology in Education, University of Pittsburgh, and Part-time Private Practice, Pittsburgh, Pennsylvania

Doris B. Baytop, R.N.
Research Associate (retired), The Newborn Project, Howard University Child Development Center, Washington, D.C.

Dwight Brown, B.A.
Deceased, was a Researcher at the Stanford Center for Research and Development in Teaching, Palo Alto, California

Angela Buchanan, Ph.D.
Child Development Specialist, Newark, California

Louis A. Castenell, Ph.D.
Dean, College of Education, University of Cincinnati, Cincinnati, Ohio

Maxine L. Clark, Ph.D.
Deceased, was Associate Professor, Department of Psychology, and Director, African American Research Institute, Center for Public Service, Virginia Commonwealth University, Richmond, Virginia

Deborah L. Coates, Ph.D.
Professor of Psychology and Associate Director, Institute for Research on the African Diaspora in the Americas and the Caribbean, The City University of New York, New York, New York

Berlinda Curbeam, M.A.
Deceased, was Instructor in Psychology, Johnson C. Smith University, Charlotte, North Carolina

William Cummings, Ph.D.
Former Director of the Gifted Program, San Francisco Unified School System, San Francisco, California

Michael Cunningham, Ph.D.
Postdoctoral Fellow, Psychology in Education Division, Graduate School of Education, University of Pennsylvania, Philadelphia, Pennsylvania

Jane David, Ph.D.
Executive Director, Connections for Children, Santa Monica, California

Harold E. Dent, Ph.D.
Research Professor, Department of Psychology and Director of Outreach, Center for Minority Special Education, Hampton University, Hampton, Virginia

William W. Dressler, Ph.D.
Professor, School of Medicine, University of Alabama, Tuscaloosa, Alabama

James Ford
Former Research Assistant, Center for Educational Research at Stanford, Stanford University, Palo Alto, California

Agnes Franklin
Training Specialist, University of Pittsburgh, Africana Studies, Institute for the Black Family, Pittsburgh, Pennsylvania

Lawford L. Goddard, Ph.D.
Director of Education and Training, Institute for the Advanced Study of Black Family Life and Culture, Inc., Oakland, California

Seward E. Hamilton, Jr., Ph.D.
Associate Professor and Coordinator of School Psychology, Department of Psychology, Florida A & M University, Tallahassee, Florida

Bruce R. Hare, Ph.D.
Professor and Chair, Department of African American Studies, and Professor of Sociology, Syracuse University, Syracuse, New York

Susan Haworth-Hoeppner, M.A.
Doctoral candidate, Wayne State University, Detroit, Michigan

William A. Hayes, Ph.D.
Deceased was consultant, Fayetteville, Georgia

Shirley Hicks, Ph.D.
Teacher of English, San Jose Unified School District, San Jose, California

Asa G. Hilliard, III, Ed.D.
Fuller E. Callaway Professor, Georgia State University, Atlanta, Georgia

Bertha Garrett Holliday, Ph.D.
Director, Office of Ethnic Minority Affairs, American Psychological Association, Washington, D.C.

Kathleen Hoover-Dempsey, Ph.D.
Associate Professor, Department of Psychology, Vanderbilt University, Nashville, Tennessee

Mary Rhodes Hoover, Ph.D.
Professor and Former Dean, School of Education, Howard University, Washington, D.C.

Anna Mitchell Jackson, Ph.D., FACIP
Professor and Assistant Dean for Student Affairs, S.O.D., Meharry Medical College, Nashville, Tennessee

Jacquelyne Faye Jackson, Ph.D.
Research Associate, Institute of Human Development, University of California, Berkeley, Berkeley, California

Deborah J. Johnson, Ph.D.
Associate Professor, Child and Family Studies, University of Wisconsin-Madison, Madison, Wisconsin

Reginald L. Jones Ph.D.
Distinguished Professor of Psychology and Director, Center for Minority Special Education, Hampton University, Hampton, Virginia; and Professor Emeritus, University of California, Berkeley, Berkeley, California

Diane Kern, Ph.D.
School/Clinical Psychologist, D.C. Public Schools, Division of Special Education, Washington, D.C.; and Part-time Private Practice, Washington, D.C.

Justin E. Levitow, Ph.D.
Professor, College of Education, Loyola University, New Orleans, Louisiana

Shirley A. R. Lewis, Ph.D.
President, Paine College, Augusta, Georgia

Grace Carroll Massey, Ph.D.
Director, African American Student Development, and Lecturer, Department of African

American Studies, University of California, Berkeley, Berkeley, California

Harriette Pipes McAdoo, Ph.D.
Professor, Michigan State University, East Lansing, Michigan

Janet L. McMaster-Olmes
Psychologist in Private Practice, Intermediate Unit and Educational Agency, State of Pennyslvania, Pittsburgh, Pennsylvania

Faye McNair-Knox, Ph.D.
Associate Professor, School of Education, Florida International University, North Miami, Florida; and Research Associate, East Palo Alto Neighborhood Study, Department of Linguistics, Stanford University, Palo Alto, California

Constance Milbrath, Ph.D.
Formerly Assistant Professor, Department of Psychology, Pacific Graduate School of Psychology, Menlo Park, California

Carolyn Bennett Murray, Ph.D.
Associate Professor, Department of Psychology, and Principal Investigator, African American Family Research Project, University of California, Riverside, Riverside, California

Wade W. Nobles, Ph.D.
Professor, Department of Black Studies, San Francisco State University, San Francisco, California, and Executive Director, Institute for the Advanced Study of Black Family Life and Culture, Inc., Oakland, California

H. M. Omotoso, Ed.D.
Head, Research Section, West African Examinations Council, Yaba, Lagos, Nigeria

Daniel J. Ozer, Ph.D.
Associate Professor, Department of Psychology, University of California, Riverside, Riverside, California

James M. Patton
Associate Professor and Associate Dean, School of Education, The College of William and Mary, Williamsburg, Virginia

M. Jean Peacock, Ph.D.
Assistant Professor, Department of Psychology, California State University, San Bernardino, San Bernardino, California

Jeanne M. Plas, Ph.D.
Associate Professor, Department of Psychology, Vanderbilt University, Nashville, Tennessee

Robert L. Politzer, Ph.D.
Professor Emeritus, Graduate School of Education, Stanford University, Palo Alto, California

Suzanne M. Randolph, Ph.D.
Associate Professor, Department of Family Studies, University of Maryland-College Park, College Park, Maryland

Pearl L. Rosser, M.D.
Professor (retired), Department of Pediatrics and Child Health, Howard University College of Medicine, Washington, D.C.

Joseph Rosenberg, A.B.
Research Associate, Research for Children, Menlo Park, California

Margaret Beale Spencer, Ph.D.
Board of Overseers Professor of Education, and Director, Center for Health, Achievement, Neighorhood, Growth, and Ethnic Studies (CHANGES), Graduate School of Education, University of Pennsylvania, Philadelphia, Pennsylvania

Howard C. Stevenson, Jr., Ph.D.
Assistant Professor, Director of Ph.D. Training, and appointment in the Policy, Research, Evaluation, and Measurement Program, Graduate School of Education, Psychology

in Education Division, University of Pennsylvania, Philadelphia, Pennsylvania

NeferkaRe Stewart, Ph.D.
Program Director, KhemRe Institute, Center for Health and Wellness, Counseling and Consultation Services, San Leandro, California

Julie E. Stokes, Ph.D.
Research Associate, Department of Psychology, University of California, Riverside, Riverside, California

Blondell M. Strong, Ph.D.
Management Consultant, Nashville, Tennessee

Lorraine S. Taylor, Ph.D.
Associate Professor, Department of Special Education, State University of New York at New Paltz, New Paltz, New York

Jerome Taylor, Ph.D.
Co-Director, Institute for the Black Family, Department of Africana Studies, University of Pittsburgh, Pittsburgh, Pennsylvania

David L. Terrell, Ph.D., Diplomate in Clinical Psychology and Fellow, ABPP
Psychologist, Psychosocial Studies & Interventions, Inc., Nashville, Tennessee

Francis Terrell, Ph.D.
Professor of Psychology, Department of Psychology, University of North Texas, Denton, Texas

Sandra L. Terrell, Ph.D.
Assistant Vice President and Associate Dean, School of Graduate Studies, University of North Texas, Denton, Texas

Lenall Thomas
Director of Programs, University of Pittsburgh, Africana Studies, Institute for the Black Family, Pittsburgh, Pennsylvania

Carrie Underwood
Retired, University of Pittsburgh, Africana Studies, Institute for the Black Family, Pittsburgh, Pennsylvania

Darlene Williams, Ph.D.
Marketing Director, Ryder Rentals, Miami, Florida

Part I

Introduction and Overview

Handbook of Tests and Measurements for Black Populations: Introduction and Overview

Reginald L. Jones

Introduction

The *Handbook of Tests and Measures for Black Populations* is a compilation of tests and measures developed or modified for use with African Americans. The two volumes include more than 100 measures and assessment approaches in 86 chapters. They were developed because of a pressing need to present tests and measures that more accurately reflect the psychological characteristics and behavior of African Americans than do conventional methods. Of particular importance is the presentation of tests and measures rarely seen in the psychological and educational literature but that are important to understanding the psychological characteristics and dynamics of African Americans. The instruments presented herein are believed to be free of many of the biases that plague tests and measures used with African Americans.

Tests and measurement textbooks focus mostly on commercially developed standardized tests. Critical reviews of these tests are reported in various editions of the *Mental Measurement Yearbook* and similar publications. In addition, a number of books describe and review tests developed for specialized populations and subject areas (for example Robinson et al.'s *Measures of Personality and Social Psychological Attitudes*, 1991; Comrey et al.'s *A Sourcebook for Mental Health Measures*, 1973; and Johnson & Bomarito's *Tests*

and Measurements in Child Development, 1971). The *Handbook* adds to the body of specialized tests and measures developed for special populations. Unfortunately, many tests and measures developed for mainstream populations do not tap important areas of the African American experience. For example, measures in such areas as cultural mistrust, African American world-view, African American racial identity, spirituality, perceived racism and responses to it, and African American acculturation styles are rarely included or discussed in psychological tests and measurements textbooks. One purpose of the *Handbook* is to make measures in the above areas, and others, available to a wide audience.

A number of issues pertinent to development of the *Handbook* are presented in the following sections. These include discussion of standards for test development and use, a brief review of the literature on culture-free, culture-fair and culture-specific tests, and the concepts of emic and etic as they relate to test development. Sections on instructions for development and use of the measures and on the content of the *Handbook* are also included.

Standards for Test Development and Use

Beginning in 1954, the American Psychological Association (APA) and later, APA and a committee representing the American Educational

Research Association and the National Council on Measurements Used in Education published a series of volumes (1955, 1966, 1974, 1985) on standards for educational and psychological testing. These volumes have guided test development and use, and the most recent volume of each edition is recognized as the definitive guide to test development available. The committee constituted to develop the 1985 standards was informed that the standards should:

1.   Address issues of test use in a variety of applications.

2.   Be a statement of technical standards for sound professional practice and not a social action prescription.

3.   Make it possible to determine the technical adequacy of a test, the appropriateness and propriety of specific applications, and the reasonableness of inferences based on the test results.

4.   Require that test developers, publishers, and users collect and make available sufficient information to enable a qualified reviewer to determine whether applicable standards have been met.

5.   Embody a strong ethical imperative, though it was understood that the *standards* themselves would not contain enforcement mechanisms.

6.   Recognize that all standards will not be uniformly applicable across a wide range of instruments and uses.

7.   Be presented at a level that would enable a wide range of people who work with tests or test results to use the *standards*.

8.   Not inhibit experimentation in the development, use and interpretation of tests.

9.   Reflect the current level of consensus of recognized experts.

10.   Supersede the 1974 *Standards for Educational and Psychological Tests* (p. v).

Each standard is followed by categorization as primary, secondary or conditional.

Primary standards are those that should be met by all tests before their operational use and in all test uses, unless a sound profes-

sional reason is available to show why it is not necessary, or technically feasible, to do so in a particular case.

Secondary standards are desirable as goals but are likely to be beyond reasonable expectation in many situations. Although careful consideration of those standards will often be helpful in evaluating tests and programs and in comparing the usefulness of competing instruments, limitations on resources may make adherence to them infeasible in many situations. Some secondary standards describe procedures that are beneficial but not often used. Test developers and users are not expected to explain why secondary standards have not been met.

The importance of some standards for test construction and validation will vary with application: These standards are designated as *conditional*. Such standards should be considered primary for some situations and secondary for others. In deciding whether to take an individual conditional standard as primary or secondary, one should consider carefully the feasibility of meeting that standard in relation to the possible consequences to all parties involved in the testing process. It may be infeasible technically or financially, for some testing programs to observe some conditional standards, particularly those programs that conduct low-volume tests. However, if the use of a test is likely to have serious consequences for test takers, especially if a large number of people may be affected, conditional standards assume increased importance (pp. 2-3).

The 1985 edition of *Standards* was developed to be responsive to new problems and issues involved in testing including, "testing advances in testing and related fields, new and emerging uses of tests, and growing social concerns over the role of testing in achieving goals..." (p. v). Given these goals, it is expected that the *Standards* will present guidelines that are responsive to the concerns of special populations, including African Americans. Readers should also expect, to the extent the standards are appropriate and utilized by test developers and consumers, that improved assessment of African Americans will result. Unfortunately, this does not appear to be the case. Existing measures used with African Americans can be faulted on many grounds. For example, rarely are African Americans included in the very beginning phases of test conceptualization, so the perspectives, styles, and attributes that might enter into test content are rarely included. (Some testing companies are attempting to overcome this shortcoming by including African American psychologists and other African American scholars as developers and reviewers of test items, but most frequently this involvemnt comes after the test has been conceptualized and the blueprint developed). Next, representative samples of African Americans are rarely included in developing test norms, so the impact of the presence of African Americans in the standardization sample is negligible. The appropriateness of the developed measures should be specifically ascertained for African Americans. This means that reliability and validity data should be obtained for each group to which the test or measure is to be applied. Where appropriate, the instrument's factor structure for the subgroup(s) with which the test is to be used should be included as well. Provisions for these and other psychometric studies are noted in the *Standards* but they are rarely applied to tests used with African American populations.

One critique of tests used in comparative studies of Black and White adolescents was undertaken by Jones (1984), who looked at unpublished tests used in ten comparative studies of Black and White adolescents. Jones was particularly interested in the psychometric properties of tests used in the studies and whether or not separate psychometric analyses were undertaken by racial group. Thus questions were asked about: (1) reliability and validity studies of the measures; (2) equivalence of test structure as revealed by factor analysis; (3) attention to examiner race; and, (4) equality of variance between the groups, among other considerations. As a result of his analyses, Jones wrote the following:

A reasonable conclusion is that the ten studies reviewed are so flawed as to render them useless as sources of information about Black-White differences. Samples and sampling were limited. The geographic location of the study was not always given. Information that would enable readers to determine whether or not the measures had equivalent meaning for the Black and White respondents was rarely given. There was no mention of the validity of any measure used in the studies. Rarely were reliability data for instruments reported, and when reliabilities were reported, separate reliabilities for Blacks and Whites were given in only a few instances. Means and standard deviations were not always reported in the studies. Therefore, it has not been possible to test for equality of variances, thereby giving the reader some assurance that the samples were drawn from the same population (p. 22).

While the tests and measures evaluated were published in professional journals and some were informal measures developed for purposes of a specific study, they are not unlike the widely used and commercially developed tests in that they rarely provide specific data on African American populations. Their value as sources of valid data for African Americans, therefore, is limited.

Sections of the *Standards* are devoted to clinical testing, educational and psychological testing in the schools, test use in counseling, licensure and employment, program evaluation, and testing linguistic minorities and people with handicapping conditions, but except for considerations for linguistic minorities, no specific standards address African Americans or other distinct cultural groups in this country. Perhaps this is as it should be; ideally, if general principles recommended for test construction and use are adhered to, standards for special sub-populations will be unnecessary. Evaluation of many existing standardized tests, as well as unpublished and experimental measures, reveals we have a long way to go before most existing tests can be judged appropriate for use with African American populations.

Culture-Free, Culture-Fair, and Culture-Specific Tests

Culture-free, culture-fair, and culture-specific tests were developed in response to dissatisfaction with tests of intelligence that were believed to be biased with respect to certain racial and socioeconomic groups. (Current terms also include culture loaded and culture reduced). Culture-free tests represented an attempt to develop a measure free of cultural influences. These tests were dismissed rather quickly as it was determined that a culture-free test was simply an impossibility since tests tend to reflect the culture in which they are devised and utilized. As Murphy and Davidshofer (1994) state, "Learned behavior is, by definition, a function of culture, and it therefore seems pointless to refer to any test as completely culture-free" (p. 269). Next came culture-fair tests which were designed to keep cultural differences from permeating the tests by selecting only those experiences, knowledge and skills common to different cultures.

Following a careful review of studies, Samuda (1975) concluded that "It is the consensual opinion of psychometricians and psychologists that culture-free or culture-fair tests have proven disappointing and have fallen short of their goals, for minority students have been shown to perform, if not more poorly, at least as badly as they do on conventional intelligence measures" (p. 142).

In a more recent discussion, Anastasi (1988) wrote:

It is unlikely...that any test can be equally fair to more than one cultural group, especially if the cultures are quite dissimilar. While reducing cultural differentials in test performance, cross-cultural studies cannot completely eliminate such differentials. *Every test tends to favor persons from the culture in which it was developed* (emphasis added) ... .Emotional and motivational factors influence test performance. Among many relevant conditions differing from culture to culture may be mentioned the intrinsic interest of the test content, rapport with the examiner, drive to do well on a test, desire to excel

above others, and past habits of solving problems individually or cooperatively.

Anastasi further states:

Each culture and subculture encourages and fosters certain abilities and ways of behaving; and it discourages or suppresses others. It is therefore to be expected that, on tests developed within the majority American culture, for example, persons in that culture will excel. If a test were constructed by the same procedures within a culture markedly different from ours, Americans would probably appear deficient in terms of test norms (pp. 357-358).

While it may appear that Anastasi is referring to studies of cultures outside this country, she is in fact referring to indigenous subcultural groups as well. She writes, "In America, the practical problems of cross-cultural testing have been associated chiefly with subcultures or minority cultures within the dominant culture" (p. 297).

Culture-specific tests were developed in response to the failure of culture-fair tests. The idea of culture-specific tests is to develop equivalents of existing tests that are expressly constructed for members of a given culture/subculture. Culture-specific tests receive very little attention in current psychological measurement textbooks. For example, the term does not appear in Cronbach (1990) or Walsh and Betz (1995) though both authors refer to issues associated with the use of such tests. A comparable term (culture-loaded) is found in Murphy and Davidshofer (1994) but actual use of the term culture-specific is found only in texts by Cohen et al. (1988) and Samuda (1975). Anastasi (1988) makes reference to the BITCH (Black Intelligence Test of Cultural Homogeneity) test, but does not actually use the term culture-specific. The BITCH test, developed by African American psychologist Robert Williams, is a vocabulary test appropriate for adolescents and adults, comprising 100 multiple choice items that deal exclusively with the Black experience. When applied to White subjects, the test is said to be a measure of their sensitivity and responsiveness to Black culture.

Following unsuccessful attempts to validate the test against traditional IQ measures, such as the Weschler Adult Intelligence Scale, the test is most often dismissed as a measure of intelligence. Some authors, Matarazzo and Wiens (1977) for example, perceived the test to be a measure of "street wiseness." A fairly typical conclusion is presented by Cohen et al., (1988), who wrote: "Although many of the culture-specific measures did yield higher mean scores for the minority group they were specifically designed for use with, they lacked predictive validity and provided little useful and practical information" (p. 279).

I believe the abandonment of culturally-specific tests has been premature: only a handful of studies were conducted and they were flawed. A major shortcoming, in my opinion, is that the dependent measures in the studies is the standard test of intelligence or achievement. The realization that these measures may themselves be flawed has not been considered as one possible explanation for the poor predictive ability of the culture-specific tests; the culturally-specific test is validated against the measure alleged to be defective! Far less work appears to have been done to develop culture-specific tests in non-cognitive areas; and in contemporary textbooks, one finds little criticism of non-cognitive tests across cultural groups, probably because these tests are often used for research purposes, and in general because stakes associated with their use are not high as is the case with tests of intelligence and aptitude. (There are, of course, exceptions to this statement. Dana [1987] for example, presents a penetrating critique of the cross-cultural use of the Minnesota Multiphasic Personality Inventory.)

Attempts to develop culture-free, culture-fair, and culture-specific tests and measures are responses to the belief that the tests were biased against certain ethnic groups and socio-economic classes. Test bias has been defined as "a factor inherent within a test that systematically prevents accurate, impartial measurement" (Cohen et al., 1988, p. 150).

Biased tests have been highly implicated in educational placement and employment testing. And while the literature is mixed, for any given test, bias can exist at the content level, where decisions are first made about what items or questions are to be included in a test or measure; at the level of standardization, where decisions are made about the populations for whom the test is appropriate; and at the level of test administration, in which tests are administered by persons unfamiliar with the pattern of language, behavior and customs of the person being tested (Jones, 1988). In-depth discussion of these issues is beyond the scope of the present work. Detailed treatment of the subject can be found in standard test and measurement textbooks (see for example, Anastasi, 1988; Cohen et al., 1988; Cronbach, 1990; Murphy et al., 1994; Samuda, 1975; Walsh & Betz, 1995) and many technical references (see for example, Berk, 1982; Butcher & Pancheri, 1976; Camilli & Sheperd, 1994; Committee to Develop Standards for Educational and Psychological Testing, 1985; Costello, 1977; Dahlstrom et al., 1986; Dana, 1987; Dent, 1976; Greene, 1987; Hilliard, 1991; Jensen, 1980; Wainer & Braun, 1988; White, 1987).

Emic and Etic in Test Development

Emic and etic are useful concepts for evaluating and developing tests for African Americans. The terms were coined by Pike (1966), a linguist, to highlight distinctions between phonetics, a generalization from different languages to all languages and phonemics, or sounds used in only a single language. As used by psychologists, these terms differentiate approaches to studying behavior whose origins are external to one particular culture (etic) or exclusively within one culture (emic). Berry (1969) has described the approaches as follows:

Emic Approach

Studies behavior from within the system.

Etic Approach

Studies behavior from a perspective outside the system.

Examines only one culture.	Examines many cultures, comparing them.
Structure discovered by the analyst.	Structure created by the analyst.
Criteria are relevant to internal characteristics.	Criteria are considered absolute or universal.

Several forms of etic have been described (Dana, 1987). "*Imposed* etic assume that a construct originating in one culture is universal, while *derived* etic requires that constructs be shared by several cultures as a basis for new constructs with cross-cultural equivalence. A *pseudo-etic* uses the middle-class Anglo-American as the standard for comparison with other groups" (p. 7).

Virtually all standardized psychological and educational tests are etic. The categories developed and the instruments designed to operationalize the categories use Caucasians as the standardization sample and frame of reference. An early articulation of the etic position vis-a-vis studies of Blacks and Whites is found in the writings of Kardiner and Ovesey (1951) in their well-known book, *The Mark of Oppression*. They wrote:

> The problem of controls is central. How do we know that our sampling is correct or representative? We do not know if we study the sample alone, but we have at hand a ready basis for comparison. Our constant control is the American White man. We require no other control. Both he and the Negro live under similar cultural conditions with the exception of a few easily identifiable variables existing for the Negro only. This means we can plot the personality differences of the Negro in terms of these variables against the known personality of the White. There is another roundabout way of controlling our conclusions. We could study the Negro in a community where he enjoys the same status as the White, as is the case, for example in Brazil. However, in order to use this control, we would first have to establish a norm for the White Brazilian, and then compare it with the Negro Brazilian–an undertaking that would destroy the unity of this book (p. 11).

I believe the views of Kardiner and Ovesey still pervade the thinking of test developers, who subscribe to an etic orientation. They appear to believe there is no need to develop separate tests and measures for African Americans or other subcultural groups. Thus we find that tests and measures developed for use with Caucasians far outweigh culture-specific tests by a significant order of magnitude. The implied rationale underlying the relative absence of culturally specific tests or even of norms for subcultural groups is that African American behavior is best understood in relationship to a White baseline. That is, in order to achieve an understanding of the behavior of African Americans, it is considered necessary to determine how Whites perform on "comparable" instruments or measures. My opinion, and the view undergirding the *Handbook* is that understanding the psychological characteristics and dynamics of African Americans requires the development of tests and measures for African Americans. The utilization of tests and measures developed for Whites is quite irrelevant for this purpose. If we aim to understand, measure, and predict the behavior of African American individuals, we need to know how African Americans are characterized psychologically. Furthermore, a principle or finding should be no less important, meaningful or reliable because it is established with tests developed on African Americans. Indeed, principles arrived at through tests and measures developed for African Americans will have the highest probability of leading to an understanding of African American characteristics, dynamics and behavior.

This is not to deny the value of tests and measures developed to understand the degree of commonalities across cultures or groups. In this way we learn about similarities as well as differences between and among groups. But it should be realized that tests and measures developed and standardized on White populations will not, in themselves, tell us about the behavior and functioning of African Americans. At best, such tests and measures developed and standardized on one group of individuals may lead to hypotheses about another group. Perhaps the best that can be said of such a strategy, at least in the context of attempts to understand the psychological characteristics and dynamics of African Americans, is that the strategy is wasteful.

My view is that a more fruitful alternative activity–at least to understand and predict the behavior of African Americans–is culture-specific tests and measures. The modified and culture specific tests and measures described in the *Handbook* address issues of especial interest in the study and assessment of African Americans. The instruments are not developed for use in comparative studies. Indeed, because of their cultural specificity, they are *inappropriate* for use in such studies just as most etically oriented instruments administered to African Americans are often inappropriate. The instruments included herein are presented as measures which enhance understanding of only a single group, African Americans.

Comparative studies which use an etic orientation will continue to be undertaken, to be sure; and many scholars will continue to seek an understanding of behaviors which are common to many cultural groups. I am not opposed to these efforts. However, because most of the behavioral and social science research on African Americans has been conducted from the outside looking in, I believe it is now time for students of the Black experience to look inward in order to identify constructs, behaviors, and ideas that explain African American culture and African American behavior on their own terms. In order to accomplish this goal, culture-specific constructs and assessment instruments will be necessary.

The development and/or modification of a test or assessment device is a major undertaking. The goal just described is admittedly the first step in what is, ideally, a two-step process: 1) test development; and, 2) test validation. All authors of measures presented herein describe some work in test validation but, as is true for virtually all tests and measures, more work is needed. The *Handbook* has been expressly developed to ensure that

measures developed for Black populations are widely available for use in validation and other research-based activities. If scholars further develop the instruments, and elaborate and expand upon the constructs underlying them, I believe the efforts will be well justified. In particular, if the instruments bear their promise, these culturally specific methods by virtue of their more accurate reflection of African American experiences, values, aptitudes, personality, abilities, and other attributes can be expected to supplant current etically oriented measurements. Indeed, when culturally specific instruments have in fact been used, as many studies in the present volumes indicate, the results have been quite rewarding. One example of the value of a culture-specific approach is demonstrated in the work of Baly.

Validating Culture-Specific Tests: The Baly Study

The litmus test of the view that culturally-specific instruments are more useful than non-culturally-specific measures must rest upon empirical demonstration that the structure of the instruments differs for Blacks and Whites even when actual test items are identical, and that the culturally-specific instruments predict relevant criteria more accurately than do culturally-non-specific measures. A limited test of these ideas was undertaken by Baly (1984) who completed her doctoral dissertation under my direction at the University of California, Berkeley.

The data for Baly's study came from the High School and Beyond (HSB), which is a continuing panel study conducted by the National Opinion Research Center (NORC) for the National Center for Educational Statistics. A thirty-five page questionnaire is employed to collect information about course content, grades, activities in school, outside employment, post-high school plans, influences on future plans, attitudes toward self, and personal and family characteristics. Each student also took a battery of tests in vocabulary, reading, mathematics, picture-number, mosaic comparison, and visualization in three dimensions.

In 1980, the first year of the survey, questionnaires were completed by 30,000 sophomores and 28,000 seniors in 1,122 public and private high schools nationwide. The data for Baly's study came from this file. Her final sample included 248 low SES Black males and 611 medium and high SES White male subjects. These two samples were drawn because they mirror, to a degree (they differ in that the typical standardization group would also include females), a not infrequent test standardization paradigm: tests and measures are standardized on White middle and upper class individuals and then applied to Black lower SES subjects. Baly hypothesized that differences would be found between the factor structures of the Black and White samples, and also that scores derived from the Black sample would be more predictive of certain external criteria (locus of control, self-concept, work orientation, and significant other influence) than would scores based on White middle and upper-class groups. Baly received partial confirmation of her hypotheses.

A test for the differences between correlation matrices was employed (Jennrich, 1970). Since factor structure is ultimately derived from the correlation matrix, the Jennrich test is also a test for the equality of factor structure from two samples using the same variables. Application of the test to the two matrices of 3,240 correlation coefficients for each sample indicated that there were significant differences (p < .01) between the matrices.

The Jennrich test only yields information with respect to whether or not a difference in pattern of correlation exists between two samples. It does not reveal information relative to the frequency and distribution of absolute value between the samples, nor about which clusters of variables show high or low coefficients for each of the two groups. Application of the Sign Test to the correlations for the samples revealed that the number of positive and negative differences for each group was not significantly different. Obviously, the differences between the groups are reflected in complex interactions among the variables and not in the similarities or differences among individual correlations between the two

samples. Thus, interpretation of the differences between the groups must be determined by interpreting the results of the factor analysis. The factor names for the two groups of subjects are the same. However, race differences existed in items that comprised the factors, and in the amount of variance explained by them (later, Baly addresses the predictive utility of information derived from the analysis in which standards are developed on the White respondents and applied to Blacks–the usual situation–as contrasted with the predictive utility of measures developed and applied to the Black population itself as the normative group).

The first factor for both samples is labeled level of Vocational/Educational Expectation. The fifteen items comprising this factor for the White sample accounted for 8.28 percent of the variance. The items include those related to a specification of the level and degree of commitment to post-high school education (represented by responses to questions such as, "As things stand now, how far in school do you think you will get?") as well as the nature of vocational activity after high school ("What is the one thing that most likely will take the largest share of your time after high school?"), self standards for success ("What is the lowest level of education you would be satisfied with?"), and parental influence on specific high school plans ("What does your mother/ father think you ought to do after school?").

Thirteen items comprised the Level of Vocational/Educational Expectations factor for the Black sample (as contrasted with 15 items for the White sample). The variance explained by the 13 items was 5.94%. There was considerable overlap among the items, but there were differences as well. The major differences appear to reside in the range of options the Black respondents considered (for example, "In the past year have you tried to enlist in any branch-of the Armed Services?"). Reported parental influence did not appear to be quite as strong for the Black sample.

As was true for the first factor, there were similarities and differences among items constituting the remaining 6 factors. Most significant, however, is that the 7 factors account for 70.3 percent of the variance for the White sample, but only 55.6 percent for the Black sample. Moreover, Baly determined that 17 factors would need to be extracted in order to explain 100 percent of the variance for the White sample, but 26 factors would be required to account for all of the variance for the Black sample. Clearly, then, factors which explain vocational educational decision-making for the two racial groups differ.

Finally, using canonical correlation procedures, Baly found the factor scores from the Black sample explained somewhat more of the variance of the five psychosocial variables (52.1 percent) than did factors from the White sample (48.6 of the variance explained).

Because of instrumentation and other methodological limitations, Baly's findings are only suggestive. A first shortcoming is the restricted range of the instrumentation. Baly commented on this shortcoming as follows:

> Perhaps the questionnaire items which tapped the respondent's attitudes, values, self-perception, aspiration, etc., ignored, at least for the low SES Black sample, other possible mediating influences on the subjects views of such factors as 1) actual or perceived racial barriers to opportunities in education and employment, 2) the influence of negative peer pressure which stems from an internalized 'sense of fatalism' about their future, and 3) the required shared reference group perspective which moderates attitudes toward work, vocational and educational aspiration, and very likely the feelings of mastery over one's environment, over and beyond class membership. There is certainly enough evidence in the literature which gives support to the influence of these variables in shaping and guiding a 'differential' response set in low SES Black subjects to a variety of stimuli (p. 121).

If the perspectives of African Americans had been included in test conception and development, it is possible that the omitted factors Baly alluded to would have been included as questionnaire items. A second limitation is that there was no cross-validation of the findings. Ideally, the results reported here should represent the basic

data/findings which are applied to comparable samples. Third, the measures were not developed explicitly for African Americans. Fourth, culturally-appropriate criterion measures were not developed. Finally, while Baly's desire was to replicate the typical test development paradigm in which there is race x class confounding, interpretation of her results are compromised by the confounding she criticizes. Future studies should use balanced race and class samples and also utilize confirmatory factor models that will pinpoint sources of reported differences. Despite limitations, the Baly study provides some support for the view that the comparability of instruments used in comparative studies needs to be determined for each comparison group, and that these culturally specific measures may be differentially predictive for their group. Obviously, additional work in this area is needed.

The cross-subcultural study of Black-White differences using various tests and measures will probably continue to be the source of data that will determine the psychological health and well-being of African Americans and provide the basis for policy and resource allocation by governmental agencies and others. The etic orientation, then, will continue to be alive and well. The challenge for scholars is to demonstrate that the definitions and instruments that reflect the African American world-view and which assess Black aptitude, attitudes, values, aspirations, and other attributes, yield a more accurate psychological portrait of African Americans than do existing instruments and measures.

Development of *Handbook* Measures

The tests and measures presented in the *Handbook* are in various stages of development. Some have existed for several years and have been the subject of a number of psychometric studies; other measures are in various stages of early development and beg further study. In conceptualizing the volume, I encouraged contributors to make their work available–whether or not it was just beginning or was fully developed. Authors were presented a checklist to assist in preparation of their chapters. I informed authors that not all checklist items had to be applied, especially if their test or measure was in an early stage of development. I expected, however, that when available, information on each checklist item would be included in the manuscript. Checklist items included the following:

1. Description of rationale and background of the instrument.

2. Citation of references related to rationale, background, concepts, and related instruments.

3. Description of concepts, constructs, abilities, aptitudes, personality, characteristics, etc. being assessed.

4. Purpose of instrument and need fulfilled by it.

5. Description of instrument (including information which includes type of measure, e.g., questionnaire, projective test, etc.).

6. Discussion of related instruments/measures, if any (this was to be included in a review of literature as presented in project rationale and background).

7. Description of procedures used in instrument development (with references when appropriate).

8. Discussion of possible uses of the instrument.

9. Age range for which the instrument is appropriate.

10. Special subpopulations, if any, for which the instrument is appropriate (e.g., candidates for psychotherapy, women only, etc.).

11. Form of administration (i.e., group or individual).

12. Approximate administration time in minutes (or time ranges).

13. Description of statistical data on measure (i.e., means, standard deviations, etc., on individual subtests, tests as a whole, etc.).

14. Standardization procedures.

15. Norms, if available.

16. Data on validity.

17. Data on reliability.

18. Discussion of instruments' vulnerability to response sets (social desirability, acquiescent, etc.).

19. Discussion of limitations of instrument or limitations of the work done to date.

20. Ideas for further research and development of instrument.

21. References to published and unpublished studies in which the instrument has been used.

22. Scoring keys and directions for their use.

The authors of *Standards for Educational and Psychological Testing* (1985) note that "Because the development of a test for widespread use is an extensive undertaking, a requirement that all relevant primary standards be satisfied at first operational use would be likely to stifle both the development of new instruments and progress in the field" (p. 3). Given this observation, it should not be surprising that many of the tests and measures reported in the *Handbook* are not yet fully developed. It can be decisively stated, however, that the tests and measures included herein meet minimum standards of initial development and are presented in a manner that encourage their use and further development. If instruments in the *Handbook* meet these criteria, I believe the value of the measures will have been established.

Handbook Content

Volume 1 includes an introductory chapter and 38 additional chapters in nine sections as follows: I. Information and Overview; II. Measures for Infants; III. Children: Cognitive Approaches and Measures; IV. Children: Self-Esteem Measures; V. Children: Race-Related Tests and Measures; VI. Measures for Adolescents and Young Adults; VII. Language Assessment and Attitude Measures; VIII. Measures of Parental Attitudes and Values; and IX. Measures of Family Structure and Dynamics. Approximately fifty instruments and approaches are presented in Volume I.

Parts I-VII of Volume 1 are arranged in developmental sequence from infancy to adolescence. Instruments for assessing parental attitudes and values as well as family structure and dynamics are also included in Volume 1. Thus instruments in Volume 1 include measures that are appropriate for infants, children, youth, and their families.

With the exception of papers by Dent on approaches to non-biased assessment, Patton on the assessment of gifted and talented learners, and Omotoso on testing in Nigeria, all remaining chapters include actual tests or measures and are data-based. A range of approaches is represented, including observational scales, experimental approaches, factor analytically derived scales, Piagetian-based approaches, projective measures, questionnaires, ecological approaches, network analysis, and structured interviews. They include pilot studies, doctoral dissertations, and national surveys. Modifications of existing instruments for use with African American populations are also included. Taken as a whole, measures in Volume 1 represent a wide spectrum of approaches to the development of tests and measures for use with African Americans.

Measures and approaches presented in Volume 2 are appropriate for late adolescents, young adults, and older age groups. The introduction and eleven other sections comprise 47 chapters arranged by topics as follows: I. Introduction and Overview; II. World-View Measures; III. Physiological Measures and Neuropsychological Assessment; IV. Spirituality Measures; V. Measures of Acculturation, Life Experiences, and Values; VI. Racial Identity Attitude Measures; VII. Other Noncognitive Measures; VIII. Stress, Racism, and Coping Measures; IX. Mental Health Delivery Measures; X. Fair Employment Testing Concepts, and Work Environment and Organizational Assessment Measures; XI. Research Program-Based Measures; and XII. Other Measures.

As in Volume 1, the chapters include discussion papers and a wide range of approaches to instrument development. Projective as well as paper-and-pencil measures are included. Some tests are derived from large data bases and others represent modifications (for African American populations) of existing measures. A number of the tests and measures were developed as masters theses or doctoral dissertations. As in Volume 1,

they vary in stage of development and invite further psychometric study and use.

Caveat: Chapters are Copyrighted

Handbook chapters are copyrighted. However, except as noted in individual chapters, most chapter authors grant non-commercial use of the tests and measures for research, service, or instructional purposes. Therefore, most *Handbook* tests and measures may be reproduced for any of the purposes listed above. However, individual items may not be included in other instruments or for other purposes, nor may the instrument be modified without the written permission of the test author whose address is listed at the end of each chapter.

Permission for inclusion of individual chapters in anthologies or other sources, whether for classroom use or for other purposes, must be secured from both the chapter author and Cobb & Henry Publishers.

Communicating with Chapter Authors

As is the case for virtually all existing tests and measures, there is need for further psychometric development. Seldom have all appropriate studies of validity and reliability been undertaken or care taken to ensure that norms for all groups to which the tests or measures are to be administered and interpreted have been developed. This failure to conduct psychometric studies on tests and measures used with African American populations is an especially noteworthy shortcoming that needs to be remedied. Many individuals need to be involved in this enterprise, not just test developers. Therefore, authors of *Handbook* chapters are anxious to communicate and network with individuals who have interest in the constructs or tests and measures the authors have developed or discussed, or who wish to use the author's measure(s) for research or other purposes. In some instances, interested parties will need to contact the author directly since full copies of the test or measure or scoring keys are not included in all *Handbook* chapters. In most chapters, however, all information required to use the test or measure is included.

To facilitate direct communication, a box is included at the end of each chapter that provides information (address, telephone, etc.) enabling interested individuals to communicate directly with authors. An example of information provided is given for the *Handbook* editor in the box below.

For additional information, contact:

Reginald L. Jones
Department of Psychology
Hampton University
Hampton, VA 23668
Telephone: (804) 727-5100 (w)
            (804) 838-1980 (h)
Fax: (804) 727-5131 (w)
      (804) 827-1060 (h)
E-mail: rjones@cs.hu.edu

References

Anastasi, A. (1958). *Differential psychology* (3rd ed.). New York: The MacMillan Company.

Anastasi, A. (1968). *Psychological testing* (1988). New York: MacMillan.

Baldwin, J. A. (1991). African psychology and Black personality testing. In A. G. Hilliard (Ed.), *Testing African American students* (pp. 56-80). Morristown, NJ: Aaron Press.

Baly, I. (1984). Assessing the vocational-education decision making of low SES Black male high school seniors: A test of two models. Unpublished doctoral dissertation, University of California, Berkeley.

Berk, R. A. (Ed.). (1982). *Handbook of methods for detecting test bias*. Baltimore: John Hopkins University Press.

Berry, J. W. (1969). On cross-cultural comparability. *International Journal of Psychology, 4*, 119-128.

Butcher, J. N., & Pancheri, P. (1976). *A handbook of cross-national MMPI research*. Minneapolis: University of Minnesota Press.

Camilli, G., & Shephard, L. A. (1994). *Methods for identifying biased test items*. Thousand Oaks, CA: Sage Publications.

Cohen, J. C., Montague, P., Nathanson, L. S., & Swerdlik, M. E. (1988). *Psychological testing*. Mountain View, CA: Mayfield Publishing Company.

Committee to Develop Standards for Educational and Psychological Testing. (1985). *Standards for educational and psychological testing*. Washington: American Psychological Association.

Comrey, A. L., Backer, T. E., & Glaser, E. M. (1973). *A sourcebook for mental health measures*. Los Angeles: Human Interaction Research Institute.

Costello, R. M. (1977). Construction and validation of an MMPI Black-White scale. *Journal of Personality Assessment, 41*, 514-519.

Cronbach, L. J. (1990). *Essentials of psychological testing*. New York: Harper Collins Publishers.

Dahlstrom, W. G., Lachar, D., & Dahlstrom, L. E. (1986). *MMPI patterns of American minorities*. Minneapolis: University of Minnesota press.

Dana, R. H. (1987, May). Culturally diverse groups and MMPI interpretation. Adapted from a paper presented at the 22nd Annual Symposium of Recent Developments in the Use of the MMPI, Seattle, Washington, titled "Culturally diverse groups and the MMPI: An etic and emic heuristic."

Dent, H.E. (1976). Assessing Black children for mainstream placement. In R.L. Jones (Ed.), *Mainstreaming and the minority child*. (pp. 77-91). Reston,VA.: Council for Exceptional Children.

Greene, R. L. (1987). Ethnicity and MMPI performance: A review. *Journal of Consulting and Clinical Psychology, 55*, 497-512.

Harrison, R. H., & Kass, E. H. (1967). Differences between Negro and White pregnant women on the MMPI. *Journal of Consulting Psychology, 31*, 454-463.

Hilliard, A. G. (1991). *Testing African American students*. Morristown, NJ: Aaron Press.

Jahoda, G. (1977). In pursuit of the emic-etic distinction: Can we ever capture it? In Y. H. Poortings (Ed.), *Basic problems in cross-cultural psychology* (pp. 55-63). Amsterdam: Swets and Zeitlinger.

Jensen, A. R. (1980). *Bias in mental testing*. New York: The Free Press.

Johnson, O. G., & Bommarito, J. W. (1971). *Tests and child development: A handbook*. San Francisco: Jossey Bass.

Jones, R. L. (1972). *Black psychology*. New York: Harper & Row.

Jones, R. L. (1980). *Black psychology* (2nd ed.). New York: Harper & Row.

Jones, R. L. (1984). *Measurement and instrumentation in cross-subcultural studies of Blacks and Whites in the United States*. Unpublished paper presented at the Invitational Conference on Racial Comparative Research, Howard University, Washington, D.C.

Jones, R. L. (1989). *Psychoeducational assessment of minority group children: A casebook*. Berkeley: Cobb & Henry Publishers.

Jones, R. L. (1991). *Black psychology* (3rd ed.). Berkeley: Cobb & Henry Publishers.

Murphy, K. R., & Davidshofer, C. O. (1994). *Psychological testing*. Englewood Cliffs: Prentice Hall.

Pike, K. L. (1966). *Language in relation to a unified theory of the structure of human behavior*. The Hague: Mouton.

Robinson, J. P., Shaver, P. R., & Wrightsman, L. S. (1991). *Measures of personality and social psychological attitudes*. New York: Academic Press, Inc.

Samuda, R. J. (1975). *Psychological testing of American minorities*. New York: Dodd, Mead, & Company.

Tannenbaum, A. J. (1965). Culture-fair intelligence test. In O. Buros (Ed.), *Sixth mental measurements yearbook, tests and reviews: Intelligence-group* (pp. 721-723). Highland Park, NJ: Gryphon Press.

Trimble, J. E., Lonner, W. J., & Boucher, J. D. (1983). Stalking the wiley emic: Alternatives to cross-cultural measurement. In S. H. Irvine & J. W. Berry (Eds.), *Human assessment and cultural factors* (pp. 259-271). New York: Plenum.

Wainer, H., & Braun, H. I. (1988). *Test validity*. Hillsdale, NJ: Erlbaum.

Walsh, W. B., & Betz, N .E. (1995). *Tests and assessment*. Englewood Cliffs, NJ: Prentice Hall.

White, W. G. (1975). A psychometric approach for adjusting selected MMPI scale scores obtained by Blacks. Unpublished doctoral dissertation, University of Missouri. *Dissertation Abstracts International, 35*, 4669B.

Williams, R. L. (1972). Abuses and misuses in testing Black children. In R. L. Jones (Ed.), *Black psychology* (pp. 77-91). New York: Harper & Row.

Part II

Measures for Infants

Observation Instruments of Toddler and Infant Experiences[1]

Grace C. Massey, Constance Milbrath, William A. Hayes, Angela Buchanan, Jane David, and Joseph Rosenberg

Abstract

This chapter presents an overview of the C-TIES and A-TIES Coding Systems. These two compatible observation systems evolved from a series of coding systems developed by the late Jean V. Carew for scoring naturalistic observations of child and caregiver behavior. The original system, the Carew-HOME Scale (1975), was used in a longitudinal investigation of home reared toddlers (age 1-3) and in a subsequent study of a similar sample attending day care centers. The scale was then revised to form the Carew-SRI Adult Behavior Codes and Child Codes used in the observation component of the National Day Care Home Study (1980). The TIES systems were developed from these two instruments using a longitudinal study of Black toddlers in Oakland, California. Both C-TIES and A-TIES were used to code the data in the National Infant Care Study (1983). The systems use a time sampling method, with a complete observe code sequence occurring every 20 seconds. The C-TIES system focuses the observation on the child and the A-TIES system focuses on the adult.

The period between age 1 and 3 is often regarded as a formative, fundamental, and even critical period of child development. It is during this two-year span that most children master a number of basic, progressively more difficult, large motor, fine motor, verbal, cognitive and social skills. Children learn to walk, run, jump, climb, ride a tricycle; they learn to manipulate tools, toys, and small objects more and more skillfully and planfully in their attempt at stacking, building, opening and closing containers, taking apart and putting things together, pouring molding, and scribbling. During this period, children learn to understand most of what is said to them and to express their thoughts more intelligibly, with more complexity, grammatically, and articulately. They also seem to acquire a great deal of knowledge about how the physical and social environment "works," how one can act upon objects and people, and how these behave when they are acted upon.

How does the child accomplish these feats of learning? Major theorists such as Piaget (1951, 1952, 1970) and White (1959) emphasize the role played by the child in acting upon the environment to create experiences from which s/he learns specific skills and develops her/his general intellectual competence. In contrast, traditional learning theory has stressed the part played by the human environment in teaching, training, modeling and guiding the child in acquisition of skills and knowledge. Central to both formulations is the idea of interaction with the environment as the basis for the development of intellectual competence but this theory focuses primarily on the child as the architect of her/his learning experiences, while learning theory centers on the other person–typically a more knowledgeable adult–as the source, provider, or mediator of such experiences.

Regardless of one's theoretical orientation, the need still exists for descriptive baseline data including detailed, longitudinal observations of children's day-to-day experiences and interactions with the environment. Developmentalists cannot expect to rely on knowledge of child or caregiver behaviors gathered in clinical or experimental settings to provide a clear understanding of the forces which influence the attainment of important social and cognitive skills during this period. Existing research, employing detailed naturalistic observations of infant and caregiver behavior, comes almost to a halt as children move into toddlerhood, become more mobile, acquire more advanced intellectual skills, and engage in more varied and complex interactions with their environments. Ironically, considerable evidence exists to suggest dramatic, qualitative shifts in the development of competence and in the behavior of caregivers in the second and third years of life (McCall, Eichorn, & Hogarty, 1977; White, Carew-Watts, Barnett, Kaban, Marmor, & Shapiro, 1973; White, Kaban, Shapiro, & Attanucci, 1977).

The few observational systems available which focus on children's behavior at this age tend to be very narrow or specialized and usually ignore the child's solitary behavior–behavior which accounts for 35 to 60 percent of the young child's time. A coding system which effectively addresses the needs of developmental research in a variety of natural settings should include the following characteristics: reliability; applicability to different care settings; freedom from cultural bias; and ability to record a wide range of behavior and to incorporate both the literal and purposive content of observed events. That is, coding categories should be reasonably broad-gauged to allow the researcher to interpret behavior rather than to simply count frequencies.

During the past decade, the late Jean Carew and her associates have developed a series of increasingly sophisticated observation procedures and coding systems which meet these requirements and have proved useful in describing the nature of infant-toddler experiences in normal, day-to-day care settings of own homes, family day care homes, and day care centers. Carew's work culminated in the set of complementary coding systems which were used to code the National Infant Care Study data, Child-focused Toddler and Infant Experiences System (C-TIES), and Adult-focused Toddler and Infant Experiences System (A-TIES). These two systems offer the following advantages: sampling of a broad array of child and caregiver behaviors, both solitary and interactive; flexibility (systems can be applied to transcripts or videotapes); high reliability; relative ease of training (video and written training materials available); cultural fairness; extensive use in data collections and coding; and complementarity. The advantage of complementarity is that a relatively small data base can be used to maximum advantage by coding it in different ways and from different perspectives. Briefly, C-TIES samples child-focused behavior, both solitary and interactive, for 5 seconds out of every 20.

Overview of C-TIES Coding System

The C-TIES system codes the child's activity and characteristics of the child's social interactions. There are 15 major coding dimensions for C-TIES: (1) Activity; (2) Mastery; (3) Source; (4) Facilitate/Control; (5) Caregiver Location; (6) Interaction; (7) Individualization; (8) What;

(9) Whom; (10) Interactor Language; (11) Interactor Emotion; (12) Child Language; (13) Child Emotion; (14) Child Mobility; and (15) Media/Music/Objects.

The C-TIES coding form is arranged in blocks of nine frames (rows) corresponding to 3 minutes of observation. The coder records the child's (C) behavior/interactions by moving from left to right on the C-TIES coding form and entering one code for each dimension. An exception is in the Edit column where two codes can be used. If the codes O (out of camera range), or V (visual problem) are used in Edit, the rest of the row is left blank. If C is not interacting with another person (as defined under Interaction, column 10), columns 10 through 19 are left blank. Each of the dimensions is described below.

Activity. This dimension describes the topic or purpose of the activity the child pursues alone or in interaction with the caregiver or other children. The codes are grouped into four areas: (1) activities that are relevant to socio-emotional development; (2) activities that seem likely to be related to the child's intellectual development and later preschool intellectual competencies; (3) codes representing activities in which the child is likely to play an active part; and, (4) codes for activities in which the child is likely to play a more passive role.

The activities considered most relevant to the child's socio-emotional state/development are:

• Negative behavior (C displays negative, aggressive, angry behavior or receives such behavior from another person)

• Controlling behavior (C controls, restricts, disapproves of, protests another person's behavior or another person does so to C)

• Distress (C displays distress of fear or another person comforts C when C is distressed or fearful)

• Prosocial behavior (C expresses kindness, sympathy, consideration for another or receives such behavior from another person)

• Affection/social games (C displays affection or receives affection from another person; C engages in social games such as peek-a-boo with another person)

• Attention-seeking (C seeks attention from another person or another person seeks attention from C)

The activities considered most likely to be related to the child's intellectual development are:

• Dramatic play (C engages in pretend play; or C attends to someone doing so in interaction with him/her)

• Language/non-routing information (C engages in an activity such as labeling objects or being read to that provides a clear opportunity for C to master a language skill or acquire non-routing, verbally-transmitted information; or C attends to someone doing so in an interaction with him/her)

• Music, singing, reciting (C plays a musical instrument, sings, recites or attends to someone doing so in an interaction with him/her)

• "Scientific" experimentation (C engages in a "scientific experiment" in an apparent attempt to understand basic laws of nature such as gravity, or attends to someone doing so in an interaction with him/her)

• Creative-artistic (C creates an "artistic" product as in crayoning or painting, or attends to someone doing so in an interaction with him/her)

• Fine motor, spatial (C engages in small muscle activities that provide clear opportunities for the learning of perceptual-spatial skills and concepts as in fitting, stacking, ordering shapes and sizes; or C attends to someone doing so in an interaction with him/her). The child's specific behaviors in attempting to master relevant skills while pursuing these activities are coded in another dimension, Mastery.

The remaining activity codes include many frequently occurring activities such as simple exploratory play (Fe), gross motor activity (Gm), physical need satisfaction (Pn), monitoring the environment (Mn), and changing location (Tr). These activities per se are not thought to have any clear significance for the child's socio-emotional or intellectual development but are included in the overall profile of the child's psychological experiences because their relative frequency changes predictably with the child's age.

Mastery. The Mastery dimension indicates whether the child (C) is actively attempting, practicing, or performing an activity that is intellectually, physically, perceptually, or otherwise challenging for C. Mastery codes do not consider how successful the child is at performing a task or understanding a concept involved in a high-level activity (that is, whether C does it correctly) but whether C is in the process of struggling with, acquiring, or attempting to perfect a skill. When the child (C) is the Source, certain activities are automatically coded as Mastery (i.e., Experimentation (Ex). These coding rules are described in the C-TIES Manual (available from author).

Source. The central activity dimension of C-TIES applies to the child's independent behavior and to his/her interactions with other people. Consequently, any one of those activities may be engendered solely by the child when s/he is on her/his own or s/he may play a more or less active role in creating them when interacting with another person. In an interactive context, the child's role ranges from being the prime creator of the activity with the other person as a passive onlooker, to being a passive observer while the other person essentially carries out the activity. The critical distinctions among the child's and interactor's role in an activity that Carew's research (1980) suggests must be made are listed under the heading Source, which is the second key dimension in C-TIES. Four sources of activity are distinguished: child, with the interactor as passive onlooker; child and interactor; interactor, with the child as a passive onlooker; and child alone. The variable Source, along with the Activity and Mastery codes, can be thought of as marking the difference between environmental stimulation (input to the child from other people) and self-stimulation (input by the child to his own development).

Facilitate/control. The fourth important dimension of C-TIES is Facilitate/Control. This variable codes distinctions among the specific behaviors that another person uses when interacting with the child. Facilitative behaviors are those that help to create, sustain, promote, or encourage

the child's activity. These include teaching, playing with, helping, directing, conversing, and looking and listening in a positive or neutral fashion. Control behaviors are those indicating that the other person wishes to prevent, restrict, or show disapproval of the child's behavior or reject, ignore, or postpone satisfying his/her demands. The distinctions made here are among routine, matter-of-fact, control behaviors with no explanation and "harsh"/strict behaviors in which the other person resorts to force, physical punishment, threats, ridicule, and so on.

Caregiver location. The caregiver's location is coded as seen, heard, or neither (absent).

Interaction type. Interactions are coded as convergent (shared focus for the interactors), divergent (different focus/purpose), or borderline (minimal involvement by one of the interactors).

Individualization. Child receives a unique, individual interaction versus child is treated as a member of a group in an interaction.

What. What is being controlled, what is the issue of the interactor's control behavior.

Who/m (Identity of Interactor). If the child is engaged in a social interaction, the interactor (caregiver, other adult, child, group) is identified.

Interactor language. Present, present but unintelligible, or not present.

Interactor emotion. Happy, sad, angry, or neutral.

Child language. Present, present but unintelligible, or not present.

Child emotion. Happy, sad, angry, or neutral.

Child mobility. Unrestricted, confined, or held.

Media/music/object. Presence in the environment (Media/Music) or type used by child (Object).

Hierarchical Coding Rules

Certain hierarchical rules are built into the C-TIES coding system which emphasize certain experiences or events for children over others, based on an underlying concept of "good quality" care experiences for children. In the course of modifying the TIES system, an important task was to evaluate its hierarchical structure, particularly for coding interactions. In previous TIES coding of children observed in their own homes, hierarchical decision rules for resolving conflicts between competing interactions in the same observation interval favored the caregiver over other interactors, and adults over children as interactors. This rule was consistent with Carew's previous research pinpointing the input of the caregivers as the most significant in the child's daily experiences at home. However, it was also understood that children attending group care could potentially receive significant input from other children attending as well as from adult caregivers; thus the existing TIES hierarchical rule for coding interactions had to be re-evaluated. A new hierarchical coding sequence was developed that emphasized the "best" experience the child was involved in by prioritizing coding in terms of the interactor's facilitation technique rather than in terms of the interactor's identity.

Activity is the principal dimension of C-TIES and it is coded at every interval in which coding takes place. The selection of the Activity Code is the first decision that the coder usually makes. In general, the main activity or interaction in which the child is engaged is the one coded under Activity. Behaviors that are clearly in the service of or incidental to another activity are not coded.

Even in an observation interval as short as 5 seconds, the coder may have difficulty in deciding which code to select when two activities occur simultaneously or sequentially and one does not seem clearly subordinate to the other. In C-TIES, a hierarchical coding rule is invoked to solve such conflicts. When behavior corresponding to two or more codes occurs in the 5-second observation interval, the code placed higher in the dimension in the coding format takes precedence over all codes placed lower.

This hierarchical coding rule was devised primarily to ease the task of decision-making when the coder has to keep up with a rapid flow of events, to ensure high levels of inter-observer agreement, and to avoid the analytic problems created by multiple coding of a single dimension. However, the hierarchical arrangement of codes within each dimension, although sometimes arbitrary, is by no means altogether so. Rather, the arrangement of codes reflects, as far as possible, best judgments about their relative importance to the child's socio-emotional, intellectual, self-expressive, and motor development.

With respect to the socio-emotional codes listed under Activity, another consideration was the infrequency with which such behaviors are typically observed in a brief time-sampling system. Thus socio-emotional behaviors are placed first in the list of Activities both because of their developmental importance and the need to guarantee that when they occur they have the maximum chance of being recorded.

The hierarchical coding rule is applied to the Activity dimension first. Here the rule instructs the coder to solve conflicts by choosing the code listed highest among the 24 activity codes. In practice, conflicts tend to arise most frequently with respect to codes for exploratory play with objects (Fe), physical need satisfaction (Pn), monitoring (Mn), and transition (Tr) because these behaviors often occur simultaneously in "real life."

Applying the hierarchical coding rule to the Activity dimension has the effect of minimizing conflicts among codes for other dimensions in C-TIES. Once the activity code is selected, the choice of codes on the remaining dimensions tend to follow automatically. For example, if Fe (fine motor) is chosen over Pn (physical needs) in a conflict case and the Fe activity involved a baby girl as an interactor whereas the Pn activity involved the caregiver (Cg) as an interactor, then the baby girl is coded as the interactor in the Who/m column, not Cg.

Overview of A-TIES Coding System

The A-TIES is an individual adult-focused coding system designed to describe the behavior and interaction of adults who care for infants and toddlers (9 to 36 months). It complements the C-TIES coding system in that it focuses on an adult caregiver while C-TIES focuses on an individual child observed in the same care setting of his/her own home, family day care home, or day care center. The A-TIES records adult behaviors as well as very basic information about child behaviors in interaction with adult caregivers, thereby making the A-TIES and C-TIES coding system both complementary and comparable.

The A-TIES system is best suited for coding adult-focused videotaped observations or transcripts of video observations. The activities, interactions, and behavior of the target adult (A) are observed on videotape for 5 seconds and coded on special A-TIES forms in the next 15 seconds, with a complete observe-code sequence occurring every 20 seconds. The 5 second/15 second observe-code sequence is recorded onto the videotape by means of audio signals transmitted to the camera microphone from a tape, recorded during the videotaping process. Alternatively, audio or visual signals may be dubbed onto duplicates of original unsignalled tapes. The adult's activities, interactions, and behavior in the 5-second videotaped observation interval are then coded in terms of A-TIES. This is the same procedure followed for the coding of C-TIES.

The A-TIES system codes the adult's activity and characteristics of the adult's interactions with children. The A-TIES coding form is arranged in blocks of nine frames (rows) corresponding to 3 minutes of observation. The coder records the adult's behavior/interactions by moving from left to right on the A-TIES coding form and entering one code for each dimension, except Edit, where two codes can be used. When an interaction between the adult (also referred to as the caregiver) and a child or children occurs in the 5-second coding interval, the coder enters the identity of the interactor(s), the type of activity in which the participants are engaged, the technique of facilitation or control used by the adult (caregiver), and the adult's use of language and type of emotional affect.

The 10 major coding dimensions for A-TIES are: (1) Auxiliary Behavior; (2) Activity; (3) Source;

(4) Facilitate/Control; (5) Interaction Type; (6) Individualization; (7) What; (8) Who/m; (9) Adult Language; and, (10) Adult Emotion. If the codes 0 (*0 = out of range) or V (V = visual problem) are used in Edit (Column 1), the rest of the coding row is left blank If the caregiver is not interacting with a child or children (as defined under Interaction, column 5), the coding ends at column 4 (Auxiliary) and columns 5 through 18 are left blank. Each of the dimensions is described below as well as in the A-TIES Manual (available from the author).

Auxiliary behavior. There are five auxiliary codes which are used for intervals in which the caregiver does not interact with any child or children. Auxiliary codes refer to "adult" activities, in contrast to child-related activities which are coded whenever a caregiver-child interaction occurs. These codes are listed hierarchically. When an auxiliary code is entered, the rest of the coding line is left blank. The five auxiliary codes are: (1) supervise; (2) preparation for children; (3) household tasks; (4) caregiver recreational activities; and, (5) other miscellaneous caregiver activities.

Activity. The principal dimension of A-TIES is activity. The codes describe the topic or purpose of the activity pursued by a child or children in interaction with the caregiver. Using activity as the primary common dimension between the two TIES systems makes it possible to compare a particular child's interactive experience during a child-focused observation (coded with C-TIES) with his/her interactive experience in an adult-focused observation (coded with A-TIES), or with the experiences of other children in their interactions with the caregiver.

The selection of the activity code is the first decision that the coder usually makes. As in C-TIES, the codes are grouped into four areas: (1) activities that are relevant to socio-emotional development; (2) activities that seem likely to be related to the child's intellectual development and later preschool intellectual competencies; (3) codes representing activities in which the child is likely to play an active part; and, (4) codes for activities in which the child is likely to play a more passive role.

The activity codes are arranged in four columns. Column 10 includes behaviors that have clear relevance to socio-emotional development. In contrast, columns 11, 12, and 13 refer to behaviors in which the socio-emotional aspect is less prominent. Column 11 is comprised of six codes that seem likely to be related to the child's intellectual development and later school achievement. Column 12 includes six codes and column 13 has one code (Tr) representing activities in which the child is likely to play an active part. The remaining five codes in column 7 refer to activities in which the child is likely to play a more passive role.

The activities considered most relevant to the child's socio-emotional state/development are:
- Negative behavior (C displays negative, aggressive, angry behavior or receives such behavior from the caregiver)
- Controlling behavior (C controls, restricts, disapproves of, protests another person's behavior or caregiver does so to C)
- Distress (C displays distress or fear, or caregiver comforts C when C is distressed or fearful)
- Prosocial behavior (C expresses kindness, sympathy, consideration for another or is taught such behavior by the caregiver)
- Affection/social games (C displays affection or receives affection from the caregiver; C engages in social games such as peek-a-boo with the caregiver)
- Attention-seeking (C seeks attention from the caregiver).

The activities considered most likely to be related to the child's intellectual development are:
- Dramatic play (C engages in pretend or attends to the caregiver doing so in an interaction with him/her)
- Language/non-routine information (C engages in an activity such as labeling objects or being read to that provides a clear opportunity for C to master a language skill or acquire non-routine, verbally-transmitted information; or C attends to the caregiver doing so in an interaction with him/her)
- Music, singing, reciting (C plays musical instrument, sings, recites or attends to the caregiver doing so in interaction with him/her)
- "Scientific" experimentation (C engages in a "scientific experiment" in an apparent attempt to understand basic laws of nature such as gravity, or attends to the caregiver doing so in an interaction with him/her)
- Creative-artistic (C creates an "artistic" product as in crayoning or painting, or attends to the caregiver doing so in an interaction with him/her)
- Fine motor, spatial (C engages in small muscle activities that provide clear opportunities for the learning of perceptual-spatial skills and concepts as in fitting, stacking, ordering shapes and sizes; or C attends to the caregiver doing so in an interaction with him/her).

The remaining activity codes include many frequently occurring activities such as simple exploratory play (Fe), gross motor activity (Gm), physical needs satisfaction (Pn), monitoring the environment (Mn), and changing location (Tr). These activities, per se, are not thought to have any clear significance for the child's socio-emotional or intellectual development but are included in the overall profile of the child's psychological experiences because their relative frequency changes predictably with the child's age.

Source. The central activity dimension of A-TIES applies to the adult's (caregiver's) interaction with children. In interactive contexts, the adult's or child's role ranges from being the prime onlooker, to being a passive observer while the other person essentially carries out the activity. The critical distinctions among the child's and adult's roles in an activity that Carew's research (1980) suggests must be made, are listed under the heading *Source*, which is the second key dimension in both C-TIES and A-TIES. Three sources of activity are distinguished in A-TIES: Adult, with the child as a passive onlooker; child and adult; child, with the adult as a passive onlooker.

Facilitate/control. The third important dimension of A-TIES is facilitate/control. This variable codes distinctions among the specific behaviors the adult uses when interacting with a child (or children). Facilitative behaviors are those that help to create, sustain, promote, or encourage the child's activity. These include teaching, playing with, helping, directing, conversing and looking and listening in a positive or neutral fashion. Control behaviors are those indicating that the adult wishes to prevent, restrict, or show disapproval of the child's behavior or reject, ignore, or postpone satisfying his/her demands. The distinctions made here are among routine, matter-of-fact control behaviors with no explanation and harsh/strict behaviors in which the adult resorts to force, physical punishment, threats, ridicule, and so on.

Interaction type. Interactions are coded as convergent (shared focus for the interactors), or divergent (different focus/purpose).

Individualization. Child receives a unique, individualized interaction from the adult versus child is treated as a member of a group in an interaction.

What. What is being controlled, what is the issue of the adult's control behavior.

Identity of interactor (who/m). If the adult is engaged in a social interaction with a child or children (or mixed group of children and other adults), the interactor is identified by descriptive characteristics including age, ethnicity, and sex.

Adult language. Present, present but unintelligible or not present.

Summary

The purpose of this chapter was to describe two observation systems, C-TIES and A-TIES. These two systems focus on documenting the experiences of the child and the caregiver through observation. The child's activities alone and in interaction with adults and other children are observed in C-TIES. The caregiver is the primary target of A-TIES. Thus, the systems can be com-

patibly used to document observed behavior from both the child's and adult's perspective. The range of behaviors of children from 12 to 36 months and the interaction between the caregiver and child can be captured through the use of these two complementary systems. In addition, links

Table 1. Average Percent Agreement of Four (4) Coders by Coding Category by Two (2) Videotapes

Coding Category	Videotape		
	Tape 1	Tape 2	Total
Edit (EDT)	96	98	97
Activity	96	97	96.5
Mastery (MAS)	96	97	96.5
Locat'n (LOC)	96	96	96
Who/m	99	99.5	99
Type of Interaction (INT)	98	99	98.5
Source (SRC)	96	93	94.5
Facilitate/Control (F/C)	98	96	97
Interactor Language (I-LAN)	99	99	99
Interactor Emotion (I-EMO)	98	99	98.5
Child Language (C-LAN)	99	98	98.5
Child Emotion (C-EMO)	98	98	98
Mobility (MOB)	95	98	97.5

can be made between key characteristics of caregivers, setting and child behaviors (as was done in the National Infant Care Study, 1983).

Based on Carew's research, certain experiences were assumed to be more valuable for the child's intellectual development than others. Specifically, cognitive experiences, such as language skills and spatial motor experiences, were considered to be most valuable for promoting intellectual development. Carew's work does not stand in isolation. Other investigators have found strong relationships between the child's early cognitive experiences and later performance on outcome measures such as IQ tests (Elardo, Bradley, & Caldwell, 1975, 1977; Golden & Birns, 1976; Heber, 1972; Wach, Uzgiris, & Hunt, 1971). Carew's systems, C-TIES and A-TIES, represent extremely valuable contributions as they capture the varied behaviors in which children engage so that these early cognitive experiences can be systematically documented. The systems offer many advantages: they sample a broad array of child and caregiver behaviors and both are solitary and interactive in a wide variety of settings; they are flexible (the systems can be applied to transcripts or videotapes); they are culturally-fair; and they can be reliably coded (see Table 1).

Carew fervently engaged in work which she believed attempted "to understand, through observation, reflection, and research, the meaning of childhood experiences–to decide which experiences are truly educative–intellectually, socially and emotionally–and how those who care for children can help bring them about" (Carew, Chan, & Halfar, 1976, p. 160). Further use of Carew's observation measures can only lead to enriching our knowledge as to how adults can facilitate positive cognitive, social and emotional growth in children.

Note

1. This chapter is taken from the Analytical and Technical report of the National Infant Care Study (Contract No. HHS 105- 80-C-041) and like the report, is dedicated to the memory of Dr. Jean V. Carew, whose vision, hard work and dedication were the primary force in the conceptualization of both the C-TIES and A-TIES instruments.

References

Ainsworth, M. (1973). The development of infant-mother attachment. In B. Caldwell & H. Ricciuiti (Eds.), *Review of child development research* (Vol. 3). Chicago: University of Chicago Press.

Ainsworth, M., & Bell, S. (1974). Mother-infant interaction and the development of competence. In K. J. Connolly & J. S. Bruner (Eds.), *The growth of competence*. New York: Academic Press.

Ainsworth, M., Bell, S., & Stayton, D. (1972). Individual differences in the development of some attachment behaviors. *Merrill-Palmer Quarterly of Behavior and Development, 18*(2), 123-143.

Arend, R., Gove, F., & Sroufe, L. A. (1979). Continuity of early adaptation from infancy to kindergarten: A predictive study of ego-resiliency and curiosity in preschoolers. *Child Development, 50*, 950-959.

Aries, P. (1962). *Centuries of childhood*. New York: Vintage Books.

Beckwith, L. (1976). Caregiver infant interaction and the development of the high-risk infant. In T. Tjossem (Ed.), *Intervention strategies for high-risk infants and young children*. Baltimore: University Park Press.

Beckwith, L., Cohen, S. E., Kopp, C. B., Parmelee, A. H., & Marcy, T. G. (1976). Caregiver-infant interaction and early cognitive development in preterm infants. *Child Development, 47*, 579-587.

Belsky, J., & Steinberg, L. D. (1978). The effects of day care: A critical review. *Child Development, 49*, 929-949.

Bloom, L. (1975). Language development. In F. Horowitz (Ed.), *Review of child development research* (Vol. 4). Chicago: University of Chicago Press.

Bloom, L., Lifter, K., & Broughton, J. (1980). What children say and what they know. In A. Reilly (Ed.), *The communication game: Perspectives on the development of speech, language, and non-verbal communication skills*. Summary of a Pediatric Round Table sponsored by Johnson & Johnson Baby Products.

Bowlby, J. (1969). *Attachment and loss* (Vol. 1). New York: Basic Books.

Brazelton, T., Koslowski, B., & Main, M. (1974). The origin of reciprocity. In M. Lewis & L. Rosenblum (Eds.), *The effect of the infant on its caregiver*. New York: Wiley and Sons.

Carew, J. V. (1980). Experience and development of intelligence in young children at home and in day care. *Monographs of the Society for Research in Child Development, 45* (6-7, Serial No. 187).

Carew, J. V., Chan, I., & Halfar, C. (1976). *Observing intelligence in young children: Eight case studies*. Englewood Cliffs, NJ: Prentice-Hall.

Carew, J. V., Massey, G., & Peters, M. (1980). *The Toddler and Infant Experiences Study (TIES)*. Unpublished report to the Institute for Developmental Studies, Oakland, CA.

Clarke-Stewart, A. (1973). Interactions between mothers and their young children: Characteristics and consequences. *Monographs of the Society for Research in Child Development, 38* (6-7, Serial No. 153).

Clarke-Stewart, A. (1977). *Early child care arrangements: Variations and effects.* Paper presented at the conference on Research Perspectives in the Ecology of Human Development, Cornell University, Ithaca, NY.

Elardo, R., Bradley, R., & Caldwell, B. (1975). The relation of infants' home environment to mental test performance from six to thirty-six months: A longitudinal analysis. *Child Development, 46,* 71-76.

Elardo, R., Bradley, R., & Caldwell, B. (1977). A longitudinal study of the relation of infants' home environments to language development at age three. *Child Development, 48,* 595- 603.

Emde, R., Gaensbauer, T., & Harmon, R. (1966). Emotional expression in infancy: A biobehavioral study. *Psychological Issues Monograph, 10* (1, Whole No. 37).

Escalona, S. (1968). *The roots of individuality.* Chicago: Aldine.

Etaugh, C. (1980). Effects of nonmaternal care on children: Research evidence and popular views. *American Psychologist, 35,* 309-319.

Garvey, C. (1977). *Play.* Cambridge, MA: Harvard University Press.

Golden, M., & Birns, B. (1976). Social class and infant intelligence. In M. Lewis (Ed.), *Origins of intelligence: Infancy and early childhood.* New York: Plenum Press.

Gratch, G. (1980). Some thoughts on cognitive development and language development. In A. Reilly (Ed.), *The communication game: Perspectives on the development of speech, language, and non-verbal communication skills.* Summary of a Pediatric Round Table sponsored by Johnson & Johnson Baby Products.

Greenspan, S. I. (1979). Intelligence and adaptation: An integration of psychoanalytic and Piagetian developmental psychology. *Psychological Issues Monograph,* (47/48).

Greenspan, S. I., & Lieberman, A. E. (1980). Infants, mothers, and their interaction: A quantitative clinical approach to developmental assessment. In *The course of life: Psychoanalytic contributions toward understanding personality development, Volume I: Infancy and Early Childhood.*

Hawkins, P., Mason, E., & Goodrich, N. (1980). *Review and testing of the Greenspan- Lieberman Observation System (GLOS): Conclusions and recommendations.* Unpublished report to the Administration for Children, Youth and Families.

Heber, R. D., Garber, H., Harrington, C. H., & Falender, C. (1972). *Rehabilitation of families at risk for mental retardation.* Unpublished Progress Report.

Kent, R. D. (1980). Articulatory and acoustic perspectives on speech development. In A. Reilly (Ed.), *The communication game: Perspectives on the development of speech, language, and non-verbal communication skills.* Summary of a Pediatric Round Table sponsored by Johnson & Johnson Baby Products.

Kessen, W., Fein, G., Clarke-Stewart, A., & Starr, S. (1975). *Variations in home-based infant education: Language, play, and social development.* Washington, DC: Final Report, Office of Child Development.

Kopp, C. (1974). Fine-motor behaviors of infants. *Developmental Medicine and Child Neurology, 16,* 629-636.

Kopp, C. (1976). Action-schemes of eight-month-old infants. *Developmental Psychology, 12,* 361-362.

Langer, J. (1980). Cognitive growth in preschoolers through verbal interaction with mothers. *American Journal of Orthopsychiatry, 40*(3), 426-432.

Lewis, M., & Freedle, R. (1973). The mother-infant dyad. In P. Plinar, L. Karnes, & T. Alloway (Eds.), *Communication and affect: Language and thought.* New York: Academic Press.

Lieberman, A. F. (1977). Preschooler's competence with a peer: Relations with attachment and peer experience. *Child Development, 48,* 192-194.

Lipsitt, L. (1966). Learning processes of newborns. *Merrill-Palmer Quarterly, 12,* 45-71.

Mahler, M. S. (1970). On the current status of the infantile neurosis. *Journal of the American Psychoanalysis Association, 23*(2), 327-333.

Matas, L., Arend, R., & Sroufe, L. A. (1978). Continuity in adaptation: Quality of attachment and later competence. *Child Development, 49,* 547-556.

McCall, R., Eichorn, D., & Hogarty, P. (1977). Transitions in early mental development. *Monographs of the Society for Research in Child Development 42*(3, Serial No. 171).

Meltzoff, A., & Moore, K. (1977). Imitation of facial and manual gestures by human neonates. *Science, 198,* 75-78.

Minifie, F. D., & Lloyd, L. L. (1978). *Communicative and cognitive abilities: Early behavioral assessment.* Baltimore: University Park Press.

Nelson, K. E., & Bonvillian, J. D. (1978). Early language development: Conceptual growth and related processes between 2 and 4 1/2 years of age.

In K. Nelson (Ed.), *Children's language* (Vol. 1). New York: Gardner Press.

Oller, D. K. (1980). Patterns of infant vocalization. In A. Reilly (Ed.), *The communication game: Perspectives on the development of speech, language, and non-verbal communication skills.* Summary of a Pediatric Round Table sponsored by Johnson & Johnson Baby Products.

Parmelee, A., & Beckwith, L. (1973). *Instructional manual for assessing infant-caretaker interaction in the home.* Unpublished manuscript, University of California, Los Angeles.

Piaget, J. (1951). *The right to education in the modern world: In UNESCO, freedom and culture.* New York: Columbia University Press.

Piaget, J. (1952). *The origins of intelligence in children* (2nd ed.). New York: International Universities Press.

Piaget, J. (1954). *The construction of reality in the child.* New York: Basic Books.

Piaget, J. (1970). Piaget's theory. In P. H. Mussen (Ed.), *Carmichael's manual of child psychology* (3rd ed., Vol. 1). New York: Wiley.

Piaget, J., & Inhelder, B. (1956). *The child's conception of space.* New York: W. W. Norten.

Ramey, C., Farran, D. C., & Campbell, F. A. (1979). Predicting I.Q. from mother-infant interactions. *Child Development, 50,* 804-814.

Ramey, C., & Finkelstein, N. (1978). Contingent stimulation and infant competence. *Journal of Pediatric Psychology, 3,* 89-96.

Reilly, A. P. (1980). *The communication game: Perspectives on the development of speech, language, and non-verbal communication skills.* Summary of a Pediatric Round Table sponsored by Johnson & Johnson Baby Products.

Rubenstein, J., & Howes, C. (1979). Caregiving and infant behavior in day care and in homes. *Developmental Psychology, 15,* 1-24.

Ruopp, R., Travers, J., Glantz, F., & Coelen, C. (1979). *Children at the center: Final report of the National Day Care Study* (Vol. 1). Cambridge: Abt Associates.

Rutter, M. (1982). Social-emotional consequences of day care for preschool children. In E. Zigler & E. Gordon (Eds.), *Day care: Scientific and social policy issues.* Boston: Auburn House.

Schachter, F. (1979). *Everyday mother talk to toddlers: Early intervention.* New York: Academic Press.

Snelbecker, G. (1974). *Learning theory, instructional theory, and psychoeducational design.* New York: McGraw Hill.

Tizard, B., Cooperman, O., Joseph, A., & Tizard, S. (1972). Environmental effects on longitudinal development: A study of young children in long-stay residential nurseries. *Child Development, 43,* 337-358.

Tuchman, B. (1978). *A distant mirror.* New York: Ballantine Books.

U.S. Bureau of the Census (1981). *Statistical abstract of the United States* (102nd ed.). Washington, DC: U.S. Government Printing Office.

Wach, T., Uzgiris, I., & Hunt, J. McV. (1971). Cognitive development in infants of different age levels and from different environmental backgrounds: An exploratory investigation. *Merrill-Palmer Quarterly, 17,* 283-317.

White, B., Carew-Watts, J. I. C., Kaban, B., Marmor, J., & Shapiro, B. (1973). *Environment and experience: Major influences on the development of the young child* (Vol. 1). Englewood Cliffs, NJ: Prentice-Hall.

White, B., Kaban, B., Shapiro, B., & Attanucci, J. (1977). Competence and experience. In I. Uzgiris, & F. Weizman (Eds.), *The structuring of experience.* New York: Plenum.

White, R. (1959). Motivation reconsidered: The concept of competence. *Psychological Review, 66,* 297-331.

Zelazo, P., & Kearsley, R. (1980). The emergence of functional play in infants: Evidence for a major cognitive transition. *Journal of Applied Developmental Psychology, 1,* 95-117.

For coding manuals and additional information, contact:

Grace C. Massey, Ph.D.
293 GBC
University of California, Berkeley
Berkeley, CA 94720
Fax: (510) 642-9078
E-mail: grace-massey@maillink.berkeley.edu

The Developmental Milestones Expectations Scale: An Assessment of Parents' Expectations for Infants' Development[1]

Suzanne M. Randolph and Pearl L. Rosser

Abstract

The Developmental Milestones Expectations Scale was specifically constructed for use with a selected group of Black mothers who were participating in the Howard University Normative Study–a study designed to establish new normative expectations for Black infants' development. The Scale addresses the empirical and practical limitations of scales used in previous research by expanding the number and types of milestones included. The Scale includes 48 items in various developmental areas: motor, cognitive, self-help, and social. A unique feature is the inclusion of activities which have potential for understanding childhood injuries (e.g., age at which parents expect children to cook or cross the street alone). The Scale is recommended for use with parents of newborns before age two months and again before the first birthday (preferably nine months). The Scale can be administered in 15-20 minutes in face-to-face interviews with parents in a variety of settings–the home, clinic, child development center, hospital, office or laboratory. Parents are asked to consider the age at which an "average" child should be able to master various social, cognitive, self-help, and motor milestones. Responses are coded as realistic or unrealistic based on whether they fall within the expected norms for the various milestones; responses can also be coded as realistically early or realistically late for use in obtaining information to guide the development of parent education programs or to assist individual parents in improving their child development knowledge. Research using the scales indicated that mothers were more realistic with the motor items than the cognitive and that few socioeconomic status differences obtained. Results also indicate that maternal developmental expectations influence patterns of development during infancy.

Background and Introduction

The Developmental Milestones Expectations Scale was specifically constructed for use with a selected group of Black mothers who were participating in a study designed to establish new normative expectations for Black infants' development. The study was entitled "The Howard University Normative Study" (HUNS) (Rosser & Randolph, 1991). A major aim of that study was to determine whether mothers' perceptions of their infants, including expectations for development, were related to the health status of the infant (full term versus preterm birth) and whether Black mothers as a group report expectations for their infants that vary from norms of standard infant assessment such as the Bayley Scales of Infant Development (1969) and the Kent Scales of Infant Development. The results of the HUNS were expected to provide new normative expectations about Black children's development and to provide information that could be used by practitioners to assist Black parents in ensuring optimal development for their children.

Several empirical and practical limitations in scales used in previous research prompted the construction of the Developmental Milestones Expectations Scale. First, previous research utilizing Black samples tended to limit mothers' interviews to their expectations of generally known motor and language milestones–(e.g., crawling, walking, sitting up, saying two-word sentences, etc.). Field (1980), for example, only used ten items in her survey of developmental milestones and interpreted total scores as an indication of adolescent mothers' knowledge about child development (the higher the score, the more knowledgeable the mother).

In attempting to use Field's scale in the HUNS with a sample of Black mothers who were older (19-37) and from a wider range of socioeconomic backgrounds, pilot data revealed that a ten-item scale was neither discriminating nor informative (in terms of mothers' expectations for their infants' development or child development knowledge in general). For example, based on the general literature on Black families, we expected to find SES differences as well as differences by sex of target infant. With respect to SES, we expected that middle class mothers would be more realistic in their expectations than lower SES mothers. With respect to sex of infant, we expected that mothers would have earlier expectations for girls than boys in the area of social development, but earlier expectations for boys in the area of motor development. The ten-item scale did not include enough items in the social, cognitive, or self-help areas to examine differences in maternal expectations associated with sex of target infant. Also, because the majority of the ten items emphasized commonly known milestones, there was little variation in responses across the sample; thus, a meaningful examination of SES differences could not be undertaken. A second limitation of previous scales is that many of the infant and toddler behaviors that are valued in Black families are not included (e.g., no finger sucking, polite manners, early weaning from bottle, early introduction of table foods, etc.). In the Developmental Milestones Expectations Scale, items were included that covered these areas as well as others that would permit an examination of a fuller range of infant and toddler behaviors.

A third observation of existing instruments also concerned the omission of milestones in other developmental areas. The cross-cultural literature on development consistently points out the motor precocity of Black infants. Some research goes so far as to suggest that this motor growth and development may be at the expense of social and cognitive development. Therefore, an instrument was needed that would permit examination of whether Black parents generally report: 1) expectations for motor milestones at ages earlier than published norms; and 2) expectations for milestones in other areas (e.g., social and cognitive) that are at ages later than published norms.

Fourth, because of the interest in the effects of birth status on maternal perceptions, an instrument was needed which would allow for an examination of the extent to which the infant serves as a stimulus for the parent in the parent-child interactive process (i.e., the extent to which an infant's health status [full term vs. preterm birth] may be associated with expectations). For example, parents of preterm infants (whose motor performance might be delayed from birth) were expected to report expectations at ages later than published norms for some motor milestones (i.e., they would expect their children to walk later than "usual"). Such information about a parent's expectations for her vulnerable newborn would be key in developing a plan to assist her in having more realistic expectations. Also, from a practical standpoint, this kind of information can provide insight into the bidirectional nature of the parent-child interaction. For example, a parent who has low expectations for an infant might not encourage growth in certain areas because she does not expect the infant to respond in developmentally appropriate ways (e.g., not encouraging walking, because the infant is perceived as "not ready"). On the other hand, a parent who has high expectations for her infant may be disappointed when the infant does not walk or talk when she expected these milestones to occur. Such situations can lead to parent-child interactive difficulty. Therefore, a scale that provided for an examination of parents' expectations in a wider variety of developmental domains was needed.

Another limitation related to the practical value of the previous scales concerns the high incidence of injuries among Black children due to fires and burns, motor vehicles, and other causes. Experience at the Howard University Child Development Center had indicated that large numbers of families (sometimes because of their social realities, other times because of lack of knowledge) left young children unsupervised for long periods, allowed them to cook their own meals, and permitted them to cross streets and play away from the home. Therefore, several items were included that would enable users of the scale to determine what kinds of additional parenting information families needed in order to ensure optimal development of young children. These items were expected to enhance the practical value of the scale.

Administration

We recommend that the Developmental Milestones Expectations Scale (See Appendix) be administered in face-to-face interviews with the parent. This allows for quick movement through the 48 items without parents taking time to study, compare responses, or try to recall specific milestones for their own child. The scale can be administered in a variety of settings–at the infant's home, in a clinic or hospital setting, or in an office or laboratory.

Parents are asked to consider the age at which an "average" child should be able to master various social, cognitive, self-help, and motor milestones. If a range is given, they are asked to give a specific week/month/year. The examiner records all responses in spaces provided on the scale. Parents' responses are then compared to the ranges designated as "expected" for a given item. These expected ranges were developed by consulting published norms on the Bayley Scales of Infant Development and the Kent Scales of Infant Development. The HUNS researchers are also developing ranges based on other data collected in the study. Responses are scored as: "earlier than expected" (i.e., an age was given which is younger than published norms); "expected" (within the range of published norms); or, "later than expected" (an age which is older than published norms). For the purposes of the HUNS analyses, expected responses were recorded as "realistic" and earlier and later than expected responses were recorded as "unrealistic." Other researchers may wish to maintain all three categories of recorded responses along some other continuum.

The following summary of results from the original use of the scale is illustrative of how the instrument can be used for research purposes.

Results from the Howard University Normative Study

The following results are based on data from a longitudinal study of 80 Black healthy full-term infants (Rosser & Randolph, 1991). The specific aims of the study were to understand the influence of infant biomedical characteristics on neonatal behavior, to describe the behavioral repertoire of a normative sample of Black neonates, and to examine the relationship between specific maternal characteristics, infant characteristics, and environmental/cultural characteristics and later cognitive motivational behaviors. To achieve these aims the HUNS proposed to follow 100 Black mother-infant pairs, 60 full-term and 40 prematurely born infants. Data were gathered from two days after birth and periodically thereafter through age three.

The following data are based on interviews with the mothers of 80 full-terms, using the Developmental Milestones Expectations Scale at two days after birth in the hospital. A description of the sample, and other measures and procedures used can be found in Rosser and Randolph (1991).

Table 1 reports the mean age at which mothers reported they expected infants to master various motor, cognitive, social, and self-help activities, for each of which is also included percentage of mothers who were realistic in their reports. Most mothers were realistic about ages at which they expected their child to smile (94%), learn numbers (75.6%), sit up alone (75.3%), and at which to send their child to nursery or preschool (72.7%). Few mothers were realistic about ages they expected babbling (7%), finger sucking (12.7%), imitating acts (20%), and weaning from the breast or bottle (23.7%). Mothers were more realistic about the ages they expected motor items (crawling, sitting up alone, taking steps alone) than they were about ages for cognitive milestones (babbling, speaking two-word sentences, learning ABCs and colors ($t(df) = 4.64$ (78), $p < .0001$).

Lower-SES mothers weaned earlier than expected (χ^2 (2) = 5.85, $p < .05$). Sex-of-infant differences appeared in mothers of males who expected holding-a-spoon-to-feed to happen later (61%), while mothers of girls were largely realistic (52%), or expected this to happen early (30%) ($\chi^2(2) = 6.06$, $p < .05$); mothers of girls expected it realistically (71%) (χ^2 (2) = 5.93, $p < .05$). These two findings suggest that mothers may expect the emergence of self-help skills to develop earlier among girls than boys.

These results were also used in examining the results of behavioral assessments of the infants which were taken at the same point in time to determine ways in which maternal childrearing perceptions influence patterns of development. The Developmental Milestones Expectations data allowed us to attribute specific neonatal behavior to environmental influences and cultural expectations rather than to genotypic influences.

Discussion and Conclusion

To understand the meaning of these findings in the general context of infant development, Sameroff's (1983) transactional model of development is considered in this discussion. Some data from the present study lend support to the notion of the infant as a dynamic interacter–a person who influences and is also influenced by the caregiving environment. In particular, support for this notion was found in the data for motor performance on the neonatal behavioral assessment scale used in this study and the mothers' expectations for motor development (Rosser & Randolph, 1991). As suggested by Lester and Brazelton (1981), the motor excitement of infants may elicit intense social handling from their caregivers which in turn promotes accelerated developmental advance in motoric skills. Mothers' early expectations for mastery of motoric milestones (as found in the HUNS) could be influenced by their experience with infants and cultural expectations for this observed motor excitement. In these ways, infants are both influencing and being influenced by the caregiving environment.

One major overall finding of the HUNS runs counter to previously established notions about Black infants and their relationships with their mothers. This finding concerns the few differences in SES found for maternal expectations. Previous research had suggested that low-income mothers would hold less realistic expectations for development (Frank & Barrett, 1980) and more inaccurate perceptions of their infants (Field, 1981) than middle-income mothers. We found only that lower SES mothers were more likely than middle SES mothers to expect weaning to occur earlier than published norms. These findings suggest that previous research which usually compared low income Black samples to middle income White samples confounds environment

Table 1. Developmental Milestones Expectations Scale: Mean Age Expected and Percentage of Mothers Having Realistic Expectations (_N_ = 80)

Milestones:

At what age would you expect child to:	Age expected (in months)		Percentage of mothers having realistic responses
	M	SD	
1. Smile	.42	1.15 ·	97.4
2. Be discouraged from finger sucking	13.21	17.10	12.7
3. Be weaned	8.00	8.83	23.7
Motor Skills			
4. Crawl	6.47	6.42	61.0
5. Sit up alone	6.51	1.99	75.3
6. Pull up using furniture	8.13	1.73	57.1
7. Step alone	10.28	1.82	43.4
8. Hold own bottle	5.49	2.60	51.1
9. Pull a toy behind	12.13	5.64	57.8
10. Hold a spoon to feed	18.64	10.10	40.0
11. Stack two blocks	13.71	6.87	35.6
12. Roll from stomach to back	3.77	4.22	46.7
13. Switch objects from hand to hand	8.60	4.22	46.7
Cognitive Skills			
14. Speak two-word sentences	13.09	4.53	31.2
15. Try to learn ABCs	18.00	9.34	39.0
16. Try to learn numbers	20.62	10.07	75.6
17. Babble	5.26	2.92	7.0
18. Imitate acts seen	18.33	12.52	20.0
19. Look for a toy dropped out of sight	12.36	9.31	28.8
20. Go to nursery or preschool	34.00	12.40	72.7
21. Try to learn color names	22.93	10.75	53.3
22. Point to common names	15.76	6.26	62.2
23. Point to parts of face named	20.44	8.59	53.3

effects. These preliminary findings with the Developmental Milestones Expectations Scale are expected to provide information useful to researchers who wish to further study maternal perceptions and infant development within a specific cultural context. Future research might explore the extent to which mother's and father's expectations coincide; mother's or father's expectations compare to actual milestone mastery; and development of normative expectations based on Black infant's development rather than published norms.

Note

1. Development of this instrument was supported in part by Grant MCJ-110461 awarded to the second author by the Division of Maternal and Child Health, Bureau of Health Care Delivery Assistance, Health Resources and Services Ad-

ministration, Public Health Service, Department of Health and Human Services; by a fellowship from the Rockefeller Foundation Research Program for Minority Group Scholars to the first author; and, by the Department of Pediatrics and Child Health, College of Medicine, Howard University.

References

Bayley, N. (1969). *The Bayley scales of infant development. New* York: Psychological Corp.

Field, T. (1980). Early development of infants born to teenage mothers. In K. Scott, T. Filed, & E. Robertson (Eds.), *Teenage parents and their offspring.* New York: Grune & Stratton.

Frank, D. A., & Barrett, D. E. (1980). Mothers' expectations of developmental milestones. *Pediatric Research, 15,* 448.

Lester, B. M., & Brazelton, T. B. (1981). Cross-cultural assessment of neonatal behavior. In H. Stevenson & D. Wagner (Eds.), *Cultural perspectives on child development.* San Francisco: W. H. Freeman.

Rosser, P. L., & Randolph, S. M. (1991). Black American infants: The Howard University normative study. In K. Nugent, B. Lester, & T. B. Brazelton (Eds.), *The cultural context of infancy.* Norwood, NJ: Ablex Publishing.

Sameroff A. J. (1983). Systems of development: Contexts and evolution. In W. Kessen (Ed.), *History, theories, and methods.* In P. H. Mussen (Ed.), *Handbook of child psychology* (Vol 4). New York: Wiley.

Appendix

Developmental Milestones Expectations Scale

Instructions: "I am going to ask you some questions concerning at what age do you think a child should do certain things. After I ask you, tell me how old (in days, weeks, months, and/or years) you think a child should be in order to do these things."

Parent's Response	Item
_____	1. At what age do you think a child should first smile?
_____	2. At what age should a child be able to crawl?
_____	3. At what age do you think a child should be able to first sit alone without support?
_____	4. At what age do you think a child should be able to pull himself up by using furniture?
_____	5. At what age do you think a child should be able to take his/her first steps without your help?
_____	6. At what age do you think a child should be able to speak in two-word sentences or phrases?
_____	7. At what age do you think a child knows you from everyone else?
_____	8. At what age do you think a child can try to learn ABC's?
_____	9. At what age do you think a child starts teething?
_____	10. At what age would you consider leaving your child all day with a babysitter?
_____	11. At what age should a child be discouraged from sucking his/her fingers?
_____	12. At what age do you think a child can try to learn numbers?
_____	13. At what age do you think a child becomes shy with strangers?
_____	14. At what age should a child be able to help dress him/herself?
_____	15. At what age should a child be able to cross the street alone?
_____	16. At what age should a child be able to start feeding him/herself?
_____	17. At what age should a child stop putting everything in the mouth?
_____	18. At what age should a child be able to sleep all night long?

Parent's Response	Item

19. At what age should a child begin to babble or jabber?
20. At what age should a child be able to hold his/her own bottle?
21. At what age would you consider buying a toy that a child can pull behind him/herself?
22. At what age do you think you will be able to tell differences in crying (e.g., hunger vs. anger)?
23. At what age do you think a child should be able to fix his/her own breakfast?
24. At what age do you think a child should be able to hold a spoon to feed him/herself?
25. At what age should a child be able to stack two blocks (one on top of the other)?
26. At what age should a child be able to wash his/her face and brush his/her teeth alone?
27. At what age should a parent not leave a child for fear that the baby will roll from stomach to back?
28. At what age should a child be able to pick up things with the index finger and thumb?
29. At what age should a child begin to realize his/her sex/gender?
30. At what age should a child be able to switch an item from one hand to another?
31. At what age do you think a child should start doing things to please you (e.g., make you smile, clap)?
32. At what age do you think a child will want to play with other children in a group?
33. At what age do you think a child should be able to imitate things he/she sees?

34. At what age do you think a child will look for a toy that is dropped out of sight?
35. At what age do you think a child should be able to play games like peek-a-boo?
36. At what age do you think a child should start eating meals with the rest of the family?
37. At what age do you think a child should be able to understand when he/she is doing something wrong?
38. At what age would you consider sending your child to a preschool or nursery school?
39. At what age should a child be weaned from the bottle/breast?
40. At what age do you think a child should show a hand preference?
41. At what age do you think a child can try to learn colors?
42. At what age do you think you can start potty-training?
43. At what age do you think a child should be able to point to common objects around the house?
44. At what age do you think a child should be able to walk downstairs while holding on?
45. At what age do you think a child should be able to learn to say "please" and "thank you" in a meaningful way?
46. At what age should a parent be able to go back to work?
47. At what age do you think a child should be able to point to parts of his/her face as you name them?
48. At what age do you think a child should be able to wave bye-bye upon request?

For additional information, contact:
Suzanne M. Randolph, Ph.D.
University of Maryland
Family Studies
College Park, MD 20742
Telephone: (301) 405-4012
Fax: (301) 314-9161
E-mail: SR22@UMAIL.UMD.EDU

Afrikan-American Normative Data for the Revised Denver Developmental Screening Test

NeferkaRe D. Stewart, Jeanne M. Plas, David L. Terrell, and Kathleen Hoover-Dempsey

Abstract

Afrikan-American normative data for the Revised Denver Developmental Screening Test (RDDST) were drawn from a sample of 250 infants, two years of age and younger. Comparisons were made between these data and the published Denver norms. In many cases, the Black infants achieved competence on developmental items at an earlier age than did the RDDST sample. Results are discussed in terms of the implications for detection of developmental delays within the Afrikan-American infant population.

The early detection of developmental delays or health problems in children is an extremely difficult and important task. The earlier a developmental or health problem can be detected, the more success can be anticipated from corrective procedures. Screening instruments such as the Revised Denver Developmental Screening Tests (RDDST) have been designed to aid psychologists, pediatricians, and other health care providers in detecting developmental delays. The RDDST is designed to identify children between the ages of two weeks and six years "who have a high probability of being developmentally impaired" (W. Frandenburg, personal communication, 1980; Dodds & Fendel, 1975). This instrument has been used as a screening measure with children who are asymptomatic, and also has been used to monitor children who are thought to

be at high risk for developmental problems, such as those born prematurely or of low birth weight. At present, this early developmental measure is one of the most widely used screening instruments in the United States.

The RDDST was standardized on 1,036 normal Denver children of both sexes between the ages of 2 weeks and 6.4 years. Children who had experienced prenatal or delivery problems were excluded, as were adopted, premature, or seriously handicapped children. The ethnic distribution included 82% European Americans, 11% Mexican-Americans (Spanish surnamed), and 7% Afrikan-American children. According to the RDDST manual (1975), the standardization sample was reflective of the ethnic and occupational characteristics of the Denver population as described by 1960 census data. However, Werner

39

(1972b) refers to an unpublished study by Frankenburg that led her to assert that "the norm group contained a significantly higher population of White children and of children whose fathers are in the professional, managerial, or sales occupation, than the census distribution would warrant" (p. 735). In a review of the RDDST, Moriarty (1972) noted that:

> In our clinical use of the DDST, we have had some reason to question the circumscribed geographical selection of the sample and the applicability of norms in screening children from the lower socioeconomic groups, especially in language areas. Furthermore, even if the standardization sample is truly representative of the Denver population, we cannot automatically assume that the established norms are appropriate for assessment of individual minority group children outside the population in the Denver area (p. 733).

Since only 7% of the standardization sample consisted of Afrikan-American children, the assessment value of the instrument when used with the Black American population is not known clearly, especially since research has revealed that Afrikan-American infants exhibit a developmental style which differs from that observed in their European and European American counterparts (Ainsworth, 1967; Bayley, 1965; Brazelton, Koslowski, & Tronick, 1971; Curti, Marshall, & Steggerd, 1935; Freedman, 1974; Geber & Dean, 1957,1958; Goldberg, 1972; Grantham-McGregor & Back, 1971; Hayes & Percy, 1975; Hindley, 1960; Kilbride, 1970; King & Seegmiller, 1973; Knobloch & Pasamanick, 1953; Leiderman, Babu, Kagia, Kroemer, & Leiderman, 1973; Lusk & Lewis, 1972; Morgan, 1976; North & MacDonald, 1977; Scott, Ferguson, Jenkins, & Culter, 1955; Stewart, 1980; Thomas, 1979; Walters, 1967; Werner, 1972a, 1979; Williams & Scott, 1953). The Black American developmental style has been observed to incorporate greater neuromuscular and sensory maturation during early infancy. It also has been noted that Afrikan and Afrikan-American children appear to decline in

development relative to White populations after ages two and three (Williams & Scott, 1953). In connection with this phenomenon it is useful to note that infant intelligence tests and the later tests of intelligence are distinctly different in their measurement emphasis. Infant tests focus on the assessment of social development, neuromuscular and sensory maturation, and the initial communication style exhibited by the child, whereas later intelligence tests often emphasize the assessment of cultural experiences, belief systems, and the cognitive, behavioral, and linguistic style of middle-class European Americans (Hilliard, 1976; Kamin, 1974).

America's Black children participate in a cultural, cognitive, behavioral, and linguistic system that is influenced by an Afrikan world-view (Dixon, 1976; Hilliard, 1976; Nobles, 1976, 1977). They also experience an ecological setting and an economic reality which differ from that of middle-class European Americans. Therefore, it is not surprising that these children, who develop differently from the European American way of being, exhibit poor performance on tests based on European American samples. As the focus of developmental instruments changes from infancy to later childhood, with tests gradually becoming more culturally influenced, Afrikan-American children move from being assessed as having advanced abilities to being labeled as "retarded" individuals. Wilson (1978) suggested that the "infant intelligence scales that are relatively unaffected by sex, birth order, parental education level, and geographical residence may be more reliable than the more culturally-biased IQ tests of late childhood and adulthood" (p. 49). Thus, it can be hypothesized that the physiological and intellectual development of Afrikan and Afrikan-American children does not decline with age, but rather that changes in instrumentation focus and design may be a major contributor to the variance.

Since the primary purpose of the RDDST is the earliest possible detection of developmental abnormalities, it is essential that the normative data employed be applicable to the children with whom the instrument is used. The very low representation of Afrikan-American children within the standardization sample of the RDDST raises serious questions as to whether the present RDDST norms are adequate for the developmental assessment needs of this population.

It is imperative that child psychologists, pediatricians, and other child care professionals be able to conceptualize what can be viewed as normal growth patterns for Afrikan-American children. Such knowledge would provide for more accurate identification of those children who are at high risk for developmental problems. At present, if a Black child performs in the normal range of infant development on a test that has been standardized on a European American sample, it cannot be said with confidence that no developmental problems exist. That is, if Afrikan-American children are typically more prepared neurologically at birth than their European American counterparts, then scoring in the normal range on a scale normed for interpretation of the performances of European American infants may suggest some type of delay in the Afrikan-American child. Currently, Black infant developmental delays may pass unnoticed, creating opportunities for the unattended development of serious and possibly uncorrectable problems. Such a situation could be physiologically, psychologically, and educationally damaging to these children.

The study presented here was designed to assess the performances of Black American infants on the RDDST in order to provide information regarding the usefulness of the current RDDST norms for the Afrikan-American infant population. Thus, the study focused on construction of Afrikan-American normative data and the comparison of those data with current RDDST norms.

Methodology

Sample and Setting

The sample was drawn from the Well-Baby Clinic of the Meharry Medical College Comprehensive Health Center, Nashville, Tennessee. The Children and Youth Department of Meharry operates a Well-Baby Clinic which conducts a comprehensive examination of all its children and continues to follow their development until 18 years of age. The sample consisted of 250 Black infants who were tested by a trained and experienced pediatric psychologist from 1975 through 1980. The sample ranged in age from 2 to 24 months with a mean number of 11 infants per 2-month age interval; the sample included 131 female and 119 male infants.

Analysis of socioecological information revealed that 37% of the sample were children of blue-collar workers, and 30% were children of professionals (including students in professional or graduate schools such as medicine, dentistry, law, and social science). The remaining 33% of the families received public assistance as their primary source of income. The data further revealed that 23% of the mothers had completed one or more years of college, 53% had completed high school, 19% had completed 9-11 years of public education, and 5% had obtained less than a 9th grade education. Twenty-six percent (26%) of the children were from single parent families (female head of household); therefore, information concerning these fathers was unavailable for analysis. Within the two parent families, 26% of the fathers had completed one or more years of college, 30% had completed high school, and 18% had completed 9-11 years of public education. Additional analyses revealed that the mean family size was three, while the average household size was found to be five; 59% of the mothers were homemakers. It should be noted that the families of children in the sample appeared to be fairly reflective of the different SES groups in which Afrikan-American families participate in America. Therefore, the sample group may be considered socioecologically representative of Black Americans. The infants were tested in a hospital setting where staff and clientele were predominantly Black. This setting provided the infants and parents with the type of comfort and security that is associated with racial and cultural familiarity. Thus, the person-environment situation approximated that used in the Denver study that employed a predominantly Caucasian setting for the administration of the instrument to the predominantly European American sample.

Procedure

The following data were collected from infant medical records: age at time of RDDST administration; all test items passed and failed; the size of the child's family; the size of the household; mother's and father's highest attained formal educational level; and the occupation of parents.

Research Questions and Analysis Strategy

The study had two research foci. The first emphasized the development of RDDST norms derived from a group of Black American infants two years of age and below. Following the lead of Frankenburg (Personal Communication), the age at which 25%, 50%, 75%, and 90% of the children passed each item was determined. This method of statistical computation was used in the development of the RDDST norms derived from the Denver sample.

The second issue concerned comparison of norms derived from the Meharry sample with the published Denver norms. The analysis strategy applied to this issue involved comparison of the distributions of the percentages passing at each successive age level. Frankenburg and Dodds (1967) reported that developmental differences of one month or more in performance of a test item during the first year of life, and two months or more during the second year of life at the 50% and 90% passing points should be viewed as noteworthy or cause for possible concern. Therefore, developmental differences of one month (2-12 months age range) and two months (12-24 months age range) in test item performance at the 50% or 90% passing points were used as the standards of comparison for the two sets of normative data.

Results

The following presentation of results is divided into two sections; the first presents the RDDST developmental norms derived from the Meharry sample, while the second focuses on comparison of these norms with the published norms drawn from the Denver sample.

RDDST Normative Data Derived from the Meharry Sample

Analysis of the performance of the Meharry infant sample on the RDDST was conducted for the Personal-Social sector, items 1-19; the Fine-Motor Adaptive sector, items 1-22; the language sector, items 1-13; and the Gross-Motor sector, items 1-24. These items constitute the 78 items (of 105) that are applicable to the age groups involved in the study. The developmental performance norms on each sector of the RDDST can be viewed in Tables 1 through 4.

In a few cases clustering at the very young infant ages, data were unavailable for construction of normative information.

Comparison of the Meharry and Denver Samples

Since Frankenburg and his colleagues have indicated that developmental differences of one month or more in performance of a test item during the first year of life at the 50% level and 90% passing points should be viewed as clinically noteworthy, as well as differences of two months or more during the second year of life at these same passing points, the study employed these criteria as standards for comparison of the Meharry and Denver samples.

Tables 1 through 4 also present norms from the Denver sample; data at the extreme left and right of the tables represent differences between the samples.

Comparison between the Meharry and Denver groups across the 78 applicable RDDST items revealed developmental differences of one month (2-12 mos. range) or two months (12-24 mos. range) on 31 of the items at the 50% passing point. The Meharry sample attained competence on 30 of these items at an earlier chronological age while the Denver sample attained competence earlier on one of the items. At the 90% passing point, 56 of the 78 items were passed at an earlier age by the Meharry sample. Earlier competence at this passing point was not attained by the Denver sample on any item. Only a few of the non-noteworthy comparisons (<1 or 2 mos. difference) favored the Denver group.

Table 1. Comparison of the Meharry Sample DDST Norms and the Published DDST Norms Derived from the Denver Sample–Personal-Social Sector

Meharry							Denver				
Grp. Diffs. 50%	25%	50%	75%	90%	100%	Item	25%	50%	75%	90%	Grp. Diffs. 90%
					2.0mo	Regards face			1.0		
					2.0	Smiles responsively		1.5	1.9		
				2.0		Smiles spontaneously	1.4	1.9	3.0	5.0	3.0*
1.3*	7.0	8.2	9.3	9.8		Initially shy with strangers	5.5	9.5	9.8	10.0	0.2
0.6	4.3	4.7	6.1	6.9		Feeds self cracker	4.7	5.3	6.2	8.0	1.1*
1.4*	3.6	4.0	5.6	6.2		Resists toy pull	4.1	5.4	6.5	10.0	3.8*
0.8	5.3	6.5	7.5	9.3		Plays peek-a-boo		5.7	7.3	9.7	0.4*
1.1*	4.3	4.7	5.4	6.3		Works for toy out of reach	4.9	5.8	7.0	9.0	2.7*
0.1	8.5	9.0	9.8	11.0		Plays pat-a-cake	7.0	9.1	9.8	13.0	2.0*
0.9	9.8	10.7	22.9	13.7		Plays ball with examiner	9.7	22.6	13.5	16.0	2.3*
1.7*	10.0	10.5	11.8	12.3		Indicates wants (not crying)	10.4	12.2	13.4	14.3	2.0*
0.2	10.5	11.5	12.4	13.0		Drinks from cup	10.0	11.7	14.4	16.5	3.5*
2.8*	10.4	11.0	12.1	13.0		Imitates housework	12.5	13.8	16.3	19.5	6.5*
1.8	11.6	12.6	14.0	15.5		Uses spoon, spilling little	13.2	14.4	18.0	23.5	8.0*
3.3**	14.8	16.0	16.9	17.8		Helps in house–simple tasks	14.8	19.3	21.8	23.5	5.7**
1.0	13.0	14.8	16.8	18.3		Removes garment	13.7	15.8	19.2	21.9	3.6**
0.1	20.8	22.4	23.5	24.0		Puts on clothes	20.1	22.3	2.6+	3.0+	12.0**
1.2	20.6	21.8	23.5	24.0		Washes and dries hands	19.0	23.0	2.5+	3.2+	14.0**
2.1**	20.8	21.9	23.6	24.0		Plays interactive games e.g., tag	20.0	2.0+	3.0+	3.3+	15.0**

* 1 or more months difference, ages 2-12 months, favoring Meharry sample; **2 or more months difference, ages 12-24 months, favoring Meharry sample; + indicates years.

Given the one and two month difference criteria at the younger and older ages, comparison across the 19 Personal-Social items revealed developmental differences on 8 items at the 50% passing point and 16 items at the 90% passing point. In all cases, the Meharry sample reached competence earlier. Within the Fine-Motor sector, Meharry children achieved competence earlier on 5 of the 22 items at the 50% passing point and 11 of the items at the 90% passing point; the Denver sample reached competence earlier on one item at the 50% passing point.

All developmental differences (1 or 2 mos.) on the Language and Gross-Motor items favored the Meharry sample. There were differential performances on 4 of the 13 Language items at the

Table 2. Comparison of the Meharry Sample DDST Norms and the Published DDST Norms Derived from the Denver Sample–Fine Motor-Adaptive Sector

Meharry							Denver				
Grp. Diffs. 50%	25%	50%	75%	90%	100%	Item	25%	50%	75%	90%	Grp. Diffs. 90%
					2.0mo	Follows to midline			0.7	1.3	
					2.0	Symmetrical movements			1.0		
					2.0	Follows past midline		1.3	1.9	2.5	
0.9	2.0	3.3	3.5			Follows 180°	1.8	2.4	3.2	4.0	
			2.0	3.0		Hands together	1.3	2.2	3.0	3.7	0.7
1.3		2.0	3.0	3.5		Grasps rattle	2.3	3.3	3.9	4.2	0.7
0.7	2.3	2.6	3.1	4.4		Regards raisin	2.4	3.3	4.2	5.0	0.6
0.8	2.4	2.8	4.2	4.5		Reaches for object	2.9	3.6	4.5	5.0	0.5
1.5*	3.5	4.1	5.3	5.7		Sit, look for yarn	4.8	5.6	6.9	7.5	1.8*
1.0*	4.6	5.1	6.3	6.8		Sits, takes 2 cubes	5.1	6.1	7.0	7.5	0.7
0.1	5.2	5.5	5.3	6.0		Rakes raisin, attains	5.0	5.6	6.2	7.8	1.8*
0.5	4.5	5.1	6.3	6.3		Transfers cube hand-to-hand	4.7	5.6	6.6	7.5	1.2*
9.5	7.3	8.0	9.1	9.7		Bangs 2 cubes held in hand	7.0	8.4	9.8	12.3	2.6*
1.2*	6.6	7.1	8.3	9.8		Thumb-finger grasp	7.1	8.3	9.1	10.6	1.8*
1.2*	9.1	9.5	11.0	12.0		Neat pincer grasp of raisin	9.4	10.7	12.3	14.7	2.7*
0.5	11.9	12.8	13.6	14.5		Scribbles spontaneously	11.9	13.3	15.8	2.1+	10.5**
1.5	11.8	12.6	13.4	13.9		Tower of 2 cubes	12.1	14.1	17.0	20.0	6.1**
2.7**	15.5	17.5	20.4	22.0		Dumps raisin from bottle-spontaneously	13.7	14.8	2.1+	3.0+	14.0**
0.6	13.0	14.0	15.0	15.7		Dumps raisin from bottle-demonstr.	12.7	13.4	16.4	2.0+	8.3**
1.2	15.7	16.6	18.0	19.0		Tower of 4 cubes	15.5	17.9	20.5	2.2+	7.0**
						Imitates vertical line within 30°	18.4	21.7	2.2+	3.0+	
0.2	23.0	24.0				Tower of 8 cubes	21.0	23.8	2.4+	3.4+	

* 1 or more months difference, ages 2-12 months, favoring Meharry sample; **2 or more months difference, ages 12-24 months, favoring Meharry sample; +indicates years.

50% passing point and on 9 of these items at the 90% point. Differences at the 50% passing point were observed on 14 of the 24 Gross-Motor items while differential performances were found on 20 of these items at the 90% point.

Discussion

The Afrikan-American sample performed the majority of RDDST items at an earlier age than the Denver sample. Developmental differ-

Table 3. Comparison of the Meharry Sample DDST Norms and the Published DDST Norm Derived from the Denver Sample–Language Sector (Age when given percent of population pass items)

Meharry						Item	Denver				
Grp. Diffs. 50%	25%	50%	75%	90%	100%		25%	50%	75%	90%	Grp. Diffs. 90%
					2.0mo	Responds to bell				1.6	
					2.0	Vocalizes–not crying			1.3	1.8	
			2.0			Laughs	1.4	2.0	2.6	3.3	
		2.0	3.4			Squeals	1.5	2.2	3.0	4.5	1.1
0.7	5.5	6.2	6.9	7.6		dada or mama, non-specific		5.6	6.9	8.7	10.0
2.4*	1.9		3.7	4.0	5.0	Turns to voice	3.8	5.6	7.3	8.3	3.3*
1.1	5.5	5.9	7.6	9.0		Imitate speech sounds	5.7	7.0	9.2	11.2	2.2*
0.9	9.0	9.2	10.9	11.6		dada or mama, specific	9.2	10.1	11.9	13.3	1.7*
0.3	11.6	12.5	12.9	14.8		Three words other than mama, dada	11.8	12.8	15.0	20.5	5.7**
2.3**	16.0	17.3	18.1	19.7		Combines 2 different words	14.0	19.6	22.0	2.3+	7.3**
0.5	14.9	16.5	17.9	19.0		Points to 1 named body part	14.0	17.0	21.0	23.0	4.0**
1.6	17.2	21.9	24.0			Names 1 picture	15.9	20.3	2.1+	2.5+	
2.5**	15.8	17.3	18.7	20.4		Follows 2 of 3 directions	14.8	19.8	22.0	2.7+	11.4**

* 1 or more months difference, ages 2-12 months, favoring Meharry sample; ** 2 or more months difference, ages 12-24 months, favoring Meharry sample; + indicates years.

ences ranged from 1 to 15 months with the largest differences appearing at the 90% passing point of comparison. One item at the 50% passing point, on the Fine-Motor sector, favored the Denver sample; all other noteworthy comparisons favored the Meharry group.

The performance results from the Language sector are of particular interest since there has been some concern over the language development and verbal abilities of Afrikan-American preschoolers (Frankenburg, et al., 1975; Sandler, Ratner, & Van Campen, 1970). The results of this study suggest that Afrikan-American infants not only develop adequate initial verbal skills, but that they display such skills at an earlier age than was reported for the Denver sample. Competence at these verbal behaviors could suggest that the Afrikan-American infant is prepared earlier to begin initial language development behaviors. The presence of an Afrikan-American examiner, coupled with a predominantly Black setting, may have facilitated the expressive abilities of these infants. Geber (1958) and Ainsworth (1967) also have reported precocious language development among their Afrikan samples when compared to European infants.

Results relative to the Fine-Motor and Gross-Motor sectors provide support for similar

Table 4. Comparison of the Meharry Sample DDST Norm and the Published DDST Norms Derived from the Denver Sample–Gross-Motor Sector (Age when percent of population pass items)

Meharry							Denver				
Grp. Diffs. 50%	25%	50%	75%	90%	100%	Item	25%	50%	75%	90%	Grp. Diffs. 90%
					2.0mo	Prone, lifts head				0.7mo	
					2.0	Prone, head up 45			1.9	2.6	
				2.0		Prone, head up 90	1.3	2.2	2.6	3.2	1.2
0.4	2.2	2.6	2.9	3.9		Prone, chest arm support	2.0	3.0	3.5	5.3	0.4
			2.5	3.0		Sits with head steady	1.5	2.9	3.6	4.2	1.2*
0.1		2.7	3.3	3.5		Rolls over	2.3	2.8	3.8	4.7	1.2*
1.4	2.5	2.8	4.3	4.6		Bears some weight on legs	3.0	4.2	6.2	7.7	3.1*
0.6	3.3	3.6	3.9	4.5		Pull to sit, no head lag	3.4	5.2	6.0	6.3	1.8*
2.0*	4.3	3.5	4.9	5.5		Sits without support	5.8	5.5	6.5	7.8	2.3*
0.2	5.3	5.6	6.2	7.5		Stands holding on	5.0	5.8	8.5	10.0	2.5*
1.2*	5.5	6.4	6.8	7.5		Pulls self to stand	6.0	7.6	9.5	10.0	2.5*
1.4*	5.5	6.2	7.4	7.9		Gets to setting	6.1	7.6	9.3	11.0	3.1*
1.8*	7.5	8.0	9.3	10.0		Stands momentarily	0.1	9.8	12.1	13.0	3.0*
1.2*	6.8	8.0	8.6	8.9		Walks holding onto furniture	7.3	9.2	10.2	12.7	3.8*
2.7*	7.7	8.8	9.7	10.4		Stands alone well	9.8	11.5	13.2	13.9	3.5*
1.6*	8.7	10.0	10.9	11.5		Stoops and recovers	10.4	11.6	13.2	14.3	2.8*
1.5*	9.9	10.6	11.4	12.0		Walks well	11.3	12.1	13.5	14.3	2.3**
1.3	12.3	12.8	13.8	15.0		Walks backwards	12.4	14.3	18.2	21.0	6.0**
2.0**	13.7	15.0	16.2	17.6		Walks up steps	14.0	17.0	21.0	22.0	4.4**
3.9**	14.8	16.1	17.6	19.0		Kicks ball forward	15.0	20.0	22.3	2.0+	5.0**
2.4**	15.7	17.4	19.4	20.3		Throws ball overhand	14.9	19.8	22.8	2.6+	9.7**
6.5**	21.5	22.5	23.4	24.0		Balance on 1 foot 1 sec.	21.7	2.5+	3.0+	3.2+	14.0**
0.3	21.4	22.0	23.3	24.0		Jumps in place	20.5	22.2	2.5+	3.0+	12.0**
0.2	22.5	23.7				Pedals trike	21.0	23.0	2.8+	3.0+	

* 1 or more months difference, ages 2-12 months, favoring Meharry sample; **2 or more months difference, ages 12-24 months, favoring Meharry sample; +indicates years

findings regarding the precocious neuromuscular development of Black infants when compared to European and European American samples. Comparison results on Personal-Social items suggest that Afrikan-American infants may become more personally self-sufficient at an earlier age than their European American counterparts.

The Meharry sample not only achieved competence on RDDST items at an earlier age, but also seemed to learn some tasks at a faster rate. The 10th and 13th language items represent examples of this phenomenon. There was a 2.3 month difference observed at the 50% passing point between the two samples on item 10 (combines two different words); the developmental difference increased to 7.3 months at the 90% point on this item. On item 13 (follows two or three directions), there was a 2.5 month difference at the 50% passing point while a 10.6 month difference was observed on the same item at the 90% passing point. Such results suggest that in some cases the Meharry sample was able to learn or perform the task under observation at a much faster rate than the Denver sample. This developmental pattern was evident across all sectors of the test.

The marked differences in the ages at which 50% and 90% of the children in the Meharry and Denver samples performed RDDST items should affect the interpretation of results of Black infant testing; the assessment value of the instrument when used with these children must be considered minimal unless normative data for Afrikan-American infants are used. The application of norms from the Denver sample to young Black children may result in under-referral of those Afrikan-American infants who may be at high risk for developmental problems. Therefore, caution is suggested in applying the RDDST as a screening device for developmentally delayed infants when testing Black children similar to the Meharry group. These results also may suggest possibly inherent limitations of the RDDST for assessment of the developmental status of infants outside the Denver area.

Limitations and Conclusion

The study's relatively small sample size ($N = 250$) prohibits broad generalization of results. The sample size precluded the presentation of data at several age levels, most notably at the youngest points. The use of test results derived by a single examiner also presents some design concerns. However, confidence in scoring is augmented by the fact that the examiner was well-trained, highly experienced, and unaware over the years of testing that results would be used for purposes other than charting the progress of individual children.

Interpretation of results of the study also must be limited somewhat by the single geographical location used. As is the case with the Denver study,

great confidence cannot be placed in the applicability of results across all American settings. Generalizability of comparison data is constrained to a degree by articulation of Afrikan-American RDDST performances from 1975 through 1980 with Denver sample performances assessed prior to that time. It could be that achievement of competence on RDDST items is occurring at an earlier age for all populations; just as norms on later intelligence tests have shifted upwards in recent years, norms for competence on early developmental tasks may be shifting in the same direction.

Generalizability of results also is limited clearly to Afrikan-American infants two years of age and younger. The performance patterns of older Afrikan-American children on the RDDST are at present unknown.

Despite the limitations just addressed, data from this study strongly suggest that published RDDST norms may be grossly inappropriate for use with Afrikan-American children who may achieve competence on initial developmental tasks at an earlier age than European American children. The developmental screening of such children must be undertaken with reference to a set of norms valid for this group if delays are to be observed and responded to clinically.

If Afrikan-American children exhibit a different developmental pattern than their European American counterparts, including earlier and more rapid rates of development during the first two years of life, scoring in the normal range on a scale designed to measure the expected performances of European American infants may suggest some type of delay in the Afrikan-American infant. The results of this study offer support for concern relative to this hypothesis. Further investigation of this issue is called for; at present, published RDDST norms should be used only with extreme caution when assessing Afrikan infants in the United States.

References

Ainsworth, M. D. S. (1967). *Infancy in Uganda: Infant care and the growth of love*. Baltimore: The John Hopkins Press.

Bayley, N. (1965). Comparisons of mental and motor tests scores for ages 1-15 months by sex, birth order, race, geographical location, and education of parents. *Child Development, 36,* 379-411.

Brazelton, T., Koslowski, B., & Tronick, E. (1971). Neonatal behavior among urban Zambians and Americans. *Journal of Child Psychiatry, 15,* 97-107.

Curti, M., Marshall, F. B., & Steggerd, M. (1935). The Gesell schedules applied to one, two, and three year old Negro children of Jamaica. *Journal of Comparative Psychology, 20,* 125-126.

Dixon, J. V. (1976). World views and research methodology. In K. Lewis & V. Dixon (Eds.), *African philosophy: Assumptions and paradigms for research on Black persons.* Los Angeles: Fanon Center Publications.

Frankenburg, W., & Dodds, J. B. (1967). The Denver Developmental Screening Test. *Journal of Pediatrics, 71,* 181-191.

Frankenburg, W., Dodds, J. B., & Fendel, A. (1975). *Denver Developmental Screening Test reference manual* (rev. ed.). Boulder, CO: University of Colorado Press.

Freedman, A. G. (1974). *Human infancy.* Hillsdale, NJ: Lawrence Erlbaum Associates.

Geber, M., & Dean, R. (1957). Gesell tests on African children. *Pediatrics, 20,* 4055.

Geber, M., & Dean, R. (1958). Psychomotor development in African children: The effects of social class and the need for improved tests. *Bulletin of the World Health Organization, 18,* 471-476.

Goldberg, S. (1972). Infant care and growth in urban Zambia. *Human Development, 15,* 17-89.

Grantham-McGregor, S., & Back, E. (1971). Gross motor development in Jamaican infants. *Developmental Medicine and Child Neurology, 13,* 79-87.

Hayes, A., & Percy, A. (1975). Suitability of the Dubowitz in assessing maturation of full-term Black infants. *Pediatrics, 9,* 259.

Hilliard, A. (1976). *Alternatives to IQ testing: An approach to the identification of gifted minority children.* (Project #75-175). Final Report. Sacramento: California State Department of Education.

Hindley, C. B. (1960). Social class influence on the development of ability in the first five years. In G. Nielson (Ed.), *Proceedings of the XIV International Congress of Applied Psychology (Vol. 3). Child and education.* London: University of London.

Kamin, L. (1974). *The science and politics of IQ.* Potomac: Lawrence Erlbaum.

Kilbride, J. E. (1970). The comparative motor development of Baganda, American White and American Black infants. *American Anthropologist, 71,* 1422-1428.

King, W., & Seegmiller, B. (1973). Performance of 14 to 22 month-old Black firstborn male infants on two tests of cognitive development. *Developmental Psychology, 8,* 317-327.

Knobloch, H., & Pasamanick, B. (1953). Further observations on the behavioral development of Negro children. *Journal of Genetic Psychology, 83,* 137-157.

Leiderman, P. H., Babu, B., Kagia, J., Kraemer, H. C., & Leiderman, G. F. (1973). African infant precocity and some social influences during the first year. *Nature, 141,* 247-249.

Lusk, D., & Lewis, M. (1972). Mother-infant interaction and infant development among the Wolof of Senegal. *Human Development, 15,* 58-69.

Moriarty, A. (1972). Review of the Denver Developmental Screening Test. In O. Buros (Ed.), *The seventh mental measurement yearbook* (Vol. 2). Highland Park: Gryphon Press.

Morgan, H. (1976). *Towards a theory of selected knowledge acquisition patterns among Black children.* Syracuse, NY: Syracuse University Press.

Nobles, W. (1976). Extended self: Rethinking the so-called Negro self-concept. *The Journal of Black Psychology, 2,* 15-24.

Nobles, W. (1977). *Changing child rearing orientations and Black child development.* San Francisco, CA: Westside Community Mental Health Center.

North, A. F., & MacDonald, H. M. (1977). Why are neonatal mortality rates lower in small Black infants than in White infants of similar birth weights? *Journal of Pediatrics, 90,* 809-819.

Sandler, L., Ratner, G., & Van Campen, J. (1970). Responses of urban preschool children to a developmental screening test. *The Journal of Pediatrics, 77,* 775.

Scott, R. B., Ferguson, A. D., Jenkins, M., & Culter, F. F. (1955). Growth in development of Negro infants: V. Neuromuscular patterns of behavior during the first year of life. *Pediatrics, 16,* 24-30.

Stewart, M. D. (1980). *Melanin and sensory-motor development during infancy.* Unpublished master's thesis, George Peabody College of Vanderbilt University, Nashville, TN.

Thomas, R. (1979). White norms skew dating of Black fetus. *Obstetrics-Gynecology News, 14.*

Walters, E. (1967). Comparative development of Negro and White infants. *Journal of Genetic Psychology, 110,* 243-251.

Werner, E. E. (1972a). Infants around the world: Cross-cultural studies of psychomotor development from birth to two years. *Journal of Cross-Cultural Psychology, 3,* 111-134.

Werner, E. E. (1972b). Review of the Denver Developmental Screening Test. In O. Buros (Ed.), *The seventh mental measurement yearbooK* (Vol. 2). Highland Park: Gryphon Press.

Werner, E. E. (1979). *Cross-cultural child development: A view from the planet earth.* Monterey, CA: Brooks-Cole.

Williams, J. R., & Scott, R. B. (1953). Growth and development of Negro infants: IV. Motor development and its relationship to child rearing practices in two groups of Negro infants. *Child Development, 24,* 103-121.

Wilson, A. N. (1978). *The developmental psychology of the Black child.* New York: United Brother Communications System.

For additional information, contact:

NeferkaRe Stewart, Ph. D.
Program Director
KhemRe Institute
Center for Health and Wellness
Counseling and Consultation Services
San Leandro, CA 94577
Telephone: (510) 568-0497

An Experimental Procedure and Scales for Assessing Attachment Relationships in African American Infants–Alternatives to Ainsworth Methods

Jacquelyne Faye Jackson

Abstract

A separation-reunion laboratory procedure and seven infant behavior rating scales for examining infant-parent attachment relationships in African American infants are presented. The scales were developed as a preliminary step in producing instruments for evaluating infant-parent relations in low, as well as middle, SES African American families. They are presented as alternatives to Ainsworth methods which were found to be inappropriate for use with middle and working class African American infants. The laboratory procedure involves an infant, two parent figures and a stranger in one session, permitting comparison of two infant-parent attachments as well as the effect of infant-parent attachment on infant responses to the stranger. Two of the seven scales, exploration and sociability, assess constructive effects of infant-parent relations that theoretically ensue from secure infant-parent attachments when an infant is in a composed affective state. Infant response to separation from a parent is assessed by a scale for distress behavior. The four scales remaining in the set of seven-proximity seeking, contact maintaining, contact resisting and inattention/avoidance-assess infant affliliative behavior toward a parent and ambivalent responses in infant-parent reunion situations, and are similar to Ainsworth methods in this respect. The need for additional research and development of the instruments is discussed, as well as prerequisites for extending the use of instruments to low SES African Americans for evaluating infant-parent relationships.

The relationships of very young African American children to their parents are increasingly the focus of public and psychologists' concern. An increasingly large percentage of African American children are born to parents who are members of "at risk" groups, such as low-income teenagers and mothers who used cocaine or other illicit drugs during pregnancy, and are also presumed to suffer inadequate parenting. This has lead to the pragmatic question of how to make culturally fair evaluative judgments about parent-child relationships in such vulnerable groups in clinical and social service circles where interventions to promote the psychosocial welfare of the child are at issue.

The procedure and scales presented in this chapter were developed as a preliminary step to devising appropriate yardsticks for assessing the affective dimension of African American infant-parent relationships. Specifically, they attempt to delineate the behavior of normal, low-risk African American infants in relation to their adult parents in a test-like situation that elicits behaviors reflecting the underlying affective quality of infant-parent relationships. The premise is that normal African American infant-parent relationships provide more appropriate yardsticks for assessing suspect African American infant-parent relationships than the frequently used and culturally alien patterns of White infant-parent relations.

The theoretical framework underlying design of the instruments is commonly utilized in clinical settings and purports to be applicable to all children. In the theory of infant-parent attachment put forth by Bowlby (1969), the function and affective quality of a sound infant-parent relationship is revealed in two situations. When the infant is with a parent and in a composed affective state, the parent functions as a secure base from which the infant explores and learns from the environment. However, when the infant is apprehensive or distressed, the parent functions as a physical refuge and source of comfort. According to Bowlby, these infant responses of venturing out from a parent when feeling secure and retreating to the parent when distressed, emerged during human evolutionary history when the parent, particularly the mother, was the facilitator of learning as well as the source of protection from environmental hazards; they emerge when infants become capable of locomotion at about

one year old and remain operationally prominent through the toddler period until infants are about three years old. Because of their evolutionary origins, these response patterns are supposed to be characteristic of all psychologically healthy human infants.

Ainsworth (Ainsworth, Blehar, Waters, & Wall, 1978) developed a structured laboratory playroom session, called the strange situation, that was designed to assess the quality of the infant-mother relationship in terms of the infant behavioral patterns detailed by Bowlby. The procedure is designed to provide the opportunity to observe infant response to mild distress brought on by several factors: the mother's departure from the room, the presence of a stranger during the mother's absence, a solitary period for the infant, and the mother's return. A two step method of evaluation of infant-mother relationships based on the procedure has subsequently been applied to infant relationships to fathers as well as mothers (e.g. Grossman, Grossman, Huber & Wartner, 1981; Main & Weston, 1981). In the first step, infant response to a returning mother, or parent figure, are rated on four ordinal scales-proximity seeking, contact maintaining, avoidance and contact resisting-that are supposed to be indices of infant defensive attachment response. Proximity seeking and contact maintaining are considered measures of uninhibited affiliative attachment responses, while avoidance and contact resisting are thought to measure apprehensive, but affectively ambivalent, attachment responses.

In the original Ainsworth system, ratings of the four behaviors are used as guides to categorize an infant in a three-type classification system without an explicitly quantitative method of linking the behavior ratings and the class assignment. Currently, a four-type classification system is employed, with type assignment based on clinical judgment primarily. On a descriptive basis, infants who actively affiliate with their parent figure when the parent figure returns to the room and/or clearly show greeting behavior are classified as securely attached. Those who appear to ignore, avoid or delay acknowledging their returning parent figure are classified insecure avoidant. The third classification group, designated insecure ambivalent, is for infants who resist physical contact with their returning parent figure even though they might also demonstrate affiliative behavior. The fourth classification is a residual category for infants who were originally hard to classify in the three-type system (Main & Soloman, 1986). It is the insecure disorganized/disoriented, for infants who exhibit a variety of atypical behaviors, that do not form a readily interpretable behavior pattern.

A major problem with the Ainsworth system is its omission of assessment of the constructive dimensions of infant-parent attachment. Exploration or other behaviors that reflect use of a parent as a security base when the infant is not distressed are not explicitly rated or used to classify an infant's attachment to a parent figure. Yet Ainsworth (Ainsworth, 1978) purports to have a comprehensive classification system, in spite of its failure to address directly the exploration dimension of infant-parent attachment as theorized by Bowlby (1969).

There has been no documented effort to establish the validity of the Ainsworth laboratory procedure and evaluation method for an African American population. Nonetheless, African American infant-mother pairs from low-income backgrounds have been evaluated using Ainsworth methods (Bell cited in Ainsworth et al., 1978; Clarke-Stewart, 1973; Kennedy & Bakeman, 1984; Lyons-Ruth, Connell, Grunebaum, & Botein, 1990; Rodning, Beckwith, & Howard, 1990; Sameroff, Seifer, & Zax, 1982) and higher percentages of "insecurely attached" African American infants relative to percentages in White samples have been reported. The possibility that the discrepancy might reflect divergent but psychologically sound differences in African American and White infant-parent attachments was never acknowledged in those reports.

In a pilot study, ten African American children from low-risk backgrounds and their mother figures were seen in the Ainsworth laboratory procedure and an effort was made to evaluate their responses using Ainsworth methods (Hansen, 1980). However, the children's response patterns were very difficult to assess within those parameters. First, exploratory activity was the most salient behavior in the strange situation procedure, not distress, even though a few children were highly upset by the procedure. In addition, few children fit the behavioral profiles of the Ainsworth classification system.

After examining ratings of the four behaviors in the first step of Ainsworth evaluation, I suspected the tentative Ainsworth class designations were spurious. Children with the most problematic health histories and the least stable experiences with mother figures were closest to the "securely attached" class profile; they were the most distressed in the strange situation and sought contact with reentering mother figures. However, the children with the best health histories and the most stable experiences with mother figures were playful rather than distressed by the session; they explored the room and interacted with the stranger, and were minimally affiliative with their mother figures when they reentered the room. Therefore, this last group was closest to the "insecure avoidant" classification in the Ainsworth system. There was a clear discrepancy in character of infant-parent relationship and the interpretive label of the Ainsworth classification group that would have been assigned. This discrepancy lead to the alternative methods for assessing African American infant-parent attachments to be presented.

The Alternative Laboratory Procedure

The primary objective was to devise methods for examining infant-parent attachments as they naturally occur in African American culture. This required addressing the fact that African American infants from a variety of backgrounds have several salient parent figures. In low-income families a mother and one or more relatives frequently share childrearing such that identification of a singular mother figure is often not possible (Stack, 1974, 1975). In addition, teenage mothers and their infants frequently live with the mother's mother (Hill, 1971) leading to extensive involvement of grandmothers as mothering figures to infants. Moreover, in economically privileged two-parent families, African American parents frequently have egalitarian roles (Billingsley,

1968; Fichter, 1967; Scanzoni, 1975; TenHouten, 1970) and fathers are extensively involved in child care. Even single parents with middle class African American backgrounds share childrearing extensively with relatives and other caretakers of children (McAdoo, 1980, 1981). For these reasons, the alternative procedure was designed to facilitate examining the functional equivalence of the two parent figures most likely to hold the position of primary attachment figure for an infant, as well as both composed and apprehensive attachment responses of infants.

Thirty-seven physically healthy African American 12 month olds were studied in a separation-reunion procedure that accommodated a child, the parents, and the stranger in one session (Jackson, 1984). To minimize probable psychopathology, infants from low-risk backgrounds were chosen. They came from two-parent working and middle class families where both parents were adults and the mothers, as well as all but one father, were employed. Five children were exceptions in that their mothers were single and a female relative participated as a father substitute.

The procedure consists of 13 three-minute episodes and is similar in separation-reunion sequence to one designed by Kotelchuck (1976). Experimental manipulation of who is in the room produces a pattern of exits and reentries of parents, resulting in cycles of two, one and no parents in the room that overlaps cycles of stranger entries and exits. The infant is alone with the stranger, who was an African American female student in the referenced study, during two episodes. The order of mothers' and fathers' exits and reentries is counterbalanced to avoid order effects as indicated in Table 1, which also shows who was present in the room during each episode. (For details on implementation of the procedure see Jackson, 1984.)

The Alternative Behavioral Measures

A set of seven ordinal scales was developed for analysis of child behavior in the alternative laboratory session. The array of behaviors represented in the set was chosen to permit analysis of composed as well as apprehensive attachment responses. The set was also chosen to cover the range of child behaviors that were salient in the pilot study. The four scales used in the first step of the Ainsworth evaluation process were used as models for formatting the alternative measures. All of the alternative scales had a seven point range with absence or virtual absence of a type of behavior at the lowest level and a very high degree of the behavior at the highest level. The alternative scales are: (a) exploration of the physical environment without an overt social element; (b) sociability with the stranger; (c) distress in response to a parent's departure; (d) seeking proximity of a reentering parent; (e) maintaining physical contact with a reentering parent; (f) resisting physical contact with a reentering parent; and, (g) inattention to or avoidance of a reentering parent (see Appendix A for complete descriptions of the scales).

Separate scales for exploration and sociability were developed to distinguish the child's inclination to explore the unfamiliar material environment from inclination to explore the unfamiliar social environment. The distress scale was added as a measure of apprehensive attachment for two reasons. First, it was response to separation from a parent that revealed apprehension in the pilot study children who exhibited distress. Second, a measure of response to infant-parent separation would provide an index of immediacy of infant defensive reaction, something that was missing in the Ainsworth assessment methods. The other four scales for rating affiliation or counter-affiliative behavior toward a parent returning to the laboratory room were essentially the same as their Ainsworth counterparts, with a few changes: a number of explicit timing guides were added to facilitate scale-point judgments and descriptions were reworded for scale-point assignments. Also, child behavior interpreted as parent figure avoidance in the Ainsworth system is considered inattention or avoidance in the proposed scale. Pilot study results indicated that redefinition of the avoidance scale to eliminate the presumption of purposeful

Table 1. Participants Present in Playroom by Episode

Episode	Mother Departs First	Father Departs First
1	infant, mother, father	infant, mother, father
2	infant, father	infant, mother
3	infant, father, stranger	infant, mother, stranger
4	infant, stranger	infant, stranger
5	infant, stranger, mother	infant, stranger, father
6	infant, mother	infant, father
7	infant, mother, father	infant, father, mother
8	infant, mother	infant, father
9	infant, mother, stranger	infant, father, stranger
10	infant, stranger	infant, stranger
11	infant, stranger, father	infant, stranger, mother
12	infant, mother, father	infant, mother, father

avoidance of a reentering parent figure by a child was appropriate and interpretively more valid.

The basic principle behind analyses using each scale entailed comparing infant behavior during episodes when an attachment response was likely to be at its peak to infant behavior during episodes when an attachment response was a less probable cause of the behavior assessed. Consequently, affiliative behavior toward a reentering parent after having been in the room without either parent–potentially the most unnerving part of the laboratory session–was compared to affiliative behavior toward a reentering parent when the other parent had been in the room and able to provide reassurance. Similarly, distress when a parent departed leaving the infant and stranger alone was compared to distress when a parent departed leaving the infant with the other parent, and sociability when the infant and stranger were alone was compared to sociability when a parent was present with the infant and stranger. Analysis of exploratory behavior adhered to the same principle but differed in format because behavior in all thirteen episodes was the basis for analysis.

Exploration of the physical environment did not require social interaction or avoidance of interaction as a point of reference to be rated. Therefore, it was rated in all episodes, and the extent of exploration examined in terms of people present or absent from the playroom. In contrast, responses to specific adults could only be rated in episodes where the adults were present to provide points of reference (e.g. sociability could only be assessed when the stranger was present). Consequently, except for exploration, each scale was used to make ratings in a subset of selected episodes to permit analyses based on comparisons of behavior according to the general principle for behavior analysis just described.

Results Obtained Using Alternative Methods

First, attachments towards mothers and towards fathers were found to be behaviorally equivalent (see Jackson, 1984 for details of statistical analyses supporting findings reported in this section). For all but one of the seven types of behaviors examined with the alternative scales, ratings associated with fathers were correlated with those associated with mothers indicating that infants' responses to their two parent figures were very similar. In addition, comparison of ratings associated with fathers and those associated with mothers, revealed no bias toward either parent group (i.e. no statistical difference) for all seven of the behaviors rated. Together these findings demonstrate that the African American children in the study sample held not only similar but functionally equivalent attachments to their two parent figures across an array of behaviors, giving readings on the full spectrum of responses reflecting underlying attachments. As shown by additional analyses, these findings cannot be discounted as the result of weak measures without the power to discriminate variations in attachment response.

Overall, this pair of findings has important theoretical and practical ramifications: African American children of the study sample and possibly African American children of similar backgrounds have the enriched psychosocial resource of two equivalent intimate bonds in early childhood. This resource potentially provides alternative sources of fundamental emotional support. Having two intimate bonds would mean that a child is less dependent on the content of a relationship to one parent for the affective experiences making up the foundation of his or her psychosocial well-being.

In a second set of analyses, the dynamics of the children's response to the laboratory sequence were examined as a reflection of the effort to manipulate their attachment responses. Essentially these were analyses of normative changes in the infants' behavior over the thirteen episodes of the alternative procedure for each of the seven types of behaviors measured. The overall pattern of response corroborated the findings of the pilot study, i.e. attachment responses theoretically attributable to feelings of security were more salient than defensive ones. Exploratory behavior, which was measured in all episodes of the alternative procedure, rose and fell in correspondence to the presence or absence of parents and was markedly lower when the stranger was present. It reached its highest levels when parents were present and its lowest levels when the stranger and child were alone. This pattern of child behavior showed that the African American infants in the sample were using their parents as a base from which to explore the physical environment of the laboratory playroom. However, no peak in sociability response was identified, revealing that parents' presence or absence had no effect on social exploration for the group as a whole.

Infants' defensive attachment responses, as a function of the experimental manipulation, were minimal. A pattern of more distress when left with the stranger than when left with another parent was identified, but no corresponding patterns of response for the four other measures of defensive reaction were found. Even for distress, the response pattern held for the girls but not the boys, and a substantial group of 16 in the total sample of 37 showed no distress throughout the session. However, the fact that a pattern of distress reaction was evident, reveals that the alternative procedure was successful in inducing a modal response of mild distress. Also, the addition of a measure of infant reaction to separation from a parent, i.e. the immediacy of defensive attachment reaction, was shown to be appropriate in studying attachment in African American children as pilot study results seemed to indicate. Nonetheless, the absence of an identifiable peak in proximity seeking, contact maintaining, contact resisting, or inattention/avoidance behaviors suggests that the distress that occurred abated quickly and was not sustained long enough to affect infants' responses when reunited with a parent, in spite of the recurring separations from parents produced by the experimental procedure.

The purpose of the last set of analyses was to delineate the pattern of individual differences in the infants' overall response to the laboratory procedure. To accomplish this, correlations among the seven behaviors rated were examined. For each of the behaviors, all episode ratings were combined and averaged. Intercorrelations of the average scores revealed two definite groupings. In the first grouping, proximity seeking and contact maintaining, the two affiliative behavior measures and distress were positively interrelated (i.e. the greater the proximity seeking and contact maintaining, the greater the distress). However, the second grouping, exploration, sociability and inattention/avoidance, was negatively correlated with proximity seeking, contact maintaining and distress (i.e. the greater the degree of each of the first three variables, the lesser the degree of the last three variables). In addition to these groupings, there was a significant positive correlation of sociability and inattention/

avoidance, and an almost significant correlation for exploration and sociability.

These patterns of correlations revealed that infants varied in their response to the session along a dimension that can be described as gregarious and self-assured on one end and wary and parent-affiliative on the other. The inverse correlation of measures of gregariousness (exploration, sociability and inattention/avoidance) with the consistently intercorrelated set of affiliative response variables (proximity seeking, contact maintaining and distress) very clearly support this conclusion. Moreover, the positive linkage of sociability and inattention/avoidance suggests that infants who were most sociable with the stranger were unconcerned about their parents' whereabouts, but those who were least sociable with the stranger were apprehensive and therefore very attentive to their parents. The positive linkage of exploration and sociability in contrast to the inverse linkage of inattention/avoidance with proximity seeking and contact maintaining give added credence to this conclusion.

Overall, the patterns of intercorrelation of variables demonstrating individual differences complement the results revealing patterns in the group's response across the episodes of the laboratory session. In conjunction, these results indicate a majority of the infants maintained a sense of security in the experimental session even though it was designed to cause distress, while a definite minority was apprehensive and sought parental reassurance. In this regard the alternative procedure and the seven variables covering a wide range of attachment responses reveal constructive effects of infant-parent attachments for African American infants, unlike the Ainsworth methods. Moreover, the alternative procedures delineate desirable infant behaviors that are not in evidence in research reported in the attachment literature based on study of White infants. If future use of the alternative procedures reveals they are equally useful with other samples of normal African American infants and if the study results are similar to those reported, an instrument for detecting valuable, positive aspects of early African American life, or the absence of such, will have been established. Then use of the proce-

dures with clinical populations, such as teenage parents abusive or maltreating parents and their offspring, would be possible and might provide culturally fair as well as clinically useful information for diagnosis and treatment.

Directions for Future Research

The most immediate need for instrument development is for the alternative procedures to be used with other samples of normal African American children to see if they appear to be as appropriate as for the sample in the study described, and to see if results can be replicated. There also is a need for other researchers to become involved in this area of study. It would thus be possible for independent researchers to compare results obtained using the alternative procedures to those obtained using the Ainsworth procedures. Replication studies with normal, low-risk African American infants as subjects would give more information about the relative utility and appropriateness of the two assessment procedures as well as establish norms. It is possible that the alternative methods are only useful for African American infants who actually have two parenting figures and that some other procedures, if not Ainsworth's, would have to be developed specifically for African American infants with only one parent figure for valid assessment of the infant-parent relationship to be possible. In any case, after a body of research on normal African American children has been generated, methods should be compared using clinical samples of African American infants to determine the clinical value of the alternative procedures that have been presented. The relatively extensive, systematic comparison of methods is deemed necessary because of the current singularity of the Ainsworth procedures as accepted tools for evaluating early social-emotional development, and the pilot study results (Hansen, 1980) indicating that they were of questionable validity with African American infant subjects.

Reliability of separation-reunion laboratory procedures is generally thought to be impossible to establish because of the problem of exercise effects. Ainsworth and her associates (1978) reported that retesting of their White infant subjects after a two week time lapse was encumbered by marked increase in distress response, as well as the question of whether, from the infants' point of view, the laboratory setting retained the unfamiliarity it was designed to have. It could be presumed that the exercise effects problem would confound efforts to establish reliability of African American infants' response in the alternative procedure. However, rather than making such a presumption, a retest study is indicated because of the apparent differences in overall response of African American and White infants. It would be worthwhile to examine African American infants' response patterns in two administrations of the proposed procedure after a short time lapse to see if reliability could be established.

Ideally, behavioral response patterns observed in the alternative procedure should be linked empirically to other contemporaneous measures of infant-parent relations and/or infant social-emotional development to validate findings and corroborate interpretations. However, such an effort would be undercut by the dearth of instruments for those purposes, other than the Ainsworth procedure, and the absence of norms for African American infants. More realistically and importantly, the results of further study using the alternative procedures could be linked to behavioral antecedents and/or sequels to provide a basis for establishing the background, and their ramifications, of the infant-parent relations observed in the laboratory context. In this way the importance of infant-parent attachment relationships for African American infant development could be either confirmed or disconfirmed even though concurrent validation of the assessment of an attachment relationship would not be achieved.

Some exploratory work in an effort to link behavior in the alternative laboratory session to antecedents in African American infants' experience was attempted with the research that has been presented. Parents were interviewed about infant experiences in the first eight months of life, and infant-parent interaction in the home during the period when infants were nine to eleven months old was observed and analyzed (Jackson, 1984). A few linkages of antecedents and labora-

tory behavior were detected, but they were too few to permit more than very tentative interpretation. It was concluded that longitudinal study should commence at a much earlier infant age, and more refined measures of antecedent behavior are needed to clearly detect connections of laboratory behavior at twelve months old and preceding experience.

Generally, long-term longitudinal study is needed, with administrations of the laboratory procedure proposed at nine months, twelve months and subsequent points up to age three or four years, to chart patterns of change or continuity of infant-parent attachment behavior for African American infants. When a substantial body of research information has been collected for normal and clinical samples and norms, antecedents, and sequels have been established for African American infants, then categorization of individual differences in response in the laboratory session and diagnosis can take place. Overall, most important is that African American norms and the character of African American infant-parent affective relations comprise the points of reference for diagnosis and intervention affecting young African American childrens' lives.

References

Ainsworth, M. D. S., Blehar, M. C., Waters, E., & Wall, S. (1978). *Patterns of attachment: A psychological study of the strange situation.* Hillsdale, NJ: Lawrence Erlbaum.

Billingsley, A. (1968). *Black families in White America.* Englewood Cliffs, NJ: Prentice Hall.

Bowlby, J. (1969). *Attachment and loss, Vol. I: Attachment.* New York: Basic Books.

Bowlby, J. (1982). *Attachment and loss, Vol. I: Attachment* (2nd ed.). New York: Basic Books.

Clarke-Stewart, K. A. (1973). Interactions between mothers and their young children: Characteristics and consequences. *Monographs of the Society for Research in Child Development, 38* (6-7, Serial No. 153).

Fichter, J. H. (1967). *Graduates from predominantly Negro colleges, class of 1964.* (Public Health Services Publication No. 1571). Washington, D.C.: National Institutes of Health, U. S. Labor Department, & National Science Foundation.

Grossmann, K. E., Grossmann, K., Huber F., & Wartner, V. (1981). German children's behavior towards their mothers at 12 months and their fathers at 18 months in Ainsworth's strange situation. *International Journal of Behavioral Development, 4,* 157-181.

Hansen, J. (1980). *Children's attachment to mother figures and the social development of African American infants and young children.* Unpublished manuscript, University of California, Berkeley.

Hill, R. B. (1971). *The strengths of African American families.* New York: Emerson Hall.

Jackson, J. F. (1984). A social ecological study of the African American infant with a working mother: Emergent attachments, sociability and cognitive maturity. *Dissertation Abstracts International, 45,* 1039B. (University Microfilms No. 84-13438).

Kennedy, J. H., & Bakeman, R. (1984). The early mother-infant relationship and social competence with peers and adults at three years. *Journal of Psychology, 116,* 23-34.

Kotelchuck, M. (1976). The infant's relationship to the father: Experimental evidence. In M. E. Lamb (Ed.), *The role of the father in child development* (pp. 329-344). New York: John Wiley & Sons.

Lambs, M. E., Thompson, R. A., Gardner, W., & Charnov, E. L. (1985). *Infant-mother attachment: The origins and developmental significance of individual differences in strange situation behavior.* Hillsdale, NJ: Lawrence Erlbaum.

Lyons-Ruth, K., Connel, D. B., Grunebaum, H. U., & Botein, S. (1990). Infants at social risk: Maternal depression and family support services as mediators of infant development and security of attachment. *Child Development, 61*(1), 85-98.

Main, M., & Soloman, J. (1986). Discovery of an insecure-disorganized/disoriented attachment pattern. In T. B. Brazelton & M. W. Yogman (Eds.), *Affective development in infancy.* Norwood, NJ: Ablex.

Main, M., & Weston, D. R. (1981). The quality of the toddler's relationship to mother and father: Related to conflict behavior and the readiness to establish new relationships. *Child Development, 52,* 932-940.

McAdoo, H. P. (1980). Black mothers and the extended family support network. In L. F. Rodgers-Rose (Ed.), *The Black woman.* Beverly Hills, CA: Sage.

McAdoo, H. P. (1981, May). *Stress and support networks of working single African American mothers.* Paper presented at conference on the African American women: Toward a humanistic context for social science research. Center for the Study, Education and Advancement of Women, University of California, Berkeley.

Rodning, C., Beckwith, L., & Howard, J. (1990). Characteristics of attachment organization and play organization in prenatally drug-exposed toddlers. *Development and Psychopathology, 1*(4), 277-289.

Sameroff, A. J., Seifer, R., & Zax, M. (1982). Early development of children at-risk for emotional disorder. *Monographs of the Society for Research in Child Development, 48*(1, Serial No. 199).

Scanzoni, J. (1975). Sex roles, economic factors, and marital solidarity in African American and White marriages. *Journal of Marriage and the Family, 37*(1), 130-144.

Stack, C. B. (1974). *All our kin: Strategies for survival in an African American community.* New York: Harper & Row.

Stack, C. B. (1975). Who raises African American children: Transactions of child givers and child receivers. In T. R. Williams (Ed.), *Socialization and communication in primary groups* (pp. 183-205). The Hague: Mouton.

TenHouten, W. D. (1970). The African American family: Myth and reality. *Psychiatry, 33,* 145-172.

Appendix A

Description of Alternative Scales

Exploration

Construct

This scale assesses exploration and play that does not have a clearly social dimension. Variations in extent of physical mobility in the room, attention to specific objects, and sustained attention to particular objects account for different rating placements on the scale. The highest ratings are assigned for high physical mobility and focused and/or sustained attention.

Very high–Exploration

a) The child is independently absorbed in activity for 60 seconds or more during the episode. He/she is highly mobile moving through a large space in the room. On his/her own initiative the child becomes very focused on one item that is at least one yard away from adults–this focus must be at least 10 seconds in duration–and/or sustains attention to independently initiated play activity (e.g. the child goes over and plays with the jumping-jack hanging on the wall or stuffed dog on the chair across from seated parent figures).

High–Exploration

The child is independently absorbed in activity not necessarily initiated by him/her for at least 30 seconds during the episode. He/she is highly mobile or physically active in his/her play for at least 15 seconds, covering moderate space in the room. The child has phases of focused attention on some item that is at least 1 yard away from an adult: definite intensity of focus is apparent.

Moderately high–Exploration

The child is independently absorbed in activity not necessarily initiated by him/her for at least 15 seconds during the episode, and is mobile or physically active also. The child also has directed attention to an object, but that object may or may not be 1 yard away from an adult (e.g. attention to cookie container). The quality of his/her attention does not appear as intense as higher ratings.

Midscale–Exploration

a) The child's activity level is moderate to highly active, covering space in the room without sustained attention to any one thing.

b) Or the child has brief phases of sustained attention (not more than 10 seconds long) totaling 30 seconds while staying within 1 yard's proximity of an adult, and without much physical activity.

Moderately low–Exploration

The child engages in very tentative movements away from an adult while staying within 1 yard's proximity of the adult. His/her activity level is very low (e.g. handling an object) and may be accompanied by intermittent glances around

the room. In total, the involvement with the object must last at least 15 seconds.

Low–Exploration

The child is quite passive and physically inactive, staying within 1 yard of an adult. He/she does, however, look around the room, and does appear to direct attention to particular objects even though that directed attention may appear fleeting.

Very low–Exploration

No exploratory or play activity independent of social interaction, or virtually none.

Sociability

Construct

This scale assesses the extent to which the child is attracted to the person who is a stranger to him/her–and is open to engaging in apparently pleasant social interaction with the stranger. The intent is to evaluate the extent of the child's willingness to explore new social opportunities. Variation in the child's efforts to establish social contact and engage in social interaction with the stranger, as well as inclination to respond positively to social overtures from the stranger, determine rating placements on the scale. The highest ratings are assigned for instances where the child initiates and sustains interactions with the stranger and/or remains receptive to interactions with the stranger in spite of minor startling events that might otherwise have caused the child to become wary of the stranger.

Very high–Sociability

a) The child approaches the stranger as she enters the room moving at least 1 yard in the stranger's direction and remains within 1 yard's proximity for 60 seconds after the approach.

b) And/or the child greets the stranger within 10 seconds of her entry into the room, by definite vocal and/or gestural means.

c) And/or the child initiates play with the stranger within 30 seconds of the stranger's entry into the room, and continues to play with the stranger for an additional 30 seconds.

d) And/or the child responds to the stranger's invitations to play by becoming involved in reciprocal play (e.g. rolling the ball back and forth), and continues to play with the stranger for at least 60 seconds.

e) And/or the child remains within 1 yard's physical proximity of the stranger after she pops the balloon and resumes social interaction with the stranger within 60 seconds after the balloon has popped.

High–Sociability

a) The child greets the stranger within 30 seconds of her entry into the room by definite vocal and/or gestural means.

b) The child remains within 1 yard's proximity of the stranger when the stranger approaches to pin the animal on his/her clothing, and allows the stranger to put the pin on. The child remains in close proximity for an additional 60 seconds.

c) And/or the child initiates contact with the stranger, which may or may not be playful, within 60 seconds of the stranger's entry into the room and continues to interact with the stranger for an additional 30 seconds.

d) And/or the child gives a departing remark to the stranger by definite vocal and/or gestural means as she departs the room within 10 seconds of noticing the stranger's approach of the door to exit.

e) And/or the child responds to the stranger's invitations to play by becoming involved in playful interaction that continues for at least 60 seconds and involves some initiative on the child's part to sustain the play.

f) And/or the child remains within 1 yard's proximity of the stranger after she pops the balloon, and remains there for 30 seconds. Also the child does not give an aversive response such as crying or leaning away from her.

Moderately high–Sociability

a) The child gives a departing remark to the stranger by definite vocal and/or gestural means, as she departs the room within 30 seconds of noticing the stranger's approach of the door to leave.

b) And/or the child approaches the stranger at some point during the episode (e.g., to get the cookie bag or a toy) and remains within 1 yard's proximity of the stranger for at least 60 seconds after the approach.

c) And/or the child initiates contact with the stranger, which may or may not be playful (e.g., seeks the stranger's assistance in opening the cookie container), at some point during the episode and continues to interact with the stranger for 30 seconds.

d) And/or the child responds to the stranger's invitations to play by becoming involved in playful interaction that continues for at least 30 seconds.

e) And/or the child remains within 1 yard's proximity of the stranger when the stranger approaches to put the animal pin on, allowing the stranger to put the pin on. The child remains in close proximity for at least 30 seconds.

Midscale–Sociability

a) The child approaches the stranger at some point during the episode and remains within 1 yard's proximity of the stranger for at least 10 seconds after the approach.

b) And/or the child initiates contact with the stranger which may or may not be playful at some point during the episode and continues to interact with the stranger for at least 10 seconds.

c) And/or the child remains within 1 yard's proximity of the stranger when the stranger approaches to put on the animal pin, even though he/she does not allow the stranger to put the pin on, for at least 30 seconds.

d) And/or the child is held by a parent when the balloon is popped and doesn't cry or make an effort to move away from stranger for 30 seconds afterwards. The parent continues to hold the child during that time.

Moderately low–Sociability

a) The child responds to the stranger's invitations to play by becoming involved in playful interaction that continues for at least 10 seconds or intermittent interaction for a total of 30 seconds.

Low–Sociability

a) After initially delaying the child responds to the stranger's invitations to play by becoming involved in a total of at least 15 seconds of interaction for the episode.

b) From a position of close proximity to a parent figure and more than 1 yard's distance from the stranger, the child looks at the stranger for at least a 30 second period of time. The child also gives some indicators of positive social response to the stranger such as smiles, laughs, etc.

Very low–Sociability

a) The child gives no signs of attraction to the stranger or positive social response to the stranger during the episode, but may watch the stranger for long periods of time from a distance (i.e. much further than 1 yard away).

Distress

Construct

This scale assesses the child's level of distress and response to adult efforts to console him/her. Because distress is not always manifest in obvious ways, only behaviors that are common signs of being upset should be evaluated. Moreover, the child is likely to respond differently to the consoling efforts of a parent figure in comparison to those of the person who is a stranger to the child. For this reason the scale point guidelines reflect a differentiation between infant response to consoling done by a parent figure in comparison to the stranger. Variations in length of time spent crying, whimpering or whining, and response to the consoling efforts of the adults remaining in the room determine scale point assignments for ratings. The highest ratings are assigned for loud, obvious distress that cannot be alleviated as long as the departed parent figure is out of the room.

Very high–Distress

a) The child begins loud crying within 5 seconds of noticing a parent figure's effort to depart the room, and the parent figure's effort to leave is aborted because of the strong distressed protests of the child.

b) Or, the child begins loud crying within 5 seconds of noticing that a parent figure has departed from the room. The child continues with loud, consistent crying in spite of the consoling efforts of the parent figure who remains in the room, for 30 seconds or more.

High–Distress

a) The child begins loud crying within 5 seconds of noticing that a parent figure has departed from the room, and continues with loud consistent crying in spite of the consoling efforts of the stranger in the room. The crying persists for 30 seconds or more until a parent figure returns.

Moderately high–Distress

a) The child begins loud crying within 5 seconds of noticing that a parent figure has departed from the room, and continues with loud consistent crying, in spite of the stranger's effort to distract the child with toys. The crying persists for 30 seconds or more until a parent figure returns.

b) Or the child begins loud crying within 5 seconds of noticing that a parent figure has departed from the room, and continues with low level crying or whimpering, in spite of the consoling or distracting efforts of the parent figure who remains in the room. The whimpering goes on continuously for 30 seconds or more.

Midscale–Distress

a) The child begins with loud crying within 5 seconds of noticing that a parent figure has departed from the room, but changes to low level, intermittent whimpering for 30 seconds or more, in response to the consoling or distracting efforts of the parent remaining in the room.

b) Or the child begins with loud crying within 5 seconds of noticing that a parent figure has departed, and continues with intermittent loud crying for 30 seconds or more in response to the stranger's effort to console or distract the child. The crying does not fully stop until a parent figure returns to the room.

c) Or the child's distress reaction is delayed, in that he/she does not begin to cry until 20 seconds or more after noticing that one parent figure has left the room. The child cries or whimpers for 30 seconds or more, in spite of the consoling or distracting efforts of the parent figure remaining in the room.

Moderately low–Distress

a) The child begins with loud crying within 5 seconds of noticing that a parent figure has departed, but continues with whimpering or low level crying for 30 seconds or more in response to the stranger's efforts to console or distract the child. The crying does not fully stop until a parent figure returns to the room.

b) Or the child's distress reaction is delayed, in that he/she does not begin to cry until 20 seconds or more after one parent figure has departed. He/she cries or whimpers intermittently for 30 seconds or more in spite of the consoling or distracting efforts of the parent figure remaining in the room. The crying may fully stop before the end of the episode.

c) Or the child's distress reaction is delayed, in that he/she does not begin to cry until 20 seconds or more after noticing that a parent figure has departed. However, the child continues with loud crying for 30 seconds or more in spite of the stranger's efforts to console or distract him/her until a parent figure returns to the room.

Low–Distress

a) The child cries briefly (no more than 10 seconds) at one or more points during the time when one parent figure is absent from the room, but stops on his/her own or in response to the consoling or distracting efforts of a parent figure or stranger remaining in the room.

Very low–Distress

a) No clear signals of distress.

b) Or one instance of 5 seconds or less of crying, whimpering, or other distressed behavior.

Proximity Seeking

Construct

This scale assesses the child's efforts to seek physical contact with the parent figure while the parent figure is entering the playroom or to seek physical contact with the parent figure during the episodes immediately after the parent figure has entered the playroom. Variation in intensity of the child's efforts, promptness and persistence in trying to attain contact account for different placements on the scale. The highest ratings are assigned for instances where the child initiates the effort to attain contact and is effective in achieving it because of his/her efforts.

Very high–Proximity Seeking

a) The child approaches the parent figure with the apparent intention of having the returning adult pick him/her up within 10 seconds of having noticed the first signal of the parent's return (i.e., having given clear response to hearing his/her own name called or seeing the parent as the door opens). The child covers the full distance needed to actually gain physical contact with the parent figure, but must cover at least a 1 yard distance, using his own motor efforts to do so. Initial contact is achieved by some effort on the child's part, such as grabbing hold of the parent figure. Once in physical contact with the parent figure, the child remains in physical contact for at least 20 seconds without any effort on the child's part to interrupt that contact.

High–Proximity Seeking

a) More than 30 seconds after having noticed the first signal of the parent's return, the child approaches the adult, with the apparent intention of having the returning adult pick him/her up. The child covers the full distance needed to actually gain physical contact with the parent figure, covering at least a 1 yard distance using his own motor efforts in the process. Initial contact is achieved by some effort on the child's part such as grabbing hold of the parent figure. Once the child has gained contact with the parent figure, there is a 10 second span of time without any effort on the child's part to interrupt the contact.

b) Or the child approaches the parent figure with the apparent intention of having the returning adult pick him/her up. He/she covers the full distance needed to achieve contact, which must be at least 1 yard, *and* gives a motor signal such as a reach that he wants to be picked up. However, initial contact is achieved by the parent figure's effort. Once the child has gained contact, there is a 10 second span of time without any effort on the child's part to interrupt the contact.

c) Or the child approaches the parent figure with the apparent intention of being picked up by the returning adult, he/she covers the full distance needed to achieve contact, which must be at least 1 yard; he/she gives a motor signal such as a reach that he wants to be picked up. However, actual physical contact is not achieved within 15 seconds of the preceding series of events because the adult does not do what would be needed to attain contact *and* the child makes no other efforts in the immediate situation that are effective in achieving contact. In addition, the child makes at least one other effort to gain contact with the reentering parent figure later in the episode, which may or may not be successful in achieving contact.

Moderately high–Proximity Seeking

a) More than 30 seconds after having noticed the first signal of the parent figure's return, the child approaches the adult with the apparent intention of being picked up; he/she covers the full distance needed to achieve contact which must be at least 1 yard; he/she gives a motor signal such as a reach indicating wanting to be picked up. The parent picks the child up or initiates some similar type of physical contact. Once in contact with the parent figure, there is a 10 seconds time span without any effort on the child's part to interrupt the contact.

b) Or the child is being held by the stranger as the parent figure returns to the room, and cannot use locomotor efforts to approach the parent figure for this reason. However, he/she, exerts clear physical effort to gain contact with the returning parent figure, involving movement of his/her torso as well as limbs in orientation to the returning parent (e.g. twisting around in the direction of the returning adult, leaning in the direction of the returning adult, etc.). Contact may or may not be achieved depending on the response of the returning adult.

c) Or the child is very close to the door, at the time he/she notices the first signal of the parent figure's return, or the child was held by the stranger then put down very close to the parent figure. For some reason he/she cannot move easily, and the child was unable to approach the parent figure. Nonetheless, the child makes definite efforts to gain contact with the returning adult by grabbing hold of the adult, reaching to be picked up, or some similar active appeal for contact.

Midscale–Proximity Seeking

a) The child approaches the parent figure with the apparent intent of having the returning adult pick him/her up within 15 seconds of having noticed the first signal of the parent's return, but does not cover a distance of greater than 1 yard before being picked up by the parent figure. The short distance covered is caused by the adult's speed in picking up the child rather than the child stopping and waiting for the adult to pick him/her up. However, once contact is attained a 10 second time span lapses without any effort on the child's part to interrupt the contact.

b) Or the child approaches the parent figure with the apparent intention of having the returning adult pick him/her up, within 15 seconds of having noticed the first signal of the parent's return. The child covers the full distance needed to actually gain physical contact with the parent figure, covering at least 1 yard distance in the process. Initial contact is achieved by some effort on the child's part, such as grabbing hold of the parent. However once the child has gained contact with the parent figure, he/she makes some effort to interrupt that contact before 10 seconds have lapsed (e.g., the child tries to get down after having been picked up by the adult and goes on to other activity).

c) Or more than 30 seconds after having noticed the first signal of the parent's return, the child approaches the adult, with the apparent intention of having the returning adult pick him/her up. The child covers the full distance needed to actually gain physical contact with the parent figure, covering at least 1 yard's distance; he/she gives a *vocal* signal such as a distinct cry or grunt of wanting to be picked up. The parent figure picks the child up or initiates some similar type of physical contact. Once in contact with the parent figure, there is a 10 second span of time without any effort on the child's part to interrupt the contact.

Moderately low–Proximity Seeking

a) The child begins to approach the parent figure within 15 seconds of having noticed the first signal of the parent's return, but does not cover a distance greater than 1 yard before stopping and waiting for the adult to pick him/her up. The adult picks the child up within 10 seconds of his/her having stopped. However, once contact is attained, a 10 second time span lapses without any effort on the child's part to interrupt the contact.

b) Or more than 30 seconds after having noticed the first signal of the parent figure's return, the child approaches the adult with the apparent intention of being picked up. However, the child stops after having gone less than 1 yards distance, and gives a motor signal or a vocal signal of wanting to be picked up. The parent figure picks the child up within 10 seconds and once contact is attained 10 seconds lapses without any effort on the child's part to interrupt the contact.

c) Or within 15 seconds of having noticed the first signal of the parent figure's return, the child gives a locomotor or nonlocomotor indicator of wanting contact with the returning parent figure such as reaching toward that adult, crying while looking at the adult, etc. The child does not make a more active effort to gain contact with the returning adult for the duration of the episode. The adult may, or may not respond to the child's appeals. If contact is attained the child may or may not attempt to interrupt contact before 10 seconds lapses.

Low–Proximity Seeking

a) More than 30 seconds after having noticed the first signal of the parent figure's return, the child approaches the adult. However, the child stops having gone less than the distance needed to achieve contact (this may or may not be more than a 1 yard distance), or changes the direction of movement toward something or someone other than the returning adult, and does not signal any intention of being picked up. The child may or may not be picked up by the returning adult.

b) Or more than 30 seconds after having noticed the first signal of the parent figure's return, the child gives nonlocomotor indicators of wanting contact with the returning parent figure by reaching toward that adult, crying while looking at that adult, etc. The child may or may not be picked up by the returning adult.

Very low–Proximity Seeking

a) The child makes no effort to seek contact with the returning adult but may accept being picked up by the returning parent figure. The child may appear to be content and smile or look at the returning adult, or very upset (e.g. crying and expressing discontent in a nonfocused way).

Contact Maintaining

Construct

This scale assesses the child's efforts to maintain physical contact with the returning parent figure once he/she has gained it. Variation in the intensity of the childrens' efforts to maintain contact, and in their acceptance of contact account for different placements on the scale. The highest ratings are assigned for instances where long periods of contact are sustained in part by the child's efforts, or long periods of contact that are fully accepted by the child.

Very high–Contact Maintaining

a) There is at least a 90 second lapse of time with continuous physical contact of the child and the returning adult; the child may be held by the adult, stand while leaning on the adult, stand while holding on to the adult, or engage in a combination of these specified behaviors. In at least *2* instances the child makes an active physical effort to prevent the adult from breaking the contact (e.g. moving closer to the adult, grabbing to hold on more tightly, etc.)

b) Or there is at least a 2 minute lapse of time with continuous contact of the child and returning adult, but neither the adult nor the child tries to break the contact within that time.

High–Contact Maintaining

a) There is at least a 60 second lapse of time with continuous contact of the child and the returning adult, in one instance the child makes an active physical effort to prevent the adult from breaking the contact.

b) Or there is at least a 90 second lapse of time with *continuous* contact of the child and the returning adult, but neither the adult nor the child tries to break the contact within that time.

Moderately high–Contact Maintaining

a) There is at least a 45 second lapse of time with continuous contact of the child and the returning adult, and the child makes 1 physically active effort to prevent the adult from breaking the contact.

b) Or there is at least a 60 second lapse of time with continuous contact of the child and the returning adult, but neither the adult nor the child tries to break the contact within that time.

Midscale–Contact Maintaining

a) There is at least a 45 second lapse of time with continuous contact of the child and the returning adult, and neither the child nor adult tries to break the contact within that time.

b) Or there is a period of contact of 10 seconds to 30 seconds length but the contact was decisively broken by the adult even though the child made one or more physically active efforts to prevent the adult from breaking contact.

Moderately low–Contact Maintaining

a) There is at least a 15 second lapse of time with continuous contact of the child and the returning adult, and neither the child nor adult tries to break the contact within that time.

b) Or there are 2 periods of brief contact of 10 seconds or less between the child and the returning adult, but each time contact was decisively broken by the adult even though the child made one or more physically active efforts to prevent the adult from breaking contact.

c) Or there is a period of contact of 10 seconds to 30 seconds length but the contact was decisively broken by the adult even though the child made one or more loud cries protesting the break in contact.

Low–Contact Maintaining

a) There is one period of brief contact of 10 seconds or less between the child and returning adult, but the contact is decisively broken by the adult even though the child makes a physically active effort to prevent the break in contact.

b) Or the child begins to cry and continues crying for more than 10 seconds after brief contact has been broken, if he/she was not crying while contact was maintained.

c) Or the child begins to cry markedly louder and continues to cry more loudly for 10 seconds after brief contact has been broken.

Very low–Contact Maintaining

a) There is no contact between the child and returning adult.

b) Or the child doesn't protest a break in contact of less than 10 seconds duration.

c) Or the child has one or more momentary contacts of less than 5 seconds duration and makes virtually no effort to extend the momentary contact.

Inattention/Avoidance

Construct

This scale assesses child behavior that might be construed as ignoring the returning parent figure. Variation in immediacy of response to a returning parent figure, lack of response to a returning parent figure who may even seek the child's attention, and inclination to avoid or avert attention away from the returning adult determine different points on the scale. The highest ratings are assigned for instances where the child ignores the returning parent figure when the adult tries to get his/her attention.

Very high–Inattention/Avoidance

a) The child gives no easily detected response to the returning adult to acknowledge the adults presence–or may even turn away or look away from the returning parent figure. Additionally there is no acknowledgment for 60 seconds after the adult's reentry. This is the case in spite of the adult's efforts to get the child's attention, which must entail more than one audible call of the child's name while opening the door to the playroom.

b) Or the returning adult picks the child up within 10 seconds of reentering the room, but the child gives no discernible attention to the adult or being picked up and continues to appear preoccupied with other interests or activities for 30 seconds in spite of being held by the returning adult. The child may even turn away or look away from the adult while being held.

High–Inattention/Avoidance

a) The child gives no more than a fleeting response to the returning adult–such as a look, smile, vocalization, or physical movement–within 10 seconds of the adult's reentry into the room. Then the child continues to give no acknowledgment of the reentering adult for 60 seconds in spite of the returning adult's efforts to get the child's attention. The adult's efforts must consist of more than one audible call of the child's name while opening the door to the playroom.

b) Or the child gives no response to the returning adult that acknowledges the adult's presence (or may even turn away or look away from the adult) and continues to give no acknowledgment for 30 seconds after the adult's reentry. This is so, *in spite* of the adult's efforts to get the child's attention, which must consist of more than one audible call of the child's name while opening the door to the playroom.

Moderately high–Inattention/Avoidance

a) The child gives no more than a fleeting response to the returning adult within 10 seconds of the adult's reentry into the room, and then continues to give no acknowledgment for 60 seconds. However, the returning adult makes no effort to get the child's attention, except in some cases where the adult has made only one audible call of the child's name while opening the door to the playroom.

b) Or the child gives no response to the returning adult for 15 seconds after the adult's reentry, in spite of the adult's efforts to get the child's attention (these efforts must consist of more than one audible call of the child's name while opening the door to the playroom). After this time, however, the child does attend to the reentering adult, but this attention is very passive and casual in nature.

c) Or the child initially acknowledges the returning adult within 10 seconds of the adult's reentry with vocalization or movement directed toward the adult. However, the child then shifts his/her focus and pursues another interest by looking at something or someone else or moving to something or someone else. The child remains preoccupied with his/her second interest for 60 seconds or more, in spite of the returning adults efforts to gain his/her attention.

Midscale–Inattention/Avoidance

a) The child gives no more than a fleeting response to the reentering adult within 10 seconds of the adult's reentry into the room, and continues to give no acknowledgment for another 30 seconds. However, the returning adult has made no effort to get the child's attention, except in some cases where the adult has made one audible call of the child's name while opening the door to the playroom.

b) Or the child does not acknowledge the returning adult for 15 seconds after the adult's reentry *or* gives a diversionary shift-of-focus response in spite of the adult's efforts to get the child's attention. After this time, however, the child does respond actively to the adult's overture (e.g., approaches the adult in response to the adult's call, or reaches in response to the adult's extended hand).

c) Or the child initially acknowledges the returning adult within 10 seconds of the adult's reentry, with vocalization or movement directed toward the adult. The child then shifts his/her focus and pursues another interest by looking at or moving to something or someone else. The returning adult makes no effort to gain the child's attention, however, and the child remains preoccupied with his/her second interest for 60 seconds or more.

Moderately low–Inattention/Avoidance

a) The child does not acknowledge the returning adult for 15 seconds after the adult's reentry, but the adult has made no effort to get the child's attention other than call the child's name once while reentering the room. However, after 15 seconds of nonacknowledgment the child takes the initiative to make distal or proximal contact with the returning adult.

b) Or the child gives no more than a fleeting response to the reentering adult within 10 seconds of the adult's reentry, and continues to give no acknowledgment for another 15 seconds. However, after that time he/she actively responds to delayed social overtures from the adult.

Low–Inattention/Avoidance

a) The child gives no acknowledgment to the returning adult for 5 seconds after the adult's reentry, but actively initiates contact with the returning adult after that time.

Very low–Inattention/Avoidance

a) The child immediately acknowledges the returning adult and continues to give indicators of acknowledgment for at least 15 seconds thereafter.

Contact Resistant

Construct

This scale assesses the child's resistance to contact and general balking to the returning adult's efforts to physically guide or direct his/her activity. The child's behaviors may vary from aggressive actions toward the returning adult to cranky fussing. The highest ratings are assigned for aggressive resistance to the returning adult's contacts with the child.

Very high–Contact Resisting

Two or more of the following:

a) Hitting or biting the returning adult, or similar aggressive behavior, 3 or more times along with screaming or loud crying.

b) Strong physical resistance to being held or having contact with the adult involving movement of the whole body such as pushing away, squirming or struggling to get out of the returning adult's hold, along with screaming or loud crying.

c) A full blown temper tantrum with loud angry screaming, sprawling on the floor, flailing arms and legs, etc. when the returning adult tries to hold onto him/her.

d) Decisive pushing away, throwing down or hitting at toys offered by the returning adult, 3 or more times, along with screaming or loud crying.

High–Contact Resisting

a) Hitting or biting the returning adult, or similar aggressive behavior, once along with screaming or loud crying.

b) Or strong physical resistance to being held or having contact with the adult involving movement of the whole body such as pushing away, squirming or struggling to get out of the returning adult's hold, with whimpering or fussing but no loud screaming and crying.

c) Or temper tantrum with sprawling on the floor, flailing arms and legs, etc. when the returning adult tries to hold onto him/her but with whimpering or fussiness rather than screaming or loud crying.

d) Or decisive pushing away, throwing down or hitting at toys offered by the returning adult, one time along with screaming or loud crying.

Moderately high–Contact Resisting

a) Hitting or biting the returning adult, or similar aggressive behavior, up to 3 times, without screaming or loud crying. Whimpering or fussing may or may not occur at the same time.

b) Or very strong resistance to being held or having contact with the adult involving movement of the whole body such as squirming or struggling to get out of the returning adult's hold *without* vocalization that would indicate discomfort such as screaming, loud crying, whimpering or fussiness.

c) Or decisive pushing away, throwing down or hitting at toys offered by the returning adult, up to 3 times, without screaming or loud crying. Whimpering or fussiness may or may not occur at the same time.

Midscale–Contact Resisting

a) Thwarting contact with the returning adult by crying loud whenever the adult approaches, tries to offer a toy or initiate play, etc.

b) Or physical resistance to being held or having contact with the returning adult that does *not* involve movement of the whole body, such as pushing away the adult's hands, kicking while being held 3 or more times with crying, whimpering or fussing.

c) Or refusing to comply with verbal requests or other social overtures from the returning adult with behavior such as shaking the head in refusal or failure to approach when asked to do so, 3 or more times, with whimpering or fussing.

d) Or one decisive instance of resistive behavior without crying, such as angry stepping when put down after being held, or kicking while in direct contact with the adult.

Moderately low–Contact Resisting

a) Refusing to comply with verbal requests or other social overtures from the returning adult with behavior such as shaking the head in refusal or failure to approach when asked to do so, up to 3 times, without vocalizations indicating protest or displeasure.

b) Or physical resistance to being held or having contact with the returning adult that does *not* involve movement of the whole body, such as pushing away the adult's hands, kicking while being held, up to 3 times, without vocalizations indicating protest or displeasure.

c) Or one decisive instance of resistive behavior, such as angry stepping when put down after being held, or kicking while not in direct contact with the adult, with whimpering or fussiness.

Low–Contact Resisting

a) One ambiguous instance of behavior easily construed as resistive, such as a singular jerk or push away from the returning adult, while otherwise appearing content, or a little kicking, etc. *without* vocalizations indicating protest.

b) One ambiguous instance of vocal behavior that might easily be construed as protest, such as an isolated vocal outburst when the returning adult approaches the child, or is holding the child, etc.

Very low–Contact Resisting

a) No resistance of physical contact is observed.

For additional information, contact:
Jacquelyne Faye Jackson
Institute of Human Development
University of California, Berkeley
1203 Tolman Hall 1690
Berkeley, CA 94720-1690
Telephone: (510) 652-3447
E-mail: jackjo@cmsa.berkeley.edu

Measuring Separation-Individuation Processes [1]

Jerome Taylor and Eileen Bartolomucci

Abstract

The concept of separation-individuation refers to Margaret Mahler's description of socioemotional development over the first three years of life and beyond. The first section of this chapter sketches the developmental sequence outlined by Mahler and the second describes an inventory designed to measure components of the separation-individuation process. The third and fourth sections summarize results of studies conducted and evaluate the reliability and validity of the inventory along with and implications for future research.

Theoretical Background

Mahler refers to the psychological birth of the individual as the separation-individuation process, the developmental sequence through which the infant moves from the sleep-like state of early neonatal life to an awareness of social reality and the achievement of separate identity. This process can be thought of as two complementary developments: "separation consists of the child's emergence from a symbiotic fusion with the mother...and individuation consists of those achievements marking the child's assumption of his own individual characteristics" (Mahler, Pine, and Bergman, 1975, p. 4). While these processes are intertwined, they are not identical and development may proceed divergently with precocity or a delay in either process. The maturation of autonomous functions and muscular abilities may lead the child into activities for which she may not be ready developmentally. "These two poles, separation-individuation and maturation-development are for Mahler, the critical determinants of developmental outcome" (Greenberg & Mitchell, 1983, p. 280).

The process of separation-individuation consists of three developmental phases: normal autism, normal symbiosis, and separation and individuation. During separation and individuation there are four subphases: differentiation, practicing, rapprochement, and libidinal object constancy (Mahler, 1968).

The negotiation of each phase is influenced by the foundation established during the earlier period of the infant's life. One subphase is not completely replaced by the next phase and there are similarities among them. From a developmental point of view, each phase can be seen as a time when "a qualitatively different contribution is made to the individual's psychological growth" (Mahler, Pine, and Bergman, 1975, p. 48).

The first phase, normal autism, occurs during the first few weeks of life. During these weeks the neonate seems almost oblivious to external stimulation, sleeping most of the time with only fleeting states of arousal. The infant generally wakens when hunger, pain, or soiled diapers cause her to cry, and again sinks into sleep when she is satisfied without any recognition of the differentiation between her attempts to reduce tension and the actions of the mother to reduce hunger and other tensions. Even when the infant is awake and demanding food or fretting, she may have her eyes closed. "Mahler characterizes this phase as 'autistic' and infers that the infant is functioning as a closed system, at considerable removal from external reality" (Greenberg & Mitchell, 1983, p. 274). The task of this phase is for the newborn to achieve a balance, a homeostatic equilibrium outside of the womb. The newborn does not have the capacity or awareness to relate to external objects. However, the infant will mold to the mother's body and make postural adjustments if held on the mother's shoulder. The infant is not entirely unresponsive and may have fleeting states of "alert inactivity" (Wolff, 1959) in which she responds to external stimuli which allows a continuity between this normal autistic phase and later phases. This can be seen when the infant coordinates her movements with the mother's speech or engages in brief eye contact.

The infant's awareness of her environment develops gradually from the autistic stage. At 3 to 4 weeks of age there is a marked increase in sensitivity to external stimulation as the infant lowers her innate stimulus barrier. Slowly, the infant starts to recognize the mother as an external object who can aid in tension reduction. This is the beginning of the normal symbiotic phase which continues until the fourth or fifth month. There are now sustained periods of alertness with a decrease in crying and an increase in contentment. The infant becomes increasingly cognizant of the environment with greater auditory, visual, and tactile awareness. She will respond to the introduction of novel objects and may kick and flail her arms and legs or try to grab and manipulate the objects. She will also turn away if overstimulated.

The essential feature of this phase is a delusional or hallucinatory fusion "in which the infant behaves and functions as though he and his mother were an omnipotent system– a dual unity with the common boundary" (Mahler, Pine, and Bergman, 1975, p. 44). A type of social symbiosis exists between the mother and child during this subphase in which the rudimentary ego of the infant is complemented by the emotional rapport of the mother's care. It is during this time that the infant persistently watches the mother's face while feeding. One of the most important experiences of this phase is the infant's total body awareness of being held and her face-to-face eye contact with the mother. The infant will explore her own body as well as her mother's and engage in social contact and protest if contact with the mother is lost. These "good enough" (Winnicott, 1956) behaviors of the mother, as she engages her child, are suggested by Mahler (1968) as the symbiotic organizers of psychological birth. This availability of the mother and the infant's innate capacity to engage in the relationship are important for the evolution of the child's "subsequent sense of the self and others, for it is the period during which the experiential precursors of self and object are laid down" (Greenburg & Mitchell, 1983, p. 275).

Around 4 to 5 months of age, at the height of the symbiotic phase, there seems to be a behavioral shift, which is one of the first indicators of the beginning of the first subphase of the separation-individuation differentiation. During the symbiotic phase the infant maintained a non-specific social smile, and spontaneously cooed and smiled at both strangers and attachment figures. Now, the infant smiles in response to the mother and may sober and withdraw when a stranger approaches. This is an important indication that a specific bond has been established between the child and the mother (Bowlby, 1958).

Also during the beginning of the differentiation subphase, the baby is increasingly alert and aware of her surroundings as she emerges from the symbiotic state of oneness with the mother. Mahler (1968) labels this increased level of alertness "hatching." With more persistent and outwardly-directed behavior the child starts to explore her mother's body and also starts to push away in order to have a better look at the mother and the environment. The infant becomes an active social participant, as the mother plays games such as "pat-a-cake" and "peek-a-boo." The dialogue between mother and child also expands as the child babbles and attempts to utilize language. During this time the baby slides down from the mother's lap and plays close to her feet. While the infant has started to move away from the mother, she monitors the mother's presence and frets if the mother disappears from view. If a stranger approaches, the infant will huddle close to the mother and soberly inspect that person.

Around 7 to 8 months the baby shows a pattern of visually "checking back" to the mother, utilizing her as a point of orientation. During this time "stranger anxiety" occurs. The baby seems to observe others and compare it to them: the familiar with the unfamiliar. This is an important sign of beginning psychic and body differentiation from the mother. It is during this stage that evolving ego capacities of the child produces significant changes in the child's relationship to the object world: "The child acquires the capacity to distinguish between contact perceptual and internal sensations; this permits for the first time a clear sensory discrimination between self and object" (Greenberg & Mitchell, 1983, p. 275). If the child shows acute distress in response to strangers this may be a danger signal. There may have been difficulties in the preceding symbiotic stage and the child may lack a sense of basic trust.

The second subphase of separation-individuation, practicing, overlaps differentiation and is a peak point of hatching. Practicing is divided into two periods: 1) the early practicing phase (around 8 to 10 months) in which the infant utilizes her ability to physically move away from the mother by crawling, climbing, and standing, but still holding on; and, 2) the practicing period proper (around 10 to 18 months) when the child achieves upright locomotion (Mahler, Pine, & Bergman, 1975). There are three interrelated developments that contribute to the child's increased ability to separate and individuate: "the rapid body differentiation from the mother; the establishment of a specific bond with her; and the growth and functioning of the autonomous ego apparatuses in close proximity to the mother" (Mahler, Pine, & Bergman, 1975, p. 65).

The expanding motor capacity of the early practicing period widens the child's world and allows for exploration at some distance from mother. But the mother continues to be needed as a stable point and the child will return to her for "emotional refueling" (Mahler, Pine, & Bergman, 1975, p. 69). The child may express her need for affection and interaction with the mother by asking for hugs and kisses or by raising her arms to be picked up. During this time the child also becomes interested in the inanimate objects of the world, one of which may become a "transition object" (Winnicott, 1953) such as a blanket or stuffed animal. The child may become deeply attached to this object and refuse to sleep or go out of the house without it. With the achievement of upright locomotion, the child enters the practicing subphase proper. Mahler (1974) notes that the child's first steps are almost inevitably taken in the direction away from the mother, which may point to an innate tendency toward separation which is response manifested at this stage of development.

The upright position gives the child a whole new perspective as she takes the greatest single step in human individuation and begins a "love affair with the world" (Greenacre, 1957). The child's narcissism and sense of omnipotence is at its peak as "the world is the junior toddler's oyster" (Mahler, Pine, & Bergman, 1975, p 71). It is characteristic of the child during this period to be impervious to falls or knocks as she explores her expanding world. The child moves rapidly from room to room and seems to get into and climb over everything. She is also able to play in an area away from the mother. However, if the mother is absent from the child's environment the child may exhibit "low-keyedness" (Mahler, Pine,

& Bergman, 1975, p. 74) in which she slows down and seems less interested in her surroundings until the mother returns.

The child is elated as she escapes from the fusion and engulfment with mother, yet while she runs off, she can also enjoy being swooped up as a way of working out autonomy and the reassurance that her mother will still want to catch her (Mahler & Gosliner, 1955). The mother must be attuned to the maturational and developmental pace of her child, and she must respond to the child's explorations and not to her own preconceived ideas of what the child should be. If the child does not move away from the mother, but stays close without evidence of pleasure or moves away but does not maintain contact with her, the child may be having difficulty negotiating this subphase.

By the middle of the second year, the infant has become a toddler and enters the third subphase, rapprochement. This is a time when the child is undergoing developmental and maturational changes as well as those involving object relationships: "It is a period of rapidly changing autonomous ego functions, most notably highlighted by rapid gains in language ability and by the appearance of reality testing" (Greenberg & Mitchell, 1983, p. 278). The child utilizes her increased language abilities to ask endless questions and to share with the mother her interest in books and other reading material. This is also the time when the child becomes aware of the anatomical differences between the sexes and her own gender identity.

As the child begins to recognize her separateness from her mother, she also experiences a decline in omnipotence, a sense of dependency, and increased separation anxiety (Mahler, Pine, & Bergman, 1975). The rapprochement subphase is ushered in by the child's realization that the mother is actually a separate person, one who will not always be available to help her deal with the world. Now the child seems to be constantly concerned with the mother's whereabouts and she seems to have a wish for the mother to share every one of her new skills and experiences as well as a great need for the mother's love. The child now involves the mother in play, bringing

the mother toys or insisting that the mother move from room to room with her. Mother is approached at a new, higher level of interaction, characterized by the child's increased use of language and the child's acceptance of physical separation. During this subphase there is a rapprochement crisis, lasting from approximately 18 to 24 months of age. Here the child works out her increased need for the mother while protecting her own autonomy. The child gradually relinquishes the delusion of her own grandeur while continuing to develop a sense of individuality and separateness. The child may be insatiable, dissatisfied, defiant, uncompromising, prone to temper tantrums, and experience rapid mood swings which are often expressed in fights with mother. The word "no" becomes the child's favorite as the child asserts herself, talks back, and may threaten to hit mother. Rapprochement is "characterized by the rapid alternating desire to push mother away and cling to her–a behavioral sequence that the word 'ambitendency' describes most accurately" (Mahler, Pine & Bergman, 1975, p. 95). The rapprochement subphase places a new set of demands on the mother who may view her child's development as regressive. The child is very sensitive to reactions of approval and disapproval by the mother since she fears the loss of her love. The mother must contend with her own conscious and unconscious feelings about symbiosis and separation as well as understand the conflicting demands of her child. Rapprochement, then, is a difficult and painful time and the manner in which the child resolves this intense struggle may determine many features of later personality development. Successful resolution of the rapprochement crisis brings to a head the conflict between the need for mother and the need for separation and individuation. Mahler (1971) saw the successful completion of this subphase as one of the central developmental requirements for the avoidance of subsequent severe psychopathology.

The fourth subphase of separation and individuation is libidinal object constancy. This subphase differs from the preceding three because it is open-ended, with the results varying throughout life. The main task of this subphase is twofold: "(1) the achievement of a definite, in certain aspects lifelong individuality, and (2) the attainment of a certain degree of object constancy" (Mahler, Pine, & Bergman, 1975, p. 109).

The emotional object constancy described by Mahler is different from Jean Piaget's (1952) object permanence, which occurs at about 18 to 20 months. Piaget focuses on the child's relations with inanimate things, and the idea of object permanence indicates that things continue to exist in the child's mind even if they are not present. The object for Mahler is the mother, an internalized image that the child develops as the result of a long process of gradual unification of "good" and "bad" aspects of the object. This internalization supplies comfort to the child in the mother's physical absence and allows the child to function separately.

The fourth subphase is also characterized by the unfolding of complex cognitive functions: verbal communication, reality testing, and fantasy. This is a period of rapid ego differentiation and individuation. The "...establishment of mental representations of the self as distinctly separate from representations of the object paves the way to self-identity formation" (Mahler, Pine, & Bergman, 1975, p. 117). It is during this time that the child begins to express a sense of pride in herself and what she can accomplish. Many self-help skills are mastered and the child begins to compare herself to others. An awareness of time also develops and the child has a sense of tomorrow and is able to wait. The child is also more amenable to the mother's requests and the mother can bargain and reason with her child. The mother now views the child as a junior member of the family who is able to play with her peers as well as other adults.

Many conflicts occur during the third year and object constancy is still a fluid and reversible accomplishment for the child as progression is often punctuated by ambivalence and regression, especially around the mother's departures. Both object constancy and the consolidation of individuality are easily challenged by the struggle around toilet training and by the awareness of the anatomical sex difference: a blow to the little girl's narcissism and a danger to the little boy's body integrity. Thus, this fourth substage "...is dependent on the context of many other develop-mental factors, the prevailing ego state, and the environmental affective response of the moment" (Mahler, Pine, & Bergman, 1975, p. 112).

Development Approach

At the outset we acknowledge the risk of simplifying psychoanalytic constructs through quantitative reductionism (Luborsky & Spence, 1971). There are three reasons, however, that led us to take this risk. First, Mahler's ideas are based upon extensive observations of normal and abnormal children and their mothers (Mahler, 1968; Mahler et al., 1975). Second, the clinical literature documents positive and negative outcomes associated with variations in quality of separation-individuation (Lax, Bach, & Burland, 1980; McDevitt & Settlage, 1971). And third, Mahler's observations are potentially suited to quantitative research by virtue of careful qualitative documentation of substages of separation–individuation (Foley, Mosey, & McCrae, 1979).

Matriculations of subphases of separation-individuation was guided by qualitative descriptions offered by Mahler (Mahler, 1968, 1971; Mahler & Gosliner, 1955; Mahler et al., 1975). We began by creating a log of behavioral attributes that characterized each subphase. By highlighting recurring attributes across studies of different populations, we hoped to capture the most stable behavioral expressions of underlying separation-individuation processes. Table 1 summarizes the results of this effort.

The major phases of separation-individuation– Differentiation, Practicing, Rapprochement, and Libidinal Object Constancy–are identified in Table 1 along with recurring behavioral attributes characterizing these phases. Sensory closure is the lead attribute of Normal Autism, sensory awakening the lead characteristic of Normal Symbiosis, and object discrimination the lead feature of Differentiation, all subphases of Differentiation. By 10 months, then, the infant has moved developmentally from symbiotic fusion to object differentiation, an important achievement relative to the separation polarity of Mahler's schema.

Practicing is divided into two subphases which continue through the 18th month. The first

Table 1. Behavioral Characteristics of Mahler's Subphases of Separation-Individuation

Phase	Behavioral Attributes

Differentiation (Birth to 8 months)

Normal Autism: birth to 4 weeks: sleeps most of the time; awakens when hungry or in pain; eyes often closed even when awake; falls asleep after feeding.

Normal Symbiosis: 1 to 5 months: smiles, gurgles, and coos to stranger and mother alike; motoric excitation with appearance of mother or introduction of novel objects; swipes at or attempts to grab objects.

Differentiation: 5 to 10 months: actively explores mother's body; plays social games such as pat-a-cake and peek-a-boo; smiles to mother but not stranger; withdraws from stranger ("stranger anxiety").

Practicing (8 to 10 months)

Practicing, Subphase 1: 8 to 10 months: explores objects while remaining in proximity of mother or while holding on to her.

Practicing, Subphase 2: 10 to 18 months: explores objects at some distance from the mother, returning periodically for hugs or kisses; expanded interest in inanimate objects in the environment; impervious to knocks or falls.

Rapproachment (18 to 24 months)

Rapproachment: 18 to 24 months: asks endless questions; shares new interests and recently acquired skills with mother; shares mother's interests in books and other materials; contests, challenges, or defies mother's authority.

Libidinal object constancy (24 months ...)

Libidinal Object Constancy: 24 months throughout life. Expresses pride in self and accomplishments; able to wait; more amenable to mother's requests and efforts to reason; functions well during physical absence of mother.

---

subphase is characterized by cautious exploration and the second by exuberant engagement. The child explores the environment while staying close to the mother in the first subphase and while periodically leaving and returning to the mother in the second subphase. This explosion of interest in the inanimate environment during Practicing advances separation and launches individuation.

The next phase, Rapprochement, is characterized initially by endless questions and shared interests and subsequently by negative responses and defiant behaviors. By the end of this phase which spans 18 to 24 months, the child has explored the limits of inanimate (Practicing) and social (Rapprochement) environments which enhance opportunities for individuation. Libidinal Object Constancy which begins at 24 months and continues throughout life is characterized by four recurring themes: sense of self-efficacy; ability to wait; ability to reason; and, ability to function autonomously; all prerequisitely related to mature expressions of individuation.

Behavioral attributes summarized in Table 1 were used to write 12 items for each of six (sub)phases: Normal Autism; Normal Symbiosis; Differentiation; Practicing; Rapprochement; and, Libidinal Object Constancy. The initial pool of 72 items was randomized and rated on a 0-10 scale by family specialists who completed the inventory on 47 children observed in home settings. These children, all from low- to low-middle income families, had a mean age of 19.30 (response sd 7.03). More than 89% were Black; sex of children was proportionately represented.

Based upon initial analyses, items were eliminated that had poor item variances, failed to correlate significantly with the subphase for which they were written, or failed to correlate more with the subphase for which they were written than with the subphase for which they were not written. These procedures led to the elimination of 4 items for each of the first five subphases and to the elimination of 2 items from the last subphase. There are, then, 8 items remaining for each of the first four subphases and 10 items for each of the last two, leaving 50 items in all. Table 2 identifies surviving items for each subphase.

A comparison of Tables 1 and 2 will reveal the degree of correspondence between recurring attributes and surviving items. In general, the level of fit between identified attributes and operational statements is good for Normal Autism, Normal Symbiosis, Differentiation, and Practicing. For Rapprochement and Libidinal Object Constancy, however, the level of fit is not as compelling. For Rapprochement, statements estimating child defiance of maternal authority did not survive psychometrically. Thus items capturing the crisis in Rapprochement described by Mahler are not represented in the current version of the inventory. For Libidinal Object Constancy, items tapping the child's autonomous functioning in the absence of the mother did not survive selection criteria. Together, these noncorrespondences suggest that the current version of the inventory may be more sensitive to the first two major phases (Differentiation and Practicing) than to the last two (Rapprochement and Libidinal Object Constancy). We bear these potential limitations in mind as we examine evidence relevant to the validity of Taylor and Dobbins' Separation-Individuation Inventory.

Validation Studies

In exploring the validity of the Separation-Individuation Inventory, three hypotheses have been evaluated. First, we hypothesized that the correlation between phases is inversely related to the distance between phases. Thus, the correlation between Normal Autism and Normal Symbiosis should be higher than the correlation between Normal Autism and Differentiation which should be higher than the correlation between Normal Autism and Practicing, and so on. This hypothesis is consistent with Mahler's idea that residual and emerging themes can be expressed conterminously with themes prototypic of the predominate phase. Second, we hypothesized that scores on the Separation-Individuation Inventory pattern with the chronological age of the child. If the mean age of the sample is six months, for example, we would expect that the score on Differentiation would be higher than scores on other phases. These predictions follow Mahler's observations that chronological age is associated with phases of separation-individuation. And third, we hypothesize that quality of caregiving environment affects level of separation-individuation outcomes. Children at risk of abuse or neglect will be compared with children enrolled in an enriched daycare environment. While Mahler has found that level of child adjustment is related to quality of separation-individuation outcomes, we expect here that quality of environment affects quality of outcomes to begin with. Results of these three studies will provide at least provisional answers to three questions: (1) Do interphase correlations confirm theoretical expectations? (2) Is the proposed inventory sensitive to maturational changes? and, (3) Is the proposed inventory sensitive to variations in quality of caregiving environment?

Table 2. Separation-Individuation Inventory (Taylor & Dobbins, 1978)

Rate each item on the following scale:

0	1	2	3	4	5	6	7	8	9	10
Not in the Least Like		Not Much Like		Somewhat Like			Very Much Like		Exactly Like	

Normal Autism (8 items)

1.　Sleeps most of the time.
7.　Falls asleep while or shortly after eating.
13.　Awakens only when hungry or in pain.
19.　Frets upon awakening.
25.　Keeps eyes closed during most of feeding.
30.　Cries only when hungry, wet, or soiled.
37.　Seems more interested in feeding than anything else.
44.　Demands food upon awakening.

Symbiosis (8 Items)

5.　When spoken to by attachment figure or stranger, primary response is quieting.
11.　Smiles vigorously to stranger and to attachment figure.
17.　Looks persistently in the face of nursing person.
24.　Coos and gurgles when stimulated by attachment figure or stranger.
29.　Awkwardly swipes at or manipulates toys and novel objects within reach.
36.　Legs kick and arms flail when presented with novel object.
43.　Spontaneously coos and gurgles.
49.　Greets attachment figure and stranger alike with smile.

Differentiation (8 items)

4.　Frets when attachment figure leaves room.
10.　Smiles at attachment figure but not at stranger.
16.　Withdraws when approached by stranger.
23.　Sobers when stranger speaks.
28.　Puts stranger through visual "customs inspection."
34.　Keeps active eye on whereabouts of attachment figure.
41.　Huddles close to attachment figure when stranger enters.
48.　Follows attachment figure around.

Practicing (8 items)

3.　Gets into everything.
9.　Bangs into furniture, knocks over objects, pulls down things.
15.　Climbs up on practically anything.

(table continues)

Rate each item on the scale:

21. Finds play in area away from attachment figure.
27. Has spills, falls, knocks.
33. Bumps into things and keeps right on going.
40. Moves from one area to the next at "astonishing" speed.
47. Seems always on the go.

Rapproachememt (8 items)

2. Insists that attachment figure share in play activities.
8. Brings toys to attachment figure for inspection and comment.
14. When child moves to different room, insists that mother tag along.
20. Seems to have a thousand questions a day for attachment figure.
26. Makes insistent requests of attachment figure for help.
32. Brings newspaper, magazines, books, or toys to attachment figure for inspection and comment.
39. Constantly asking "What's this?" or "What's that?" type of questions.
46. Always wants to show attachment figure something.

Libidinal object constancy (10 items)

6. Following chastisement, quick to make up with attachment figure.
12. Parent more often than not is able to get child to wait for things without blowing up.
18. Expresses pride in accomplishments through phrases such as "Look!" "See!" "Watch me!" or "Mommie!"
22. Responds appropriately with "no" and "yes" to requests made by attachment figure.
31. Expresses pride in self through phrases like "I'm a big girl!"
35. Has sense of time; knows what "after nap" or "tomorrow" means and usually is able to wait.
38. Open to bargaining and negotiation with attachment figure.
42. Attachment figure more often than not is able to reason things out with child.
45. Child tries to talk through conflicts with attachment figure.
50. Child tries to "reason" with attachment figure.

Hypothesis 1: Interphase correlations. The Separation-Individuation Inventory was completed by two teachers and two instructional aides on 24 children enrolled in an enriched daycare center operated by Right Start at the University of Pittsburgh. Individualized lesson plans were implemented with each enrollee, and their school-age adolescent mothers were involved in response structured parenting activities and counseling sessions on a daily basis within the center. More than 83% of the mothers were Black, and their children ranged in age from 4 weeks to 15 months (mean of 6.03).

Inventories were scored by summing ratings associated with each of the six phases identified in Table 2. The pattern of interphase correlations based on these summations is given in Table 3.

As hypothesized, the pattern of correlations between phases tends to be inversely related to the distance between phases. At one extreme, Autism is positively correlated with Symbiosis (0.70) and negatively correlated with the remain-

Table 3. Intercorrelation Patterns Among Components of Separation-Individuation Inventory

Sample 1: Infants of Adolescent Mothers; $N = 24$, Mean Age of 6.03 Months*

	AUT	SYM	DIF	PRA	RAP	LIB
AUT	1.00	0.70	-0.68	-0.68	-0.54	-0.33
SYM		1.00	-0.64	-0.66	-0.54	0.40
DIF			1.00	0.65	0.47	0.33
PRA				1.00	0.55	0.48
RAP					1.00	0.70

*All children, ranging in age from 4 weeks to 15 months, were enrolled in an enriched daycare center operated by Right Start. Their adolescent mothers were involved in structured parenting activities and counseling sessions within the center. The Separation-Individuation Inventory was completed by Teachers and Instructional Aides assigned to infants rated.

ing phases. At the other extreme, Libidinal Object Constancy is positively correlated with Rapprochement (0.70), Practicing (0.48), and Differentiation (0.33) while being negatively correlated with Symbiosis (-0.40) and Autism (-0.33). Of interest is not only the magnitude but also the sign of interphase correlations. Autism and Symbiosis share common variance of similar sign. In contrast, Autism and the remaining phases share common variance of dissimilar sign. Together, this pattern suggests that Autism and Symbiosis have socioemotional roots different from those linking Autism and the remaining phases. Application of this logic also suggests that Objectal Libidinal Constancy, Practicing, and Differentiation may share similar latent structures which are different from those linking Object Libidinal Constancy to Autism and Symbiosis. Attention, then, to magnitude *and* sign of interphase correlations adds important interpretive nuance. Under the theory (cf. Table 1), Differentiation peaks during the 5 to 10 month period which brackets the mean age of the present sample, 6.03 months. For this reason the pattern of interphase correlations involving Differentiation is of special interest. Differentiation correlates negatively with Symbiosis (-0.64) and Autism (-0.68) and posi-

tively with Practicing (0.65), Rapprochement (0.47), and Libidinal Object Constancy (0.33). Consistent with Mahler's theory, Differentiation which shares common variance with Practicing, Rapprochement, and Libidinal Object Constancy is radically different from Autism and Symbiosis.

Theoretically, all results summarized point in one direction: the inventory successfully differentiates pre-separation from separation and individuation processes. This conclusion is supported by (a) negative correlations between pre-separation processes (Autism and Symbiosis) and separation processes (Differentiation) and (b) negative correlations between pre-separation processes and individuating processes (Practicing, Rapprochement, and Libidinal Object Constancy). That separation is also somewhat distinguishable from individuating processes is suggested from the decreasing magnitude of correlations between Differentiation and Practicing (0.65), Differentiation and Rapprochement (0.47), and Differentiation and Libidinal Object Constancy (0.33). Thus while the sign of interphase correlations is useful in characterizing distinctions between pre-separation, separation, and individuating processes, the magnitude of interphase correlations is useful in differentiating the continuum of separation-individua-

Table 4. Basic Descriptive Statistics on Components of Separation-Individuation Inventory

Sample 1: Infants of Adolescent Mothers*; $N = 24$, Mean Age of 6.03 Months

Phase	Mean	S.D.	Range	Split-Half Reliabilility	Interrater** Reliability
AUT	13.58	6.69	0-56	.94	.88
SYM	22.88	16.56	0-56	.74	.87
DIF	34.58	22.18	0-75	.87	.93
PRA	23.38	25.87	0-78	.87	.99
RAP	12.29	16.58	0-49	.96	.85
LIB	3.03	5.47	0-18	.77	1.00

* See footnote in Table 3. Split-half reliability was determined using the Spearman-Brown method and interrater reliability using the Pearson correlation coefficient. ** $N = 6$ pairs.

tion processes. Overall, evaluation of signs and magnitudes of interphase correlations provides provisional evidence that the proposed inventory is theoretically consistent in its differentiation of pre-separation, separation, and individuation processes.

Hypothesis 2: Developmental changes. Since 10 items survived for Libidinal Object Constancy and 8 items for the first five subphases, it was necessary to prorate the set of scales prior to evaluating our developmental hypothesis. This we did by multiplying summed ratings on the 10-item scale by 0.80 and using unmodified sums on 8-item scales.

Table 4 provides descriptive and reliability statistics for each phase on Sample 1 described under Hypothesis 1. Since the mean chronological age of Sample 1 was 6.03 months, we would expect that the highest score would fall in Differentiation which brackets the mean age of this sample. Table 4 indicates that the expected pattern is precisely what we found. The mean associated with Differentiation is 34.58 with adjacent means being 22.88 for Symbiosis and 23.38 for

Practicing. While split-half and interrater reliabilities are all within an acceptable range, standard deviations for all but Differentiation are large in relation to reported means. Keeping in mind that *all* items were rated for each child in the sample, children for instance, in Practicing were also rated on items for Autism, large standard deviations outside the model phase Differentiation are expected. Because of striking variations in variances across phases, the assumption of homoscedasticity is violated and formal evaluation of differences is not defensible.

We further evaluated our developmental hypothesis on a sample of 62 cases, 20% of whom were offspring of low-income families referred to Right Start for child abuse or neglect. Remaining families were referred by public health nurses, community mental health centers, and local hospitals for suspected or documented problems in parenting. Table 5 provides descriptive and reliability statistics on this older sample of children rated by four Family Specialists who visited each home at least once per week for three months prior to rating items on the Separation-Individuation Inventory.

Table 5. Basic Descriptive Statistics on Components of Separation-Individuation Inventory

Sample 2: Children of Mothers Referred for Problems in Parenting*; $N = 62$, Mean Age of 23.14 Months

Phase	Mean	S.D.	Range	Split-half Reliability
AUT	4.80	10.81	0-78	.65
SYM	13.74	14.10	0-77	.72
DIF	21.62	16.15	0-74	.81
PRA	32.84	21.58	0-76	.88
RAP	27.34	17.13	0-70	.82
LIB	22.09	16.96	0-58	.92

* Children ranged in age from 11 to 36 months. The Separation-Individuation measure was completed by Right Start Family Specialists who made home visits at least once per week. Interrater reliability was not available because of the service delivery context within which ratings were made. Split-half reliability was estimated using the Spearman-Brown method.

Since the mean age of the sample is 23.14 months, we would expect that the highest mean score would fall in Rapprochement which brackets this chronological age. However, the highest mean score of 32.84 falls in the preceeding subphase, Practicing. While this pattern suggests possibly a degree of developmental lag associated with this sample at risk (a relationship which we do not evaluate formally for reasons indicated above), it could be related as well to our previous note that the Inventory may not measure advanced stages of separation-individuation as well as earlier stages. Which of these alternative explanations is more plausible is the subject of our third hypothesis.

Hypothesis 3: Caregiver environment. In estimating quality of caregiving environment on separation-individuation, it is important initially to adjust separation-individuation scores to accommodate variations in child age. Otherwise, there is the risk of misinterpretation, particularly where chronological age and caregiver quality are confounded as in Samples 1 and 2. A procedure for scoring separation-individuation is proposed to facilitate comparison of the effects of caregiver environments on separation-individua-

tion processes for children of various ages. The assumptions, application, and limitations of this procedure are now reviewed.

There are eight items for each subphase except for the last which contains ten items. Each of the first five subphases has a possible range of 0-80 since each item is rated on a 0-10 scale. The last subphase is prorated by multiplying its sum by 0.80 so that it, too, has a possible range of 0-80.

While it is possible to take a child's Subphase Score X over the maximum 80 and multipliy the result by 100 to obtain a substage score, this procedure disregards the age of the child. This problem may be corrected in part by multiplying the preceding product by the Theoretical Upper Age Limit L of the subphase in question over the Chronological Age C of the child. All values of L are given in Table 1, except for the value of L for Libidinal Object Constancy which we have set to 36 months in this study. With C and L in hand, Separation-Individuation scores may be estimated from

$$S_i = (L/C) \times (X/80) \times 100,$$

where S_1 will represent Delayed Separation -Individuation, S_2 Appropriate Separatio--

Individuation, and S_3 Advanced Separation-Individuation. Total Separation-Individuation is estimated from

$$S_t = (S_2 + S_3) - S_1,$$

where the Delayed component is subtracted from the sum of Appropriate and Advanced components.

An infant of 4 months presents the following profile: 17 (AUT), 22 (SYM), 30 (DIF), 12 (PRA), 9 (RAP), and 2 (LIB). Under the theory presented by Mahler, the *prototypic subphase* for a 4 month old child should be Differentiation (DIF). Residual themes from the prior period Symbiosis (SYM) and anticipatory movement toward the next phase Practicing (PRA) are developmentally expected. Components of Separation - Individuation are estimated as follows:

$$S_1 = (5/4) \times (22/80) \times 100$$
$$= 34.38$$

for the Delayed component defined on $L = 5$ months for Symbiosis (cf. Table 1),

$$S_2 = (10/4) \times (30/80) \times 100$$
$$= 93.75$$

for the Appropriate component defined on $L = 10$ months for Differentiation,

$$S_3 = (18/4) \times (12/80) \times 100$$
$$= 67.50$$

for the Advanced component defined on $L = 18$ months for Practicing. Total Separation- Individuation, then, is estimated from

$$S_t = (93.75 + 67.50) - 34.38$$
$$= 126.87,$$

suggesting that the child in question may be somewhat advanced, given a theoretically expected score of 100 under stipulations of the model and its estimation by the Separation-Individuation Inventory. This inference is conditioned by the validity of four assumptions which will be explored in future research:

1. Theoretical Upper Age Limits L in Table 1 are defensible empirically;

2. The summed child score X is linearly related to progress on the phase being evaluated;

3. Subphases contiguous to the prototypic subphase (S_1, S_3) are relatively more important in judging separation-individuation process than noncontiguous phases; and

4. Overall separation-individuation progress should be estimated net delayed separation-individuation outcome (S_3).

In evaluating recommended scoring procedures, we used measures developed by Taylor, Underwood, Thomas, & Franklin (1988) to subdivide Sample 2 into three subsamples: 2A families which are at low risk of abuse or neglect; 2B families at high risk of neglect; and 2C families at high risk of abuse. Mean chronological age of subsamples was within 1.21 months of the mean age of 23.14 months for the parent sample. Sample 1 together with Subsamples 2A, 2B, and 2C provide a continuum of quality in caregiving environments: enriched daycare; low risk of abuse or neglect; high risk of neglect; and high risk of abuse. While some investigators regard neglectful environments as more deleterious than abusive environments, our research using the recommended measure to classify risk status indicates that abuse is more deleterious than neglect (Long, 1981; McDonough, 1983).

Table 6 presents mean Delayed, Appropriate, Advanced, and Total separation-individuation scores across the continuum of caregiving environments.

The most striking and systematic differentiation of caregiving environments is reflected in total separation-individuation scores: 120 for Daycare; 103 for Low Risk of Abuse or Neglect; 85 for High Risk of Neglect; and 65 for High Risk of Abuse. Systematic difference in total scores associated with Sub-samples 2A, 2B, and 2C cannot be accounted for by age alone since children in these groups fall within 1.21 months of the mean age of Sample 2. The overall implication from Table 6 is that quality of caregiver environment is directly related to separation-individuation outcomes. However suggestive these differences

Table 6. Comparison of Separation-Individuation Scores Across Four Samples Varying in Quality of Caregiving Environment*

		Separation-Individuation Scores			
Sample	N	Delayed S_1	Appropriate S_2	Advanced S_3	Total S_t
#1: Daycare	24	24.72	72.33	72.81	120.42
#2A: Low Risk	29	32.39	69.24	66.12	102.97
#2B: High Neg	17	27.09	60.19	51.76	84.86
#2C: High Abuse	16	30.89	58.54	37.27	64.92

* Sample #1 children were exposed to enriched daycare experiences. Samples #2A, #2B, and #2C are disaggregated from Sample 2 families. Based upon measures developed by Taylor, Underwood, Thomas, & Franklin (1988), Sample #2A families are at low risk of abuse or neglect, Sample #2B families at high risk of neglect, and Sample #2C families at high risk of abuse.

might be, it is premature to evaluate them formally until the validity of assumptions underlying the method of scoring is examined further. Until such time, the evidence linking caregiver quality with separation-individuation outcomes is regarded as provisional. It is reasonable to argue, however, that the hint of developmental delay in Table 5 is not primarily a function of measurement limitation.

Summary and Conclusion

The developmental sequence through which the infant moves from the sleeplike state of early neonatal life to an awareness of social reality and the achievement of separate identity has been labeled the separation-individuation process by Mahler. Six developmental subphases have been identified: 1) Normal Autism, where the infant sleeps most of the time; 2) Normal Symbiosis, where the infant smiles and coos to mother and stranger alike; 3) Differentiation where the infant smiles to mother but not strangers; 4) Practicing, where the infant explores the inanimate environment often at some physical distance from the mother; 5) Rapprochement, where the child asks endless questions of the mother whose authority is frequently challenged; and 6) Libidinal Object Constancy, where the child displays increasing

patience, pride in self accomplishments, and ability to function well during the absence of mother.

On the basis of salient behavioral attributes characterizing each subphase, Taylor and Dobbins (1978) developed an initial pool of items to operationalize the separation-individuation process. Items were eliminated which had restricted variance, correlated poorly with the subphase for which they were written, or correlated more with the subphase for which they were not written than with the subphase for which they were written. The revised Separation-Individuation Inventory consists of 8 items for each of the first five subphases and 10 for the last.

Three hypotheses were evaluated on the revised Separation-Individuation Inventory. First, we hypothesized that the correlation between Subphases is inversely related to the distance between subphases. Thus, we expected that Differentiation would be more highly correlated with adjacent subphases Normal Symbiosis and Practicing than with nonadjacent subphases Normal Autism and Rapprochement. The data were generally consistent with expectations. Second, we hypothesized that scores on the Separation-Individuation measure pattern with the chronological age of the child. This hypothesis was evaluated on one sample of infants enrolled in an enriched daycare center with structured programs for infants and their adolescent mothers and on a second sample of infants and toddlers of mothers referred for problems in parenting. In the first sample, the pattern of separation-individuation scores was consistent with chronological age, and in the second sample, the pattern of separation-individuation scores suggested a degree of developmental delay. The possibility that separation-individuation scores might vary across quality of caregiving environments was evaluated further under our third hypothesis. The second sample was subdivided into three subsamples: low risk of child abuse or neglect; high risk of child neglect; and high risk of child abuse. There was support for the third hypothesis which predicted that quality of caregiving environment affects level of separation-individuation: the mean was highest for infants enrolled in the enriched daycare center and next highest for infants and toddlers in the low risk of abuse or neglect subsample. Infants and toddlers in the high risk subsamples for neglect and abuse had relatively low mean totals on separation-individuation, the mean for the high abuse subsample being the lowest. Overall, the results suggest that subphases of the Inventory are correlated in the manner expected, sensitive to maturational changes in children, and sensitive to variations in quality of caregiving.

There are two immediate implications for future research. First, there is need for further developmental work with the instrument itself. We need more extensive studies of interrater reliability and systematic evaluation of assumptions underlying the method of scoring. Moreover, we need to explore the possibility of supplementing Rapprochement with items reflecting oppositional behaviors characterizing this period. Second, there is need for studies that focus on the validity of the Separation-Individuation Inventory. To what extent do variations in parental style influence quality of separation-individuation outcomes? To what extent do variations in parental affect or mood influence quality of separation-individuation outcomes? To what extent do child temperament influence these outcomes? To what extent does child age and sex influence these outcomes? To what extent do separation-individuation outcomes vary by so-

cioeconomic status? The future research agenda, then, must evaluate the inventory itself as well as the implications of the inventory for other constructs.

Note

1. This research was supported in part from grants from the Center for Minority Groups Mental Health of MIMH, the Allegheny County Mental Health Retardation Program, the Commonwealth of Pennsylvania Department of Welfare, and Allegheny County Children and Youth Services.

References

Bowlby, J. (1958). The nature of the child's tie to the mother. *International Journal of Psychoanalysis, 39*, 350-373.

Foley, G., Mosey, A., & McCrae, M. (1979). *The attachment separation-individuation (A-S-I) scale–experimental edition.* Reading, PA: Family Centered Resource Project, Pennsylvania Department of Education.

Greenacre, P. (1957). The childhood of the artist: Libidinal phase development and giftedness. In R. S. Eissler, A. Freud, H. Hartmann, & M. Kris (Eds.), *The psychoanalytic study of the child* (Vol. 12, pp. 27-72). New York: International Universities Press.

Greenberg, J. R., & Mitchell, S. A. (1983). *Object relations in psychoanalytic theory.* Cambridge, MA: Harvard University Press.

Lax, R. F., Bach, S., & Burland, J. A. (1980). *Rapprochement: The critical subphase of separation-individuation* New York: Jason Aronson.

Long, L. G. (1981). *The effect of parental abuse and neglect upon the quality of separation and individuation in the child.* Unpublished doctoral dissertation, University of Pittsburgh.

Luborsky, L. B., & Spence, D. P. (1971). Quantitative research on psychoanalytic therapy. In A. E. Bergin & S. L. Garfield (Eds.), *Handbook of psychotherapy and behavior change: An empirical analysis* (pp. 408-437). New York: Wiley.

Mahler, M. (1963). Thoughts about development and individuation. In R. S. Eissler, A. Freud, H. Hartmann, & M. Kris (Eds.), *The psychoanalytic study of the child* (Vol. 18, pp. 307-324). New York: International Universities Press.

Mahler, M., & Gosliner, B. J. (1955). On symbiotic child psychosis: Genetic, dynamic and restitutive aspects. In R. S. Eissler, A. Freud, H. Hartmann, & M. Kris (Eds.), *The psychoanalytic study of the child* (Vol.10, pp. 195-212). New York: International Universities Press.

Mahler, M., Pine, F., & Bergman, A. (1975). *The psychological birth of the human infant.* New York: Basic Books.

McDevitt, J. B., & Settlage, C. F. (Eds.). (1971). *Separation-individuation: Essays in honor of Margaret S. Mahler.* Madison, CT: International Universities Press.

McDonough, M. C. (1983). *Relationships among lashing out, neglect, affiliation and control in primary parent-to-child relations.* Unpublished doctoral dissertation, University of Pittsburgh.

Piaget, J. (1952). *The origins of intelligence in children.* New York: International Universities Press. (Original work published 1936.).

Taylor, J., Dobbins, J. (1978). *Separation-Individuation Inventory.* Unpublished manuscript, University of Pittsburgh, Institute for the Black Family.

Taylor, J., Underwood, C., Thomas, L., & Franklin, A. (1996). Measuring psychological maltreatment of infants and toddlers. In R. L. Jones (Ed.), *Handbook of tests and measurements for Black populations* (Vol. 1). Hampton, VA: Cobb & Henry.

Winnicott, D. W. (1953). Transitional objects and transitional phenomena: A study of the first not-me possession. *International Journal of Psychoanalysis, 34,* 89-97.

Wolff, P. H. (1959). Observations on newborn infants. *Psychosomatic Medicine, 21,* 110-118.

For additional information, contact:

Jerome Taylor
University of Pittsburgh
Institute for the Black Family
Department of Africana Studies
Pittsburgh, PA 15260
Telephone: (412) 648-7217
Fax: (412) 648-5656

Measuring Psychological Maltreatment of Infants and Toddlers[1]

Jerome Taylor, Carrie Underwood, Lenall Thomas, and Agnes Franklin

Abstract

A multistage strategy was used to develop measures of abusive and neglecting dispositions on six successively drawn samples of mothers referred by a child protective service agency for child abuse or neglect or by mental and public health agencies for problems in parenting. Six validation studies are described along with formal psychometric properties of the revised inventory.

Background

Psychological maltreatment has been defined in terms of acts which "...deny or frustrate efforts on the part of an individual to satisfy...basic psychological needs to the degree that the individual's functioning becomes maladaptively deviant" (Hart, Germain, & Brassard, 1987, p. 8). Based on the feedback from scholars and practitioners, the Office for the Study of the Psychological Rights of the Child at Indiana University identified seven attributes of psychological maltreatment:

1. Rejection: actively refusing to acknowledge a child's needs or requests for help;

2. Degradation: publicly denigrating or humiliating a child;

3. Terrorization: threatening to harm or kill the child;

4. Isolation: denying social contact with others inside or outside the home;

5. Corruption: teaching antisocial behaviors or prejudicial attitudes;

6. Exploitation: encouraging participation in pornographic or sexual activities or forcing the child to play the role of surrogate parent rather than attend school; and

7. Denial of Emotional Responsiveness: passively ignoring the child's attempts to interact or mechanical handling of the child (Hart et al., 1987).

From this inclusive definition of psychological maltreatment, it would appear that traditional concerns with child abuse are related to attributes 1 (Rejection), 2 (Degradation), and 3 (Terrorization) while traditional concerns with child neglect are related to attributes 4 (Isolation), and 7 (Denying Emotional Responsiveness). This leaves, then, attribute 5 (Corruption) which may be regarded as a form of child abuse and attribute 6 (Exploitation) which may be regarded as a form of sexual abuse. In combination, the attributes summarized by Hart et al. (1987) seem primarily to reflect aspects of child abuse, child neglect, and sexual abuse, although physical aspects of child neglect and sexual abuse are more often implied than stated. Nonetheless, physical abuse is also assigned to the more inclusive category of psychological maltreatment (Erickson & Egeland, 1987).

While recent studies and reviews indicate that psychological maltreatment impairs cognitive, social, and emotional functioning (Aber & Allen, 1987; Augoustinos, 1987; Brassard & Gelardo, 1987; Lyons-Ruth, Connel, Zoll, & Stahl, 1987) and that psychological maltreatment during childhood increases the risks of suicide during adolescence (Oliver, 1984), personality disorders during adulthood (Bryer, Nelson, Miller, & Krol, 1987) and abusive behaviors as an adult (Deykin & Alpert, 1985), the field has not yet progressed to the point of affirming interval measures of psychological maltreatment.

In the literature, nominal categorizations of abuse and neglect abound. Based upon agency referral (Aber & Allen, 1987), interview routines (Bailey & Bailey, 1986), or home observation (Erickson & Egeland, 1987), cases are classified as maltreated or nonmaltreated, as verbally abused, physically abused, sexually abused, physically neglected, or some combination or further differentiation of these nominal categories. Most measurement schema differentiate *types* of maltreatment but not *magnitude* within types or *magnitude of differences* between types. In consequence, the continuum of risk within types and the implication of differences between types are still underdeveloped areas of inquiry. To address these shortcomings, the development effort described here was undertaken with four objectives in mind: (a) to operationalize abusive disposition as a continuous rather than a categorical variable; (b) to operationalize neglecting disposition as a continuous rather than a categorical variable; (c) to

differentiate the risk of abuse from the risk of neglect; and (d) to operationalize overall psychological maltreatment as a continuous rather than a categorical variable; and, (e) to evaluate the construct validity of resulting measures.

Objectives (a) through (d) are taken up in the next section on Development Approaches, and objective (e) in the section Summary and Conclusion. We note at the outset that measures were developed on predominantly Black metropolitan samples of low-income families with children 36 months of age or younger.

Development Approach

A multistage strategy was used to develop measures of abusive and neglecting dispositions on six successively drawn samples of mothers referred by a child protective service agency for child abuse or neglect or by mental and public health agencies for problems in parenting. Altogether, 480 mothers with children from 2 to 36 months of age were evaluated, each being either an adjudicated case of abuse or neglect or at risk of abuse or neglect. All cases were referred to the Right Start Program for Family Development, University of Pittsburgh, directed by the senior author. This program provides unique opportunities to develop or apply theoretical, measurement, and intervention innovations to problem families of a wide range. Data for studies reported here were collected by trained professional and paraprofessional members of the Right Start staff.

In the initial effort, four items were written for each of four scales: Lashing Out (physical or psychological assault on the child); Externalization (attribution of blame to the child); Escape (leaving the child unattended); and Removal (isolating the child for extended periods of time). The first two scales were intended to measure aspects of abusive disposition and the last two aspects to measure neglecting disposition. Each item was rated on a 0 (Not in the Least Like) to 10 (Exactly Like) scale by trained observers who had visited each home at least once per week for a period of at least three months prior to rating the four scales identified. On a sample of 20 mothers referred by a child protective agency, item and scale variances were unacceptably restricted for our purpose of estimating the continuum of risk within the sample. Two decisions were made to enhance item and scale variances. First, noun-verb combinations such as "Parent beats" were softened to "Parent spanks" to spread item and scale variances. Second, some of the items were positively keyed ("Parent is gentle with child") and some negatively keyed ("Parent yells at child"). The revised item set was administered under conditions identical to the original item set to a second sample of 25 mothers referred by a child protective service agency. Item variances were appreciably improved under Revision 1. The interscale correlation between Lashing Out and Externalization was sufficiently high to justify combining these scales into a magnum scale which we called Lashing Out. Likewise, the correlation between Escape and Removal scales was sufficiently high to justify combining these into a magnum scale which we called Neglect.

For Revision 2, the number of items for Lashing Out was extended from 8 to 28 and the number of items for Neglect from 8 to 21. In each instance, items were written to fill conceptual gaps identified from the literature on abuse and neglect and from our experience in working with families at risk of abuse and neglect. Revision 2 was administered by trained raters to 98 mothers referred for abuse and neglect under conditions identical to those described for Revision 1. On this sample of 98 mothers with children between 2 and 36 months (mean of 22.3), more than 75% were Black, 71% single, and less than 50% high school graduates.

On the set of 28 Lashing Out and 21 Neglect items defining Revision 2, two analytic strategies were used. First, the internal homogeneity of each scale was evaluated by examining the Pearson correlation between each item and its scale total. Each item failing to correlate significantly with scale for which it was written was eliminated. Second, the differential validity of each item set was evaluated under procedures proposed by Taylor (1973). Each item which failed to correlate significantly more with the scale for which it was written than it did with the scale for which it was not written was eliminated. The correlation

obtained between Lashing Out and Neglect scales was .52 before and .32 after differential validity and item homogeneity procedures were applied. Following application of these procedures, item-total correlations ranged from .57 to .85 for Lashing Out , with a median of .73, and .46 to .79 for Neglect, with a median of .67. The number of items for Lashing Out was reduced from 28 to 21 and the number of items for Neglect from 21 to 17. The Spearman-Brown split–half reliability was .95 for Lashing Out and .93 for Neglect on Revision 2 for the sample of 98. The mean and median of the Lashing Out Scale were 76.48 and 72.50, with a standard deviation of 28.03 and range of 5 to 123. On a subsample of 72, test-retest reliability over a two-week period was .92 for Lashing out and .88 for Neglect.

In summary, then, Revision 2 of Lashing Out and Neglect exhibited psychometrically acceptable dispersion characteristics and internal reliability. However, in a subsequent replication sample of 86 families referred for child abuse and neglect, the correlation between Lashing Out and Neglect increased from .33 to .64. To reduce covariation between these scales, the same item strategies used to develop Revision 2 were reapplied to form Revision 3. This resulted in the elimination of five additional items from the Lashing Out Scale, bringing the total number of items for each scale to 17. Since the resulting correlation between scales was .46 on this sample and .53 in a subsequent sample, we concluded that there is an irreducible communality between the scales which is not subject to further reduction. The set of items for Revision 3 of Lashing Out are given in Table 1.

Instructions for scoring negatively (A) and positively (B) keyed items of Lashing Out are given along with instructions for calculating the total (LO). For the negatively keyed set, items 2 (P is impatient with C's progress), 4 (P's expectations of C are unrealistic), 10 (P insists that C do things a certain way), 12 (P gets annoyed when C doesn't follow instructions), and 16 (P prefers C to play quietly) all seem related to the Rejection attribute of psychological maltreatment described by Hart et al., (1987). Items 3 (P has verbal blowups on C), 6 (P gets angry at C), 11 (P scolds C), and 17 (P yells

Table 1. Items for Measuring Parental Lashing Out (LO). (Jerome Taylor and Barbara Sourkes)

Rate each item using the following scale:

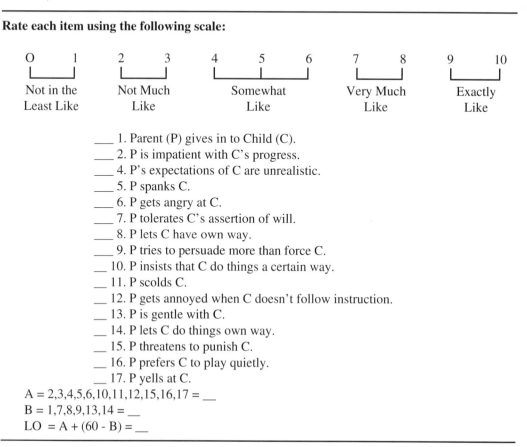

O 1	2 3	4 5 6	7 8	9 10
Not in the Least Like	Not Much Like	Somewhat Like	Very Much Like	Exactly Like

_____ 1. Parent (P) gives in to Child (C).
_____ 2. P is impatient with C's progress.
_____ 4. P's expectations of C are unrealistic.
_____ 5. P spanks C.
_____ 6. P gets angry at C.
_____ 7. P tolerates C's assertion of will.
_____ 8. P lets C have own way.
_____ 9. P tries to persuade more than force C.
__ 10. P insists that C do things a certain way.
__ 11. P scolds C.
__ 12. P gets annoyed when C doesn't follow instruction.
__ 13. P is gentle with C.
__ 14. P lets C do things own way.
__ 15. P threatens to punish C.
__ 16. P prefers C to play quietly.
__ 17. P yells at C.

A = 2,3,4,5,6,10,11,12,15,16,17 = ___
B = 1,7,8,9,13,14 = ___
LO = A + (60 - B) = ___

at C) appear related to varying degrees of the Degradation attribute of psychological maltreatment, while items 5 (P spanks C) and 15 (P threatens to punish C) seem related to the Terrorization component. For the positively keyed set, items 1, 7, 8, and 14 are negative images of the Rejection component, and item 9 and 13 are negative images of the Degradation component. Rejection, Degradation, and Terrorization, then, are integral aspects of the Lashing Out measure. Revision 3 items for the Neglect measure are given in Table 2.

Instructions for scoring the Neglect measure are given in the foot of Table 2. For the negatively keyed set (A), items 10 (P leaves C unattended), 13 (P sleeps when C is awake), and 17 (P takes off when things get rough) are related to the Isolation component of psychological maltreatment (Hart et al., 1987). Items 3 (P permits C to watch T.V. late into the night), 5 (P doesn't feed C at predictable times of the day), and 14 (P is more attentive to T.V. than to C) are directly related to the Emotional Underresponsiveness attribute of psychological maltreatment, and items 8 (P doesn't keep herself up) and 12 (P doesn't make realistic plans are related indirectly to this component. For the positively keyed set (B), all items are directly or indirectly related to the attribute of Emotional Underresponsiveness except item 16 which is related to the Isolation component. Altogether, then, the Social Isolation and Emotional Underresponsiveness attributes of psychological maltreatment are operationalized in the Neglect measure.

Table 2. Items for Measuring Parental Neglect (NEG). (Jerome Taylor and Barbara Sourkes)

Rate each item on the following scale:

0	1	2	3	4	5	6	7	8	9	10

Not in the Like	Not Much Like	Somewhat Like	Very Much Like	Exactly Like

___ 1. Parent (P) is responsive to Child's (C) verbal or nonverbal requests.

___ 2. P considers C's needs to be top priority.

___ 3. P permits C to watch T.V. late into the night.

___ 4. P keeps a constant eye on C.

___ 5. P doesn't feed C at predictable times of the day.

___ 6. P keeps house orderly.

___ 7. P maintains a regular nap and bedding down time for C.

___ 8. P doesn't keep herself up.

___ 9. P is attentive to C's crying.

__ 10. P leaves C unattended.

__ 11. P keeps C's clothes reasonably clean.

__ 12. P doesn't make realistic plans.

__ 13. P sleeps when C is awake.

__ 14. P is more attentive to the T.V. than to C.

__ 15. P keeps C clean.

__ 16. P thinks twice before leaving C with someone else.

__ 17. P takes off when things get rough.

A = 3,5,8,10,12,13,14,17 = __

B = 1,2,4,6,7,9,11,15,16 = __

NEG = A + (90 - B) = __

Data from mothers used in forming Revisions 2 ($N = 98$) and 3 ($N = 86$) were combined into a single file with $N = 184$. On this combined sample, 71% of the mothers were Black, 74% were single, and less than 50% reported completion of high school. The mean child age was 22.91 (SD 8.47), with a range of 2 to 44 months. Fifty-five percent of the children were male. Descriptive statistics associated with Revision 3 of Lashing Out, Neglect, and Psychological Maltreatment (the sum of Lashing Out and Neglect) are presented in Table 3.

The distribution of scores around the mean for LO, NEG, and PM indicate considerable variability in parenting within the age range specified in the study. That dispersion characteristics noted are not simply a function of the child's age is reflected in the fact that correlations between age and LO, NEG, and PM are .27, -.09, and .22, respectively. At most, then, age accounts for less than 9% of the variance in this set of measures. Another way of expressing this is to say that considerable variations in abusive and neglecting dispositions occur at all age levels used in this study. Findings in Table 3 suggest, then, that LO provides a provisional method for operationalizing abusive disposition as a continuous rather than categorical variable (Objective a), that NEG provides a provisional method for operationalizing neglecting disposition as a continuous rather than categorical variable (Objective c), and that PM provides a provisional method for operationalizing

Table 3. Descriptive Statistics and Reliabilities Associated with Taylor and Sourkes' Revision 3 Measures of Lashing Out (LO), Neglect (NEG), and Psychological Maltreatment (PM)*

Measuring	Mean	Median	S.D.	Range	Alpha	Inter-rater Reliability**
LO	44.96	40.10	25.08	3-138	.92	.81
NEG	34.79	28.83	25.61	0-123	.87	.88
PM	80.27	68.75	44.92	7-229	.93	.87

* N = 184; **Based upon home observation of nine families.

psychological maltreatment as a continuous rather than categorical variable (Objective d).

Application of differential validity procedures in the construction of Revisions 2 and 3 removed those items from either scale which patterned more with the scale for which they were not written, a strategy of direct relevance to Objective c, differentiating the risk of abuse from the risk of neglect. A more compelling demonstration of conceptual separation would entail evidence that items written to measure components of abusive and neglecting potential loaded uniquely on factors reflective of these components. A fresh sample of 141 mothers sociodemographically similar to previous samples was drawn to evaluate the dimensionality of LO and NEG items taken together. Table 4 provides a summary of the results.

The five factors in Table 4–Coercion, Permissive, Neglectful, Attentive, and Orderly–account for 91.6% of the total variance obtained under an initial rotation using a principal components procedure and final rotation by Varimax criterion. Of the total variance accounted for, 62.7% is associated with abusive disposition (51.4% for Coercive and 11.3% for Permissive) and 28.9% is associated with neglecting disposition (5.7% for Neglectful, 4.9% for Attentive, and 18.3% for Orderly). Careful inspection of item numbers associated with each factor reveals, with exception of LO 16 on Factor III, that items written to measure abusive disposition loaded on factor dimensions reflecting polarities of that disposition–Coercive and Permissive. For neglecting disposition, all items written loaded on factors reflecting components of that disposi-

tion–Neglectful, Attentive, and Orderly. This evidence of factorial separation of abusive and neglecting dispositions provides provisional support for the metrical separability of abusive and neglecting dispositions (Objective c). In a real sense, this evidence of factor separability validates the success of Revision 2 and 3 procedures designed by Taylor (1973) to eliminate items which correlated significantly more with the scale for which they were not written.

It is possible, however, to specify the continua of abusive, neglecting, and maltreatment dispositions even further through the use of standard error statistics derivable from Table 3. Theoretically, the standard error of measure is the standard deviation of the distribution of individual scores sampled over a very large number of occasions (Magunusson, 1966). It is estimated from

$$S_m = S_i \sqrt{1 - r_i}$$

where S_i = standard deviation of test i and r_i = reliability of test i.

From Table 3, the standard error of measure for LO is

$$S_m = 25.08 \sqrt{1 - .92}$$

$$= 7.09,$$

which is standard deviation of the theoretical distribution of true LO scores generated from a very large number of ratings on the same individual. If a given parent obtains a LO score of 60

Table 4. Factor Structure of Taylor and Sourkes' Revision 3, Measures of Lashing Out (LO) and Neglect (NEG)

Factor I: Coercive (51.4%, eigenvalue = 10.86)

LO 3	(.74)*	Verbal blow ups
LO 5	(.69)	Spanks
LO 6	(.77)	Gets angry at C
LO 11	(.88)	Scolds
LO 12	(.72)	Gets annoyed when instruction not followed
LO 15	(.83)	Threatens to punish
LO 17	(.75)	Yells

Factor II: Permissive (11.3%, eigenvalue = 2.38)

LO 1	(.79)	Gives in
LO 7	(.66)	Tolerates assertion of will
LO 8	(.84)	Lets C have own way
LO 9	(.56)	Persaudes more than forces
LO 13	(.47)	Gentle
LO 14	(.79)	Lets C do things own way

Factor III: Neglectful (5.7%, eigenvalue = 1.2)

LO 16	(.43)	Prefers C to play quietly
NEG 5	(.68)	Irregular feeding times
NEG 10	(.59)	Leaves C unattended
NEG 14	(.63)	More attentive to T.V. than C
NEG 16	(-.48)	Careful about who leaves C with
NEG 16	(.49)	Takes off when difficulties arise

Factor IV: Attentive (4.9%, eigenvalue = 1.04)

NEG 1	(.58)	Responsive to requests
NEG 2	(.48)	C's needs are top priority
NEG 9	(.54)	Attentive to C's crying

FACTOR V: Orderly (18.3%, eigenvalue = 3.87)

NEG 4	(.40)	Keeps constant eye on C
NEG 6	(.82)	Orderly house
NEG 7	(.41)	Regular nap time for C
NEG 8	(-.64)	Doesn't keep herself up
NEG 11	(.63)	C's clothes reasonably clean
NEG 13	(-.54)	Sleeps when C is awake
NEG 15	(.74)	Keeps C clean

* Item factor loadings are in parenthesis.

before treatment and a LO score of 48 following treatment, how shall we evaluate this magnitude of change? Since the magnitude of difference divided by the standard error of measure can be interpreted as a z-score,

$$(60 - 48)/7.09 = 1.69,$$

we would conclude that the magnitude of change is significant at $p < .05$ level under a one-tail hypothesis. In fact, z-scores of 1.65 or higher would be associated with magnitudes of change at the $p < .05$ level. We hasten to add that this would be considered a liberal estimate of significance since the reliability is based upon an alpha coefficient taken at a given point in time rather than a test-retest reliability established on the term of intervention. Technically, this increases the risk of Type I statistical error, which could be decreased somewhat by reducing the alpha criterion from .05 to .01. With this caveat in mind, the z-score can provide at least a provisional gauge of treatment impact associated with an individual case. Rather than speaking strictly in categorical terms of abuse vs. nonabuse, the standard error of measure statistic permits us to speak of the continuum of risk for abusive disposition. As such it might provide a more sensitive gauge of intervention impact as well as diagnostic status.

In like manner, the standard error of measurement can be calculated for NEG and PM– 9.23 and 11.88, respectively. If we apply a one-tail hypothesis to LO scores, magnitude of change at $p < .05$ would be 7.09 x 1.65 = 11.70. Analogously, pre-intervention to post-intervention changes equal to or greater than 16 for NEG and 20 for PM would be associated with $p < .05$ under the caveat already mentioned. We emphasize again the potential diagnostic and treatment advantage of speaking in terms of risk continua rather than nominal categories.

And finally, it is possible to evaluate with greater precision the magnitude of difference between abusive and neglecting dispositions (cf. Magnusson, 1966). If a parent obtains a LO score of 60 and a NEG score of 40, is the 20 point magnitude of difference sufficient to infer that abusive disposition is significantly greater than neglecting disposition? Key to estimating an answer to this question is determining the standard error of difference which structurally is analogous to finding the standard error of measurement:

$$S_d = S_{de} \sqrt{1 - r_{de}}$$

where S_{de} = standard deviation of random differences between tests d and e and r_{de} = reliability of the difference between tests d and e. It can be shown in the present instance that

$$S_{de} = S_{mLO} + S_{mNEG}$$
$$= 7.09 + 9.23$$
$$= 16.23,$$

and that

$$r_{de} = (r_i + r_j - 2r_{ij})/2(1 - r_{ij})$$

where r_i = reliability of test i
r_j = reliability of test j
and r_{ij} = correlation between tests i and j.

From Table 3, r_i = .92 for LO and r_j = .87 for NEG. Using the highest obtained correlation of .53 between LO and NEG (r_{ij}) in conjunction with the preceding estimates, r_{de} = .78. It is now possible to estimate the standard error of difference adjusted for the reliability of difference scores:

$$S_d = 16.32 \sqrt{1 - .78}$$
$$= 7.65$$

Using this adjusted standard error of difference, we can evaluate the difference (60 - 40) associated with LO and NEG. As before, we divide the magnitude of difference by the standard error of difference 7.65, giving 2.61 which is interpretable directly as a z-score. We would conclude under a two-tail hypothesis that a difference of this magnitude between LO and NEG would occur by chance at $p < .01$ under a two-tailed hypothesis which appears appropriate here since magnitudes of difference may be positive or negative. With the S_{de}, then, it is possible to evaluate magnitudes of difference between types of psychological maltreatment. As before, this moves us beyond simple categorization by types to evaluation of magnitude of difference between types.

Available data on Revision 3, then, indicate that measures of LO, NEG, and PM reliably and differentially map the continuum of risk in childrearing. The following section summarizes results of studies bearing on the validity of these measures.

Validation Studies

Six validation studies have been conducted on LO, NEG, and PM measures. Two of these studies identify differences in parenting style associated with components of psychological maltreatment: one explores the association between components of psychological maltreatment and socioemotional adjustment of the child, and three examine the association between components of psychological maltreatment and systemic factors within and outside the home.

Parenting Style

Davis (1976) conducted a study of four mothers presenting contrasting LO ratings obtained from home observation. Mother A had an LO score of 21, Mother B a score of 63, Mother C a score of 85, and Mother D a score of 107. Maternal age was 28, 22, 25, and 27 for A, B, C, and D, respectively, and the corresponding ages of their children were 35, 36, 35, and 36 months. All children were male except for Mother C's child.

Each mother-child pair was observed in a laboratory setting for a 38 minute period segmented in the following way: 10 minutes of mother and child alone without toys; 10 minutes of mothers instructing child how to perform a shape sorting task; 8 minutes of mother's instructing the child how to assemble tinker toy pieces to replicate four different patterns; and, 10 minutes of mother and child alone without toys. All inter-

actions were videotaped, and scripts of each session were typed.

Verbal statements of mothers were classified reliably as positive or negative, 17 subcategories for the former and 18 for the latter. Davis found that:

1. Mother A produced a total of 443 messages, B a total of 421, C a total of 309, and D a total of 232, suggesting therefore that quantity of interaction is inversely related to abusive disposition;

2. During the free interaction segments (first and last 10 minutes), 75% of mother A's messages were positive, 59% of Mother B's, 44% of Mother C's, and 54% of D's, suggesting (except for Mother D) that the continuum of abusive disposition is associated with decreasing levels of positive statements;

3. During instructional segments, 52%, 48%, 52%, and 37% of the messages were positive for Mothers A, B, C, and D, respectively, suggesting that the highest level of abusive disposition (Mother D) is associated with diminished positivity within an instructional context;

4. Overall, the positivity of statements was significantly higher for Mother A than for Mothers B, C, and D and the positivity of statements was higher for Mother C than D.

Within the laboratory context of Davis' study, mothers did not differ in level of negative statements made. The most striking disturbance in behavioral pattern was quantity of statements, followed by diminished positivity during instruction for the highest level of abusive disposition. It may be that this quantitative reduction of verbal statements in general diminished quality of verbal statements during instruction in particular are related to widely reported impairments in cognitive and linguistic performance of abused children. Whatever the precise explanatory mechanism, evidence from this study suggests that the continuum of abusive disposition is primarily related to quantity of verbal engagements throughout the range of LO and secondarily to quality of parental instruction at extreme levels of LO.

Since affiliation and control have been identified as primary dimensions of interpersonal relationships, McDonough (1983) conducted a study to evaluate the extent to which these dimensions covary with LO, NEG, and PM. Parental affiliation was measured by Taylor's (1988a) Affiliation Inventory which estimates levels of warmth, support, and helpfulness of relationships. Parental control was measured by Taylor's Control Inventory (Taylor & McMillian, 1996a) which estimates levels of coerciveness, restrictiveness, and rigidity of relationships. On the sample of 96 described under Development Approach, each observed in the home setting, McDonough found the following relationships between dimensions of affiliation and control and the continuua of LO and NEG:

1. Mothers low on LO *and* low on NEG had significantly higher means on affiliation (128.53) than mothers high on LO and high on NEG (88.18);
2. Mothers low on LO *and* low on NEG had significantly lower scores on control (37.20) than mothers high on LO *and* high on NEG (66.71);
3. Various combinations such as high LO-low NEG versus low LO-high NEG were not significantly different on measures of affiliation or control;
4. The correlation between LO and affiliation and LO and control were -.56 and .59, respectively; and,
5. The correlation between NEG and affiliation and NEG and control were -.45 and .42, respectively.

Dividing the continuum of PM scores into thirds–High (H), Moderate (M), and Low (L)–McDonough reported the following relationships between psychological maltreatment and the dimensions of affiliation and control:
6. H, M, and L means on affiliation were 129.64, 115.64, and 89.46, H and L as well as M and H being significantly different; and
7. H, M, and L means on control were 66.34, 45.09, and 34.93, with H and L means as well as M and H means being significantly different.

The relative success of PM in differentiating control and affiliation throughout the range (Findings 6 and 7) and the failure of NEG and LO in differentiating these dimensions except at the extremes (Findings 1 and 2) suggest that the combined measure PM may be useful as an initial screening device. For PM scores at the extreme, it might be useful clinically to disaggregate components of PM into LO and NEG.

Together the Davis (1976) and McDonough (1983) studies provide complementary evidence supporting quantitative and qualitative variations in parenting style associated with LO and strong qualitative variations in affiliation and control are associated with PM and with extremes in LO and NEG. In general, these findings are supportive of the nomological validity of these measures of psychological maltreatment.

Socioemotional Adjustment

Under the definition of psychological maltreatment offered by Hart et al. (1987), there should be corresponding evidence that the child's functioning has become "maladaptively deviant." Long (1981) explored whether children at risk of abuse and neglect would be "maladaptively deviant" on a measure of separation-individuation structured around the theory of socioemotional development introduced by Margaret Mahler (1969). LO and NEG were administered to a sample of 62 families. The mean child age was 23 months and the range was from 11 to 36 months. Although most of these low-income families were at risk of abuse and neglect, only 20% of the sample had been referred to Right Start for these reasons. Two findings are especially relevant to the "maladaptively deviant" criterion.

First, children whose mothers were rated above the median of LO were more impaired on the measure of separation-individuation than children whose mothers were rated below the median of LO. While developmental delay on the separation-individuation measure was not significantly different between groups, age-appropriate development on the separation-individuation measure was more impaired for children of mothers scoring above the median than for children of mother scoring below the median on LO. In these analyses, the effects of child age and NEG score were sources of confounding.

Second, children whose mothers were rated above the median NEG were less delayed developmentally than were children whose mothers were rated below the median on NEG. While these groups did not differ significantly on age-appropriate development on the separation-individuation measure, the delayed score of 27 for children of mother above the median was significantly less than the delayed score of 35 for children of mothers below the median. That this pattern of pseudomaturity among children whose mothers were high on NEG was not found for a younger subsample of 33 children with a mean age of 16.8 months suggests that pseudomaturity may be more characteristic of the second and third years.

In summary, Long's study suggests that developmentally appropriate separation-individuation processes are impaired among children whose mothers are rated relatively high on abusive disposition. Further, older children (24-36 months) whose mothers are rated relatively high on neglecting disposition exhibit a pattern of pseudomaturity that is uncharacteristic of children whose mothers are rated relatively low on neglecting disposition. These results are all the more remarkable since only 20% of families referred were for reasons of abuse or neglect. One implication, then, is that the proposed measures of abusive and neglecting dispositions may be sensitive to variations in behaviors considered "maladaptively deviant" in subclinical populations.

System Factors

Studies reviewed have shown that the continuua of risk as operationalized by LO and NEG measures are associated with quantitative and qualitative disturbances in parenting. In turn these disturbances are associated with selective impairments in the child's socioemotional development. Here, we will review additional studies which identify child, parent, social, and structural variables that covary with abusive and neglecting dispositions. As such, the interest here is in evaluating the extent to which systemic variables possibly contribute to the risk of psychological mal-

treatment and its untoward effects upon child development.

Given the importance of child effects on parenting behaviors, Sourkes (1976) examined the relationship between the Carey Infant Temperament Scale and LO as well as NEG measures. She found in a sample of 30 families that infant temperament as rated by mothers significantly correlated with LO (.31) and NEG (.33) as independently rated by Right Start staff. A more recent view is that ratings of child temperament provide more information about maternal attitudes toward the child than they do about temperamental attributes of the child. Unfortunately, we are unable to determine from Sourkes' study whether significant correlations noted are primarily child or maternal effects. In the second instance, we would conclude that maternal attitude was the basis for the covariation and in the second that child temperament was the basis. Either view is of theoretical value but for different reasons.

We have evaluated the relationship between several parent variables–self-efficacy, dysphoria, anxiety, and anger–and components of psychological maltreatment. Sourkes (1976) examined associations between maternal perception of control over her life and scores on LO and NEG. Impairment in self-efficacy was significantly correlated with NEG (.37) but not with LO (.01). This suggestion of differential impact on components of psychological maltreatment was not altogether supported by Ruback (1976) who, on a sample of 22 Right Start families, found significant correlations of .45 between externality and NEG and .36 between externality and LO. That staff observers rated maternal self-efficacy in Sourkes' study and mothers themselves completed Rotter's Locus of Control in Ruback's study may account for reported differences in covariation with LO scale. What is clear in both studies, however, is that different methodologies applied to different samples yielded significant correlations between efficacy and NEG. Although sample sizes are small, there is tentative support for a direct relationship between impaired efficacy and neglecting disposition. Whether the same relationship obtains for LO must await future replication.

Taylor and Asbury (1984) explored the relationship between maternal affective experience and abusive as well as neglecting disposition. Using a median split criterion, mothers were divided into Highs and Lows on three of Taylor's (1996b) measures of maternal affect: Dysphoria, Anxiety, and, Anger. Highs on Dysphoria had significantly greater means on LO, NEG, and PM than Lows on Dysphoria, indicating that mothers reporting many depressive symptoms were at higher risk of psychological maltreatment than mothers reporting few depressive symptoms. Surprised that Highs and Lows on Anxiety and Anger were not significantly different on LO, NEG, or PM total scores, we decided to generate the factor structures and loadings given in Table 4. We reasoned that this procedure might provide a more fine-grained analysis of covariation between affective experience and psychological maltreatment. We found that Highs and Lows for each affect were significantly different on Factor III Neglectful and on this factor only. In other words, mothers falling above the median on Dysphoria, Anxiety, and Anger tended to be more neglectful than mothers falling below the median on these measures. They tended to feed their children at irregular times, leave their children unattended, take off during difficult times, and watch T.V. more attentively than their children. They tended to prefer that their children play quietly and were less concerned about persons with whom they left their children. At high levels of affective arousal, then, whatever the experienced content, psychological or physical withdrawal, disengagement, flight, or distractibility were common responses. Together with the previous results, it appears that high affective arousal in general may influence physical or psychological withdrawal and that depressive affective arousal in particular may influence abusive parenting. Dysphoric affect, then, may influence neglecting and abusive dispositions. Since it is also possible that problem child behaviors may contribute to maternal affects, it is important in future studies to evaluate the relative contributions of child affects and maternal affects.

Finally, we have found that social structural variables correlate significantly with components of psychological maltreatment. Sourkes (1976) found that maternal isolation from family members and outside friends covaried significantly with NEG (.34) but not with LO (-.17). She also reported that a composite index of socioeconomic status correlated significantly with NEG (-.41) but not with LO (-.11). Recent evidence that accord with patterns summarized adds to the construct validity of the proposed measures of psychological maltreatment.

While development and validation work continues on LO, NEG, and PM, the evidence thus far indicates that these measures successfully differentiate quantity and quality of maternal behaviors as well as social emotional processes in young children. Further, these measures covary meaningfully with a continuum of potential systemic variables–child, parent, social, and structural.

Summary and Conclusion

This paper reviews development efforts to create interval measures that would: (a) operationalize abusive disposition as a continuous rather than categorical variable; (b) operationalize neglecting disposition as a continuous rather than categorical variable; (c) differentiate the risk of abuse from the risk of neglect; and, (d) operationalize overall psychological maltreatment as a continuous rather than categorical variable. Essential also to this development effort was the demonstration that resulting measures would pattern meaningfully with child, parent, and systemic variables.

Development efforts in relation to objectives (a) through (d) were described. The Lashing Out and Neglect measures were developed to estimate the continuum of abusive and neglecting dispositions, respectively, in children 36 months of age or younger. The Psychological Maltreatment measure was defined as the sum of Lashing Out and Neglect total scores. Available data on Revision 3 of these measures indicate that they reliably and differentially map the continuum of risk in childrearing. Further, we found that high levels of Lashing Out were associated with quantitative and qualitative disturbances in parenting and that high levels of Lashing Out and Neglect were associated with impairments in the child's socioemotional adjustment. Both Lashing Out and Neglect measures correlated significantly with maternal ratings of child temperament, and the Neglect measures correlated significantly with maternal and observer ratings of self-efficacy. High levels of maternal affective arousal–dysphoria, anxiety, and anger–were associated with physical or psychological withdrawal. Dysphoric affect seemed to be particularly damaging since it was associated with neglecting and abusive dispositions. In relation to social and structural variables, we found that a composite index of socioeconomic status and observer ratings of maternal social isolation correlated significantly with Neglect but not with Lashing Out. Finally, we found that the Psychological Maltreatment measure might be useful as an initial screening instrument to identify children at risk, Lashing Out and Neglect scores being disaggregated when Psychological Maltreatment scores are high.

While finding that objectives (a) through (d) have been met relatively well and that measures of abusive and neglecting dispositions correlate with a range of child, parent, social, and structural variables, we have yet to investigate the contribution of cultural variables to psychological maltreatment. Taylor (1996) and Taylor and Grundy (1996) summarized a program of research at the University of Pittsburgh which examines the role of cultural identity upon mental health and social variables of a wide range. Since the evidence suggests that Blacks internalizing White stereotypes about Blacks are less charitable and accepting in their relationship with other Blacks, a new line of research will entail examining how this cultural variable influences quantitative and qualitative patterns of parenting. This is an urgent item for investigation in future studies since it is at least possible that psychological maltreatment by Black parents may be related to psychological maltreatment of Blacks.

Note

1. The research reported here was supported in part from grants from Allegheny County Children and Youth Services, Allegheny County Mental Health/Mental Retardation Program, and the Center for the Study of Minority Groups Mental Health of NIMH.

References

Aber, J. L., & Allen, J. P. (1987). Effects of maltreatment on young children's socioemotional development: An attachment theory perspective. *Developmental Psychology, 23*, 406-414.

Augoustinos, M. (1987). Developmental effects of child abuse: Recent findings. *Child Abuse & Neglect, 11*, 15-27.

Baily, T. F., & Baily, W. H. (1986). *Operational definitions of child emotional maltreatment: Final report.* (Contract #90-CA-0956). Washington, DC.: National Center on Child Abuse and Neglect.

Brassard, M. R., & Gelardo, M.S. (1987) Psychological maltreatment: The unifying construct in child abuse and neglect. *School Psychology Review, 16*, 127-136.

Bryer, J. B., Nelson, B. A., & Krol, P. A. (1987). Childhood sexual and physical abuse as factors in adult psychiatric illness. *American Journal of Psychiatry, 144*, 1426-1430.

Davis, E. E. (1976). *An investigation of the communication of mothers with assessed abuse potential to their children.* Unpublished doctoral dissertation, University of Pittsburgh.

Deykin, E. Y., Alpert, J. J., & McNamara, J. J. (1985). A pilot study of the effect of exposure to child abuse or neglect on adolescent suicidal behavior. *American Journal of Psychiatry, 142*, 1299-1302.

Egeland, B., & Erickson, M. F. (1987). Psychologically unavailable caregiving. In M. R. Brassard, R. Germain, & S. N. Hart (Eds.), *Psychological maltreatment of children and youth* (pp. 110-120). NY: Pergamon and Press.

Erickson, M. F., & Egeland, B. (1987). A developmental view of the psychological consequences of maltreatment. *School Psychology Review, 16*, 156-168.

Hart, S. N., & Brassard, M. R. (1987). A major threat to children's mental health: Psychological maltreatment. *American Psychologist, 42*, 160-165.

Hart S. N., Germain, R. B., & Brassard, M. R. (1987). The challenge: To better understand and combat psychological maltreatment of children. In M. R. Brassard, R. Geramin, & S. N. Hart (Eds.), *Psychological maltreatment of children and youth* (pp. 3-24). New York: Pergamon Press.

Long, L. G. (1981). *The effect of parental abuse and neglect upon the quality of separation-individuation in the child.* Unpublished doctoral dissertation, University of Pittsburgh.

Lyons-Ruth, K., Connel, D. B., Zoll, D., & Stahl, J. (1987). Infants at social risk: Relations among infants maltreatment, maternal behavior, and infant attachment behavior. *Development Psychology, 23*, 223-232.

Magnusson, D. (1966). *Test theory*. Reading, Mass: Addison-Wesley.

Mahler, M. S. (1969). *On human symbiosis and the vicissitudes of individuation*. London: Hogarth Press.

McDonough, M. C. (1983). *Relationships among lashing out, neglect, affiliation, and control in primary parent-to-child relations*. Unpublished doctoral dissertation, University of Pittsburgh.

Oliver, J. E. (1985). Successive generations of child maltreatment. *British Journal of Psychiatry, 147*, 484-490.

Ruback, B. (1976). *Perceptions of societal institutions and locus of control as factors in child abuse*. Paper presented at Eastern Psychological Convention.

Sourkes, B. (1976). *Parental neglect and lashing out: Maladaptive styles of coping*. Unpublished doctoral dissertation, University of Pittsburgh.

Taylor, J. (1973). Comments on the paper by Dr. Shipman. In W. Coffman (Ed.), *Frontiers of educational measurement and information systems*. Boston: Houghton Mifflin.

Taylor, J. (1996). Cultural conversion experience: Implications for mental health research and treatment. In R. L. Jones (Ed.), *African American Identity Development*. Hampton, VA: Cobb & Henry.

Taylor, J., & Asbury, J. (1984). *Differential effects of maternal anxiety, dysphoria, and aggression on patterns of maladaptive caregiving: An exploratory investigation*. Paper presented at the Second Annual Conference for Family Violence, University of New Hampshire.

Taylor, J., & Grundy, C. (1996). Black internalization of White stereotypes about Blacks: The Nadanolitization Scale. In R. L. Jones (Ed.), *Handbook of tests and measurements for Black populations* (Vol. 2). Hampton, VA: Cobb & Henry.

Taylor, J., & McMillian, M. (1996a). Taylor's measures of affiliation and control. In R. L. Jones (Ed.), *Handbook of tests and measurements for Black populations* (Vol. 2). Hampton, VA: Cobb & Henry.

Taylor, J., & McMillian, M. (1996b). Taylor's measures of dysphoria, anxiety, anger, and self-esteem. In R. L. Jones (Ed.), *Handbook of tests and measurements for Black populations* (Vol. 2). Hampton, VA: Cobb & Henry.

For additional information, contact:

Jerome Taylor
University of Pittsburgh
Institute for the Black Family
Department of Africana Studies
Pittsburgh, PA 15260
Telephone: (412) 648-7217
Fax: (412) 648-5656

Part III

Children: Cognitive Approaches and Measures

Non-Biased Assessment or Realistic Assessment?

Harold E. Dent

Abstract

Since IQ tests were first introduced at the turn of the 20th century, educators, psychologists and other scholars have waged an ongoing battle over the question of bias of standardized psychometric tests. The history of that debate is summarized in the following chapter. The contributions made by African American scholars to the debate, seldom mentioned in textbooks, is also described. The chapter also gives an update on the continuing legal battle concerning the cultural bias in IQ testing and the application of these instruments to African American students. There is a discussion of the sources of inherent bias which enters the construction, administration, and interpretation of the standardized tests of intelligence, achievement, scholastic ability, and cognitive ability. Criteria established by African American educators, special educators, and psychologists to achieve a realistic assessment of the cognitive functioning of African American school age children are defined. Dynamic assessment approaches to cognitive assessment appear to be the only alternatives which meet those criteria. Three dynamic assessment models are described.

The debate over bias in standardized tests has been conducted in the psychological literature and the public media since formal efforts to measure intelligence were first introduced into this country at the turn of the century. Almost immediately following their introduction, the African American scholar, W.E.B. DuBois, initiated an unrelenting campaign in *The Crisis*, the NAACP monthly magazine which he edited, to alert the African American community to the inherent bias of intelligence tests. Over the years the debate has shifted, and test makers and advocates now admit that test bias exists. However, they offer a variety of technically sophisticated explanations, some of which appear as simplistic as others are complex, to justify continued use of these instruments with populations against whom the bias operates.

There is a legacy of research by early scholars (Block & Dworkin, 1976; Guthrie, 1976) and a plethora of data from contemporary research critical of the practice of applying standardized tests to African Americans and other minority populations (Dixon, 1977; Kamin, 1978; Laosa, 1989; Williams, 1974). Historical accounts and documentation of the racist motivations, the unprofessional and even unethical activities of unscrupulous proponents of the mental measurement movement, both past and present, are appearing in the literature with alarming frequency (Chase, 1977; Gould, 1981; Guthrie, 1976; Hernshaw, 1979; Mensh & Mensh, 1990). The fact that these exposés have been reported in books with limited readership, even among professionals, explains why they have had no damaging effect on the popularity of standardized tests; standardized testing has not only survived, it is flourishing.

Two national commissions recently issued reports, [the National Commission on Testing and Public Policy's *From Gatekeeper to Gateway: Transforming Testing in America* (1990), and the National Council on Education Standards and Testing's *Raising Standards For American Education* (1992)], which place heavy emphasis on the discriminatory impact standardized tests have on minorities in education and employment. These reports will help raise public awareness of the true value of standardized testing which the general public has come to believe to be scientifically objective and fair.

In addition, federal legislation requiring the use of non-discriminatory procedures in psychoeducational assessment has been in force for more than a decade (P.L. 94-142, the Education For All Handicapped Children Act of 1975). Also, litigation which challenged the use of standardized tests of intelligence in special education placement of African American students has been successful up through the appellate court level (*Larry P. v. Riles*, 1986). The Association of Black Psychologists, the American Personnel and Guidance Association, and the National Education Association, the nations largest and oldest teacher organization, are among a long list of professional organizations which have gone on record expressing dissatisfaction with standardized testing in education. Nevertheless, the educational community's reliance on standardized tests has not diminished, despite the fact that the

overrepresentation of minority group students, particularly African American and Hispanic-American, in special education programs across the country is attributable to this reliance on standardized tests. The evidence that more than half of these placements are inappropriate continues to grow (Collins & Camblin, 1983; Dent, 1990; Mercer, 1973).

Continued use of traditional methods of assessment would appear reasonable at least in some degree if, as many advocates maintain, these techniques are the best available means for determining the appropriate educational placements for children experiencing problems in learning in public schools. They are not the best available means of determining educational placement nor are they the best available measures for identifying learning problems. As will be discussed later in this chapter, appropriate techniques for reducing test bias do exist (Laosa, 1989; Schmitt & Bleistein, 1987; Schmitt & Doran, 1987; Shapiro, Slutsky, & Watt, 1989), and descriptions of new approaches to cognitive assessment are appearing in the literature with increasing frequency (Budoff, 1974; Feuerstein, Rand, & Hoffman, 1979; Jones, 1988; Tucker, 1985; Ysseldyke & Regan, 1980).

Nevertheless, this chapter is not the appropriate forum for a discussion of institutional resistance to change. Instead, in this chapter I will provide the reader with an update on the status of the debate about bias, discuss the sources of bias in standardized tests, and describe different approaches to the assessment of cognitive ability which this writer believes offer realistic prospects for providing accurate information about the cognitive functioning of African American children who experience problems in learning.

Assessment

For purposes of this discussion, assessment is a process through which information reflecting the behavior, performance or functioning of an individual is collected, analyzed, interpreted and summarized, usually in response to a specific request or referral. Although assessment usually involves gathering information from a variety of sources and not exclusively in the cognitive domain, a great deal of emphasis is placed on the nature of the relationship between the assessee and the assessor. Rapport is crucial to this relationship. In other words, the assessor strives to establish rapport to ensure the assessee is comfortable and at ease. Every effort is put forth to reduce the perceived threat which is usually associated with a formal testing situation. Assessment is distinctly different from testing, although assessment may include testing.

Testing refers to the administration, either individually or in a group, of a test (or battery of tests) in a systematic, prescribed manner to ensure that the administration is conducted in as similar a fashion as possible to all who take them. Group administration of achievement, aptitude, employment, and civil service tests are examples of psychological testing in which there is little or no emphasis on the relationship between the examiner and the examinee, except that everyone receives the same, standardized instructions.

The Debate

At the turn of the century, the French Ministry of Education commissioned a noted psychologist, Alfred Binet, who had gained recognition for his research in mental retardation, to assist the Paris public schools address the problem of teaching the mentally retarded. Binet and his colleague published the first version of their scale for measuring intelligence in 1904 (Binet & Simon, 1911). American psychologists, eager to advance a popular belief that intelligence was genetically transmitted, translated the Binet scale and proceeded to apply it to masses of people in the United States. H. H. Goddard, a psychologist and director of research at the Vineland Training School for Feebleminded Girls and Boys in New Jersey, was one of the most active and influential proponents of the mental measurement movement in this country at that time. As a staunch eugenicist he advocated the colonization of the mentally retarded to preserve society from the 'menace of the feebleminded' because of the belief that deficient intelligence and immorality were linked (Gould, 1981). Binet's original discussions of

intelligence did not include the notion of the inheritability of intelligence, nor did he believe intelligence to be a fixed entity (Binet & Simon, 1911).

While Goddard was testing large numbers of retarded residents of the Vineland school, Lewis Terman of Stanford University was busy exploring modifications of the Binet-Simon Scale, which he administered to different populations in the Western United States, specifically Mexican-Americans, American Indians and African Americans. Terman's modification, which he ultimately called the Stanford-Binet Test of Intelligence, included items representative of formal and informal educational and cultural activities and community experiences of native born White Americans. When Terman's testing resulted in lower IQ scores of American Indians, Mexican-Americans and African Americans than White Americans, he concluded:

". . .their dullness seems to be racial, or at least inherent in the family stock from which they come. The fact that one meets this type with such extraordinary frequency, in Indians, Mexicans, and Negroes, suggests quite forcibly that the whole question of racial differences in mental traits will have to be taken up anew by experimental methods. The writer predicts that when this is done, there will be discovered enormously significant racial differences in general intelligence, differences which cannot be wiped out by any scheme of mental culture" (Terman, 1916, p. 92).

One of the first critics of the mental measurement movement was the outspoken African American scholar, W.E.B. DuBois. While editor of *The Crisis* magazine from 1910 to 1934, he engaged in an ongoing discourse to warn African Americans of ". . .the new technique of psychological tests, which were quickly adjusted so as to put Black folk absolutely beyond the possibility of civilization."

World War I provided an opportunity for the measurement movement to make giant strides, the mobilization of millions of men who needed to be trained for a variety of jobs provided psychologists, including Terman and Goddard, the opportunity to develop new IQ tests, the Army ALPHA and the Army BETA. These tests were administered to almost 2 million soldiers and were intended to measure native intellectual ability. Following World War I, volumes were published describing the results of this massive testing of American men from all walks of life throughout the country. In essence, the reports of the army testing indicated that the average American man had the mental equivalent of a fourteen year old (Mental Age 14), and that did not bode well for the future of the nation. In order to improve standards of living, health and education, it was recommended that these IQ tests be administered in the public schools throughout the country. This triggered the most publicized debate in the annals of psychological history, a debate between the renowned literary critic of the day, Walter Lippmann, and Lewis Terman. (The Lippmann-Terman debate is reported in its entirety in Block & Dworkin, 1976). Lippmann challenged the scientific basis of the claim that intelligence tests measured intelligence and raised the spectrum of the potential abuse to which these tests could be used:

> "One has only to read around in the literature of the subject, but more specifically in the work of popularizers like McDougall and Stoddard, to see how easily the intelligence test can be turned into an engine of cruelty, how easily in the hands of blundering or prejudiced men it could turn into a method of stamping a permanent sense of inferiority upon the seal of a child" (Block & Dworkin, p. 19).

During the 1920's and 1930's, African Americans began to filter into the ranks of academic psychologists. In 1920, Francis C. Sumner, was the first African American to receive a Ph.D. degree in Psychology from an American university. Others who followed him continued the campaign to raise the issue of the bias in psychological testing which was based on the differences in cultural experiences between ethnic and cultural groups in this country. Notable among the African Americans to criticize the mental measurement movement was the African American educator, Horace Mann Bond, who criticized the practice of White psychologists generalizing to the African American population, based on comparison of unequal social groups. It was the practice of the day for psychologists to compare the IQ test sores of White middle-class Americans with African Americans with no regard for differences in socio-economic status (Bond, 1924). Bond pointed out that in assessing White children, the examiner would place particular emphasis on establishing rapport. However, such was not the case when testing African American children. He also observed that African American children were often criticized for being withdrawn during the testing and for being docile due to hereditary influences (Bond, 1927).

Bond conducted an extensive study in which he selected African American children from middle-class homes and administered the Stanford-Binet Test of Intelligence to these children. It was reported that he leaned over backwards to maintain scientific methodology in administering the tests (Guthrie, 1976). His results were similar to the findings of the recent research on race of examiner as a factor in student performance. Bond found that forty-seven percent (47%) of the African American students that he assessed exceeded an IQ of 122 points, and twenty-two percent (22%) achieved scores over 130, which is considered 'genius' classification. The reassessment of the plaintiffs in the *Larry P.* case by African American psychologists found that these students who were assigned to special education classes for the mentally retarded, increased their IQ scores between 17 and 34 points (*Larry P. v. Riles*, 1979). Like Bond before them, the psychologists who retested the student plaintiffs in the *Larry P.* case adhered strictly to standard administration procedures. Another African American psychologist, Herman Canady (1936), conducted the seminal work on race of the examiner as a factor in establishing rapport in IQ testing, which comprised his masters thesis.

In the mid 1970's an African American psychologist, Robert Williams developed a culture specific test to demonstrate the inherent bias of traditional standardized tests. Williams (1974) named his test the BITCH Test (Black Intelligence Test for Cultural Homogeneity). The items in the BITCH test were drawn exclusively from the African American experience, in contrast to the items of standardized IQ tests, which are drawn from the White middle-class experience.

Barnes (1972), pointed out that the two most frequently used IQ tests, the Stanford-Binet Intelligence Test and WISC (Wechsler Intelligence Scale for Children) are cultural specific tests,

"Perhaps a potentially more fruitful approach lies in the development of 'culture specific tests'. If this suggestion seems far out, then ponder this. The model for culture specific tests already exists, and when appropriately used, displays considerable effectiveness. Consider for example, the Stanford Binet and the WISC, these are examples of 'culture specific tests'. The culture in this instance, is what is frequently referred to as 'White middle-class'. . ." (p. 6).

Culture-specific tests have the advantage of dealing with content material which is familiar to members of a specific culture. Thus, an example of cultural specificity would be an item such as on the BITCH test in which an African American child from a low income family living in an inner-city would probably have no difficulty understanding, What is an alley apple? Likewise, a culture-specific item which a middle-class child from suburban America would have no difficulty with would be a WISC item, Why is it better to pay bills by check than with cash? The term 'alley apple' represents the same degree of cultural discontinuity for the child from suburbia as the concept of 'paying bills by check' would for a child from a low income family.

The latest chapter in the conflict concerning the bias of standardized tests is being waged in federal court. In 1971, a class action suit was filed in the U.S. District Court of the Northern District of California (*Larry P. v. Riles*), which claimed that standardized tests of intelligence were culturally biased, and their use resulted in the dispro-

portionate placement of African American children in special education classes for the educable mentally retarded of the San Francisco Unified School District. During a highly publicized trial which extended over eight months, and is contained in 10,000 pages of transcripts, all of the test industry experts, with one exception, agreed that there is inherent bias in standardized intelligence tests. However, they argued that these same instruments were the best available techniques for assessing the abilities of children. During the course of this litigation, two significant pieces of legislation were enacted which had a major bearing on the trial. One was The Rehabilitation Act of 1973 (P.L. 92-113) which included a provision in Section 504 that instruments used in the assessment of handicapped individuals must be validated for the specific purpose for which they were being used. The other was P.L. 94-142, the Education for All Handicapped Children Act of 1975, which contained the provision that instruments used in the assessment of handicapped children must be selected and administered in a fashion which was nondiscriminatory. The evidence presented during this lengthy *Larry P.* litigation convinced the Presiding Federal District Judge, Robert Peckham, that individual standardized tests of intelligence were culturally biased, and had not been validated for the specific purpose of placing African American children in special education programs. He ruled that such tests should not be used in the evaluation of African American students being considered for EMR placement in California public schools (*Larry P. v. Riles*, 1979).

After two appellate court rulings upheld the decision of the Ninth District Court, the California Department of Education agreed to a settlement which called for discontinuing the use of standardized tests for placement of African American students in all categories of special education (*Larry P. v. Riles*, 1986). Current data on the enrollment of African American students in special education programs in the state of California reflects the impact of the ban of IQ tests in the psychoeducational assessment process. When the *Larry P.* class action suit was filed in 1971, African American students comprised 9.1% of the public school enrollment in the state of California, and 27.5% of the enrollment of one category, the Educable Mentally Retarded (EMR) category of special education. In 1979, when Judge Peckham issued his decision, African American student enrollment in public schools was still 9.1%, but the African American special education student enrollment had decreased to 23.5%. However, this percentage included four categories of special education, the EMR category plus the new categories which came into being with the passage of P.L. 94-142. The new categories were Learning Disabilities (LD), Seriously Emotionally Disturbed (SED), and Speech and Language Impaired (SLI). In other words, instead of one category where African American students were overrepresented (EMR), the passage of this new legislation increased the number of categories in which African American students were overrepresented to four (EMR, LD, SED, and SLI). By then the proportion of African American students in all four categories was nearly twenty-four percent (23.5%), slightly down from twenty-seven percent in the EMR category eight years earlier. In 1986, when the final settlement was signed, African American student enrollment in California public schools had dropped to 9.0%, and special education enrollment of African American students had dropped to 19.6%. In December 1989, three years later, African American student enrollment in California public schools was 8.9%, and the special education enrollment in all categories was 12.%. This partly reflected a national trend toward reduction of the proportion of all students in special education. However, the size of the decrease between 1986 and 1989 in California was far greater than the decrease reported by any other state during the same period. Reviewing these data from a different perspective, there was a four percent drop in enrollment during an eight year period between 1971 and 1979, and another four percent drop during the next seven years between 1979 and 1986. But in a three year period between 1986 and 1989, there was a drop of almost eight percent. This is a clear, direct indication of the impact of the federal court order banning the use of standardized IQ tests in the assessment of African

American students for special education placement in the state of California (see Table 1).

Bias in Standardized Tests

To assist the reader gain a thorough understanding of what is meant by cultural bias in standardized testing, we must begin with the discussion of the assumptions which underlie standardized tests and then we will turn to the process employed in test construction. For purposes of this discussion, the phrase standardized tests refers to the commercially developed, norm-referenced, group or individual tests of achievement, ability, intelligence, and scholastic ability. Jones (1988) maintains that bias in testing is multifaceted. Bias enters at the content level that is, the content of the items included in the test; at the administration level, when a test is administered by a person unfamiliar with the language, behavior, and culture of the person(s) being examined; at the standardization level; and at the validation level.

Assumptions

One of the fundamental principles underlying psychological testing is that in order for the obtained scores to be valid, certain assumptions must be met In the discussion of these assumptions it will become apparent to the reader that when applying standardized tests to African American and other minority groups, the basic assumptions on which they rest cannot be met

The first assumption is that there is commonality of experiences shared by all those who take the test. Stated differently, it is assumed that all people have equal opportunity to share similar experiences tapped by the questions on the test. The reality is that cultural backgrounds and cultural values are distinctly different among and between different ethnic groups, and that an array of social, economic and geographic conditions impact different ethnic groups differentially. These factors operate to make this assumption of commonality of experience virtually impossible to meet. The fact is that the educational opportunities and experiences available to children in dif-

Table 1. African American Student Enrollment in California Special Education Programs

	California Public School Enrollment	Special Education Enrollment
1971	9.1%	27.5%[a]
1979	9.1%	23.5%[b]
1986	9.0%	19.6%[b]
1989	8.9%	12.0%

Notes. [a]EMR (Educable Mentally Retarded) Program; [b] MR - Mental Retardation (includes EMR); LD - Learning Disabilities; SED - Seriously Emotionally Disturbed; SI - Speech Impaired. These categories were introduced in 1975 with the passage of the California Master Plan in Special Education and the Education for All Handicapped Children Act of 1975 (P. L. 94-142). These data were obtained from the California Department of Education.

ferent geographic and socio-economic communities cannot remotely be considered comparable. Knowledge of cultural differences tells us that this assumption cannot be met.

Another assumption is that test takers have equal facility with the English language; that is, they speak, read, and understand the language to the same degree. However, it is not difficult to understand that in a pluralistic society such as ours, the use of standard English is not the mode. Standard English is not spoken in every household. When confronted with a standardized test where fluency in the English language is required, students from non-traditional English-speaking backgrounds are at a disadvantage. In other words, it is assumed that a child whose parents have not completed an elementary school education will have the same facility with the English language and will have been exposed to the same quality of verbal communication as a child whose parents have completed college.

When developing vocabulary tests, word frequency counts were conducted in the middle-class communities to determine the frequency with which certain words were used. However, there has been no effort to conduct word frequency counts in ethnic minority communities. Thus, minorities are expected to be as familiar with the words used in vocabulary tests as are members of the rest of the population in whose community these words are used most frequently.

Still another assumption is that all who take the test will understand the questions equally. It is presumed that all test takers comprehend the word usage and context of the question in exactly the same way, without regard to differential background experiences. However, research conducted by ETS (The Educational Testing Service), one of the largest producers of standardized tests in the world, provides definitive information that this assumption cannot be met Their research points out that sentence structure, word usage, question format and even position of items in the total examination have differential influence on the performance of minority group members (Rogers & Kulick, 1986; Schmitt, 1988; Schmitt & Bleistein, 1987). For example, understanding of the key words used in analogies was found to represent a serious problem for all minority groups in the sample: African Americans; Hispanic Americans; and, Asian Americans. Without familiarity with the primary words used in the stem of an analogy, the ability of the examinee to correctly identify the other elements of that analogy will be impaired. The use of homographs, words that are spelled alike but have different English meanings, i.e., 'nail,' is another source of difficulty for minority populations. The inability to meet these assumptions when applying standardized tests to minority populations seems to have no deterrent effect on the continued inappropriate use of standardized tests and their proliferation.

Sources of Bias in Test Construction

As was mentioned earlier, there are at least three sources of bias in the test construction process: content, standardization, and validation. While administration is a definite source of bias, it is separate from the construction process per se. Nevertheless, administration will also be discussed in this context.

Content

Items which comprise a given test, whether it be an IQ test, an achievement test, or any other formal standardized test, are contributed by experts in the field. These experts are individuals who have contributed to the field through research, teaching and practice, who have authored books and articles, and gained recognition among their colleagues in their respective professions. It is not unrealistic to assume that this group represents middle-class America, and that the items they contribute reflect the middle-class experience. Asking an African American child who has lived in the inner-city, a Hispanic youngster, brought up in a barrio, or a refugee child who recently arrived from another country questions that reflect White American middle-class values and experiences will reveal very little about that child's cognitive ability or intellectual functioning. For example, to ask an inner-city child, "If you were lost in the forest in the day time, how would you find your way out?", is outrageously inappropriate without assurance that child has had an opportunity to learn that moss grows on a particular side of a tree in a forest, and to use that as a reference point to find direction out of the forest. Similarly, is it unrealistic to ask a child who has only experienced island living, i.e., Hawaii or Puerto Rico, " In what direction does the sun set?" The reference points on an island are the sea and the mountains (or the core of the island). East, West, North, and South are not the customary reference points for islanders, as they are for mainlanders. Nevertheless, the only appropriate answer on a standardized test to the question, "In what direction does the sun set?" is, "the West."

These are but a few examples of how bias operates to the disadvantage of minority group children when dealing with standardized tests.

Special Interest Content

There should be little wonder that the research indicates that test questions with subject matter content of particular interest to gender or ethnic groups yield scores which favor those groups. In other words, there is a positive relationship between content of interest and the score of individuals from different gender or ethnic groups (Schmitt & Doran, 1988).

Standardization

The term *standardized* test has two distinctly different meanings in psychometric parlance. One use of the term implies that the test is administered to all who take the test in a neutral, objective fashion. In this sense, standardized means there is a prescribed method for administering the items of a test. The same wording of the instructions is used with each administration. The instructions are read from a manual by the examiner or read from a test booklet by the examinee. Standardized tests can be administered individually, as are most IQ tests, or in large groups, as is the SAT.

When used in relation to the norming of tests, *standardized* means the process by which norms or standards have been established for the test by administering the test to a representative sample of the population. The standardization process begins with the selection of individual items. Each item is administered to a small representative sample (called a try-out sample) of the population. Items selected for the test will be those that will yield a normal distribution of the scores from this sample. Test makers assume that all traits, skills, and abilities measured by a test are normally distributed in the general population. Consequently, a distribution of scores from a representative sample of the population will be expected to approximate a normal curve. After the items have been selected (from the try-out samples), they are compiled into the complete test. The next step in the process is to administer the completed version of the test to a large representative sample of the population, referred to as the standardization sample. If African Americans and other minorities are included in these samples, their scores will be dispersed throughout the distribution of obtained scores. Minority group scores will not cluster within the distribution in large enough numbers to have any influence on the norms. Likewise, they will not have any influence in determining which items are selected for inclusion in the test from the responses of the tryout samples. The largest segment of the population represented in the tryout samples and the standardization sample will be the White, middle class. This is the group which will control the greatest influence on item selection and on the norms or the standardization of a norm-referenced test.

The developer of one of the most frequently used IQ tests, David Wechsler, in his book, *The Measurement of Intelligence* (1944), expressed caution about mixing populations in the standardization sample:

> "[We] have eliminated the colored vs. White factor by admitting at the outset that our norms cannot be used for the colored population of the United States. Though we have tested a large number of colored persons, our standardization is based upon White subjects only. We omitted the colored population from our first standardization because we did not feel that norms derived by mixing the population could be interpreted without special provisos and reservations" (p. 107).

In a monograph entitled, *Racial and Ethnic Bias in Test Construction*, Green (1972) made a similar observation.

> "Just as the degree of minority representation in standardization samples can have only a small influence on norms, minority group presence in tryout samples dominated by some solid majority will not accomplish much" (p. 14).

In recent years, many test producers have emphasized in their marketing literature that Af-

rican Americans and other minority groups are represented in the standardization samples. Despite these proclamations, there has been no evidence reported in the literature which refutes Green and Wechsler's conclusions.

The point of this discussion is to emphasize that norm-referenced tests should be applied to the population on which the test was standardized, the group that dominates the standardization sample.

With respect to the applicability of standardized norm-referenced tests to African American and other minority-group children, the evidence is quite clear: tests must be normed on the populations on which they will be used. The increase in the number of immigrant and refugee children and the substantial number of at-risk school age minority-group children who are referred for special education dramatically emphasizes the need for accurate assessment information and appropriate assessment tools.

Validation

Validity refers to the extent to which a test measures what it was intended to measure. In other words, do standardized tests provide accurate measures of the abilities of African Americans and other minorities, when in fact they were standardized on different populations?

A common practice in the test industry is to validate one test against another test reported to measure the same thing. In other words, if the standardization sample of test "A" is similar to the standardization sample of test "B" (given these tests measure the same content domain), whatever bias exists in test "A" would operate in a similar fashion in test "B" thus raising the question, does this test provide an accurate measure of the abilities of individuals on whom the test was not standardized?

As part of a continuing effort to provide explanation of the validity of standardized tests when applied to minority populations, the American Psychological Association appointed a blue ribbon committee composed of experts in psychometrics. The committee's report, *The Educational Use of Tests with Disadvantaged Students*,

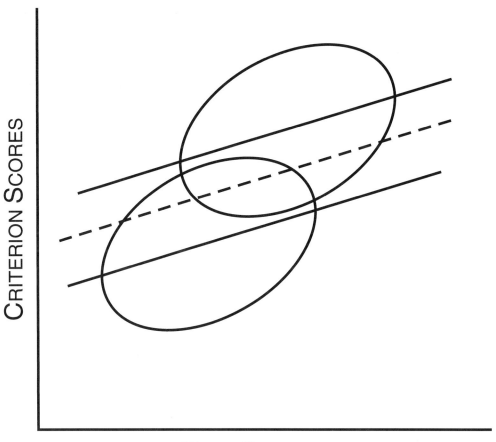

TEST SCORES

Figure 1.
Note. From "Educational Uses of Tests with Disadvantaged Students" by Cleary, A. T., Humphreys, L. G., Kendrick, S. A., and Wesman, A., 1975, *American Psychologist, 30*(1), pp. 15-41. Copyright 1975 by the American Psychological Association. Reprinted by permission of the author.

(Cleary, Humphreys, Kendrick, & Wesman, 1975), received a great deal of attention and was a major factor used by the defense in *Larry P. v. Riles*. The essence of the Cleary et al., report affirmed that a test was fair and could be used with different populations if three conditions were met (See Figure 1). Those conditions were:

1. The regression lines of the distributions of the scores (on the same standardized test) of the different groups were parallel;

2. The slope of the regression lines of these separate distributions was similar; and,

3. The correlation between the criteria and the test scores were similar for the two groups.

Applying these criteria to a set of data obtained in a major study, Mercer (1979) reported that the correlation coefficients between IQ test scores and grade point averages for African American students and White students, grades kindergarten through sixth, were significantly different. The correlation coefficient for White students was .46, whereas the correlation coefficient for African American students was .20. The regression lines for

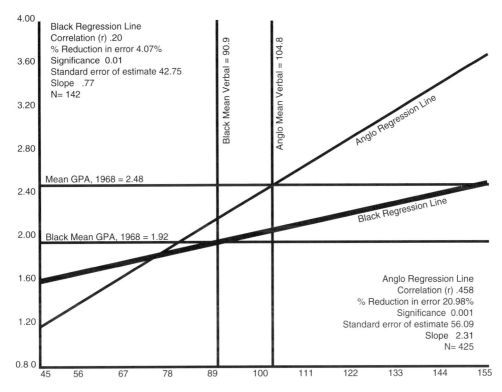

Figure 2. Anglo and Black Students: Kindergarten Through Sixth Grade
Note. Depicts Academic GPA, 1968 from WISC Verbal Score in 1967.

the distributions of these sets of data are presented in Figure 2 and reveal clearly that the regression lines for these distributions are not parallel; and, the slope of the regression lines of these distributions are not similar. In fact, the regression lines intersect.

These data clearly indicate that when using the criteria established by the American Psychological Association Task Force on the Educational use of Tests with Disadvantaged Students, the Wechsler Intelligence Scale for Children does not meet the criteria established for test fairness.

Administration/Interpretation

In addition to the problems associated with meeting the basic test assumptions and the problems of inherent bias in test construction, there are problems related to test administration and interpretation of test results. Standardized procedures for administration were designed to eliminate the influence of subtle questions, hints, etc., of asses-

sor bias. Mehan (1986) found that examiner influence operated to increase IQ test scores by as much as twenty-seven (27) points. He also found that examiner influence was more evident in the assessment of middle-class students than in the assessment of low-income, minority-group students.

All too often the scores obtained on standardized tests are interpreted as indicators of the individual's maximum ability. In the education arena particularly, the score is interpreted as indication of the individual's ability to learn. A low score carries with it the implied assumption that one cannot expect the student to achieve because of limited ability. Thus, a self-fulfilling prophesy may be established. The teacher expects little, requires little, and the student accommodates these expectations by producing little.

The interpretation that a low score on an IQ test is an indication of ability to learn is grossly inaccurate. In fact, a standardized testing situation does not offer the student an opportunity to demonstrate ability to learn. Standardized test results are in reality a sample of behavior which, at best, is representative of the student's average performance. Learning is demonstrated over time and there is no opportunity to demonstrate ability to learn in a single standardized testing session. Thus, the estimate of ability to learn attributed to an IQ score is in reality an interpretation.

Classification

Space does not permit opportunity to delve into the reasons why the educational assessment system employs medically-oriented diagnostic classifications. The use of terms such as Learning Disability and Learning Disorder are simply metaphorical analogies to physical illness. Application of the disease model and use of diagnostic terminology are, in the opinion of this writer, totally inappropriate in education. Use of the disease model draws attention to a supposed illness of the child. In medicine there is some degree of objectivity and some degree of consistency in a diagnosis. In other words, if a child contracts a disease, e.g., measles, the symptoms of that illness will be manifest wherever the child happens to be, whether the child is on the playground, in church, in school or at home. The disease or illness will be with the child 24-hours of the day, and there will be a high degree of consistency in the diagnosis among practitioners who see the child.

However, a Learning Disability is more often than not manifest only in the school. Standardized tests do not sample the range of activities and the variety of situations in which learning occurs. But, the standardized test is only conducted to assess learning which occurs in the school. Some years ago the phrase, the *Six-Hour Retarded Child*, was used frequently to refer to a child who was observed to function as though he/she was retarded only during the 6 hours the child was in school.

Another problem associated with the classification system employed in psychoeducational assessment is the inconsistency in the use of these classifications, or the lack of agreement among

professionals in the use of these classifications. Ysseldyke et al., (1983) indicated that eighty percent (80%) of the students in regular education would be classified learning disabled depending upon the method or definition of learning disabilities employed. Mercer (1986) pointed out there were as many definitions for learning disabilities as there were states. The inconsistency in use of this diagnosis is also reflected in its growth rate, specifically in the increase in numbers of students classified Learning Disabled over the years. The number of students classified Learning Disabled, has increased by one hundred forty percent (140%) in a ten-year period between 1975 and 1985, compared to an increase of sixteen percent (16%) in all other educational diagnostic categories in the same period (Wang, Reynolds, & Walberg, 1986). The growth rate for the Learning Disabilities classifications also varies across states, ranging from an increase of 1.5% in one state (Utah), to an increase of 40% in another jurisdiction (Washington, D.C.).

According to Heller, Holtzman, and Messick (1982), classification should lead to a distinctive prescription for educational practice, and lead to improved educational outcomes. However, present practices fall far short of this standard (Wang et al., 1986). It is apparent that classification and placement are influenced by factors other than student needs. In my experience, classification and practice are more directly related to the availability of program services and professional staff than to student needs. In a project which this author conducted involving two school districts serving adjacent communities, where crossing the street literally meant going from one district to another, the impact of availability of services was apparent. One district (which shall be nameless), employed a large staff of ancillary pupil personnel specialists, including speech therapists. In that district, children classified learning disabled represented 38% of the special education population and children identified as having speech problems represented 37% of the students in special education. The other district, which was much smaller, did not employ a staff of speech therapists. Speech therapy was provided by the county. In that district, students labelled learning disabled constituted 67%

of the special education enrollment, and students with speech problems, only 8% of the special education population. Empirical research also reveals that classification does not necessarily influence the nature of remediation provided in special education classrooms (Ysseldyke, 1992). Remediation that takes place in the classroom is in fact also influenced by the availability of staff and service programs.

Criteria

From the discussion in the preceding pages there is ample basis for the criticisms waged against IQ tests. From the time they were introduced into the education arena, teachers have criticized them for their failure to accurately assess students' ability to learn, and their failure to link classification with remediation (Hilliard, 1987; Tyler & White, 1979). Minority groups have challenged IQ tests because of cultural bias (Dent & Williams, 1972; Laosa, 1977). In the search for appropriate methods of assessment in education, these concerns must be given serious consideration. In conjunction with a statewide project conducted in California, a committee of school psychologists, administrators, and special educators established the following criteria for selection of alternative assessment models (Dent, 1991):

1. The first criterion establishes the standard that assessment models must meet the federal and state legislative mandates requiring that instruments used are properly validated and do not have a discriminatory impact on those being assessed.

As mentioned earlier in this chapter, Section 504 of the Rehabilitation Act of 1975 requires that instruments employed in the evaluation of the handicapped be validated for the specific purpose for which they are used; and the Education for All Handicapped Children Act (P.L. 94-142) requires that instruments be selected and administered so as not to be discriminatory. Both of these provisions have been incorporated into the Individuals with Disabilities Education Act of 1990 (IDEA).

Prior to the enactment of P.L. 94-142 and the California Master Plan in Special Education, the IQ score was accepted as the primary source of information in special education placement decisions throughout the country. Until revised to coincide with that legislation, the California Educational Code (sec 56507) required that the IQ score substantiate all other data gathered in the placement process, which in essence meant the IQ score was the most important factor in special education eligibility determination. Even today, and despite the fact that P.L. 94-142 also contains a provision designed to eliminate reliance on a single measure of general intelligence, the IQ score is accepted as the measure of ability in the ability/achievement discrepancy ratio employed in determining learning disabilities. This is not only contradictory to the intent of the legislation, but it is contradictory to research which indicates: A) that IQ measures and measures of learning ability tap distinctly different variables (Lidz, 1987); and, B) that discrepancy models are invalid procedures for differentiating handicapped learning disabled students from the rest of the student population (Brown, 1984; Ysseldyke et al., 1983).

2. The second criterion requires that assessment models be sensitive to the cultural experiences of African American children, particularly to the linguistic cultural style of African Americans.

After examining the data presented in the *Larry P.* case, a federal court found that standardized individual tests of intelligence (IQ tests) were culturally biased because they did not account for the cultural background and experiences of African American children. Another factor which prompted the inclusion of this criterion is the lack of understanding of the phonological and syntactical patterns of African American language which are frequently mistaken and diagnosed as a speech disorder. Consequently, large numbers of African American youth are perceived as having speech problems and placed in special education programs for the speech impaired.

3. The third criterion requires that assessment models yield data which will lead to the

identification of a specific problem or problems in learning, or lead to the identification of a handicapping condition which impedes learning; and that will identify specific remediations or modifications in the instruction that will positively impact the learning problems or handicapping condition identified.

In the absence of definitive data about a problem in a learning or handicapping condition, the assessment procedures must yield data which will relate specifically to the student's ability to learn, rather than provide a single index of intelligence. Traditional psychoeducational assessment focuses on classification and diagnosis rather than on intervention and remediation. Except in those instances where the referral is based on disruptive behavior, the teacher is aware that a learning problem exists. The teacher's concern is, What can be done to remediate that problem? Remediation should be the focus of the assessment rather than classification.

4. The fourth criterion requires that the assessment procedures employed cannot include standardized tests nor rely on normative data drawn from a representative sample of the population.

In summary, the criteria for selecting non-biased assessment procedures are:

• The assessment model must meet the validity and non-discriminatory requirements of IDEA;
• The assessment model must be sensitive to differences in cognitive and linguistic styles of diverse cultural groups;
• The assessment model must identify a specific problem and relate the results to specific instructional interventions; and,
• The assessment model must not involve standardized norm-referenced tests.

With these criteria as guidelines for selection of non-biased assessment models for determining the educational needs of African American students, we will proceed with a discussion of models.

Assessment

A variety of assessment methods are being proposed by their advocates as alternatives to traditional psychometric testing, i.e., authentic assessment (Taylor, 1990), cognitive assessment (Sternberg, 1982), criterion assessment (Campbell, 1992), curriculum-based assessment (Tucker, 1985), and dynamic assessment (Lidz, 1987).

Dynamic assessment is one approach to assessment which meets the criteria cited above, and which this writer believes offers the greatest potential for serving students from diverse cultural backgrounds. Dynamic assessment theorists make only one assumption and that is, *all children can learn*. Dynamic assessment looks at the process of learning, how the student learns, as compared with traditional assessment which focuses on the content of learning, and what the student has learned.

Dynamic assessment techniques employ the test-teach-test paradigm, which permits the examiner to actually document learning which occurs during the assessment process. In the test-teach-test model, the difference between the pre-test and the post-test performance is evidence of learning. In an extensive review of the test-teach-test method, the post-test performance was reported to be the best predictor of teacher ratings and future learning (Lidz, 1987). The test-teach-test paradigm reduces, if not eliminates, the cultural bias which is of major concern when employing standardized tests with students from diverse backgrounds.

Dynamic assessment does not assume universality of previous experience. The pre-test provides the baseline for comparing the student's subsequent performance. The teaching phase of this paradigm is intended to eliminate that differential experience factor. The teaching phase provides the opportunity for all students to start at a comparable level. The teaching phase provides the opportunity to introduce learning strategies and the opportunity to directly observe the student's response to the teaching. The post-test provides the opportunity to see how the student applies the strategies just introduced. In sum, this basic paradigm provides direct, accurate information on student's learning potential, i.e., the student's ability to benefit from instruction.

Two dynamic assessment approaches with which this writer has had considerable experience include the Learning Potential Assessment (LPA), which employs a well-developed training regimen (Budoff, 1970), and the Learning Potential Assessment Device, which focuses on mediated learning experiences (Feuerstein et al., 1979). A third model which meets the aforementioned criteria and appears to offer prospects for utilization, but has yet to be put to an empirical test will also be described. It is an approach designed by Richard Figueroa, The Six Stage Model for Non-Discriminatory Cognitive Assessment (Dent, 1987). The Six Stage Model focuses particular emphasis on the nature of and sources from which assessment data are gathered. It requires utilization of data from a variety of sources in addition to the data obtained from the assessment of cognitive functioning.

The Learning Potential Assessment

The Learning Potential Assessment (LPA) was developed by Milton Budoff, founder and president of the Research Institute for Educational Problems, Cambridge, Massachusetts. Dissatisfaction with the psychometric model and the misclassification of poor and minority-group children in special education via the use of IQ tests motivated Budoff to search for an alternative. He observed that many low-income, non-White, low IQ scoring children were competent problem solvers in non-school situations and showed mastery of skills to adjust and survive in their often times hostile environments.

The Learning Potential Assessment was developed as an alternative strategy for assessment of cognitive functioning. Rather than restricting testing to the child's ability to respond to information already acquired or to information the child has not been exposed to, the Learning Potential Assessment embeds training into a test-teach-test sequence. The intent of the Learning Potential Assessment is to obtain an estimate of the child's ability derived from reasoning problems in which the child has had opportunity to learn to solve. If the child can demonstrate, following training, the ability to perform at a level approximating aver-

age peer performance, the interpretation should be that the child is not mentally retarded nor mentally handicapped. Budoff developed training procedures that would help children solve the diversity of tasks employed. The training procedures attempt to sensitize students to the strategies required to solve the four types of problems found in this test: Simple and Complex Pattern Completions; Complex Visual Perceptual problems; and, Double Classification problems. The training helps equalize the differences in experience.

In applying LPA techniques, Budoff consistently found three patterns of responses from students whose IQ scores fell within the EMR classification range. *Non-gainers* performed poorly initially and did not profit from the instructional procedures. *Gainers* performed poorly on the pre-test administration, but improved markedly following training. *High scorers* demonstrated excellent understanding of the task prior to training and did not improve significantly on the post-test.

Research on the LPA by Budoff and others (Lidz, 1987) over the years has consistently documented the stability of the post-test measure over time as the best predictor of teacher ratings and the student's future performance.

Careful scrutiny of the student's reaction to the different strategies introduced during the teaching phase of an LPA administration will enable the assessor to determine which strategies were most effective for this student and in what specific areas of cognitive functioning. These strategies can then be translated into appropriate cognitive instructional strategies (Pressley et al., 1991) which can be applied in the classroom.

Learning Potential Assessment Device

The Learning Potential Assessment Device (LPAD) is a system of assessing cognitive functioning developed by Reuven Feuerstein and his colleagues of the Hadassah WIZO-Canada Research Institute in Israel. Feuerstein believes the human organism is an open system susceptible to influences which produce structural changes in cognitive processes. The LPAD is based on Feuerstein's *theory of structural cognitive modifiability*. The theory advances the belief that learning is facilitated through mediated learning experiences (MLE). Mediated learning takes place through a dynamic relationship between the mediator and the learner, one in which the mediator intentionally filters, screens, and interprets stimulus to the learner, and provides the opportunity for the learner to understand and comprehend the stimulus in such a way as to formulate appropriate meaning and responses. Individuals who, for whatever reason, did not receive adequate mediated learning experiences, will perform as though they were incapable, as though they were of marginal or limited ability. Feuerstein refers to them as the mentally retarded performers. Feuerstein believes that appropriate mediation facilitates the development of the individual's cognitive structure. He also believes that inadequate or deficient cognitive development can be modified significantly, thus, improving deficient functioning. He also believes there is no critical stage, before which or after which, modification can or cannot be accomplished. Of course, some individuals will require more MLE than others, and some will require less to accomplish similar advances along the continuum of learning.

For more than 25 years, Feuerstein and his colleagues have engaged in research which has explicated the components of the mental act which comprises learning. For purposes of this discussion, I will simplify the description of the mental act, but it is important to remember that analyzing the mental act enables the assessor to be very precise in the identification of the problem in learning which the student experiences. According to Feuerstein, there are three phases of the mental act: the *Input Phase*, in which the student gathers or takes in information; the *Elaboration Phase*, in which the student processes, develops, and analyzes the information; and, the *Output Phase*, in which the student produces a response.

Feuerstein has identified 27 specific areas of problems associated with the Input, Elaboration, and Output phases of learning. There are eight specific difficulties which may appear in the input phase, eleven specific difficulties which may appear in the elaboration phase, and, eight which may appear in the output phase. The goal of assessment is to determine the areas of difficulty which interfere with learning and also how accessible the cognitive structure is to modifiability. For example, some students encounter difficulty in problem-solving not because they lack the capacity, but because they have developed habits which impede the collection of the information needed to understand and/or solve the problem. This is a problem at the *Input Phase*. Unplanned, impulsive, and unsystematic exploratory behavior can cause a student to select and to utilize the wrong information, even though the problem-solving processes may be appropriate. Another frequently encountered problem is one in which the student has not developed the skill to utilize two or more sources of information at the same time. The student takes the first piece of information and attempts to solve the problem without considering another piece of critical information. In the elaboration phase, some students fail to engage in spontaneous comparative behavior. They do not automatically recognize that one thing may be related to another in some specific fashion, e.g., in size, one object may be larger or smaller than another or may be positioned opposite another, etc. This lack of spontaneous comparative behavior will severely curtail effective elaboration.

In the process of identifying these areas of cognitive deficiency, Feuerstein and his colleagues developed a series of exercises or drills that can be employed in the classroom to remediate these deficiencies, or which will facilitate development of the student's cognitive structure. Mediation strategies which are found to be most effective in the assessment process, can be communicated to the teacher to apply in the classroom. Feuerstein and his colleagues have also developed a complete program which can be employed as a supplement to an existing curriculum. Instrumental Enrichment (1980) is currently being used as a remedial program in some districts and as a preventive program in others, with extremely favorable results.

Six Stage Model for Non-Discriminatory Cognitive Assessment

This model of non-discriminatory cognitive assessment was designed by Richard Figueroa, a professor in the School of Education, University of California, Davis. This approach was designed specifically to address the problem of the over-representation of minority group students in special education. It was reasoned that, if almost all students referred for testing were ultimately placed in special education, then attention must be directed toward reducing the number of false positives in the referral process. False positives refers to students determined to be eligible for special education when in fact they are not in need of special education services. This six stage model focuses on the referral process as well as the assessment of the student's cognitive abilities.

This approach places heavy emphasis on gathering the appropriate information from a variety of sources, and using this information as a basis for making sound educational decisions. As the name implies, there are six critical points in the data gathering process. The stages in this process are not sequential. It is not necessary to progress through each stage of the model in sequence. If the data gathered at any stage clearly lead to the decision that the student is not eligible for special education, the assessor can stop the process and return the student to the regular class program with appropriate recommendations for remediation. In other words, a child's assessment can be terminated at any stage because the problem has been resolved by appropriate intervention or explained by other factors.

This non-discriminatory assessment program focuses on: A) The Referral Process; and, B) The Assessment of Cognitive Abilities.

A. The Referral Process is considered a key factor affecting the disproportionate representation of African American students in special education. The following six stage model for non-discriminatory assessment of cognitive skills (Figueroa, 1984) emphasizes the need to examine all aspects of the referral process:

• Review of the referrals and placements in the district by school, grade, age, sex, ethnicity, etc.;

• Review of the referral data on the child in question;

• Review of the modifications undertaken in the regular classroom;

• Observations of the classroom and instructional style;

• Observations of the home curriculum (mediation strategies employed by the family); and,

• Assessment of student's cognitive abilities.

B. Assessment of Cognitive Abilities. Figueroa did not advocate for a specific assessment method as a component of the Six Stage Model. He did acknowledge the conceptual framework for assessment of cognitive abilities discussed by Campione, Brown, and Ferrara (1982). Campione, Brown, and Ferrara identified five determinants of performance which their extensive review of research in learning revealed as areas which differentiate between the performance of the mentally retarded and their non-retarded counterparts. These determinants of performance are:

• *Speed* or *efficiency* with which the elementary information processing operations are carried out;

• The subject's *knowledge base*, the extent and organization of relevant knowledge available to the learner;

• The role of various learning *strategies* in dealing with memory and problem-solving situations. (Many complex learning situations require planned, active processing for optimal performance.);

• *Executive control* or the regulation of cognitive activities (the choice, timing, sequencing, and monitoring of cognitive activities); and,

• *Metacognition* or a person's knowledge of their own cognitive system. (How much does a person know about their own thinking processes?)

Summary

This chapter was intended to provide the reader with a fundamental awareness of the need for alternatives to the traditional, time-worn approaches to assessment, specifically assessment of the cognitive functioning of African American and other minority-students. The brief descriptions of alternatives included here were intended to alert the reader to approaches which, in the opinion of the writer, offer the greatest prospects for providing accurate information about the problems which students encounter in the learning process and how these problems can be remediated in the context of the classroom where these problems occur. Finally, this discussion was intended to encourage creative exploration and experimentation with alternatives in the struggle to find effective means of enhancing the educational experiences of all children, not just the *Larry P*.s'.

References

Barnes, E. (1972). *IQ testing and minority children: Imperatives for change.* (Technical Paper, pp. 1-8). Storrs: University of Connecticut, National Leadership Institute Teacher Education/Early Childhood.

Binet, A., & Simon, T. (1911). *A method of measuring the development of intelligence of young children.* Lincoln, IN: Courier.

Block, N. J., & Dworkin, G. (Eds.). (1976). *The IQ controversy: Critical readings.* New York.: Pantheon.

Bond, H. M. (1924). Intelligence tests and propaganda. *The Crisis, 28*(2), 61.

Brown, A. (1978). Knowing when, where and how to remember: A problem of metacognition. In R. Glaser (Ed.), *Advances in instructional psychology.* Hillsdale, NJ: Erlbaum.

Brown, D. K. (1984, July). *Discrepancies as predictors within a learning disabled population.* Paper presented at the Annual Convention of the American Psychological Association Conference, Toronto, Canada.

Budoff, M. (1970). Learning potential: A supplementary procedure for assessing the ability to reason. *Acta Paedopsychiatrics, 37,* 293-309 (ERIC Document Reproduction Service No. ED 048, 723).

Budoff, M., & Friedman, M. (1964). Learning potential as an assessment approach to the adolescent mentally retarded. *Journal of Consulting Psychology, 28,* 434-39.

Campbell, P. (1992, March). *Criterion assessment.* Paper presented at Advisory Committee Meeting on Reform in California Assessment, Sacramento, CA.

Campione, J. C., Brown, A. L., & Ferrara, R. A. (1982). Mental retardation and intelligence. In R. J. Sternberg (Ed.), *Handbook of human intelligence.* Cambridge: Cambridge University Press.

Canady, H. G. (1936). The effect of rapport on the IQ: A new approach to the problem of racial psychology. *Journal of Negro Education, 5,* 209-219.

Chase, A. (1977). *The legacy of malthus: The social costs of the new scientific racism.* New York: Knopf.

Cleary, A. T., Humphreys, L. G., Kendrick, S. A., & Wesman, A. (1975). Educational uses of tests with disadvantaged students. *American Psychologist, 30*(1), 15-41.

Collins, R., & Camblin, L. D. (1983). The politics and science of learning disabilities classification: Implications for Black children. *Contemporary Education, 54,* (2), 113-18.

Dent, H. E. (1990). *Preschool assessment project.* (Contract No. 7203) Sacramento, CA: Final report to the California Department of Education.

Dent, H. E. (1991). The San Francisco public school experience with alternatives to IQ testing: A model for non-biased assessment. In A. G. Hilliard (Ed.), *Testing African American students.* Morristown, NJ: Aaron Press.

Dixon, N. R. (Ed.). (1977). Testing Black students [Special Issue]. *The Negro Educational Review, 28*(3, 4).

Feuerstein, R., Rand, Y., & Hoffman, M. B. (1979). *The dynamic assessment of retarded performers: The learning potential assessment device: Theory, instruments, and techniques.* Baltimore, MD: University Park Press.

Figueroa, R. A. (1984). *The non-psychometric assessment of children's intelligence.* Unpublished manuscript. University of California, Davis.

Goddard, H. H. (1912). *The Kallikak family: A study in the heredity of feeblemindedness.* New York: MacMillan.

Gould, S. J. (1981). *The mismeasure of man.* New York: Norton Press.

Green, D. R. (1972). *Racial and ethnic bias in test construction.* (Contract No. OEC 9-70-0058 (057))

Final report of the United States Office of Education, Washington, DC.

Guthrie, R. V. (1976). *Even the rat was White: A historical view of psychology.* New York: Harper & Row.

Heller, K. A., Holtzman, W. H., & Messick, S. (Eds.). (1982). *Placing children in special education: A strategy for equity.* Washington, DC.: National Academy Press.

Hernshaw, L. S. (1979). *Cyril Burt psychologist.* London: Hodder & Stoughton.

Hilliard, A. G. (1987). The learning potential assessment device and instrumental enrichment as a paradigm shift. *Negro Educational Review, 36*(2-3), 200-208.

Jones, R. L. (Ed.). (1988). *Psychoeducational assessment of minority group children: A casebook.* Berkeley, CA: Cobb & Henry.

Kamin, L. J. (1978). *The science and politics of IQ.* Potomac, MD: Erlbaum.

Laosa, L. M. (1989). *Population generalizability, cultural sensitivity, and ethical dilemmas.* (Research Report 89-26). Princeton, NJ: Educational Testing Service.

Larry P. v. Riles, 495 F. Supp., (N. D. CA, 1979).

Larry P. v. Riles (1986, September). C-71-2270 RFP, Order modifying judgment.

Lidz, C. S. (1987). *Dynamic assessment: An international approach to evaluating learning potential.* New York: Guilford.

Lippmann, W. (1976). The Lippmann-Terman debate. In N. J. Block & G. Dworkin (Eds.), *The IQ controversy: Critical readings* (pp. 4-44). New York: Pantheon.

Mehan, H., Hertweck, A., & Meihls, J. L. (1986). *Handicapping the handicapped decision making in students' educational careers.* Palo Alto: Stanford University Press

Mensh, E., & Mensh, H. (1991). *The IQ mythology: Class, race, gender, and inequality.* Carbondale, IL: Southern Illinois University Press.

Mercer, C. (1986). Personal Communication.

Mercer, J. R. (1973). *Labeling the mentally retarded.* Berkeley, CA: University of California Press.

Mercer, J. R. (1979). Expert testimony in the Larry P. trial (*Larry P. v. Riles*). 495 F. Supp., Northern District CA.

National Commission on Testing and Public Policy (1990). *From gatekeeper to gateway: Transforming testing in America.* Chesthill, MA: Boston College.

National Council on Education Standards and Testing (1992, January). *Raising standards for American education*: A report to Congress, the Secretary of Education, the National Education Goals Panel, and the American People, Washington, DC.

Pressley, M., & Associates. (1990). *Cognitive strategy instruction that really improves children's academic performance.* Cambridge: Brookline Books.

Rogers, J., & Kulick, E. (1986, April). *An investigation of unexpected differences in item performance between Blacks and Whites taking the SAT.* Paper presented at the annual meeting of the National Council on Measurement in Education, San Francisco, CA.

Schmitt, A. P. (1988). Language and cultural characteristics that explain differential item functioning for Hispanic examinees on the scholastic aptitude test. *Journal of Educational Measurement, 25*, 1-13.

Schmitt, A. P., & Bleistein, C. A. (1987). *Factors affecting differential item functioning for Black examinees on scholastic aptitude test analogy items* (RR-87-23). Princeton, NJ: Educational Testing Service.

Schmitt, A. P., & Dorans, N. J. (Eds.). (1987, March). Differential item functioning on the scholastic aptitude test. Research Memorandum, Princeton, NJ: Educational Testing Service.

Shapiro, M. M., Slutsky, M. H., & Watt, R. F. (1989). Minimizing unnecessary differences in occupational testing. *Valparaiso University Law Review, 23*(2).

Sternberg, R. J. (Ed.). (1982). *Handbook of human intelligence.* Cambridge: Cambridge University Press.

Taylor, D. (1992, March). *Authentic assessment.* Paper presented at Advisory Committee Meeting on Reform of California Assessment, Sacramento, CA.

Terman, L. M. (1916). *The measurement of intelligence: An explanation of and a complete guide for the use of the Stanford revision and extension of the Binet-Simon intelligence scale.* Boston: Houghton-Mifflin.

Tucker, J. A. (Ed.). (1985). Curriculum-based assessment [Special Issue]. *Exceptional Children, 52*(3).

Tyler, R. W., & White, S. H. (1979). *Testing, teaching, and learning.* Report of a Conference on Research and Testing. Washington, D.C.: National Institute of Education, U.S. Department of Health, Education and Welfare.

Wang, M. C., Reynolds, M. C., & Walberg, H. J. (1986, September). Rethinking special education. *Educational Leadership, 44,* 26-31.

Wechsler, D. (1944). *The measurement of intelligence.* Baltimore, MD: Williams & Williams.

Williams, R. L. (1974). *Contemporary issues in Black psychology*. St. Louis, MO: Washington University Press.

Ysseldyke, J. E., Algozzine, B., & Epps, S. (1983). A logical and empirical analysis of current practice in classifying students as handicapped. *Exceptional Children, 50*, 160-66.

Ysseldyke, J. E., & Regan R. R. (1980). Non-discriminatory assessment: A formative model. *Exceptional Children, 46,* 465-466.

For additional information contact:
Harold E. Dent, Ph.D.
Director of Outreach
Center for Minority Special Education
Hampton University
Hampton, VA 23668
Telephone: (804) 727-5107
Fax: (804) 727-5131

Identifying and Assessing the Gifts and Talents of Young African American Learners: Promising Paradigms and Practices

James M. Patton

Abstract

After reviewing and critiquing the European roots of contemporary psychoeducational testing, this chapter presents an African centered axiological and cosmological schema designed to guide the development of authentic assessment of young African Americans with gifts and talents. Screening and assessment practices, instruments, identification systems, and intervention assessment approaches found effective in the discovery of intellectual, creative, and psychosocial gifts and talents among African American youths are identified and emerging alternative assessment approaches are offered. A comprehensive empowerment oriented intervention model that involves collaboration among school, families, communities, businesses, churches, and Black self-improvement organizations is also presented. Finally, additional research directions are offered.

Background

A host of African American researchers (Baldwin, 1984; Frasier, 1990; Harris & Ford, 1991; Hilliard, 1991; Nobles, 1987; and Patton, 1992) have recently called for the modification of traditional practice in the assessment of gifts and talents of young African Americans. Using conventional assessment models and practices continues to depress the gifts and talents of African Americans unabatedly in the field of gifted education. In fact, a recent study found that 88.5% of the states responding to a national survey indicated use of traditional, norm-referenced, tests in the identification of "at-risk," gifted learners (Van Tassel-Baska, Patton, & Prillaman, 1989).

Oftentimes, the identification and selection of students for gifted programs is based heavily on the use of assessment measures that rely on a single construct of intelligence, usually reflected in a single intelligence or achievement test score, and to some extent the nominations of teachers (Frasier, 1990; VanTassel-Baska, Patton, & Prillaman, 1989). Clearly, this mono-operational view of intelligence and concomitant monomodal assessment approach have not resulted in the identification of young, gifted, and talented African Americans at the levels thought to exist in society. Although *some* acculturated or assimilated African Americans are identified as gifted

123

through conventional means, especially over-looked through the use of these Eurocentric de-rived assessment approaches are those truly gifted African American youth who engage in culturally distinct and oppositional cultural forms of behav-iors and those from lower socioeconomic envi-ronments who, for whatever reasons, do not dis-play gifted and talented behaviors that are indica-tive of traditional White, middle class environ-ments. It is these truly gifted and talented African Americans whose appearances and manifesta-tions of giftedness are often obscured and obfus-cated by culture and differential expressions of giftedness who are often overlooked through con-ventional tests and procedures. Zappia (1989) reported that while African Americans comprise approximately 16.5% of the population of public school age children, they make up only 8.4% of those identified as gifted. A reality such as this is not acceptable in a nation that professes to be a world leader in talent identification and develop-ment. Further, creating and utilizing definitions of giftedness and assessment theories, method-ologies, and tests that consider alternative, plural-istic identification systems based upon philo-sophical world views and cultural and behavioral systems of African Americans should contribute to increasing the numbers of African Americans identified as gifted, especially those not easily identified by traditional means. Once identified, these talented students should contribute indi-vidually and collectively to the progression of African Americans, as well as to positive change in American society as a whole.

Several elements of an identification system that should yield more gifted and talented African American learners have been identified in the research and literature base. Listed below are three emerging attributes of such a system:

1. The utilization of a philosophical orienta-tion to assessment and identification that recog-nizes the important influence of African and African American culture in the manifestation of giftedness (Hilliard, 1991; Patton, 1992). This orientation values the use of norms in the identi-fication and selection process of gifted and tal-ented learners that are based upon the world views, values, experiences, and culture of Afri-can Americans (Gay, 1978; Harris & Ford, 1991).

2. The use of a multidimensional construct of intelligence (Gardner, 1983; Sternberg, 1985) in defining expressions of intelligence and gifted-ness.

3. The use of multimodal assessment proce-dures (Baldwin, 1989; Frasier, 1987; Patton, 1992; Renzulli, 1977) in the gifted and talented assess-ment identification and selection process.

Unfortunately, there has not been enough attention paid to the use of African centered philosophical and conceptual frameworks in the design of assessment theory and practices to identify young, gifted African Americans. The purpose of this chapter is to offer a schema, based clearly on the strengths of people of African ancestry, that may be used to guide theory build-ing and the development of assessment method-ology and tests that should enhance our capacities to identify gifts and talents among African Ameri-can learners. Many scholars believe that a focus on theory building in this regard will allow for the creation of a belief system that inspires and rein-forces the authentic identification of the gifts and talents of truly gifted and talented African Ameri-cans. Second, existing traditional and non-tradi-tional assessment instruments and practices proven to be effective in this authentic identification process will be presented. Additionally, emerg-ing alternative identification systems whose ef-fectiveness in the identification of gifted African Americans are being recognized will be offered. Finally, ways for moving beyond assessment and identification to the design of empowerment ori-ented programmatic practices needed in the pro-gressive education and development of the gifts and talents of young African American learners will be suggested.

The following review of the philosophical and theoretical origins of contemporary psychoeducational testing should provide an his-torical context for the proposed African centered schema offered later in this chapter.

Eurocentric Roots of Contemporary Psychoeducational Testing: A Critique

Gordon (1985) has reminded us that one's set of philosophical assumptions or world-views is reflected in theory, methodology, and practice in the social sciences. He notes that this world-view shapes one's inquiry method, modes of obtaining knowledge, and ways of organizing and verifying knowledge, all of which are culture specific. More recently, Gordon, et al., (1990) informed us that the communicentric and a priori prejudices traditionally held by many Euro-American social scientists have generated false and distorted theories, paradigms, and methodologies which deny the cultural integrity of African Americans and affirm and exalt Eurocentric culture and world-views. The thought provoking and studied critiques of the philosophical and conceptual origins of conventional intelligence tests offered by Gould (1977, 1981), Hilliard (1984, 1991), Kamin (1974, 1975) and Nobles (1983) have demonstrated the shared cultural, philosophical, and sociopolitical world-views held by the early European and Euro American developers of so-called intelligence tests. Chief among the shared paradigms advanced by these early assessment theorists and test developers such as Galton (1884), Goddard (1919) and Terman (1916) were notions of the unidimensional and static construct of intelligence and the accuracy of measuring intelligence through the use of intelligence tests. These tests were thought to tap deep structure, universal mental aptitudes and abilities. Some have argued, however, (Cole, & Scribner, 1973; Hilliard, 1984,1991; Nobles, 1987; Ogbu, 1988; Sattler et al., 1981; and Vernon, 1969) that I.Q. tests more closely identify specific middle class-oriented, culturally and linguistically cognitive skills, not global cognitive capacities and processes.

Continuing this analysis, Ogbu (1988) has demonstrated the difference between intelligence as cognitive capacities which are global, and cognitive skills which are relative and vary from culture to culture. Accordingly, Ogbu claims that intelligence tests measure specific, Eurocentric oriented cognitive skills which are associated with Western culture. Therefore, since these tests are based on samplings of cognitive universes and behaviors valued by "the middle class in Western societies, they inevitably discriminate against members of other cultures" and cannot adequately measure "intelligence" of African Americans (Ogbu, 1988, p. 29).

The works of Terman, Galton, Goddard, and others who shared European oriented conceptual universes influenced current assessment theory, methodology, and practice. Relatedly, their research has been seen also as a strong source of influence to several generations of politicians, social scientists, educators, and researchers. Today, the testing and measurement assault on African Americans is not as openly and crudely advanced as the earlier craniometrists or hereditarian pioneers (Nobles,1987). Modern approaches have called for different types of assault–more subtle in their conceptual and psychometric manifestations. Gould (1981) has stated, "the crudities of the cranial index have given way to the complexity of intelligence testing" (p. 143). Relatedly, Kamin (1975) observed that the pseudo-objective "scientific" approaches of contemporary practice in psychometry have disguised many biases still inherent in much of today's intelligence and standardized testing paradigms. While traditional tests based upon oppressive oriented paradigms sometimes have the power to identify those African Americans who have been successfully assimilated into so-called mainstream American culture, many assimilated and non-assimilated truly gifted African Americans still have not been identified as such. Further, the identification of non-assimilated African American learners whose appearances and manifestations of giftedness are often missed through the use of approaches designed to identify young, gifted, middle-class Whites has been clearly lacking.

As more African American and other theorists increase their challenges to the theoretical precision, purposes, goals, and decision-making processes around conventional intelligence tests, in particular, and certain standardized measures of achievement, in general, new theories of intelligence and talent identification must be utilized that emanate from and are connected with deep structure African American culture and world-views and the strengths these youth bring to America's schools. The following thoughts advance several key philosophical and conceptual attributes needed to guide assessment theory and practice designed to equitably identify the gifts and talents of young (ages 4-15) African American learners, especially those not easily identified through conventional methodologies and instruments.

Toward the Development of a Schema for Assessing Young African Americans with Gifts and Talents

Kaplan (1964) defined theory as the symbolic representation of experience. Accordingly, theory can serve as a mediator for reconstructing experiences that can be subsequently analyzed, synthesized, measured, interpreted, and criticized. The methodological processes utilized in conventional psychoeducational assessment are guided, shaped, and influenced, in part, by theory. Therefore, the use of a specific methodological approach or test assumes some type of implicit or explicit *prior* theorizations about the construct or attribute of the thing or person to be measured and the inquiry method to be utilized. These theory building and methodological selection processes, as shown earlier, flow from one's culturally based philosophical world-views and can, as a result, influence results.

The exploration and creation of psychoeducational assessment theory, methodologies, and tests that are consistent with and advance the philosophical world-views and cultural systems and styles of African Americans, should enhance our abilities to identify increased numbers of gifted African Americans. Stated differently, what is being advanced is the development and use of multimodal, culturally specific and sensitive assessment and identification approaches in attempts to locate and educate young, gifted and talented African American learners.

Perhaps the first and most essential consideration in the design of systems that assess and identify gifted African American learners is the construction of a belief system which will undergird and define the identification protocol. It would be postulated that such a value system would assume that large numbers of gifted and talented African Americans exist; that many are often overlooked; and that most can be identified with the use of proper instruments, techniques, and approaches. Second, this value system must include the belief that, while African American learners possess some values and behavioral characteristics similar to all gifted and talented learners, they also manifest characteristics unique to African American culture. It is important, then, to establish assessment and identification systems that include norms which recognize this reality. Also, assumed in this belief system is a pluralistic view of giftedness that recognizes the existence of multiple domains for manifesting gifts and talents, e.g., aptitude, achievement, creativity or psychosocial characteristics, that can be displayed through various manifestations of gifts and talents. Relatedly, such a system acknowledges the possibility of manifestations of giftedness in one specific domain of intelligence and the possibility of slightly above average or average performance in additional domains of giftedness. Plainly speaking, one can be gifted in one traditional area of giftedness and not in others.

Accordingly, the following represents the presentation of a schema needed for conceptualizing and understanding the needed inter-relatedness and connections among African American culture and world-views, accepted theories of intelligence and giftedness, and accepted assessment methodology and practice, that might serve to guide the psychoeducational assessment of African American learners with gifts and talents. This schema is followed by examples of screening, assessment and identification instruments and approaches *more* consistent with African American cultural norms, ethos, and conventions.

Table 1 identifies selected aspects of a "pure" and classical African American philosophical and theoretical system which could be used in relating constructs of intelligence and giftedness to culturally distinct assessment methodologies and approaches suggested in Table 2. The selected African–centered cosmology presented in

Table 1. Selected Dimensions of Classical African American Oriented Philosophical World-Views

Metaphysics	Axiology	Epistemology	Logic of Inquiry
Use of a Dualism/ Holism View of Reality	Person-to-Person Relations are Deemed Important	Affective Orientation	Diunital
The individual views the whole field and then understands the interconnectedness of its parts.	Interpersonal relationships and strong social bonds with people hold the highest value.	One uses the affect and emotional cues to know through symbolic imagery and rhythm.	The individual thinks through viewing the union of opposite ideas or realities: the individual views something apart and united at the same time.

Note. The information obtained in the metaphysics, axiology, and logic sections of this table are drawn from the philosophical and conceptual works of Baldwin (1991), Dixon (1976), Maurier (1979), Nichols (1976), and Nobles (1991). That included in the epistemology section is drawn from these same authors and the theoretical work of Boykin (1983). This table is adopted from previous work of Patton (1992, 1993).

Table 1 is defined as "pure" and "traditional" because it sketches historical, deeply embedded cultural characteristics of African Americans which provide the foundation for the cultural uniqueness of African Americans. It is understood that all African Americans do not correspond to this "pure" type of philosophical system or cosmology. Intragroup behavioral differences exist and have been identified, understood, and discussed elsewhere (e.g., Frasier, 1989). While within group variations are important variables to consider in any type of cultural/ecological theoretical analysis, space however will not allow a detailed discussion of these differences. Differences in degrees of actualizing this cosmology exist but do not disprove the fact that many African Americans relate strongly to the cosmological system outlined in Table 1. Accordingly, many reconstruct life experiences through lenses reflected by fundamental realities presented in this table.

Concepts and questions of ultimate reality and values are by nature metaphysical and axiological. The left side of Table 1 outlines briefly a schema for understanding some funda-mental metaphysical and axiological orientations of African Americans as a group. These metaphysical and axiological systems include notions of context, continuous time, verve, and the value of developing personal relationships with individuals groups. The overriding ontological principle of "survival of the group" and the general, relational and corporate consciousness of the individual governs this African centered cosmology (Baldwin, 1991). Relatedly, the holistic view of reality and approach to problem solving utilized by many African Americans reflects a metaphysical and axiological orientation that values harmony or oneness with nature; while perceiving and interpreting reality through uniting seemingly opposite information. This schema also suggest that emphases on emotions and feelings are valued in this epistemology.

Imperatives for Appropriate Assessment

The search for overlooked populations of young, gifted, and talented African Americans

Table 2. Interaction Between Giftedness Constructs and Assessment Approaches More Likely to Identify Gifts and Talents of Young African Americans

Constructs of Intelligence and Giftedness	Culturally Affirming Assessment Approaches and Procedures
1. Using an intelligence and giftedness construct that employs multiple domains for manifesting intelligence (Gardner, 1983; Sternberg, 1991).	1. Using assessment approaches and instruments grounded in identifying and interpreting cognition, behavior, and creativity emanating from a normative structure of African American culture, and experiences (Baldwin, 1991; Hilliard, 1976; Nobles, 1987; Ogbu, 1988).
2. Employing a pluralistic view of intelligence that recognizes the giftedness construct within the context of African American and other cultural forms (Hilliard, 1984; Patton, 1992).	2. Utilizing an open assessment system that employs multiple criteria within multiple contexts. Employing both quantitative and qualitative data in the data collection process, Such a system requires assessing-traits such as motivation, leadership, and affective development in addition to measures of aptitude, achievement, and creativity. These systems employ peer, community, and parent nominations, as well as student product evaluations. (Frasier, 1989; Patton, 1992; Renzulli, 1973; Torrance, 1987).
3. Recognizing the dynamic nature of intelligence (Feuerstein, 1980).	3. Utilizing action-oriented and dynamic assessment methodology that are instructionally oriented (Feuerstein, 1980; Hilliard, 1991).
	4. Use of curriculum-based assessment approaches that employ a test, teach, retest, teach approach (Fuchs, L. S. & Fuchs, 1986).

would be better understood and implemented if undertaken within the context of the framework presented herein. Frasier (1990), Gardner (1983), Sternberg (1991) and others have reminded us that the use of multidimensional screening and assessment instruments and procedures that are qualitative as well as quantitative, provides additional avenues in the search for gifted African Americans. The work of these individuals and that of Baldwin (1984), Harris and Ford (1991), Hilliard (1976), Renzulli (1973), and Torrance (1977) suggest the need to develop more fluid views of intelligence and assessment belief systems, instruments, and practices which are culturally specific and multimodal.

As previously stated, philosophical worldviews inform the method of inquiry employed to investigate, assess or measure certain phenomena. Accordingly, cosmological orientations, culture, language, values and behaviors are complex and interrelated phenomena. It is important, then, for these phenomena to be congruent with intelligence and gifted constructs and assessment instruments and methods. The concept of multiple manifestations and forms of intelligence, gifts, and talents, as presented by

Gardner (1983) and Sternberg (1991), is consistent with the world-view set forth in Table 1. In order to more appropriately assess and identify gifted and talented African Americans, the information in Table 2 suggests the use of a multiple construct of intelligence and giftedness and selected assessment approaches and procedures more consistent with African Americans' worldviews suggested in Table 1. The information outlined on the right side of Table 2 contains characteristics of assessment designs that could be useful in building assessment systems for identifying giftedness among African American learners. The proposed design elements provide a close fit to the basic philosophical orientations of African Americans postulated in Table 1.

Within the past 20 years, a modicum of advances have been made toward the appropriate assessment and identification of gifted African American learners. A 1981 National Identification Conference (Richert et al., 1982) attempted to catalog a comprehensive listing of practices that would advance the identification of "disadvantaged" gifted. While probably well intended, this effort was flawed because it employed a deficit philosophical orientation and confused definitions related to the "disadvantaged" construct. A body of literature based on theory, research, and practice has advanced which suggests that certain instruments and procedures have power in assessing and identifying young, gifted African American learners. While space does not permit a detailed description of all of these tests and procedures, a sample of those most often identified in the literature as effective in assessing and identifying gifted African Americans follows.

Screening

While local school districts may vary among their procedures for identifying and selecting students for gifted and talented programs, most engage in an initial pre-screening and/or screening phase in order to establish a pool of potentially eligible students. An assessment phase follows during which time instruments are used to collect additional and more discrete data. Most school systems conclude with the selection of individuals for gifted programs. The number of African American children identified as gifted and talented has been seen to increase if a teacher nomination procedure is augmented during the screening phase with nominations from multiple data sources within and outside the school setting (Blackshear, 1979; Davis, 1978; Kitano & Kirby, 1986; Van Tassel-Baska, Patton, & Prillaman, 1989). It is suggested that these additional data sources include peer nominations, parent nominations and nominations from community leaders, as well as samples of student products.

Two decades ago both Hilliard (1976) and Torrance, (1977) developed screening checklists and rating scales based upon assessing the distinct social, cultural, and psychological indicators of giftedness and creativity within the normative context of African American culture. Frasier (1989) has found that the inclusion of these rating scales and checklists in the process of screening gifted and talented learners will likely increase the number of African Americans subsequently identified as gifted (Frasier, 1989).

Hilliard devised pre-screening devices which recognized the "basic African American cultural contributions to patterns of human behavior" (1976, p. 14). Accordingly, his resulting checklists, the "Who" and "O," were grounded in the uniqueness and commonalities in the deep structure culture of African Americans. It has been purported that these checklists emphasize synthetic-personal stylistic characteristics of African American learners such as creative improvisation, divergent experimentation, inferential reasoning and harmonious relationships with nature and one's environment (Hilliard, 1976).

While the use of the "Who" and the "O" scales represents an excellent opportunity to gain culturally relevant information, these scales have been designed as pre-screening devices to be used in concert with post-screening tests and procedures. Presently, as suggested by Hilliard, cultural and behavioral style information resulting from the use of the "Who" and "O" should be collected in order to utilize it as a base for developing *new* culturally sensitive second level screening instruments. This culturally sensitive information could be integrated also into existing post-screening instruments.

Torrance (1969) identified a set of behaviors thought to be central to African Americans. These behaviors provided the basis for the development of the Checklist of Creative Positives (CCP) (Torrance, 1977). He identified a "set of characteristics that helped to guide the search for strengths of culturally different students for giftedness among such students" (p. 25). The subsequent 18 characteristics have became known in the literature as "creative positives." Torrance postulated that indicators of these creative positives, such as articulation and spontaneity in role playing situations, the creative type of parables and story-telling, use of expressive speech, responsiveness to the kinesthetic, originality of ideas in problem solving, to name a few, could best be measured through observational techniques with responses recorded on a checklist. The CCP has been widely used and represents another pre-screening measure which has the capacity to increase the numbers of African Americans considered for gifted and talented programs (see Patton, 1992; VanTassel-Baska, Patton, & Prillaman, 1989).

Identification

The heavy reliance on using traditional, norm referenced intelligence tests, as previously discussed, have not resulted in the numbers of identified gifted African American students that are thought to exist in this nation's schools. Non-assimilated African American learners are especially not identified by traditional approaches and tests. Some intelligence tests, as a result of their conceptual, technical and cultural sensitivity attempts, however, show some promise. Baska (1986a, 1986b), Frasier (1989), and VanTassel-Baska, Patton and Prillaman (1989) have found that the Coloured, and Standard Progressive Matrices (Raven, 1938, 1947a, 1947b) are frequently used intelligence tests by school systems attempting to increase the number of African American learners in gifted programs. While the popularity of these tests is not sufficient to recommend their use, their high-to-moderate positive correlations with other intelligence and achievement tests and

their high concurrent validity in use with African Americans (Court & Raven, 1982; Sattler, 1982; and Valencia, 1979) is noteworthy. Additionally, the predominant nonverbal administration and content of these tests make them appealing for use with potentially gifted African American learners. Other attractive features consist of their quick and easy untimed administration and the option of individual or group administration. These tests have been faulted, however, because of the unidimensional definition of intelligence upon which they have been built.

Another aptitude measure, the Matrix Analogies Test-Expanded and Short Form (MAT-EF and MAT-SF) has been developed recently and is purported to be normed on a large, current and nationally representative sample of individuals in terms of gender, race, ethnicity, socioeconomic status, and geographic region. This test has been reported to have a high level of internal reliability and validity (Naglieri & Prewett, 1990). It measures nonverbal ability through the use of figural matrices and is purported to be useful with individuals whose scores may be influenced by speed (Naglieri & Prewett, 1990).

The MAT-EF was utilized recently as part of a profile assessment approach used in a federally funded Jacob Javits project designed to identify and educate gifted African American learners who are often not identified through the use of conventional assessment and identification processes. This program, Project Mandala (Patton et al., 1989), has been the subject of several studies designed to validate the efficacy of the assessment protocol used in the identification process. One of these recent studies conducted by Ward, Ward, and Patton (1992) found that large numbers of heretofore unidentified gifted African American learners (aged 4-13) were identified through the use of the MAT-EF. These researchers found that the results of the MAT-EF proved to be the highest estimate of general intellectual ability for a significant portion of African Americans than any other aptitude measure employed in the profile protocol. The MAT-EF correlated significantly with the WISC-R and the PIAT-R resulting in validating the MAT-EF as a non-verbal measure of general intellectual ability (Ward et al., 1992).

Frasier (1989) reported that the Kaufman Assessment Battery for Children (K-ABC) (Kaufman & Kaufman, 1983), "is fair to minorities" (p. 281). Collectively, African Americans have generally scored higher on the K-ABC than on other intelligence tests. The developers attribute these higher scores to the test's emphasis on a concept of multiple intelligence and "deemphasis of applied skills and verbal expression" (Kaufman & Harrison, 1986, p. 151). While African Americans have scored higher on these tests, they have been criticized for their low ceiling for gifted populations (Sattler, 1982) and lack of evidence of validity (Salvia & Ysseldyke, 1988).

An assessment system consistent with the concept of multiple intelligences would include measures of creativity. Accordingly, it would be appropriate to include the use of the Torrance Test of Creative Thinking (TTCT) in assessment efforts designed to identify gifted African American learners (Torrance, 1987). This test measures creativity and has been found to be culturally fair, particularly the figural form of the test. It enjoys moderate levels of reliability according to data obtained from longitudinal studies designed to "predict quantity and quality of public personal creative achievements" (Torrance, in press). The test's quick and easy administration (30 minutes), and wide application (individual or group; grades K through graduate school) make it appealing, particularly in light of the paucity of valid tests of creativity.

The Group Inventory for Finding Talent (GIFT) and The Group Inventory for Finding Interests I (GIFFI I) and II (GIFFI II) represent self-report inventories developed by Rimm, 1976; Rimm and Davis, 1976 & 1980; and Davis and Rimm, 1983, respectively. These inventories have been recently reported by Torrance (in press) as being technically sound and are psychometrically designed to allow their use with learners from diverse cultural groups and socioeconomic levels. These instruments have been developed for use with individuals from preschool to senior high school. Some of the attributes measured by these instruments include independence, flexibility, curiosity, and perseverance. Validity and reliability evidence of these inventories with Afri-

can American learners has not been reported in the literature.

Matrix and Profile Approaches

Several assessment models exist which view giftedness as a multidimensional construct and employ a comprehensive approach at *identifying, selecting,* and *nurturing* the development of gifted, African American learners. An earlier matrix assessment model (Baldwin, 1984) and a present profile assessment model (Frasier, 1990) appear to represent a holistic orientation and, thus, more closely fit the appearances and manifestations of giftedness within an African American context. The Baldwin Identification Matrix (BIM) (Baldwin, 1984) and modifications thereof (Dabney, 1983, 1988) have been reported to be effective approaches to identifying large numbers of gifted African American learners, many of whom would not have been identified through the more conventional approach of viewing isolated, and discrete test score results. These matrix approaches have been designed in a way that allow decision makers to display the results of multiple, objective and subjective data sources and juxtapose these results in a matrix format. This allows for data from these multiple sources to be collected, reviewed, and analyzed collectively *prior to* making decisions about the selection of individuals for inclusion in programs for the gifted.

Frasier's work related to the development of assessment "profiles" appears promising for enhancing the capacity for identifying gifted African American learners. The K-ABC Frasier Talent Assessment Profile (F-TAP) (Frasier, 1990) requires that the user collect both quantitative and qualitative data on individual students that provide information from multiple sources. The resultant individual profile includes information from which collected identification and selection decisions can be made. Selection decisions are based, therefore, upon multiple and broad areas of indicators of giftedness or potential giftedness rather than narrow and discrete indicators (Frasier, 1990).

The reliability of a profile identification approach was reported in a recent study (Ward, Ward,

Landrum, & Patton, 1992). This research also found that a profile approach, which considered, at the same time, achievement, and creativity measures, was not influenced by race or culture.

Intervention Planning

Some curriculum–based assessment approaches have been used in attempts to increase the number and kind of African Americans included in programs for the gifted and talented. Based primarily upon "dynamic assessment" models Feuerstein (1968, 1977) and Haywood (1988), an "identification through teaching" approach (a test, teach, retest approach) has been utilized as the basis for assessment, identification, selection and instruction. This approach allows potentially gifted students to develop and display cognitive and affective abilities over time and subsequently refine these skills while project staff suspend their decision on the selection of students for program inclusion (Johnson, Starnes, Gregory, & Blaylock, 1985). Students selected for the program are those who have the strongest response to curriculum exposure. Responsiveness to differentiated classroom curricula, therefore, becomes a part of the assessment and identification paradigm thus providing for a close link between identification and curriculum (Johnson et al., 1985). Further, the Program of Assessment, Diagnosis and Instruction (PADI) , as reported by Johnson et al., (1985), operationalizes the belief that the giftedness construct should include those students who demonstrate evidence of high performance and also those with giftedness potential.

The PADI Program and the Potentially Gifted Minority Student Project, recently described by Alamprese and Erlanger (1988), represent examples of the effectiveness of using a curriculum based approach to identify gifted and talented or potentially gifted African American learners. In addition to the "identification through teaching approach," both of these programs employ several psychometric features which reflect practices that result in increasing numbers of African Americans identified as gifted and talented. First, the conceptual orientation of these programs that undergirded the selection of instruments and pro-

cedures consisted of using those diagnostic instruments *known to be able* to measure the reasoning and creativity potential of African American learners (Johnson, Starnes, Gregory, & Blaylock, 1985). Thus, the ability of selected instruments and procedures to identify and diagnose the strengths, skills, and needs of potentially gifted, African American learners guided project personnel in the selection of measures and procedures used in the projects' assessment protocols. Second, both programs used multidimensional diagnostic instruments that were reflective of an expanded vision of the giftedness construct. Third, both programs emphasized early identification and intervention approaches, perspectives often found to be effective with African Americans. Last, the curriculum-based measurement (CBM) emphasis of both programs, allows teachers to use assessment data to teach students, rather than rank them.

Emerging Alternative Assessment Approaches

In spite of the suggestions and recommendations made in the last fifteen years to change the way school divisions search for and identify young, gifted or potentially gifted African Americans, school systems continue to heavily rely on norm referenced intelligence tests and teacher nominations (VanTassel-Baska, Patton, & Prillaman, 1989). In practice, some intelligence test is normally used as the single criterion for entrance into gifted programs. Other measures, approaches, and perspectives are required. The dissonance that often exists between the culture of African Americans and that of assessment practices normally used in schools must be bridged. There is a need for continued modification of conventional measures of general aptitude by removing tasks not appropriate for African American children and by adding tasks based upon the previously discussed ethos and culture of African Americans. Alternative assessment approaches to the identification of gifted and talented African American children that incorporate techniques other than standardized pencil and paper tests that use multiple choice formats must continue to be explored. Continued research which emphasizes the use of alternative forms of measuring performance, i.e., portfolio assessment which asks students "to perform tasks that closely emulate the mental tasks of life" (Archambault, 1992, p. 5) hold promise for use in identifying gifted African Americans.

If those responsible for creating authentic educational systems for young and gifted African American learners are serious in their charge, it is imperative to cast as wide a net as possible in the initial process of nominating students for gifted programs. This would require schools to link more closely not only with parents but also with social and community organizations known to have power and facility in identifying gifts and talents of African Americans. Neighborhood settlement houses, community action agencies, social service agencies, Black fraternities and sororities, etc., must be contacted in this early nomination process and networks should be established within the social, political and economic structures of African American communities. School/business partnerships that focus on talent identification and development of young African Americans, especially males, would benefit schools, businesses and industry, and ultimately the economy of African Americans and this nation. African American entrepreneurs themselves should lead the way in the development of coalitions among schools, African American communities, and social and political organizations for the express purpose of identifying and empowering the gifts and talents of young African American students.

Empowerment Oriented Programmatic Practices for Young, Gifted African American Learners: A Comprehensive Approach

To empower a student to learn assumes that the learner has some level of strengths or skills to begin with. He or she, in essence, "brings something to the table." All too often it is assumed that African American learners have little to bring to the academic and instructional transaction table. This assumption has been consistently proven to be invalid. It is important that the search for gifted and talented African American students not end with assessment and identification. Assessment should lead to intervention. The assessment process must be empowering and lead to the identification of the strengths, skills, and needs of these gifted learners in order to design appropriate empowering interventions. In order, to accomplish individual and collective empowerment goals, a comprehensive approach is required. While space does not allow for a detailed explication of such an approach, the designs of the components of a comprehensive assessment and intervention system will be discussed next.

Towards a Comprehensive Model

It is important that efforts aimed at assessing and identifying gifted and talented African Americans advance within the context of a comprehensive, dynamic, and culturally mediated model. This model should include the following components: assessment, curriculum and instruction, family involvement and interagency collaboration and consultation. Recognition of the dynamic nature of factors within and across the components of this model and the interrelationship of these components is important for program development and implementation. Equally important is the linkage of efforts in each program component with one another. Once students are identified, viable, culturally mediated curricula are required in order to be effective and accepted by African American communities.

Program and Curriculum Planning and Development

The use of assessment data to design curricula for the gifted and talented has been previously established (Gallagher, J. J., 1985; Van Tassel-Baska, 1988). Other social scientists (Anderson, 1988; Hilliard, 1976; Nobles, 1987) inform us of the need to consider cultural factors unique to African American learners in the curriculum development and delivery process. These researchers point to additional assumptions that should be embraced in order to develop a more comprehensive curriculum development and delivery system. Suggested by this research is a curriculum development and intervention focus that should: 1) be interdisciplinary; 2) possess an infusion of affective experiences; 3) involve teachers, students, and significant others (e.g. mentors) actively in the learning process; 4) utilize teaching-learning strategies found effective in working with African American learners; 5) have a future tense orientation by focusing on career goals and enhanced career possibilities; and, 6) involve the formal and fictive families of the students.

Family Empowerment and Involvement

Attempts to identify and enhance the gifts and talents of African American learners must include the involvement of formal and extended family members. The importance of supportive family structures in the lives of eminent adults has been chronicled by others (Comer, 1988; Perino & Perino, 1981). Family nurturance of gifted learners no doubt has a significant impact on the development of talent and the future accomplishments of these learners. The need for positive nurturance of gifted African Americans by family members is most significant. Thus, the following assumptions are thought to be useful in an effective family involvement component of a comprehensive identification and intervention system:

• Socialization in African American families is an interactional, multi-directional process whereby family members influence the gifted child's behavior and are influenced by the child's behavior.
• Systems theory and knowledge of African American formal and informal extended family structure should guide family interventions with these populations of gifted learners.
• Formal as well as informal social ties must be considered in the analysis and understanding of family interactions with gifted learners.
• Organized and functional families exist in both low and high income family structures. Understanding and respect for the centeredness of

the culture of African American families must be maintained.
• Facilitative family value systems for talent development focus on the importance of education and the work ethic.
• Important roles for families of gifted learners to perform include: monitoring the child's progress; encouraging learning; and direct involvement in the support structure for learning (Patton et al., 1989).

Guided by these assumptions, research and experience suggest that a comprehensive family empowerment and involvement plan should be developed for family members of gifted and talented African American learners. This plan should contain elements which approach family empowerment and involvement at both collective and individual levels. The primary goals of this family involvement component must include the following objectives:

1. To ensure the participation of significant family members in the education of their gifted child.
2. To increase the family's understanding of the gifts and talents of its child.
3. To enhance family/school interaction through understanding and respect for the centeredness of African American families.
4. To maintain and advance family interpersonal relationships supportive of the cognitive and affective development of the gifted child.
5. To empower families to propel their gifted learners into a career and aspirational path of excellence and progression.

Two approaches could be taken to accomplish these objectives. First, at the collective level, a series of family involvement sessions could be organized around several basic themes. Some suggested themes include focusing on 1) understanding the characteristics of gifted and talented students, 2) understanding the school's gifted curriculum, 3) accessing and extending school and community resources, 4) monitoring and advancing the child's progress in school, 5) organizing and advocating for appropriate education of the gifted child's learning, and 6) supporting enhanced career paths for gifted children.

The second approach should consist of the development and implementation of an Individualized Family Support Plan (IFSP) for each family. Each plan, while individualized, would focus on 1) involvement of the family in the gifted educational program, 2) child enrichment activities, 3) family/school interactions, 4) family interpersonal relationships, and 5) educational and vocational goal setting[1].

Interagency Collaboration

Efforts aimed at identifying and empowering young, gifted and talented African Americans will yield greater results if they are linked with activities of important economic, religious, social, political, and neighborhood networks existing in African American communities. These identification and intervention efforts should begin with the establishment of a pool of candidates for gifted programs and continue through the intervention and empowerment stage.

In urban and suburban areas, contact should be made with African American Greek-letter fraternities and sororities; educational organizations; Masonic organizations; social and professional organizations; political organizations; and self-help community based organizations. It should be observed that all Black Greek-letter fraternities and sororities and African American social organizations require their members to pursue very active individual and collective social action agendas. These organizations are always looking for an education project" which will promote the development of young African Americans, especially those who have gifts and talents. Efforts to build the candidate pool and to nurture the gifts and talents of African American learners once identified should also include establishing contact with individuals and groups such as African American spiritual leaders and ministers, African American owners of major print and nonprint media, Boy's Clubs, and Y.W.C.A.s, and so on (Patton & Baytops, 1995).

Identifying gifted African American learners in rural communities poses additional challenges. Many rural communities in the South reflect the roots of African adaptations to American culture. Traditional family values, a sense of community, religion, and hard work are readily apparent in African American communities in the rural South. In addition to the type of contacts previously discussed, relationships should be built with the leadership and members of Ruritan Clubs, 4-H Clubs, the Agriculture Extension Service, and the formal and informal communication networks in existing rural African American communities (Patton & Baytops, 1995).

Summary Remarks and Additional Research Directions

This chapter has sought to offer an African American centered philosophical and conceptual framework to guide the assessment of young African Americans with gifts and talents.

It should be acknowledged that while some progress has been made in contemporary psychometric theory and instrumentation, more work remains. The historical Western fixation upon pseudo-scientific testing approaches (Nobles, 1987) continues to hinder the development of more progressive and solid conceptions concerning the assessment and identification of African Americans with gifts and talents. Assessment paradigm shifts must be forthcoming if progress is to occur.

It is essential to understand that tests are not neutral in their context or effect. They reflect the predominant culture of their developers and interpreters. This fact has resulted in the political use of psychoeducational assessment and testing to the disadvantage of African Americans (Nobles, 1987). Ways exist that can overcome this problem:

1. Broader and more dynamic visions about intelligence and gifted constructs have emerged (Asante, 1988; Gardner, 1983; Ogbu, 1988; Sternberg, 1985, 1991) and should serve as a foundation for future research and development.

2. Pluralistic procedures for identifying gifted African Americans have emerged (Harris & Ford, 1991) and should be built upon. Special attention should focus on the search for gifted African American males for they are truly

underrepresented in gifted programs.

3. Curriculum–based measurement (CBM) approaches hold promise in that they have been found to improve the correspondence between testing and teaching the school's curriculum (Fuchs & Fuchs, 1986) and in enhancing the communication of assessment data (Deno & Fuchs, 1987). Increased use of pluralistic procedures and CBM approaches should move the psychoeducational assessment process towards assessing for the purpose of teaching and student empowerment rather than ranking students.

4. Alternative, qualitative assessment approaches must be researched and address reliability and validity issues.

5. A focus of all assessment efforts should be on the identification of strengths of African Americans, as these strengths are manifested in diverse ways, and recognize the unique traits and psychosocial characteristics of achieving African Americans. Shade's (1978) research and that of Frasier (1990) related to psychosocial traits of gifted African American learners point the way to identifying diverse indicators of giftedness among African Americans from diverse socioeconomic circumstances.

6. While aspects of the deep structure culture of African Americans is both unique and common to people of African descent, there exists some diversity in its sociopsychological manifestations. Recognizing and understanding within-group differences should lead to the development of psychoeducational assessment theories, methodology, instruments and practice based upon intra-group research and study. Additional research is needed that uncovers intra-group differences in cognition, behavior, and motivation (Gordon, 1985).

7. An assessment approach is needed which is comprehensive in its design and delivery. Assessment of gifted and talented African American learners must lead to appropriate curriculum planning and delivery, family intervention and involvement and eventually neighborhood and community empowerment.

8. It is necessary that educators move beyond the current discussions of identification and intervention issues related to gifted learners and instead become more inclusive by creating ways to use similar gifted and talented treatments for *all* African American learners. One could wonder what would be so horrible if African American learners, as a rule, were treated as if they were gifted or potentially gifted? What could be the damage done by this approach? Enrichment and other types of empowering interventions designed for gifted African Americans would undoubtedly prove helpful to all African American learners, their families, and communities. Gifted interventions for all should be the rallying call for the future.

Note

1. Some of the concepts included in the family empowerment section have been drawn from work associated with Project Mandala. The author wishes to acknowledge the work of Mrs. Joy Baytops, Dr. Vicki Damiani, and Dr. Kathy Evans in this particular regard.

References

Alamprese, J. A., & Erlanger, W. J. (1988). *No gift wasted: Effective strategies for educating highly able disadvantaged students in mathematics and science Vol. I: Findings.* Washington, DC: Cosmos.

Anderson, J. A. (1988). Cognitive styles and multicultural populations. *Journal of Teacher Education, 39*(1), 2-9.

Archambault, F. X. (1992). *Alternative assessment and the evaluation of programs for the gifted and talented.* Unpublished manuscript, University of Connecticut, National Research Center on the Gifted and Talented, Storrs.

Asante, M. K. (1988). *Afrocentricity.* Trenton, NJ: Africa World Press.

Baldwin, A. Y. (1984). *The Baldwin Identification Matrix 2 for the identification of the gifted and talented: A handbook for its use.* New York: Trillium.

Baldwin, A. Y. (1989). The purpose of education for gifted Black students. In C. J. Maker & S. W. Schiever (Eds.), *Critical issues in gifted education* (pp. 237-245). Austin, TX: Pro Ed.

Baldwin, J. A. (1991). African psychology and Black personality testing. In A. G. Hilliard (Ed.), *Testing African American students* (pp. 56-66). Morristown, NJ: Aaron.

Baska, L. (1986a). Alternatives to traditional testing. *Roeper Review, 8* , 181-184

Baska, L. (1986b). The use of the Raven advanced progressive matrices for the selection of magnet junior high school students. *Roeper Review, 8*(3), 181-184.

Blackshear, P. (1979). *A comparison of peer nomination and nomination of the academically gifted Black primary level student.* Unpublished doctoral dissertation, University of Maryland, College Park.

Boykin, A. W. (1983). The academic performance of Afro-American children. In J. Spence (Ed.), *Achievement and achievement motives.* San Francisco: W. H. Freeman.

Comer, J. P. (1988). Educating poor minority children. *Scientific American, 259*(5), 42-58.

Cole, M., & Scribner, S. (1973). Cognitive consequences of formal and informal education. *Science Education, 182,* 553-559.

Court, J. H., & Raven, J. (1982). *Research and references: 1982 update.* London: H. K. Lewis.

Dabney, M. (1983, July). *Perspectives and directions in assessment of the Black child.* Paper presented at the meeting of the Council for Exceptional Children, Atlanta, GA.

Dabney, M. (1988). An alternative model for identification of potentially gifted students: A case study. In R. L. Jones (Ed.), *Psychoeducational assessment of minority group children: A casebook* (pp. 273-294). Berkeley, CA: Cobb & Henry.

Davis, G. A., & Rimm, S. (1983). Group inventory for finding interests (GIFFI) I and II: Instruments for identifying creative potential in the junior and senior high school. *Journal of Creative Behavior, 16,* 50-57.

Davis, P. (1978). *Community efforts to increase the identification of the number of gifted minority children.* Ypsilanti, MI: Eastern Michigan College of Education.

Deno, S. L., & Fuchs, L. S. (1987). Developing curriculum-based measurement systems for data-based special education problem solving. *Focus on Exceptional Children, 19*(8), 1-16.

Dixon, V. J. (1976). World views and research methodology. In L. M. King, V. J. Dixon, & W. W. Nobles (Eds.), *African philosophy: Assumptions and paradigms for research on Black persons* (pp. 51-102). Los Angeles: Fanon Center Publication.

Feuerstein, R. (1968). *The learning potential of assessment device: A new method for assessing modifiability of the cognitive functioning of socioculturally disadvantaged adolescents.* Unpublished manuscript, Israel Foundation Trustees, Tel Aviv.

Feuerstein, R. (1977). Mediated learning experience: A theoretical basis for cognitive human modifiability during adolescence. *Research to practice in mental retardation: Proceedings of the 4th Congress of IASMD: Vol 2. Education and training* (pp. 105-116). Baltimore, MD: University Park Press.

Feurstein, R. (1980). *Instrumental Enrichment.* Baltimore, MD: University Park Press.

Frasier, M. M. (1987). The identification of gifted Black students: Developing new perspectives. *Journal for the Education of the Gifted, 10*(3), 155-180.

Frasier, M. M. (1989). A perspective on identifying Black students for gifted programs. In C. J. Maker & S. W. Schiever (Eds.), *Critical issues in gifted education: Defensible programs for cultural and ethnic minorities* (Vol. 2, pp. 213-255). Austin, TX: Pro Ed.

Frasier, M. M. (1990, April). *The equitable identification of gifted and talented children.* Paper presented at the annual meeting of the American Educational Research Association, Boston, MA.

Fuchs, L. S., & Fuchs, D. (1986). Curriculum-based assessment of progress toward long and short term goals. *Journal of Special Education, 20,* 69-82.

Gallagher, J. J. (1985). *Teaching the gifted child.* Boston: Allyn & Bacon.

Gardner, H. (1983). *Frames of Minds.* New York: Basic Books.

Galton, F. (1884). *Hereditary genius.* New York: D. Appelton.

Gay, J. E. (1978). A proposed plan for identifying Black gifted children. *Gifted Child Quarterly, 22*(3), 353-360.

Goddard, H. H. (1919). *Psychology of the normal and abnormal.* New York: Dodd, Mead.

Gordon, E. W. (1985). Social science knowledge production and minority experiences. *The Journal of Negro Education, 54*(2), 117-133.

Gordon, E. W., Miller, F., Rollock, D. (1990). Coping with communicentric bias in knowledge production in the social sciences. *Education Researcher, 19*(3), 14-19.

Gould, S. J. (1977). *Ever since Darwin.* New York: Norton.

Gould, S. J. (1981). *The mismeasure of man.* New York: Norton.

Harris, J. J., & Ford, D. Y. (1991). Identifying and nurturing the promise of gifted Black American children. *Journal of Negro Education, 60*(1), 3-18.

Haywood, H. C. (1988). Dynamic assessment: The learning potential assessment device. In R. L. Jones (Ed.), *Psychoeducational assessment of minority group children: A casebook* (pp. 39-63). Berkeley, CA: Cobb & Henry.

Hilliard, A. G. (1976). *Alternative to I. Q. testing: An approach to the identification of "gifted" minority children.* Sacramento, CA: Final Report, Sacramento Division of Special Education, California State Department of Education. (ERIC Document Reproduction Service No. ED 147 009)

Hilliard, A. G. (1984). I. Q. thinking as the emperor's new clothes: A critique of Jensen's bias in mental testing. In C. R. Reynolds & R. T. Brown (Eds.), *Perspectives in mental testing* (pp. 139-169). New York: Plenum.

Hilliard, A. G. (1991). The learning potential assessment device and instrumental enrichment as a paradigm shift. In A. G. Hilliard (Ed.), *Testing African American students* (pp. 200-216). Morristown, NJ: Aaron Press.

Johnson, S. T., Starnes, W. T., Gregory, D., & Blaylock, A. (1985). Program of assessment, diagnosis, and instruction (PADI): Identifying and nurturing potentially gifted and talented minority students. *The Journal of Negro Education, 54*(3), 416-430.

Kamin, L. J. (1974). *The science and politics of I. Q.* Potomac, MD: Lawrence Erlbaum.

Kamin, L. J. (1975). Social and legal consequences of I. Q. tests as classification instruments: Some warnings from our past. *Journal of School Psychology, 13*(4), 317-323.

Kaplan, A. (1964). *The conduct of inquiry.* San Francisco: Chandler.

Kaufman, A. S., & Harrison, P. L. (1986). Intelligence tests and gifted assessment: What are the positives? *Roeper Review, 8*(3), 154-159.

Kaufman, A. S., & Kaufman, N. L. (1983). *Kaufman Assessment Battery for Children (KABC).* Circle Pines, MN: American Guidance Service.

Kitano, M. K., & Kirby, D. F. (1986). *Gifted education: A comprehensive view.* Boston: Little, Brown.

Maurier, H. (1979). Do we have an African philosophy? In R. A. Wright (Ed.), *African philosophy: An introduction.* Washington, DC: University of America Press.

Naglieri, J. A., & Prewett, P. N. (1990). Nonverbal intelligence measure. A selected review of instruments and their use. In C. R. Reynolds & R. W. Kamphaus (Eds.), *Handbook of psychological & educational assessment of children: Intelligence and achievement* (pp. 348-370). New York: Guilford.

Nichols, E. J. (1976). [The philosophical aspects of cultural difference]. Unpublished table, University of Ibadan, Nigeria.

Nobles, W. W. (1983). *Critical analysis of scholarship on Black family life.* Washington, DC: Final report, United Church of Christ Commission for Racial Justice.

Nobles, W. W. (1987). Psychometrics and African American reality: A question of cultural antimony. *The Negro Educational Review, 38,* 45-55.

Nobles, W. W. (1991). African philosophy: Foundations for Black psychology. In R. L. Jones (Ed.), *Black psychology* (3rd ed, pp. 47-63). Berkeley, CA: Cobb & Henry.

Ogbu, J. (1988). Human intelligence testing: A cultural-ecological perspective. *National Forum, 68*(2), 23- 29.

Patton, J. M. (1992). Assessment and identification of African American learners with gifts and talents. *Exceptional Children, 59*(2), 150-159.

Patton, J. M. (1993). Psychoeducational assessment of gifted and talented African Americans. In J. H. Stanfield, II & R. M. Dennis (Eds.), *Race and ethnicity in research methods.* Newbury, CA: Sage.

Patton, J. M., & Baytops, J. L. (1995). Identifying and transforming the potential of young, gifted African Americans: A clarion call for action. In B. A. Ford, F. E. Obiakor, & J. M. Patton, *Effective education of African American exceptional learners: New perspectives* (pp. 27-67). Austin, TX: Pro Ed.

Patton, J. M., Prillaman, D., Laycock, V., & VanTassel-Baska J. (1989). *A research and demonstration project for culturally diverse, low income, and handicapped gifted and talented learners.* Washington, DC: Office of Educational Research and Improvement, U.S. Department of Education.

Perino, J., & Perino, S. C. (1981). *Parenting the gifted: Developing the promise.* New Providence, NJ: R. R. Bowker & Co.

Raven, J. C. (1938). *Standard progressive matrices.* London: H. K. Lewis.

Raven, J. C. (1947a). *Coloured progressive matrices.* London: H. K. Lewis.

Raven, J. C. (1947b). *Advanced progressive matrices.* London: H. K. Lewis.

Renzulli, J. S. (1973). Talent and potential in minority group students. *Exceptional Children, 39,* 437-444.

Renzulli, J. S. (1977). *The enrichment triad model: A guide for developing defensible programs for the gifted and talented.* Mansfield Center, CT: Creative Learning Press.

Richert, E. S., Alvino, J., & McDonnel, R. (1982). *The national report on identification: Assessment and recommendations for comprehensive identification of gifted and talented youth.* Sewell, NJ: Educational Improvement Center-South.

Rimm, S. (1976). *GIFT: Group inventory for finding talent.* Watertown, WI: Educational Assessment Service.

Rimm, S., & Davis, G. A. (1976). GIFT: An instrument for the identification of creativity. *Journal of Creative Behavior, 10,* 178-182.

Rimm, S., & Davis, G. A. (1980). Five years of international research with GIFT: An instrument for the identification of creativity. *Journal of Creative Behavior, 14,* 35-46.

Salvia, J., & Ysseldyke, J. E. (1988). *Assessment in special and remedial education.* Boston: Houghton & Mifflin.

Sattler, J. M. (1982). *Assessment of children's intelligence and special abilities.* Boston: Allyn & Bacon.

Sattler, J. M., Hilliard, A., Lambert N., Albee, G., & Jensen, A. (1981, August). *Intelligence test on trial: Larry P. and PASE.* Paper presented at the annual meeting of the American Psychological Association, Los Angeles.

Shade, B. J. (1978). Social-psychological characteristics of achieving Black children. *The Negro Educational Review, 29*(2), 80-86.

Sternberg, R. (1985). *Beyond I.Q.* Cambridge, MA: University Press.

Sternberg, R. (1991). Giftedness according to the triarchic theory of human intelligence. In N. Colangelo & G.A. Davis (Eds.), *Handbook of gifted children* (pp. 45-53). Boston: Allyn & Bacon.

Terman, L. M. (1916). *Human nature and the social order.* New York: Macmillan.

Torrance, E. P. (1969). Creative positives of disadvantaged children and youth. *Gifted Child Quarterly, 13*(2), 71-81.

Torrance, E. P. (1977). *Discovery and nurturance of giftedness in the culturally different.* Reston, VA: Council for Exceptional Children.

Torrance, E. P. (1987). *Using tests of creative thinking to guide the teaching of creative behavior.* Bensville, IL: Scholastic Testing Service.

Torrance, E. P. (in press). *The blazing drive: The creative personality.* Buffalo: Bearly.

Valencia, R. R. (1979). Comparison of intellectual performance of Chicano and Anglo third grade boys on the Raven's coloured progressive matrices. *Psychology in the Schools, 16*(3), 448-453.

VanTassel-Baska, J., Patton, J., & Prillaman, D. (1989). Disadvantaged gifted learners at-risk for educational attention. *Focus on Exceptional Children, 3,* 1-16.

Vernon, P. E. (1969). *Intelligence and cultural environment.* London: Methuen.

Ward, T., Ward, S., Landrum, M., & Patton, J. (1992). *Examination of a new protocol for the identification of at-risk gifted learners.* Paper presented at the annual meeting of the American Educational Research Association, San Francisco.

Ward, T., Ward, S., & Patton, J. (1992). *An analysis of the utility of the matrix analogies test with at-risk gifted learners.* Paper presented at the annual meeting of the American Educational Research Association, San Francisco.

Zappia, I. A. (1989). Identification of gifted Hispanic students. A multidimensional view. In C. J. Maker & S. W. Schiever (Eds.), *Critical issues in gifted education* (pp. 19-26). Austin, TX: Pro Ed.

For additional information, contact:

Dr. James M. Patton
Office of Academic Programs
School of Education
P. O. Box 8795
The College of William and Mary
Williamsburg, VA 23187-8795
Telephone: (804) 221-2317
Fax: (804) 291-2988

Optimal Performer Locator for Parents and Teachers

Seward E. Hamilton, Jr.

Abstract

The Optimal Performer Locator Scales (OPL) are behavioral rating scales for determining the outstanding behavioral characteristics of African American children. The purpose of the scales is to serve as a criterion measure for the identification of gifted African American children. The scales assess diverse behavior characteristics of African Americans based upon cognition, creativity, language, liberal arts, leadership, and psychomotor skills, and attributes of outstanding accomplishments and outstanding achievers within the African presence. There are four different developmental levels of the Optimal Performer Locator-Parents and Teachers (OPL-P & OPL-T) scales: (1) preschoolers (age 3-6); (2) elementary (grades 1-5); (3) middle school (grades 6-8); and (4) high school (grades 9-12). Pilot and psychometric analyses, including reliability, content, and construct validity studies at the preschool level are reported.

Purpose and Rationale

The Optimal Performer Locator (OPL) for Parents (OPL-P) and Teachers (OPL-T) scales are the renamed Gifted Children Locator (GCL) for Parents (GCL-P) and Teachers (GCL-T) (Hamilton, 1983, 1987, 1991). The OPL-P & T consist of preschool, elementary, middle, and high school scales which are primarily behavioral assessment observational-interview rating scales used to identify African American preschool through high school aged children as optimal (gifted) performing children. The OPL is a rating of the pupil by one or both parents and his/her teacher, counselor or school psychologist.

The purpose of the OPL is to serve as a criterion measure for identifying optimal performing children to provide multicultural/multiethnic, critical thinking, and advance curriculum enrichment education. These childrens' outstanding abilities and talents can be promoted and transformed so that they may eventually contribute their genius to craftsmanship, engineering, leadership, liberal arts, mathematics, medicine, the sciences, and other fields.

The OPL is different at each developmental level for age and grade behavioral performance. The descriptions of specific behavioral traits and total number of items varies from form to form. The OPL is designed to identify children with optimal performance demonstrated by exhibiting behavioral abilities in various activities which are rated as outstanding by their parents and teachers.

Definition of Terms

Culturally Diverse African American Children refers to African American children whose socialization process differs from that of the dominant European American culture resulting in the development of generally distinct behavior patterns, responses and learning styles.

Giftedness is used to describe children whose intellectual functioning is at or above two standard deviations above the mean on any one of the major intelligence tests (i.e., Kaufman Assessment Battery for Children (1983), Stanford-Binet Intelligence Test-Fourth Edition (1986), Wechsler Intelligence Scale for Children-Revised III (1991), & Wechsler Preschool and Primary Scale of Intelligence-Revised (1989).

Multicultural/Multiethnic Enrichment refers to education curriculum resources that include creative project development, critical thinking, and research investigations to promote optimal experiences to enhance children's precocious abilities. These educational experiences are to prepare students to increase their mental prowess. Enrichment provides students with a knowledge base that enables them to contribute, learn, live and function in a culturally diverse and technically advanced society by fostering respect, appreciation, and tolerance for people of other ethnic and cultural backgrounds.

Optimal Performer refers to children whose performance rating yield's a score 1 1/3 standard deviation above the mean on either the Optimal Performer Locator for Parents (OPL-P), the Optimal Performance Locator for Teachers (OPL-T), or a composite score on both instruments.

Description of Instruments

Optimal Performer Locator for Parents and Teachers: Preschool Scale

The Gifted Children Locator (GCL) for Parents (GCL-P) and Teachers (GCL-T) Preschool Scale which were used in the initial research on this instrument (Hamilton, 1983;1987) have been renamed the Optimal Performer Locator (OPL) for Parents (OPL-P) and Teachers (OPL-T): Preschool Scale (Hamilton, 1991). All GCL items are retained in the OPL, either intact or with substantial modification and fourteen items were added to the new scale. A teacher should have at least a six month period of observing and working with the child to adequately assess the school performance of the child.

The first component of this scale consists of sixty-five items that are evaluated on a Likert scale. The preschool scales are used to ascertain the degree to which parents and teachers have observed the child exhibiting various behavioral acts and to determine how these acts relate to behavioral statements which were identified in gifted children. Response alternatives and sample items are presented in Sample 1.

Items are scored from one to five. A total score can be as high as 325. Standardized raw scores yield a mean of 100 and a standard deviation of 15 for the national population, to measure optimal performance. Each item is described in a manner to illustrate descriptively the outstanding behavioral skills of preschool children (2 1/2 years to 5 years, 11 months) with respect to learning styles, interests, environments, activities and experiences.

The second component of the preschool scale is supplemental and consists of open-ended questions which ascertain from parents and teachers the child's precocious behavioral characteristics as they perceived them to be related to giftedness. Additionally, for the purpose of the research, the OPL-P preschool form includes information on the child's demographics, health, and parental background.

A diagnostic profile analysis based upon rating scale behavior descriptions, is used to identify students' weaknesses and strengths. The rat-

Sample 1. The Optimal Performer Locator for Teachers (Preschool - Kindergarten Scale)

Administration Booklet

Name _____   Date Rated _____
School _____   Date of Birth _____
Rated By _____   Age _____
Relationship to Student _____

Directions: Please indicate the degree to which the child can demonstrate abilities of each and every item listed by encircling the appropriate number. The numbers represent the following values:

1	2	3	4	5
Never	Seldom	Occasionally	Frequently	Always
(0-20%)	(21-40%)	(41-60%)	(61-80%)	(81-100%)

	1	2	3	4	5
1. The child figures out the answers to problems without the help of others.	1	2	3	4	5
2. The child asks questions about Black people's past history and differences from other racial groups.	1	2	3	4	5
3. The child likes to be the center of attention.	1	2	3	4	5
4. The child likes to make quick decisions.	1	2	3	4	5
5. The child is good at guessing.	1	2	3	4	5
6. The child appears to know how people feel.	1	2	3	4	5

ings for the five point scale are as follows: 1 - Well Below Average; 2 - Below Average; 3 - Average; 4 - Above Average; and, 5 - Optimum. Prescriptive activities are provided for weaknesses (ratings of 1 to 3) and strengths (ratings of 4 to 5). This analysis is used to provide parents and/or teacher(s) with educational prescriptive activities to enhance the child's movement toward superior functioning.

Optimal Performer Locator for Parents and Teachers: Elementary School Scale

The Optimal Performer Locator (OPL) for Parents (OPL-P) and Teachers (OPL-T) Elementary School Scale (Hamilton, 1988) are individually administered by parents and teachers who rate children they believe demonstrate outstanding academic, cognitive, psychomotor, leadership, creative skills, and/or talents in the liberal arts. A teacher should have at least a six month period of observing and working with the child to adequately assess the child's school performance.

The first component of the scale consists of sixty-four items that are evaluated on a 5-point Likert scale. The elementary instrument is used to ascertain the degree to which parents and teachers have observed the child exhibiting various behaviors indicative of outstanding performances and to determine how these behavioral performances relate to the descriptive behavioral statements which have been identified as characteristic of gifted children. Response alternatives and sample items are presented in Sample 2.

Sample 2. The Optimal Performer Locator for Teachers (Elementary School Scale, Grades 1-5)

Directions: Please indicate the degree to which the child can demonstrate abilities of each and every item listed by encircling the appropriate number. The numbers represent the following values:

1 Never (0-20%)	2 Seldom (21-40%)	3 Occasionally (41-60%)	4 Frequently (61-80%)	5 Always (81-100%)

1. The child uses words which are at a higher level than used by his or her age group.	1	2	3	4	5
2. The child recognizes information presented to him which reflects his cultural heritage.	1	2	3	4	5
3. The child likes to be recognized for what he or she knows.	1	2	3	4	5
4. The child makes problem–solving decisions readily.	1	2	3	4	5
5. The child is good at developing clues to to solve problems.	1	2	3	4	5

Items are scored from one to five. The total score can be as high as 320, with scores at or above 15 percent of the local, state, and national standardization population indicating optimal performance or giftedness. The OPL-P and OPL-T Elementary School Scale contain seven subscales with varying numbers of items from six to ten. The subscales measure creativity, psychomotor ability, cognition/intellectual ability, leadership, mathematics, science, language arts, and liberal arts skills. Subscale reliability will be determined in future studies. Each item describes the outstanding behavior or skill exhibited by the child that corresponds specifically to the child's grade level and age, with consideration of learning styles, interests, environment, activities and experiences.

The second component of the Elementary School Scale is supplemental and consists of open-ended questions which are administered to ascertain from parents and teachers the child's outstanding behavioral performances as they have been observed. The OPL-P Elementary School Scale also includes demographic information on health, and parental background.

As was noted for the preschool scale, a diagnostic profile analysis and prescriptive activities are used to identify students' weaknesses and strengths. The ratings for the five point–scale are as follows: 1 - Well Below Average; 2 - Below Average; 3 - Average; 4 - Above Average; and 5 - Superior. Prescriptive activities are provided for weaknesses (ratings of 1 to 3) and for strengths (ratings of 4 to 5). This analysis is used to provide parents and/or teacher(s) with educational prescriptive activities to enhance the child's performance.

Optimal Performer Locator for Parents and Teachers: Middle School Scale

The Optimal Performer Locator (OPL) for Parents (OPL-P) and Teachers (OPL-T) Middle School Scale (Hamilton, 1988) are also individually administered to parents and teachers who rate children they believe demonstrate outstanding

Sample 3. The Gifted Children Locator for Teachers (Middle School Scale, Grades 6th - 8th)

Directions: Please indicate the degree to which the child can demonstrate abilities of each and every item listed by encircling the appropriate number. The numbers represent the following values:

1 Never (0-20%)	2 Seldom (21-40%)	3 Occasionally (41-60%)	4 Frequently (61-80%)	5 Always (81-100%)

1. The student has a positive view of himself or herself and strives to perform with high esteem in exercising mental tasks.	1	2	3	4	5
2. The student demonstrates a common sense approach to life.	1	2	3	4	5
3. The student strives to be the center of attention.	1	2	3	4	5
4. The student makes spontaneous decisions.	1	2	3	4	5
5. The student demonstrates concrete hypothesis in problem-solving.	1	2	3	4	5

academic, cognitive, psychomotor, leadership, creative skills, and/or talents in the liberal arts. Here again, a teacher should have at least a six month period of observing and working with the child to adequately assess the child's school performance.

The first component of this scale consists of fifty items that are evaluated on a 5-point Likert scale. The middle school scale is used to ascertain the degree to which parents and teachers have observed the child exhibiting various behavioral acts and to determine how these acts relate to the descriptive behavioral statements which have been identified as characterizing gifted children. As well, a high achieving student's self-rating may indicate his/her belief he/she is demonstrating optimal skills. Response alternatives and sample items are presented in Sample 3.

Items are scored from one to five. Total scores can be as high as 250, with standardized scores that yield a mean of 100 and a standard deviation of 15 for local, state, and national populations to measure optimal performance. The OPL-P and OPL-T Middle School Scale contains eight subscales with varying numbers of items. These subscales measure outstanding creativity, cognition/intellectual ability, leadership, mathematics, science, psychomotor/athletic ability, language arts, and liberal arts skills. Subscale reliability will be determined in future studies.

The second component of the middle school instrument is supplemental and consists of open ended questions which are administered to ascertain from parents and teachers the child's outstanding performance characteristics as they have been observed. Information on demographics, health, and parental background are also included.

Again, a diagnostic profile and educational prescriptive activities were developed from the behavior descriptions.

Optimal Performer Locator for Parents and Teachers (High School Scale)

The Optimal Performer Locator (OPL) for Parents (OPL-P) and Teachers (OPL-T) High School Scale (Hamilton, 1988) are individually administered to parents and teachers to rate chil-

Sample 4. The Optimal Performer Locator for Teachers (Senior School Scale, Grades 9th -12th)

Directions: Please indicate the degree to which the child can demonstrate abilities of each and every item listed by encircling the appropriate number. The numbers represent the following values:

1	2	3	4	5
Never	Seldom	Occasionally	Frequently	Always
(0-20%)	(21-40%)	(41-60%)	(61-80%)	(81-100%)

1. The student has a positive view of himself or herself and strives to perform with high esteem in exercising mental tasks.   1   2   3   4   5
2. The student demonstrates a commonsense approach to life.   1   2   3   4   5
3. The student strives to be the center of attention.   1   2   3   4   5
4. The student makes spontaneous decisions.   1   2   3   4   5
5. The student demonstrate concrete hypothesis in problem-solving.   1   2   3   4   5

dren who they believe demonstrate outstanding academic, cognitive, psychomotor, leadership, creative skills, and/or talents in the liberal arts. Again, a teacher should have at least a six month period of observing and working with the child to adequately assess the child's school performance. Also, a high achieving student's self-rating may indicate his/her belief that he/she demonstrates optimal performance.

The first component of this scale consists of sixty items that are evaluated on a 5-point Likert scale. Characteristics of gifted children, response alternatives and representative items are presented in Sample 4.

Items are scored from one to five. A total raw score can be as high as 360, with standardized scores that yield a mean of 100 and a standard deviation of 15 for local, state, and national populations to indicate optimal performance. The OPL-P and OPL-T High School Scale contains eight subscales. These subscales measure outstanding creativity, cognition/intellectual, leadership, mathematics, science, psychomotor/athletic ability, language arts, and liberal art skills.

Open-ended questions ascertain from parents and teachers the child's behavioral characteristics; and information on demographic, health, and parental background is obtained. As indicated in previous sections, a diagnostic profile is developed.

Administration and Scoring

The Optimal Performer Locator is administered individually to the parents and teachers of a particular child. Administration time is approximately 30 to 60 minutes. The scales can be self administered for parents and teachers or administered by a school psychologist or counselor. Adolescent high achieving students can be administered the rating scale by counselor or school psychologist. Each descriptive statement on the scale is directly related to a behavioral trait. No training is necessary for parents or teachers to evaluate a child. Exceptions must be made for parents who have less than a high school education. In such cases, the items should be read to the parents and detailed examples should be given to provide clarity.

The scoring of OPL instruments consists of totalling the items to compute the sum of the scale scores. The Z-score transformation method will be used to convert the OPL scores into seven standard units to yield a mean of 100 and standard deviation of 15. This will provide a descriptive classification table for the range of scores on the instrument for each respective form.

Reliability and Validity of OPL-P & T

Reliability

There have been no reliability studies of the Optimal Performer Locator elementary, middle and high school scales to date, but pilot and standardization data are now being gathered. However, reliability and validity were conducted on the Optimal Performer Locator for Parents and Teachers Pre-school Scale via the Gifted Children Locator for Parents and Teachers (Hamilton, 1985). Utilizing Cronbach Alpha, coefficients of .93 were obtained for the OPL-P, and .95 for the OPL-T.

Content Validity

The Optimal Performer Locator instruments were developed from a synthesis of items taken from several different instruments and related research which is pertinent to the gifted. Some items were developed from the "Who" and "O" prescreening checklist by Hilliard (1976), and a rating scale developed by Malone (1974); other items were created from biographies of outstanding achieving African American men and women (Baldwin, 1978; Brown 1863; Jenkins, 1943). Hilliard (1976) suggested that synthetic personal behavioral style characteristics could identify gifted children among cross-cultural groups. The Behavioral Identification of Giftedness (BIG) questionnaire was developed by Malone (1974). The BIG questionnaire uses biographical, behavioral, and life history information to identify the gifted among low socio-economic and minority populations. These tests were used to form some of the behavioral traits for the OPL instruments. Other behavioral characteristic items were developed from the writings of Hildreth (1954), Jenkins (1936, 1948, 1950), Laycock and Caylor (1964), Marland (1972), Roedell, Jackson, and Robinson (1980), Sullivan (1973), Torrence (1973), Williams and Addison (1978), and Witty and Jenkins (1936).

Construct Validity

Construct validity was assessed to establish that the construct, optimal performance behavioral traits, that were presumed to be reflected in the OPL-P and OPL-T rating score actually accounted for differences in ability traits. The OPL-P and T behavioral traits were highly intercorrelated. This validity check was based on a correlation between parents and teachers' observational

Table 1. Eigenvalues and Percentage of Variance

Factor	Eigenvalue Variance	Percentage of Percentage	Cumulative
1	14.76	54.5	54.5
2	2.85	10.5	65.0
3	2.35	8.7	73.7
4	1.54	5.7	79.4
5	1.18	4.4	83.8
6	1.05	3.9	87.6

Table 2. Varimax Rotation Factor Matrix

OPL-P Item		Factor* 1	2	3	4	5	6	Communality
28	Long Term Memory	.52						.60
29	Problem Solving/Competition	.60						.61
30	Independence	.54						.55
31	Creativity/Inventiveness	.52						.58
32	Positive Self-Concept	.64						.62
33	Assertiveness	.62						.65
34	Breadth of Knowledge/Elaboration	.44						.60
35	Analysis	.65						.61
37	Exploration	.69						.67
38	Judgement	.61						.54
39	Perception	.51						.64
40	Advance Vocabulary	.51						.50
41	Power of Concentration	.54						.52
12	Verbal Concentration Activity	.55						.53
13	Verbal Reasoning of Similarities		.60					.58
16	Inquisitive with Intuition		.43					.58
21	Color in Visual Perception		.66					.57
22	Immediate Recall		.54					.60
23	Motor Control Ability		.67					.62
24	Organization Sequence Ability		.58					.53
25	Organization of Relationships		.76					.65
26	Numerical Reasoning		.68					.55
6	Emotional Empathy Perception			.46				.46
9	Verbal Recall/Voice Modeling			.57				.43
10	Extroversion			.53				.39
11	Creativity			.48				.46
15	Calculative Problem Solving			.42				.25
16	Inquisitive with Intuition			.49				.58
17	Verbal Assertiveness			.48				.52
19	Aggressiveness with Curiosity			.40				.50
8	Distinguishing Differences				.40			.36
18	Self-Identity/Keen Observation				.44			.40
20	Verbal Comprehension				.57			.50
36	Verbal Recall				.57			.65
42	Visual Motor Skills/Concentration				.48			.29
43	Verbal Expressiveness				.42			.50
46	Alertness/Factual Recall				.51			.53
47	Social Judgment				.57			.61
48	Verbal Creativity					.56		.53
49	Creativity/Imagination					.53		.64
4	Alertness of Judgement						.62	.46
5	Risk with Problem Solving						.47	.42

(table continues)

Note. Factor loadings less than .40 are not reported.
*Description of Factors: 1) Verbal Perceptual Problem Solving Ability Function; 2) Perceptual Organization Ability Function; 3) Assertive Verbal Expressive Ability Function; 4) Verbal Memory with Concentration Ability Function; 5) Differential Evaluation Ability Function; 6) Spontaneous Mental/Perceptual Problem Solving Function.

judgment of gifted behavioral functioning traits. In each instrument, OPL-P and OPL-T items 1-51 were intercorrelated ($N = 284$) and factor analysis (with varimax rotation) was utilized to highlight behavioral trait clusters that defined relationships among the items. This procedure resulted in the extraction of six factors whose eigenvalues were above 1.0 (principal factor solution, see Table 1). The principal factors solution accounted for 87.60 percent of the variance. Table 2 presents the factors and their loadings (loadings less than .40 are not reported). Factor 1 has loadings from .44 to .69 on the OPL-P. Factor labels are presented at the bottom of Table 2 (verbal/perceptual problem solving function). Factor 2, labelled perceptual organization function (see Table 2) had loadings ranging from .43 to .76. Factor 3 had loadings of .40 to .57. This factor was labelled assertive verbal expression function. Factor 4 had the highest loadings ranging from .40 to .57. This function was labelled verbal memory with concentration function. Factor 5 had loadings as low as .42 to as high as .57. This factor was labelled differential evaluation ability function. Factor 6 had two items (Item 4 and 5) that yield loadings at a low of .47 to a high of .62. This factor was labelled Spontaneous Mental/Perceptual Problem Solving Function.

Principal component factoring (with varimax rotation) was applied to the fifty one items ($N = 284$) of OPL-T (see Table 4). This procedure resulted in the extraction of six factors whose eigenvalues were above 1.0 (see Table 3). The solution accounted for 88.30 percentage of the variance.

Factors with loadings of less than .40 were ignored. Behavioral traits for the OPL-T that describe the factors and the factor names are also presented in Table 4.

The OPL-P and the OPL-T rating scales factored the same items and behavioral traits for both scales in evaluating children's potential gifted ability. However, the OPL-T eigenvalues for the factors were higher than those for the OPL-P. As well, the OPL-T yielded higher loadings than those of the OPL-P.

In addition to the factor structure and loadings reported in Table 4, there is another validating feature of this analysis. The findings reported here suggest that the OPL-P and the OPL-T items for potentially gifted children ability tended to load onto many corresponding factors, yet the OPL-T had higher communalities than the OPL-P, both having corresponding high uniqueness. This finding supports the idea that even though specific high ability potential may be seen better

Table 3. Eigenvalues and Percentage of Variance

Factor Number	Eigenvalue	Percent of Variance	Cumulative Percentage
1	17.44	58.9	58.9
2	3.34	11.3	70.2
3	1.66	5.6	75.8
4	1.45	4.9	80.7
5	1.13	3.8	84.5
6	1.11	3.7	88.3

Table 4. Varimax Rotation Factor Matrix

OPL-T Item		1	2	3	4	5	6	Comm unality
				Factor				
5	Risk with Problem Solving	.42						.58
13	Verbal Reasoning of Similarities	.48						.63
16	Inquisitive with Intuition	.55						.62
19	Aggressiveness with Curiosity	.58						.63
22	Immediate Verbal Recall	.43						.76
27	Curiosity/Interest in New Ideas	.58						.64
28	Long Term Memory Skills	.63						.67
29	Problem Solving/Competition	.65						.68
30	Independence	.72						.71
32	Positive Self-Concept	.58						.60
33	Assertiveness	.69						.71
34	Breadth of Knowledge/Elaboration	.68						.69
35	Analysis	.67						.61
39	Perception	.50						.60
40	Advanced Vocabulary	.51						.57
43	Verbal Recall	.44						.61
13	Verbal Reasoning of Similarities		.41					.63
21	Color in Visual Perception		.82					.74
22	Immediate Recall		.54					.76
23	Motor Control Ability		.64					.72
24	Organization Sequence Ability		.64					.68
25	Organization of Relationship		.66					.59
26	Numerical Reasoning		.80					.70
31	Creativity/Inventiveness		.43					.51
44	Verbal Memory /Recall		.59					.70
45	Verbal Recall/Factual Memory		.41					.76
47	Social Judgment		.40					.54
3	Alertness/Attentiveness			.53				.50
9	Verbal Recall/Voice Modeling			.63				.61
10	Extroversion			.63				.51
17	Verbal Assertiveness			.66				.63
50	Verbal Assertiveness			.65				.58
20	Verbal Comprehension				.71			.65
36	Verbal Recall				.66			.71
44	Verbal Memory/Recall				.44			.70
45	Verbal Recall/Factual Recall				.68			.76
6	Emotional Empathy Perception					.62		.63
12	Verbal Concentration Activity					.46		.49
46	Alertness/ Factual Recall						.46	.55
48	Verbal Creativity						.41	.51

(table continues)

Optimal Performer Locator for Parents and Teachers 151

Note. Factor loadings less than .40 are not reported.

*Description of Factors: 1) Verbal Perceptual Problem Solving/Verbal Knowledge Function; 2) Perceptual Organizational Skills /Memory Orientation Function; 3) Facility of Expression/Active Responsiveness Function; 4) Verbal Facility/Memory Function; 5) Intuitive Perception/Verbal Concentration Function; 6) Verbal Recall Ability Function)

by teachers, parents of children with gifted ability are similarly able to identify their potentially gifted children.

Standardization of the OPL-P and OPL-T

The average score of the OPL-P rating scale is 193, with a standard deviation of 27. The rating scale was converted into seven standard units to enable the comparison of the P and T scores.

From the results obtained, based on the OPL-P mean of 193 and the standard deviation of 27, it was found that classification as an Average child and a Well Above Average child required scores between 220 and 247 and above, respectively. From the data, 15.1% of the children had a score between 247 and 255. For the OPL-T the results obtained indicate a mean of 169 and a standard deviation of 39. Classification as an Average child and a Well Above Average child, required a score between 169 and 247 and above, respectively. The higher ratings of the children provided by teachers may reflect teachers' greater familiarity with attributes that go into a definition of high ability. The results of the distribution of the OPL-P and the OPL-T are presented in Table 5.

Summary

The development of the Optimal Performer Locator for Parents and Teachers and previous findings were presented in this chapter. Several statistical procedures were employed to determine reliability and validity of the OPL-P and the OPL-T preschool scale for African American culturally diverse gifted children pilot and research study.

Table 5. The Classification Proportions by Percentages for the OPL-P and OPL-T

Descriptive Category	OPL-P		OPL-T	
	N	Percent	N	Percent
Upper Extreme	2	0.7		
Well Above Average	41	14.4	41	14.4
Above Average	95	33.5	99	34.9
Average	85	29.9	85	29.9
Below Average	39	13.7	50	17.6
Well Below Average	15	5.3	9	3.2
Lower Extreme	4	1.4		
Total Number	284			

Further, research is presently being undertaken to pilot and standardize the OPL-P and OPL-T revised preschool scale and the recently developed elementary, middle, and high school scales. Southeastern regional data are being gathered for standardization procedures. Projected future studies include the following:

1. Reliability studies using Cronbach Alpha and/or the split-half method;

2. Validity studies, using factor analytic and correlational procedures.

3. Stratified sampling by region, parent, and education and occupation at half years intervals ages between 2 1/2 and 18 years. An attempt will be made to have at least 200 boys and 200 girls in each age group in the standardization sample who have been identified as gifted or who are participating in a gifted program.

4. Development of standard scores for each scale.

References

Baldwin, A. Y. (1977). Tests do underpredict: A case study. *Phi Delta Kappan, 58*(8), 620-621.

Brown, W. W. (1863). *The Black man: His antecedents, his genius, and his achievements.* New York: Thomas Halton.

Gay, J. E. (1978). A proposed planned for identifying Black gifted children. *The Gifted Child Quarterly, 22(3)*, 353-359.

Gibbon, C. T. (1974). The identification of mentally gifted, disadvantaged students at the eight grade level. *The Journal of Negro Education, 42,* 53-66.

Hamilton, S. E. (1983). *The gifted children locator for parents.* Unpublished Instrument. Howard University, Washington, DC.

Hamilton, S. E. (1985). *A report on the identification of gifted African American children: A pilot study.* Unpublished paper, Howard University, Washington, DC.

Hamilton, S. E. (1987). *The identification of gifted culturally diverse pre-school children.* Unpublished doctoral dissertation, Howard University, Washington, DC.

Hamilton, S. E. (1988). *Optimal performer locator for parents and teachers (Elementary School Scale).* Unpublished instrument, Fort Lauderdale, FL.

Hamilton, S. E. (1988). *Optimal performer locator for parents and teachers (Middle School Scale).* Un-

published instrument, Fort Lauderdale, FL.

Hamilton, S. E. (1988). *Optimal performer locator for parents and teachers (Senior High School Scale).* Unpublished instrument, Fort Lauderdale, FL.

Hamilton, S. E. (1991). *Optimal performer locator for parents and teachers (Preschool Scale).* Unpublished instrument, Florida A & M University, Tallahassee, FL.

Hildreth, G. (1954). Characteristics of young gifted children. *The Journal of Genetic Psychology, 85,* 239-311.

Hilliard, A. G. (1976). *Alternatives to IQ testing: An approach to the identification of gifted "minority" children.* Sacramento: California State Department of Education.

Jenkins, M. D. (1936). A socio-psychological study of Negro children of superior intelligence. *The Journal of Negro Education, 5,* 175-190.

Jenkins, M. D. (1948). The upper limit of ability among American Negroes. *The Scientific Monthly, 66*(5), 399-401.

Jenkins, M. D. (1950). Intellectually superior Negro youth: Problems and needs. *The Journal of Negro Education, 19,* 322-332.

Kaufman, A. S., & Kaufman, N. L. (1983). *Kaufman assessment battery for children (KABC).* Circle Pines, MN: American Guidance Service.

Laycock, F., & Caylor, J. S. (1964). Physiques of gifted children and their less gifted sibling. *Child Development, 35,* 63-74.

Malone, C. E. (1974). *Identification of educationally deprived gifted children.* Unpublished doctoral dissertation, United States International University, San Diego, CA.

Marland, S. (1972). *Education of the gifted and talented.* Report to the Congress of the United States by the U.S. Commissioner of Education. Washington, DC: U.S. Government Printing Office.

Roedell, W. C., Jackson, N. E., & Robinson, H. B. (1980). *Gifted young children.* New York: Teachers College Press.

Sullivan, A. R. (1973). The identification of gifted and academically-talented Black students: A hidden exceptionality. *Journal of Special Education, 7*(4), 353-379.

Thorndike, R. L., Hagen, E. P., & Sattler, J. M. (1986). *Guide for administering and scoring the Stanford-Binet Intelligence Scale* (4th ed.). Chicago: Riverside.

Torrence, E. P. (1973). Non-test indicators of creative talent among disadvantaged children. *Gifted Child Quarterly, 17*(4), 243-249.

Wechsler, D. (1989). *Manual for the Wechsler Preschool and Primary Scale of Intelligence* (rev.

ed.). New York: The Psychological Corporation, Harcourt Brace Jovanovich.

Wechsler, D. (1991). *Manual for the Wechsler Intelligence Scale for Children* (3rd ed.). New York: The Psychological Corporation, Harcourt Brace Jovanovich.

Williams, J. H., & Addison, L. (1981). *Training teachers to work with gifted minority students. In Bal-ancing the scale for the disadvantaged gifted.* Paper presented at the National State Leadership Training Institute, Ventura, CA.

Witty, P. A., & Jenkins, M. D. (1936). The education achievement of a group of gifted Negro children. *Journal of Educational Psychology, 24,* 583-597.

For additional information, contact:

Seward E. Hamilton, Jr., Ph.D.
Gore Education Complex-Building-D
Room #305
Department of Psychology
Florida A & M University
Tallahassee, FL 32307
Telephone: (904) 599-3014 or 3468
Fax: (904) 561-2540

.

The "WHO" and the "O": Contextually Situated Vehicles for the Assessment of Pupil Potential

Asa G. Hilliard and William Cummings

Abstract

Two checklists for assessing characteristics of gifted minority children are described. The "O" test is an inventory of characteristics of an individual child, while the reference population for the "WHO" test is all of the students in a specified classroom. Results of factor analyses of self, peer, and parent ratings are presented, issues discussed, and recommendations for further study of the instruments proferred.

Revision of Pre-Screening Checklist and Procedures for Administration

It can be noted here that the utilization of Paul Torrance's items in the checklist for creativity was a significant step forward for the San Francisco Unified School District. When this device was adopted, it signaled recognition that a *broad range of behaviors* must be considered in any identification program, and that information not normally included on standard assessment procedures must be considered as well. Paul Torrance has done pioneer work in the assessment of intelligence based upon *actual observations of children.* It became clear to him very early that traditional definitions of intelligence were unnaturally limiting. As a result, he found it both more realistic and practical to speak of "creativity" than to think of high level mental functioning as an expanded definition of "intelligence." The checklist which sum-

marizes characteristics that Paul Torrance has identified and has associated with "creative behavior," are presented in Hilliard (1976).

This checklist is fine as far as it goes. However, Paul Torrance has failed to make the next fundamental refinement which observations of human behavior would dictate. That refinement is to deal with the matter of style. Essentially the implicit assumption in the use of the Torrance checklist is similar to the assumption in the use of standardized tests, that being that one "norm" can be used in thinking of all children. There is little or nothing in Paul Torrance's formulations (Torrance 1972a, 1972b, 1973, 1975), to account for cultural and stylistic variations in any systematic way. In a sense, to move from traditional standardized variables to those characteristics which Paul Torrance has identified, represents an embryonic move to come to terms with or to face the matter of style. Torrance does this through an argument over the definition of "intelligence." With him, it is as if the only problem in assessment of intelligence is that the range of behaviors which constitute the "norm" of cognitive functioning is not broad enough to encompass some of the behaviors which students in a standard culture exhibit. Any in-depth study of the cultural roots and expressions of specific groups will illustrate clearly that a person's experience is situated in a cultural milieu which exists with its own integrity, and that this may or may not overlap the cultural milieu of others.

Our revision of the existing pre-screening checklist and the revision of procedures for administration are designed to integrate what we know about the origin and expression of behavioral style and the difficulty an observer will have seeing stylistic differences in behavior. The following important points describe the revised basic checklist:

1. The revised checklist is *not* to be used as a complete assessment for the identification of "gifted" children. It is to be considered only as a rough screening device which seems to identify talented students who are missed by traditional assessment practices.

2. No attempt has been made here to specify the character of the remainder of the assessment process for the identification of gifted children, nor has there been any attempt here to specify procedures or principles related to the articulation of this assessment procedure with later final assessment procedures.

3. The revised checklist contains items which have been designed to be more characteristic of the "synthetic-personal" style. Several of the items are quite similar to those on Torrance's checklist for creativity. However, it should be pointed out that the use of this particular checklist requires a more global conceptualization of "pre-screening" than was the case with the Torrance checklist. To be specific, not only are the specific *items important, it is also important who does the rating using the items.*

4. The checklist has been revised so as to depend upon several assessments of the same child from different points of view. A single teacher may or may not have enough information about a given child to be able to rate what that child actually does.

Furthermore, a single teacher has his or her own behavioral style which will condition how the behavior of a child is perceived. Therefore, multiviews of a single child must be garnered.

5. The checklist as now administered provides an opportunity to minimize potential misperceptions in cross-style assessments by a single observer by including peer assessment, self-assessment, and parental assessment. The more sophisticated extension of this principle would be to include the ratings of other individuals, particularly those who had extensive information about the experiences of the student being rated.

6. The checklist calls for observations on "thematic" behaviors with the specific content cited or used being free to vary. The assessment uses the child's experience in a variety of settings but with a special opportunity to include behavior in natural settings. These behaviors, most likely, are to be observed by parents and peers. The more sophisticated extension of this principle would include the use of relatives, peers in addition to those in the same classroom, and other adults who are familiar with the experience of a given child. For example, on the item "is very funny sometimes," what we expect is the *observer's impression* of the behavior of the observee, without spelling out specific jokes or even joking behavior as an index of funniness. The intent here is to determine if, *in the eyes of the observer,* the student appears to be funny, *not* if the person who develops a standardized test thinks a particular joke in a test would characterize a student as being funny.

7. The checklist can be applied in any setting where the raters are familiar with the ratee. The most sophisticated use of the checklist, therefore, would call for the raters to indicate the level of familiarity they felt with the ratee. Further research would have to be conducted in order to determine the weightings of items or to determine how to take into account the rater's degree of familiarity with the subject in some systematic way.

In general, it is important to keep in mind that the list is not an "instrument" in the sense that some investigators seem to accept traditional standardized tests. It is instead, *an instrument to "structure observations or recollections" which does not utilize preconceived content, but which does utilize preconceived themes.* The list represents our expression of the fact that in the assessment of human behavior, the state of the art is such that *the most dependable observations come from skilled observers with cross-cultural sophistication and demonstrated familiarity with the subject being observed, when these observers use the experiences which the child has and analyzes those meanings in order to make a determination about ability and style.*

How the Checklist Was Developed

The items on the "WHO" and the "O" checklist were developed based upon an in-depth review of the literature on the assessment of intelligence, cognitive and behavioral style, culture, and world-view. In addition to this review, in-depth interviews were conducted with "experts": teachers; psychologists; sociologists; social workers; linguists, and others who have had *ongoing, intensive contact with children in their daily practice,* primarily African American children. Experts were also selected according to their ability to articulate their observations about their clinical practice.

We would have preferred to be more broad-ranging and have more structured in-depth involvement with an even broader range of expert clinicians, utilizing structured observations to corroborate their clinical assessments. However, the limitations of the scope of this investigation precluded such an approach. In interviews, the clinical experts were advised that we were interested in the development of alternative procedures for the identification of gifted minority children. Specific inquiries were focused to elicit from these experts their articulation of how gifted behavior was expressed, utilizing as much anecdotal material as possible. Expert opinion on the conditions under which accurate observations could be made were also sought.

In addition to the above, key project staff were selected based upon their own broad range of experiences in working with children at a variety of levels. The project staff were used to assist the principal investigator to analyze literature and interview material in order to identify characteristics to be investigated.

Finally, a small group of consultants were interviewed and appropriate literature reviewed in order to refine the theoretical framework on behavioral style and assessment procedures. The data which were synthesized from interviews and literature, as well as from our own observations, were then examined to determine their fit with the hypothesized categories of "atomistic-objective" and "synthetic-personal." For example, Dr. Buford Gibson, child psychiatrist, provided vivid anecdotal information about the behavior of African American children who were referred to his clinic for treatment. Dr. Gibson noted that many of the Black children who were referred to him as "learning problems" and later proved to have high ability, often were characterized as having a "mature playfulness": "They would have a joke for me every time they came to the clinic"; "They would build humorous situations out of mutual experiences that we had in the interview"; "They sometimes hide their talents"; "They know they are gifted and will tell you if you ask them"; "It is necessary to have a rapport before information will be revealed"; "The inquirer must be perceived by the student as 'smart' enough to understand in order for the student or gifted child to reveal important information."

Mr. Rudy Smith, Director of the Crisis Clinic at Mount Zion Hospital, emphasized that the interpretation of behavior as gifted must include the evaluation of that behavior as "appropriate" to a given situation. Mr. Smith added an additional dimension which was also highlighted by Dr. Orlando Taylor, a linguist. They both spoke of "code switching" which we later saw as "by-stylistic" behavior, or what Ramierez and Castaneda have called "bi-cognitive development." That is to say, the truly gifted child is able to function under a variety of conditions, including being able to function with people who have more than one style and who can, themselves, function in more than one style. This is an important consideration in the definition of gifted behavior, in that many children now labeled as gifted are really nothing more than highly practiced "monostylistic" people and, consequently, may be presumed to be inappropriately assessed as "gifted."

Once the behavioral indicators of style were identified, the indicators were extracted which seemed to be congruent with the synthetic-personal style, and, therefore, with many of the "missing" gifted students. In view of the fact that behavioral styles have been variously referred to by different investigator, and with no intent deliberately to add to confusion by the introduction of still another set of descriptors, it is necessary for this study to offer labels for two polar styles and to relate the discussions of behavioral styles by other investigators to them.

Basic behavioral styles may be thought of as "atomistic-objective" and "synthetic-personal." These styles represent two fundamentally opposite approaches to the organization of human experience and to the use of one's environment. No serious attempt will be made here to speculate regarding the origins of these two styles. However, the speculations of other investigators will be cited as appropriate.

Atomistic-objective style. Atomistic-objective behavioral style is one in which habitual patterns of approach to experience involve an attempt to break down the experience into components which can be understood. The observer who uses this style tends to feel himself or herself to be separate from the phenomena being observed. Among atomistic-objective style users is a decided preference for permanence, regularity, predictability, uniformity, and environmental control. There is a general distrust of feeling, a low tolerance for uncertainty, and the placement of little or no value on matters of "meaning" or purpose in events. A more complete description of this behavioral style will merge through the presentation of the alternative perspectives which follow.

Synthetic-personal style. The users of this style tend to approach the world in a way so as to bring together divergent experiences and to distill them to discover the essence of a matter without undue concern for the small pieces which go to make up a given experience. These style users tend to perceive themselves as an integral part of the phenomena which are being observed. Values tend to be placed on such things as divergent experimentation, expression, improvisation, and harmonious interaction with the environment. A more detailed description of the synthetic-personal behavioral style will emerge in the discussion which follows.

It can be shown that high level cognitive functioning is a property of both of these behavioral styles and of other styles, including a combination of these two. There is some evidence that styles may be changed or expanded. While ethnicity seems to be associated with stylistic variations, all styles transcend cultural groupings to some degree.

How Was the Checklist Administered?

The checklist was first administered in the usual way, that is, the teacher was asked to identify students who might be gifted and then was asked to fill out the "O." (See Appendix.)

Pilot Process for Checklist Development

Three third grade and three sixth grade classes were selected in the San Francisco Unified School District during the middle of the second semester of 1976. The procedures for the administration of the checklist were as follows:

1. The teachers were asked to identify children in their classes whom they thought might be gifted, and for further evaluation. They were then instructed to fill out the "O" form of the new checklist on those students.

2. Following the completion of that task, teachers were then asked to think of the entire class and to fill out the "WHO" form (see Appendix). Teachers were advised that a student might be named more than one time or that on a given item it would be possible that only one would be named.

3. The "O" forms were passed out to students in the class and each student was asked to check

Table 1. Factor Analysis of Self Ratings

Factor Loading*		Item Number
1	.78	Remembers a lot about T.V.	(31)
	.75	Can always find something to do	(34)
	.72	Really knows what they want to do	(29) *ALERT*
	.63	Is really hard to con	(25)
	.51	Can talk more than one way	(28)
	.45	Can make quick decisions	(17)
	.43	Is good at guessing	(18)
2	.76	Has a quick temper	(4)
	.78	Is very impatient	(11) *ENERGY*
	.52	Is always getting excited about new things	
3	.80	Can talk to grown–ups easily	(13)
	.48	Has lots of different ideas	(7) *CONFIDENCE*
	.47	Can make quick decisions	(17)
4	.74	Is really funny sometimes	(2) *HUMOR*
	.62	Gets along well with all different kinds of people	(16)
5	.72	Can really dance	(12) *EXPRESSIVE*
	.68	Knows the words to lots of songs	(15)
6	.68	Always asks the best questions	(20)
	.53	Always tries new styles of clothes	(9) *EXPERIMENTATION*
	.45	Seems to know what I am thinking	(30)
	.43	Does lots of different kinds of things	(19)
7	.66	Can get children to do things	(23)
	.65	Knows how to put people down real fast	(32)
	.51	Is good at fooling people	(3) *SOCIAL CONTROL*
	.48	Can get grown–ups to do things	(24)
	.46	Can tell some of the biggest lies	(8)
	.44	Is really hip	(26)
8	.74	Can make up good stories	(6)
	.52	Can make stories really interesting	(5) *VERBAL CREATIVITY*
	.47	Can get grown–ups to do things	(24)
9	.76	Is always bragging about different things	(27) *ATTENTION*
	.54	Is good at making up things	(14) *SEEKING*
10	.80	Seems to know how people feel	(21) *SYMPATHY*
	.45	Seems to notice everything	(22)

(table continues)

Factor Loading*			Item Number
11	.56	Is too nosey	(33)
	.52	Likes to use different or new words	(10) *RISK*
	.41	Is good at guessing	(18)

*Includes only loadings of .40 or higher

those items which the student felt were descriptive of himself or herself.

4. Following that, the students were then asked to think of the entire class and to name the individuals in the class who seemed to fit the description on the "WHO" form. Students were advised that any student could be named more than one time, or that there might be items for which the student would have no nominee. Students were not told that their ratings were associated in any way with selection for a gifted program.

5. Parents were surveyed by mail to determine if they would permit their children to be involved in the study and also if they would be willing to fill out the "O" form on their own child. Parents were advised that the information would be used in order to assist school personnel in identifying children for the gifted program. Only one parent, either parent, for a given child, was asked to respond.

In view of the fact that not all parents responded to the questionnaire, it was decided to give primary weight to peer ratings as a basis for identifying students to be assessed further. The ten students with the highest peer ratings were then selected and evaluated by the District's normal processes. Based upon that description, three children were identified as gifted.

The checklist was factor analyzed. Since there were too few teachers to provide a meaningful factor analysis, three sets of responses to the instrument were factored: the child's self ratings, the child's peer ratings, and the parent's ratings. See Tables 1 - 3.

While we have no test retest reliability for the instrument, both the high factor loadings and expert judgment by staff and consultants of the internal consistency and face validity of the factors seem to indicate that the factors identified are substantive. To the extent that reliability does exist or can be accepted, it is interesting to note that one of our major points is supported. That is that the "instrument" is really not the checklist but the observer. For example, when taking an internal view, eleven factors emerge in our sample (self-ratings). However, with the same instrument when taking a view of peers, twelve factors emerge, but significantly, twelve different factors with some overlapping. Finally, when parents used the same instrument, only six factors emerged, and once again, the six factors are different from either the eleven or the twelve. This seems to suggest an hypothesis that the checklist serves a slightly different function depending upon who is looking, and what is being looked at!

Results/Suggested Issues

This study has been largely exploratory. It would be presumptuous indeed to suggest, on the basis of the pilot of this instrument, that "results" in any final sense have been obtained. It would be more appropriate to say that strong evidence suggesting basic questions to be investigated has been discovered. The results, therefore, seem to be that the following hypotheses are highly worthy of further investigation:

1. Factor analyses seem to show that the "instrument" is the person doing the observation.

2. There may be a relationship between the grade level of the student and the average score obtained on the instrument.

3. There may be relationships between ethnic group membership and the scores obtained, overall, on the checklist.

Table 2. Factor Analysis of Peer Ratings

Factor Loading*		Item Number
1 .79	Always asks the best questions	(20)
.76	Can make stories really interesting	(5)
.70	Can make up good stories	(6) *EXPERIMENTATION*
.59	Can talk more than one way	(28)
.51	Gets along well with all different kinds of people	(16)
.47	Can make quick decisions	(17)
.46	Can always find something to do	(34)
2 .77	Is good at fooling people	(3)
.67	Knows how to put people down	(32) *DECEPTION*
.43	Can tell some of the biggest lies	(8)
.42	Is really funny sometimes	(2)
3 .71	Can get children to do things	(23)
.68	Has a quick temper	(4) *SOCIAL CONTROL*
.54	Can talk to grown–ups easily	(13)
4 .80	Is always bragging about different things	(27) *SELF PROJECTION*
.67	Is too nosey	(33)
.56	Can tell some of the biggest lies	(8)
5 .76	Knows the words to lots of songs	(15)
.69	Is hip	(26) *SOCIAL AWARENESS*
.44	Can really dance	(12)
.43	Always tries new styles of clothes	
6 .73	Remembers a lot about T.V. programs	(31) *CREATIVE*
.68	Is good about making up things like games	(14)
7 .62	Likes to use different or new words	(10)
.57	Has lots of different ideas	(7) *EXPLORATION*
.51	Does lots of different kinds of things	(19)
.47	Can talk to grown–ups easily	(13)
8 .78	Is really funny sometimes	(2) *EXTROVERSION*
.57	Can really dance	(12)
9 .67	Is good at guessing	(18) *EMPATHY*
.67	Seems to know what I am thinking	(30)
10 .68	Is very impatient	(11)
.63	Really knows what they want to do	(29) *SELF-DIRECTED*
.50	Is always getting excited about new things	

(table continues)

Factor Loading*			Item Number
11	.78	Seems to know how other people feel	(21) *SYMPATHY*
12	.75	Seems to notice everything	(22) *AWARENESS*

Includes only loadings of .40 or higher

4. There may be significant geographical differences in results when this checklist is used.

5. Teachers did not nominate any child as gifted whose peers rated him or her at ten or lower. No child with ten or lower peer scores got more than one teacher rating in the "WHO." Therefore, teachers' judgments on the low end of the scale seem to coincide with those of a student's peers.

6. There may be a high relationship between the teacher's rating and a child's self-rating.

7. There may be a low relationship between the teacher's rating and the peers' rating.

8. The very highest peer ratings seem to be of students who are "overlooked" by teachers. Teachers may tend to overlook the most gifted synthetic-personal students.

9. There may be a moderate positive relationship between the parent's rating of the child and the child's self-rating.

Conclusion and Recommendations

The following tentative conclusions seem to be warranted from our investigation:

1. The use of the "WHO" and the "O," employing the procedures which have been described, will identify previously overlooked students who, with the regular post-screening procedure, will be identified as "gifted."

2. Among the students so identified will be previously excluded minorities.

3. Some of the students so identified will be previously excluded White students.

4. No single pre-screening rating of a student will be sufficient to insure that large groups of talented students are not overlooked.

5. This total assessment approach is more valid than previously utilized assessment procedures for any cultural group. However, in view of the fact that the "WHO" and the "O" checklist have been designed deliberately to emphasize synthetic-personal stylistic characteristics, and in view of the fact that such characteristics are thought to be associated with particular ethnic, economic or cultural groups, it is necessary that other investigations be carried out with other ethnic groups in order to determine if the stylistic variations which have been identified are sufficient to account for the range of behavior in a given cultural group, or if further explications of stylistic behavior are required.

6. One thing that becomes abundantly clear is that while it may be possible to identify previously excluded or overlooked students who have high "ability," "talent," "aptitude," or "intelligence," such identification would be virtually useless if the instructional program of the school remains tailored so that only a narrow atomistic-objective style is reflected in the school program. Style in behavior is real. No particular style is better or worse than another. The schools have an obligation as a service institution for the public to provide an appropriate education for every child. Therefore, it would seem imperative that existing school curricula be examined from the point of view of the various behavioral styles that exist, that the training of assessment personnel reflects what is known about style, and that extensive training of teachers is required to utilize data which comes from an examination of the interaction of behavioral styles in educational settings.

Table 3. Factor Analysis of Parent Ratings

Factor Loading*		Item Number
1	.75	Likes to use different or new words	(10)
	.73	Can talk to grown–ups easily	(13)
	.72	Seems to notice everything	(22)
	.71	Can get children to do things	(23)
	.70	Is good at guessing	(18)
	.70	Has lots of different ideas	(7)
	.69	Gets along well with all different kinds of people	(16)
	.68	Always asks the best questions	(20)
	.67	Knows the words to lots of songs	(15)
	.65	Can make quick decisions	(17) *SOCIAL*
	.64	Seems to know how other people feel	(21) *DESIRABILITY*
	.62	Does lots of different kinds of things	(19)
	.61	Really knows what they want to do	(29)
	.60	Can always find something to do	(34)
	.59	Can make stories really interesting	(5)
	.59	Is good at making up things	(14)
	.56	Is always getting excited about new things	(1)
	.56	Can make up good stories	(6)
	.55	Is hip	(26)
	.53	Remembers a lot about T.V.	(31)
	.52	Is really hard to con	(25)
	.51	Can talk more than one way	(28)
	.45	Has a quick temper	(4)
	.44	Is really funny sometimes	(2)
	.41	Can get grown-ups to do things	(24)
2	.80	Always tries new styles of clothes	(9)
	.73	Can really dance	(12)
	.44	Is always getting excited about new things	(1) *SOCIAL EXPRESSION*
	.43	Knows the words to lots of songs	(15)
	.43	Remembers a lot about T.V. programs	(31)
	.42	Can always find something to do	(34)
	.40	Is hip	(26)
3	.81	Is too nosey	(33)
	.70	Can tell some of the biggest lies	(8) *INTRUSION*
	.49	Is good at fooling people	(3)
4	.75	Is very impatient	(11)
	.73	Has a quick temper	(4) *ENERGY*
	.61	Is always bragging	(27)
	.40	Can get grown-ups to do things	(24)

(table continues)

Factor Loading*			Item Number	
5	.75	Seems to know what I am thinking	(30)	
	.46	Can get grown–ups to do things	(24)	
	.44	Can talk more than one way	(28)	*EMPATHY*
	.42	Seems to know how other people feel	(21)	
	.40	Can make up good stories	(6)	
6	.85	Knows how to put people down	(32)	
	.50	Is really hard to con	(25)	*ASSERTIVE*
	.45	Can make stories really interesting	(5)	

*Includes only loadings of .40 or higher

Further Study

Much further study is needed! The surface barely has been scratched in this vital area. It seems clear from recent activity in the area of standardized test development and recent criticisms of standardized tests, that the public will demand much greater sophistication, equity, reality, and accountability in all assessment procedures. From what we have learned, that process can be aided by further study of the following:

1. A complete description of the identification process which has been used to select students for the Gifted Program in the San Francisco Unified School District and elsewhere.

2. Further in-depth study of behavioral style as manifested in school settings is required.

3. Further in-depth study of the potential for cross-cultural assessment of student behavior which takes into account the impact of the assessor as a style user as well as the impact of student style in educational activities is required.

4. Further investigation is needed to determine the impact on students' ratings of their awareness of the purposes for the ratings that they make of themselves and other students.

5. An in-depth study of the "second level of assessment," after students have been identified by a checklist such as the "WHO" or the "O," is required. For example, what is known about behavioral style must be reflected in the use of existing standardized tests.

6. The curriculum for students must be examined systematically to determine the extent to which one style may be favored over another. Otherwise, there is no point in identifying the range of stylistic behavior among students.

7. There is a need to investigate the relationship between the behavioral styles of out-of-school minority students and those who remain in school. There is a strong possibility that many dropouts and many students who are suspended or expelled for "behavior problems" may be so situated because of the school's failure to accommodate to basic stylistic differences.

8. There is a need for extensive investigation of the interaction between assessor style and pupil style in the assessment setting.

9. There is a need to investigate the relationship of style and learning for specific content areas. For example, both analytic-objective and synthetic-personal style users can learn mathematics. Both can also learn art, however, both *approach* these subjects in different ways. More precision is required in order to understand how this happens.

10. There is a need for an in-depth investigation of the impact that the assessor's degree of knowledge about or familiarity with a given child has on the accuracy of the assessment of that child's "intelligence."

11. There is a need for a large scale study, with sufficient sample size to determine the impact of ethnic and sex differences on assessor judgments and student behavior.

Summary

Our investigations have shown that far from being a simple and easy process, the assessment of student "ability" is a highly complex process which required highly prepared *observers*. The assessment processes must be built by a multidisciplinary group of assessors who have a demonstrated cross-cultural sophistication. The assessment process must account for stylistic differences among observers. The assessment process must account for stylistic differences among children. The assessment process must utilize a variety of levels of information and must utilize information from many sources external to the classroom, as well as including behavior in the classroom. Finally, the assessment process must utilize information about the child over time.

The conclusion seems clear. Traditional approaches to the assessment of "intelligence" have proceeded as if the dynamic behaviors which we have described do not exist. We feel that the evidence is compelling that these dynamics do exist and that to proceed in ignorance of them is equivalent to ignoring the wind on a rifle range, the weather, and movement of heavenly bodies on a missile range, or temperature, heart beat, and pulse rate in a physical examination. A sophisticated assessment model requires that every conceivable influential variable be accounted for to the extent that it is possible to do so. Our approach is far from complete. We do not know everything about children from these data. But we do know that there is much more of vital importance to know.

Therefore, traditional assessment can proceed only by doing violence to children if the minimal data which comes from unsophisticated IQ tests is presented as complete, and is regarded as "scientific."

Cautions and Interpretation

It is critically important that those who would use the information presented here be aware of the following points:

1. We do not regard style as in any way equivalent to IQ or "intelligence." *We simply regard style as the vehicle through which intelligence is expressed.*
2. We do not posit the notion of style as an excuse to explain why some children do not learn some subjects. In fact, we believe that there is evidence to indicate that any content may be learned by any style user. The question is simply one of *how* a given style user will approach the task and whether the approach that a given style user uses is compatible with that of the teacher or the institution which provides instruction.
3. Finally, it is our opinion that the evidence indicates that style *is*. However, there is no intent here to take sides in any debate over whether style should or should not exist. That would be a separate discussion and would be resolved in terms of the aims of society and education.

The acceptance of the notion of style in behavior would, of necessity, affect assessment practice, educational priorities, teaching strategies, and counseling activity. These areas must take into account the individual and group differences among students. The simple industrial model may be perfect for industry. However, for schools, it is a disaster. "Standardized assessment" as traditionally conceived will do violence to the human spirit.

References

Hilliard, A. (1976). *Alternatives to IQ. testing: An approach to the identification of gifted "minority" children.* San Francisco: Frederic Burk Foundation for Education, San Francisco State University. (ERIC No. ED 147 009).

Hilliard, A. (1987). (Ed.). Testing African American students. *Special issue of the Negro Education Review, 38*(2 and 3), April - July.

Torrance, E. P. (1972a). *Identification of gifted and creative children and youth among Black disadvantaged groups.* Paper presented at the Southeastern Invitational Conference on Measurement in Education, Athens, GA.

Torrance, E. P. (1972b). Training teachers and leaders to recognize and acknowledge creative behavior among disadvantaged children. *The Gifted Child Quarterly, 16,* 1.

Torrance, E. P. (1973). Non-testing indicators of creative talent among disadvantaged children. *The Gifted Child Quarterly, 17*(1), 4-5.

Torrance, E. P. (1975). What kind of person are you? A brief screening device for identifying creatively gifted adolescents and adults. *Gifted Child Quarterly, 14*(2), 71-75.

Appendix

The WHO and O

The testing procedure involves two instruments, for convenience labeled "O" and "Who". These two instruments are inventories of characteristics of gifted children. The "O" test is an inventory of characteristics for an individual child. In taking the test, the teacher, child or parent marks only those statements which fit a specified child. The reference population for the "Who" test is all of the students in a specified classroom. The answer to each item is the name of one (*only* one) child in the classroom. Any child's name may be used on any number of items, but only one child per item. If the teacher or child taking the "Who" test cannot think of anyone for a given question, that item should be left blank.

The atmosphere for the testing should be a comfortable, relaxed one. Words appearing in parentheses at the end of some items may be used by the teachers to explain the meaning to the questions or items. It is essential that the students comprehend the meanings of the items, thus, other clarification of item meanings should be offered by teachers as deemed necessary without fear of confounding results.

"Who"

Name _____

Age ____

Grade ____

Male ____ Female ____

You do not have to mark if you cannot think of anyone for a given question. You can name someone more than once. You can use the words in parentheses to explain the test taker.

1. Who is always getting excited about new things?
2. Who is really funny sometimes?
3. Who is good at fooling people ("shining people on")?
4. Who has a quick temper?
5. Who can make stories really interesting?
6. Who can make up good stories?
7. Who has lots of different ideas?
8. Who can tell some of the biggest fibs (lies)?
9. Who always tries new styles of clothes?
10. Who likes to use different or new words?
11. Who is very impatient?
12. Who can really dance?
13. Who can talk to grown-ups easily (is not afraid to talk to grown-ups)?
14. Who is good at making things up like games, dances, jokes, music, and pictures?
15. Who knows the words to lots of songs?
16. Who gets along well with all different kinds of people?
17. Who can make quick decisions?
18. Who is good at guessing?
19. Who does lots of different kinds of things?
20. Who always asks the best questions (interesting, different)?
21. Who seems to know how other people feel?
22. Who seems to notice everything?
23. Who can get children to do things?
24. Who can get grown-ups to do things?
25. Who is really hard to con (to shine, to fool, to hype)?
26. Who is "hip" (really knows what is going on)?
27. Who is always bragging about different things?
28. Who can talk more than one way (really talk proper, everyday talk, talk to different groups)?
29. Who really knows what they want to do (makes up their own mind)?
30. Who seems to know what I am thinking?
31. Who remembers a lot about T.V. programs?
32. Who knows how to put people down real fast (call down, insult)?
33. Who is too nosey (always in everybody's business)?

34. Who can always find something to do?

"O"

Name _____

Age ____

Grade ____

Male ____ Female ____

Mark each one which fits.

1. Is always getting excited about new things.
2. Is really funny sometimes.
3. Is good at fooling people (shining people on).
4. Has a quick temper.
5. Can make stories really interesting.
6. Can make up good stories.
7. Has lots of different ideas.
8. Can tell some of the biggest fibs (lies).
9. Always tries new styles of clothes.
10. Likes to use different or new words.
11. Is very impatient.
12. Can really dance.
13. Can talk to grown-ups easily (is not afraid to talk to grown-ups).
14. Is good at making things up like games, dances, jokes, music, and pictures.
15. Knows the words to lots of songs.
16. Gets along well with all different kinds of people.
17. Can make quick decisions.
18. Is good at guessing.
19. Does lots of different kinds of things.
20. Always asks the best questions (interesting, different).
21. Seems to know how other people feel.
22. Seems to notice everything.
23. Can get children to do things.
24. Can get grown-ups to do things.
25. Is really hard to con (to shine, to fool, to hype).
26. Is "hip" (really knows what is going on).
27. Is always bragging about different things.
28. Can talk more than one way (can really talk proper, everyday talk, talk to different groups).
29. Really knows what they want to do (makes up their own mind).
30. Seems to know what I am thinking.
31. Remembers a lot about T.V. programs.
32. Knows how to put people down real fast (call down, insult).
33. Is too nosey (always in everybody's business).
34. Can always find something to do.

For additional information, contact:

Asa G. Hilliard
Department of Education Policy Studies
Georgia State University
Atlanta, GA 30303
Telephone: (404) 651-1269

Informal Assessment of Intellectual Ability Using Piagetian Tasks

Lorraine Taylor

Abstract

Informal assessment of intellectual ability in African American students was undertaken using Piagetian tasks. In contrast to traditional assessment devices, Piagetian tasks are less dependent upon mainstream English usage. The tasks offer another dimension to African American students in which their potential for learning can be demonstrated. Two case studies are presented which illustrate important uses of the Piagetian tasks in assessing intellectual potential. Johnny's case illustrates the use of the tasks in a situation where a formal referral for special education is under consideration. The case of B.P. involves a student who has been classified mentally retarded on standardized tests. B.P.'s performance on the Piagetian tasks supports his math teacher's position that the student's ability appears higher than indicated by the traditional test score. The use of Piagetian tasks in the assessment process can raise questions about the results of standardized tests, prevent inappropriate referrals to special education, and provide African American youth another dimension for the demonstration of intellectual ability.

Background

The approach to be described in this chapter is based upon Piaget's view of intellectual development in children and adolescents. The emphasis is upon the selection and administration of Piagetian-derived tasks within the context of informal assessment procedures. The tasks provide the opportunity for students to demonstrate characteristics of their thinking. The developmental view of intelligence described by Piaget and Inhelder (1958) includes characteristics of thinking at different ages and stages of development. Thus, careful observation of a child's performance and questioning by the examiner to determine how the child arrives at an answer can indicate ability to think at the appropriate developmental level.

According to Piaget and Inhelder (1958), adolescents are at the stage of formal operations, a stage attained in the 12 to 15 age period. This stage is characterized by the ability to solve complex verbal and other types of problems and to think scientifically (Wadsworth, 1978). Combinatorial thinking, hypothetical thinking, and logical thinking are descriptions of thinking that differentiate children from adolescents. Children of different cultures vary in the ages at which they reach the stage of formal operations. Piaget attributes this variation to the influence of experience and social interactions. However, the important role of maturation in Piaget's theory makes his approach distinctly different from the traditional, additive view of intelligence on which most traditional tests are based (Inhelder, 1968). A Piagetian-based approach to assessment is more optimistic and less biased.

Because Piagetian measures are less influenced by formal school learning and mainstream cultural experiences, De Avila and Havassy (1974) compared Mexican-American and White middle class children on Piagetian and non-Piagetian measures. They found significant differences between the groups in achievement and intelligence on traditional measures, but not on Piagetian measures. De Avila and Havassy indicated that language, cultural, and school learning experiences influenced traditional scores but these factors did not influence Piagetian scores.

The original inspiration for the author's use of Piagetian tasks as an informal measure of intellectual assessment of adolescents came from the work of Furth (1966, 1974), Furth and Youniss, (1969), and Elkind (1966, 1974), Elkind, Barocas, and Rosenthal (1968) and Elkind and Johnson (1969). In his work with children with hearing impairments, Furth found that linguistic competence was not a prerequisite for intellectual development. He was able to verify propositional thinking in adolescents with hearing impairments who had severe language handicaps (Furth, 1971). Furth used such tasks as combinations, probability, and displaced volume. Elkind compared combinatorial thinking in students from graded and ungraded classes. His use of the combinations task will be described later as one measure of the author's informal assessment approach. Other studies by Elkind (1966, 1969) verified differences in the thinking of adolescents as compared with that of children.

Piagetian tasks were explored with Black adolescents because of the author's responsibility to plan curriculum and instruction in an alternative high school program for dropouts and students at risk for dropping out. Students enrolled in the program had low scores on traditional achievement and intelligence tests, restricted verbal language, and hostility toward school and teachers. Many of the students had been enrolled in special education classes in public, inner city schools. However, informal observations revealed that a significant number of them had far more potential than was evident in their formal test scores which ranged from second to sixth grade in reading and math. Their mastery of chess, management of family affairs, informal responses in discussion, and problem-solving at school functions indicated such potential. As a curriculum planner, this author needed to identify measures which could accurately distinguish individual differences in ability in order to provide realistic guidance and counseling for curriculum choices and post-secondary educational planning.

Samples of Piagetian tasks were collected from various sources. They were selected on the basis of the type of thinking elicited, ease and simplicity of administration, wide use in the literature, and interest in the tasks–as demonstrated by Black adolescents' performance in preliminary trials. The tasks represent only samples of the many possible choices available (See Wadsworth, 1978, for additional tasks to be used).

The combinations task, for example (Elkind, et al., 1968), assesses the student's ability to explore all possible combinations when presented with red, blue, black and white poker chips. Variations of this task include combining four playing cards, and short girl, tall girl, short boy, and tall boy. The response is evaluated in terms of the number of combinations found and the process by which the student arrives at his answer. The student who demonstrates the use of formal operational thinking will systematically explore all possible combinations. This involves holding one or more elements constant while combining it with others. There are sixteen possible combinations (see Appendix).

The second type of task assesses the student's understanding of probability. A recent description of this task can be found in Wadsworth (1978). This author has used coins instead of small blocks. Ninety-six coins of four types–pennies, nickels, dimes and quarters–are divided into two groups. One group is used as a reference set and is placed on the table in view of the student. The second set is placed in a bag (or box). Two coins at a time are withdrawn after the bag has been shaken. The student is asked to predict what the coins will be each time. The use of the reference set, which increases the accuracy of the predictions, is indicative of the understanding of probability (see Appendix).

The third type of task includes a set of formal reasoning items. In order to avoid penalizing students with reading difficulties, the items are read to the subject. This task assesses the adolescent's ability to reason and to do hypothetical thinking. The items are based on several models. One of these is described by Wadsworth (1978) and another is based upon the work of Morf (1973).

The adolescent's response on formal reasoning tasks as well as the other Piagetian measures, must be interpreted cautiously. Success is interpreted as age-appropriate thinking. Failure is more difficult to explain since it may be due to normal stage mixtures, inadequate assessment, and age variations in the acquisition of certain concepts (Wadsworth, 1977). The influence of interest also is important. However, Bart (1971), for example, examined the effect of interest on horizontal decalage. He explains that this is similar to "the notion of generalizability of formal operational skills." Interest was doubtful as a key factor in his study. Racial/cultural background may also influence development of the stages, but there is little research on such influence. Piaget has stated that cultural/environmental influences are important determinants of the age at which a given stage is reached.

A variety of criticism of Piaget's theories is found in the research literature. They include discussions of the adequacy of his logical model (Isaacs, 1951), inadequacies in his discussion of adolescents' thinking (Parsons, 1960), and in-

sufficient explanation for the shift from concrete to formal operational equilibrium (Ausubel, 1956).

Two important problems in the interpretation of performance on Piagetian tasks are discussed in Siegel and Brainerd (1978). In their preface to *Alternatives to Piaget: Critical Essays on the Theory,* the editors introduce the performance-competence problem and the role of learning as two areas of criticism of Piaget's work. They characterize the performance-competence problem with the question, "When a child fails a certain Piagetian test that is supposed to tap some given underlying concept, what does this mean?" (p. xii). The competence explanation favored by Piaget is that the child does not possess the concept. The performance explanation is that failure was a result of task difficulty or that Piagetian tests invariably measure attributes other than the intended ones. Failure, therefore, should not be interpreted to mean the respondent does not possess the underlying concept.

The role of cognitive development in learning involves readiness. Piaget's position is that children must be developmentally ready to learn what we want to teach. Therefore, we should not attempt to teach content or concepts for which the cognitive structures are not present. When the Piagetian task is failed, do we refuse to teach adolescents content which requires the use of formal operations? The reverse question should also be considered. When there is evidence that the student is ready, based on successful completion of Piagetian tasks, can we refuse to teach the appropriate level of content? Can we refuse to teach content which requires the use of formal operations? Siegel and Brainerd describe Piaget's ideas about learning as "a classic readiness model in which learning is subordinated to development. Some incipient competence (concept, operation, structure, etc.) is supposed to develop before learning occurs" (p. xiii).

Wadsworth (1978), who discusses the readiness problem, points out there is a difference between memorizing and learning. Children can memorize correct responses even when they do not have the underlying structures or necessary readiness, but they cannot truly learn. Ennis

(1978) also challenges Piaget's propositional logic. He provides an excellent discussion which includes valuable clarification of the nature of such tasks. Questions are raised about the validity of characteristics which separate the thinking of children from that of adolescents. Ennis' evidence supports the use of abstract thinking and logic by children while Piaget reserves this ability for adolescents.

Despite criticism of the theory and its application, the author found Piagetian tasks can reveal distinct differences in the nature and quality of thinking among Black adolescents. The characteristics of their thinking can closely resemble characteristics identified and described by Piaget at the stage of formal operations–and the dimensions of mental ability tapped by these tasks are not available on traditional intelligence tests.

In using Piagetian tasks for practical purposes, a decision must be made about the number of tasks which must be successfully completed to demonstrate formal operational thinking. Some students will complete one; others will complete all. The criterion for passing is open to discussion. Furth and Youniss (1969) accept a single task. This author accepts two of the three informal assessment tasks. Because combinatorial thinking has been identified as an early stage of formal operations (Martorano, 1973), it appears that this task must be passed. However, some students in graduate courses of this author have had difficulty in their approach and have not "passed" combinatorial thinking items.

The total number of tasks to be included in an informal assessment is another practical consideration. The number included in this approach has been developed on an empirical basis. Trials with difficult students have indicated that the time, attention, and thinking involved in this group of three tasks have been close to the limit of their tolerance.

The informal approach described in this chapter represents initial work involving the author's efforts to use Piagetian tasks to assess evidence of age-appropriate intellectual capability in Black adolescents. There is much work to be done, but the author believes application of the results from informal assessment using Piagetian tasks in educational planning and curriculum decisions can be made at the present time.

The problem of readiness discussed earlier represents a dilemma for curriculum areas important to adolescents. Curriculum content in this area is difficult to justify until certain "stage-related" evidence is available. The problem of failure also is difficult to resolve. If Inhelder's (1968) conclusion that students with mental retardation do not reach the stage of formal operations is accepted, success on Piagetian measures offers important contributions to the entire special education decision-making process. Can we justify a label of mental retardation for an adolescent who succeeds on these tasks as well as on more formal Piagetian measures? If Piagetian measures are failed, can we accept mental retardation with confidence?

The focus on how the student arrives at his answer represents a major value of the Piagetian approach. The teacher can learn important information about how the student thinks and how the student can be taught. Incorrect responses are better understood when the explanation is provided by the student in his process of finding the answer. When the response is correct, the teacher learns about the strategies used in the process; when it is incorrect, the teacher learns what can go wrong, detract, or distract the student from the correct outcome in the thinking process. Some students will explain their choice of a name as correct because "You said it last." Others, in response to some of the formal reasoning items, have responded to questions about "Who is tallest?," "None of them because I don't know any boys named Sam or Mike." This focus on the answer and its explanation is most needed by teachers to understand better the nature of thinking and learning and to differentiate ultimately among students and their needs. Correctives may then be more appropriately and effectively selected.

Interestingly, the responses quoted above are from students classified as mildly mentally retarded. Other students in their classes correctly responded to all of the tasks administered. Piagetian measures, which can supplement scholastically-based measures comprising most test batteries, offer Black students the unique opportunity to express intellectual capability in different and important dimensions. The developmental view of intelligence appears particularly useful in evaluating Black school-aged children and youth.

Two case studies are presented. Both are male adolescents who attend a public middle school. One student was classified mildly mentally retarded and placed in a departmentalized special education program with mainstreamed art, music, and physical education. The second student was enrolled in a regular sixth grade program but was being considered for referral because he was very slow and completed little schoolwork each day. The special education student was described by his teachers as "having behavior problems." The regular class student was described as polite, courteous, and likeable.

Case 1

Name:	Johnny
Age:	13
Grade:	6–regular classes, departmentalized program
School:	Public, middle school

Reason for referral. This student has not been referred for formal evaluation. Rather, his mother was referred to me, by the reading teacher, for outside evaluation and tutoring. The student is failing all of his sixth grade classes except physical education. His teachers complain that he is "slow," has poor work habits, daydreams, and completes little work each day. The reading teacher commented that he has not been referred for formal evaluation or retained thus far because his behavior is exemplary.

Educational evaluation. Because his formal school records were not available, the author administered the following tests in addition to the Piagetian tasks: Wide Range Achievement Test [(WRAT) Jastak, 1965; Connolly, A.J. Nachtmen, & Protheet, 1972)]; Key Math Test; and the Slosson Intelligence Test. Informal classroom

work samples were also collected. The results were as follows:

Slosson		83
WRAT	Reading: Grade	3.5
	Spelling: Grade	1.7
Key Math Grade Level:		5.3

Johnny was cooperative and pleasant during testing. However, distraction was a problem; several times he yawned and complained that the tests were difficult. He was encouraged to continue and was praised. While most students require about 30-40 minutes to complete the Key Math test, Johnny completed it in 90 minutes (the examiner allowed him as much time as he required to complete the test). Because he counts on his fingers for all of his computation problems, this section required most of the total testing time. However, given the time he required, few computation errors occurred. In regular classes of 45 minutes, it is easy to understand that a student who works so slowly will have great difficulty. Johnny's failing math grade in the regular sixth grade math class is due to his poor completion of assignments.

Johnny's low reading and spelling scores reflect poor word attack skills. Even when his responses are correct, he expresses uncertainty. He explains his difficulties in reading, spelling, and pronunciation as resulting from the fact that he is "half from the South and half from the North." (Since he spends vacations with relatives of his mother in the South, perhaps this is what he is describing). Many of the grammatical forms he uses appear to be modeled by his mother.

Health. Johnny's health is described by his mother as excellent. He has had no serious illnesses. However, he did recently have a growth removed from his neck and an obvious scar remains from the surgery. His mother reported that Johnny has normal vision and hearing although he has a hearing impaired sister. The sister, who is nonverbal, attends a special school. The mother did not reveal in the interview that her daughter also has mental retardation.

Family history. Johnny resides with his mother and ten year old sister. His sister is transported each day by special bus to a special school. Johnny's father died when he was seven years old. His mother is employed full-time at a post office. She has made provisions for the management of her daughter in the after-school period during the hours when she is at work.

Interviews in the home revealed the mother has provided encyclopedias, games, dictionaries, and outside tutoring to help Johnny. She describes her son as "slow" and disinterested in school. With respect to school during the past six years, she described him as "having problems." She also noted that teachers are too quick to decide that Johnny should be in special education when they learn about his sister.

Student interview. Johnny's perceptions of his school problems were explored in an interview. He described school as being difficult. He views his problems as due to not completing his work and, sometimes, to not understanding his teachers. He reported that his average in his classes is 50 and that 50 is the lowest grade most teachers will give. He also described the grouping of students in his school in the following manner: "There are the smart kids at the top. Then there are the kids who are half smart and half dumb. They are called the 'academics.' Then there are the kids who are dumber than they are smart, or just dumb. They are called the 'generals.' That's the group that I am in. Then there are the special education kids at the bottom and they are 'all dumb,' the dumbest." He explains much of his school problems as caused by his "slowness." His favorite subject is Math Lab where he receives extra help. The subject he dislikes most is English. He worries a great deal about discipline problems at his school and also about being retained next year in sixth grade.

Recent Report Card Grades and Comments.

Social Studies	65
Math	50
Science/Health	65
Reading	65

(Teacher comment: word attack skills are below grade level)

Math Lab	75

(Teacher comment: wastes time and performs inconsistently)

Band	78

(Teacher comment: insufficient practice time)

Exploratory	6 P
Physical Education	100

(Teacher comment: outstanding; a pleasure to have in class)

The sixth grade students attend classes in ability groups. Johnny is in the lowest group . In oral reading of a grade 6 paragraph from the Durrell Analysis of Reading Difficulty (1955), Johnny did not recognize the following words: "yield, subtonic, drying, gradually, sort, determined, pure, ever, weighed." Recognition is based on the correct pronunciation of the word. He appears to comprehend through the skillful use of context clues. In several comic books which he read to the author, the vocabulary appeared quite difficult. However, Johnny's use of picture and context clues facilitated his reading of several of the stories.

Personal social observation. Johnny is described by his teachers as courteous, pleasant, and likeable. The author also found him to be cooperative, humorous, and eager to please. Since his mother is employed full-time, Johnny shares many of the management chores of their home. He must carefully record telephone messages, and he must phone his mother at work if an emergency arises concerning any member of the family, particularly his sister who is cared for by a babysitter after school. Johnny must also start dinner according to his mother's directions. Saturday is devoted to routine household tasks. He must remember when his mother will work late, when he is to report to the babysitter, when he must care for his sister (if the babysitter is unavailable), and many other family matters. Preparations for a recent trip to the south required that he plan for his necessary clothing, school books, hobby materials, and the special activities he would engage in during his visit there. He is frequently in charge at home. He describes the "worst day in my life" as the day that his sister was born. He must frequently manage her when his mother is at work, and he must share his mother's time and attention with his sister. On a recent visit to his home, the author waited while Johnny made several calls to his mother, wrote messages received for his mother, prepared a cup of tea for the author, checked the date on a kitchen calendar, and reviewed the week's events at school.

Classroom observation. Johnny was recently observed in his reading class. The teacher asked the class to write an imaginary story about "The worst day in my life." Johnny wrote 42 words in 32 minutes. He lost time when he retrieved a pencil from the floor, stared at the ceiling, listened to other students as they read their stories aloud before he had finished, and asked the teacher for the date. His handwriting appeared labored and difficult.

Summary. Johnny is a 13-year old Black male adolescent who is in regular sixth grade in a public middle school. He has been placed in the lowest group on the basis of achievement and "ability." His basic skills are approximately at the third grade level, and his school grades are usually from 50 to 65. He appears to be easily distracted and slow in his classroom responses compared with his peers. He has problems completing tasks, handwriting assignments, and activities which involve short-term memory. He often forgets dates, books, papers, recent events and important messages. Some of his teachers believe he is more capable than his performance and grades indicate; others disagree. His teachers and parent are at a loss to explain the nature and cause of his problems and the means to correct them. His IQ score obtained on the Slosson is 83. Formal school data are not yet available. There is increasing pressure by some of his teachers for a formal referral to evaluate Johnny for a handicap-

ping condition. His mother continues to refuse consent.

Piagetian Tasks

Combinatorial thinking. As a variation of the combinations task, Johnny was asked to find all the possible combinations of:

tall girl   short girl   tall boy   short boy

Four circles at the top of the page were labeled in this way:

tall girl   short girl   tall boy   short boy

The author wrote Johnny's responses as he dictated them. His responses were as follows:

short boys, short girls
tall boys, tall girls
short boys, tall boys
tall girls, short girls
tall boys, tall girls
short boys, short girls
tall boys, short girls
tall girls, short boys

Results. Johnny neither systematically explored all possible combinations nor identified all 16 possible combinations. He used contiguity mainly as the basis for completing this task. That means the choices were made on the basis of position—what was close to, next to, or near. Thus, "short boys" is next to/contiguous with "short girls." "Tall girls" and "tall boys" are contiguous. Some students use this approach when combining poker chips. They will place them and then name the combination on the basis of what is closest to what other color. This is *not* considered systematic exploration of all possible combinations in which one or more elements are held constant and systematically paired with others.

Probability. In order to assess Johnny's understanding of probability, he was asked to tell what he thought the coins were going to be each time the examiner first shook the bag and then withdrew two coins.

For the first five predictions, he made wild guesses. He appeared to be distracted, looking at the ceiling and a light fixture. He observed neither the reference group nor the group of coins as they were withdrawn and placed on the table. Upon making an error, guessing the wrong coins, he expressed disappointment in "Oh, wrong again," etc... After the examiner observed him staring at the opposite wall, she asked Johnny, "Are you looking at the table?" He responded, "Yes," although it was obvious that he was "not" looking. He made two more wild guesses, and suddenly, as if realizing what the task involved and what he should do, he looked carefully at the coins which had been withdrawn from the bag and counted each type–pennies, nickels, dimes and quarters. Then he examined the reference group and counted all of the coins in the reference group. He then examined the reference group after each drawing. Sometimes he counted the coins of each type in the withdrawn group before making his prediction. His predictions improved dramatically. He continued to predict based upon observations and counting. He accurately predicted the final four coins as pennies since his count probably indicated that there were more pennies in the bag. The examiner sat quietly through the observations and counting. When asked, "How did you get the answer?" He did not respond verbally. However, the answer was obvious. Johnny performed well on this task once he began to attend to the reference group and count the coins. He demonstrated an understanding of probability.

The same question posed to other children, "Are you looking at the table, or the coins?" will not result in this type of performance if they have no understanding of probability. The author uses this question routinely for that assurance.

Reasoning items. The following series of items comprises the third type of task administered in this informal assessment. The purpose is to assess the student's ability to reason, to do hypothetical thinking. A piece of scratch paper is provided. Each item was read to Johnny and,

when necessary, he was asked to explain (or draw) how he arrived at his answer.

Johnny appeared to enjoy these tasks. His response came quickly and easily. When given the first item, "Jane is taller than Susie. Jane is shorter than Mary. Who is tallest? Who is shortest?" Johnny quickly sketched three stick figures and responded correctly. For each of the other items, his response was based on the sketch. There were six items based on this model. The seventh item involves hypothetical thinking: "Suppose I ask you to agree that if an animal has long ears, it can be either a donkey or a mule; and if an animal has a big tail, it can be either a mule or horse. If I want an animal with long ears and a big tail, what can it be?" Johnny quickly answered, "A mule."

The author also administered the *Cartoon Conservation Scales* (De Avila, 1980) in order to compare the results with that of the informal assessment. (See Appendix for results and interpretation.)

Interpretation and recommendations. Johnny demonstrated evidence of formal operational thinking on the probability task and the formal reasoning items. His thinking appears to be age-appropriate. He is distractible and must be constantly reminded to stay "on task," and he wastes a great deal of time getting started. Johnny describes his poor achievement as "due to not completing much work." His problems appear to be due less to lack of ability than to lack of organization and concentration. This author has recently begun to tutor him and to work with his regular teachers in order to identify informal assessment techniques and strategies which can be used by the regular teachers. Thus far, teachers have been pleased by his performance on the Cartoon Conservation Scale (De Avila, 1980), and Piagetian tasks and now are concerned about motivating him to do more. Since he enjoys comic books, his reading teacher will try to identify materials in that format for reading. A simple behavior modification technique has been implemented to try to increase the percentage of tasks he completes each school day. The author suggested that a timer be placed on Johnny's desk as a reminder of the time available to complete his tasks. Each week a report is required on the number of tasks completed in each class. If the figure represents an increase of at least 20% over the previous week, he earns a free Saturday. (It has been arranged with his mother to free him from his Saturday chores.). A recommendation for the use of a program such as the Glass Analysis for Decoding Skills has been made to his reading teacher. However, it is difficult for the regular reading teacher to obtain special materials or to find time to use them with individual students. Perhaps a "skills center" can be organized in her room for independent work in this area. Curriculum activities which may challenge and stimulate him in math and science can be planned and developed as learning activity packets to individualize his instruction. Learning centers in the regular classrooms can facilitate this individualization. Johnny's teacher hopes he can remain in the mainstream classes without retention and improve his performance and they are shifting their interest from the cause of his "problem" to stimulation and motivation. Additional behavior modification techniques will also be tried to increase the percentage of tasks completed and the rate of responses. Johnny will continue to receive after-school tutoring. Thus far, we have avoided referral for formal evaluation, the first step in removal from the mainstream and placement in special education classes.

Case 2

Name: B.P.
Age: 14.5
Sex: Male
School Status: Grade 7, special class.

B.P. is classified educable mentally retarded and has been in a departmentalized program within the special education classes. Four special education teachers share the schedule, which consists of math, science, social studies and English. The students are mainstreamed for art, music and physical education.

Reason for referral. The parents consented to a special assessment for a school project conducted by this author. According to his current teacher, the original referral was based on severe behavior problems.

Available Test Scores.

Reading: Grade level 4.0, Stanford Achievement Test
Key Math Test: 3.7 grade level
Full Scale WISC-R IQ: 76

Reasoning items. The verbal reasoning items were read to B.P. and he was asked to answer each question and tell how he decided on his answer. On the first item, "If Jane is taller than Susie and Jane is shorter than Mary, who is tallest? Who is shortest?" B.P. first responded, "Susie is tallest." He had a question mark in his voice and asked that the item be repeated. He was told that he could draw the problem to show how he figured it out and also to help remember what was said. He sketched the three stick figures and quickly corrected his responses. "Mary is tallest. Susie is shortest." B.P. then sketched each of the reasoning items and quickly responded without questions in his voice. He was alert and his responses were accurate.

Several authors have pointed out that children at the stage of concrete operations cannot correctly respond to these items. They also noted that it is more difficult to answer, "Who is shortest?" than "Who is tallest?" I have found that students who are able to answer one form of this question do not usually have difficulty with the reverse. Nevertheless, in an effort to be certain that the use of formal operational thinking is being tapped, both forms are administered. Obviously, B.P. is able to figure out these problems. Although his verbal responses consisted of "Na," "Yeh," "Uh-uh," "Huh?," his drawings and quick responses communicated his understanding. He would either repeat his answer or shrug his shoulders and smile when asked, "How do you know? Prove it." Disadvantaged Black students have often been unable to verbalize how they get their answers on Piagetian tasks (La Rue, 1974).

When the student is allowed to draw or sketch his/her understanding of the problem, it offers several advantages. First, the task's memory requirements are reduced; the student does not have to remember the details once they are drawn. Second, the verbal aspects of the task are reduced for the student of limited expressive language, particularly standard vocabulary. The sketching aspect of the tasks has only created a problem when the student has been so interested in the artwork that too much time was invested in the details of the "picture."

Probability. To assess B.P.'s understanding of probability, 96 coins were divided into two equal groups and the same procedure was followed as in the case of Johnny. B.P. was asked to predict what he thought the two coins were going to be each time the examiner withdrew them. Before the first two coins were withdrawn, B.P. counted all the coins on the table. As the coins were withdrawn each time, he would check the reference group and those already taken from the bag. Occasionally the examiner would say, "I'll bet that it's going to be a penny and a nickel" or some other combination. This was done to maintain interest and also to maintain friendly rapport. Since it is possible to predict coins which are most unlikely, if not impossible, it also serves to verify the student's understanding. For example, after the quarters are withdrawn (there are only 2), the examiner said, "I'll bet that it's going to be a quarter and a dime," B.P. replied, "It can't be because there's no more quarters in there. It's going to be two pennies because there are more pennies." B.P. predicted very well as he carefully observed and counted from the beginning of the procedure. He matched the group of drawn coins constantly with the reference group. At one point he said, "All the dimes are out, all the pennies are out, it must be nickels." Thus he accurately predicted the last two coins before the examiner shook the bag to withdraw them. He was alert, involved, and accurate throughout this task. His responses came quickly and with confidence.

Combinations. In order to assess ability to do combinatorial thinking, the student is asked to find or make all possible combinations of four items. The student is given four poker chips–red, blue, black and white–and may manually place them in patterns or arrangements or combinations or simply keep them in view. Older students usually write their combinations on a piece of paper; younger students dictate them and the list is kept in view so they can refer to it. Combinations cannot be repeated. There are 16 possible combinations if "none" is included as a choice. The systematic, orderly exploration of all possible combinations as well as the number made are two aspects of the performance which are evaluated.

B.P. was asked to do two examples of this task. First, he was asked to make all the different combinations possible of the four poker chips. Secondly, he was asked to combine four playing cards. B.P. dictated the following combinations for the cards:

diamond, club
heart, spade
spade, club
heart, diamond
heart, club
diamond, spade
spade, heart,
club, spade,
club, heart

Although B.P. found eight of the 16 possible combinations, he did not use a systematic, orderly exploration of all possible task combinations. The combinations do show some organization, however, in that the same card appears to be held constant through some of the combinations above, for example, the diamond with the club and then with the heart. The heart is paired with the spade and then with the club. When this task is performed easily and competently, systematic exploration is obvious. Students who possess good verbal ability can provide an explanation such as, "I took the heart and used it with each of the others, one by one."

Interpretation and recommendations. Teachers found B.P.'s performance on the Piagetian-derived tasks supported their perceptions that he was brighter than his test scores revealed. His special education math teacher believed he was more capable than the mentally retarded label implied. The main question raised by the special education teachers was, "How could the results of Piagetian tasks be applied in their classrooms?" The math and science teachers expressed the opinion that it was probably going to be easier to derive curriculum applications in those areas than in other content areas. It was decided that we would explore the "Finding Out" curricula developed by De Avila, et al. (1981) in the areas of math and science and select instructional objectives at the level of formal operations which appeared appropriate for B.P. Although B.P.,'s Key Math Score of 3.7 is considerably below grade level, his teachers believed it was possible to attempt to enrich his math program with "thinking or word problems" which involved the use of reasoning or hypothetical thinking. The teachers were also interested in the possible use of Feuerstein's (1981) Instrumental Enrichment Program for students like B.P. who appear to be more capable than his standardized scores indicate. These teacher discussions took place at the end of the previous school year. Several additional resources were recommended to the teachers for their use in selecting learning tasks which were designed for students at the formal operational stage.

Several months into the next school year, the author visited the school to check on B.P.'s progress and his possibilities for being mainstreamed. B.P.'s behavior was described as deteriorating. He had been removed from the departmentalized special education arrangement with mainstreamed art, music, and physical education classes. He is now in a self-contained, special class for educable mentally retarded students. The specific incident which precipitated this decision appears to be that B.P. threw a chair in the classroom. In discussions concerning B.P.'s academic needs and intellectual potential, teachers remarked that "His behavior is unmanageable in a mainstreamed situation" and that recommendations concerning his academic needs must wait until his behavior improves.

B.P. appears to be a student who could have remained in the mainstream classes if a behavior management plan had been available to his regular teachers. B.P.'s previous special education teachers also agree that he appears to have more ability than his test scores reveal. His problem does not appear unique. The likelihood of removal from the mainstream classes is much greater if disruptive behavior is involved. Although B.P.'s achievement scores are below grade level, they are not too different from those of students who remain in the mainstream classes at his school.

While neither B.P. nor Johnny was successful on the combinations task, they were both successful on the reasoning task and the probability task. B.P., in particular, whose verbal language was restricted to "yeah" and "Na" and shrugs and other nonverbal gestures, was very alert and enthusiastic in his performance on the Piagetian tasks (other disadvantaged Black students have also performed well on the combinations task). The author has found these tasks to be simple, easy and dependable in the differentiation of the characteristics of thinking in the adolescents with whom they have been used.

Further research and development are needed. Evaluation of this informal assessment approach on a broader scale is important. Since individual administration is required, time is an important factor in the use of Piagetian assessment. Questions concerning the number of tasks to be included and the criteria for passing are also important and practical issues. Nevertheless, the important contribution that this type of assessment can make in the evaluation of intellectual capability in Black and other minority students deserves special attention and effort.

Follow-up. Although several of his teachers insisted on referral for a possible handicapping condition, Johnny continues to function in the mainstream. His current average in math is 80 and in English 85. Improvement in reading and spelling have occurred as well as in math. He continues to have difficulty in social studies and science. These averages are currently 60 and 50 respectively. Again, there are mainstream teachers who insist that he is a candidate for special education. Johnny describes his problems in science and social studies as due to boredom. The informal Piagetian tasks as well as the Cartoon Conservation Scales have been critically important in establishing a more accurate estimate of Johnny's potential to learn and to function in regular classes. A recent conference which included this examiner, the school psychologist, Johnny's mother, the school principal and guidance counselor confirmed that recent test results by the school psychologist also did *not* support Johnny's referral for a formal evaluation. Johnny participated in this conference at the end of our meeting and agreed that his problems might be solved with an "in-school" homework room, a "Big Brother," and increased motivation to succeed in school.

References

Bart, W. (1971). The effect of interest on horizontal decalage at the stage of formal operations. *Journal of Psychology, 78,* 141-150.

Connolly, A. J., Nachtman, W., & Pritchett, E. M. (1972). *Key Math Diagnostic Arithmetic Test.* Circle Pines, MN: American Guidance Service.

De Avila, E. (1980). *Cartoon Conservation Scales.* Corte Madera, CA: Linguametrics Press.

De Avila, E. (1981). *Finding out.* Corte Madera, CA: Linguametrics Press.

De Avila, E., & Havassy, B. E. (1974). *Intelligence of Mexican-American children: A field study comparing neo-Piagetian and traditional capacity and achievement measures.* (Multi-lingual assessment project.) Stockton, CA: Stockton Unified School District.

Durrell, D. D. (1955). *Durrell analysis of reading difficulty.* New York: Harcourt, Brace, Jovanovich.

Elkind, D. (1966). Conceptual orientation shifts in children and adolescents. *Child Development, 37,* 493-498.

Elkind, D. (1974). *Children and adolescence.* New York: Oxford University Press.

Elkind, D., Barocas, R., & Rosenthal, B. (1968). Combinatorial thinking in adolescents from graded and ungraded classrooms. *Perceptual-Motor Skills, 27,* 1015-1018.

Elkind, D., & Johnson, P. (1969). Concept production in children and adolescents. *Human Development, 12,* 10-21.

Ennis, R. H. (1978). Conceptualization of children's logical competence: Piaget's propositional logic and an alternative proposal. In L. Siegel & C. Brainerd (Eds.), *Alternatives to Piaget: Critical essays on the theory* (pp. 201-257). New York: Academic Press.

Feuerstein, R. (1981). *Instrumental enrichment.* Baltimore: University Park Press.

Feuerstein, R. (1981). *Dynamic assessment of retarded performers: Learning potential assessment device.* Baltimore: University Park Press.

Furth, H. (1970). On language and knowing in Piaget's developmental theory. *Human Development, 13,* 241-257.

Furth, H. (1970). *Piaget for teachers.* Englewood Cliffs, NJ: Prentice-Hall.

Furth, H. (1974). *Thinking goes to school: Piaget's theory in practice.* New York: Oxford University Press.

Furth, H., & Youniss, J. (1969). Thinking in deaf adolescents: Language and formal operations. *Journal of Communication Disorders, 2,* 195-101.

Harris, A., & Moore, T. (1978). Language and thought in Piagetian theory. In L. Siegel & C. Brainerd (Eds.), *Alternatives to Piaget: Critical essays on the theory* (pp. 131-150). New York: Academic Press.

Inhelder, B. (1968). *The diagnosis of reasoning in the mentally retarded.* New York: John Day.

Jastak, J. F., & Jastak, S. (1965). *Wide Range Achievement Test.* Wilmington: Guidance Associates of Delaware.

Larue, G. (1974). The acquisition of concepts of conservation of matter in Black adolescents. In G. I. Lubin, J. F. Magary, & M. K. Poulsen (Eds.), *Proceedings of the fourth interdisciplinary seminar: Piagetian theory and its implications for the helping professions.* Los Angeles: University of Southern California.

Martorano, S. C. (1973). The development of formal operations thinking. *Dissertation Abstracts International, 35,* (I-B), 515-516.

Mogdil, S., & Mogdil, C. (1976). *Piagetian research: Compilation and commentary.* Highlands, NJ: Humanities Press.

Modgil, S., & Mogdil, C. (1982). *Jean Piaget: Consensus and controversy.* New York: Praeger.

Morf, A. (1973). Les relations entre la logique et la langage lors du passage du raisonnement concret au raisonnement formal. Etudes D'Epistemologie Genetique, 1957, 3, 173-203. In Bart, W., *Development of a formal reasoning instrument.* Unpublished monograph.

Piaget, J., & Inhelder, B. (1958). *The growth of logical thinking from childhood to adolescence.* New York: Basic Books.

Siegel, L., & Brainerd, C. (Eds.) (1978). *Alternatives to Piaget: Critical essays on the theory.* New York: Academic Press.

Slosson, R. L. (1963). *Slosson Intelligence Test.* East Aurora, NY: Slosson Educational Publications.

Wadsworth, B. (1971). *Piaget's theory of cognitive development.* New York: McKay.

Wadsworth, B. (1978). *Piaget for the classroom teacher.* New York: Longman.

Recommended Sources for the Selection of Tasks for Informal Assessment

Copeland, R. (1974). *Diagnostic and learning activities in mathematics for children.* New York: Macmillan.

Copeland, R. (1979). *How children learn mathematics.* New York: Macmillan.

Ducksworth, E. (1972). The having of wonderful ideas. *Harvard Educational Review, 42,* 217-231.

Formanek, R., & Gurian, A. (1976). *Charting intellectual development: A practical guide to Piagetian tasks.* Springfield, Ill.: Charles C. Thomas.

Pulaski, M. (1971). *Understanding Piaget.* New York: Harper and Row.

Schwebel, M., & Ralph, J. (1973). *Piaget in the classroom.* New York: Basic Books.

Wadsworth, B. (1971). *Piaget's theory of cognitive development.* New York: McKay.

Wadsworth, B. (1978). *Piaget for the classroom teacher.* New York: Longman.

Appendix

Combinations

The combinations task was described by Elkind (1968) in a study with combined combinatorial thinking in adolescents from graded and ungraded classrooms.

Purpose: To assess the student's ability to do combinatorial thinking; to explore all possible combinations. Piaget described the adolescent's approach based upon his use of formal operations as systematic, holding one element constant while systematically combining it with others (Piaget and Inhelder, 1958). For a group of four elements, there is a constant of 16 possible combinations.

As Elkind noted, since one of these possibilities is "None, 15 combinations are more likely to be identified."

Materials. Red, blue, Black and white poker chips and for any four objects with which the student is familiar. This author has used boys and girls, short and tall, and numbers.

Procedure. Establish that the child understands the word combinations and that one, two, three or more may be used to make these. Elkind provided a brief training example in his study cited earlier. The student is told to combine the objects in all the possible ways. Responses are easily recorded on scratch paper or the students may write them. Some students sketch a matrix or other scheme with which they "solve the problem." The scratch paper becomes a valuable record of the student's approach to the problem.

Evaluation. The number of combinations are evaluated. The student who demonstrates combinatorial thinking will use a systematic, orderly approach to naming possible combinations. He/she will also identify most if not all of the 16 possible combinations. The examiner must remember that this is an informal approach to the identification of adolescents who are thinking in age-appropriate ways based upon performance on these tasks. One may view this as a screening process which can be very helpful in the evaluation of ability in Black, disadvantaged students whose verbal language is limited and whose achievement and intelligence scores on traditional measures are below average. Obviously, additional evaluation is important and required in decisions concerning retardation.

red
blue
black
white
red, blue
red, black
red, white
red, blue, black
red, blue, white

blue, black
blue, white
blue, black, white
black, white
black, white, red
black, white, red, blue
none

The second type of task involves assessment of the child's understanding of probability. This task has been described by Wadsworth (1979). In this author's adaptation of the probability task, blocks are replaced by coins.

Purpose. To assess the student's understanding of probability.

Materials: 96 coins, four different types–pennies, nickels, dimes and quarters–in the following quantities:

36 pennies   36 nickles   20 dimes   4 quarters

Procedure: Divide the coins into two equal groups as follows:

18 pennies   18 nickels   10 dimes   2 quarters

Place one group of coins (total number is 48) into a paper bag or box. Place the other group of 48 coins in front of the child on the table to be used as a reference group. Tell the child that you are going to take two coins at a time from the bag without looking. Shake them up or mix them before each drawing. Ask the child to guess what the coin will be each time. Continue until all coins have been drawn. From time to time ask the child how or why he gives that answer. Each time you draw two coins, place them on the table in view, but separated from the reference set.

Evaluation. Probability is understood if the child uses the reference to make predictions. He may actually count the coins or describe the numbers. According to Piaget, the ability to make predictions based on probability appears to occur around 12 years of age.

Cartoon Conservation Scales Performance

Johnny

The Cartoon Conservation Scales, developed by Edward De Avila and published by Linguametrics Group, Corte Madera, California, is described in the administration manual as a "measure of intellectual development derived from the theory of Jean Piaget." It consists of 32 test items which assess the student's understanding of the following:

Conservation of number, length, substance, distance, and volume. Horizonality of water, probability, and egocentricity/perspective.

The format consists of pictures (Cartoon format) and three answer choices which are presented in "bubbles."

Johnny answered all four items correctly for the following: conservation of number, length, substance, horizonality, volume, egocentricity, and probability. He answered two of the items on conservation of distance. (This is a somewhat difficult item to present and the language may have been a problem.) However, the student's performance on this test is impressive and supports and confirms his performance on the informally administered probability task as well as his ability to do formal operational, age-appropriate thinking. While the developmental scales for comparison end at 150 months, and the test author notes that guessing may be involved, a simple addition of Johnny's correct responses across subscales demonstrates sufficient ability.

For additional information, contact:

Lorraine S. Taylor, Ph.D.
Old Main 115
Educational Studies Dept.
State University of New York
New Paltz, NY 12561
Telephone: (914) 257-2918 or 2830
Fax: (914) 257-2799

Problems of Educational Research on Tests and Measurements in Nigeria

H. M. Omotoso

Abstract

The history of formal testing and measurement activities in Nigeria is traced and foreign and indigenous tests and measures used in educational and other settings are described. Problems and issues in test development and use are also discussed. These include ethnic/cultural problems, sociological problems, data collection and analysis and manpower and communication. Finally, suggestions for improving test and measurement activities in Nigeria are proffered.

Introduction

The use of tests and other measurements to assess or diagnose educational achievement, personal capability, personal traits, interest, etc. has been in existence from time immemorial. The techniques for such assessment vary from one culture to another. The format may be oral, written, or observational, and for individuals or groups.

The Ephesians and Greeks in pre-Christian times used oral tests to assess abilities. Even though this method has been widely criticized, it is still being used in many cultures and even in graduate schools. While the Spartans were interested in evaluating how every boy could demonstrate his mastery of the required manhood skills, the Athenians stressed the more intellectual educational pursuits, and Socrates used tests to stimulate and enrich learning by throwing a series of lead questions to learners to discover the truth about a subject-matter. These procedures have raised vital issues and there is concern about testing that continues to this day.

Today, the concern of the critics of testing programs covers:

(1) the use and misuse of test scores;

(2) the fairness of tests to minority groups in employment and education–a typical problem of cross-cultural testing;

(3) nature and quality of tests;

(4) effects of testing on pupils in terms of pupils' anxiety and their being categorized and labeled for testing purposes;

(5) sex bias–that is, use of different norms for males and females; and,

(6) the invasion of privacy.

The result is that educators have begun to reassess the purpose of testing and the kind of procedure to be adopted in the assessment of pupils.

There is now increased use of criterion referenced measurement, and a growing shift in the nature of aptitude and achievement tests. Tests are now being used for the improvement of instruction with an expanding use of computers in testing.

As an illustration of the foregoing trend, the Joint Matriculation Board (MB) of London (Forest & Williams, 1980) conducted studies on its grade award procedure with the aim of making their assessment more objective and close to reality. They sought proper definition of grades attached to physics scores.

In most developed countries one short state examination is being abandoned in favor of internal assessment or its combination with external examinations. Individual countries' assessment procedures reflect their experience, political background, and educational aspirations.

In the indigenous African setting before the advent of Western education, assessment of an individual's ability was mostly informal and in the form of oral interviews and observations. In Nigeria, even today, test of strength is measured by the observation of the two contestants in action.

The strong man usually overpowers the weak man and throws him down thrice in a row. A man's acquired knowledge, mastery of manhood skills and mental ability were often assessed through his creativity, foresight, and wisdom. The measurement of distance between two points is taken by use of strides of legs or the stretch between the thumb and the seconds finger–a sort of non-standardized measurement procedure. Measurement procedures vary from one ethnic group to another.

Written examinations were first introduced in Cape Coast (Ghana) of West Africa in 1800 A. D. with the advent of Western education. This was done with a view to carefully observing indigenous education in West Africa where Western education had just been introduced with its formal written examination system (Ohuche & Akeju, 1977).

Even with the introduction of Western education a measure of mental maturity before selecting children into primary school was based on "if the left hand, when passed over the head, can reach the right ear." An older child with short hands would fail to be accepted into the school.

Apart from the fact that this kind of maturity test was primitive, it was considered highly subjective. The system allowed younger children with big stature to be admitted into school before the older children.

This study traces the history of formal testing and measurement procedures in Nigeria and reviews the work of educational researchers. Problem areas are identified with emphasis on cultural differences facing test developers and administrators in Nigeria today. The aim is to offer possible solutions based on the new Federal Government National Policy on Education (FGNPE).

History of Educational Testing in Nigeria

In the introduction, testing and measurement procedures in Nigeria in the pre-colonial era were discussed. This section will trace the history of formal testing in Nigeria.

The advent of Western education ushered in formal educational measurement. The London and Cambridge Overseas examining bodies initially managed the school external examination while classroom teachers carried out the internal assessment of pupils using teacher made tests.

The ordinance establishing the West African Examinations Council (WAEC) became effective in Nigeria from 1952 when the WAEC (Nigerian Status) ordinance was enacted by the Nigerian Central Legislature. The Council was charged with the responsibility of determining the examinations required in the public interest in West Africa, and was also empowered to conduct such examination and award certificates with a proviso that "these certificates shall not represent a lower standard of attainment than equivalent certificates of other examining authorities."

With the birth of the WAEC, the overseas examining bodies only prepared the syllabus, developed and marked the examination papers and awarded grades and certificates. The WAEC was then used in the organization and administration of examinations such as the School Certificate of Cambridge Local Examination Syndicate, the General Certificate of the University of London, City and Guild of London Institute, and the

Royal Society of Arts. While some of the West African Examination Council staff members were being trained locally as organizers and administrators of the examinations, others were trained as examiners and tests developers overseas.

By 1969, the tutelage was over. The gradual takeover by the WAEC of the Secondary School G. C. E. (O and A Levels) Commercial and Technical examinations began. These examinations are now developed and administered to both the sited and blind candidates by the WAEC.

In addition to the above-mentioned achievement tests, the Council administers some National and Miscellaneous Examinations which could be used to measure achievement and also serve selection purposes. The Council also gives aptitude test services for placement into jobs or school. It also administers other tests of aptitude, or achievement for international testing organizations such as the Educational Testing Service (ETS) (U.S.A.).

Since 1976, the Nigerian Government has asked WACE to shed some of its responsibilities. The Administrative Staff College of Nigeria, (ASCON) now conducts the public service commission examination. The National Institute for Technical and Business Education has taken over the technical and commercial examinations while the National Teachers Institute now conducts the National Common Entrance Examinations (NCEE).

At present, the council conduct four categories of examinations: national examinations; collaboration with other examining bodies; and, examinations conductd on behalf of their examining bodies. The National Examinations are restricted to the specific member countries for which they are developed and reflect their local policies, needs and aspirations. The international examinations are centrally divided for candidates in all the five member countries–Nigeria, Ghana, Sierra Leone, Liberia and Gambia.

The last two are yet to be implemented. To date, WAEC remains the only established institution involved in various kinds of educational measurement, achievement, aptitude, selection, etc. with adequate research capabilities and facilities for that purpose. At present, the Council conducts a total of 29 examinations involving a population of about 1.3 million in Nigeria alone, using the objective, essay, practical, oral and short answer questions types.

The Federal Government has just reviewed and liberalized its educational and assessment procedure from one short national and final examination to a combination of final examination and continuous assessment of the progress of the individual. In the view of this, The WAEC examination structure is being reviewed.

In addition to the West African Examinations Council, the Joint Admission and Matriculations Board (JAMB) was set up by the Federal Government in 1978 to select candidates for admission into universities. One of the motives was to balance ethnic representation of students in the universities. The Board prepares its own syllabuses and the questions used are multiple choice.

The examining bodies discussed above concentrate on achievement, selection, and aptitude testing. The affective and psychomotor domain are rarely used in the educational system in Nigeria except for clinical purposes in guidance and counseling. These, however, are being used in the universities guidance and counseling units, and the hospital mental health sections. The introduction of the continuous assessment in school systems highlights an urgent need for tests and measures in these two domains.

The International Centre for Educational Evaluation (ICEE) came into formal existence in 1979 at the University of Ibadan Institute of Education. The Centre was set up to look into the problems of educational innovation in Africa, and its objectives were to:

(i) train evaluators;
(ii) conduct research on evaluation techniques and instruments; and,
(iii) evaluate specific educational projects–on contract.

The existence of ICEE has definitely put new life into the field of tests and measurements in Nigeria by producing post-graduate students (Nigerians and other Africans) in the field of tests and measurements and in carrying out various educational research studies.

Method

Problems encountered by test developers across the country were identified through the use of questionnaires, personal interviews and library study. Forty-five university lecturers from eight well established universities in the country were interviewed. They responded to questionnaires developed to identify their testing research. They were also asked to state the problems encountered in carrying out their research. Similar information was collected through library study of students' dissertations in all eight universities to give insight into the problems encountered by the students.

Results

A total of 117 studies were reviewed (published and unpublished). Results indicated that researchers concentrated mostly on the following areas:

1. Development of new instruments from scratch or from an existing one (adaptation);
2. Reliability and validity studies–of local or foreign instrument and their adaptation for local use;
3. Causality and correlational–with a view to solving educational problems;
4. Predictive validity of an instrument–for selection and placement, achievement purposes, etc.;
5. Diagnostic–of attitude, interest, personality, achievement, etc.;
6. Comparison of groups–across cultural, age, sex, nature and nurture, etc.;
7. Assessment of cognitive abilities;
8. Grading, weighting, and item analysis;
9. Evaluation of educational programs (summative and formative); and,
10. Tests and measurement issues.

Table 1 summarizes all foreign tests being used in or adapted for use in Nigeria.

The tests cover the areas of measurement of intelligence, aptitude, interest, achievement, attitude, self-concept, and personality.

Table 1. Some Foreign Measuring Instruments Used in Nigeria

Test	Publisher
Intelligence	
1. Stanford-Binet Intelligence Scale	Houghton Mifflin Co. Boston, USA
2. Wechsler Intelligence Scales	Psychological Corporation, New York
3. Concept Assessment Kit-Conservation	Educational and Industrial Testing Service, USA
4. Culture Fair Intelligence Test	Institute of Personality and Ability Testing (IPAT)
5. Goodenough Harris Drawing Tests	Psychological Corporation New York, USA
6. Otis-Lennon Mental Ability Test	Psychological Corporation, New York, USA
7. Coloured Progressive Matrice (RAVEN)	H.K. Lewis & Co., U.K. and Psychological Corporation, New York, USA
8. Tests ML and MQ	Australian Council for Educational Research
9. Pictorial Test of Intelligence	Riverside Publishing Company, USA
10. Children Embedded Figures Test	Consulting Psychologists Press, California, USA
11. Lorge Thorndike Intelligence Test	Houghton-Mifflin Boston, USA

(table continues)

Test	Publisher	Test	Publisher
Aptitude		**Interest**	
12. Miller Analogies	Psychological Corporation, New York, USA	23. Lex and Thorpe Occupational Interest Inventory	California Test Bureau, USA
13. I-D Batteries	TEDRO, WAEC Nigeria and American Institute for Research, Pittsburgh, USA	**Achievement**	
		24. Graduate Record Examinations (GRE)	Educational Testing Service, Princeton, USA
14. California Mental Maturity Test	CTB/Mcgraw-Hill Monterey, California, USA	25. Progressive Achievement Test	New Zealand Council of Educational Research
15. Cadwell Preschool Inventory	Educational Testing Service, Princeton, USA	26. Test of English as a Foreign Language (TOEFL)	Educational Testing Service Princeton, USA
16. Differential Aptitude Test (DAT)	Psychological Corporation, New York, USA	27. College Entrance Aptitude Test (SAT)	Educational Testing Service Princeton, USA
Interest		**Aptitude**	
17. Kuder Preference	Science Research Record Vocational Associates, USA	28. Minnesota Teacher Attitude Inventory	Psychological Corporation New York, USA
18. Kuder Preference Record Vocational	Science Research Associates, USA	29. Shaw and Wright Scales for the Measurement of Attitude	McGraw-Hill Publishing Company, USA
19. Minnesota Vocational Interest Inventory	Psychological Corporation, New York, USA	**Self-Concept and Personality**	
20. Strong Vocational Interest Blank (SVIB)	Stanford University Press, California, USA	30. Piers and Harris Self-Concept Scale	Counselor Recordings and Tests, USA
21. Kuder Occupational Interest Inventory	Science Research Associates, USA	31. Minnesota Multiphasic Personality	Psychological Corporation, USA
22. Kuder Interest Scales	Science Research Associates, USA		

Table 2 shows the 17 published tests developed or adapted for Nigerian use after they have

Table 2. Adapted and Locally Developed Tests in Use in Nigeria

No.	Test/Developer	Author
University of Ibadan		
1.	Student Problem Inventory (SPI)	C.M.G. Bakare
2.	Vocational Interest Inventory (VII)	C.M.G. Bakare
3.	Motivation for Occupational Preference Scale (MOPS)	C.M.G. Bakare
4.	Student Habit Inventory (SHI)	C.M.G. Bakare
5.	Obanya French Achievement Test (OFAT)	P.A.I. Obanya
6.	French Language Achievement Test (FLAT)	P.A.I. Obanya
7.	Test of Principles and Strategies of Second Language Teachers (TEPSET)	P.A.I. Obanya
8.	Adolescent Personal Data Inventory (APDI)	J.O. Akinboye
Ahmadu Bello University		
9.	Biology Diagram Perception Test (BDPT)	O.J. Jegede
10.	A. B. U. Design Test	Sister Halligan
University of Ife		
11.	Self-Concept Test	A.A. Olowu
University of Lagos		
12.	Scholastic Aptitude Test	E.O. Obe
13.	Personality Questionnaire Inventory	Akin Odebunmi

No.	Test/Developer	Author
University of Benin		
14.	Awaritefe Psychological Index (API)	Awaritefe
University of Jos		
15.	Somatization Scale	A. Nwezeh
16.	Students Needs and Problem Inventory	A. Nwezeh
West African Examinations Council		
17.	29 Advancement Tests for Assessment of School Children and Private Candidates	West African Examination Council
Joint Matriculation Board		
18.	Selection Test for University Admission	Joint Admission Matriculation Board

met appropriate psychometric standards. There are forty-four other tests which are being developed but have not reached the stage of publication. The guidance and counseling and mental health units, as well as students from the various universities have attempted to develop diagnostic instruments often for local research or counseling purposes but not for publication. Very few of such instruments reach the stage of publication for the following reasons:

(1) Most fail to meet minimum psychometric standards and the samples are too small for meaningful generalization;

(2) Tests that met minimum psychometric standards for initial use were never followed up to develop norms for a particular group (for lack of funds and manpower); and,

(3) Those who publish their work often do so for research and economic reasons.

This study has revealed that at present Nigeria can hardly boast of very good locally developed instruments in any of the three required domains that are standardized and normed for any individuals, moreover, there exists no clearinghouse to attest to the quality of such instruments.

The results also indicate widespread abuse of tests in Nigeria. A review of the large number of published achievement tests on school subjects are teacher made. They are mass produced for commercial reasons, tailored to the content of WAEC syllabus and questions, and are made for the consumption of students preparing for one kind of terminal or selection examination at the primary, secondary, vocational, or college level.

The tests neither have the same quality controls which WAEC gives its tests before final use, nor do the tests meet minimum psychometric standards. In addition, these never pass through any quality control (clearinghouse) to allow for the assessment of their quality and appropriateness.

Discussion

The above listed research topics and the information on test development in Table 1 point to the fact that Nigeria is at an embryonic stage in tests and measurements compared to developed nations.

Identification of problem areas in education require the use of valid and reliable instruments for improvement. The problem of developing suitable instruments for conducting research activities has faced Nigeria for some time.

Schwartz (1961) who an American Institute for Research (AIR) team, was the first crusader to develop and adapt tests for use in educational and vocational selection in Nigeria. The I-D test battery (with concurrent validity of .56 to .64) was developed through AIR. This battery of tests was used in East and West African countries and is still being used by WAEC to date, with slight modification.

In Nigeria, great premium is placed on certificates and paper qualification. Admission to universities and other post primary and secondary institutions are usually based on one-short national examination which usually records high failure rates. The public, employers and even educators have made many allegations against examiners in terms of examination irregularities, difficulty of tests, examining system (test) development and administrative procedures, award of grades, and uses made of test results, to list a few. There is no doubt that the examiners are faced with many problems–social, political, economic, cultural, etc.

The results of this study have revealed a number of problems which are classified as Ethnic/Cultural, Sociological, Data Collection and Analysis, and Manpower and Communication.

Ethnic/Cultural Problems

There are three major ethnic groups in Nigeria–Yoruba, Ibo, and Hausa with Yoruba, Igbo, and Hausa as their respective medium of expression. However, English is the official language in Nigeria. Within each of the three major groups, there are hundreds of tribes. They differ in tribal dialects, cultural heritage, religious affiliations, personal attributes, and social structure. Paul Boski (1983) observed some of these differences which have been found to affect each group's attitude toward life.

The ethnic/cultural problems arising from the multiplicity of ethnic groups are language, political, tribal, religious, sociological and geographical. They pose the greatest challenge to Nigerian educators as well as test developers and administrators. Research into test uses and development started out by using and adapting foreign tests before attempting to develop tests from scratch. Our experiences indicate serious cultural bias when foreign tests are used on any Nigerian ethnic group.

Daramola (1971) and Yoloye (1974) conducted studies on the suitability of the Lorge Thorndike Intelligence Test for use in Nigerian schools. These researchers discovered that the test required slight modification before use with Nigerian children. The results of these studies encouraged other educators who were already convinced that many of the existing foreign test inventories were unsuitable for use with African subjects.

The first attempt at adaptation was made by Bakare (1974). Bakare emerged with the Vocational Interest Inventory (VII). VII was an adaptation of the Kuder Preference Record Vocational Form C, Lee and Thorpe Occupational Interest Inventory, and Strong Vocational Interest for men and women. Following Bakare's effort, many Nigerian educators have attempted to adapt foreign tests or develop one from scratch to suit Nigerian cultural needs (Table 2). In the process of adapting foreign tests for Nigerian use, many cultural problems which militate against test development and administration surfaced. Bakare discovered that the unsuitability of foreign tests for African subjects was accounted for by their foreign occupation content, relatively different vocabulary, and the high level of sophistication required for their administration, scoring, and interpretation.

Obemeata (1974), in his attempt to determine predictive validity of three foreign tests, discovered that the English language content of the tests needed to suit Nigerian pupils with rather little knowledge of the English language. He advocated simplification of English content and substitution of local proverbs for English metaphors. This was also the view of Maurean McCarthy (1974) who administered the Kuder General Interest Survey (KGIS) to Nigerian subjects.

Awaritefe and Ebie (1982) used the Jordan and Massey (1967) School Readiness Survey Test on Benin Emotan Nursery School children. They observed consistently that certain cultural influences on the test performance of Nigerian children on the (SRST) were due to the use of objects not locally available in Nigeria.

Awritefe (1982) on the same problem said that foreign tests standardized outside Africa are partially lacking in educational and cultural relevance for Africans. Awaritefe maintains that the use of such tests without validation or modification is a questionable practice.

Tests developed by Nigerians for Nigerians face similar complaints. Awaritefe (1982) in using his Awaritefe Psychological Index (API) on

his patients pointed out the aspects of Nigerian culture which militate against the use of personality inventories in hospitals and other mental health facilities. He claimed most patients have no experience with questionnaire type tests. Such patients are shocked and are often uncooperative. He explained his patients reaction to be associated with their ethnic customs and experience with local traditional healers who have conditioned them to contrary expectations. They see themselves as guinea pigs and they cannot understand how use of tests could solve their problems. Although Awaritefe believed that translation of existing tests into indigenous languages would help, he was still worried about the problem of accurate translation of tests to well over 100 indigenous languages, especially when the languages do not have detailed written grammar and lexicography.

Poor understanding of English Language has compelled secondary school candidates taking the WAEC GCE (O/L) examinations sometimes to respond to questions written in English, in their own tribal language, despite the fact that classroom instruction is officially in English. This situation creates serious difficulty for proper assessment of candidates. As a solution to this problem, Ojerinde (1983) asserted that the Yoruba child will learn better in school if the language of instruction is the mother tongue throughout the six years of primary education. As a result of his various research projects, he maintained that the use of local language as the medium of instruction in schools has contributed to the higher performance of his experimental groups.

Sociological Problems

Obemeata (1967) discovered that pupils from low socioeconomic backgrounds tended to do better in Yoruba (local language of the pupil), while those from high socioeconomic background tended to do better in the second language due to their exposure. He concluded that no matter what language was used in constructing and administering tests, pupils from high-socioeconomic backgrounds tended to have an advantage. In another study, Obemeata (1980) confirmed that socioeconomic status of people, quality of school, level of sophistication, and the rural environment, all combined to effect test performance. Similar results were obtained by Okonkwo (1983) when he administered the Modern Language Aptitude Tests (MLAT) developed by Carrol and Sapon (1959) to 202 secondary students.

Examination irregularities such as examination leakage, cheating, and certificate racketeering is another serious sociological malady facing Nigeria. The control and complete eradication of examination leakage is of greatest concern to WAEC, JAMB, and other examining bodies. Nwana (1982) stated that the problem is a fundamental issue on which validity of the certificates and result sheets depend. He further indicated that leakage and forging of certificates had made the universities skeptical of the paper qualifications presented by applicants. As a result, the Nigerian Federal Government took a positive step to combat these irregularities by promulgating the "West African Examinations Council Decree." Decree No. 27 in 1973 and "Examination Malpractice's Decree," Decree No. 20 in 1984 prescribed various jail terms for offenders. Nwana (1982) also implied that the Joint Admissions Matriculation Board was formed partly to screen candidates for admission to the university. The establishment of JAMB was a political move by the federal government to balance admission into the universities on an ethnic basis. Admission into the federal government secondary schools (Unity Schools) after taking the National Common Entrance Examination and interviews was also based on the ethnic balancing theory.

Data Collection and Analysis

Record keeping is a major problem in test development in Nigeria. Because the country lacks automation or computerization of personal data, researchers are faced with poor sampling and large mortality of subjects due to difficulty in retrieving information. Ezewu and Okoye (1981) expressed their fears that once the keeping of assessment records is faulty, decisions made on them cannot be immune to inconsistency.

Inadequate sampling of subjects or content have militated against validity and reliability of most of the developed tests. Nwana (1982) stressed the need for representative items. He gave an example that was in developing questions on geography, political division, ethnic groups, physical features, climatic zones, and economic geography must be considered for a test to be valid. Also, Obemeata (1980) blames differences between urban and rural children performance on poor sampling and the tendency of test developers to validate tests mostly on urban children. This gives urban children an advantage over rural children. Inadequate sampling disallows generalization of result and does not encourage confidence in the findings.

Similarly, Iwuji (1982) stressed the need to norm tests according to class and sex as well as rural and urban locations of schools. Such tasks require large sampling.

To have a viable test developed one needs good machinery to process data–computers and necessary programs to carry out data analysis on sizeable samples. These facilities are non-existent in most institutions. For this reason, sample sizes are small and limited to manual analyses.

Manpower and Communication

The development of measuring instruments and research activities require inter-institutional cooperation for extensive and adequate data collection. Such cooperation encourages division of labour in terms of financial and manpower needs, data collection and analysis, as well as other operations in the process of standardization of instruments. The needed cooperation among academics or institutions is more or less non-existent in Nigeria today. One of the reasons for this lack of cooperation is the fact that Nigerian researchers tend to be secretive, unlike their overseas counterparts who share and compare opinions. The current practice is for academicians to develop instrument solely for research purposes and produce papers which may enhance their promotion chances. This attitude has affected following up of development of such tests to standardization and validation stages.

To date, most educational institutions in Nigeria have no tests and measurements unit. The few established ones still find it difficult to have post-graduate programs for lack of interested students and qualified lecturers who themselves lack basic knowledge of tests and measurements. This has hampered proper assessment of primary and secondary school pupils as most teachers are not trained in the field of testing. This lack of expertise has equally affected production of locally written text books that are technical enough for university students. Books used in the universities are still foreign.

Another unfortunate observation is inadequate communication between the researchers and the users of research results. This has resulted in a huge waste of resources that would have been useful in nation building.

Sending questionnaires by post to non-literate subjects creates data collection problems. This means that the subject will have to look for an interpreter to be able to respond to the questionnaire. None of the researchers in this study claim to have tried this method. In such cases, the method they usually employ is observation and personal interviews which will allow the researcher to translate and record responses.

Problems of data collection and administration of test or questionnaires is compounded by the high illiteracy rate which stands at no less than 80%. Even among the literate population, many psychological tests are not understood because the subjects' level of English is poor. Illiteracy has crippling effects of blocking communication between the testee and tester almost completely.

Conclusion

In Nigeria, as in other countries of the world, there is a continuing reassessment of the purposes of testing and the procedure to be adopted in designing well validated tests. A review of the history of educational testing in Nigeria has revealed the great role being played by the various examination bodies, universities and other government educational institutions.

Although efforts have been made by researchers in test and measurements in Nigeria, fundamental problems still exist. Major among

these are ethnic/cultural problems arising from the multiplicity of ethnic groups in Nigeria, coupled with the high illiteracy rate and the use of the English language as a medium of instruction. These problems pose the greatest challenge to Nigerian tests and measurements researchers. The use of foreign test on Nigerians does not help the situation either, as such tests require proper validation. Indeed, there is now a great need to develop tests exclusively for local use–bearing in mind ethnic/cultural problems.

There needs to be better communication among tests and measurements researchers . With proper cooperation among researchers, tests could be developed which would be standardized and normed for at least the major Nigerian ethnic groups. Such tests could be translated into the three main languages. It is believed that if Nigerians are made to learn at least one major Nigerian language in addition to their own, language and communication problems in test development and administration will be partially solved.

Finally, there is immediate need to intensify staff training in test and measurement procedures especially for school teachers who will implement the newly introduced continuous assessment in both primary and secondary schools. Thus, training also calls for improvement in publishing more technical books, locally produced by Nigerians, for use by university students.

References

Awaritefe, A., & Ebie, J. C., (1982). Nigerian norms on the school readiness survey. *Nigerian Journal of Clinical Psychology, 1*(1), 119-128.

Awaritefe, A. (1982). The Awaritefe Psychological Index (API). *Nigerian Journal of Clinical Psychology, 1*(2), 42-51.

Bakare, C. G. M. (1974). The construction and validation of a vocational interest inventory for use in Africa *WAJEVM, TEDRO, WAEC, 2*(1), 7-15.

Daramola, S. F. (1981). *Adaptability of Lorge-Thorndike Intelligence Test for use in Nigerian secondary schools*. Unpublished master's thesis, University of Ibadan, Nigeria.

Esezebor, S. A. (1981). *Nigerian education trends and issues: Tests evaluation and performance in Nigeria*. University of Ilorin, Ilorin.

Ezewu, E. E., & Okoye N. W. (1981). *Principles of practice of continuous assessment*. Lagos, Lagos State, Nigeria: Evans Brothers.

Federal Republic of Nigeria (1981). *Federal republic of Nigeria national policy on education*. Lagos, Nigeria: Federal Government Press.

Forest, G. M., & Williams C. A. (1981). Report of the Interboard Study in G. C. E. Physics (Ordinary). Joint Matriculation Board Manchester.

Iwuji, V. B. C. (1982). Aptitude testing: In search of appropriate aptitude test to be used in Nigerian schools. *Education and Development, NERC Mainland Bureau, 2*(1), 390-403.

Nwana, O. C. (1979). *Educational Measurement for Teachers*. Nelson: Africa.

Obemeata, J. O. (1971). *Some problems of intelligence testing in Nigeria*. Unpublished master's dissertation, University of London.

Obemeata, J. O. (1980). A verbal intelligence test in the mother tongue as a predictor of success in the school certificate examination. *WAJEVM WAEC, 5(1)*, 7-12.

Ohuche, R. O., & Akeju S. A. (1977). *Testing and evaluation in education*. Ikeja: Nigeria Skyway.

Ojerinde, A. (1983). *Six year yoruba primary project primary six evaluation institute of education*. Ileife, Oyo: University of Ife .

Okokwo, A. (1983). *Some problems of foreign language aptitude testing in Nigeria*. Unpublished master's thesis, University of Ibadan.

Roski, P. (1984). A Study of Person Perception in Nigeria Ethnicity and Self Versus other Attributions for Achievement Related Outcomes. *Journal of Cross Cultural Psychology, 14*(1), 85-106.

Schwatz, P. (1961). *Aptitude Test for Use in Development Nations*. Pittsburgh: American Institute of Research.

Yoloye, E. A. (1966). *Performance of bilingual Nigerian students on verbal and non-verbal tests of intelligence*. Doctoral dissertation, Columbia University. (University Microfilms).

Yoloye, E. A. (1983). The predictive validity of Lorge-Thorndike Intelligence Tests for Achievement in Nigerian grammar school. *Waejevm, WAEC, 1*(1),

For additional information, contact:

Dr. H. M. Omotoso
OMOT Industries Ltd.
(Educational Toys and Joy Division)
P. O. Box 1551
Ikeja, Lagos, Nigeria
Telephone: 521991

Part IV

Children: Self-Esteem Measures

The HARE General and Area-Specific (School, Peer and Home) Self-Esteem Scale

Bruce R. Hare

Abstract

The HARE General and Area-Specific (School, Peer and Home) Self-Esteem Scale is described. This chapter provides a critique of the shortcomings of prior measures, offers a detailed account of the development of this new measure, and assesses the advantages it brings to the study of self-esteem. Along with the scale and coding instructions, the author provides information on the validity (construct and concurrent) and reliability of the measure. Results of a factor analysis, tests of association with related measures and constructs, and means and standard deviations from a survey of a representative sample of fifth (10 and 11 year old) and eighth (13 and 14 year old) graders are also provided. In addition to being more detailed than similar general measures, this thirty–item measure consists of three ten item subscales that allow for the separate assessment of self-esteem in each of the subject's significant arenas of interaction (at home, in school and with peers). Finally, evidence is presented in support of the author's argument that the scale is both more robust and less biased than the currently established measures.

How people view themselves (self-concept) and how they feel about that self-view (self-esteem) are among the more frequently studied sociopsychological questions. Variation in everything from attainment to general mental health is posited to be related to self-esteem, both at the individual level (as through the assumed connection between self-confidence and subsequent individual motivation and performance) and at the aggregate level (as, for example, through the assumption of lower self-esteem among outgroup members). While the exact nature of the relationship between attainment and esteem might be debated, there exists a highly regarded tradition which posits that lower self-esteem leads to lower subsequent performance, and that people of color, people of lower class status, and women are more likely to suffer from low self-esteem than successful "White," middle class, or male counterparts. There have been at least two major flaws in this tradition: 1) biased ethnocentricity, classism and sexism inherent to most measures; and, 2) the level of generality of the measures. Put simply, most measures, having been normed on ingroup

199

members, are biased against outgroup members, and most measures either assess a vague general sense of self-worth or overemphasize the school arena as the source of self-esteem at the neglect of the peer and home arenas. In response to these concerns, the HARE General and Area-Specific (School, Peer and Home) Self-Esteem Scale was devised.

In order to better investigate general and area-specific self-esteem among school age youngsters ten years old and above, the author constructed a thirty–item general self-esteem scale. The scale combines ideas from the Rosenberg (1965) and Coopersmith (1967) scales with the author's in an attempt to create a measure that is sensitive, and both general and area- specific. The necessity for creating such a new measure derived from an inability to assess area-specific (i.e., school, home and peer) self-esteem from the Rosenberg general measure, and concern that the reported failure of the Coopersmith measure to detect differences in self-evaluation by children across different areas of experience may be due to a lack of sensitivity in the items and the failure of the measure to sufficiently emphasize the specific context in which the respondent is to answer the question.

The devised measure is both general and area-specific (See Appendix 1 for full copy of the measure and Appendix 2 for coding key.). It is area-specific in that it is composed of three ten item subscales, (peer, school, and home) which unlike the Coopersmith subscales are not diffused and separated, but are presented as distinct units. The reasoning is that if the objective is to assess how a child feels about himself/herself at home, for example, the clustering of questions with specific directions to reflect upon that arena are not prejudicial but conducive to an accurate report of the subject's self-evaluation in that arena. On the other hand, the measure is general in that the sum score on any ten item subscale is treated as a general self-evaluation for that arena, and the sum score of thirty items (or the three subscales) is viewed as the general self-esteem measure. The assumptions are that for each subscale a variety of questions are asked so as to be reasonably representative of the universe of questions within that

specific arena, and that the addition of the three subscales, in reflecting the subject's three significant arenas of interaction, can cohere to elicit an accurate reflection of general self-esteem.

With regard to the composition of the subscales, questions were chosen to include both self-evaluative and other evaluative items. Thus, the "I" (self-evaluative) items can be distinguished from the "my parents," "my teachers," or "my friends" (other-evaluative) statements. This provides theoretical possibilities of distinguishing between whether a subject's self-evaluation is in accord or disagreement with his or her perception of the evaluations of significant others in the specific arenas, and provides a theoretical safeguard against reports simply based on self-assessments. In addition, the questions are constructed so as to induce the subjects to report a general sense of the self-feeling within the specific arenas and assure face validity.

There are two reasons for assuming that the sum of the three subscales (or thirty items) may be construed as a general self-esteem scale. The first, a theoretical justification, is that since school, peer, and home are the major arenas of interaction for the child, there is little room for the adolescent or preadolescent to develop a sense of self-worth independent of, or outside them. Unlike the adult, the possibilities for the child to develop other significant arenas of interaction and/or other significant others is minimal. Thus, these three arenas can be argued to represent something close to the child's universe for self-evaluation and thus, in combination, become a general self- esteem measure. The other reason is grounded in recent studies in statistics which suggest that the average score from a series of subscores equally weighted are as good if not a better predictor of a general trend as any intuitive judgment or aggregate measure.

The measure was pretested and correlated highly with two established self-esteem measures. In fact, the Hare general self-esteem scale (the sum of thirty items) was found to correlate 0.83 with both the Coopersmith self-esteem schedule and the Rosenberg general self-esteem measure. These two established measures correlated less highly at 0.74. In addition, each of the Hare subscales correlated most highly with its

Table 1. Test-Retest Reliability: HARE Self-Esteem Scale ($N = 32$)

Esteem	r	Significance
Home	.56	< .01
School	.61	< .01
Peer	.65	< .01
General	.74	< .01

Coopersmith counterpart. The two home subscales correlated 0.65 and the school and peer social subscales 0.75. Thus, at the very least, the Hare measure can be argued to be measuring processes similar to those assessed by these two recognized measures, and to have combined aspects of both.

In short, based on pretest findings, the Hare measure is both general and area-specific, and therefore capable of serving as both an indicator of general and area-specific self-esteem. The reliability of the Hare general and area-specific self-esteem scale was found to be high and significant. It was tested on a stratified sample of White and Black male and female fifth grade subjects. Three months elapsed between the test and retest of the thirty-two subjects. Although there is debate as to the amount of time one should wait between testing and retesting, it is generally thought that there is more error associated with too short, as opposed to too long a wait. The problem associated with too long a wait is, of course, the possible impact of maturation and other real occurrences which might account for changes in scores. On the other hand, too short a period endangers the test-retest validity by increasing the problem of memory. Thus, the three month interval is acceptable. Results of the reliability test (Pearson) are presented in Table 1.

Factor analysis (see Table 2) and tests of association between the subscale scores and area-specific life events by Shoemaker (1980) provide information on the construct validity of both the general scale and the area-specific subscales.

The Shoemaker factor analysis yielded three distinct factors with the peer, school and home items loading appropriately on different factors

(see Table 2). Shoemaker also reported home self-esteem to be significantly associated with social class, peer self-esteem with recent family moves, and school self-esteem with test anxiety and reading and math achievement. Hare (1980) reports a significant correlation between social class and general self-esteem and no significant racial difference in general self-esteem when social class is controlled. Hare (1984) reports a significant rise in peer self-esteem, a simultaneous significant drop in school self-esteem and no change in general self-esteem as children move from preadolescence (ten and eleven years old) to adolescence (thirteen and fourteen years old). Thus the subscore changes cancel each other out and demonstrate that there may be changes in the area-specific sources of general self-esteem that need not result in changes in the level of general self-esteem.

Table 3 presents the mean and standard deviation results elicited from a 1977 survey of a representative sample of ten and eleven year old fifth graders and a follow-up 1980 survey of the same youngsters as thirteen and fourteen year old eighth graders.

Finally, the Scale administration may be individually or group administered. It is suggested that the interviewer read the survey aloud (in order to reduce the effect of variations in reading ability), while the subjects follow along and mark their own copies of the instrument. When appropriate, subjects should also be assured of the confidentiality of their answers. The scale takes less than thirty minutes to administer, appears to have no adverse effects on the subjects, and is argued to be less biased and more robust than other similar measures.

Table 2. Factor Loadings for the HARE Self-Esteem Scale*

Item		Factor	
p1 I have at least as many friends as other people my age.	0.05	0.57	-0.02
p2 I am not as popular as other people my age.	0.03	0.52	-0.08
p3 In the kinds of things that people my age like to do, I am at least as good as most other people.	-0.01	0.50	0.02
p4 People my age often pick on me.	0.07	0.38	0.02
p5 Other people think I am a lot of fun to be with.	0.02	0.57	-0.04
p6 I usually keep to myself because I am not like other people my age.	0.09	0.47	0.00
p7 Other people wish that they were like me.	0.04	0.52	-0.04
p8 I wish I were a different kind of person because I'd have more friends.	0.14	0.45	0.03
p9 If my group of friends decided to vote for leaders of their group, I'd be elected to a high position.	-0.07	0.60	0.09
p10 When things get tough, I am not a person that other people my age would turn to for help.	0.00	0.31	0.02
h1 My parents are proud of the kind of person I am.	0.66	0.09	-0.10
h2 No one pays much attention to me at home.	0.58	0.06	-0.03
h3 My parents feel that I can be depended on.	0.51	0.17	0.01
h4 I often feel that if they could, my parents would trade me in for another child.	0.66	0.05	0.04
h5 My parents try to understand me.	0.55	-0.07	0.03
h6 My parents expect too much of me.	0.46	-0.11	0.08
h7 I am an important person to my family.	0.48	0.06	0.11
h8 I often feel unwanted at home.	0.51	0.05	0.08
h9 My parents believe that I will be a success in the future.	0.36	0.11	0.20
h10 I often wish I had been born into another family.	0.55	0.04	-0.05
s1 My teachers expect too much of me.	0.15	-0.10	0.42
s2 In the kinds of things we do in school, I am at least as good as other people in my classes.	-0.06	0.42	0.30
s3 I often feel worthless in school.	0.07	0.29	0.39
s4 I am usually proud of my report card.	0.14	0.06	0.48
s5 School is harder for me than most other people.	-0.03	0.24	0.50
s6 My teachers are usually happy with the kind of work I do.	0.18	0.18	0.35
s7 Most of my teachers do not understand me.	0.17	0.02	0.39
s8 I am an important person in my classes.	-0.08	0.25	0.49
s9 No matter how hard I try, I never get the grades I deserve.	-0.02	-0.10	0.56
s10 All in all, I feel I've been very fortunate to have had the kinds of teachers I've had since I started school.	0.00	-0.12	0.56

*From Shoemaker, 1980. It is worth noting that the home self-esteem items load most heavily on Factor 1, peer items on Factor 2, and the school items on Factor 3.

Table 3. Means and Standard Deviations on the Hare Self-Esteem Scale for Longitudinal Sample in 1977 (5th Grade) and 1980 (8th Grade)

Measures	1977		1980	
	μ	SD	μ	SD
Hare General Self-Esteem				
Blacks	91.7	10.4	95.0	10.3
Whites	91.0	12.1	90.4	10.8
Boys	92.0	9.9	92.4	10.7
Girls	90.4	13.2	90.1	10.9
Total	91.1	11.8	91.1	10.8
Hare School				
Blacks	30.6	5.0	29.5	4.1
Whites	30.0	4.9	28.8	4.9
Boys	30.1	4.3	28.7	4.8
Girls	30.2	5.4	29.1	4.7
Total	30.1	4.9	28.9	4.8
Hare Peer				
Blacks	28.4	4.1	30.9	5.0
Whites	28.4	4.5	29.4	3.9
Boys	29.0	4.5	30.5	4.4
Girls	27.9	4.4	28.9	3.7
Total	28.4	4.8	29.6	4.1
Hare Home				
Blacks	32.7	4.5	34.6	4.4
Whites	32.6	5.3	32.2	4.7
Boys	33.0	4.8	33.2	4.8
Girls	32.2	5.6	32.1	4.7
Total	32.6	5.2	32.6	4.7
Blacks ($N = 41$) Whites ($N = 207$) Boys ($N = 115$) Girls ($N = 133$) Total ($N = 249$)				

References

Bandura, A. (1964). The stormy decade: Fact or fiction? *Psychology in the Schools, 1,* 224-231.

Banks, W. C. (1976). White preference in Blacks: A paradigm in search of a phenomenon. *Psychological Bulletin, 83*(6), 1179-1186.

Brookover, W., LePere, J., Hammacher, T., & Erickson, E. (1965). *Self-concept of ability and school achievement, II.* East Lansing: Michigan State University.

Coleman, J., Campbell, E., & Hobson, C. (1966). *Equality of educational opportunity.* Washington, DC: Department of Health, Education and Welfare. U.S. Government Printing Office.

Coopersmith, S. (1967). *The antecedents of self-esteem.* San Francisco, CA: Freeman.

Dawes, R. M., & Corrigan, B. (1974). Linear models in decision-making. *Psychological Bulletin, 81*(2), 95.

Dusek, B., & Flaherty, J. F. (1981). The development of the self-concept during the adolescent years. *Monographs of the Society for Research in Child Development, 46*(4).

Epps, E. (1975). Impact of school desegregation on aspirations, self-concept and other aspects of personality. *Law and contemporary problems,* 300-313.

Erikson, E. H. (1968). *Identity, youth and crisis.* New York: Norton.

Freud, A. (1958). Adolescence. *Psychoanalytic study of the child, 13,* 255-278.

Hall, G. S. (1904). *Adolescence* (Vols. 1 and 2). New York: Appleton.

Hardy, C., & Petrinovich L. (1969). *Introduction to statistics for the behavioral sciences.* Philadelphia: Saunders.

Hare, B. R. (1975). *The relationship of social background in the dimensions of self-concept.* Unpublished doctoral dissertation, University of Chicago.

Hare, B. R. (1984). Development and change among desegregated adolescents: A longitudinal study of self-perception and achievement. In D. E. Bartz & M. L. Maehr (Eds.), *Advances in motivation and achievement, Vol. 1* (pp. 173-201). Greenwich, CT: JAI Press.

Hare, B. R. (1977a). Black and White self-esteem in social science: An overview. *Journal of Negro Education, 46*(2), 141-156.

Hare, B. R. (1977b). Racial and socioeconomic variations in preadolescent area-specific and general self-esteem. *International Journal of Intellectual Relations, 1,* 31-51.

Hare, B. R. (1980). Self-perception and academic achievement variations in a desegregated setting. *American Journal of Psychiatry, 137,* 683-689.

Hare, B. R. (1985). Reexamining the adjustment central tendency. In J. McAdoo & H. McAdoo (Eds.), *Black children: Their social, emotional and family environments.* Beverly Hills: Sage.

McCall, R. B., Eichorn, D. H., & Hogarty, P. S. (1977). Transition in early mental development. *Monographs of the Society for Research in Child Development, 42,* (3, Serial No. 171).

McDill, E., Meyer, E., & Rugby, L. (1966). *Sources of educational climate in high schools.* Baltimore: Johns Hopkins University.

Monge, R. H. (1973). Developmental trends in factors of adolescent self-concept. *Developmental Psychology, 8,* 382-393.

Nobles, W. W. (1973). Psychological research and the Black self-concept. A critical review. *Journal of Social Issues, 29,* 11-31.

Rosenberg, M. (1965). *Society and the adolescent self-image.* Princeton, NJ: Princeton University Press.

Shoemaker, A. L. (1980). Construct validity of area-specific self-esteem: The Hare self-esteem scale. *Educational and Psychological Measurement, 40,* 495-501.

Simmons, R. G., Rosenberg, F., & Rosenberg, M. (1973). Disturbance in the self-image at adolescence. *American Sociological Review, 38,* 553-568.

Spencer, M., Brookins, G., & Allen, W. (Eds.) (1985). *Beginnings: The social and affective development of Black children.* Hillsdale, NJ: Lawrence Erlbaum.

Wylie, R. (1961). *The self-concept.* Lincoln: University of Nebraska Press.

Appendix A

Peer Self-Esteem Scale

Please circle the letter in front of the answer which best describes how you feel about the sentence. These sentences are designed to find out how you generally feel when you are with other people your age. There are no right or wrong answers. (The questions for each of the following scales are of the same format as question 1 of the Peer Self-Esteem Scale. To conserve space, therefore, only the actual test questions, without the options, will be presented for questions 2-10).

1. I have at least as many friends as other people my age.
   a. Strongly Disagree
   b. Disagree
   c. Agree
   d. Strongly Agree
2. I am *not* as popular as other people my age.
3. In the kinds of things that people my age like to do, I am at least good as most other people.
4. People my age often pick on me.
5. Other people think I am a lot of fun to be with.
6. I usually keep to myself because I am *not* like other people my age.
7. Other people wish that they were like me.
8. I wish I were a different kind of person because I'd have more friends.
9. If my group of friends decided to vote for leaders of their group, I'd be elected to a high position.
10. When things get tough, I am *not* a person that other people my age would turn to for help.

Home Self-Esteem Scale

Please circle the letter in front of the answer which best describes how you feel about the sentence.

These sentences are designed to find out how you generally feel when you are with your family. There are no right or wrong answers.

1. My parents are proud of the kind of person I am.
   a. Strongly Disagree
   b. Disagree
   c. Agree
   d. Strongly Agree
2. No one pays much attention to me at home.
3. My parents feel that I can be depended on.
4. I often feel that if they could, my parents would trade me in for another child.
5. My parents try to understand me.
6. My parents expect too much of me.
7. I am an important person to my family.
8. I often feel unwanted at home.
9. My parents believe that I will be a success in the future.
10. I often wish that I had been born into another family.

School Self-Esteem Scale

Please circle the letter in front of the answer which best describes how you feel about the sentence. These sentences are designed to find out how you generally feel when you are in school. There are no right or wrong answers.

1. My teachers expect too much of me.
   a. Strongly Disagree
   b. Disagree
   c. Agree
   d. Strongly Agree
2. In the kinds of things we do in school, I am at least as good as other people in my classes.

3. I often feel worthless in school.
4. I am usually proud of my report card.
5. School is harder for me than most other people.
6. My teachers are usually happy with the kind of work I do.
7. Most of my teachers do not understand me.
8. I am an important person in my classes.
9. It seems that no matter how hard I try, I never get the grades I deserve.
10. All and all, I feel I've been very fortunate to have the kinds of teachers I've had since I started school.

Appendix B

Scoring Key for the Hare General and Area-Specific Self-Esteem Scale*

Peer Self-Esteem

Question Numbers	*Score Values*
1, 3, 5, 7, 9	A(1), B(2), C(3), D(4)
2, 4, 6, 8, 10	A(4), B(3), C(2), D(1)

Home Self-Esteem

Question Numbers	*Score Values*
1, 3, 5, 7, 9	A(1), B(2), C(3), D(4)
2, 4, 6, 8, 10	A(4), B(3), C(2), D(1)

School Self-Esteem

Question Numbers	*Score Values*
1, 3, 5, 7, 9	A(4), B(3), C(2), D(1)
2, 4, 6, 8, 10	A(1), B(2), C(3), D(4)

*The sum of the scores for each ten item sub-scale is the area specific measure. The sum of the sub-scales is the general self-esteem measure.

Optimal Extended Self-Esteem Scales

Seward E. Hamilton, Jr.

Abstract

The Optimal Extended Self-Esteem Scales (OESES) assess African Americans from their perception and cultural value perspectives. The measures consider the cultural norms, experiences, and values of the African American community, while traditional measures define self-esteem according to a European cultural value standard. A brief theoretical overview is presented concerning the redefinition of self-esteem from an African cultural centered perspective of extended self-esteem. There are four different developmental levels of the Optimal Extended Self-Esteem Scales (OESES) that include preschool (ages 3-6), children (1st - 6th grades), adolescent (grades 6-12) and an adult scale (ages 18 and above). The purpose of the OESES scales is to serve as a criterion measure for determining the holistic African principles of Kwanzaa by Maulana Karenga (1989). Some validity and reliability data are reported.

Introduction

The Optimal Extended Self-Esteem Scales (OESES) represent the culmination of over two decades of research by African scholars (Baldwin, 1981; Ben-Jochannan, 1971; Brown, 1863; Carruthers, 1984; Diop, 1974; James, 1954; Karenga, 1988; Van Sertima, 1985; Williams, 1976; Woodson, 1933) exploring the nature of African peoples' cultural ways of viewing themselves. From ancient times to the present, African peoples have been noted to perceive themselves from an extended self-identity perspective. The cardinal point in understanding the traditional African conception of self is noted through the belief "I am because we are, and because we are, therefore I am" (Mbiti, 1970;

Nobles, 1976). This essentially means that for African peoples, individual identity is always subsumed under one's group collective identity/consciousness. The conception of the self means that African people express their being (self-concept) in terms of a fundamental interdependence.

The Optimal Extended Self-Esteem Scales were developed from traditional African cultural history, philosophy and values. Akbar (1980), Asante (1980), Baldwin (1976), Karenga (1988), Nobles (1976), and Williams (1981) have presented substantial definitive information on the collective concept of African peoples' self-concept and identity. Africans have more common experiences than differences which are shared

207

throughout the African diaspora (Baldwin, 1981; Karenga, 1988; Williams, 1981). Extended self-esteem and identity can be observed through Africans' collective self activities that have been represented in their cultural practices and psychosocial functioning from ancient to contemporary times.

Rationale and Purpose of the Optimal Extended Self-Esteem Scales

The Optimal Extended Self-Esteem Scales are instruments for assessing the extended self-concept of African Americans' self-racial/cultural identity and values. These instruments evaluate the manner in which Africans in the American context maintain the practice and reverence for the collective self-orientation in identification with the philosophy, traditions and values of their culture. African culture, philosophy and values view the African individual's condition as interdependent with the survival of the group and one with nature (Baldwin, 1976; Carruthers, 1984; Karenga, 1988; Mbiti, 1970; Nobles, 1976). This describes the African individual's philosophy and values as interdependent with the group, a strong kinship bond to cooperate, and an extended corporate community orientation and ties in their survival thrust. African self-identity is defined as interdependent diunitally (I-me) with the group (we) conception (Nichols, 1986). Here the individual has an extended self-concept of his/her being (Nobles, 1976).

The African American Optimal Extended Self-Esteem Scales' purpose is to serve as a culturally-oriented measure for the assessment and diagnosis of extended self-esteem and identity. When the optimal functioning of African American extended self-esteem and identity is exemplified through a high self-rating on the scales' affirmative attributes, the person should manifest optimal African centeredness in extended self-esteem and identity.

Definition of Terms

Extended Self-Esteem/Identity is defined as a person's self-concept yielding interdependence toward oneness of being; feeling oneself as part of all other African people.

In *African Self-Consciousness,* the African person exhibits: (1) awareness of his/her identity, cultural heritage and sees value in the pursuit of knowledge of self; (2) priority value in the recognition of African survival and proactive development; (3) respect for African life and institutions with active perpetuation of all things African; and, (4) a standard of conduct toward all things, peoples, etc., that are "anti-African," and toward all things "non-African" (Baldwin, 1987).

Collective Self describes the African person in their striving to live in connection with family, the community, and the nation as a racial-cultural people.

Diunitally describes something apart and together at the same time; the connection of apparent opposites (Nichols, 1986).

Interdependent means working together as a unit or a member in the group and having co-dependence on each other in survival.

MAAT means order, balance, truth, justice, and righteousness in the highest ethical divine human way: the natural order and social behavior of reciprocity for human beings in the universe.

Psychological/Cultural Misorientation describes believing, behaving and thinking in ways that are socially antithetical to one's African racial-cultural heritage and orientation (or Eurocentric) (Baldwin, 1985).

Nguzo Saba consists of the seven principles of Kwanzaa that relate to African values in the following Kiswahli terms: 1. *Umoja* (unity); 2. Ku–*jichagulia* (self-determination); 3. *Ujima* (collective work and responsibility); 4. *Ujamaa* (cooperative economics); 5. *Nia* (purpose); 6. *Kuumba* (creativity); and, 7. *Imani* (faith) (Karenga, 1989).

Description of the Instruments

Separate scales are developed for Preschool and Primary Pupils (43 items), Children (50 items), Adolescents (50 items) and Adults (60 items). (See Samples 1-4).

Sample 1. The Optimal Extended Self-Esteem Scale for Pre-school and Primary Pupils
(Age Levels 4 to 6)

Administration Booklet

Developed by Seward E. Hamilton Jr. Ph.D.

Name _____	Date of Rating _____
Nick name _____	Date of Birth _____
Sex: Male Female	Teacher's Name _____
Parent(s) name _____	Occupation _____
Education Level(s) _____	Religion _____
Address _____	
Child Development Center _____	Examiner's Name _____

Directions: I want to know some things about you. Listen to my statements and tell what you think about them. Tell me if you believe the statement I said is true about you by saying "*I Do.*" Or tell me if you believe the statement is not true about you by saying "*I Do Not.*" Tell me the answer that you believe to be your answer to all of the statements. (The Teacher or Examiner may allow the child to answer the statements through conversation to gather the answer).

I like myself.	I DO	I DO NOT	IDK
I like being Black.	I DO	I DO NOT	IDK
I like being happy.	I DO	I DO NOT	IDK
I believe that Black people like me.	I DO	I DO NOT	IDK
I like to do the right things.	I DO	I DO NOT	IDK

Sample 2. The Optimal Extended Self-Esteem Scale for Children
(Grades 1- 6)

Directions: Here is a set of statements that tell how a person thinks about himself or herself. Read each statement and decide whether or not it describes how you think about yourself. If it is true or mostly true for you, circle the word "yes" next to the statement. If it is not true for you, circle the word "no." Answer every question as best you can. Do not circle both "yes" and "no" for the same statement. Remember, there are no right or wrong answers. Only you can tell us what you think about yourself.

1. I like being joyful.	YES	NO
2. I like to make up my own games.	YES	NO
3. I like to ask questions.	YES	NO
4. I look good.	YES	NO
5. I like to tell the truth.	YES	NO
6. I like being a quiet person.	YES	NO

Sample 3. The Optimal Extended Self-Esteem Scale for Adolescents
(Grades 7 - 12)

Directions: Here is a set of statements that tell how a person thinks about himself or herself. Read each statement and decide whether or not it describes how you think about yourself. If it is true or mostly true for you, circle the word "True" next to the statement. If it is not true for you, circle the word "False." Answer every question as best you can. Do not circle both "True" and "False" for the same statement. Remember, there are no right or wrong answers. Only you can tell us what you think about yourself.

1. I like being a good person.	True	False
2. I am an honest person.	True	False
3. I am an intelligent person.	True	False
4. I like being a leader in groups.	True	False
5. I like respecting my parents.	True	False
6. I care about my family.	True	False

Sample 4. The Optimal Extended Self-Esteem Scale For Adults
(Ages 18 and Older)

Directions: Here is a set of statements that tell how a person thinks about himself or herself. Read each statement and decide whether or not it describes how you think about yourself. Circle the number that indicates the degree to which you believe each item statement is true. Only circle one answer for each item. Remember, there are no right or wrong answers. Only you can tell us what you think about yourself.

1 Almost Never True (0-20%)	2 Seldom True (21-40%)	3 Occasionally True (41-60%)	4 Frequently True (61-80%)	5 Almost Always True (81-100%)

1. I love being who I am.	1	2	3	4	5
2. I would like to have more books written by authors of my own race.	1	2	3	4	5
3. I believe that people of my race should have leaders from other racial groups in society.	1	2	3	4	5
4. I believe that other people are more intelligent than my people.	1	2	3	4	5

Items on each scale vary based on the age group for the respective developmental level. Each scale has common categories for assessing the central value orientation of the Nguzo Saba (Karenga, 1988) and some principles of African self-consciousness (Baldwin and Bell, 1985). Categories on the scales are labeled and defined in terms of the principles of Nguzo Saba:

1. Umoja (social relationship/interaction);
2. Kujichagulia (self-determination and commitment to tasks);

3. Ujima (extended family relationship/ interaction);
4. Nia (African American cultural con– sciousness/recognition identity);
5. Kuumba (cognitive ability and prob- lem solving perception);
6. Imani (beliefs, faith and practices);
7. Maat (moral ethical values); and,
8. M-Scale (lie scale).

For each scale a diagnostic profile of strengths and weaknesses is developed and intervention-prescriptive activities are provided to encourage culturally centered activities and exercises for promoting optimal extended self-esteem and remediating areas of weakness. When validated, these programs can help counselors, clinical/ school psychologists, parents and teachers en- hance ego and identity development and ex- tended self-esteem.

Validity and Reliability

The scales' content validity has been estab- lished by creating items congruent with African peoples' cultural values and practices in psycho- social development. African scholars have indi- cated essential knowledge of African peoples behavioral, mental and spiritual functioning through their in-depth studies of the literature, experiences of the peoples cultural practices, and understanding of African peoples beingness from ancient to contemporary times (Baldwin, 1981; Ben-Jochannan, 1971; Brown, 1863; Carruthers, 1984; Diop, 1974; James, 1954; Karenga, 1988; Van Sertima, 1985; Williams, 1976; Woodson, 1933). Further, they have provided essential knowledge of the culture, folkways, values, his- tory and philosophy of Black peoples' ways of life. These perspectives by African scholars are viewed as the African cultural centered world- view paradigm.

To date, one empirically based validity and reliability study has been completed. Subjects were 95 males and 95 female regular class 9 - 12 grade students who were enrolled in the Florida A & M University's Developmental Research School. All subjects completed the OESES Ado- lescent Scale and the Rosenberg Self-Esteem Scale (RSES). Cronbach Alpha Coefficient were .82 and .76 for the OESES -A, and the Rosenberg, respectively. Concurrent validity (Pearson Prod- uct Moment Correlation between OESES-A and RSES) was .29, $(p < .001)$. These results show acceptable reliability and some evidence of valid- ity of the OESES-A. Additional validity and reliability studies utilizing OESES-A and the remaining OESES scales are in progress.

References

Akbar, N. (1980). *Community of self.* Tallahassee, FL: Mind Productions and Associates.

Asante, M. K. (1980). *Afrocentricity: The theory of social change.* Buffalo, NY: Amulefi.

Baldwin, J. A. (1976). Black psychology and Black personality: Some issues for consideration. *Black Books Bulletin, 4* (3), 6-11, 65.

Baldwin, J. A. (1981) Notes on an Africentric theory of Black personality. *The Western Journal of Black Studies, 5* (3), 172-179.

Baldwin, J. A., & Bell, Y. R. (1985). The African self-consciousness scale. An africentric personality questionnaire. *The Western Journal of Black Stud- ies, 9* (2),61-68.

Baldwin, J. A. (1987). African psychology and Black personality testing. *The Negro Educational Re- view, 18* (2-3), 56-66.

Ben-Jochannon, Y. (1971). *Africa: Mother of western civilization.* New York: Alkebulan.

Ben-Jochannon, Y. (1978). *Black man of the Nile and his family.* New York: Alkebulan.

Brown, W. W. (1963). *Black man: His antecedents genius and his achievements.* New York: Thomas Hamilton.

Carruthers, J. H. (1984). *Essays in ancient EaYDtain studies.* Los Angeles: University of Sankore Press.

Diop, C. A. (1974). *African origins of civilization.* New York: Lawrence Hill and Co.

James, G. G. M. (1988;1954). *Stolen legacy.* (2nd ed.). San Francisco: Julian Richard.

Karenga, M. R. (1989). *The African-American holiday of Kwanzaa: A celebration of family, community, and culture.* Los Angeles: University of Sankare Press.

Mbiti, J. S. (1970). *African religions and philosophy.* New York: Anchor Books.

Nichols, E. J. (1986). *Teaching mathematics, Volume I: Culture, motivation, history, and classroom management*. Washington, DC: Institute for Independent Education.

Nobles, W. W. (1980). Extended self: Rethinking the Negro self-concept. *Journal of Black Psychology, 2*(2) 15-24.

Van Sertima, I. (1985). *Egypt revisited*. New Brunswick, NJ: Transaction Books.

Williams, C. (1976). *The destruction of Black civilization: Great issues of a race from 4500 B.C. to 2500 A.D.* (Rev. ed.). Chicago, IL: Third World Press.

Williams, R. L. (1981). *The collective Black mind: An Afrocentric theory of Black personality*. St. Louis, MO: Williams and Associates.

Woodson, C. G. (1933). *The miseducation of the Negro*. Washington, DC: Associated.

For additional information, contact:

Seward E. Hamilton, Jr., Ph.D.
Gore Education Complex-Building-C
Room #305
Department of Psychology
Florida A & M University
Tallahassee, FL 32307
Telephone: (904) 599-3014 or 3468
Fax: (904) 561-2540

Part V

Children: Race-Related Test and Measures

Race Awareness and Racial Stereotyping Assessment: Cultural (Racial) Cognition

Margaret Beale Spencer

Abstract

The Racial Cognition Assessment Battery (RCAB) is composed of two subtests that assess the awareness of race as a stable, physically-based human characteristic and a second subtest that assesses children's knowledge of color and racial stereotypes. The former, then, assesses the *awareness* of race and the latter assesses knowledge of stereotypes which are associated with color and race. Although the race awareness subtest uses a sorting format, the measure requires that children offer a reason or explanation for their particular sorting pattern. Race awareness is assumed to be maturationally determined. The measure's rationale implies the use of cognitive schema for making correct placements. The second subtest assesses the child's knowledge of racial and color based stereotypes. Three component tasks make up the color and racial stereotypes subtest and include knowledge of or exposure to (1) color concept connotations, (2) racial attitudes/beliefs, and (3) racial preferences. Because we believe that color concept connotations operate quite differently from racial attitudes/beliefs and preference stereotypes, the subtest obtains discrete measures of each. The measure, although indicative of aspects of psychosocial processes, is *not* a measure of personal identity or self-esteem; it represents group identity processes which are, themselves, influenced by broadening social experiences and indirectly by cognitive maturation.

Introduction

Stereotypic racial attitudes and preference stereotypic response patterns continue to serve an important function for theorizing about Black personality organization by majority group researchers. Only recently has developmentally focused research refined the understanding of racial attitudes, preferences and color-stereotyping behavior for personality functioning for African Americans by integrating the role of social cognitive processes (see Spencer, 1982b, 1985, 1988, 1991; Spencer & Markstrom-Adams, 1990). Parental childrearing efforts serve an important potential

215

function by offering a compensatory cultural emphasis given the prevalence of Eurocentric imagery; recent research demonstrates consistent and salient relationships between parenting perceptions, beliefs and strategies and children's cultural cognition (see Spencer, 1983; Spencer, 1990; Spencer, Swanson, & Glymph, in press).

Research findings for preschool and early school age youth suggests that cultural cognition variables (i.e., race awareness and Eurocentric stereotypes) represent important factors for more positive achievement outcomes and for stress reactivity(see Spencer, 1986a; Spencer, Cunningham, & Swanson, 1995; Spencer, Dobbs & Swanson, 1988; Spencer, Kim, & Marshall, 1987; Swanson & Spencer, 1991). More recent research integrates cognitive processes with stereotypic response patterns; cultural cognition assessment allows a discrete examination of the role of race awareness, and cultural stereotypes: color connotations, racial attitudes, and racial preferences (Spencer & Markstrom-Adams, 1990).

From this more contemporary perspective, race awareness is conceptualized as a developmental phenomenon that, like gender awareness, obtains a ceiling as a consequence of social knowledge and social experiences. That is, given a specific level of experience in the differentiation of racial groups, no further exposure increases children's differentiation of race as a social-physical category.

Racial and color stereotyping are not developmental phenomena; they merely reflect an individual's exposure to a specific type of knowledge: stereotypes concerning color and racial concepts. The separation of color concept stereotyping from racial attitudes and preferences stereotyping is important since each does not necessarily show a similar or consistent pattern over time.

The purpose of the racial cognition measure differs by component or subtest. First, the purpose of the *race awareness measure* is for assessing the child's awareness of race as a stable social-physical attribute or characteristic of an individual. The second subtest, for assessing stereotyping, measures exposure to or *knowledge of color* (White versus Black) *and racial social*

stereotyping and finally an assessment of racial preferences. The purpose of the three component tasks of the color and racial stereotyping subtest is to assess the child's color connotations and knowledge of stereotypic responses for racial attitudes and racial preferences; accordingly, the child's evaluative judgments concerning Black people and their preferences for social relationships as a function of racial group membership are assessed.

Measure Description

I. The Race Awareness Subtest

The measure has been used in several studies conducted in both the North and the South with Black preschool through middle-childhood youth ages 3 through 12 (see Spencer, 1976, 1982b, 1984, 1985). Scoring of the original research protocol (Spencer, 1976) was modified in subsequent studies for obtaining a race awareness score, gender awareness score and cognitive functioning score. The instructions and stimuli remained the same in the modification; the modified scoring technique reflects a more differentiating method of scoring the sorting patterns. The original and modified scoring techniques are significantly correlated ($p < .0001$).

For this subtest of the racial cognition measure, children are required to sort four paper doll cut-outs of Black and White, male and female children into groups that are identified with four pictures; the four pictures are presented to the children as pairs. The attribute that distinguishes the first pair of pictures presented is gender. That is, one picture of this first pair shows two groups of *female* children–one Caucasian group and one African American group. The second picture of the pair contains two groups of *male* children– one Caucasian group and one African American group. Thus, the children have the option of not only sorting by gender between pictures, but also the option of categorizing stimuli by race *within* the all female pictures or within the all male pictures. Therefore, a double dimension placement is possible: race placement within gender categorization.

The same categorization option applies to the second pair of picture stimuli presented. For this second case, the distinguishing characteristic between the pair of pictures is race. However, after sorting the four paper doll cut-outs between pictures, each subject has the option of further categorizing *within* each picture by sex since each picture shows two groups of children. That is, within the Caucasian children picture grouping there is a group of White males and a group of White female children. In the African American grouping of children, there is a group of Black females and a group of Black males. Thus, again, a double dimension placement (i.e., sex placement within racial stimuli categorization) is possible. Each child is requested to offer a reason for the particular sorting pattern which results in three possible scores for: (1) race awareness; (2) gender awareness; and, (3) cognitive awareness.

Race awareness score: indicates a correct placement by race (either alone or race and sex) and the child's ability to explain with accuracy the reasons for placement patterns.

Gender awareness score: represents a correct placement by sex (either by sex alone or sex and race) and the child's ability to explain with accuracy his or her response.

Cognitive functioning score: suggests the child's skill in sorting two dimensionally (i.e., sex and race as opposed to a one-dimensional (i.e., sex or race) pattern.

II. Color Connotations and Racial (Eurocentric) Attitude/Preference Subtest

The two component tasks of the second subtest assess Eurocentric or White-biased color connotations or racial attitudes/preferences. Scores range from Afrocentric response patterns (low scores) to Eurocentric response rates (high scores). This picture-card procedure was originally designed by Williams and Roberson (1967) and was revised and modified to obtain measures of color connotations about the colors White and Black

and for ascertaining racial attitudes and preferences for "light-skinned" (European or Caucasian) vs. "dark-skinned" (African American) persons. The subtests have been used with Black and White preschoolers in the Midwest, with Black preschoolers in the North and with Black preschool and primary school children in the South (see Spencer, 1970, 1976, 1982a, 1982b, 1983, 1985, 1984; Spencer, in press; Spencer & Horowitz, 1973). See Spencer (1990) and Spencer and Markstrom-Adams (1990) for a review.

Description: Two sets of picture stimulus materials are used. The first set is used to assess color connotations and is a modification of the revised picture-meaning procedure (Williams & Edwards, 1969); it is used for determining the child's connotative meanings associated with the colors Black and White. On each of six picture cards are drawings of two identical animals which differ only by color: one animal is Black and the other is White.

The second set of picture cards was originally designed by Williams and Roberson (1967) and was revised and used to provide a measure of attitude or preference toward "dark-skinned" (Black) persons and "light-skinned" (White) persons. In this set, each stimulus picture shows two children in full-length drawings; each child is engaged in an identical play context. Each brightly colored drawing is identical except for hair (texture) and skin color (White children are depicted as having pinkish-tan skin, while Black children are medium-dark brown). Thus, each of the eight cards contains a Black child and a White child. Both children depicted are of the same sex.

In both sets of stimulus materials (i.e., color connotation assessment and racial attitude/preference subtasks), the order of presentation is varied but preset in order to control for possible left-right response biases.

For both the six cards of the color connotations task and the racial attitudes/preference task, stories accompany each card. For color connotations, the story might state: "Here are two ducks. Everyone says that one duck is ugly. Which is the ugly duck?" For the racial attitude/preference component task, a story that elicits attitudinal

Figure 1.

responses might state: "Here are two girls. Everyone thinks that one girl is pretty. Which is the pretty girl?"

For obtaining an indication of each child's racial preference, a story might state: "Here are two boys. Everyone thinks that one would make a nice playmate. Who would you choose to play with?" Similar stories are included, using the same racial attitude stimuli for classmate, study mate, and friend. Accordingly, separate scores for Eurocentric racial attitudes, racial preferences and color connotations are generated. The Spearman-Brown correlation coefficient is 0.80 for this subtest.

Studies conducted with this measure to date for preschoolers through 12 year olds indicate a consistent Eurocentric pattern for *color connotations*. For African American and Caucasian preschool children, the Eurocentric response pattern is consistent with the children's egocentric developmental stage. However, children's Eurocentric pattern becomes more neutral of Afrocentric with increasing age and social experiences (see Spencer, 1985, 1988; Spencer & Dornbusch, 1990; Spencer & Markstrom-Adams, 1990 for a review of the studies to-date).

The race awareness task and components of the racial stereotypes task are appropriate for children between 3 and 12 years of both lower- or middle-socioeconomic status families. Administration time for the race awareness subtask is approximately 8 minutes: it must be *individually* administered. For older children (i.e., 10-to-12 year olds) the racial stereotyping subtask may be administered in small groups. Administration time for the second subtask is approximately 10 to 12 minutes[1].

Reliability. The Spearman-Brown split-half reliability coefficient for the racial stereotyping subtask is 0.81. Test-retest reliability for the race awareness subtask measure is 0.65. For young children, no significant and persistent correlation coefficients are apparent between cultural (racial) stereotyping and personal identity or self-esteem.

Note

1. A new version of this measure which is *not* a forced–choice procedure is currently being piloted. It includes other ethnic groups in addition

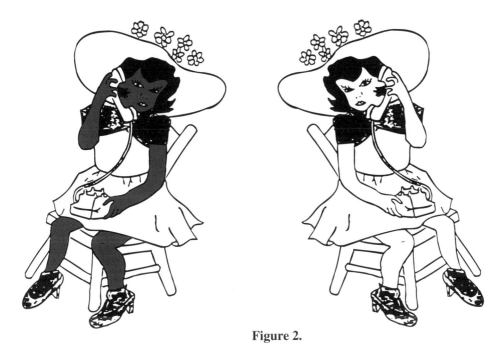

Figure 2.

to African American preschoolers and early school-age youngsters.

References

Spencer, M. B. (1970). *The effects of systematic social (puppet) and token reinforcement on the modification of racial and color concept attitudes in preschool aged children.* Unpublished master's thesis, University of Kansas, Lawrence.

Spencer, M. B. (1976). The social-cognitive and personality development of the Black preschool child: An exploratory study of developmental process. University of Chicago, *Dissertation Abstracts International, 38.*

Spencer, M. B. (1982a). Personal and group identity of Black children: An alternative synthesis. *Genetic Psychology Monographs, 103,* 59-84.

Spencer, M. B. (1982b). Preschool children's social cognition and cultural cognition: A cognitive developmental interpretation of race dissonance findings. *Journal of Psychology, 112,* 275-286.

Spencer, M. B. (1983). Children's cultural values and parental childrearing strategies. *Developmental Review, 3,* 351-370.

Spencer, M. B. (1984) Black children's race awareness, racial attitudes and self concept: A reinterpretation. *Journal of Child Psychology and Psychiatry, 25*(3), 433-441.

Spencer, M. B. (1985). Cultural cognition and social cognition as identity factors in Black children's personal-social growth. In M. B. Spencer, G. K. Brookins, & W. R. Allen (Eds.), *Beginnings: The social and affective development of Black children* (pp. 215-230). Hillsdale, NJ: Erlbaum.

Spencer, M. B. (1986a). Risk and resilience: How Black children cope with stress. *Social Science, 71*(1), 22-26.

Spencer, M. B. (1990). Parental values transmission: Implications for Black child development. In J. Steward & H. Cheatham (Eds.), *Interdisciplinary perspectives on Black families* (pp. 111-130). New Brunswick, NJ: Transactions.

Spencer, M. B., Dobbs, B., & Swanson, D. (1988). Afro-American adolescents: Adaptational processes and socioeconomic diversity in behavioral outcomes. *Journal of Adolescence, 11,* 117-137.

Spencer, M. B., & Horowitz, F. D. (1973). Racial attitudes and color concept-attitude modification in Black and Caucasian preschool children. *Developmental Psychology, 9,* 246-254.

Spencer, M. B., Kim, S., & Marshall, S. (1987). Double stratification and psychological risk: Adaptational processes and school experiences of Black children. *Journal of Negro Education, 56*(1), 77-86.

Spencer, M. B., & Markstrom-Adams. (1990). Identity processes among racial and ethnic minority children in America. *Child Development, 61*(2), 290-310.

Williams, J. E., & Edwards, C. D. (1969). An exploratory study of the modification of color and racial concept attitudes in preschool children. *Child Development, 40,* 737-750.

Williams, J. E., & Roberson, J. K. (1967). A method for assessing racial attitudes in preschool children. *Educational and Psychological Measurement, 27,* 671-689.

For additional information, contact:

Margaret Beale Spencer, Ph. D.
Graduate School of Education
University of Pennsylvania
3700 Walnut St.
Philadelphia, PA 19104-6216

The Development of the Children's Racial Attitude and Preference Test

Maxine L. Clark[1]

Abstract

The Children's Racial Attitude and Preference Test was constructed to measure three variables: preference for own race, attitudes about own race, and perception of being a member of that race. The test is composed of thirteen items. The first six items assess racial preference, the next six items assess racial attitudes, and the last item determines the child's racial self-perception (whether the child could identify his/her racial group membership). The racial attitude items include three positive and three negative attributes. Each question is accompanied by a Black and White illustration displaying a Black and White person similar except for skin color, facial dimensions, and hair type. Zipitone was used to shade the skin of the Black figures. The scale was designed as a group test for use with children in grades 3 through 6. It could possibly be used with younger children (grades 1, 2) if it is individually administered. Three scores are calculated from the Children's Racial Attitude and Preference Test. The racial preference and racial attitude subscales both have scores that can range from 0 to 12; high scores indicate Black preferences or positive own-race attitudes. Racial self-perception was scored as correct if the child was able to select the stimulus figure that represented his/her racial group. The test was pretested on 210 Black children in grades 3 through 6 (88 males, 122 females) attending integrated or desegregated schools. The overall Cronbach's alpha for the racial preference subscale was 0.57 and 0.79 for the racial attitude subscale. The split-half reliability coefficients were 0.57 for the racial preference subscale and 0.77 for the racial attitude subscale. The two subscales were significantly correlated, $(r = 0.43, < .001)$, but were clearly measuring different concepts. A factor analysis was performed on the racial preference and racial attitude items. All of the racial attitude items loaded on Factor I and five of the six racial preference items loaded on Factor II. All children in the present study identified their racial group membership correctly (racial self-perception).

For close to 50 years there have been numerous attempts to measure the racial preferences and racial attitudes of young children. In one widely-cited study, Kenneth and Mamie Clark developed a doll test for the purpose of assessing the racial identification and racial preferences of children (Clark & Clark, 1947). The doll technique required that a child be shown four dolls (Black male, Black female, White male, White female). They were then asked four identification questions (e.g., Give me the doll that looks like a White child) and four racial preference questions (e.g., Give me the doll you would like to play with; Give me the doll that is a nice doll). Preference for one racial group was interpreted as a rejection of the other group. There have been many modifications of this basic technique (for review, see Wylie, 1979).

There are a number of problems with using the doll technique and similar measures to assess racial preferences. The technique uses a forced-choice format and thus has no response option for the child who has no preference. Twenty-four percent of the Black children tested by Clark and Clark (1947) said "I don't know" or did not respond to the request by the experimenter to "Give me the doll that looks bad." Therefore, "no preference" should be a valid response option. Another limitation of the doll technique is that it provides too few questions to assess racial preferences. Only one of the questions assumed to assess racial preference is truly a preference question. This question, "Give me the doll that you like to play with" assesses an expressed liking for one's racial group over others. The remaining three questions, "Give me the doll that is a nice doll...looks bad...is a nice color," assess racial attitudes and measure positive and negative evaluations of racial groups.

Racial attitudes have been more accurately measured by the Preschool Racial Attitude Measure (PRAM II) (Williams, Best, Boswell, Mattson, & Graves, 1975). The PRAM II presents evaluative statements with photographs of two stimulus figures. The subject must select the stimulus figure that is best described by each statement. The illustrated people vary by skin color only with one light and one dark-skinned stimulus figure for each of the statements. The test is scored by counting the number of light-skinned choices. A high score indicates a pro-White bias whereas a low score is interpreted as a pro-Black bias.

The PRAM II uses the forced-choice format and thus no option is available for children who do not think that an attribute is more characteristic of one of the stimulus figures than the other. Another limitation of the PRAM II is that it assesses attitudes toward light and dark skin. The dark-skinned figures have the same features as the White stimulus figures and thus may not be perceived as a representation of Black Americans. The dark-skinned figure could represent any brown-skinned ethnic group with straight black hair. Finally, attitudes about Blacks and attitudes about Whites are linked in this type of measure. The PRAM II and the Doll Test do not allow for independent assessment of preference for or attitudes toward Blacks and toward Whites. Instead, a preference for or positive evaluation toward one ethnic group is interpreted to mean a rejection or negative evaluation of the other ethnic group. This methodological error of confounding own-group with other-group racial evaluations has been noted by Aboud and Skerry (1984).

The weaknesses in the current racial attitude and racial preference techniques resulted in a need for a measure that could yield independent scores for racial attitudes and racial preferences. It also seemed desirable to develop an instrument that gave children an option to say "I don't know" or "I don't have a preference." In addition, it seemed necessary to make sure that the stimulus pictures possessed features that could distinguish them as either Black or White Americans. Finally, because most of the previous tests were developed to be given individually, it appeared advantageous to have a test that could be administered in a group setting. The Children's Racial Attitude and Preference Test was developed to include these features.

Table 1. Individual Items for the Racial Preference and Racial Attitude Subscales

Racial Preference
1. Which man would you like to help carry his groceries?[1]
2. Which baker would you like to work for?
3. If you were lost, which policeman would you like to walk you home?
4. If your mother was going to adopt a baby, which baby would you like her to adopt?
5. If you were having a party at your house and inviting all of your friends, which child would you invite to your party?
6. Which school teacher would you like to invite to dinner?

Racial Attitude
7. Which boy do you think picks on other kids?
8. Which lady is mean?
9. Which girl do you think plays fair?
10. Which boy do you think has many friends?
11. Which girl do you think is lazy?
12. Which boy do you think helps other children?

Racial Self-Perception
13. Put a check by the child that looks most like your racial group.

Note. [1] These items have been shortened for ease of presentation.

Method

Subjects

The subjects were 210 Black children (88 males, 122 females) in grades three through six. The children attended eight different public schools in two small midwestern cities with a Black population of 12% and 14%. Three schools were integrated because of their location in racially heterogeneous neighborhoods and the remaining six were desegregated with the majority of Black students bused to schools in predominantly White areas. Only 26% of the Black children lived in neighborhoods with a mean neighborhood income level above $10,000. The majority lived in neighborhoods with mean incomes from $6,000 to $10,000 (47%). In addition, 70% of these children lived in neighborhoods with more than 75% Black population and 26% lived in predominantly White neighborhoods (less than 25% Black population).

Scale Construction

The Children's Racial Attitude and Preference Test was constructed to measure three variables: preference for own race, attitudes about own race and perception of being a member of that race. The test was composed of 13 items (see Table 1). The first 6 items assessed racial preference, the next 6 assessed racial attitudes, and the last item determined the child's racial self-perception (whether the child could identify his/her racial group membership). The racial attitude items included three positive and three negative attributes. Each question was accompanied by a Black and White illustration displaying a Black and White person similar except for skin color, facial dimensions, and hair type (see Figure 1). Zipitone was used to shade the skin of the Black figures. The scale was designed as a group test for use with children in grades 3 through 6. It could possibly be used with younger children (grades 1, 2) if it is individually administered.

Figure 1. Picture to accompany Item 9. "Which one of these girls always plays fair?" Illustrated by Al Mitchell/Umbasi.

Procedure

The Black children who participated in this study were part of a larger study to assess the relationship between racial identity and self identity (Clark, 1982). The children were taken from their classroom and assembled in a testing room by two Black female experimenters. The groups varied in size from 10 to 20 children. The children were given several measures. The last measure was an illustrated booklet for the Children's Racial Attitude and Preference Test. They were instructed to fill in the demographic information on the front page. They were then asked to turn to page one and listen while the following instructions were read:

I will read some short stories to you about the people on each page of your answer booklet. Listen while I read each story. Then choose one of the people in your booklet by putting a check by the person of your choice. If for some reason you cannot decide which person you want to choose, you should then put your check mark in the circle beside the words "don't know" at the bottom of the page. Be careful that you make only one check mark on each page.

The experimenter then began by reading the 13 short captions allowing the children several minutes to make their choices. The test took 10 to 15 minutes to administer. All data were collected during the 1975-1976 school year.

Scoring

Three scores were calculated from the Children's Racial Attitude and Preference Test. For the preference items (1-6) two points were given for each Black choice, one point for each don't know choice and no points for White choices. The racial preference score could range from 0 to 12 with high scores indicating Black preferences

Table 2. Item-Total Correlations and Alphas for Racial Attitude and Racial Preference Subscales

Subscale		Item-Total Correlation	Alpha if Deleted
Racial Preference			
1.	Grocer	.33	.51
2.	Baker	.19	.58
3.	Policeman	.41	.47
4.	Baby	.12	.59
5.	Child	.40	.47
6.	Teacher	.41	.47
Cronbach Alpha			.57
Racial Attitude			
7.	Pick on others	.54	.76
8.	Mean lady	.40	.79
9.	Play fair	.67	.72
10.	Have friends	.46	.78
11.	Lazy	.50	.77
12.	Help others	.69	.72
Cronbach Alpha			.79

(and low scores indicating non-Black preferences). The racial attitude items consisted of three positive (items 9, 10, 12) and three negative (items 7, 8, 11) attributes. Two points were given if a Black choice was made for a positive attribute or a White choice was made for a negative attribute. One point was given for don't know answers. No points were given if a Black choice was made for a negative attribute or a White choice for a positive attribute. These points were totaled to yield a racial attitude score ranging from 0 to 12; high scores indicated positive own-race attitudes and low scores indicated negative own-race attitudes. Racial self-perception (item 13) was scored by giving one point for a Black choice (correct racial identification) and no point for a White choice (incorrect racial identification).

Results

Cronbach Alphas were computed for the racial attitude and racial preference subscales.

Table 2 presents the item-total correlations for each item in each subscale and the alphas for the subscales. The overall alpha for the racial preference subscale was 0.57 and 0.79 for the racial attitude subscale. The split-half reliability coefficients were 0.57 for the racial preference subscale and 0.77 for the racial attitude subscale.

The two subscales were significantly correlated, ($r = 0.43$, $p < .001$), but were clearly measuring different concepts. A factor analysis was performed on the racial preference and racial attitude items (see Table 3). All of the racial attitude items loaded on Factor I and five of the six racial preference items loaded on Factor II. Item 2 (Which baker would you like to work for?) was not significantly loaded on either factor. Item 10 (Which boy has many friends?) loaded almost equally on both factors.

The means and standard deviations for the racial preference and racial attitude subscales are presented in Table 4 for the total sample and by sex and grade level. Separate 2 (Sex) x 2 (Grade)

Table 3. Varimax Factor Loadings for Racial Attitude and Racial Preference Items

Items		Factor Loadings	
		Factor 1	Factor 2
9.	Play fair	.77	
7.	Pick on others	.74	
12.	Help others	.74	.31
11.	Lazy	.63	
8.	Mean lady	.63	
10.	Have friends	.50	.44
2.	Baker	—	—
5.	Child		.70
1.	Grocer		.59
3.	Policeman	.37	.58
6.	Teacher		.56
4.	Baby		.46
	Percentage of Variance	31%	12%

ANOVAS were calculated for the two subscales. There was a significant sex effect on the racial preference subscale, $F(1, 206) = 5.17, p < .02$: the males made more Black choices than the females. In addition, there was a significant grade effect, $F(1, 206) = 10.74, p < .001$: the third and fourth graders made more Black choices than the fifth and sixth graders. There was a significant grade effect on the racial attitude subscale, $F(1, 206) = 4.11, p < .04$. The younger children had more positive own-race attitudes than the older children. The fifth and sixth graders had lower scores on both subscales than the third and fourth grader because the older children used the "don't know" response category more frequently than the younger children. The older children were not making more White preference choices than the younger children.

Additional ANOVAS were performed to determine if the racial preference and racial attitude scores varied according to either the mean income and the proportion of Blacks in the neighborhood where each child lived. No significant differences were found.

The responses to each racial attitude and racial preference item are presented in Table 5.

The majority of the children made Black choices for each of the preference items. More than half of the children made Black choices for the positive racial attitude questions (e.g., play fair, have friends, and help others). More White choices than Black were made for the negative racial attitude items (e.g., mean lady, lazy). When asked which child picks on other children, almost equal numbers of Black and White choices were made.

The last item in the Children's Racial Attitude and Preference Test was designed to determine if each child knew their own racial group membership (racial self-perception). All of the children in the present study identified their racial group membership correctly.

Discussion

The results of this study provide some support for the reliability of the Children's Racial Attitude and Preference Test. The racial attitude subscale appears to have better reliability than the racial preference subscale. The split-half reliability of 0.77 for the racial attitude subscale is very similar to the 0.79 to 0.88 range of split-half reliabilities reported for children in kindergarten

Table 4. Means and Standard Deviations for Racial Attitude and Racial Preference Subscales

Subscale	Sex		Grade		
	Male	Females	3-4	5-6	Total
Racial Preference					
Mean	10.47	9.93	10.66	9.83	10.16
SD	1.63	2.19	1.77	2.06	1.99
Racial Attitude					
Mean	8.43	8.08	8.77	7.87	8.23
SD	3.02	3.48	3.41	3.18	3.29
N	88	122	83	127	210

through the third grades on the Preschool Racial Attitude Measure II (Williams & Morland, 1976). Reliability data have not been reported for any of the commonly used racial preference measures; thus, there is no way to determine if the reliability for the racial preference subscale is within the range of reliabilities for other racial preference measures.

The Children's Racial Attitude and Preference Test has an acceptable level of internal consistency. Nevertheless, the items in the racial attitude subscale appear to be more highly correlated than those comprising the racial preference subscale. Further support for the internal structure of the test comes from the factor analysis. According to these findings, two distinctive sub-

Table 5. Responses to Subscale Items, in Percents

		Responses		
		Black	Don't Know	White
Racial Preference				
1.	Grocer	79	16	5
2.	Baker	77	13	10
3.	Policeman	77	16	7
4.	Baby	85	8	7
5.	Child	66	29	6
6.	Teacher	74	20	6
Racial Attitude				
7.	Pick on others	39	18	43
8.	Mean lady	17	24	59
9.	Play fair	57	21	22
10.	Have friends	67	21	11
11.	Lazy	14	23	63
12.	Help others	56	26	18

Note. Chi-squares calculated for each item were significant at $p < .001$.

scales exist. All of the six racial attitude items clustered around Factor I and five of the six racial preference items clustered around Factor II. Only one item, "Which baker would you like to work for?" was not loaded on either factor and thus could be dropped from the scale or replaced.

Early research reported that the majority of Black children made White doll choices and thus preferred Whites over Blacks (e.g., Clark & Clark, 1947; Stevenson & Stewart, 1958). More recent reviews of racial preference research have provided contrary results. Black children either make Black preference choices or exhibit no racial preferences when given an opportunity to make a preference choice between a Black and a White stimulus figure (Aboud & Skerry, 1984; Banks, 1976). Black children also evaluate Blacks more positively than Whites or express no difference in their evaluation of the two ethnic groups (Aboud & Skerry, 1984). The findings from the present study are consistent with these more recent findings.

The younger children (third and fourth graders) had higher racial preference and racial attitude scores than the older children (fifth and sixth graders). The older children were less ethnocentric than the younger children but not because the former preferred Whites or had more positive attitudes about Whites than Blacks. The older children were more likely than the younger children to avoid expressing a racial preference by picking the "don't know" category. It is for this reason that forced-choice measures may not accurately assess racial preferences or racial attitudes. Hraba (1974) has shown that when these techniques are used (e.g., Doll Test), children do not consistently choose one ethnic group over the other. Instead, they change their preference choices "to express a liking for both races" (p. 527). The forced-choice technique was originally developed to control social desirability, which is the tendency to choose socially desirable response alternatives (Anastasi, 1982). Nevertheless, when used with racial preference and racial attitude measures the technique may not inhibit social desirability and may encourage other undesirable response sets. Any measure that gives a child the option of indicating "no preference" appears to offer a more accurate assessment of racial preferences or racial attitudes than tests with forced-choice formats.

The grade level differences on the racial preference and racial attitude subscales support some developmental theories of racial attitude formation which suggest that as age increases children acquire the ability to evaluate individuals based on a person's disposition and not merely their group membership (Aboud & Skerry, 1984; Katz, 1976). As children reach pre-adolescence, we might expect them to become less ethnocentric, especially those who have positive interracial contacts.

Conclusion

The present study has focused on establishing the reliability of the Children's Racial Attitude and Preference Test. However, studies are needed to establish the validity of this measure. Several modifications seem necessary in order to improve the present test. The illustrations should be updated and the Black and White figures should be counterbalanced on each consecutive page, and it may be advantageous to increase the number of questions in each subscale. In the future, the developers of racial preference and racial attitude scales must do more to establish the reliability and validity of their instruments. In addition, researchers must be careful to treat racial attitudes and racial preferences as separate variables. Finally, a preference for one racial group should not be interpreted as a dislike for other racial groups. It is possible to have differential levels of liking for people from various racial/ethnic groups and not dislike any of these groups. Future racial preference measures should be designed to assess this pattern.

Note

1. A portion of the data presented in this article is based on a doctoral dissertation submitted to the University of Illinois. Champaign-Urbana. This research was reported (in part) by U.S. Public Health Service Grant No. HD-00244 from the National Institutes of Child Health and

Human Development. The author would like to thank Al Mitchell/Umbasi for providing illustrations for the measure.

References

Aboud, F., & Skerry, S. (1984). The development of ethnic attitudes. *Journal of Cross-Cultural Psychology, 15,* 3-34.

Anastasi, A. (1982). *Psychological testing* (5th ed.). New York: MacMillan.

Banks, W. (1976). White preference in Blacks:: A paradigm in search of a phenomenon. *Psychological Bulletin, 83,* 1179-1186.

Clark, K., & Clark, M. (1947). Racial identification and preference in Negro children. In T. Newcomb & E. Hartley (Eds.), *Readings in social psychology* (pp. 602-611). New York: Holt, Rinehart & Winston.

Clark, M. (1982). Racial group concept and self-esteem in Black children. *Journal of Black Psychology, 8,* 75-88.

Hraba, J. (1972). The doll technique: A measure of racial ethnocentrism? *Social Forces, 50,* 522-527.

Katz, P. (1976). The acquisition of racial attitudes in children. In P. Katz (Ed.), *Towards the elimination of racism* (pp. 125-154). New York: Pergamon Press.

Stevenson, H., & Stewart, E. (1958). A developmental study of racial awareness in young children. *Child Development, 29,* 399-409.

Williams, J., Best, D., Boswell, D., Mattson, L., & Graves, D. (1975). Preschool Racial Attitude Measure II. *Educational Psychological Measurement, 35,* 3-18.

Williams, J., & Moreland, J. (1976). *Race, color, and the young child.* Chapel Hill: University of North Carolina Press.

Wylie, R. (1979). *The self-concept, Vol. 2: Theory and research on selected topics.* Lincoln: University of Nebraska Press.

The Perceived Racial Stress and Coping Apperception Test

Deborah J. Johnson

Abstract

The PRSCAT is a projective test designed to elicit child and adult conceptualizations of race-related stressors and the racial coping strategies available to cope with those stressors. The PRSCAT consists of five pictures. Card 1 depicts an African American boy in a White classroom. Card #2 depicts an African American girl and an angry White woman. Card #3 depicts a Black man in an office with a Black woman and two African American children. Card #4 depicts a tug-of-war game in which an African American and White team are competing against one another. Card 4 depicts Black children engaged in play on a playground. The respondent is shown each picture and asked to tell a story about it. For the first four pictures, the examiner points to the African American child in the picture and asks the respondent to tell a story about the picture. The story should have a beginning , a middle, and an end (to determine race-related stress). The examiner then asks the respondent how the child in the picture feels (further exploration of race-related stress) and then proceeds to ask what (s)he is going to do (racial coping strategies). For the fifth picture the respondent need only tell a story about it. Responses are coded from 0 to 4 depending on the intensity of the racial conflict expressed. The time required to administer this measure is approximately 10–15 minutes. Interrater reliability coefficients for racial conflict ratings and racial coping stategies were .83 and .75, respectively.

Introduction

The problem of instrumentation and Black populations has somewhat inhibited the development of empirically based knowledge among Black social scientists. It impedes production of these works in at least two ways: a) culturally inappropriate or insensitive instruments may be difficult to interpret or irrelevant to the context and realities of the population; and, b) agenda setting (development of central themes or research questions, hypothesis testing issues) in research is

231

restricted by the availability and utility of appropriate measures. These critical issues are no less prevalent among researchers contributing to the expanding empirical and theoretical base of Black psychology. Recently, researchers' interests have encompassed the study of the race-related socialization of Black children. This paper describes the rationale and instrumentation of one measure, the Perceived Racial Stress and Coping Apperception Test (PRSCAT), which contributes to the alleviation of problems in the study of race-related socialization of Black children.

Many studies of racial socialization have in common the goal of identifying parental racial socialization strategies but differ in their notion of which child outcomes to emphasize. Much has been learned through the variations studied. Peters and Massey (1983) observed the indirect effects of racial stress experienced by Black parents on the behavior of their 12–26 month old children. Two studies (Bowman & Howard, 1985; Thornton, Chatters, Taylor, & Allen, 1990) identified the race-related socialization orientations of Black parents through the recall of Black youth. Bowman and Howard (1985) determined that certain of these orientations were related to important aspects of school achievement among these youth. Spencer (1983) found that specific racial socialization strategies of Black parents correspond to racial preference patterns of young children. Finally, Holliday, Hennings, and Johnson (1992) and McAdoo (1982a) found that parental beliefs about race-related socialization of their children were linked to child functioning, responsibility, and future vulnerability.

Yet, despite these variations, within this area of inquiry empiricists have been limited with regard to the child outcomes they could focus on by the lack of appropriate instrumentation, particularly for children. Child outcomes focused on in the previously mentioned studies reflect the researchers' desires to understand something about how parental racial socialization strategies ultimately influence the competencies in children, their developing world-view(s), and issues of social mobility within Black communities. However, investigators in this area have been forced to make a critical conceptual and empirical leap by

overemphasizing child outcomes. Perhaps as a consequence of the aforementioned restraints in instrumentation, considerably less time has been devoted to the study of process. Studying race-related strategy development among children begins to touch upon process. Typically, behaviors of children in varying contexts (e. g., integrated settings, schools, stressed family circumstances) and parental perspectives on rearing Black children have been associated with other aspects of the child's personality or "success" outcomes (usually achievement). With the exception of the Spencer (1982) study, racial socialization strategies and goals of parents have not previously been linked to development in their children. The complexity of personality variables associated with skills and racial attitudes useful in school achievement and toward upward social mobility have been important in understanding the experiences of Black children and their families, but appear to be a sophisticated second, not first, step. Simply stated, previously there has been attention given to the important assessment of outcomes and consequences of both excellent and poor race-related socialization. This paper describes one measure which has been and can be utilized to fill this gap by focusing on the perception of racial conflict and the articulation of racial coping strategies.

Presentation and method have been particular problems facing instrumentation that addresses racial coping in children of elementary school age. Multiple methods were favored in this instance. The author has initiated the development of two such methods, the Racial Stories Task (Johnson, 1988) which is described elsewhere, and the Perceived Racial Stress and Coping Apperception Test (PRSCAT), a projective test which is described in this chapter.

The projective technique has been used successfully in getting children to articulate various aspects of their intrapsychic states as well as solutions to problem states. The Thematic Apperception Test (TAT) (Bellak, 1986) is one such test that challenges respondents with a variety of themes to which they respond. The Thematic Apperception Test for Urban Hispanic Children (TEMAS) (Malgady, Constantino, & Rogler, 1984) also has multiple themes. TEMAS provides Hispanic children with stimuli which include culturally relevant settings and non-White characters. When TEMAS was used, Hispanic children were likely to articulate more elaborate responses as compared with similar themes on the TAT. The Separation-Attachment Apperception Test (SAAT) (Savage, 1979) is a projective test used to identify separation anxiety in Black children of incarcerated mothers. The SAAT used Black characters exclusively and focused on the one theme of separation anxiety.

The race-related socialization of children is an issue having particular importance for Black families (Carew, 1980; Comer, 1985). Traditional methods employed to investigate this issue have begun the process; however, new methods are required to further these endeavors. The PRSCAT, while designed for use with children, is appropriate for adults as well. The question of racial socialization, addressed in the next section, required the development of new measure(s) using proven techniques.

Background

The social and economic ecologies of Black Americans have been defined as contexts of mundane extreme environmental stress (MEES) (Pierce, 1975) to which Blacks are particularly vulnerable. It is therefore reasonable to argue that the ecology of the Black child is one pervaded by these same forces. Despite their vulnerability to ecological stressors related to race (Dohrenwend, 1973; Dressler, 1985; McAdoo, 1982), Black families of various economic strata and their children develop strategies to cope with the exigencies of racism and discrimination.

Pierce's (1975) notion of MEES provided for the sustained effects of both chronic and mundane life stressors, or alternatively overt and subtle stressors. This concept is central to the study of racial coping strategies. Furthermore, racial coping skills must be understood given the particular nature of a child or family's vulnerability (Garmezy & Rutter, 1983; Lazarus & Folkman, 1984; Murphy & Moriarty, 1974) to racial stress and overall stress, and their crises-meeting resources (Hill, 1982).

Whether a child employs racial coping strategies in response to an event is dependent upon that child's perception of the event as race-related in his or her operationalized definition. It is therefore important to consider whether the child is capable of perceiving racial differences. The literature on racial awareness in young children assures us that color differences are detectable by children as young as three years of age (Clark & Clark, 1939; Goodman, 1964; Horowitz, 1939; Williams, Best, Boswell, Mattson & Graves, 1975). Moreover, at the ages of four and five years old Black children have been shown to have a rudimentary understanding of the concept of race (Alejandro-Wright, 1985; Clark & Clark, 1939; Goodman, 1964; Johnson, 1983; Semaj, 1980; Spencer, 1982).

This chapter focuses on the extent to which elementary school aged Black children perceive racial stress in response to stimuli on a projective test and their ability to articulate racial coping strategies to cope with it. Children's use of racial coping strategies (RCSs) was explored. It was expected that RCSs would vary by school type. The importance of the school as a major socializing agent can be demonstrated through evidence of the influences the varying school philosophies and ecologies on children's racial coping.

Methods and Procedures

Subjects

Forty-one elementary school children between the ages of 5 and 14 years old participated in the study. Fifty-four percent ($n = 22$) of the children were male and 46% were female ($n = 19$). Children were enrolled in one of three all-Black private schools in large urban areas. The schools were selected to be representative of small, stable, Black independent institutions for children. Among the institutions selected were a parochial school ($n = 14$), a traditional school ($n = 17$), and an alternative school ($n = 10$). The alternative school in this study had a Pan African sociocultural orientation.

Within the three schools there was some variation in educational attainment and family income. Overall, 58.5% of mothers had completed 4 years of college or more. By comparison, 35.3% of fathers had obtained a baccalaureate or more. Cross-tabulations of school with educational level resulted in significant differences in mother's education (X^2 (39) = 0.82, p = .00), but not in father's education (X^2 (32) = 0.38, p = .67). In 1986 dollars, the median family income in the traditional school, Chaucer, ranged between $45,000 and $65,000 (58.8%); at the alternative school, Watoto, the range was between $15,000 and $35,000 (40.0%); and the median range at the parochial school, St. Benedito, was between $25,000 and $35,000. However, about 69% of annual incomes reported were $35,000 or less.

Perceived Racial Stress and Coping Apperception Test (PRSCAT)

Description. The PRSCAT is a projective test which focuses on various aspects of one central theme, racial stress and coping. The PRSCAT has five pictures depicting similar themes of racial stress and coping. Children were presented with the stimuli by a same-race interviewer and asked to tell a story about each picture. The story was to have a beginning, a middle, and an end (Part A). On the first four pictures they were asked how the central character or Black child in the picture feels (Part B) and what they were going to do (Part C). Part C is generally considered the coping statement.

The PRSCAT pictures were photographed copies of black-and-white sketches drawn by a talented and experienced artist. The pictures were of two types. Three of the pictures showed Black and White children in situations of subtle but potential racial conflict. These cards are described below.

Card 1 - Black boy in White classroom
Card 2 - Black girl and White woman
Card 4 - Tug-of-war game; Black vs. White team

Two pictures showed only Black people; these stimuli were considered to have very low potential for racial conflict.

Card 3 - Two Black children in an office with a Black woman and a man behind a desk.

Card 5 - Black children engaged in various forms of play (For availability of cards, contact author).

Scoring. The response to each stimulus card of the PRSCAT was scored and coded in two interdependent parts. Each card received a Racial Conflict Rating (RCR), which described the intensity of the racial conflict expressed. If RCR equal one or more, then racial coping strategies (RCSs) were coded. Table 1 contains the intensity ratings.

The baseline level of racial conflict for Cards 1, 2, and 4 is racial conflict identified (2). A story devoid of race, therefore, is an indication that the storyteller has either missed or ignored the contradictory racial conflicts depicted in the picture and was coded as no racial conflict identified (0). Other times this same code was used, but only in cases where there was clearly a non-racial conflict created by the storyteller. Below are two examples of children's responses on the PRSCAT. The first two are exemplary of a no racial conflict identified (0) rating, and the next two were scored as having a clear racial conflict (2).

Often storytellers told stories which made assumptions about the cultural understanding of the Black interviewer. Sometimes, then, as is traditional in the vernacular of Black storytellers, the actual topic or theme of their story was not explicit. In these instances, storytellers acknowledged racial content but expressed no explicit conflict. In such stories where no overt or unequivocal declaration of racial conflict was made, stories were coded as implied racial conflict identified (1).

A story imbued with intense racial conflict (3) is one where the storyteller clearly makes a strong declaration and is passionate about the conflict identified. Furthermore, the category "intense racial conflict" extends to stories that go beyond a discussion of the characters within the picture to a more generalized discussion of racial discrimination or of the condition of Blacks in society.

Cards 3 and 5 have a baseline of *no racial conflict* because all the characters are Black in these scenes.

A *racial conflict* for Cards 3 and 5 is one in which the storyteller not only identifies the race of

Table 1. Intensity Ratings

RCR	Sample Statements
0 = No racial conflict identified	Story about a race. Feels happy, wants a chance to race.
1 = Implied racial conflict identified	Both Black and White (children) they look friendly. Look like they don't treat each other in a bad way. . . He looks sad 'cause no one is talking with him.
2 = Racial conflict identified	Bunch of Black and White kids playing together on the playground. Black boy found a rope. Let's play tug-of-war! Everybody say "yeah." Then it was Black against White.
3 = Intense racial conflict identified	The teacher and the girl are Black. She either did something wrong or the teacher is being mean to her because she is Black.

the characters, but develops a story of conflict and makes the link to race. An *intense racial conflict* is a story that not only includes racial conflict but goes further to remark on the status of Blacks as a group and the problems that arise when these individuals interface with the larger social system. The category is also appropriate when the stories reflect some deeper analysis of the problems of Blacks in America or when a Black/White conflict is alluded to even though no White characters appear in the picture. Following are examples of children's "no racial conflict" and "intense racial conflict" responses to PRSCAT Cards 1 (classroom scene) and 4 (tug-of-war scene).

No Racial Conflict	Intense Racial Conflict
Card #1	
"Picture reminds me of a classroom. Mostly everybody is paying attention...one boy is not paying attention (#513)."	"...There are a lot of White people in his (Black child) class and nobody paid attention to his raised hand because he was Black (#103)."
Card #4	
"They are playing tug-of-war and they	"...Black school and White school, compet-

are all happy (#523)." ing...One of Black boys was struggling so hard... Black girl cheering for them. White girl cheering for the other team. He concentrated on African people (#316)."

Reliability. Reliability was calculated from the percent agreement coded between two independent raters. If a rater coded strategies not coded by the second rater, those racial coping strategies (RCSs) figured negatively into the percent agreement calculated. Reliability for the racial conflict rating (RCR) was calculated in the same manner. Both raters coded each of 41 cases. Interrater reliability was established at .74 (RCSs) and .83 (RCR).

Findings

Racial Conflict Rating

High-potential stimulus cards differed somewhat in their effectiveness to elicit perceived racial conflict from children (Table 2). On Card 1, 65.1% (23), on Card 2, 36.6% (15), and on Card

4, 65.1% (23) of children perceived a racial conflict. Cards 1 and 4 elicited the greatest amount of racial stress from children. Card 2 created the greatest amount of ambiguity for children 63.4% (26) most of whom described no racial conflict in their stories. Often the stories revealed the children's tendency to regard the White adult as the Black child's mother. In stories of this kind the child had to be quite explicit about race in order for racial conflict to be scored. Otherwise, any conflict expressed in the story was regarded as something other than *racial* conflict.

Racial Stress and School Ecology

There was some variation among schools in the intensity with which children perceived racial conflict. Children attending the Pan African school (Watoto) appeared to be at higher risk for perceived stress related to race. Watoto children were consistently more likely to perceive racial conflict in both the high-and-low potential cards of the PRSCAT. Indeed, Table 2 shows that in response to any one stimulus PRSCAT card, Watoto children were from about 1/3 to 10 times more likely to perceive racial conflict as their counterparts at other schools.

The variances in the intensity of perceived racial conflict among children attending the different schools is partially explained by school, sex, and age effects. However, these effects vary by card.

Cards 2 and 5 show Watoto children to be at extreme odds with Chaucer and more so with St. Benedito in perceiving racial conflict. On both these cards there is a pronounced school effect (RCR2 - [r (41) = - 0.34, p = 0.015) and RCR5 - (r (41) = - 0.27, p < 0.05)]. On these cards, St. Benedito children perceived virtually no racial conflict. Chaucer children have a unique pattern whereby most perceived no racial conflict, but of those who did, the conflict expressed was very intense. By contrast, Watoto children were more likely to exhibit varying degrees of intensity.

Sex and age effects were apparent for Cards 3 and 4. As with Cards 2 and 5 similar effects were shown for both high-and-low potential cards. Older children [RCR3 - (r (40) = 0.30, p < 0.05) and RCR4 - (r (40) = 0.32, p < 0.05)) and boys

[RCR3 - (r (41) = -0.35, p < 0.01) and RCR4 - (r (41) = -0.37, p < 0.01)] were more likely to project racial stress on these cards.

Despite the absence of White figures in Cards 3 and 5 of the PRSCAT, Watoto children viewed racial stress as something that could be experienced without the presence of visible White characters. Other children were more likely to perceive no racial stress in these cards.

There were no school, age, or sex effects for Card 1 of the PRSCAT. Children who perceived racial conflict in this card could not be distinguished by these factors. While Watoto has a greater percentage of respondents scoring between 1 and 3 on this card, the overall intensity of conflict is comparable if not greater at Chaucer.

Racial Coping Strategies

Identifying racial coping strategies (RCSs) was a three-fold process. The 17 RCSs identified in the adult pilot study (Johnson, Slaughter, & Schneider, 1984) were (a) re-identified, (b) amplified, and then (c) applied to the child data. Eleven new RCSs were identified and 11 were either maintained or amplified from the pilot study (Johnson et al., 1984). Table 3 shows the results of this process.

The percentage of individual RCSs utilized for each high-potential card was computed. Strategies were grouped in three ways: (a) Tier 1–strategies tallied at more than 10% of responses on that card; (b) Tier 2–RCSs at 5%-10%; and (c) Tiers 3 and 4–RCSs less than 5% of total number of responses.

Twenty-three children generated a total of 90 responses on the PRSCAT (Table 4). Across the 5 stimulus cards several RCSs were prominent. Children most preferred RCSs, change or choice of environment, persist, assert personal self-hood, physical confrontation, and verbal confrontation.

The stimulus cards also inspired some RCSs use unique to individual cards. For Card 1, children primarily used RCSs, support, persist, and choice or change of environment (Table 4).

In response to Card 2, children employed RCSs choice or change of environment, defer, and engage authority most often. Children who

Table 2. Frequency Distribution of the Child Racial Conflict Rating by Intensity on the PRSCAT[a] by School

	Chaucer (N = 17)		Watoto (N = 10)		St. Benedito (N = 14)		Total (N = 41)	
RCR1	%	n	%	n	%	n	%	n
0	47.1	8	30.0	3	50.0	7	43.9	18
1	0.0	0	20.0	2	21.4	3	12.2	5
2	23.5	4	30.0	3	21.4	3	24.4	10
3	29.4	5	20.0	2	7.1	1	19.5	8
RCR2								
0	58.8	10	20.0	2	92.9	13	63.4	26
1	5.9	1	30.0	3	7.2	1	12.2	5
2	5.9	1	20.0	2	0.0	0	7.3	3
3	29.4	5	30.0	3	0.0	0	19.5	8
RCR3								
0	94.1	16	60.0	6	85.7	12	82.9	34
1	0.0	0	10.0	1	0.0	0	2.4	1
2	0.0	0	10.0	1	14.3	2	7.3	3
3	5.9	1	20.0	2	0.0	0	7.3	3
RCR4								
0	47.1	8	10.0	1	64.3	9	43.9	18
1	5.9	1	20.0	2	0.0	0	7.3	3
2	23.5	4	50.0	5	35.7	5	34.1	14
3	23.5	4	20.0	2	0.0	0	14.6	6
RCR5								
0	82.4	14	70.0	7	100.0	14	85.4	35
1	0.0	0	20.0	2	0.0	0	4.9	2
2	0.0	0	10.0	1	0.0	0	2.4	1
3	17.6	3	0.0	0	0.0	0	7.3	3

[a]Scale 0 = no racial conflict; 1 = implied racial conflict; 2 = racial conflict; 3 = intense racial conflict.

perceived racial conflict in this card were generally prosocial in their use of RCSs.

A "tug-of-war" scenerio between Black and White teams was depicted on Card 4. Four RCSs accounted for almost 60% of the RCSs used by children in response to card 4. In order of priority, strategies, superiority, assert personal self-hood, verbal confrontation, and moral reasoning (nonracial).

Children felt compelled to suggest the superiority of the Black children in Card 4. Young children were no more likely to invoke verbal confrontation than older children. Still, some children were more likely to go beyond verbal confrontation and to suggest the use of physical confrontation. Overall, when responding to the tug-of-war scene, children were generally actively assertive in their use of RCSs.

Table 3. Comparison of Parent RCSs (1984/85)[a] with Child/Adult RCSs (1985/86)

Parent Pilot[a] 1984/85	Child/Adult Data 1985/86
0. No elaboration	1. Defer to authority[c]
1. Ignore	2. Engage authority[c]
2. Project to others	3. Physical confrontation[c]
3. Project superiority	4. Verbal confrontation[c]
4. Meet problem on own terms	5. Authoritative directive[c]
5. Can't protect	6. Moral reasoning (nonracial)[c]
6. Internalization of stereotypes	7. Moral reasoning (race-related)[14,2][b]
6a. Select educational environment	8. Legal reasoning[c]
7. Build self-esteem/confidence	9. Strategic planning [4]
8. Positive Black role models	10. Explore the problem [10, 12]
9. Extended family interaction	11. Develop support systems [9, 11, 15]
10. Exploration of child events	12. Project racial pride [8,11,13]
11. Family activities	13. Project superiority [3]
12. Exploration of contemporary politics & events	14. Project inferiority [6]
	15. Assert personal self-hood [7]
13. Exploration of family history & struggles	16. Persist[c]
14. Racial awareness	17. Conform[c]
15. Involvement in helping others	18. Change or choice of environment [6a]
16. General discussion	19. Ignore/do nothing [1, 5]
	20. Avoid or withdraw[c]
	21. Negate racial group[c]
	22. No racial coping [0]

[a] Johnson, Slaughter, & Schneider, 1984. [b] [ ] RCS reidentified/amplified from 1984/85 data. [c] New RCS identified from child/adult 1985/86 data.

Children's preferred RCSs differed somewhat by school. Table 5 shows that while there is overlap in children's articulated racial coping strategies, the specific configurations differ by school. At St. Benedito, children primarily use persist (18.8%) and assert (12.5%). At Watoto and Chaucer, children articulated a greater variety of strategies. At Watoto the configuration of preferred RCS included inferiority (11.4%), verbal confrontation (8.6%), persist (8.6%), and ignore (8.6%). Chaucer's pattern had very little in common with the other schools; change of environment (15.4%) and physical confrontation (10.3%) were articulated often, while defer to authority (7.7%), inferiority (7.7%), and assert personal selfhood were critical but articulated less often. Given the small number of participants at Watoto ($n = 10$), children there generated a disproportionately greater number of RCSs than children at either of the other two schools. Yet, many of their RCSs overlap with those used by children attending Chaucer, though with a different emphasis. Children at St. Benedito were much less likely to project racial conflict into their stories/responses. Those few children who did project racial conflict had few RCSs to address

Table 4. Children's Frequency of Response by Racial Coping Strategies on High-Potential Racial Conflict Cards of the PRSCAT

Card 1 (n = 32)	%	Card 2 (n = 27)	%	Card 4 (n = 32)	%	Total (n = 91)	%
Support	15.8	Environ	22.2	Super	18.7	Environ	10.9
Persist	12.5	Defer	14.8	Assert	15.6	Persist	8.8
Environ	12.5	Engage	11.1	Verbal	12.5	Infer	8.8
		.		Moral(N)	12.5		
Physic	9.4	Plan	7.4	Physic	9.4	Assert	7.7
Infer	9.4	Infer	7.4	Infer	9.4	Super	6.6
Defer	6.3	Persist	7.4	Persist	6.3	Defer	6.6
Avoid	6.3	Conform	7.4	Ignore	6.3	Physic	6.6
Assert	6.3	Ignore	7.4			Verbal	5.5
						Moral(N)	5.5
						Support	5.5
						Ignore	5.5
Engage	3.1	Moral(N)	3.7	Explore	3.1	Engage	4.4
Verbal	3.1	Legal	3.7	Pride	3.1	Avoid	4.4
Moral(R)	3.1	Pride	3.7	Avoid	3.1	Conform	3.3
Legal	3.1	Avoid	3.7			Legal	2.2
Explore	3.1					Plan	2.2
Conform	3.1					Explore	2.2
Ignore	3.1					Pride	2.2
						Moral(R)	1.1
Directive	0.0	Directive	0.0	Directive	0.0	Directive	0.0
Negate	0.0	Negate	0.0	Negate	0.0	Negate	0.0
Moral(N)	0.0	Verbal	0.0	Defer	0.0		
Plan	0.0	Moral(R)	0.0	Engage	0.0		
Pride	0.0	Explore	0.0	Moral(R)	0.0		
Superior	0.0	Support	0.0	Legal	0.0		
		Superior	0.0	Plan	0.0		
		Assert	0.0	Conform	0.0		
				Environ	0.0		

the problem. Most often, however, these children chose a road of quiet nonconfrontational persistence which did not compromise their sense of self.

Discussion and Conclusion

One of the most important findings of this study is reflected in the perceptions of children as young as 5 years old who not only perceived racial conflicts but were able to articulate RCSs to address them. Older children were more likely to perceive racial conflict in situations where there was little potential for racial tension to arise. Maturity may be a factor in children's ability to determine and understand the impact of institutional racism in their daily lives. While

Table 5. Frequency of Articulated RCSs of Children on the PRSCAT by School

	School						
Chaucer $(n = 39)$[a]		Watoto $(n = 35)$		Benedito $(n = 16)$		Total $(n = 90)$	
	%		%		%		%
Environ	15.4	Inferior	11.4	Persist	18.7	Environ	11.1
Physical	10.3	Superior	8.6	Assert	13.5	Persist	8.8
		Verbal	8.6			Infer	8.8
		Persist	8.6				
		Environ	8.6				
		Ignore	8.6				
Defer	7.7	Defer	5.7	Defer	6.3	Assert	7.7
Engage	7.7	Assert	5.7	Engage	6.3	Super	6.6
Moral(N)	7.7	Physical	5.7	MoralN	6.3	Defer	6.6
Superior	7.7	Support	5.7	MoralR	6.3	Physical	6.6
Inferior	7.7	Pride	5.7	Legal	6.3	Verbal	5.5
Assert	7.7	Avoid	5.7	Explore	6.3	Moral(N)	5.5
Verbal	5.1			Support	6.3	Support	5.5
Support	5.1			Inferior	6.3	Ignore	5.5
Avoid	5.1			Conform	6.3	Engage	4.4
Persist	5.1			Environ	6.3	Avoid	4.4
				Ignore	6.3		
Legal	3.9	Moral(N)	2.9			Conform	3.3
Plan	3.9	Explore	2.9			Legal	2.2
Conform	3.9	Conform	2.9			Plan	2.2
		Plan	2.9			Pride	2.2
						Explore	2.2
						Moral(R)	1.1
Direct	0.0	Direct	0.0	Physical	0.0	Direct	0.0
Moral(R)	0.0	Moral(R)	0.0	Verbal	0.0	Negate	0.0
Explore	0.0	Legal	0.0	Direct	0.0		
Pride	0.0	Negate	0.0	Plan	0.0		
Ignore	0.0	Engage	0.0	Pride	0.0		
Negate	0.0			Superior	0.0		
				Avoid	0.0		
				Negate	0.0		

N of responses does not include RCS, no racial coping strategy, which accounted for 50.0% at Chaucer, 38.6% at Watoto, and 65.2% at Benedito of the total responses.

boys and girls appear to use reactive and proactive RCSs in general, boys were somewhat more vulnerable or predisposed to use confrontational and self-denigrating coping strategies. The slightly greater use of these strategies by boys may indicate sex role constraints that limit the development of a wide array of RCSs and the utilization of more proactive coping styles. These limitations may increase the vulnerability of Black boys to racial stress and other stressful life events.

Among the children in all three schools a wide variety of racial coping strategies were articulated, the majority of which may be described as proactive or an orientation toward self-development. Nevertheless, emerging patterns of children's preferred RCSs differed by school. While there was overlap in use of racial coping strategies on the PRSCAT, individual schools were distinguished by unique patterns consistent with the expressed philosophy of the school. The greater articulation of RCSs by children associated with particular school philosophies versus those who were limited in their coping options suggests that the ecologies of some schools encourage the development of a multiple array of RCSs whereas the ecologies of other schools are less conducive to this kind of development. In these schools fewer options for coping are articulated by children.

The PRSCAT appears to be a useful tool for determining the extent to which children perceive racial stress in their daily environments and how they may be prepared to cope. However, as a developing tool the PRSCAT is not without its weaknesses and problems. Presently, despite the unity in theme, the degree of racial stress perceived by any individual child often varied unexpectedly by stimulus card. That is, children who may have perceived intense racial stress on high-potential Cards 1 and 4 may perceive no racial stress on high-potential Card 2 (Black female child and White woman). There should be greater consistency within individuals on the high-potential cards. Card 2 may simply be too ambigu-

ous. In the future, an expanded number of stimulus cards may allow for more consistency within the individual. Expanding the number of stimulus cards may also be useful in assessing racial stress with better accuracy. By offering children more coping opportunities, the child can better demonstrate his or her true coping pattern. This improvement may enhance our confidence and reduce error in the measurement of racial stress and the identification of racial coping strategies among children. The usefulness of the PRSCAT could be expanded by alternative scoring techniques of a more clinical nature. These developments could further enhance the applicability of the instrument for use with Black clinical populations. In addition, a clinical scoring method may be more useful in assessing the more subtle aspects of racial stress not addressed in the present scoring method. That is, racial conflict which is not explicitly referred to by the individual is ignored in the present study for reasons of validity. It is hoped that in the future valid methods will be developed for understanding the more subtle aspects of racial stress expressed.

The PRSCAT is one tool which has been successful in accessing some information about the vulnerability of Black children of elementary school age to race-related stressors. The precise identification of both resilient and vulnerable coping patterns is necessary if we are to reduce the impact of racial stress on the quality of life for Black children and their families. The continued development of this kind of instrument will contribute to the attainment of this goal.

References

Alejandro-Wright, M. N. (1985). The child's conception of racial classification: A socio-cognitive developmental model. In M. B. Spencer, G. K. Brookins, & W. R. Allen (Eds.), *Beginnings: The social and affective development of Black children* (pp. 185-200). Hilldale, NJ: LEA Publishers.

Bellak, L. (1986). *The Thematic Apperception Test: The children's senior apperception technique in clinical use* (4th ed.). Orlando, FL: Grune and Stratton.

Bowman, P. J., & Howard, C. (1985). Race-related socialization, motivation, and academic achievement: A study of Black youths in three generation families. *Journal of the American Academy of Child Psychiatry, 24*, 131-141.

Bronfenbrenner, U. (1979). *The ecology of human development.* Cambridge: Harvard University Press.

Carew, J. (1980). Effective caregiving: The child from birth to three. In M. D. Fantini & R. Cardenas (Eds.), *Parenting in a multicultural society* (pp. 170-180). New York: Longman.

Comer, J. P. (1985). Black children and child psychiatry. *Journal of the American Academy of Child Psychiatry, 24*, 129-133.

Costantino, G., Malgady, R., & Rogler, L. (1985). *Cuento therapy: Folktales as a culturally sensitive psychotherapy for Puerto Rican children.* (Hispanic Research Center Monograph No. 12). Maplewood, NJ: Waterfront Press.

Cross, W. E., Jr. (1985). Black identity: Rediscovering the distinction between personal identity and reference group orientation. In M. B. Spencer, G. K. Brookins, & W. R. Allen (Eds.), *Beginnings: The social and affective development of Black children* (pp. 155-172). Hillsdale, NJ: LEA Publishers.

Dohrenwend, B. S. (1973). Social status and stressful life events. *Journal of Personality and Psychopathology, 28*, 225-235.

Dressler, W. W. (1985). Extended family relationships, social support and mental health in a southern Black community. *Journal of Health and Social Behavior, 26*, 39-48.

Garmezy, N., & Rutter, M. (1983). *Stress, coping, and development in children.* New York: McGraw-Hill.

Goodman, M. (1958). *Race awareness in young children.* New York: Crowell and Collins.

Gurin, P., & Epps, E. (1975). *Black consciousness, identity, and achievement.* New York: John Wiley and Sons.

Holliday, B., Henning, R., & Johnson, D. J. (1992). *Black maternal beliefs.* Unpublished manuscript.

Hill, R. (1958). Generic features of families under stress. *Social Casework, 39*, 139-150.

Hill, R. (1972). *The strengths of Black families.* New York: Emerson Hall.

Horowitz, R. (1939). Racial aspects of self-identification in nursery school children. *Journal of Psychology, 7*, 91-99.

Johnson, D. J. (1983). *Racial preference and biculturality in interracial preschoolers.* Unpublished master's thesis, Cornell University.

Johnson, D. J., Slaughter, D. T., & Schneider, B. (1984). *Parental coping and identity formation in Black children: Coding manual IV. Newcomers: Blacks in private schools.* Unpublished manuscript, Northwestern University.

Johnson, D. J. (1988). Identity formation and racial coping strategies of Black children and their parents: A stress and coping paradigm. (Doctoral Dissertation, Northwestern University) *Dissertation Abstracts International, 48*, 2581A.

Lazarus, R. S., & Folkman, S. (1984). *Stress, appraisal and coping.* New York: Springer Publishing Co.

McAdoo, H. P. (1982a). Stress absorbing systems in Black families. *Family Relations, 31*, 479-488.

McAdoo, H. P. (1982b). Levels of stress and family support in Black families. In H. I. McCubbin, A. E. Cauble, & J. M. Patterson (Eds.), *Family stress, coping and social support* (pp. 239-252). Springfield, Il: Thomas.

Murphy, L. B., & Moriarty, A. E. (1974). *Vulnerability, coping, and growth.* New Haven, CT: Yale University Press.

Peters, M. F., & Massey, G. (1983). Mundane extreme environmental stress in stress family theories: The case of Black families in White America. In, H. I. McCubbin & C. Figley (Eds.), *Stress and the family: Advances and developments in family stress theory and research* (pp. 193-218). New York: Haworth.

Pierce, C. (1975). The mundane extreme environment and its effect on learning. In S. G. Brainerd (Ed.), *Learning disabilities: Issues and recommendations for research.* Washington, DC: National Institute of Education.

Peters, M. F. (1981). Parenting in Black families with young children: A historical perspective. In H. P. McAdoo (Ed.), *Black families* (pp. 211-224). Beverly Hills, CA: Sage Publications.

Savage, J. E. (1979). Separation and its effects on female prisoners and their children. In W. E. Cross, Jr. & A. Harrison (Eds.), *Fourth conference on empirical research in Black psychology* (pp. 152-165). Washington, DC: Association of Black Psychologists.

Scanzoni, J. (1971). *The Black family in modern society.* Boston, MA: Allyn and Bacon.

Semaj, L. T. (1980). Reconceptualizing the development of racial preference in children: A sociocognitive approach. *Journal of Black Psychology, 6*(2), 59-79.

Semaj, L. T. (1985). Afrikanity, cognition, and extended self identity. In M. B. Spencer, G. K. Brookins, &

W. R. Allen (Eds.), *Beginnings: The social and affective development of Black children* (pp. 173-184). Hilldale, NJ: LEA Publishers.

Slaughter, D. T., & Schneider, B. L. (1986). *Newcomers: Blacks in private schools* (Project no. 2-0450). Washington, DC: ERIC Document Reproduction No. ED 274768.

Spencer, M. B. (1982). Personal and group identity of Black children: An alternative synthesis. *Genetic Psychology, 106*, 59-84

Spencer, M. B. (1983). Children's cultural values and parental childrearing strategies. *Developmental Review, 3*, 351-370.

Staples, R. (1974). The Black family revisited: A review and preview. *Journal of Social and Behavioral Sciences, 20*, 65-78.

Taylor, R. (1976). Black youth and psychological development. *Journal of Black Studies, 6*, 353-372.

Thornton, M., Chatters, L., Taylor, R., & Allen, W. (1990). Sociodemographic and environmental correlates of racial socialization by Black parents. *Child Development, 61*(2), 401-409.

Williams, B. E., Best, D. L., Boswell, D. A., Mattson, L. A., & Graves, D. J. (1975). Preschool Racial Attitude Measure II. *Educational and Psychological Measurement, 35*, 3-18.

For additional infomation, contact:

Deborah J. Johnson, Ph.D.
Department of Child and Family Studies
1430 Linden Drive
University of Wisconsin-Madison
Madison, WI 53706
Telephone: (608) 263-4066
Fax: (608) 262-5335
Email: DEBOJOHN@MACC.WISC.EDU

An Inventory for Assessing Cultural Mistrust in Black Children

Francis Terrell and Sandra L. Terrell

Abstract

An inventory designed to measure the extent to which Black children as young as 3 years of age mistrust Whites was developed. Based upon a review of the literature and interviews with Black parents, items which seemed to describe areas in which Black children mistrust Whites were written to form the initial Children's Cultural Mistrust Inventory (CCMI). The psychometric properties of this inventory were then explored. Items with low reliability and validity estimates were eliminated. Suggestions for future research are discussed.

Grier and Cobbs (1968) suggested that many Blacks have a tendency to mistrust Whites and this characteristic plays a major role in the way they behave. The tendency by Blacks to mistrust Whites has been referred to as cultural mistrust and is defined as suspiciousness by Blacks of Whites and those holding White values. Cultural mistrust is assumed to develop as a result of either directly or vicariously experiencing unfair treatment by Whites. Recently, a measure designed to assess this trait in adolescent and adult populations has been developed and this measure has been shown to correlate with previous exposure to racism and intelligence test scores of Black students (Terrell & Terrell, 1981).

Several authors have suggested that the tendency to distrust Whites often begins early in childhood (Barnes, 1972). Empirical evidence supports this contention. For example, Terrell, Terrell, and Golin (1977) found that Black children tend to talk less in the presence of White children than they did in the presence of other Black children. The authors implied that this finding, at least in part, may have been due to a lack of trust by Black children of White children.

While evidence exists that Black children also tend to acquire a distrust of Whites, no assessment technique currently exists to measure this tendency in Black children. Such a measure would be of value for longitudinal studies in this area. Therefore, the purpose of the present project was to develop a measure to assess cultural mistrust in Black children.

From a consideration of the literature, items (controlled for acquiescence) were written which were designed to measure this construct. Next, five Black advanced graduate students in clinical and social psychology independently rated each statement for clarity and content validity. Items which raters considered inappropriate or unclear were either rewritten or eliminated. Modified items were then resubmitted to all judges who again independently evaluated the items for clarity and domain appropriateness. This procedure was repeated until total agreement was obtained from all judges. In all, a total of 94 statements were written upon which all judges agreed. These items composed the initial Child Cultural Mistrust Inventory (CCMI).

Method

Subjects

The initial CCMI was administered to 163 Black male children ranging in age from seven to fourteen years. Children were also administered Crandall, Crandall, and Katkovsky's (1965) Social Desirability Scale, and a background information questionnaire. In addition, where possible, the parent of each child was administered the Terrell and Terrell (1981) Cultural Mistrust Inventory (CMI) and a background information questionnaire.

Procedure

A sequential psychometric strategy was next used to examine the internal construction of the CCMI. This consisted of first performing an item discrimination analysis to eliminate items which were frequently or infrequently endorsed by the majority of participants. This consisted of taking each statement, one at a time, and dividing the total scores into quartiles. Then, using subjects who responded in the highest versus subjects responding in the lowest quartile, a t-test of the difference between means was computed for each item. Items which did not discriminate significantly at the 0.05 level were eliminated. Second, an index of homogeneity among the surviving items was examined by computing a Pearson correlation between each item and its own total scale score. Items which did not correlate significantly with its own total scale score were eliminated. Third, the remaining items were tested for contamination with social desirability using a

procedure developed by Jackson (1971). Here items which correlated significantly at the 0.05 level with scores on the Social Desirability scale were eliminated. This completed the procedures used to examine the internal properties of CCMI. Of the initial 94 items, a total of 19 items remained to form the final CCMI (see Appendix).

The external validity of the CCMI was also explored. We reasoned that if mistrust of Whites is acquired vicariously, then a major contributor to children's level of mistrust would be the parents. Therefore it was hypothesized that parents of children scoring high on the CCMI would score high on the Terrell (1980) Cultural Mistrust Inventory. To examine this prediction, Pearson correlations were computed between Children's scores on the CCMI and parents' scores on the CMI. A value of 0.63 was obtained between children's scores on the CCMI and their mother's scores on the CMI while a value of 0.57 was obtained between children's scores on the CCMI and their father's scores on the CMI.

Summary and Discussion

An inventory designed to measure cultural mistrust in Black children was developed. The reason for developing this measure was to facilitate longitudinal studies in the area of cultural mistrust. However, the development of this inventory should be considered to be in its infancy. Additional research is needed in order to further investigate and refine the inventory. As a preliminary step, an estimate of the temporal stability of the CCMI is needed. We are currently in the process of collecting test-retest reliability data. These findings should be available in the near future. Also, although there is preliminary evidence which seems to support the construct validity of this measure, more research in this area is needed to further explore the utility of the measure. Finally, the collection of normative data would be helpful for interpreting scores. Until such research is conducted in the areas described, any findings obtained using this scale should be interpreted with caution.

References

Barnes, E. J. (1972). Cultural retardation or shortcomings of assessment techniques. In R. L. Jones (Ed.), *Black psychology* (pp. 66-76) New York: Harper and Row.

Crandall, V. C., Crandall, V. J., & Katkovsky W. (1965). A children's social desirability questionnaire. *Journal of Consulting and Clinical Psychology, 29*, 27-36.

Grier, W. H., & Cobbs, P. M. (1968). *Black rage.* New York: Bantam Books.

Terrell, F., & Terrell, S. L. (1981). An inventory to measure cultural mistrust among Blacks. *Western Journal of Black Studies, 5*, 180-185.

Terrell, F., Terrell, S. L., & Golin, S. (1977). Language performance of Black and White children in Black and White situations. *Language and Speech, 20,* 377-383.

Appendix

Children's Cultural Mistrust Inventory (CCMI)**

Directions: Rate the extent to which you agree with each of the statements using the following scale:

"1= No"; "2 = sometimes"; "3 = Yes."

1. Most White children will give your toys back if you lend them to him or her. (C-)
2. Most White teachers can be trusted to give you the grade you deserve. (A-)
3. White policemen will help you if you need it. (A-)
4. A White child will pay your money back if you lend him or her some. (C-)
5. A White store owner will try to cheat you. (A+)
6. Most White children do not keep their promise. (C+)
7. Most White people will promise you one thing and then do something else. (A+)
8. A White child will keep a secret. (C-)
9. White children can not be trusted. (C+)
10. White children usually do not tell the truth. (C+)
11. Most White children usually cheat when they play games. (C+)
12. A White child will accuse you of something you didn't do. (C+)
13. A White child will try to steal your toys. (C+)
14. Most White people are honest. (A-)
15. Most White people do not keep their promises. (A+)
16. White policemen will accuse you of something you didn't do. (A+)
17. Most White people tell fibs. (A+)
18. If you work for a White person and they promise to pay you for the work, they will keep their word. (A-)
19. If you lose something and a White child finds it, he or she will try to return it. (C-)

**Key to the CCMI
C refers to mistrust of White children. A refers to mistrust of White authority figures. Items followed by a positive (+) are positively keyed. Items followed by a negative sign (-) are negatively keyed.

For additional information, contact:

Francis Terrell
Psychology Department
University of North Texas
Denton, TX 76203
Telephone: (817) 565-2678
Fax: (817) 565-4682

Measures of Attitudes Toward School, Physical Self, Blacks, Whites, and Neighborhood[1]

James A. Banks

Abstract

Measures of attitudes toward school, physical self, Blacks, Whites, and neighborhood were developed and administered to a sample of African American children who lived in a predominantly White suburban community in the Pacific Northwest. Scale reliabilities (Cronbach alphas) ranged between .67 and .81. A variety of analyses of the investigator's scales' relationships to demographic variables and other existing measures were undertaken. Predicted and unexpected relationships were found.

Introduction

The measures described herein were developed as part of a larger study of Black families who live in selected, predominantly White suburban communities of a large metropolitan area in the Pacific Northwest, the population of which exceeds one million. The study was designed to describe the self-concepts of ability, general self-concepts, levels of externality, and the attitudes toward physical characteristics, neighborhoods, and schools of the children in the larger study who were ages eight to eighteen.

The variables selected for examination in this study were chosen because of their possible relationship to socialization within a predominantly White suburban community. Several variables, such as self-concept of ability and internality, were selected because they are important correlates of academic achievement.

Many researchers who have studied the self-concepts and racial attitudes of Blacks have studied low-income Black students, Blacks in artificially integrated situations, or have not sufficiently controlled for social class, i.e., they have treated Blacks as a monolithic group without determining the effects of social class on their behavior. The conflicting results from various studies of the self-concept, locus of control, and racial attitudes of Black youths may result in large part from the fact that social class, degree of assimilation, region, and the racial composition of the community in which the students live are not adequately controlled or examined. Most of the youths who participated in this study have upper middle-class and highly educated parents. These parents, because of their attitudes and socio-economic status, have voluntarily chosen to live in predominantly White suburban communities and to send their children to the public schools in their neighborhoods. Because of the unique characteristics of the Black children in this study, its findings should contribute to a better understanding of the complex relationship between race, social class, racial attitudes, and externality. The children in this study are among the very few Blacks in their classes and/or schools. Consequently, an examination of their attitudes and self-concepts will help us to understand better the social and psychological characteristics of individuals whom social scientists have described as "marginal."

Method

Subjects

A method was developed to identify Black families with school-age children who lived in selected predominantly White suburban communities of a metropolitan area in the Pacific Northwest. This method consisted primarily of asking members of Black churches, social and civic organizations, and community groups to identify families with the above characteristics. The identified families were then asked to name other such families. Sixty-four of the identified families participated in this study. The 98 children (55 boys; 43 girls) who became subjects were members of 57 of the 64 participating families. The children had a mean age of 12.8 years and were in grades three through twelve.

There are inherent difficulties in identifying Black families who live in predominantly White suburban communities. This study required all members of the family (parents and school-age children) to participate during what is normally their leisure time, a Saturday afternoon. These constraints eliminated both the possibility of a larger sample as well as a random selection of the subjects. However, the nature and size of the sample was adequate to satisfy the major goals of this exploratory study.

Procedures

The families who participated in this study had the option to complete the questionnaires at a central site on a university campus or to request that a member of the research staff administer the questionnaires in their homes. Half of the 98 children in this study completed the questionnaires in each of the two sites. At the central testing site, questionnaires were administered in standardized group situations by staff members trained in the technique. In the home settings, the same staff members administered the questionnaires to the children individually or with other family member subjects.

Instruments

The children were administered the following scales: The Brookover Self-Concept of Ability Scale, the Rosenberg Self-Esteem Scale, the Stephan-Rosenfield Racial Attitude Scales, the Nowicki-Strickland Locus of Control Scale, and a 45-item questionnaire developed by the investigator with subscales that measure (a) Attitudes Toward School, (b) Physical Self-Concept, (c) Attitudes Toward Blacks, (d) Attitudes Toward Whites, and (e) Attitudes Toward Neighborhood. These latter scales are the primary focus of the present chapter (see Appendix). The internal consistency reliabilities (Cronbach's Alpha) for each of the scales and subscales are presented in Table 1.

The Brookover Self-Concept of Ability Scale is an 8-item questionnaire in which students estimate their academic ability. The Rosenberg Self-Esteem Scale is a measure of general self-concept, in which individuals indicate the extent of their agreement or disagreement with statements such as, "I feel that I have a number of good qualities," and, "On the whole, I am satisfied with myself."

The Stephan-Rosenfield Racial Attitudes Scales consist of two parallel parts. The two parts measure attitudes toward Blacks and Whites, respectively. Each part includes 10 items. Each item consists of two paired adjectives, such as, "happy; sad." For each adjective pair, the students

Table 1. Internal Consistency Reliabilities (Cronbach's Alpha) of Scales

The Brookover Self-Concept of Ability Scale	.77
The Rosenberg Self-Esteem Scale	.73
The Stephan-Rosenfield Racial Attitude Scales	
Attitudes Toward Whites Scale	.74
Attitudes Toward Blacks Scale	.84
Nowicki-Strickland Locus of Control Scale	.77
Banks Scales	
Attitudes Toward School	.77
Physical Self-Concept	.67
Attitudes Toward Blacks	.80
Attitudes Toward Whites	.76
Attitudes Toward Neighborhood	.81

are asked to judge Blacks or Whites as groups by circling the response closest to their opinion. These two subscales will hereafter be referred to as *Step White* and *Step Black*. Both *Step White* and *Step Black* are scored in a *negative* direction, i.e., the higher the score, the more negative the respondent's attitudes are toward the ethnic group. *It is important to note this scoring method since the other measures in this study are scored in a positive direction.*

The Nowicki-Strickland Locus of Control Scale measures the extent to which individuals attribute their success or failure to themselves or to others. Individuals who are externally oriented tend to attribute their success or failure to others. Internal individuals tend to attribute their success or failure to their own efforts. This scale consists of 40 items, such as "Are some kids just born lucky?" to which individuals are asked to respond either "yes" or "no." Internality has been found to correlate positively with academic achievement and other behavior usually associated with success. Research indicates that ethnic minority youths tend to be more external than White youths.

The 45 items that comprised the investigator's attitude scale are declarative statements. The subjects indicated their extent of agreement or disagreement with each statement. Sample items from each of the subscales follow. The numbers in parentheses indicate the number of items in each subscale.

Attitudes Toward School (11): I like school.

Physical Self-Concept (10): I like the color of my skin.

Attitudes Toward Blacks (8): I like to spend a lot of my time with my Black friends.

Attitudes Toward Whites (8): I sometimes feel uneasy around Whites.

Attitudes Toward Neighborhood (8): I wish I lived in another neighborhood.

Hereafter, these scales will be referred to as *School, Physical, Ban Black, Ban White,* and *Neighborhood.*

Measurement of the Two Derived Variables

In addition to the measures of the ten attitude and self-concept variables described above, two measures of what Stephan and Rosenfield have described as ethnocentrism were computed, using scores obtained by the subjects on *Step White* and *Step Black* and *Ban White* and *Ban Black.* In each case, this measure indicated how much more positively the subjects evaluated their own ethnic group than they evaluated Whites. The ethnocentric score was computed by finding the difference between a respondent's sum of scores on Black and White measures of attitudes. The ethnocentric measure derived from the Stephan-Rosenfield Scale will be hereafter referred to as *Ethnic Step.* The one derived from the investigator's scales will be referred to as *Ethno Ban.*

Intercorrelations of the Stephan-Rosenfield Scales and the Investigator's Scales

In this study, two different scales were used to measure attitudes toward Blacks and Whites. This was done, in part, because intercorrelations among racial attitude measures tend to be low. The Stephan-Rosenfield Racial Attitude Scales are designed for use with a general population of students. An additional scale was needed that would more directly measure the racial attitudes of Black children who lived and went to school in unique sociocultural environments. When the results from these different measures are viewed collectively, a more complex view of the racial attitudes of the children in this study is attained.

The *Ban White* and the *Step White* scales correlated substantially ($r = -.55, p < .001$). The *Ban Black* and *Step Black* correlated significantly but only moderately ($r = -.27, p < .01$). This correlation may be moderate rather than high because the Stephan-Rosenfield Scales measure global racial attitudes, while four of the eight items on the *Ban Black* scale relate to Blacks in a school setting. Only one of the items on *Ban White* relate to the school setting. This probably explains why *Ban White* and *Step White* correlate much more highly than *Step Black* and *Ban Black*.

Results

Relationship Between the Demographic and the Attitudes and Self-Concept Variables

The 98 children who participated in this study lived in ten different suburban communities and went to school in 14 separate districts. A one-way analysis of variance indicated that neither suburb nor school district was significantly related ($p < .05$) to any of the attitude and self-concept variables.

A two-tailed t-test indicated that site was related to only one of the attitude and self-concept variables; children who completed the questionnaires at home scored significantly more positively toward Whites on the *Ban White* scale than did children who completed the questionnaires at the central testing site (Group means= 23.25 and 21.16; $t = 2.53, p < .01$). Because it was not possible to assign subjects to the two different sites randomly, it is not possible to determine whether the differences in the scores on *Ban White* resulted from differences in the characteristics of the subjects or from differences in the two sites.

However, because *Ban White* was the only variable in which the two groups of subjects differed significantly, it is reasonable to hypothesize that the all-Black setting of the central testing site may have reinforced positive attitudes toward Blackness and caused the youths in that setting to express fewer pro-White feelings than the youths who

completed the questionnaires at their homes in predominantly White suburban communities.

Sex, age, grade, and family type (whether children lived in two-parent or one-parent families) were correlated with the ten primary and the two derived attitude and self-concept variables. As Table 2 indicates, there were few significant correlations between these variables and the attitude and self-concept variables. Sex correlated significantly but only moderately with attitudes toward neighborhood and attitudes toward Blacks (*Step Black*). Girls had slightly more negative attitudes ($r = -.16, p < .05$) toward their neighborhoods than boys, and slightly more negative attitudes toward Blacks ($r = .25, p < .01$) when attitudes were measured with *Step Black*. Age and self-concept of ability were negatively related; however, this correlation was not significant ($r = -12, p > .05$). Family type did not correlate significantly with any of the attitude and self-concept variables. Whether the children in this study were members of families with one or two family heads was not significantly related to the attitude and self-concept variables.

Age correlated moderately and negatively with attitudes toward neighborhood ($r = -.24, p < .01$), indicating that the older children in this population were slightly less positive toward their neighborhoods than were the younger children. Age also correlated rather substantially with attitudes toward Blacks (*Step Black*), ($r = .40, p < .01$), indicating that as the age of the children in this study increased, they scored significantly more negatively toward Blacks on the Stephan-Rosenfield Scale. This relationship between age and attitudes toward Blacks is also revealed in the negative correlations between age and ethnocentrism on the investigator's ethnocentrism measure ($r = -.10, p > .05$) and the ethnocentrism measure derived from the Stephan-Rosenfield Scales ($r = -.24, p < .01$).

Age correlated moderately and negatively with externality ($r = -.32, p < .01$), indicating that externality decreases as children get older. This finding is consistent with the findings of most researchers who have investigated the relationship between externality and age in school-age populations. As might be expected because of the

Table 2. Relationship Between the Demographic and Attitude and Self-Concept Variables (Pearson Correlation Coefficients)

	Concept	Esteem	School	Physical	Ban Black	Ban White	Neigh-borhood	Step White	Step Black	Locus	Ethno ban	Ethno step
Sex	.07	.06	-.06	-.03	.05	-.13	-.16*	.12	.25**	-.06	.10	-.11
Family	.11	.02	-.07	-.08	-.06	-.06	-.07	.01	-.11	-.04	.09	.10
Age	-.12	.10	.04	-.06	-.08	.09	-.24**	.12	.40**	-.32**	-.10	.24**
Grade	-.10	.10	.02	-.06	-.07	.08	-.27**	.15	.44**	-.34**	-.08	.25**

$n = 98; *p < .05; **p < .01$

strong positive relationship between age and grade, grade correlated significantly with the same variables as age: attitudes toward neighborhood, attitudes toward Blacks (*Step Black*), and externality. As their grades increased, the children in this study became moderately more negative toward their neighborhoods and toward Blacks, and less external.

Intercorrelations of the Attitude and Self-Concept Variables

A discussion of the interrelationships among the attitude and self-concept variables follows. These interrelationships, as determined by a Pearson correlational analysis, are given in Table 3.

Self-Concept of Ability and Self-Esteem. Self-concept of ability is a strong correlate of academic achievement; consequently, it is an important research variable. In this study, self-concept of ability was not related to most of the measures of racial attitudes. However, it was significantly related to most of the other attitude and self concept variables and moderately related ($r = .16, p < .05$) to racial attitudes toward Blacks when racial attitudes were measured by *Ban Black*. Self-concept of ability was significantly related, in a positive direction, to self-esteem, attitudes toward school, physical self-concept, and internality. As the self-concepts of ability of the children in this study increased, their self-esteem increased, their evaluation of their Black physical characteristics became more positive, their attitudes toward school and Blacks became more positive, and their sense of control over their fate increased.

Self-esteem consists of a person's generalized evaluation of self, while self-concept of ability is a measure of an individual's opinion of his or her ability to do academic work successfully. Consequently, it was expected that these two variables would be substantially related, as was found to be the case in this study. Self-esteem was also substantially related to attitudes toward school ($r = .50, p < .001$), and physical self-concept ($r = .46, p < .001$), and moderately related to attitudes toward Blacks (*Ban Black*) ($r = .19, p < .03$). However, self-esteem and attitudes toward Blacks were not significantly related when attitudes were measured with *Step Black*. There was a small but significant relationship between self-esteem and attitudes toward Whites (*Step White*) ($r = -.22, p < .01$). However, this relationship was not significant when attitudes were measured by *Ban White*.

Self-esteem and attitudes toward neighborhood were moderately related ($r = .21, p < .01$). The more the children in this study liked their neighborhoods, the higher was their self-esteem. Self esteem was negatively related to externality ($r = -.33, p < .001$). The children in this study who had high self-esteem tended to be internal.

Attitudes Toward School. Attitudes toward school and physical self-concept were not significantly related. How the children in this study felt about their Black physical characteristics was not related to whether they liked or disliked school. These findings may mean that the school setting is having a rather neutral impact on how the children in this study view their physical characteristics.

Table 3. Intercorrelations of the Attitude and Self-Concept Variables ($n = 98$)

Variable	1	2	3	4	5	6	7	8	9	10	11	12
1. Self-Concept of Ability	1.0											
2. Self-Esteem	.41**	1.0										
3. Attitudes Toward School	.32**	.50**	1.0									
4. Physical Self-Concept	.30**	.56**	.15	1.0								
5. Attitudes Toward Blacks (BAN)	.16*	.19*	-.23**	.30**	1.0							
6. Attitudes Toward Whites (BAN)	.08	.10	.56**	-.15	-.40**	1.0						
7. Attitudes Toward Neighborhood	.12	.21**	.57**	.09	-.19*	.60**	1.0					
8. Attitudes Toward Whites (STEP)+	.00	-.22**	-.55	-.02	.30**	-.55**	-.48**	1.0				
9. Attitudes Toward Blacks (STEP)+	.02	-.01	-.04	-.07	-.27**	.01	-.14	.22**	1.0			
10. Externality	-.25**	-.34**	-.34**	-.12	.04	-.25**	-.15	.07	-.21**	1.0		
11. Ethnocentrism (ETHNO-BAN)	.03	.05	-.50**	.25**	.83**	-.84**	-.47**	.50**	-.16	.17*	1.0	
12. Ethnocentrism (ETHNO-STEP)	.01	-.18*	-.38**	.04	.46**	-.44**	-.25**	.60**	-.70**	.23**	.17*	1.0

+ High scores on this scale indicate negative attitudes. All other measures are scored in a positive direction. *$p < .05$. **$p < .01$

There was a moderate but significant negative relationship between attitudes toward school and attitudes toward Blacks (*Ban Black*) (*r* = -.23, *p* < .001). This relationship was not significant when racial attitudes were measured by *Step Black*. Half of the eight items on *Ban Black* relate directly to the school setting, while none of the items on the *Step Black* relates uniquely to the school situation. *Ban Black* includes these items: I wish more Black children were in my school," and "I wish I could go to a Black school." Consequently, this negative relationship between attitudes toward Blacks and toward school means, in part, that the more the children liked their schools, the less they wanted them changed by integrating them with more Blacks.

Attitudes toward Whites and attitudes toward school were substantially related. This relationship was significant when attitudes toward Whites were measured by both *Ban White* (*r* = .56, *p* > .001) and by *Step White* (*r* = - .55, *p* < .001). The more the children in this study liked school, the more positive they felt toward Whites. This is an expected relationship because most of the teachers and students in the schools attended by these students were White.

There was a substantial positive relationship between attitudes toward school and attitudes toward neighborhood (*r* = .57, *p* < .001). Since the socio-cultural and racial worlds of the schools and neighborhoods in which these students lived were highly similar, it is to be expected that their attitudes toward their schools and neighborhoods would be highly related.

Attitudes toward school and externality were negatively related (*r* = -.34, *p* < .001). Consequently, the more the children in this study liked their schools, the more internal they were. Children who like school the most probably experience success in school because they have high academic self-concepts and high academic abilities. Both high academic self-concept and academic achievement are correlates of internality. The relationship between attitudes toward school and externality found in this study is consistent with both theory related to externality and previous research findings that relate internality to academic success.

Physical Self-Concept. Black children who are socialized within predominantly White suburban communities beginning at an early age experience many situations in which they are a small minority. Consequently, they are likely to internalize White standards of physical beauty and to evaluate their own color and physical characteristics negatively. Previous research on children's racial attitudes suggests that this may be the case. The ten-item scale in this study, the Physical Self-Concept Scale, was designed to measure how Black youths evaluated their physical characteristics and race and to determine how physical self-evaluation related to other variables.

The predominantly White communities in which the children in this study lived do not seem to have had a significantly negative effect on their evaluations of their physical characteristics and race. These children gave positive evaluations of their physical characteristics and Blackness. The mean physical self score was 33.14, out of a possible score of 40 (*SD* = 3.51, *n* = 98). Over 92 percent of the children agreed with this statement: "I like the way I look;" 98 percent agreed with this statement: "I like the color of my skin." Only 8.2 percent of the children agreed with the statement: "My looks bother me."

Even though the children in this study had high opinions of their physical characteristics, physical self-concept was significantly related to only four of the other attitude and self-concept variables: self-concept of ability, self-esteem, attitudes toward Blacks (*Ban Black*), and ethnocentrism (*Ethno Ban*). The children who had positive attitudes toward their physical characteristics tended to have high self-concepts of ability, high self-esteem, positive attitudes toward Blacks, and to be more pro-Black than pro-White when ethnocentrism was measured with *Ethno Ban*.

Locus of Control. Rotter (1966) and Nowicki and Strickland (1973) have done pioneering conceptual and empirical research on the concept of internality. Internality has been found to correlate in a positive direction with a number of important variables, such as higher academic achievement (Nowicki & Strickland), persistence (Gordon, 1977), greater popularity (Nowicki & Barnes, 1973), and self-esteem (Roberts) .

A goal of the present study was to describe the extent to which the children in this study were internal and the correlates of internality in this population. The children's mean score (11.99) on the Nowicki-Strickland Locus of Control Scale is lower (more internal) than the norms reported for this scale. Internality was related positively to self-concept of ability, self-esteem, attitudes toward school, and attitudes toward Whites, and negatively to attitudes toward Blacks (*Step Black*) and ethnocentrism as measured by both *Ethno Ban* and *Ethno Step*.

The more internal the children were in this study, the higher were their self-concepts of ability, self-esteem, attitudes toward school, and attitudes toward Whites. However, internality and positive attitudes toward Blacks, and internality and ethnocentrism, were negatively related.

Ethnocentrism and the Other Attitude and Self-Concept Variables

The relationship between ethnocentrism (pro-Blackness) and the other attitude and self-concept variables is summarized in Table 3. Self-concept of ability is not significantly related to ethnocentrism as measured on either *Ethno Ban* or *Ethno Step*. Self-esteem is not significantly related to ethnocentrism as measured by *Ethno Step*, but is negatively related to ethnocentrism as measured by *Ethno Step*. This finding is perplexing and seems inconsistent with some of the other findings in this study. Self-esteem, for example, is positively related to racial attitudes toward Blacks when attitudes are measured by *Ban Black*. However, self-esteem is not related to attitudes toward Blacks when attitudes are measured with *Step Black*.

This finding indicates that ethnocentrism, as derived from mean scores on the Stephan-Rosenfield Racial Attitudes Scales, is moderately but negatively related to self-esteem ($r = -.18$; $p < .05$). However, this negative relationship between ethnocentrism and self-esteem is not revealed by the other correlations in this study; yet it warrants further discussion.

This finding indicates that children who evaluated Blacks more positively on the Stephan-Rosenfield Scales tended to score slightly lower on the Rosenberg Self-Esteem Scale. What factors can explain this unexpected finding? Assimilationist theory can help provide some possible answers to this question. The children who evaluated Blacks more positively on the Stephan-Rosenfield Scales might be more culturally Black, have a stronger Black identity, be more external, and may have experienced more discriminatory situations that have negatively influenced their self-esteem than the children who evaluated Blacks less positively. Consequently, the experiences that have caused children to evaluate Blacks more positively than Whites might be related to the experiences that have caused them to have slightly lower self-esteem. The assimilation process that causes Black youths to acquire more positive self-esteem might also cause them to evaluate Blacks less positively than Whites. The factors and experiences that enable Black youths to become more internal, discussed earlier, may also cause them to acquire higher self-esteem and to evaluate Blacks as a *group* less positively, but themselves more positively. The fact that self-esteem correlated positively with attitudes toward Whites (*Step White*) lends support to the explanation presented here. However, the positive correlation between self-esteem and attitudes toward Blacks does not.

Ethnocentrism correlated negatively with attitudes toward school (*Ethno Ban* and *Ethno Step*). This finding indicates that positive attitudes toward school and pro-Blackness are inversely related. This finding is consistent with the earlier reported correlation which shows a negative relationship between attitudes toward school and attitudes toward Blacks.

Ethnocentrism and physical self-concept are positively related when pro-Blackness is measured with *Ethno Ban*. However, these two variables are not related when ethnocentrism is measured with *Ethno Step*. Ethnocentrism and attitudes toward Blacks are substantially related when ethnocentrism is measured by both scales. Ethnocentrism (both *Ethno Ban* and *Ethno Step*) is correlated negatively and substantially with *Ban White*. This is an expected relationship.

On both ethnocentrism measures, pro-Blackness correlated negatively with attitudes toward neighborhood. The more the children in this study liked their neighborhood, the less pro-Black they were. Ethnocentrism (both measures) correlated with attitudes toward Whites (both measures) in the expected direction: high ethnocentrism scores were negatively related to scores on racial attitudes toward Whites. Ethnocentrism (both measures) was significantly related to externality: the more pro-Black the children were in the study, the more external they were.

Conclusion

The findings of this exploratory study must be interpreted with caution because of the sample size (*n* = 98), the non-random selection of the subjects, and because the study was conducted in only one geographic region. However, the design enabled us to study a population that is extremely di ficult to identify and convince to participate in social research. While this study has limitations, it raises important questions and provides fruitful hypotheses that merit further study by researchers.

The predominantly White suburban communities in which the children in this study were being socialized have not prevented them from developing positive attitudes toward themselves, their communities, and their schools. These children were biracial in their attitudes–they had positive attitudes toward both Blacks and Whites–although they were slightly more positive toward Blacks (mean = 26.15) than toward Whites (mean = 22.20). The findings suggest that Black children socialized within predominantly White suburban communities are likely to become highly attitudinally assimilated into White society and that this kind of assimilation may have complex effects on their racial attitudes toward Blacks and their levels of ethnocentrism. As attitudinal assimilation increased, these children became increasingly more positive toward their schools and neighborhoods and more positive toward Whites, but less positive toward Blacks.

The findings of this study suggest, however, that attitudinal assimilation may have some desirable educational consequences: The children in this study who had highly positive attitudes toward Whites and toward their schools and neighborhoods were also more internal. Internality is positively related to academic achievement and to other success-related behavior. Internality was negatively related to positive attitudes toward Blacks and to ethnocentrism. This latter finding raises a question about whether Black children can remain ethnic in their racial attitudes and attain high levels of internality. This question warrants study within a wide range of populations in which Black youths are socialized.

Several findings in this study suggest that the experiences of Black females in predominantly White suburban communities may be slightly more difficult than those of Black males. Girls not only liked their neighborhoods less than boys did but had slightly more negative attitudes toward Blacks as measured by *Step Black*. This study also suggests that life in White suburbia may be a bit more difficult for children as they grow older. The older children in this study had significantly more negative attitudes toward their neighborhoods and toward Blacks. These two findings, which must be interpreted cautiously because of the limitations of this study, merit further study and investigation.

Many of the findings of this exploratory study are consistent with those of other researchers. However, a number of questions are raised about the relationship between race, social class, and sociocultural environment. These variables warrant further study so that a more accurate picture of Black life and culture can be described.

Note

1. A version of this chapter was published in the *Journal of Negro Education*, 1984, 53, pp. 3-17, titled "Black youths in predominantly White suburbs: An exploratory study of their attitudes and self concepts." It is reprinted here with permission.

References

Brookover, W., Paterson, A., & Thomas, S. (1962). *Self-concept of ability and school achievement*. (Project No. 845). East Lansing: Michigan State University, U.S.O.E. Cooperative Research Report.

Brookover, W., Paterson, A., & Thomas, S. (1979). *School social systems and student achievement.* New York: Praeger.

Carlson, E. (1981, October 20). Blacks increasingly head to suburbs. *Wall Street Journal*, p. 25.

Gordon, M. (1964). *Assimilation in American life.* New York: Oxford University Press.

Gordon, D. A. (1977). Children's beliefs in internal-external control and self-esteem as related to academic achievement. *Journal of Personality Assessment, 41*, 383-386.

Jordan, T. J. (1981). Self-concepts, motivation, and academic achievement of Black adolescents. *Journal of Educational Psychology, 73*, 509-517.

Jordan, T. J. (1963). *Self-concepts, motivation, and achievement.* Unpublished master's thesis, East Lansing: Michigan State University.

Katz, P., & Zalk, S. (1978). Modification of children's racial attitudes. *Developmental Psychology, 14*, 447-461.

Lake, R. W. (1981). *The new suburbanites: Race and housing in the suburbs.* New Brunswick, NJ: Rutgers University Center for Urban Policy Research.

Leftcourt, H. M. (1976). *Locus of control: Current trends in theory and research.* New York: Wiley.

Morse, J. R. (1963). *Self-concept of ability, significant others, and school achievement of eighth grade students: A comparative investigation of Negro and Caucasian students.* Unpublished master's thesis, East Lansing, Michigan State University.

Nowicki, Jr., S., & Barnes, J. (1973). Effects of a structured camp experience on locus of control orientation. *Journal of Genetic Psychology, 122*, 247-252.

Nowicki, Jr., S., & Strickland, B. (1973). A locus of control scale for children. *Journal of Consulting and Clinical Psychology, 40*, 148-154.

Nowicki, S. (1976). The factor structure of locus of control at three different stages. *Journal of Genetic Psychology, 129*, 13-17.

Roberts, A. (1971). *The self-esteem of disadvantaged third and seventh graders.* Unpublished doctoral dissertation, Emory University, Atlanta, GA.

Rotter, J. (1966). Generalization expectancies for internal versus external control of reinforcement. *Psychological Monographs, 80*, Whole number 609.

Samuels, D., & Griffore, R. (1979). Ethnic and sex differences in self-esteem of preschool children. *Journal of Genetic Psychology, 135*, 33-36.

Schweitzer, J., & Griffore, R. (1981). A longitudinal study of students and parents coincident with court-ordered school integration. *Urban Review, 13*, 111-119.

Williams, J., & Morland, J. K. (1976). *Race, color, and the young child.* Chapel Hill: University of North Carolina Press.

Wilson, W. J. (1978). *The declining significance of race: Blacks and changing American institutions.* Chicago: University of Chicago Press.

Appendix

Banks' attitudes toward school scale

1. I like school.
2. The children at school make me feel different.
3. My teachers like me.
4. I get along well with other children.
5. I feel left out of things in class.
6. I wish I could go to a different school.
7. The children at school leave me out of things.
8. The teachers at school make me feel different.
9. The children at school like me.
10. I don't like to be called on in class.
11. My classmates make fun of me.

Banks' attitudes toward Whites

1. I sometimes feel uneasy around Whites.
2. I sometimes wish that I were White.
3. Schools with a lot of Whites are good schools.
4. I like to spend a lot of time with my White friends.
5. My White friends treat me like everyone else.
6. A White can be as good a friend to me as a Black.
7. I trust White people.
8. I spend as little time with Whites as possible.

Banks' attitudes toward Blacks scale

1. I wish more Black children were at my school.
2. I wish more Black teachers were at my school.
3. I wish more Black people lived in my neighborhood.

4. I wish I could go to a Black school.
5. I feel uneasy when I am around a lot of Blacks.
6. A Black school is as good as a White school.
7. I like to spend a lot of time with my Black friends.
8. I wish I had more Black friends.

Banks' physical self-concept scale

1. I like the way I look.
2. I like the color of my skin.
3. I have a nice nose.
4. I have pretty eyes.
5. My hair is nice looking.
6. I look different from other children.
7. I like my lips.
8. My classmates at school think I look different.

9. My looks bother me.
10. I am proud to be Black.

Banks' attitudes toward neighborhood scale

1. I like my neighborhood.
2. The children in my neighborhood like to play with me.
3. The children in my neighborhood think I am important.
4. The children in my neighborhood leave me out of things.
5. The grown-ups in my neighborhood make me feel different.
6. I get along well with the other children in my neighborhood.
7. I spend as much time with the children in my neighborhood as possible.
8. I wish I lived in another neighborhood.

For additional information, contact:

James A. Banks
Professor and Director
Center for Multicultural Education
115 Miller Hall, D Q 12
University of Washington
Seattle, WA 98195

Part VI

Measures for Adolescents and Young Adults

Assessing Achievement Motivation in Black Populations: The Castenell Achievement Motivation Scale

Louis A. Castenell and Justin E. Levitow

Abstract

This chapter explores the hypothesis that achievement motivation is multidimensional and varies by race. A theoretical argument is that the formation of achievement orientation is primarily a function of the social self and not any single psychological variable. A new scale is introduced which attempts to provide empirical evidence that Blacks perceive success differently than Whites though both groups possess the need to achieve. Results supported the hypothesis, especially when Home Influence is considered as an achievement variable.

Introduction

The mismeasurement of African Americans is a persistent problem in the field of psychology. For the most part, primary responsibility lies in the operational definition of many psychological constructs that are based on ethnocentric assumptions, the design of inappropriate instruments for cross-cultural research, and the subsequent biased generalization of the theoretical paradigm to African Americans. The history and measurement of achievement motivation are a case in point. In this chapter, we will attempt to correct past misconceptions and offer a new instrument for review.

Review of Literature

Early researchers generally defined achievement motivation as a drive in which behavior should involve competition, with a standard of excellence, and if successful, produce a positive effect; or if unsuccessful, a negative effect (Atkinson & Raynor, 1974). Furthermore, achievement motivation is formed early in childhood training eventuating in some children having a need to achieve and others not. McClelland (1961) bluntly concluded that American Blacks as a group possess low levels of achievement motivation due to their past slave status and childrearing practices. Based on his ideas, McClelland rescored the Thematic Apperception Test that has become the most widely used projective technique to measure achievement motivation (Castenell, 1980). A plethora of studies ensued. They concluded that Blacks have a lesser need to achieve than Whites (McClelland, 1961; Mingione, 1965; Mussen, 1953; Ramirez & Williams, 1976).

Other research on cross-cultural achievement motivation differences is based on an attributional framework. It is argued in this research that those who believe that success is attributable to ability and failure to a lack of effort or some other unstable factor are most likely to expect success in the future. A commonly used technique is self-report. Self-report measures (e.g., Rotter I-E scale, Bialer scale and Nowicki-Strickland Locus of Control) assume the individual is capable of responding accurately to the questionnaire. Unlike the traditional projective measures, self-report measures assume that behavior involves cognition and thus we can understand constructs at the conscious level. Research has generally supported these hypotheses (Weiner, 1974). However, only a few studies attempted cross-cultural analyses and these were usually limited to evaluating perceived racial differences in a set of tasks. Results from these reports remain inconclusive (Castenell, 1984). In addition, most measures of this kind are standardized on a White non-urban population (Guttentag & Klein, 1976).

New Measure

The idea that achievement motivation is multifaceted and is common to all groups has been with us for some time (Katz, 1969; Maehr, 1974). However, an investigation of exactly how and in what way adolescents perceive success has not been empirically tested. Coleman (1961) identified three major arenas for such possible interactions: home, peer groups and school. Consequently, a new self-report instrument was constructed to test the hypothesis that achievement motivation is perceived differently by African Americans than Whites across the three arenas. That is, African Americans' life experiences would shape their achievement behavior in all arenas; unlike Whites whose life experiences at this de-

velopmental stage would focus primarily on school success. Thus, it was posited that an area-specific approach, in addition to a general measure, will provide more information regarding group differences than a single general achievement measure. Results supported this premise (Castenell, 1983).

The new measure, the Castenell Achievement Motivation Scale (CAMS) is a nine–item general and area-specific scale. It is area-specific in that it is composed of three three-item subscales (peer, home school) which are components of the general measure. That is, the first three items are peer achievement questions, the middle three questions are home achievement questions, and the last-three questions are school achievement questions. A response of either "not important" or "somewhat important" is scored as low achievement motivation, and a response of either "quite important" or "very important" is scored as high achievement motivation. The logic is that if the objective is to assess achievement motivation of an adolescent within a specific arena, such as school, then it becomes necessary to cluster questions with specific directions to reflect the subject's perceived achievement motivation in that arena. At the same time, the measure is general in that the sum score on any three-item scale is treated as a general self-evaluation for that arena, and the sum score of nine items (all three subscales) is viewed as a measure of general achievement motivation for adolescents. Dawes and Corrigan (1974) demonstrated that the average score from a series of equally weighted sub scores are good predictors of a general trend (Dawes & Corrigan, 1974).

Validity

The CAMS was administered in a single sitting to groups of one or more classes (without teacher participation) of eighth graders in a mid-sized midwestern city. The subjects were told the investigator was doing a study of their beliefs and needed their help. To prevent social-approval responses, the investigator did not use the term achievement or motivation. The students were asked to be honest and were encouraged to seek clarification of the meaning of individual CAMS

Table 1. Pearson Correlation Matrix

Item Number

	1	2	3	4	5	6	7	8	9
1	1.00	0.42	0.41	0.23	0.28	0.27	0.28	0.03	0.13
2	0.42	1.00	0.54	0.28	0.27	0.20	0.29	0.08	0.09
3	0.31	0.54	1.00	0.16	0.13	0.15	0.29	-0.03	0.22
4	0.23	0.28	0.16	1.00	0.36	0.20	0.33	0.36	0.25
5	0.28	0.27	0.13	0.36	1.00	0.32	0.31	0.21	0.04
6	0.27	0.20	0.15	0.20	0.32	1.00	0.28	0.06	0.03
7	0.28	0.29	0.29	0.33	0.31	0.28	1.00	0.27	0.24
8	0.03	0.08	-0.03	0.36	0.21	0.06	0.27	1.00	0.39
9	0.13	0.09	0.22	0.25	0.04	0.03	0.24	0.39	1.00

questions. The interviewer read the instructions and questions with all subjects.

A nine by nine Pearson correlation matrix (Table 1) was generated and factor analysis (varimax) was used to evaluate the structure of CAMS. Table 2 presents the three factor varimax rotated factor matrix.

Factor scores were calculated for all 310 subjects on each of the three factors. A two-group discriminant analysis was utilized to determine whether Black student motivation could be differentiated from White student motivation by their factor scored on three factors shown in Table 2. The following discriminant equation resulted:

$$V = 0.231X1 = 0.300X^2 + 0.94\ 0X^3$$

The Chi-squared test was used to determine the level of significance of the computed discriminant equation ($X^2 = 32.085$, $df = 3$, $p < .05$). The discriminant equation was statistically significant. Means for both groups on each factor are reported in Table 3.

Results

Three factors were hypothesized to exist in the CAMS and results of the factor analysis

Table 2. Varimax Rotated Factor Matrix Factors

Items	Factors			Communality
	I	II	III	h^2
1	0.58	0.02	0.37	0.49
2	0.78	0.06	0.23	0.67
3	0.86	0.09	-0.05	0.75
4	0.14	0.54	0.46	0.53
5	0.09	0.15	0.77	0.62
6	0.15	-0.05	0.71	0.53
7	0.34	0.41	0.41	0.46
8	-0.15	0.81	0.17	0.71
9	0.22	0.78	-0.20	0.69

Table 3. Means on Three Factors for Two Groups

Group	I	II	III	N
White	-0.03	-0.04	-0.13*	257
Black	0.15	0.20	0.65*	53

*Statistically significant difference between group means ($F = 29.17$, $p < .05$).

confirmed this hypothesis. Factor I was interpreted as "Peer Influence"; Factor II was interpreted as "Academic Influence" and Factor III was interpreted as "Home Influence." These results and conclusions were consistent with expectations. The discriminant analysis shows that the scale is useful in assessing differential achievement motivational forces in Black versus White student populations. Factor III, "Home Influence," seems to make the strongest contribution to differentiating the two groups. Specifically, Black students tended more to perceive achievement motivation as something that might impact positively and directly on their family or home life.

Conclusion

The need to reassess achievement motivation in African American populations is based largely on the too often stated inconclusive findings that African American possess less achievement motivation than Whites. The statistical results of our investigation support the notion that achievement motivation is multidimensional. In addition, the significant difference between group means gives support to the idea that one's perception of achievement is influenced more by variables such as group membership, sex and class than any single psychological phenomenon as ego, drive, or locus of control. This tendency to overestimate the importance of the individual is particularly problematic for cross-cultural research. Past and present failure to take into consideration the social context of African Americans is largely responsible for many researchers developing measures that are inappropriate for race, sex or class comparisons.

We believe the new measure described in this chapter is a step in the right direction. The field of area-specific analysis applied to African American populations is relatively new. Yet it promises a more accurate reading of behavior than the single dimensional approach. The work of Hare (1977) is credited with providing many of the major hypotheses used in this type of research.

Finally, we hope results from this research will encourage increased dialogue among investigators who are interested in group differences and achievement outcomes.

References

Atkinson, J., & Raynor, J. (1974). *Personality, motivation, and achievement.* New York: John Wiley & Sons.

Castenell, L. (1980). *Achievement motivation: An area specific analysis.* Unpublished doctoral dissertation, University of Illinois, at Urbana-Champaign.

Castenell, L. (1983). Achievement motivation: An investigation of adolescents' achievement patterns. *American Educational Research Journal, 20*(4), 503-510.

Castenell, L. (1984). A cross-cultural look at achievement motivation. *Journal of Negro Education, 53*(4), 435-443.

Coleman, J. (1961). *The adolescent society.* New York: The Free Press.

Dawes, R. M., & Corrigan, B. (1974). Linear models in decision making. *Psychological Bulletin, 81*, 95.

Guttentag, M., & Klein, I. (1976). The relationship between inner versus outer locus of control and achievement in Black middle school children. *Educational and Psychological Measurement, 36*, 1101-1109.

Hare, B. R. (1977). Racial and socioeconomic variation in preadolescent area-specific and general self-esteem. *International Journal of Intercultural Relations, 1*, 31-51.

Katz, I. (1969). A critique of personality approaches to Negro performance, with research suggestions. *Journal of Social Issues, 25*, 13-27.

Maehr, M. (1974). *Sociocultural origins of achievement.* Belmont, CA: Brooks/Cole.

McClelland, D. (1961). *The achieving society.* New York: Free Press.

Mingione, A. (1965). Need for achievement in Negro and White children. *Journal of Consulting Psychology, 29*, 108-111.

Ramirez, M. III, & Price-Williams, D. R. (1976). Achievement motivation in children of three ethnic groups in the United States. *Journal of Cross-Cultural Psychology, 7*, 49-61.

Weiner, B. (Ed.). (1974). *Achievement motivation and attribution theory.* Morristown, NJ: General Learning Press.

Appendix

Achievement Motivation Area-Specific Measure

Please circle the letter in front of the answer which best describes how you feel about the sentence. These sentences are designed to find how you generally feel about the importance of success in life. There are no right or wrong answers.

a) not important, b) somewhat important, c) quite important, d) very important

1. How important is it to you that you be good at sports and games in order to be successful in life?
2. How important is it to you that you be pretty or handsome in order to be successful in life?
3. How important is it to you that you are popular in order to be successful in life?
4. How important is it to you that your parents be proud of you in order to be successful in life?
5. How important is it to you that you work hard around the house in order to be successful in life?
6. How important is it to you that you get a job as soon as possible to help out your family?
7. How important is it to you that you that your teachers like you in order to be successful in life?
8. How important is it to you that you be a good student in order to be successful in life?
9. How important is it to you that you that you go to college in order to be successful in life?

For additional information, contact:

Louis A. Castenell
College of Education
University of Cincinnati
P.O. Box 210002
Cincinnati, OH 45221-0002
Telephone: (513) 556-2338
Fax: (513) 556-4283
E-mail: CASTENELA@UC.EDU

The Social Network Record

Deborah L. Coates

Abstract

The role of family, peers, and other social relationships in development has been demonstrated extensively. The characteristics of these relationships can be designated as a social network. A social network refers to individuals' links to persons to whom they feel, or are significantly connected, and to other somewhat less important social contacts. It also refers to the interrelationships among these social contacts. This chapter presents an instrument designed to measure the social networks of African American adolescents. The *Social Network Record* (SNR) is a multi-dimensional, paper-and-pencil inventory that presents the respondent with graphics, check-list grids and questionnaire materials that help to describe the content of a social network. Both structural and functional or support aspects of the network are measured. Preliminary reliability and validity data are presented and example stimulus materials are included.

Rationale and Background

The role of family and peers as a source of influence on development in early childhood has been demonstrated and discussed extensively (e.g., see Cairns, 1979; Cochran & Brassard, 1979; Dunn, 1993; Laursen, 1993; Levitt, Guacci-Franco, & Levitt, 1994; Lewis & Feiring 1978; Piaget, 1954). These relationships can be characterized as a social network. Social network refers to an individual's links to persons to whom they feel significantly connected and to other somewhat less important social contacts. The social network has emerged as a psychological construct that refers to an individual's perceptions of the characteristics of a broad array of social relationships. A personal social network includes family, peers, and non-familial adults who are seen in home, school, community, and other settings. These social structures, social experiences, and social interactions are assumed to influence the development of self-identity. Some empirical evidence supports the view that social environment acts as an influence on behavior by serving as a mirror through which individuals view themselves and shape their social expectations, perceptions, identity, and behavior (Cooley, 1902; Margolin, Blyth, & Carbone, 1988; Mead, 1934; Merton, 1957; Shrauger & Schoeneman, 1979).

A growing number of studies have examined how available social networks including family, peers, and nonfamilial adults, are organized and

269

how these relationships are perceived by the children and adolescents (e.g., Blyth, Hill, & Theil, 1982; Coates, 1985, 1987, 1990, 1991; Coates & Kern, 1993; Cochran, Larner, Riley, Gunnarson, & Henderson, 1990; Fischer, 1981; Galbo, 1983; Garbarino, Burston, Raber, Russell, & Crouter, 1978; Hinde, Perret-Clermont, & Stevenson-Hinde, 1985; Sarason, Sarason, & Pierce, 1990; Serafica & Blyth, 1985; Shade, 1983). Looking at the specific organizational features of networks, and at the way in which adolescents perceive social relationships, may be useful in demonstrating precisely which aspects of social relations influence development during adolescence. At any period in a person's life, a social context or network exists that can be viewed as a collection of social contracts and an index of that person's social world or life space (Feiring & Coates, 1987). Adolescence is a period of increased social contacts and the adolescent's social relationships are of paramount importance to him/her. The social network concept provides a useful conceptual tool for exploring the nature of emerging social relationships during adolescence. In both research and service applications of the personal social network paradigm, social relationships can be schematically or summarily represented. The representations indicate how the individual's social world is organized, how persons function to provide the individual with desired or necessary social interactions, and how they are interrelated. These social contacts can be based on blood or marital kinship, sentiment, the need to exchange material, emotional, or informational resources, or other less well-defined social functions. The social network paradigm operationalizes social relations by allowing a schematic representation of how "significant others" in an individual's social system are organized, interrelated and function.

The social network construct has been discussed extensively in the adult sociology and family socialization literature (see Boissevain, 1974; Boissevain & Mitchell, 1973; Bott, 1971; Leinhart, 1977; Levitt, Weber & Guacci, 1993; Whitten & Wolfe, 1973).

Coates (1991) describes the application of the social network construct to adolescent development. Both the structure and perceived function of social networks are important.

Network structure refers to the discernible and persistent organization of positions and roles within the network. Structural dimensions also refer to the characteristics of persons and their associations and roles within a network system (Boissevain, 1974).

Network function refers to the social support the network provides. Social support is the way in which the network functions to allow for the exchange of resources. The relationship between psychological well-being and the availability of social support for adults has been well documented (Brownell & Shumaker, 1984; Kaplan, Cassal, & Gore, 1977; Thoits, 1986; Tolsdorf, 1976). Social support is assumed to provide a buffer against negative stress outcomes by facilitating social problem solving. The functional dimensions of networks are the interactions which occur between the individual embedded in a network and the social support they provide. These interactions involve exchanges or transactions between key individual and network members. Interactions in networks are supportive or functional when they achieve some goal or offer emotional or material benefits to the individual. The situations in which social exchanges occur, or in which members' interactions are observed in relation to the individual, are also stressed in the social network analysis.

The *Social Network Record* (SNR) characterizes the important social relationships in adolescence. The SNR generates scale scores which describe qualitative and quantitative aspects of adolescent social networks. The SNR has been used primarily with African American adolescent populations. It is a way to obtain comprehensive and objective measures of their interpersonal relationships. It also highlights the diversity, homogeneity, and heterogeneity of the environmental backgrounds seen in African American families and communities.

Description

The *Social Network Record* is a multi-dimensional, paper-and-pencil inventory that presents the respondent with graphics, check-list grids, and questionnaire stimulus materials. These help the adolescent to describe the characteristics of their social contacts. Six major structural subscores are derived to describe overall network and an additional six are used to describe each of six subnetwork groups–Family, Friends, Others, Closest Persons, Material Resources, Emotional Resources. Scale definitions are based on previous network literature (Boissevain, 1974; d'Abbs, 1982). Appendix A outlines the main subscales which are described below. In the SNR subscale definitions which follow, the terms "network member" and "persons identified" are used to refer to entries made by adolescent respondents:

(a) *size*–total number of persons identified;

(b) *durability*–"age of the network" or the average length of time network members have been known;

(c) *frequency of contact*–the average number of contacts per week with members of the network;

(d) *multiplicity*–the degree to which members of a network are seen in one or multiple settings. The number of settings in which an identified person is seen is summed and these numbers are then averaged. A high score indicates that more members are seen in multiple rather than one setting;

(e) *proximity*–geographic proximity of identified persons; the average rating of the travel time it would take the respondent to reach members' homes. A high score indicates that most members are geographically close to the respondent;

(f) *density*–the number of pairs of persons identified who know each other.

The structural scales, with the exception of density are based on social network "maps" which the respondent completes (See Appendix B). Each respondent is given a list of target group members: (a) family; (b) friends; and, (c) other persons. The respondent is shown a list of relationships typically found in each of these three groups and then asked to list *all the persons* they can who are similar to those in each respective group.

Respondents first list all the persons they know in each group with whom they have had at least one contact in the past five years. They then use a checklist grid to describe several characteristics of each person listed and the nature of their contact with each person. These characteristics include sex, age, how frequently they are in touch with the person, places of contact, physical proximity of person, relation of person to subject, and the length of time they have known each person.

The *density score* is based on a separate item which measures the 'ties' or links between members by asking the respondent to indicate *who knows whom* among a predetermined group of persons comprised of parents, closest peers and non-peer friends (See Appendix C).

The support or functional scales are based on social network maps that are very similar to those referred to in the structural dimensions (See Appendix B). Some of these maps target groups that offer material or emotional support to the respondent. For example, adolescents are asked to complete grids to identify:

- closest friend and family;
- to whom they could go if they needed money; and,
- to whom they could go to discuss an argument with a friend.

In addition to these maps, there are other support scales used to measure respondents' perceptions of support. Items ask respondents to: (a) explain what it means to be close to someone; (b) identify role models and their characteristics; (c) define success; (d) indicate whom they prefer for support and how satisfied they were with the support they received from that person; and, to (e) rate how satisfied they were with the support they received for help with different types of problems (See Appendix D).

The *Success Scales* require the respondent to ordinally rate definitions of success. These definitions were derived from the responses given by 35 pilot-test adolescents to an open-ended question about what success meant to them. A *Problem Checklist* asks adolescents to identify problem areas in their lives from a predetermined list of 33 problems. These problems were selected from a list of problems identified and nominated most often by 40 pilot-tested adolescents. Using their own problem list, they then are asked to identify the degree of support, availability, and satisfaction with that support on a 5-point Likert scale. Problems listed in this measure represent nine domains and include: (a) family conflict; (b) interpersonal conflict; (c) material or interpersonal loss; (d) emotional resource needs; (e) information/counseling needs; (f) material resource needs; and (g) transitions.

The *My Largest Problem Scale* requires the adolescent to describe his or her biggest problem at the moment and to provide descriptive information on the characteristics of persons who helped them resolve the problem.

Using these maps, several additional subscales are derived from the SNR which measures the social support characteristics of the network. These social support scales are:

(a) *quality of closeness*–the adolescent's definition of what it means to be close is coded for reciprocity (e.g., Youniss, 1990); that is, mutual exchange of friendship activities and level of closeness which can range from simply sharing a mutual activity to communication which includes confiding and trust; a score is derived which is a weighted average of these two rating systems multiplied by the number of persons identified to whom the adolescent feels close; a high score indicates a greater degree of reciprocal sharing of trust and confidence;

(b) *size of chum group*–number of persons identified as being a part of special group friends;

(c) *closeness resource*–number of persons identified as "persons I feel especially close to," using the adolescent's definition of closeness;

(d) *emotional resource*–number of persons identified as possible sources of help with the hypothetical problem of having an argument with a friend;

(e) *material resource*–number of persons identified as source of help with the hypothetical problem of needing money desperately;

(f) *support satisfaction*–adolescent's report of the degree to which they found the help they received helpful for a problem they identified, which occurred within the last week. A high score indicates satisfaction with the adequacy of the help for resolving the problem.

Administration

The SNR can be administered in a small group setting or on an individual basis. The ideal size for group administration when only one interviewer is available is between 2 and 8 subjects. Part One of the SNR, which includes demographic and structural scales, takes roughly 30 minutes to complete. Part Two, which includes structural and support scale items, requires about one hour to complete.

Reliability and Validity

The SNR was pilot tested on separate samples of 40 African American college students, 32 African American junior and senior high school students, and 60 European-American high school students. The results of the pilot administrations improved the psychometric properties of the protocol. About a third of each pilot group was administered revisions of the SNR individually, with the tester recording difficulties with interpretation of items. These participants were also interviewed following the SNR administration and asked what aspects of their relationships are most important to them and what they found difficult or interesting about the protocol. This information was used to improve the face validity of the protocol by eliminating portions and clarifying the instructions for some tasks. The interviewed participants were tested and retested after a two-week period using the revised measure, and test-retest reliability indices were computed. Several tasks with reliability indices below .50 were deleted from the protocol. These items had to do primarily with density, multiple role functions and group membership reporting.

Three-week test-retest reliability indices for the structural subscores were computed and ranged from .69 for multiplicity to .97 for size. The SNR functional subscores were validated using a 3-times per week phone interview over a three-week period on a random sample drawn from previous participants. Availability of social support and social contact were determined using Wellman's (1981) system. Intercorrelations between structural subscores derived from the SNR and similar structural subscores derived from day-to-day structured phone-interviews were examined to explore the validity of the SNR. These intercorrelations ranged from .67 for multiplicity to .89 for size. Three-week test-retest reliability indices for the support or functional subscales range from .68 for support satisfaction to .86 for size of chum group.

Means and standard deviations for the standardization sample ($n = 343$) on the overall network structural dimensions and functional dimensions of family and peer interactions have been published (Coates, 1985). Two indices of social desirability were administered–the Crowne Marlowe Social Desirability Scale and the Self-Criticism subscore of the Tennessee Self-Concept Scale. Using these scores, data from 11 subjects were eliminated from further analyses because of scores which indicated excessively defensive responses.

This protocol has been used with a number of different samples. These different samples included African American middle-income adolescents; African American college-age freshmen; unmarried White females who were one to five years out of high school; and low and high achieving African American adolescents living in a low-income neighborhood. This previous research was performed with population samples whose respondents had no known physical, mental or emotional handicaps. These adolescents' social network data have been intercorrelated with many other self-concept and identity indices used to measure adolescent psychosocial development such as the Tennessee Self-Concept Scale; Coopersmith Self-Esteem Inventory; Ziller Nonverbal Self-Esteem Scale; Rosenberg Self-Concept Scale; Rotter Internal-External Locus of Control; Adams and Groterant's Objective Measure of Ego Identity Status; Tanner Scale of Sexual Development and the California Achievement Test. Measures of family socioeconomic levels were determined for all samples through Siegel-Hodge-Rossi prestige ranks of parental occupation (Siegel, 1971). Prestige ranks provide a more continuous measure of SES than the often used Hollingshead/Two-Factor Index of Social Position (Myers & Bean, 1968). This research is described in Coates (1985, 1987, 1990) Kern and Coates (1993); Kern (1989); and Kinney (1988).

Limitations of Use

The SNR may be somewhat limited in its applicability for samples whose reading comprehension levels are low. However, this instrument can be orally administered by the interviewer. Standardization with special populations who demonstrate visual or auditory dysfunctions has not been done. Adolescents with attention-deficit dysfunctions may have difficulty completing this protocol within one administration and thus may require two, but not more than three, interview sessions.

Potential Use and Future Research

Uses of the SNR as a research tool have been documented. However, this scale could be used diagnostically to help a clinician understand the social interactions of adolescents at risk for such problems as teen pregnancy, juvenile delinquency, and stress related disorders. The scale might serve to identify those areas within the at-risk adolescent's network system where intervention is needed. Coates (1990) discussed the social network construct as an emerging intervention strategy with African American adolescents.

Social network intervention may be especially relevant for adolescents since they often experience the stress of separating from parents and emerging adolescent social relationships. During early adolescence, tension between emerging biological development and lagging social skill development produce a number of support needs for this group (Price, 1988). A key developmental task during this period is the development of self-esteem. This requires the availability of close and mutually self-disclosing relationships that can provide stable and sustaining support. This focus on social relationships may be particularly difficult for adolescents from dysfunctional families or those who experience few social opportunities. These groups may require social intervention to create appropriate systems of support (Speck & Speck, 1985). The Carnegie Council on Adolescent Development (Price, 1988) has suggested that current demographic trends indicate a pressing need for considering how to use social network support to address many problems facing adolescents today. The Council has suggested that many adolescents lack meaningful social relationships within and/or outside of their immediate families and feel unconnected to traditional American values and life goals. In addition, some African American adolescents must cope with difficult school and work transitions, blended families, and living in environments where the risk of substance abuse is high.

Evaluating the efficacy of network intervention. Efforts to evaluate the efficacy of network intervention/prevention efforts should be fairly straightforward. Using specific observable, behavioral outcomes one can examine the pre-intervention, intermediate, and post-intervention frequency of desired behavior. Subjective determinations of how relationships function between adults and adolescents and between pairs or within groups of adolescents will also help to provide some formative evaluation data. It also may be useful to test the adolescent's knowledge regarding the critical functions of support. Gottlieb (1988) has suggested that evaluation research in this area needs to involve comparisons between different programmatic elements offered in a specific intervention. These comparisons should focus on differences in attracting and sustaining participation of adolescents, in providing meaningful help to meet supportive needs, and in effecting desirable adjustment outcomes.

Psychometric limitations. A major psychometric problem, that has not been addressed with adolescent populations, concerns item scaling of social support item responses. The issue involves determining whether social competence outcomes can be expected to vary as a function of social support. Donald and Ware (1984) underscore the importance of further investigating the psychometric properties of social network assessments that are conceptually linked to adolescent competence. In addition, we have little data available for adolescents that provide details on: (a) the stability of social network characteristics; (b) the derivation of scale values for measures of social contact and resources that generalize across population subgroups; or (c) the conceptually and empirically distinct aspects of social network characteristics. An additional validity issue involves determining the veridicality of social support. Antonucci and Israel (1986) have provided some data, from a study of adults over 70, on the relationship between responses about the network provided by a focus adult and those provided by members of this adult's network. Congruence in the perception of supportive functions between those with whom an adolescent interacts and the target adolescent is useful in planning a clinical intervention program. The psychometric properties of this congruence need to be explored further. This may greatly improve the quality of assessments available to those providing intervention or prevention services. Studies conducted in natural settings are needed to identify specific component features of the adolescent social network. Once identified, these factors can be examined to determine which are effective stress buffers for adolescents. These buffers can also be linked to specific stress reactions.

Other potential applications. Further study is also needed to examine how effective these network characteristics are as a function of cultural, ethnic, gender, and developmental variation. Based on this information, randomized quasi-experimental trials should be conducted, where ethically possible, to determine whether these naturally occurring network buffers work to reduce stress and whether they are related to any of the generally accepted developmental tasks required to achieve adult status. It is also important to find out whether or not some of these naturally occurring buffers can be introduced to adolescents who do not use them. An additional question central to this line of inquiry involves testing the efficacy of the intervention for long-term and short-term outcomes.

The examination of individual differences in perceptions of support, reactions to stress, and susceptibility to efforts at intervention is also required as a basis for the design of sensitive implementation strategies. A concurrent line of inquiry is needed that will produce practical case studies utilizing small clinical trials. These studies would help to offer clarity regarding this source of variation by examining the resiliency and attachment patterns of very high-risk youngsters, early in life and during adolescence.

Longitudinal studies of social networks are also very important for understanding high-risk behavior. Block, Block, and Keyes (1988) have demonstrated that distinct social and personality antecedents of adolescent drug use can be identified. This suggests that it might be important to determine which characteristics of the social network are linked to drug use, delinquency, or other risk-taking behavior. These studies may help to understand when and how to intervene to prevent these negative outcomes. There is also a need to explore how children learn coping behaviors or how to use their networks to garner support. As Compas (1987) suggests, it is not clear whether children learn their coping behavior through observations of parents or other significant figures. This learning process has received very limited empirical investigation. Likewise, as Gottlieb (1981) suggests, we need to examine whether one type of support is perceived as more helpful if offered by one network member rather than another. In this context, Gottlieb (1981) also points out that it is important to pursue research that helps to shed light on how support is communicated to others and on what basis networks need to be organized to facilitate the transfer of support from network members to the target adolescent. It is also important, Gottlieb (1988) suggests, to identify the processes by which their aid is used when necessary. Answers to these questions are critical to our understanding of how to intervene with vulnerable adolescents and with well functioning adolescents.

Note

1. The development of the *Social Network Record* was supported by a grant from NICHD (R23 HD16844-03) to the author and by the Center for the Study of Youth Development and the Computer Center at Catholic University.

References

Antonucci, T. C., & Israel, B. A. (1986). Veridicality of social support: A comparison of principal and network members responses. *Journal of Consulting and Clinical Psychology, 54*, 432-437.

Block, J., Block, J. H., & Keyes, S. (1988). Longitudinally foretelling drug usage in adolescence: Early childhood personality and environmental precursors. *Child Development, 59*, 336-355.

Blyth, D. A., Hill, J. P., & Theil, K. S. (1982). Early adolescents' significant others: Grade and gender differences in perceived relationships with familial and nonfamilial adults and young people. *Journal of Youth and Adolescence, 11*, 425-450.

Boissevain, J. (1974). *Friends of friends: Networks, manipulators, and coalitions.* Oxford: Basil, Blackwell & Mott.

Boissevain, J., & Mitchell, J. (1973). *Network analysis: Studies in human interaction.* Hague, Netherlands: Mouton.

Bott, E. (1971). *Family and social network: Roles, norms and external relationships in ordinary urban families* (2nd ed.). New York: Free Press.

Brownell, A., & Shumaker, S. A. (1984). Social support: An introduction to a complex phenomenon. *Journal of Social Issues, 40*, 1-10.

Cairns, R. (1979). *Social development: The origins and plasticity of interchanges.* San Francisco: Freeman.

Coates, D. L. (1985). Relationships between self-concept measures and social network characteristics for Black adolescents. *Journal of Early Adolescence, 5*, 319-338.

Coates, D. L. (1987). Gender differences in the structure and support characteristics of Black adolescents' social networks. *Sex Roles, 17*, 667-687.

Coates, D. L. (1990). The use of social network analyses in clinical intervention with African American adolescents. In F. C. Serafica, A. I. Schwebel, R. K. Russell, D. D. Isaac, & L. J. Meyers (Eds.), *Mental health of ethnic minorities.* New York: Praeger Press.

Coates, D. L. (1991). Social networks. In R. Lerner, A. Petersen, & J. Brooks-Gunn (Eds.), *Encyclopedia of Adolescence*. Garland.

Cochran, M., & Brassard, J. A. (1979). Child development and personal social networks. *Child Development, 50,* 601-616.

Compas, B. (1987). Coping with stress during childhood and adolescence. *Psychological Bulletin, 98,* 393-403.

Cooley, C. H. (1902). *Human nature and the social order*. New York: Scribner.

d'Abbs, P. (1982). *Social support networks. A critical review of models and findings*. Institutes of Family Studies. (Monograph No. 1) Melbourne: Institute of Family Studies.

Donald, C., & Ware, J. (1984). The measurement of social support. *Research in Community and Mental Health, 4,* 325-370.

Feiring, C., & Coates, D. L. (1987). Social networks and gender differences in the life space of opportunity: Introduction. *Sex Roles, 17,* 611-620.

Fischer, J. (1981). Transitions in relationship style from adolescence to young adulthood. *Journal of Youth and Adolescence, 10,* 11-24.

Galbo, J. (1983). Adolescents' perceptions of significant adults. *Adolescence, 18,* 417-427.

Garbarino, J., Burston, N., Raber, S., Russell, R., & Crouter, A. (1978). The social maps of children approaching adolescence: Studying the ecology of youth and development. *Journal of Youth and Adolescence, 7,* 417-428.

Gottlieb, B. (Ed.). (1988). *Social networks and social support*. Beverly Hills, CA: Sage.

Hinde, R., Perret-Clermont, A., & Stevenson-Hinde, J. (Eds.). (1985). *Social relationships and cognitive development*. Oxford: Clarendon Press.

Kaplan, B. H., Cassel, J. C., & Gore, S. (1977). Social support and health. *Medical Care, 15,* (Suppl.), 47-58.

Kern, D., & Coates, D. L. (1987). *Social networks, academic support and personal traits as correlates of achievement motivation and achievement in African American early adolescents*. Paper presented at the annual meeting of the American Educational Research Association.

Laursen, B. (1993). The perceived impact of conflict on adolescent relationships. *Merrill-Palmer Quarterly, 39,* 535-550.

Leinhart, S. (1977). Social networks: A developing paradigm. In S. Leinhart (Ed.), *Social networks: A developing paradigm* (pp. 13-34). New York: Academic Press.

Levitt, M., Guacci-Franco, N., & Levitt, J. (1994). Social support and achievement in childhood and early adolescence: A multicultural study. *Journal of Applied Developmental Psychology, 15,* 207-222.

Lewis, M., & Feiring, C. (1978). The child's social world. In R. M. Lerner & G. Spanier (Eds.), *Child influences on marital and family interaction: A life-span perspective*. New York: Academic Press.

Margolin, L., Blyth, D., & Carbone, D. (1988). The family as a looking glass: Interpreting family influences on adolescent self-esteem from a symbolic interactionist perspective. *Journal of Early Adolescence, 8,* 211-224.

Mead, G. H. (1934). *Mind, self and society*. Chicago: University of Chicago Press.

Merton, R. (1957). *Social theory and social structure*. Glencoe, IL: Free Press.

Myers, J., & Bean, L. (1968). *A decade later: A follow-up of social class and mental illness*. New York: Wiley.

Piaget, J. (1954). *The construction of reality in the child*. New York: Basic.

Price, R. H. (1988). *Chairman's overview*. Comments presented at the Carnegie Council on Adolescent Development Workshop on the Potential of Social Support.

Serafica, F., & Blyth, D. (Eds.). (1985). Contemporary approaches to friendship and peer relations in early adolescence [Special issue]. *Journal of Early Adolescence, 5.*

Shade, B. (1983). The social success of Black youth: The impact of significant others. *Journal of Black Studies, 14,* 137-150.

Shrauger, J. S., & Schoeneman, T. J. (1979). Symbolic interactionist view of self-concept: Through the looking glass darkly. *Psychological Bulletin, 86,* 549-573.

Siegel, P. S. (1971). *Prestige in the American occupational structure*. Unpublished doctoral dissertation, Department of Sociology. University of Chicago. (Available from Photoduplication Department. University of Chicago Libraries. Chicago, IL 60637).

Speck, J., & Speck, R. (1985). Social network intervention with adolescents. In M. Mirkin & S. Koman (Eds.), *Handbook of adolescence and family therapy* (pp. 149-160). New York: Garner.

Thoits, P. A. (1986). Social support as coping assistance. *Journal of Consulting and Clinical Psychology, 54,* 416-423.

Tolsdorf, C. C. (1976). Social networks, support and coping: An exploratory study. *Family Process, 15*, 407-417.

Wellman, B. (1981). *East York interview codebook.* Toronto: Center for Urban and Community Studies, University of Toronto.

Whitten, N., Jr., & Wolfe, A. (1973). Network analysis. In J. Honingman (Ed.), *Handbook of social and cultural anthropology* (pp. 717-746). Chicago: Rand-McNally.

Appendix A

Adolescent Social Record: An Outline

I. Social Network Record, Pt. I
    A. *Demographic Profile*
       1. Subject's age, job status, grade
       2. Site living group (family size, composition, birth order, extended family, etc.)
       3. Subject's social affiliations
       4. Subject's network size
       5. Parent's travel
       6. Parent's education and occupational prestige score
       7. Neighborhood descriptives
       8. Denominational affiliation and attendance
       9. Girl/boy friend status
       10. Hourly breakdown of time spent w/ parents, siblings, friends, and other adults.

II. Social Network Record, Pt. II–(see Appendices)
    A. *Social Maps* (see Appendix A for the format used for all maps. There are 7 in all.)
       1. Maps: family, friends, closest friend/ family; significant others; argument with a friend; needs money.
          a. each map has subject indicated for each person listed; sex, age relational status, length of time known, place of contact, amount of contact, and geographical proximity.
    B. *Network Density Measures*
       1. Density Subgroups a. mother, best friend, father and peer; density interactions are examined by subgroup and overall.

2. Overall Intimate Network Density Measure a. number of close ties, b. closeness density, c. intimate density
    C. *Closeness Definition Measure*
       1. Definition given by subject; coded for
          a. complexity
          b. reciprocity
          c. levels of closeness
    D. *Role Model Measure*
       1. Total role models given by subject; coded for
          a. total number given
          b. status descriptives and characteristics such as age, sex, peer/adult status, relational status, occupation, famous vs. nonfamous status, etc.
          c. reason given for admiration, broken down into constructs and characteristics
    E. *Success Measure*
       1. Success categories are rank ordered by subjects for an overall score and by subgroup categories.
    F. *Support Projection Measure*
       1. Problem Identification Checklist
          a. subscales coded for orientation outlook on family, interpersonal conflict, loss, emotional resource, information counseling, transitions, material resources.
          b. also examined: support availability, support satisfaction, support characteristics, overall and for each subscale.
       2. Measure (2): Largest Problem Measure
          a. subjective listing of largest problem given by subject.
          b. coded by subscale groupings as listed in measure (1) and overall for: problem characteristics, support availability, supporter characteristics, support projections.
       3. Support Preference Measure
          a. coded for overall support preference and categorical support preference given for categories of trouble with school, argument with friend, need a job and feeling depressed.

Appendix B: Sample Network Maps

YOUR SOCIAL MAP

Family and Relatives

HOW I AM IN TOUCH:

- my home
- their house
- a personal get-together
- away from home
- social activities
- through sports
- at church
- on vacation
- by phone
- through letters
- at school
- at work
- other:

YOU MAY CHECK SEVERAL IN HERE

HOW OFTEN I AM IN TOUCH:

- daily or hourly
- a few times a week
- once a week
- twice a month
- once a month
- 3-4 times a year
- twice a year
- once a year
- summers only
- once every 2 years
- once every 5 years
- other:

CHECK ONLY ONE HERE . . . . . .

HOW NEAR IS THIS PERSON

- same house
- half-hour or less away
- about 1 hour away
- more than 2 hours away

AND HERE

RELATION TO ME   HOW LONG

Y = Year
M = Month

SEX INITIALS
AGE

1. M F ___
2. M F ___
3. M F ___
4. M F ___
5. M F ___
6. M F ___
7. M F ___
8. M F ___
9. M F ___
10. M F ___
11. M F ___

Appendix B: Network Maps

YOUR SOCIAL MAP

HOW NEAR IS THIS PERSON

RELATION TO ME | HOW LONG

	same house	half-hour or less away	about 1 hour away	more than 2 hours away	AGE
1.					
2.					
3.					
4.					
5.					
6.					
7.					
8.					
9.					
10.					
11.					

AND HERE . . . . . .   CHECK ONLY ONE HERE.

Y = Year
M = Month

HOW OFTEN I AM IN TOUCH:

daily or hourly · a few times a week · once a week · twice a month · once a month · 3-4 times a year · twice a year · once a year · summers only · once every 2 years · once every 5 years · other:

CHECK ONLY ONE HERE. . . . . .   AND HERE

HOW I AM IN TOUCH:

my home · their house · a personal get-together · away from home · social activities · through sports · at church · on vacation · by phone · through letters · at school · at work · other:

YOU MAY CHECK SEVERAL IN HERE

SEX INITIALS

M F	1.	
M F	2.	
M F	3.	
M F	4.	
M F	5.	
M F	6.	
M F	7.	
M F	8.	
M F	9.	
M F	10.	
M F	11.	

Other People

Appendix C: Density Item

II. Directions:

On the next page you will see three circles with letters in them. The "M" in the first circle stands for your mother. The "BF" in the second circle stands for your Best Friend. The "F" in the last circle stands for your father.

We want you to use the empty circles around the "M" circle first. Fill in the initials of *your friends* whom your mother knows. Next, do the same for your father. Finally, do the same thing for your best friend. Next, you will draw *a line between each of the people on the page who know* each other. "To know" means they know the name of the person you listed and would recognize them and maybe say hello if they met them and you were not there.

Remember, you are going to put the initials of *your* friends in the circles.

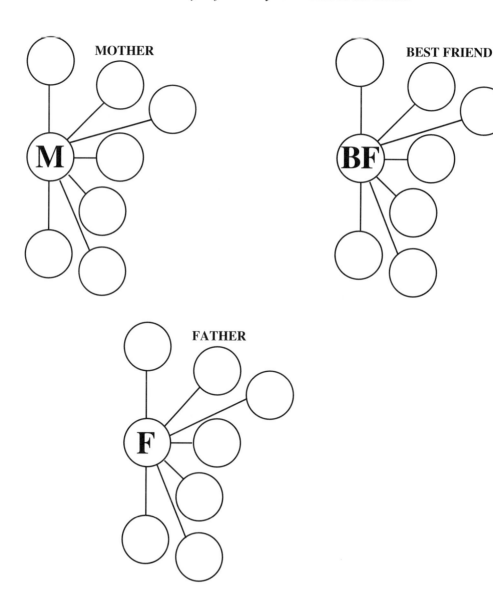

Appendix D: Other Items

Directions: We want to know about people you think of who really fit the image of what you want to be like. These persons could be living or dead, famous, or not famous, persons whom you know or they could be persons whom you only know about. The persons you admire could be sports figures, movie actors, musicians, writers, politicians, teachers, friends, or a parent or grandparent. In other words, they could be just about anyone. List the people whom you admire by name or by their initials and then check off the words which describe these persons.

Who do you admire or who would you like to be like?	If adult, what do they do or did they do for a living?	Make a check or circle for each word which describes each person.				
List them by name or initials below: (if famous, use a full name)	(fill in below)	Living	Not Living	Sex (Circle one)	Relation to you (if you know the person)	Famous Person I don't know
	(age)					
1. _____	_____ ( )	____	____	M F	_____	_____
2. _____	_____ ( )	____	____	M F	_____	_____
3. _____	_____ ( )	____	____	M F	_____	_____
4. _____	_____ ( )	____	____	M F	_____	_____

What is it that you like or admire most about the *first* person you listed? _____

_____

_____

Appendix D: Other Items

A	B	C			D	E
Which ones are problems which, if they happened to you, would cause you to want someone's help?	**Did this happen to you in the last 2 weeks?**	**If someone helped you with this problem, who was it?** (Fill in about the major person)			**Were you happy with the help you got from this person?**	**How many people do you know who could have helped you with this problem?**
(Check as many as you want)	(Circle one)	Relation	Age	Sex	(Circle one)	(Circle one)
1. ___ can't do school work	1. Yes No	1. ___	___	M F	1. Yes No	1 2 3 4 5 or more
2. ___ fight with mother	1. Yes No	1. ___	___	M F	1. Yes No	1 2 3 4 5 or more
3. ___ fight with father	1. Yes No	1. ___	___	M F	1. Yes No	1 2 3 4 5 or more
4. ___ fight with sister	1. Yes No	1. ___	___	M F	1. Yes No	1 2 3 4 5 or more
5. ___ fight with brother	1. Yes No	1. ___	___	M F	1. Yes No	1 2 3 4 5 or more
6. ___ fight with a friend	1. Yes No	1. ___	___	M F	1. Yes No	1 2 3 4 5 or more
7. ___ hassles at school with adults	1. Yes No	1. ___	___	M F	1. Yes No	1 2 3 4 5 or more
8. ___ being worried about being sick	1. Yes No	1. ___	___	M F	1. Yes No	1 2 3 4 5 or more
9. ___ going to a new school	1. Yes No	1. ___	___	M F	1. Yes No	1 2 3 4 5 or more
10. ___ losing a friend	1. Yes No	1. ___	___	M F	1. Yes No	1 2 3 4 5 or more
11. ___ death in the family	1. Yes No	1. ___	___	M F	1. Yes No	1 2 3 4 5 or more
12. ___ death of a friend	1. Yes No	1. ___	___	M F	1. Yes No	1 2 3 4 5 or more
13. ___ needing money desperately	1. Yes No	1. ___	___	M F	1. Yes No	1 2 3 4 5 or more
14. ___ deciding about your future life	1. Yes No	1. ___	___	M F	1. Yes No	1 2 3 4 5 or more
15. ___ planning a trip or vacation	1. Yes No	1. ___	___	M F	1. Yes No	1 2 3 4 5 or more
16. ___ feeling depressed or very sad	1. Yes No	1. ___	___	M F	1. Yes No	1 2 3 4 5 or more
17. ___ feeling upset because you did something wrong	1. Yes No	1. ___	___	M F	1. Yes No	1 2 3 4 5 or more

(table continues)

Appendix D: Other Items (cont'd)

Imagine that you have a problem like the ones listed in the boxes below and that you want someone to help you solve the problem. Look at the pairs of persons listed beneath the first problem. **Trouble with school work,** and pretend that you could only get help from one of the persons listed in each pair. For example, if you could only choose to get help from your mother or your father which one would you choose. Imagine that you could only get help from one person in each pair and that you wanted and needed help. *Force yourself to choose one and* put a circle around the one that you would choose. Do this for each of the pairs listed in the column under **trouble with school work,** go on to the next column and imagine that you have this problem. Again, look at each pair of persons and choose the one you would want to help you with this problem if you could only choose one of these people to help you and needed and wanted help with this problem. Do this for the other two problems also.

Try this example:

Trouble with school work	Argument with best friend	Need to find a job	Feeling down or generally upset
mother father	father teacher	father counselor	boss counselor

For additional information, contact:

Professor Deborah L. Coates
CUNY/CCNY, Dept. of Psychology
138th and Convent Avenue
New York, NY 10031
Telephone: (212) 650-5690
Fax: (908) 754-4472
E-mail: DEBORAHLC@AOL.COM

The How I Learn Scale and the How My Child Learns Scale

Diane Kern and Deborah Coates

Abstract

The *How I Learn Scale* and its parent version, The *How My Child Learns Scale,* were devised to assess adolescent and parent perceptions of achievement support in a study of the predictors of multidimensional or area specific achievement motivation in Black adolescents. Both the adolescent and parent versions of this achievement support measure consist of two subscales: one measuring student initiated resources; and one assessing externally provided resources. Scores are obtained for both the student and external resources subscales, as well as for the combined resources. Reliability data consisted of inter-item consistency coefficients, obtained for the items for each subscale and the total test scores. These ranged from .36 to .63 for the student version and .51 to .72 for the parent version. Validity data in the form of interscale correlations for each version of the achievement support measure yielded moderate correlations between the two subscale scores and high correlations between each subscale score and the total test score. Additional validity data consisted of several significant correlations between student ratings of external and total achievement support with overall achievement motivation, some specific achievement motivation areas, and certain academic achievement subscores. Results for the parent version were relatively weaker. Other findings obtained through regression analyses yielded several significant associations between the student and parent perceptions of either external or total achievement support and various forms of achievement motivation.

Rationale and Background

The *How I Learn Scale* was devised to measure adolescent perceptions of achievement support in a study of the predictors of multidimensional or area specific achievement motivation in Black adolescents (Kern, 1987). The term "achievement support" was originally suggested by Coates and Kern (1986) and refers to the interpersonal and structural resources available to encourage the pursuit of educational and achievement goals. Achievement support also can be considered to include verbal and emotional encouragement and rewards which underscore the value of achievement. The concept of achievement support is similar to that of learning environment, but focuses more on the availability and use of interpersonal resources. There are two important aspects to achievement support. The first is the child's and the second is the parent's perception of available resources. Achievement support should be higher in adolescents where both adolescents and parents can identify multiple resources which encourage and support achievement tasks and activities. Achievement support should also be related to several types of academic achievement.

The hypothesized relationships between achievement support and academic achievement motivation and academic achievement are derived from literature on the importance of parental behaviors and home environmental factors in promoting academic striving. Lightfoot (1978) stresses the mutual relationship between parents and schools as critical in the educational and achievement process. She notes that there has been a tendency in the literature to construe the Black family's influence upon the achievement orientations of Black children in a negative light. One example of this negative focus includes findings that Black parents tend to foster greater dependence, as opposed to autonomy and mastery in their socialization practices, relative to White parents (e.g. Rose, 1959; Feld, 1967).

Scheinfeld (1983) criticizes the approach of many studies that focus upon demographic factors (i.e., family structure, income level, family size, etc.) to explain the influence of families upon the achievement behaviors of Black children. Scheinfeld emphasizes the process of relationships between parents and children in a study comparing low income Black families with high versus low achieving male children. The findings suggested that the parents of the high achievers espoused views which encouraged the children's pursuit of their own interests and competence gained through active engagement with the environment. In contrast, Scheinfeld (1983) found that the parents of low achieving students stressed isolation from the environment to avoid feared

and negative outcomes, and neglected the children's interests. This study also found evidence of a positive association between children's school achievement and involvement with the community, through which competency and motivation enhancing experiences may be obtained.

Another study (Amato, 1986) found that reading ability was related to structural and interpersonal process resources in the families of adolescents. The structural resources consisted of the economic and social status attributes, whereas the process resources were defined as the parents' expectations, help and attention.

Research on preschool children has indicated the importance of parental behaviors and home environment to intelligence (Bradley & Caldwell, 1984; Bradley, Caldwell & Elardo, 1979). Academic achievement has also been related to parental achievement promoting behaviors in elementary aged (Amato, 1986; Clark, 1984) and adolescent (Amato, 1986) students. Achievement related behaviors, such as self-initiated reading behavior, was positively associated with parental encouragement among a sample of fifth grade students (Neuman, 1980). The relationship between parental process variables and academic achievement was weaker for adolescents in comparison to the elementary aged schoolchildren in one study (Amato, 1986).

Some researchers indicate the need to consider the influence of the larger social context of parent-child relationships, such as the various cultural institutions and range of other persons with whom the child interacts, that encourage achievement oriented behaviors (e.g. Scott-Jones, 1984). The existing research on the process variables related to achievement oriented behaviors focuses primarily upon the home environment and parental attitudes or behaviors. Such studies have not examined the role of the larger social context in providing achievement support. The social network construct may also be useful as an intervention paradigm to improve the achievement orientation of youngsters (see Coates, 1990).

It is also important to examine how students martial the resources that are available to assist them in academic pursuits. Clearly, some achievement support is obtained as the result of the student's action or initiative. For instance, a student may seek out help with homework from another person, or may join community organizations that instill positive achievement orientation. While there are many studies on achievement motivation and achievement orientation, little systematic research is available on some of the specific attitudes and behaviors of adolescents that may further academic achievement. The present study differs from others in that achievement support is defined as having a self-initiative component and an environmental resource aspect which extends beyond the immediate family.

A notable paucity of research exists that focuses upon the achievement processes of academically successful Black adolescents. Some research supports the notion that achievement motivation is a multidimensional, rather than a unidimensional construct for Black students (Banks, McQuater & Hubbard, 1978; Castenell, 1983). This measure was developed to examine the self-initiative component of achievement support and the interpersonal resource aspect, which extends beyond the immediate family.

Description of the Achievement Support Scales

The *How I Learn Scale* was developed to assess adolescent perceptions of achievement support. This measure consisted of two subscales. One scale measured student resources and student initiated behaviors such as requesting assistance with homework and going to the library voluntarily. The other subscale assessed externally provided resources from parents or others in the environment such as the availability of educational materials and books at home and the availability of someone to answer school related questions.

The instrument utilized the structured alternative format, originally described by Harter (1982). This format was devised by Harter (1982) in her perceived competence measure in order to minimize socially desirable responses. Each of the 14 items presented the student with pairs of opposing statements regarding either the student initiated behaviors that facilitate learning or the externally provided resources. The students were

asked to select one of the statements which best described them or their situation, and to rate their selections as being either "really true" or "sort of true" for them. For example, those students who selected a statement that described resourcefulness, rather than non-action on their part, and rated this statement as being "really true," earned a higher score (4 points), as opposed to those students who selected the option that described non-activity in learning related behavior and rated that statement as "really true" for themselves (1 point). Scores were totaled for each subscale and for the total instrument, to reflect the total number of achievement resources. Higher scores reflected a higher number of perceived resources.

The *How My Child Learns Scale* was devised to assess parental perceptions of student initiated and externally provided achievement support resources. This instrument was similar to the *How I Learn Scale* in all respects, except for the wording of the rating statements, which were "really" or "sort of true for my child," as opposed to "really" or "sort of true for me."

Procedures

Other Measures

Several measures were administered to the students, which purportedly assessed perceived competence, self-regulation style, social support, achievement support, multidimensional achievement motivation, and demographic characteristics. The *California Test of Basic Skills (CTBS)*, published by the California Test Bureau/McGraw Hill (1975), is a standardized achievement test which consists of four subscales–reading, mathematics, language, and reference skills, as well as a total score. Scores were obtained from the *CTBS,* which had been previously administered by the schools in June, 1984, and were used as measures of academic achievement. The parents were administered an instrument to assess their perceptions of their children's competence in various skill areas, as well as the measure of their perceptions of achievement support available to their children. For the purposes of this chapter, only the achievement support measure will be described in detail and discussed in relation to the dependent variables, multidimensional achievement motivation and academic achievement.

The *Life Profile Questionnaire* was devised by Coates (1981). Demographic data were obtained from this measure. The Siegel-Hodge-Rossi prestige rating scale (Siegel, 1971) was applied to the reported occupations of the parents as an index of social status.

Multidimensional Achievement Motivation. This scale was developed for use in the present study, based upon the *Multidimensional Motivation Questionnaire* constructed by Uguroglu, Schiller, and Walberg (1981). The present study's version consisted of six subscales, which measured achievement motivation in reading, mathematics, science, art/music, sports, and in general. Each item consisted of a five-point Likert scale, which varied in the intensity to which the participant either agreed with the statement or was committed to behave according to the description presented. A total score was the combination of the subscale scores. Inter-item consistency coefficients obtained for the subscales of this test ranged from .73 to .90.

Achievement Motivation by Domain. This scale, reported by its author, Castenell (1983), was originally developed in 1980. A revised version of this scale was used in this study, so that it consisted of three subscales designed to assess achievement motivation in the peer, home, and school domains. The items were rated on a five-point Likert scale. Inter-item consistency coefficients obtained in this study ranged from .64 to .81.

The *How I Learn Scale* was administered to the student participants along with the other measures in group sessions, which ranged from 1-1/2 hours to two hours and 15 minutes. The testing took place between October and mid-December, 1984 at schools attended by the students. Each session was monitored by one to three Black female testers, depending on the size of the group. The group size varied from 13 to 30 students per session.

The *How My Child Learns Scale,* along with a measure of parent perception of perceived competence, was sent home by the students for the parents to complete. Those parents who completed their questionnaires were requested to re-turn them to the school by their child participants in sealed envelopes.

Sample

Data were analyzed for 119 Black eighth and ninth grade students from the District of Columbia Public Schools. These students were classified as either high achievers, with grade point averages of "B" or better, and average achievers who held a "C" average. The student sample consisted of 57 high achievers (18 males and 39 females) or 62 average achievers (25 males and 37 females). In addition, 53 parents of high achievers and 53 parents of average achievers completed achievement support questionnaires.

Reliability Data for the Achievement Support Scales

Inter-item consistency coefficients were obtained for both the student and parent versions of this instrument from this study. Intercorrelations were performed among the items within each subscale and for the total test. These coefficients obtained for the student version, the *How I Learn Scale,* were as follows: .42, the student resources subscale; .36, the external resources subscale; and .63, the total test. The coefficients, obtained for the parent perception version, the *How My Child Learns Scale,* were as follows: .67, student resources; .51, external resources; and .72, the total test.

Validity Data for the Achievement Support Scales

Content Validity

Interscale correlations were obtained among the subscale scores for each version of this instrument from the present study. For the *How I Learn Scale,* the student resources subscale correlated positively with the external resources subscale ($r = .40, p < .01$) and the total resources score ($r = .78, p < .01$). The external subscale score correlated positively with the total resources score ($r = .86, p < .01$). For the *How My Child Learns Scale,* the student resources subscale correlated positively

Table 1. Correlations Between Achievement Support, Achievement Motivation and Achievement Measures for the Total Sample

	1	2	3	4	5	6	7	8	9	10	11	12
Achievement Support: External Resource	—	0.86**	0.30**	0.07	0.33*	0.31**	0.19*	0.16*	0.21**	-0.01	0.23**	0.13
Achievement Support: Total Resource			0.50**	0.04	0.38**	0.36**	0.19*	0.13	0.23**	0.10	0.38**	0.26**
Achievement Support: Parent Rating: External Resource				-0.07	0.14	0.09	0.11	-0.08	0.09	0.14	0.40**	0.31**
Sports Achievement Motivation					0.40**	0.68**	0.20*	0.20*	0.28**	-0.09	-0.19*	-0.11
General Achievement Motivation						0.82**	0.36**	0.47**	0.48**	-0.04	0.11	0.07
Total Multidimensional Achievement Motivation							0.38*	0.46**	0.51**	0.02	0.04	0.07
Peer Domain Achievement Motivation								0.39**	0.78**	0.05	0.06	0.14
Home Domain Achievement Motivation									0.72**	-0.12	-0.12	-0.07
Total Domain Achievement Motivation										-0.02	-0.01	0.04
CTBS Reading Percentile											0.71*	0.86**
CTBS Language Percentile												0.82**
CTBS Total Percentile												——

$* p < .05.; ** p < .01.$

with the external resources subscale ($r = .51, p < .01$) and with the total resources score ($r = .87, p < .01$). The external subscale correlated positively with the total resources score ($r = .84, p < .01$).

Construct Validity

Intercorrelations were computed between achievement support, area specific achievement motivation and academic achievement. Table 1 presents the significant intercorrelations between the achievement support subscores, the area specific achievement motivation, and the academic achievement subtest scores. Both the students' ratings of external achievement support and total achievement support resources were significantly and positively correlated with general achievement motivation, the total score of the *Multidimensional Achievement Questionnaire,* the total score of the *Achievement Motivation by Domain Scale* ($p < .001$), and peer domain achievement motivation ($p < .01$). Adolescents who reported greater numbers of external and total achievement support resources were more likely to have higher general and overall achievement motivation, as well as higher motivation in the peer domain. Student rating of external sources of achievement support was significantly and positively correlated with home domain achievement motivation ($p < .001$). The higher the number of perceived achievement resources in the home and larger environment, the higher the achievement motivation in the home domain. The parents' perceptions of the childrens' achievement support resources were not significantly associated with adolescent achievement motivation.

The student rating of external achievement support was significantly and positively correlated with only the language percentile score of the *CTBS* ($p < .001$). Student perceptions of total achievement support were significantly and positively correlated with the language and total percentile

CTBS scores ($p < .001$). Students who identified greater sources of overall achievement support were more likely to obtain higher academic achievement scores in language and on the total achievement test. This pattern was identical to that found for the parent rating of the child's external achievement support resources and the language and total percentile scores of the *CTBS*, e.g., the higher the parent's rating of the child's external achievement support resources, the higher the adolescent's language and overall achievement ($p < .001$).

Other Findings for the Achievement Support Scales

Significant mean differences were found between the high and average achievers in their ratings of total achievement support resources ($\overline{X}$ = 47.2 and 45.4, respectively; $p < .05$). The high achievers reported a greater number of total resources that aid in academic performance. No mean group differences were obtained for the student perceptions of student or external achievement support resources. The parents of high achievers reported a significantly greater number of achievement support resources than did parents of the average achievers of the student resource type (X = 20.4 and 18.0, respectively; $p < .01$), the external resources type (X = 28.0 and 26.3, respectively; $p < .01$), and in total (X = 48.0 and 44.5, respectively; $p < .01$).

Z-score transformations were performed on the correlations between the independent and dependent variables to test the significant differences between the high and average achievers. These analyses yielded fewer than 10% significant differences between the two groups. Therefore, a decision was made to perform subsequent analyses on the combined sample of high and average achievers. No significant differences were obtained between the group means among the demographic variables.

Achievement Support as a Predictor of Achievement Motivation and Academic Achievement

Table 2 presents the results of the regression analyses in which achievement support was found to be a significant predictor of either area specific achievement motivation or academic achievement scores. Regressions were run for each of the dependent variables, the specific achievement motivation measures and the *CTBS* subscale scores. The selection of predictor variables was based on their zero-order correlation with each of the dependent variables. Independent variables that intercorrelated with each other too highly were not entered into the regression equations in order to reduce multicollinearity. Up to 10 predictor variables were selected for each regression equation. The SPSSX (1986) multiple regression analysis computer program was used. The stepwise method of variable entry was selected. The SPSSX program set a minimum tolerance level of .050, after which no additional variables were entered. Table 2 contains the means, standard deviations, simple r, beta, multiple R, R^2, R^3 change, F ratio, and p significance for the change in variance from one step to another.

Student perception of total achievement support resources was one of five variables that accounted for a significant portion of the variance in science achievement motivation. It accounted for the largest amount, 16% of the total variance, along with the number of females identified as resources in the event of an argument with a friend, the preference for the father for overall interpersonal support an internalized integrated self-regulation style, and the student self-rating of cognitive competence.

Of the two predictors that accounted for a significant portion of the variance in art/music achievement motivation, the student perception of the total achievement support resources accounted for the largest amount, 21% of the total variance. The second significant predictor of art/music achievement motivation was the internalized/integrated self-regulation style, which accounted for an additional 7% of the variance.

Student perception of the total achievement support resources also accounted for a significant portion of the variance in the total score of the *Multidimensional Achievement Motivation Scale* (18%). This was the second most powerful predictor. Two other variables emerged as significant predictors of this total achievement motiva-

Table 2. Regression Analyses for Personality, Social Support, and Achievement Support Variables as Predictors of Area Specific Achievement Motivation for the Total Sample

Variable	μ	SD	r	β	R	R^2	multiple R^2 Δ	F	p
Science Achievement Motivation									
Achievement Support: Total Resources	46.24	5.20	0.40	0.28	0.40	0.16	0.16	20.90	<0.01
Argument Resources: Total Females	4.11	2.25	-0.31	-0.28	0.51	0.26	0.11	19.78	<0.01
Support Preference: Father	9.07	4.18	0.28	0.19	0.57	0.33	0.06	17.85	<0.01
Self-Regulation: Internalized Integrated	18.23	1.80	0.38	0.19	0.60	0.36	0.04	15.69	<0.01
Cognitive Competence: Self-Rating	23.32	3.33	0.37	0.17	0.62	0.39	0.02	13.75	<0.05
Art/Music Achievement Motivation									
Achievement Support: Total Resources	46.24	5.20	0.46	0.38	0.46	0.21	0.21	13.72	<0.01
Self-Regulation: Internalized Integrated	18.23	1.80	0.38	0.27	0.53	0.28	0.07	9.72	<0.05
Total Multidimensional Achievement Motivation									
Homework Res.: 3 or > Places of Contact	3.89	2.29	0.54	0.39	0.54	0.29	0.29	13.70	<0.01
Achievement Support: Total Resources	46.24	5.20	0.48	0.45	0.69	0.48	0.18	14.64	<0.01
Largest Problem: Support Satisfaction	3.64	0.57	0.45	0.30	0.74	0.55	0.07	12.70	<0.05
School Domain Achievement Motivation									
Achievement Support: Parent Perception: External Resources	27.14	3.32	0.72	0.72	0.72	0.52	0.52	30.17	<0.01

tion score, as follows: 1) having contact with interpersonal resources who help with homework in several different settings (variance = 29%) and 2) the degree of satisfaction with the interpersonal support received while experiencing a large problem (variance = 7%).

The parent perception of the external achievement support resources emerged as the sole significant predictor of achievement motivation in the school domain. It accounted for 52% of the variance in school domain achievement motivation.

Regression analyses on the *CTBS* subscale scores failed to yield significant findings for the achievement support variable.

Discussion

The student's perceptions of the both the external and total achievement support resources were related to several domains of achievement motivation. Therefore, students whose environments provided them with greater material and interpersonal learning related assistance were more likely to strive in the general, peer, and home achievement motivation domains than students with less perceived external achievement support. The strong correlations between student perceptions of external achievement support and the total scores on both achievement motivation measures in this study further suggest the importance of the availability of support and resources both within the family and in the larger community upon overall achievement motivation.

Student perceptions of total achievement support resources were also found to be significant predictors of achievement motivation in science, art/music, and overall, across domains. Therefore, a wide array of specific achievement motivation domains is associated with externally provided and overall achievement support resources.

It is notable that student initiated achievement support was not significantly associated with any area of achievement motivation. However, it appears to be influential in combination with external sources of achievement support, as evidenced by the significant findings between perceived total achievement support and various areas of achievement motivation. Perhaps students learn to take initiative in securing academic assistance or seeking out learning related resources through the externally provided assistance from parents and other social agents.

Also noteworthy is the relatively weaker association between parent perceptions of achievement support and student achievement motivation. The one significant finding, that parent perception of external achievement support predicted student achievement motivation in the school domain, is consistent with the predictions of this study. Apparently, students' perceptions of achievement support have a more direct impact upon their achievement motivation than the parents' perceptions, particularly in nonacademic areas.

The findings concerning academic achievement indicated that student perceptions of external achievement support were significantly associated with language achievement, while total achievement support was related to overall achievement. These findings appear consistent with the expectations of this study, although the relationship between achievement support and academic achievement was not specifically predicted.

The finding that parents' perceptions of the externally provided achievement support resources was strongly associated with language and overall achievement scores was also in accordance with the expectations of this study and other research. While previous research on the relationship of family environment and process variables with achievement behavior focused only upon home environment and the immediate family (e.g. Amato, 1986; Clark, 1984), the present study's notion of achievement support extended to the larger social environment. Thus, the findings suggest the utility of examining the influence of institutions and other persons who may promote learning.

Limitations of the Study

Some limitations of this study may have adversely influenced the findings. Moderate reliability data were obtained in this study for the *How I Learn* and *How My Child Learns* scales. The intertest reliabilities were higher for the total test, the combination of the two subscales, than for either subscale. In addition, the student resources subscale contained fewer items than did the external resources subscale. The subscales consisted of six and eight items, respectively. This apparent weakness in the test's construction may have accounted for the relatively weaker relationships obtained between the student resources subscale and the various achievement motivation measures and achievement scores. Therefore, further research is needed in order to create scales of equal length and higher reliability.

Another possible shortcoming in this study may have been the failure to directly assess social desirability in the participants' responses for the various measures used. This may have contributed to the weak differentiation of the two subsamples, the high versus the average achievers. Future use of these measures should be accompanied by the measurement of response bias; and adjustments made if bias is found.

Sampling posed another possible in this study. The criteria for the classification of the high achievers may have been too broad in range. This resulted in very few significant group differences. Therefore, powerful comparisons of the two groups and conclusions regarding how they differed in scope of achievement support and in areas of specific achievement motivation could not be made.

One solution to this sampling problem might be the restriction of the grade point average range to the upper limits for the high achievers (grade point average of 3.5 or above). The average achievers should then be defined as those students with grade point averages of 2.0 through 2.5, or solid "C's." Then stratified random sampling might be performed between those two groups.

This strategy may eliminate the apparent overlap that occurred between the low high achievers and the high average achievers.

In addition, males were underrepresented in this study. The disproportionately lower number of males was particularly evident among the high achievers. This problem was generally reflected in the schools. Some research has suggested a higher vulnerability of Black male adolescents to social pressures that impede academic striving (Edwards, 1976). Therefore, it is critical that closer investigation be conducted of possible gender differences in achievement support processes among Black adolescents. This would necessitate a more deliberate effort to recruit larger samples of high achieving Black male adolescents.

Implications for Future Research

Recent research illustrates the importance of family communication and behavioral dynamics to aspects of adolescent psychosocial development (Bell & Bell, 1983; Reiss, Oliveri & Curd, 1983) by utilizing observational assessment techniques in addition to self-report data. While there is some research which employs observational assessments of the influence of parental behaviors upon achievement processes (e.g. Amato, 1986), a greater number of studies are needed using such methods. In addition, such techniques might be useful in further exploring and identifying the interpersonal dynamics, activities and material resources in the larger social environment that promote achievement motivation and actual achievement.

Marjoribanks (1988), in a longitudinal study, reported on the use of a scale developed to assess the perceptions of 310 Australian adolescents of their parents' support for learning. The 1988 study examined the relationship between the perceptions of these late adolescents, aged 16 and 21 to their occupational aspirations and attainment, in the case of the 21 year olds. The findings indicated that the scale had predictive validity for occupational outcomes, although less so for the male than female participants. Unfortunately, little detail was provided on the structure of this scale.

Despite the limited information provided in the Marjoribanks (1988) study, it has implica-

tions for the use of a scale, such as the achievement support measure used in the present study. The use of the *How I Learn Scale* may have implications for the predictive power of resources provided to adolescents in both the home and in the larger community. Future research, using an expanded version of this achievement support instrument, may help delineate not only the specific resources parents and the community provide to enhance academic learning, but may also identify those resources that aid in the development of occupational interests or prevocational skills. Such information could have immense value to educators and parents who seek to provide educational and occupational guidance to adolescents.

References

Amato, P. R., & Ochiltree, G. (1986). Family resources and the development of child competence. *Journal of Marriage and the Family, 48,* 47-56.

Banks, W. C., McQuater, G. V., & Hubbard, J. L. (1978). Toward a reconceptualization of the social-cognitive bases of achievement orientations in Blacks. *Review of Educational Research, 48,* 381-397.

Bell, D. C., & Bell, L. G. (1983). Parental validation and support in the development of adolescent daughters. *New Directions for Child Development, 22,* 27-42.

Bradley, R. H., Caldwell, B. M., & Elardo, R. (1979). Home environment and cognitive development in the first two years: A cross-lagged panel analysis. *Developmental Psychology, 15,* 246-250.

Bradley, R. H., & Caldwell, B. M. (1984). The relationship of infants' home environments to achievement test performance in first grade: A follow-up study. *Child Development, 55,* 803-809.

Castenell, L. A. (1983). Achievement motivation: An investigation of adolescents' achievement patterns. *American Educational Research Journal, 20,* 503-510.

Clark, R. M. (1984). *Home interaction and children's school learning.* Manuscript submitted for publication.

Coates, D. L. (1990). Social network analysis as a mental health intervention with African American adolescents. In F. C. Serafica, A. I. Schwebel, B. K. Russell, D. D. Isaac, & L. J. Myers (Eds.), *Mental health of ethnic minorities.* New York: Praeger.

Coates, D. L. (1981). *The Social Network Record.* Washington, DC: Catholic University, Center for the Study of Youth Development.

Coates, D., & Kern, D. (1986, April). *Social networks, academic support and personal traits as correlates of achievement motivation and achievement in Black adolescents.* Paper presented at the annual meeting of the American Educational Research Association, San Francisco, CA.

Edwards, O. L. (1976). Components of academic success: A profile of achieving Black adolescents. *Journal of Negro Education, 45,* 408.

Feld, S. (1967). Longitudinal study of the origins of achievement strivings. *Journal of Personality and Social Psychology, 7,* 408-414.

Harter, S. (1982). The Perceived Competence Scale for Children. *Child Development, 53,* 87-97.

Kern, D. (1987). *Perceptions of competence, self-regulation and social support as predictors of achievement motivation in academically successful Black adolescents.* Unpublished doctoral dissertation. Catholic University, Washington, DC.

Lightfoot, S. L. (1978). *Worlds apart.* New York: Basic Books.

Marjoribanks, K. (1988). The predictive validity of a parents' support scale in relation to occupational aspirations and attainment. *Educational and Psychological Measurement, 48,* 155-159.

Neuman, S. B. (1986). The home environment and fifth grade students' leisure reading. *The Elementary School Journal, 86,* 334-343.

Reiss, D., Oliveri, M. E., & Curd, K. (1983). Family paradigm and adolescent social behavior. *New Directions for Child Development, 22,* 77-92.

Rosen, B. (1959). Race, ethnicity, and the achievement syndrome. *American Sociological Review, 24,* 47-60.

Scheinfeld, D.R. (1983). Family relationships and school achievement among boys of lower-income urban Black families. *American Journal of Orthopsychiatry, 53,* 127-143.

Scott-Jones, D. (1984). Family influences on cognitive development and school achievement. In E. W. Gordon (Ed.), *Review of education.* Washington, DC: American Educational Research Association.

Siegel, P. S. (1971). *Prestige in the American occupational structure.* Unpublished doctoral dissertation, Department of Sociology, University of Chicago. (Available from Photoduplication Department, University of Chicago Libraries, Chicago, IL 60637).

Uguroglu, M. E., Schiller, D. P., & Walberg, H. J. (1981). A multidimensional motivation instrument. *Psychology in the Schools, 18,* 279-285.

Appendix

How I Learn Scale

Directions: The items on the following pages will help us understand some ways by which you may learn. People learn things in different ways. Therefore, there are no right or wrong answers.

1. First, go to number 1. You will see two descriptions near the center of the page, which are separated by the word, "but." Read these two descriptions.

2. Decide which description is most like you, the one on the right or the one on the left side of the word, "but".

3. Then decide whether the description you chose is really like you or sort of like you and *make an X* in the space underneath either the "Sort of True for me" or "Really True for me" column.

4. Be sure to *pick only one description* that best fits you and *mark an X in only one space,* to show how much that description is like you *for each numbered item.*

For Example:

Really true for me	Sort of true for me	Sort of true for me	Really true for me
1. ____	____	X	____

Some kids often study.   but   Other kids never study.

If you study only occasionally you would place an X in the "Sort of True" column.

1. ____	____	____	____

Some kids do their homework on their own.   but   Other kids need to be reminded.

2. ____	____	____	____

Some kids do not ask for help when they have problems with homework.   but   Other kids ask for help when they have problems with homework.

Really true for me	Sort of true for me		Sort of true for me	Really true for me

3.____ ____   ____ ____
Some kids get help from their parents with homework.   but   Other kids get no help from their parents with homework.

4. ____ ____   ____ ____
Some kids have no place at home to study.   but   Other kids have a place at home to study.

5. ____ ____   ____ ____
Some kids enjoy going to museums to learn new things.   but   Other kids do not enjoy going to museums.

6. ____ ____   ____ ____
Some kids are not sure of what they want to be when they grow up.   but   Other kids know what they want to be when they grow up.

7. ____ ____   ____ ____
Some kids have things (i. e. encyclopedia, other books, computer, etc.) at home that help them learn.   but   Other kids do not have things at home that help them learn.

8. ____ ____   ____ ____
Some kids do not know anyone personally who has gone to college.   but   Other kids know someone personally who has gone to college.

9. ____ ____   ____ ____
Some kids' parents want them to attend college after high school.   but   Other kids' parents want them to do something else after high school.

10. ____ ____   ____ ____
Some kids seldom visit the library.   but   Other kids visit the library often.

11. ____ ____   ____ ____
Some kids have a place besides home where they can get help with schoolwork.   but   Other kids have no other place where they can get help with school work.

12. ____ ____   ____ ____
Some kids are happy just to get by in school.   but   Other kids have a strong desire to do well in school.

13. ____ ____   ____ ____
Some kids know an adult besides their parents whom they can talk to about school and future plans.   but   Other kids do not an adult besides their parents whom they can talk to about school and future plans.

14. ____ ____   ____ ____
Some kids do not belong to a club or organization at school or in the community (i.e. church choir, scouts, band, etc.).   but   Other kids belong to a club or organization at school or in the community.

Scoring Key

Title of Measure: How I Learn
Variable: Achievement Support
Title of Measure: How My Child Learn
Variable: Achievement Support (Parent Scale)
Description: Consists of 2 subscales which differentiate sources of achievement support as follows:

Subscales	Item Numbers
1. Student Resources	1,2,5,6,10,12
2. External Resources	3,4,7,8,9,11,13,14

Scoring: A total score for the amount of achievement support may be obtained by combining the ratings for each of the items in the following manner:

1. Assign a numerical value for each of the ratings for each of the odd numbered items as follows:

A.	Really True	Sort of True	Sort of True	Really True
	4	3	2	1

for the following items:

1. Student Resources   1,5
2. External Resources   3,7,9,11,13

2. Assign to the even numbered items:

A.	Really True	Sort of True	Sort of True	Really True
	1	2	3	4

for the following items:

1. Student Resources   2,6,10,12
2. External Resources   4,8,14

The higher the score, the greater the number of achievement support resources available. The lower the score, the fewer the number of achievement support resources available.

For additional information, contact:

Diane Kern, Ph.D.
2420 Newton Street, N. E.
Washington, D.C. 20018
Telephone (202) 526-3609

The Jackson Competency Scales

Anna Mitchell Jackson

Abstract

Item construct-based self-report competency scales were developed to assess perceived academic ability for 10-17 year old African American males. Two forms were constructed: Form A for 10-14 year old youth and Form B for 15-17 year old youth. In developing the scales, standardized tests and pertinent literature pertaining to academic success perceptions were reviewed. On the basis of that review, four categories were delineated: 1) Self-Reliance; 2) Independent Action; 3) Goal Persistence; and 4) Objectivity. Specific items were derived for each category. A three point Likert Scale (1 = Rare/Never, 2 = Sometimes, 3 = Almost all of the time), was used to measure perceived participant attitudes. The alternate forms were administered to 182 African American youth participating in the Community Coalition Intervention Project at The Meharry Medical College School of Dentistry, and to youth at Churches and Community agencies in the Greater Nashville, Tennessee Metropolitan area. Split-half reliability coefficients were computed. A .88 reliability coefficient was obtained for Form A (10-14 year old youth) and a .81 coefficient for Form B (15-17 year old youth). A validity correlation of .24 was obtained between the two scales and the Self-Concept of Ability Test General (Form A, $r = .24$, $p < .05$).

Moderate to high correlations have been reported between self-ability perceptions and achievement motivation (Byrne, 1986; Byrne, 1990; Gerardi, 1990; Graham, 1994; Wilhite, 1990). African American populations exhibit consistently high achievement expectations in a number of the reported investigations (Graham, 1994). The identification and reinforcement of competency perceptions held by African American Youth, a form of achievement motivation, offers a potentially productive avenue for achievement motivation enhancement. Given the above premise, a project to develop reliable and valid competency instruments was conceived and initiated by the author. The target population was low to middle income 10-17 year old African American males in the Nashville Metropolitan Area. The project was a component of the Minority Male Initiative Grants activated by the U.S. Department of Health and Human Services. The project funding agency was The Office of Minority Health.

297

Prior to the intervention, item construct based self-report competency scales were developed: Form A for 10-14 year old youth and, Form B for 15-17 year old youth. In developing the tests, literature on academic perceptions and attitudes was reviewed. On the basis of that review, four categories were delineated: 1) Self-Reliance; 2) Independent Action; 3) Goal Persistence; and 4) Objectivity. Specific items were derived for each category. A three point Likert Scale (1 = Rare/Never, 2 = Sometimes, 3 = Almost All of The Time) was used to measure the perceived relevance of each item. The scales were administered to 182 African American youth participating in the Community Coalition Intervention Project based at The Meharry Medical College School of Dentistry, and to youth at Churches and Community agencies in the Greater Nashville, Tennessee Metropolitan area. The scales were administered as part of a battery of tests in which self-concept of ability, self-esteem, and school perception were assessed. Possible test scores for the Jackson Competency Scales range from 35 to 114 (See Appendix for sample items). Mean scores and standard deviations for the sample are presented in Table 1. A .88 reliability coefficient (split-half) was obtained for Form A (10-14 year old youth) and a .81 for Form B (15-17 year old youth). A validity correlation of .24 was obtained between the two scales and the Self-Concept of Ability Test General Form (Form A) ($r = .24$, $p < .05$). Therefore the test would appear to be both valid and reliable. The reliability coefficient (split-half) for males in the standardization sample for the concept of ability test was computed at .95 (Gerardi, 1990). Validity coefficients ranged from .63 to .88 for the same population. For females in the standardization sample, reliability coefficients of .96 and validity coefficients of .52 to .68 were reported (Gerardi, 1990). The Jackson Competency Scales will be administered to a wider group of African American youth (males and females) as a further test of its reliability and validity. Reinforcement regimens will then be undertaken to determine the effect of identified competency areas on achievement motivation and performance.

Table 1. Means and Standard Deviations of the Jackson Competency Scales

Form A	M	Sd
10-14 year olds	86.97	19.71
Form B		
15-17 year olds	88.00	11.83

References

Byrne, B. M. (1990). Concept and academic achievement: Investigating their importance as discriminators of academic Track membership in high school. *Canadian Journal of Education, 15*(2) 173-182.

Byrne, B. M. (1986). Self-concept academic achievement relations: An investigation of dimensionality, stability, and causality. *Canadian Journal of Behavioral Science, 18*(2), 173-186.

Gerardi, S. (1990). Academic self-concept as a predictor of academic success among minority and low socio-economic status students. *Journal of College Student Development, 31*(5), 402-407.

Graham, S. (1994). Motivation in African Americans. *Review of Educational Research, 64*(1), 55-117.

Wilhite, S. C. (1990). Self-efficacy, locus of control, self-assessment of memory ability, and study activities as predictors of college course achievement. *Journal of Educational Psychology, 82*(4), 696-700.

Appendix

Jackson Competency Scale (Ages 10-14)

Be sure to select a choice for each statement.

Example: Doing homework even on Christmas. ■ [2] [3]

Scale: [1]   [2]   [3]
        rare/never   sometimes   almost/all time

Keeping at things I start.
Doing things by myself.
Being able to understand why things happen.

Checking on the success of things done.
Seeing things through to the end.
Reviewing things I have learned.
Making sure things done are correct.
Depending on myself to do things.
Knowing who I am as a person.
Starting again which things go wrong.

Continuing tasks after let downs.
Working alone.
Understanding why things happen.
Having different plans for the same goal.
Dependence on own resources.
Self knowledge.
Self-reliance.
Bouncing back after disappointments.
Practice assignments.

Jackson Competency Scale (Ages 15-17)

Be sure to select a choice for each statement.

Example: Doing homework
        even on Christmas.   ■   [2]   [3]

Scale: [1]   [2]   [3]
       rare/never   sometimes   almost/all time

For additional information, contact:

Anna M. Jackson, Ph.D.
School of Dentistry, Box 2A
Meharry Medical College
1005 D.B. Todd Boulevard
Nashville, TN 37208
Telephone: (615) 327-6076
Fax: (615) 327-6213

The Black Male Experiences Measure

Michael Cunningham and Margaret Beale Spencer[1, 2]

Abstract

The Black Male Experiences Measure examines the social experiences and perceptions of African American males in public places. The five-point Likert-type questionnaire has four reliable factors. Each factor examines males' perceptions of environmental situations. The measure's theoretical background considers youths' phenomenological experiences in social contexts and their linkages to adolescent symbolic processes and abstract thinking.

Adolescence is a potentially difficult time period for any youth. It is a period when youth go through a normative "identity crisis" (Erikson, 1968). But the difficulty of this developmental period is exacerbated when the adolescent is African American, male, and poor. As an economically disadvantaged minority group member, stressful encounters are highly probable. Cumulative adverse and unwarranted ex–periences are often linked to race and gender associated prejudice, discrimination, and are barriers to full opportunity for personal growth (Erikson, 1959; Gibbs & Huang, 1989; Spencer, 1995, 1985). In general, the life experiences of minority adolescents in the United States are complicated by issues not faced by majority youth. Complex political, cultural, economic, and social forces interact in ways that exacerbate normative adolescent concerns such as identity and self-image (Spencer & Markstrom-Adams, 1990), increased autonomy, relations with peers, school achievement and career goals (Spencer & Dornbush, 1990). Most importantly, complex

interactive forces impact the ecological-cultural context in which normative processes occur (Spencer, 1995).

Many researchers have shown that the process of maturation is universal and occurs with minor variations across racial and cultural groups. They also acknowledge that individuals are subject to wide ethnic variations in their behavioral manifestations, their symbolic meanings, and their societal responses (Phinney & Rotheram, 1987). By adolescence, given normal cognitive maturation, minority youth are well aware of the values of the majority culture and its standards of performance, achievement, and beauty. In contrast to younger children, adolescents evaluate their personal opportunities for attaining valued goals (Spencer, 1985; Spencer & Dornbush, 1990). Accordingly, coping processes, identity outcomes, and behavioral outcomes may vary because of adolescents' use of hypothetical abstract reasoning that results in different phenomenological processes (Spencer, 1995). Because the life goals of young people and the developmental stages

301

these pursuits represent are quite different from those expected of adults, it is critical to examine African American adolescent males from a perspective that considers both their unique and social structural experiences. Moreover, the literature on identity formation suggests the need for more empirical research on African American adolescent males in many areas (Cunningham, 1993). Recent theorizing suggests that identity processes, especially for visible minority group members, are linked to risk experienced, stress encountered, coping methods employed, adaptive identity processes, and patterned outcomes (Spencer, 1995). Accordingly, alternative theorizing (Spencer, 1995) introduces an Identity and Cultural-Ecological perspective (ICE) that invites *new constructs.* The Black Male Experiences Measure (BMEM) provides a construct which examines phenomenological processes as linked to youth's social stresses, identity, and adaptation as associated with their unique cultural-ecological niche.

Too frequently, research efforts on African American adolescent males have generally been conducted in response to negative outcomes such as high incarceration rates, high school drop-out rates, and morbidity and mortality rates. Consequently, many theories of adolescent development foster an incomplete picture of developmental processes for African American males. As indicated, current efforts emanate from a cultural-ecological phenomenological theoretical framework (Spencer, 1995).

Background

Much of the research on African American male development lacks the incorporation of contextual variables (e.g., poverty, ethnicity, family structure) that influence life-course outcomes. Since adolescence is a point of transition, the contextual experiences of African American male adolescents (like all youth) are heavily influenced by their environment (Spencer, 1986) in addition to cultural patterns and normal psychological processes (Spencer, 1995). Developmental outcomes, then, are unavoidably linked to adolescent-sensitive contextual experiences (Spencer, Swanson, & Cunningham, 1991).

Theorizing about the conception of Black male experiences was influenced and is supported by culturally-sensitive perspectives and programmatic research efforts (Chestang, 1972; Connell, Spencer, and Aber, 1994; Cunningham, 1993, 1994; Spencer, 1986, 1995; Spencer, Cole, Dupree, Glymph, and Pierre, 1994; Spencer, Cunningham, and Swanson, 1995; Spencer, Swanson, and Cunningham, 1991). These works consider adolescent male experiences in different contexts. Spencer (1986) and Spencer, Dobbs, and Swanson (1988) examine the effects of poverty and youth victimization as life stressors. Spencer (1985) and Spencer, Cunningham, and Swanson (1995) explore normal identity processes under high race-stigmatizing conditions. Spencer, Cunningham, and Swanson (1995) and Cunningham (1993, 1994) include peer group experiences as significant variables that influence adolescent development. Connell, Spencer, and Aber (1994), Spencer, Cole, Dupree, Glymph, and Pierre, (1994) and Spencer, McDermott, Burton, and Cole (in press) examine neighborhood and parenting effects on adolescent development. Spencer and Markstrom-Adams (1990) explore the effects of minority status and identity. Chestang (1972) depicts the consequences of development in a "hostile environment" and its potential contribution to vulnerability. Spencer (1995) incorporates and extends research and theorizing into a theory that represents a phenomenological variant of ecological systems theory. In sum, her perspective represents an identity focused and cultural ecological developmental framework (i.e., ICE) which has generally been ignored in theorizing about African Americans.

The Black Male Experiences Measure (BMEM) is best used as an indicator of African American males' daily stressors. Its content examines perceived implicit and explicit events. The measure's utility garners contextual experiences of African American male's negative and positive imagery. Often the contextual experiences of African Americans, generally, are not considered (Cunningham, 1993, 1994; Spencer, 1935, 1995; Spencer & Dornbush, 1990). This measure is useful in attempts to understand precursors to negative outcomes.

Table 1. Proximal Negative Experiences Factor 1 Loadings (alpha = .92)

Question	Factor loading
1. When hanging out, do police/security stop and ask what you are doing?	.61
2. How often do people you don't know think you are doing something wrong(like selling drugs, preparing to rob somebody, preparing to steal something, etc.)?	.67
3. How often do teachers think you are doing something wrong?	.72
4. How often do school administrators think you are doing something wrong?	.73
5. How often do neighbors think you are doing something wrong?	.75
6. How often do sales people think you are doing something wrong?	.72
7. How often do police think you are doing something wrong?	.77
8. How often do people on the street think you are doing something wrong?	.70
9. How often do "White Americans, generally" think you are doing something wrong?	.61
10. How often do "Black Americans, generally" think you are doing something wrong?	.67
11. Are these experiences reported by your brothers?	.59
12. Are these experiences reported by your sisters?	.58
13. Are these experiences reported by your male friends?	.43

Table 2. Distal Negative Experiences Factor 2 Loadings (alpha = .84)

Question	Factor loading
14. Do police stop you for minor driving offenses?	.48
15. Are you harassed by police?	.45
16. Have you been stopped when driving, riding or walking in a White neighborhood?	.48
24. Do you receive "hate stares" from Black men?	.56
26. Do you receive "fear stares" from Black women?	.64
27. Have you been rejected from a job due to your appearance?	.63
28. Do sales people tend to ignore you when enter a store?	.54
32. Do Whites ask you questions as if you were an expert on all Black issues?	.43
35. Do you ever feel invisible when you walk into a group?	.44

Cunningham's (1995) findings indicate one aspect of the measure's usefulness. He examined contextual influences on reactive identity outcomes. The Black Male Experiences factors were statistically significant predictors of reactive identity development. Specifically, proximal experiences were an indicator of reactive identity that was potentially harmful to self. In contrast, distal experiences were an indicator of reactive identity that was potentially harmful to others, attitudes toward females especially. Therefore, the measure can be used as one indication of contextual stress that influences reactive coping and emergent identity styles (Cunningham & Spencer, 1995). In turn, the reactive coping and emergent identity styles influence negative life stage outcomes (i. e., adjudication, mental illness, poor health and lack of intimacy) (Spencer, 1995).

Method

The Black Male Experiences Measure (BMEM) was developed to examine the social experiences of Black males in public places. The thirty five question instrument was administered as one component of an adolescent interview. Students were instructed to circle one of five responses for each question: (a) "never" if the event did not happen; (b) "almost never" if the event happened 1-3 times; (c) "sometimes" if the event happened 4-6 times; (d) "almost always" if the event happened 7-9 times; or (e) "always" if

Table 3. Negative Inferences Factor 3 Loadings (alpha = .74)

Question	Factor Loading
17. Do White people tend to lock their car doors when you pass?	.48
21. When in conversation with a White person do they try to use "Black" lingo or jargon to communicate?	.46
23. Do you receive "hate stares" from White men?	.49
25. Do you receive "fear stares" from White women?	.52
29. Do sales people tend to follow you when enter a store?	.48

the event happened 10 or more times during the last year. Boys and girls answered the same form. However, the girls were asked to answer about their knowledge of their Black male peers' experiences.

The questionnaire items were subjected to a principle components factor analysis. Thirty-three of the original thirty-five questions comprised four reliable factors. (See tables, 1-4) Factor 1 (Proxi-mal Negative Experiences) is made up of 13

Table 4. Positive Inferences Factor 4 Loadings (alpha = .67)

Question	Factor Loading
19. How often do people that you don't know smile when you approach them?	.53
20. How often do people that you don't know speak or greet you as you approach them?	.45
30. Do you generally feel welcome when you walk into a place of business?	.47
31. Are sales people courteous to you when shopping in a store?	.58
33. Do Black professional men talk to you about career options?	.57
34. Do White professional men talk to you about career options?	.54

Table 5. Black Male Experiences Questionnaire

This set of questions asks your opinion about the experiences of Black males in public places. Circle "never" if the event did not happen, "almost never" if the event happened 1-3 times, "sometimes" if the event happened 4-6 times, "almost always" if the event happened 7-9 times, or "always" if the event happened 10 or more times during the last year.

1. When you are hanging out (like in the park, playground, street corner, etc.), how often do police/security guards stop to ask what you are doing?
2. How often do people you don't know think you are doing something wrong (like selling drugs, preparing to rob somebody, preparing to steal something, etc.)?
3. How often do teachers think you are doing something wrong?
4. How often do school administrators think you are doing something wrong?
5. How often do neighbors think you are doing something wrong?
6. How often do sales people think you are doing something wrong?
7. How often do police think you are doing something wrong?
8. How often do people on the street think you are doing something wrong?
9. How often do "White Americans, generally" think you are doing something wrong?
10. How often do "Black Americans, generally" think you are doing something wrong?
11. How often are these experiences reported by your brothers?
12. How often are these experiences reported by your sisters?
13. How often are these experiences reported by your males friends?
14. How often do police stop you for minor driving offenses (like not using your signals, not coming to a full stop at stop signs, etc.)?
15. How often are you harassed by police (physically and/or abusive language)?

(table continues)

16. Have you been stopped when driving, riding, or walking in a White neighborhood?
17. Do White people tend to lock their car doors when you pass?
18. Do people go out of their way to speak when you pass?
19. How often do people that you don't know smile when you approach them?
20. How often do people that you don't know speak or greet you as you approach them?
21. When in conversation with a White person do they try to use "Black" lingo or jargon to communicate?
22. Do White people always bring up sports or women in their conversations with you?
23. Do you receive "hate stares" from White men?
24. Do you receive "hate stares" from Black men?
25. Do you receive "fear stares" from White women?
26. Do you receive "fear stares" from Black women?
27. Have you been rejected from a job due to your appearance?
28. Do sales people tend to ignore you when entering a store?
29. Do sales people tend to follow you when you enter a store?
30. Do you generally feel welcome when you walk into a place of business?
31. Are sales people courteous to you when shopping a store?
32. Do White people ask you questions as if you were an expert on all Black issues?
33. Do Black professional men talk to you about career options?
34. Do White professional men talk to you about career options?
35. Do you ever feel "invisible" when you walk into a group?

questions and has a standardized alpha of .92. As listed in Table 1, the general theme of the questions addresses experiences with actual or potential significant others. These situations can be viewed as incidents with people with whom one has a potential or actual proximal (close) relationship. Because of the actual or potential closeness of the relationship between the perpetrator and the incident's focal person, the respondent may misinterpret the situation's cause as due to one's own personal attributes as opposed to larger group membership.

Factor 2 (Distal Negative Experiences) is made up of nine questions and has a standardized alpha of .84 (see Table 2). The general theme of the questions addresses situations that are not individual specific. The respondent may assume that these experiences, although personal in nature, occur because of membership in a larger devalued group. Thus, experiences are perceived as psychologically distant (i.e., group membership-linked) although personally experienced.

Factor 3 (Negative Inferences) is made up of five questions and has a standardized alpha of .74. As listed in Table 3, the questions' general theme addresses projected negative imagery toward African American males generally.

Factor 4 (Positive Inferences) is comprised of six questions and has a standardized alpha of .67. The questions' general theme addresses potentially beneficial positive African American male perceptions (see Table 4).

Scoring

The Black Male Experiences Measure was designed to assess males' everyday experiences in potentially dissonance producing social contexts. As indicated in Table 5, the measure consists of 35 five-point Likert-type responses. Four factors were generated using each factor's standardized score (z-score). Because of the different number of questions in each factor, a standardized score is necessary. There are four reliable factors:

1. Proximal Negative Experiences (Proxneg) = questions 1, 2, 3, 4, 5, 6, 7, 8, 9, 10, 11, 12, 13;
2. Distal Negative Experiences (Distneg) = questions 14, 15, 16, 24, 26, 27, 28, 32, 35;
3. Negative Inferences (Neginfer) = questions 17, 21, 23, 25, 29; and,
4. Positive Inferences (Posinfer) = questions 19, 20, 30, 31, 33, 34.

Notes

1. The research reported was supported by funds awarded to the second author from several sources: The Commonwealth Fund, Spencer, W. T. Grant and The Social Science Research Council, and Ford Foundations. In addition, supplemental support from the Annenberg Foundation was provided.

2. The authors wish to thank several research assistants and graduate students of Project PAC (Project for the Promotion of Academic Competence) for their significant skill, sensitivity and efforts in bringing the first phase of work to a tremendously successful completion. During the second phase, Post-doctoral support and University of Pennsylvania support afforded through the Center for Health, Achievement, Neighborhood, Growth, and Ethnic Studies (CHANGES), have been sincerely appreciated. The authors wish to thank the significant financial assistance provided by the Spencer Foundation, Commonwealth Fund, the W. T. Grant Foundation, and the supplemental support from the Children's Trust Fund of Georgia, Annenberg Foundation and the Social Science Research Council which supported statistical analysis activities. Most importantly, we wish to thank the respondents for sharing their personal thoughts and experiences.

References

Chestang, L. (1972). The dilemma of biracial adoptions. *Social Work, 17,* 100-105.

Connell, J., Spencer, M. B., & Aber, L. (1994). Educational risk and resilience in African American youth: Context, self, action, and outcomes in school. *Child Development, 65,* 493-506.

Cunningham, M. (1993). Sex role influences of African American males: A literature review. *Journal of African American Male Studies, 1*(1), 30-37.

Cunningham, M. (1994). *Expressions of manhood: Predictors of educational achievement and African American adolescent males.* Unpublished doctoral dissertation, Emory University, Atlanta.

Cunningham, M. (1995, March). *Perceived contextual experiences' influence on reactive identity devel-*

opment. Paper presented at the Black Caucus Preconference of the Society for Research in Child Development, Indianapolis, IN.

Cunningham, M., & Spencer, M. B. (1995). *Perceived contextual experiences' influence on reactive identity development in adolescent African American males.* Manuscript submitted for publication. University of Pennsylvania.

Erikson, E. (1959). Identity and the life cycle. *Psychological Issues, 1,* 1-171.

Erikson, E. (1968). *Identity: Youth, and crisis.* New York: Norton.

Gibbs, J. T., Huang, L. N. (Eds.). (1989). *Children of color.* San Francisco: Jossey-Bass.

Phinney, J. S., & Rotheram, M.J. (Eds.). (1987). *Children's ethnic socialization.* Newbury Park, CA: Sage.

Spencer, M. B. (1985). Cultural cognition and social cognition as identity factors in Black children's personal-social growth. In M. B. Spencer, G. K. Brookins, & W. R. Allen (Eds.), *Beginnings: The social and affective development of Black children* (pp. 215-230). Hillsdale, NJ: Erlbaum.

Spencer, M. B. (1986). Risk and resilience: How Black children cope with stress. *Journal of Social Sciences, 71*(1), 22-26.

Spencer, M. B. (1995). Old issues and new theorizing about African American youth: A phenomenological variant of ecological systems theory. In R. L. Taylor (Ed.), *Black youth: Perspectives on their status in the United States* (pp. 38-69). Westport, CT: Praeger.

Spencer, M. B., Cole, S. P., Dupree, D., Glymph, A., & Pierre, P. (1993). Self-efficacy among urban African American early adolescents: Exploring issues of risk, vulnerability, and resilience. *Development and Psychopathology, 5,* 719-739.

Spencer, M. B., Cunningham, M., & Swanson, D. P. (1995). Identity as Coping: Adolescent African American males' adaptive responses to high-risk environments. In H. W. Harris, H. C. Blue, & E. H. Griffith (Eds.), *Racial and ethnic identity* (pp. 31-52). Routledge, NY.

Spencer, M. B., Dobbs, B., & Swanson, D. P. (1988). African American adolescents: Adaptational processes and socioeconomic diversity in behavioral outcomes. *Journal of Adolescence, 11,* 117-137.

Spencer, M. B., & Dornbush, S. M. (1990). Challenges in studying minority youth. In S. S. Feldman & G. R. Elliott (Eds.), *At the threshold: The developing adolescent* (pp. 123-146). Cambridge, MA: Harvard University Press.

Spencer, M. B., & Markstrom-Adams, C. (1990). Identity processes among racial and ethnic minority children in America. *Child Development, 61*(2), 290-310.

Spencer, M. B., McDermott, P., Burton, L., & Cole, S. P. (in press). An alternative approach for assessing neighborhood effects on early adolescent achievement and problem behavior. In J. Brooks-Gunn & G. Duncan (Eds.), *Neighborhood, poverty and youth outcomes.* New York: Sage.

Spencer, M. B., Swanson, D. P., & Cunningham, M. (1991). Ethnicity, ethnic identity, and competence formation: Adolescent transition and cultural transformation. *Journal of Negro Education, 60,* 366-387.

For additional information, contact:

Michael Cunningham, Ph. D.
University of Pennsylvania
Graduate School of Education
3700 Walnut Street
Philadelphia, PA 19104-6216
Telephone: (215) 898-4610

Development of the Scale of Racial Socialization for African American Adolescents

Howard C. Stevenson, Jr.

Abstract

This chapter seeks to broaden the definition and measurement of racial socialization and to integrate it with the current debate about racial identity development and African American cultural characteristics and strengths. The development and validation of the Scale of Racial Socialization for Adolescents (SORS-A) is described. A principal components analysis was conducted following administration of the SORS-A and measures of demographics, family communication about racism, and perception of skin color's influence on haughty behavior to 200 African American urban teenagers. Four factors were found to be very meaningful and moderately reliable: Spiritual and Religious Coping, Extended Family Caring, Cultural Pride Reinforcement, and Racism Awareness Teaching. A second-order factor analysis to identify underlying themes was also conducted. Themes of protective and proactive racial socialization were found to be supportive of a theoretical framework for racial socialization that is multidimensional and inclusive of both socially oppressive and culturally empowering experiences.

Introduction

Family socialization processes that contribute to the healthy racial identity development of African American men, women, and children have been and continue to be of clinical and research interest (Boyd-Franklin, 1989; Greene, 1992; Sanders, 1994; Spencer, 1983; Stevenson, 1993a, 1993b; Stevenson & Renard, 1993). Various psy-chological disciplines including counseling, developmental, and survey research psychology have made a substantial contribution to our understanding of ethnic and racial identity processes of children and adolescents (Burlew & Smith, 1991; Cross, Parham, & Helms, 1991; Clark & Clark, 1947; DeVos, 1990; Jackson, McCullough, & Gurin, 1988; Jackson, McCullough, Gurin, & Broman, 1991; Phinney & Rotheram, 1987; Smith, 1989,

1991; Spencer, 1984; 1987; Spencer & Markstrom-Adams, 1990). Interest in racial identity development apart from family socialization influences has centered on the life experiences of college-age students, although interest in understanding the ethnic identity development of young children and adolescents has increased (Phinney & Rotheram, 1987; Ponterotto, 1989). Differences between use of the terms racial identity and ethnic identity development have been debated (Smith, 1991), and modifications and criticisms of the theories of racial/ethnic identity development have been grounded in epistemologies ranging from logical positivism to Afrocentricity (Myers, Speight, Highlen, Cox, Reynolds, Adams, & Hanley, 1991; Reynolds & Pope, 1991).

For the most part, the racial identity development process of adults has been studied as a function of racist and discriminatory experiences, the respondent's perceptions of Whites, or as an acceptance of pro-African American cultural styles and affiliation. Very little has been written regarding the influence of family communication and preparation on the racial identity of African American adolescents. The present research emphasizes the importance of viewing racial identity as a multidimensional construct that is precipitated by family socialization processes (Phinney & Rosenthal, 1992). One reason the link between racial socialization and racial identity attitudes has not been solidified is due to the paucity of sophisticated and psychometrically sound measurement of racial socialization processes. The present chapter will describe the development of a measure of racial socialization attitudes for African American adolescents and present information on the scale's multidimensionality and reliability.

Family Racial Socialization: A Multidimensional Construct

The process whereby children develop a sense of their unique ethnic and racial identity has been identified with several terms. Those terms include racial socialization, cultural transmission, socialization environment, race-related messages, parental values transmission, cultural parenting, ethnic socialization and others (Bowman &

Howard, 1985; Jackson et al., 1988; Peters, 1985; Rotheram & Phinney, 1987; Spencer, 1990). African American scholars have begun to acknowledge the importance of childrearing in a racially hostile world (Boykin & Toms, 1985; Hale, 1991; Harrison, 1985; Johnson, 1988; McAdoo, 1988; Peters, 1985; Powell-Hopson & Hopson, 1992; Spencer, 1983, 1984; Thornton, Chatters, Taylor, & Allen, 1990). Ethnic socialization has been defined by Rotheram and Phinney (1987) as "developmental processes by which children acquire the behaviors, perceptions, values, and attitudes of an ethnic group, and come to see themselves and others as members of such groups" (p. 11). Racial socialization is defined by Peters (1985) as the "tasks Black parents share with all parents–providing for and raising children . . . but include the responsibility of raising physically and emotionally healthy children who are Black in a society in which being Black has negative connotations" (p. 161). Cultural transmission of values and beliefs has long been a factor in understanding effective African American family functioning. This socialization process is believed to be a protective buffer against societal antagonism towards people of color. Like all parents, many African American parents fear the effects of misinterpretation, helplessness, and ignorance on their children (Franklin & Boyd-Franklin, 1985).

While the definitions are varied, the concept that African American families have a special role in buffering the impact of racism and promoting a sense of cultural pride for their children is an important one. In the clearest example to date of the link between socialization and racial identity, Demo and Hughes (1990) found that "group identity is shaped by the content of parental socialization" (p. 371). They found that adults who had received racism preparation messages from parents while growing up were more likely to have stronger feelings of closeness to other Blacks and to hold stronger support for Black separatism.

Edwards and Polite (1992) interviewed successful Black men and women and identified a positive sense of racial identity as a primary reason for their survival of racism. Jeter (1994) found a relationship between the racial socialization messages given by parents to their college-age children and the racial socialization messages the children reported that they received from the parents. Bowman and Howard (1985) found that African American adolescents who received positive messages about their racial identity were better prepared academically than African American adolescents who did not receive these direct messages. Asking adolescents about the racial socialization messages they have received is an important strategy in understanding how they see this phenomenon.

Reactive, Evolutionary, and Bicultural Views of African American Culture

Three models of African American culture have been proposed to give meaning to the substance of African American beliefs and behaviors (Boykin, 1983; Cole, 1970; Jones, 1991). A reactive model of African American culture is one that views racial oppression as the substance of African American motivation, identity development, and achievement. Several authors have contrasted this model with an evolutionary or reactive model of African American culture. The proactive model views African American culture as substantive apart from oppression experiences and in fact has origins in an African cultural ethos. A bicultural model of African American culture combines the essence of the proactive and protective models. Cole's (1970) distinction between the American mainstream experience, minority experience, and the Blackness experience typifies the three models. Jones' (1992) TRIOS model represents a "bicultural integration" in that cultural dimensions of African American experience are identified as unique. The TRIOS model represents five dimensions of human experience and stands for time, rhythm, improvisation, oral expression, and spirituality. Burlew and Smith (1991) categorized racial identity measures according to four models: developmental, Africentric, group-based, and racial stereotyping. What is useful from this discussion for the development of racial identity measures is the increased support for models of racial identity development that move beyond dichotomous or "either-or" thinking. I am proposing that we develop more measures

with a diunital logic framing the item selection and analysis. That is, it is possible for an African American individual to experience *both* protective and proactive attitudes toward family socialization of African American culture and not either-or. It is this thinking that underlies the development of the Scale of Racial Socialization for adolescents and parents that is described in the present chapter.

Measurement of Racial Socialization

Measuring the degree of racial socialization is difficult for several reasons. First, definitions vary across studies and thus no single body of knowledge is comparable across studies. Second, including and excluding certain information must be informed by a theoretical base. To date, no theoretical base has existed from which to develop a consistent set of domains and subsequently construct an instrument that captures the totality of those domains. It is quite possible to assess the degree of racial socialization among parents and/or adolescents but still not have an understanding of which aspects of racial socialization are more likely to lead to improved personal- and group-esteem. Some studies have found little correlation between cultural values and personal identity (Spencer, 1983, 1984).

There is considerable variance in what constitutes a measure of racial socialization. Previous studies have used descriptive and survey interviews primarily to ascertain this information. It is proposed that there are several domains from which to assess family racial socialization processes. These include:

1. Parental perceptions of the importance of racial socialization;
2. Adolescent or child perceptions of the importance of racial socialization;
3. Parental socializing behaviors (i.e., verbal and nonverbal) to race;
4. Adolescent receptivity or experience of parental socializing behaviors;
5. Correspondence among family members regarding the prevalence and importance of racial socialization behaviors.

The research data on race-related messages gathered from the National Study of Black Americans (Bowman & Howard, 1985; Demo & Hughes, 1990; Jackson et al., 1991; Thornton et al., 1990) were gathered from asking three questions:

1. When you were a child, were there things your parents, or the people who raised you did or told you to help you know what it is to *be Black?* (If yes, to the above question, then . . .)

2. What are the most important things they taught you? Are there any (other) things your parents or the people who raised you told you about how to *get along with White people?* (If yes, then . . .)

3. What are the most important things they taught you?

Parham and Williams (1993) asked a demographically diverse sample of African Americans one question related to racial socializing experiences. That question asked what "predominant race-specific messages" were received by the respondents from parents while they were growing up. The authors found no relationship between parental messages and racial identity attitude and concluded that "the question regarding messages received from parents is not sensitive enough to capture the actual differences" (p. 19).

Jeter (1994) has developed a measure called the Jeter Attitudes of Racial Socialization which has been found to have four reliable subscales: Pro-dominant Culture Socialization, Pro-ethnic Socialization, Confounded Culture Socialization, and Raceless Culture Socialization. Two forms of the measure were developed, one for parents and the other for adult children (e.g., undergraduates). All four subscales were found to have moderate to good alpha reliability for both forms (ranging from .47 to .85). Using dyads of parents and their adult child counterparts, Jeter (1994) measured the correspondence between parental and adult child ratings of racial socialization and found there to be significant and positive correlation between parents and children across all four subscales. This work shows considerable promise for broadening future measurement research in the area of family racial socialization.

To date there are few studies that measure racial socialization in a large scale manner and that consider a multidimensional understanding of the African American life experience. In addition, while there is considerable reference to racial socialization as an important variable in the psychological adjustment of African American children and families, there is no consensus about the definition of the concept of racial socialization or how to measure it. Third, to date no single study has attempted to develop an instrument that seeks to combine the existing literature's varied themes of cultural values transmission. Fourth, the struggle of racial identification and socialization are equally crucial issues for teenagers as they are for young Black children or young adults and there has been no specific research agenda on racial socialization for this population.

Stevenson (1993a) has developed an instrument (two versions, one for adolescents and one for parents) called the Scale of Racial Socialization (SORS) that seeks to address some of the measurement dilemmas in the area of racial socialization. While pilot data on the parent version are being analyzed, some validation studies have begun with the adolescent version. The SORS-A is the Scale of Racial Socialization for Adolescents and is a 45 item scale designed to assess the degree of acceptance of racial socialization attitudes or race-related messages of childrearing in a number of domains of central interest within African American culture. Each item is scored on a five-point Likert scale ranging from strongly disagree to strongly agree. Item development was conducted by using several key areas germane to African American family socialization. The content areas include perception of education, extended family, spirituality, racism and society, childrearing, and African American heritage and pride. The selection of these domains was based upon a review of literature on African American family functioning and strengths and the literature on racial socialization (Bowman & Howard, 1985; Boykin & Toms, 1985; Franklin & Boyd-Franklin, 1985; Harrison, 1985; Hayles, 1991; Hill, 1972; Nobles, 1974; Peters, 1985; Semaj, 1985; and Spencer, 1983). One hundred items were developed from the following domains and then revised to the 45-item scale utilized in this study:

Perception of education. This domain relates to the importance of preparing African American children for subtle and blatant experiences and messages of racism that occur in educational environments. It also relates to the impact that African Americans ascribe to education in attaining societal and professional advancement for them. Items in this area represent attitudes about whether the school environment is racist and whether Black children would be more or less comfortable in a mostly White or Black school setting. Other items represent attitudes about the curriculum content in schools and beliefs about whether information on African American culture should be used by teachers.

Awareness of racism in society. This content domain consists of items that epitomize societal interactions between Blacks and the larger society. It represents the attitudes regarding the type of racist societal attitudes and behaviors that Black children are likely to face as they grow up and their awareness of it as a social reality.

Appreciation for spirituality and religion. Religiosity and spirituality are key areas of strength and empowerment for many African Americans. This domain is made up of items to tap beliefs in God, dependence upon religion, family teaching about religion, and family practice of spirituality through participation in organized religious institutions.

Promotion of Black heritage and culture. This content area assesses whether parents should actively engage in teaching their children about Black culture and history in order for them to grow and survive in American society. Other items tap into attitudes toward inclusion of African cultural elements in family teaching as well as the importance of teaching pride in one's heritage.

Appreciation of extended family involvement. Items from this content area investigate the important roles that relatives (blood and nonblood) can play in child rearing and family management. Respondents are asked to express their level of agreement regarding how much children benefit from the involvement of these fictive and blood kin relationships.

Acceptance of child rearing. This domain consists of items that investigate the importance of the childrearing task to Black parents as it relates to survival of the family for the future. The literature identified child rearing in and of itself as a strength as much as past struggles and blocked opportunity could be eradicated through the success of one's posterity. In this sense, raising one's children to be aware of racism and discrimination contributes to survival.

In a pilot study, Stevenson (1993a) administered a 35-item, four-point Likert version of the SORS-A to 120 African American adolescents (52 males and 58 females) enrolled in a summer youth jobs preparation program in a Northeastern U.S. city. The mean age of the group was 14.3 years. A factor analysis of the instrument revealed the presence of two factors with 10 items loading high on the two factors. One factor, *spiritual appreciation* represented socialization messages that promote the discussion and awareness of religious and cultural expression in the context of the family. The spiritual appreciation dimension related to items that mention religious involvement, church participation or some reference to God (e.g., "A belief in God can help a person deal with tough life struggles."). Items on this dimension represent family teaching of Black history as well.

The other dimension was called *societal apprehension* which includes socialization messages that warn children in the family about possible negative societal experiences. The societal apprehension dimension consists of items that involve childrearing and family teaching in the face of societal barriers and untrustworthy institutions (e.g., "teaching children about Black history will help them to survive a hostile world").

The two factors were found to be uncorrelated as evidenced by a correlation coefficient of .10 and seemed to be measuring different phenomena. Each of the factors was found to be moderately reliable with alphas of .72 and .71, respectively. Test-retest reliability (two-week interval) yielded a stability correlation of .50.

In addition to preliminary support for the predictive validity of the SORS-A, there is evidence of criterion validity. Stevenson (1993a) investigated the relationship between the SORS-A and a modified version of the African Self-Consciousness Scale (ASC) (Baldwin & Bell, 1985) in a teenage population. The 35-item SORS-A was found to be significantly correlated to the ASC which demonstrates that it does measure some level of African American racial attitudes (r = .34, p < .001). Ten items (with more of them worded in reverse) were added to improve the measure's coverage of the domain areas and to inhibit socially desirable responding. The scale was also changed from a 4-point scale to a 5-point scale to allow for greater variability in responding.

The purpose of this chapter is to contribute to the literature on racial identity development for adolescents by reporting on the development of the Scale of Racial Socialization for Adolescents (SORS-A) and determining if the factors of the measure relate to each other in any meaningful way that supports a theory that views racial socialization attitudes among youth as evolutionary or proactive as well as protective. Additional results of studies that relate the identified factors of the SORS-A to other relevant psychosocial variables will be presented and discussed.

Method

Sample

Two hundred and thirty-six inner city African American adolescents (mean age = 14.6 years, 156 females and 80 males) who were students in a summer jobs preparation program participated in a larger study to assess the relationship between kinship support, racial socialization, and racial identity attitudes. Permission for participation in the program and the study was granted by parents of the teenagers. Only 200 of the students were selected for analyses due to inadequate completion of the measures. During the administration, the measures were read aloud to control for reading difficulties among the youth.

Measures

Demographic questions. Questions on age, mother and father educational level, family size, and gender were asked of the respondents to determine basic descriptive information.

Scale of racial socialization. The SORS-A is a 45-item measure designed to assess an adolescent's opinion about the appropriateness of racial socialization processes in educational, family, and societal venues (See Appendix). This method of asking the teenager about a process usually within the domain of parenting is viewed as vicariously assessing one's experience of racial socialization and fulfilling the notion that the self of African American youth are experienced as extended. This view of extended self fits the ideas proposed by Nobles (1991), Burke (1980), and Semaj (1985). Not only is the teenager responding "for his community"; he or she is responding for herself or himself.

Family teaching of racism and skin color concern variables. Two items from the SORS-A, labelled Family Teaching of Racism (FTR) and Skin Color Concern (SKIN) variables, respectively (Items 45 and 36) were utilized. Item 45 (e.g., "My family taught me very little about racism and what it means to be Black living in America") was taken from the Racism Awareness Factor while item 36 (e.g., "Light skin Black persons often think they are better than darker skinned Blacks") did not load adequately on any factor. Differences in racial identity between persons with and without histories of family racial socialization are supported by previous research (Jackson et al., 1991). Concerns about skin color have often been at the base of psychological distress for African Americans, have accounted for considerable past and present within-race discrimination, and continue to be a phenomenon of African American family communication and socialization (Russell, Wilson, & Hall, 1992).

Procedures

Factor Analysis of the Scale of Racial Socialization. A principal components analysis

(SPSS) was conducted on the SORS-A (completed by 200 adolescents) using a varimax rotation and squared multiple correlations as initial communality estimates. The factors were expected to correlate with each other because they were related components of the model of racial socialization. Four factors from a five factor solution were deemed to be the most meaningful and most psychometrically sound compared to other multi-factor solutions. Several other extractions and rotations were conducted including a principal axis factor analysis with oblique and equamax rotations. The five factor solution yielded similar factor item composition and order.

Results

Factor Analysis of the SORS-A Scale

Factor analysis of the SORS-A revealed that a four factor model derived from a five factor solution was the most meaningful for interpretation. The fifth factor is described because of its potential meaningfulness to the proposed multidimensional model of racial socialization and due to its repeated appearance across various extractions and rotations of multi-factor models. While it was deleted from the Stevenson (1994) article due to its low internal consistency, it is included in this current chapter for future research purposes. Caution is urged regarding the use of this factor at this time until further evidence can be gathered to prove it's fit within the construct of racial socialization. The correlation matrix used squared multiple correlations in the analyses. The four-factor model was based upon its ability to (a) satisfy Cattell's (1966) screen test, (b) retain five or more items with salient loadings, where loadings greater than or equal to .30 are considered adequate (Boyle, 1985), (c) yield adequate internal consistency for items within factors, (d) include only items found to load exclusively on one factor, and (d) make psychological sense according to the model of racial socialization proposed earlier. This four-factor solution accounted for 28% of the variance. Table 1 describes the five factors, their loadings, their respective eigenvalues, and Alpha coefficients. Items with loadings under .30 were not included. The five factors were identified as corresponding closely to the literature domains mentioned earlier. Factor 1 is labeled *Spiritual and Religious Coping (SRC)* and includes items that represent messages about recognizing spirituality as one survives life's experiences. Factor 2 is labelled *Extended Family Caring (EFC)* and includes items that express attitudes and interactions that promote the role of extended and immediate family as serving child rearing and caring functions. Factor 3 represents items and attitudes that endorse the teaching of African American history and culture to children and is labelled *Cultural Pride Reinforcement (CPR)*. Factor 4 is labeled *Racism Awareness Teaching (RAT)* and is a subscale of items that focus on messages and attitudes that promote cautious and preparatory views regarding the presence of racism in society and the need to discuss racism openly among all family members. The final factor is called *Life Achievement and Struggling (LAS)* and emphasizes attitudes that are realistic toward the burden of achieving and surviving as an African American in school and work settings.

Factor Reliability

Cronbach's alpha for the entire SORS-A scale (e.g., Global Racial Socialization) was .75 ($n = 200$). The mean and standard deviation for the total scale were, respectively, 170.1 and 16.2. The reliability for most of the factors are moderate with only one subscale below an Alpha of .60. Means, standard deviation and Alphas associated with each factor are as follows: Spirituality and Religious Coping, Alpha = .74; $M = 26.8$, $SD = 4.9$; Extended Family Caring, Alpha = .70, $M = 44.4$, $SD = 5.9$; Cultural Pride Reinforcement, Alpha = .63, $M = 27.7$, $SD = 4.3$; Racism Awareness Teaching, Alpha = .60, $M = 38.8$, $SD = 6.7$; Life Achievement Struggling, Alpha = .48; $M = 18.4$, $SD = 3.7$.

Demographic Analyses

Several multiple regression analysis were performed with age, mother and father's educa-

Table 1. Item Loadings, Eigenvalues, and Reliabilities of Principal Components Analysis of SORS-A

Items	Factor Loadings

Spiritual and Religious Coping Eigenvalue = 5.44: Alpha coefficient = .75)

Families who talk openly about religion or God are helping their children to grow.	.74
A belief in God can help a person deal with tough life struggles.	.73
Depending on religion and God can help a person make good life decisions.	.73
Black children should be taught early that God can protect them from racial hatred.	.63
Religion is an important part of a person's life.	.52
It's important for families to go to church or mosque where spiritual growth can happen.	.42
Spiritual battles that people fight are more important than the physical battles.	.30

Extended Family Caring (Eigenvalue = 2.61; Alpha coefficient = .70)

Children should be taught that all races are equal.	.56
Racism and discrimination are the hardest things a Black child has to face.	.51
Getting a good education is still the best way for a Black child to survive racism.	.52
Families of Black children should teach them to be proud to be Black.	.45
Spending good time with relatives is as important for parents as for their children.	.45
Having large families can help many Black families survive life struggles.	.44
Children who have good times with their relatives become better people.	.43
"Train up a child in the way he should go, and he will not turn away from it."	.40
Relatives can help Black parents raise their children.	.31
"Don't forget who your people are because you may need them someday."	.33
Grandparents help parents to make decisions.	.19

Cultural Pride Reinforcement (Eigenvalue = 2.10: Alpha coefficient = .63)

Relatives can teach children things that parents may not know.	.55
Schools should be required to teach all children about Black history.	.53
Teachers should make it so Black children can see signs of Black culture in classrooms.	.54
If Black parents teach their children that Blacks have fewer opportunities than Whites, it may help them to survive racism and be successful.	.47
Parents can teach children to be proud to be Black without saying a word.	.40
Teaching children about Black history will help them to survive a hostile world.	.40
More job opportunities would be open to African Americans if people were not racist.	.40
Spiritual battles that people fight are more important than the physical battles.	.36
Black parents should talk about their roots to African culture to their children.	.36
Black parents should teach their children about racism.	.37

Racism Awareness Teaching (Eigenvalue = 1.96; Alpha coefficient = .60)

Whites do not think of Black people as lazy or aggressive today like they used to believe 30 or more years ago.	.52

(table continues)

Items	Factor Loadings
Families who talk about racism to their children will lead them to doubt themselves.	.52
Black parents should not teach their children to speak their mind because they could be attacked by others in society.	.53
Whites do not have more opportunities than Blacks.`	.46
Our society is fair toward Black people.	.46
Black children will feel good about being Black in a school with mostly White children.	.40
When children are younger than 5, racism doesn't bother them.	.42
A Black child or teenager will not be harassed simply because s/he is Black.	.39
My family taught me very little about racism in America.	.36

Life Achievement Struggling (Eigenvalue = 1.82; Alpha coefficient = .48)

A mostly Black school will help Black children learn more than a mostly White school.	.52
African American children who go to a mostly Black school will feel better about themselves than those who go to a mostly White school.	.49
Watching parents struggle to find work makes many African American children believe it is not worth it to try and succeed in the world.	.48
A Black child has to work twice as hard in order to get ahead in this world.	..46
Parents should talk about the history of Black slavery with their children.	.30

$N = 200$

tional level, family size, and gender entered as independent variables with each of the SORS-A factors as dependent variables for each analysis. None of these variables was found to be significantly related to the five factors.

Relationship Between Racial Socialization Factors

A review of Table 2 reveals that correlations between the Extended Family Caring, Spiritual and Religious Coping, and Cultural Pride Reinforcement factors (when the total sample is included) are significant but in the moderate range. This suggests that the three factors reflect a common theme between them but still measure uniquely different aspects of racial socialization. The Racism Awareness Teaching factor is uniquely different from the other three in that it does not significantly correlate with any of them. The Life Achievement Struggling factor appears to be related to all of the factors.

The data were then subjected to a intercorrelation analysis categorized by gender (see Table 3). The results support the intercorrelation pattern identified for the entire sample in Table 2 with one slight difference. Males responded differently to the Racism Awareness Teaching factor than females. For males, the relationship of the RAT to the other three factors was nonsignificant or significantly negative in the case of Spiritual and Religious Coping attitudes (e.g., $r = -.21, p < .01$). Females are able to integrate perceptions of racism awareness views within their understanding of other forms of racial socialization attitudes while attitudes about racism in society are viewed as separate for males. Because the results pointed to a multidimensional nature to the construct of racial socialization, a higher order factor analysis was conducted.

Second Order Factor Analysis

The five factors were subjected to a higher order principal axis factor analysis similar to the

Table 2. Intecorrelations and Second-Order Principal Factors for Racial Socialization Factors Using a Five Factor Solution

Factors	SRC	EFC	CPR	RAT	LAS	GRS	Com-munal[a]	Speci-ficity[a]	Rotated Loadings Pro-active[RS]	Pro-tective[RS]
1. Spir./Relig. Coping	-	-	-	-	-	-	.40	*.35*	*.63*	-.03
2. Ext. Family Caring	.38**	-	-	-	-	-	.48	.22	*.66*	.22
3. Cultural Pride Reinforcement	.36**	.44**	-	-	-	-	.44	.18	*.65*	.09
4. Racism Awareness Teaching	-.01	.12	.04	-	-	-	.13	*.47*	.00	*.50*
5. Life Achievement Struggling	.23*	.32**	.25**	.19*	-	-	.26	.22	*.36*	*.36*
6. Global Racial[c] Socialization	.64**	.72**	.65**	.50**	.65**					
Eigenvalue	-	-	-	-	-	-			1.48	.34
% Variance	-	-	-	-	-	-			29.7	7.0
Cumulative	-	-	-	-	-	-			29.7	36.7

Note. [a]Communality equals the total proportion of common variance expressed by a factor. Specificity reflects the proportion of variance which is both reliable and unique to a factor. Specificity is obtained by subtracting communality for a factor from its alpha coefficient. Specificity values that are in excess of error variance (where error variance = 1-alpha) are considered significant and are underlined. [b]Rotated Loadings are significant if they exceed 35 for a particular higher order factor and are italicized. [c]Global Racial Socialization is a total score of all 45 items of the Scale of Racial Socialization. *p < .02. **p < .001. N = 200

earlier factor analysis. Results are displayed in Table 2. This was conducted to identify meaningful underlying but distinct themes and to test the hypothesis that the four factors represented both proactive and protective perceptions of racial socialization. The results presented in Table 2 indicate that, in fact, two distinct higher order factors are underlying the Scale of Racial Socialization for Adolescents. The two factors accounted for 35% of the variance. This information coincides with the low factor intercorrelations and lends support to the idea that the unique variance of the factors (i.e., specificity) is substantial. A specificity value of a factor is determined significant if it is higher than the error variance (where error variance = -1 alpha). Table 2 reveals that the spiritual and religious coping and the racial aware-

ness teaching factors are significant with respect to specificity. This further validates the proposition that the racial socialization construct is multidimensional. These two higher order factors are meaningfully identified as proactive and protective forms of racial socialization processes. Second order Factor 1 (Protective Racial Socialization) is comprised of the Extended Family Caring, Spiritual and Religious Coping, and Cultural Pride Teaching factors. Second order Factor 2 (Protective Racial Socialization) is comprised only of the Racism Awareness Factor. The moderate reliability of the Racism Awareness Teaching factor and it's significant specificity as a factor are proposed as support for constituting this higher order factor as reliable, and for accepting the hypothesis of two core underlying dimen-

Table 3. Intercorrelation of Racial Socialization Factors by Gender

Factors	SRC	EFC	CPR	RAT	GRS
			Males		
1. Spiritual/Religious Coping	-	.47***	.46***	-.21*	.60***
2. Extended Family Caring	-	-	.46***	.00	.77***
3. Cultural Pride Reinforcement	-	-	-	-.11	.60***
4. Racism Awareness Teaching	-	-	-	-	.28**
			Females		
1. Spiritual/Religious Coping	-	.35***	.37***	.15*	.68***
2. Extended Family Caring	-	-	.46***	.21**	.68***
3. Cultural Pride Reinforcement	-	-	-	-.21**	.70***
4. Racism Awareness Teaching	-	-	-	-	.51**
5. Global Racial Socialization	-	-	-	-	-

$+p < .05.; *p < .01.; **p > .001$, Males, $n = 72$, Females, $n = 128$.

sions to racial socialization attitudes from an adolescent's perspective. Because the LAS factor loaded equally on both second order factors it was not included in these two underlying themes.

Variables Relevant to Racial Socialization and Identity

Both questions, family teaching of racism (FTR) and skin color concern (SKIN) were written according to a five-point Likert format with responses ranging from "disagree a lot" (1) to "agree a lot" (5). The FTR variable yielded a mean score of 3.58 and standard deviation of 1.46 while the SKIN variable yielded a mean of 3.08 and standard deviation of 1.63.

Correlations of these two questions with the five factors can be found in Table 4. Reverse scoring was applied to the family teaching of racism question such that a high score on this question represented a disagreement with the statement that little discussion of racism had occurred in the respondent's family. With respect to the family teaching of racism variable, it was found to be positively related to overall racial socialization ($r = .20, p < .01$) and racism aware-

ness teaching ($r = .41, p < .0001$). The more that one's family talked about racism, the more the respondent endorsed the importance of overall racial socialization attitudes and specifically in the area of racism awareness. The skin color concern variable was negatively related to racism awareness teaching ($r = -.17, p < .01$), suggesting that persons who endorsed strong racism awareness teaching messages tended to disagree that light-skinned Blacks thought of themselves as better than dark-skinned Blacks. These results tend to support the construct validity of the racism awareness teaching factor.

Other support for the construct of adolescent racial socialization attitudes comes from research relating the construct to the racial identity model of William Cross, Janet Helms, and Thomas Parham. Stevenson (1995) modified the 50-item version of the Racial Identity Attitudes Scale (RIAS) to be appropriately applied to an adolescent audience and then factor analyzed the measure using 287 African American teenagers. The results indicated that the Nigrescence model remained intact despite the lack of empirical support for the encounter stage of the model. The other three stages were identified and followed an expected progression

Table 4. Correlation among Independent Variables

						Second-Order Factors[a]		
	Spiritual Religious Coping	Extended Family Caring	Cultural Pride Reinforc.	Racism Aware. Teaching	Life Achvm't Strug.	Global Racial Socializ.	Proactive Racial Socializ.	Protec. Racial Social.
1. Family Racism Teaching	.00	.11	.07	.43**	-.04	.20*	.12+	.43**
2. Skin Color Concern	.08	.05	.01	-.17*	.09	.14+	.08	-.17*

Note. [a]Neither of these second order factors includes the Life Achievement Struggling factor score given its double loading on both second order factors.
+$p < .05$.; *$p < .01$.; **$p < .001$; $N = 200$.

from pro-majority culture to pro-African American cultural attitudes. Table 5 describes the relationship between the two measures. Stevenson (1995) found a significant relationship between some of the SORS-A factors and the adolescent version of the RIAS. Moreover, multiple regression analyses revealed that the protective factors were negatively correlated with the pre-encounter stage attitudes while they were positively correlated with internalization stage attitudes (Stevenson, 1995). This work extends the significance of adolescent opinions about how child-rearing in their community and the subsequent impact these group-identity values have upon personal racial identity attitudes.

Discussion

This work supports the growing body of literature that seeks to view African American socialization cultural practices as rich and multidimensional. It provides a beginning for the development of improved measurement of the construct of racial socialization, which has previously varied across studies and has consisted primarily of one to five question formats. This study is the first to apply factor analytic procedures to the area of racial socialization and con-

tributes to the measurement of culturally relevant African American experiences (Montgomery, Fine, & Myers, 1990; Sanders-Thompson, 1992; Stokes, Murray, Peacock, & Kaiser, 1994).

Specific nuances of this research include the emphasis on the extended view of self and how one's view of self can be inferred through one's view of his or her community. A unique aspect of this emphasis is the increased congruence with Africentric thinking regarding the adolescent self-report method. The process of asking teenagers about family communication and socialization activities within their communities implicitly expects the teenager to express self-views through his or her reporting about one's community. This research has taken the perspective that attitudes about racial socialization can be asked of adolescents as well as parents. While work on the relationship between parental views of racial socialization and their offspring's views of racial socialization is necessary, adolescent views are examined here in their own right.

The use of the adolescent perspective of racial socialization (which usually is known to be the domain of parents) is a unique angle within this area of research. I believe this to be an initial step toward understanding how each member in a family views childrearing. The use of self-report

Table 5. Correlations of Racial Socialization Factors to Racial Identity Stages

Factors	Preencounter	Immersion	Internalization
1. Spiritual and Religious Coping	-.16*	.01	.18*
2. Extended Family Caring	-.09	-.14+	.22**
3. Cultural Pride Reinforcement	-.13+	.12+	.30**
4. Racism Awareness Teaching	-.38**	-.01	.10
5. Life Achievement Struggling	-.01	.17+	.21*
6. Global Racial Socialization	-.22*	-.00	.34**

$+p < .05.; *p < .01.; ** p < .001; N = 287.$

data in this research is simply the beginning. Future research should diversify investigative strategies. Behavioral observations of racial socialization processes will help to complement and validate the use of self-report data. As skin color issues are so complex within African American communities, perhaps more questions regarding the perception of skin color issues need to be developed. Future research might examine how the self-perceived identification of one's skin color affects one's response to the skin color concern question raised in this study. In addition, other concerns regarding the impact of skin color on behavior [e.g., increased health risks for darker skinned African Americans (Dressler, 1993)] might be assessed. Despite these concerns, it is believed that this work promotes a more enriched understanding of culturally relevant psychological phenomena for African American youth.

Adolescent attitudes about racial socialization consists of more than telling children that they should beware of racial hostilities that exist in a White supremacist world. A robust racial socialization agenda may require discussions about spirituality and religion and how one's identity is not fully shaped by hostile societal influences. It may suggest that children be reinforced to learn about how their cultural heritage is unique and not solely developed out of socially oppressive experiences. Enslavement is a reality of the history of being Black in America, but it does not solely concretize one's cultural identity. Blood and non-blood extended family members play a crucial role in teaching children about their character and in raising children to be responsive

to the inner community concerns about racism and cultural pride development (Sanders & Thompson, 1994). The extended family caring factor parallels the extended family strength so often discussed as central to African American cultural resilience and survival (Wilson, 1986; Wilson & Tolson, 1990).

Racism awareness teaching appears to significantly differ from the other factors of racial socialization. This raises several interesting implications for adolescent perceptions of how families should rear their children. Contrary to the common misperception that talking to youth about racism may reflect some racial hatred themes, the racism awareness factor derived in this study seems to reflect a wariness of various psychological expressions of racist thinking. That is, racism awareness teaching may be protective in that it challenges the recipients of the teaching to reject traditional opinions about Black culture that are also influenced by racist, inferior-based rhetoric. That the racism awareness teaching factor was negatively correlated with a disparaging view of lighter skin color further frames this factor as protective and necessary in order to counteract forces of inferiority thinking that rests within as well as outside of the Black community. The different gender perspectives regarding this factor are interesting. For females, awareness of racist experiences is not incompatible with one's attitudes of socializing children to race. The questions raised from these data suggest that males are socialized differently to respond and interpret racist experiences with more sensitivity. Perhaps it relates to the differential fears and negative perceptions of African American males in racially hostile situations. Future research should investigate these experiences more specifically. The findings here support research that investigates gender and racial identity development processes and how these processes are prioritized and synthesized by African American youth.

Socializing children to race from solely a protective stance is called into question by the results of the second order factor analysis. These results point to the importance of proactive aspects of racial socialization that often gets ignored. It supports the work of James Jones (1992) and other authors who have discussed the various psychological representations of Black culture (Cole, 1970, Boykin & Toms, 1985). The protective and proactive components of racial socialization are not meant as dichotomies, a result that pushes this work back into the inferior-based "either-or" thinking it was developed to upend. This distinction has implications for how one interprets the scores of the SORS-A. Persons scoring high on either of these dimensions are not perceived to be protective versus proactive, but some combination of both. In fact, low scores on either or both dimensions are just as reflective and important to track.

More work is needed to bolster the reliability and validity of the LAS factor. It appears to be an important factor as it is tapping elements of both protective and proactive socialization. Perhaps additional items that are specific to achievement will prove beneficial to the quality of this subscale.

Adequate diversity among African American youth is present on factors of racial socialization such that the factors are not simply wishes regarding how life should be in the Black community. Some families do not engage in active verbal discussion of racism, cultural pride, and spiritual growth (Stevenson, 1993b). This fact alone helps to put in perspective the obvious: some aspects of racial socialization may be realized by an adolescent and others may not. Again, the implications for scoring are implicit. A profile analysis of the scores on the four factors of the SORS-A may give credence to the multidimensionality of the measure but more accurately depict what occurs with racial socialization practices since one area

(e.g., spirituality and religion) in some families may be stressed more than another. The questions raised here for future research relate to the differential influences of the various factors on mental health and behavior. Future research must address which factors, if any, are most likely to relate directly to healthy coping behaviors or mentally healthy attitudes (Spencer, Swanson, & Cunningham, 1991).

Other implications for future research include the importance of gathering parental perceptions of racial socialization and assessing the degree of agreement with adolescent perceptions of racial socialization (Jeter, 1994). A key question raised here is what is the relationship between actual family racial socialization practices and communications to parental and adolescent racial socialization attitudes? What relationships exist between adolescent racial socialization attitudes and existing theories of racial identity (e.g., the theory of Nigrescence and African Self-Consciousness) or academic achievement? Some research is underway to assess these relationships as well as the construction of theoretical ideas to undergird this assessment (Bowman & Howard, 1985; Demo & Hughes, 1990; Sanders Thompson, 1994; Stevenson, 1993b, 1994; Stokes et al., 1994). Currently, qualitative interviewing of families that is underway to determine if these processes exist across socioeconomic groups may provide added dimension to the self-report data.

In summary, racial socialization attitude measurement has been initiated for African American teenagers through the use of the Scale of Racial Socialization for Adolescents (SORS-A). The acronym is meant to be pronounced as "source" in order to reflect the potential utility of racial socialization processes in being the center of support from which identity development and self-esteem and psychological integrity spring forth. It is hypothesized that these processes represent the source of meaning and self-protection for African Americans in America. While more research is necessary, this step toward a multidimensional understanding of adolescent racial socialization processes has considerable promise for broadening our vision within which African American adolescent psychology can develop.

References

Baldwin, J. A., & Bell, Y. R. (1985). The African self-consciousness scale: An African personality questionnaire. *The Western Journal of Black Studies, 9*(2), 61-68.

Bowman, P., & Howard, C. (1985). Race related socialization, motivation, and academic achievement: A study of Black youths in three-generation families. *Journal of American Academy of Child Psychiatry, 24*, 134-141.

Boyd-Franklin, N. (1989). *Black families in therapy: A multisystems approach.* New York: Guilford Press.

Boykin, A. W. (1983). The academic performance of Afro-American children. In J. Spence (Ed.), *Achievement and achievement motives* (pp. 323-371). San Francisco: Freeman.

Boykin, A. W., & Toms, F. D. (1985). Black child socialization: A conceptual framework. In H. P. McAdoo & J. L. McAdoo (Eds.), *Black children: Social, educational, and parental environments* (pp. 33-51). Newbury Park: Sage.

Boyle, G. J., (1985). A reanalysis of the higher-order factor structure of the Motivation Analysis Test and the Eight State Questionnaire. *Personality and Individual Differences, 6*, 367-374.

Burke, P. J. (1980). The self: Measurement requirements from an interactionist perspective. *Social Psychology Quarterly, 43*, 18-29.

Burlew, A. K, & Smith, L. R. (1991). Measures of racial identity: An overview and a proposed framework. *Journal of Black Psychology, 17*, 53-71.

Cattell, R. B. (1966). The screen test for the number of factors. *Multivariate Behavioral Researcher, 1*, 245-276.

Clark, K. B., & Clark, M. P. (1947). Racial identification and preference in Negro children. In T. M. Newcomb & E. L. Hartley (Eds.), *Readings in social psychology* (pp. 169-178). New York: Holt, Rinehart & Winston.

Cole, J. (1970). Negro, Black, and nigger. *Black Scholar, 1*, 40-44.

Cross, W. E., Parham, T. A., & Helms, J. E. (1991). The stages of Black identity development: Nigrescence Models. In R. Jones (Ed.), *Black psychology* (3rd ed., pp. 319-338). Hampton, VA: Cobb & Henry.

Demo, D. H., & Hughes, M. (1990). Socialization and racial identity among Black Americans. *Social Psychology Quarterly, 53*, 364-374.

DeVos, G. A. (1990). Self in society: A multilevel psychocultural analysis. In G. A. DeVos & M. M. Suarez-Orozco (Eds.), *Status inequality: The self in culture* (pp. 17-74). Newbury Park, CA: Sage.

Dressler, W. W. (1993). Health in the African American community: Accounting for health inequalities. *Medical Anthropology Quarterly, 7*, 325-345.

Edwards, A., & Polite, C. (1992). *Children of the dream: The psychology of Black success.* New York: Doubleday.

Franklin, A. J., & Boyd-Franklin, N. (1985). A psychoeducational perspective on Black parenting. In H. P. McAdoo & J. L. McAdoo (Eds.), *Black children: Social, educational, and parental environments* (pp. 194-210). Newbury Park: Sage.

Greene, B. A. (1992). Racial socialization as a tool in psychotherapy with African American children. In L. A. Vargas & J. D. Koss-Chioino (Eds.), *Working with culture: Psychotherapeutic interventions with ethnic minority children and adolescents* (pp. 63-84). New York: Jossey-Bass.

Hale, J. (1991). The transmission of cultural values to young African American children. *Young Children, 46*, 7-15.

Harrison, A. O. (1985). The Black family's socializing environment: Self-esteem and ethnic attitude among Black children. In H. P. McAdoo & J. L. McAdoo (Eds.), *Black children: Social, educational, and parental environments* (pp. 159-173). Newbury Park: Sage.

Hayles, V. R. (1991). African American strengths: A survey of empirical findings. In R. Jones (Ed.), *Black psychology* (pp. 379-408). Hampton, VA: Cobb & Henry.

Hill, R. (1972). *The strengths of Black families.* New York: Emerson Hall.

Jackson, J. S., McCullough, W. R., & Gurin, G. (1988). Family, socialization environment, and identity development in Black Americans. In H. P. McAdoo (Ed.), *Black families* (2nd ed., pp. 242-256). Newbury Park, CA: Sage Press.

Jackson, J. S., McCullough, W. R., & Gurin, G., Broman, C. L. (1991). Race identity. In J. S. Jackson (Ed.), *Life in Black America* (pp. 238-253). Newbury Park, CA: Sage.

Jeter, R. F. (1994). *Racial socialization: The effectiveness of the transmission of messages about race by Black parents to their college-aged children.* Unpublished dissertation manuscript, University of Pennsylvania, Philadelphia.

Johnson, D. J. (1988). Racial socialization strategies of parents in three Black private schools. In D. T. Slaughter & D. J. Johnson (Eds.), *Visible now: Blacks in private schools* (pp. 251-267). New York: Greenwood Press.

Jones, J. (1991). The politics of personality: Being Black in America. In R. L. Jones (Ed), *Black psychology* (pp. 305-318). Hampton, VA: Cobb & Henry.

McAdoo, J. L. (1988). The roles of Black fathers in the socialization of Black children. In H. P. McAdoo (Ed.), *Black families* (2nd ed., pp. 257-269). Newbury Park, CA: Sage.

Montgomery, D. E., Fine, M. E., & James-Myers, L. (1990). The development and validation of an instrument to assess an optimal Afrocentric world view. *Journal of Black Psychology, 17,* 37-54.

Myers, L, J. Speight, S. L., Highlen, P. S., Cox, C. I., Reynolds, A. L., Adams, E. M., & Hanley, C. P. (1991). Identity development and world-view: Toward an optimal conceptualization. *Journal of Counseling and Development, 70,* 54-63.

Nobles, W. (1991). African philosophy: Foundations for Black psychology. In R. L. Jones (Ed), *Black psychology* (pp. 47-63). Hampton, VA: Cobb & Henry.

Nobles, W. (1974). Africanity: Its role in Black families. *The Black Scholar, 5,* 9.

Parham, T. A. (1993, August). *Discussant in cultural contexts of identity formation—Some international perspectives.* Paper presented at the 101st Convention of the American Psychological Association, Toronto, Ontario, Canada.

Parham, T. A., & Williams, P. T. (1993). The relationship of demographic and background factors to racial identity attitudes. *Journal of Black Psychology, 19,* 7-24.

Peters, M. F. (1985). Racial socialization of young Black children. In H. P. McAdoo & J. L. McAdoo (Eds.), *Black children: Social, educational, and parental environments.* Newbury Park, CA: Sage.

Phinney, J. S., & Rosenthal, D. A. (1992). Ethnic identity in adolescence: Process, context, and outcome. In G. R. Adams, T. P. Gullotta, & R. Montemayor (Eds.), *Adolescent identity formation* (pp. 145-172). Newbury Park, CA: Sage.

Phinney, J. S., & Rotheram, M. J. (1987). *Children's ethnic socialization: Pluralism and development.* Newbury Park, CA: Sage.

Ponterotto, J. G. (1989). Expanding directions for racial identity research. *The Counseling Psychologist, 17,* 264-272.

Powell-Hopson, D., & Hopson, D. S. (1992). Implications of doll color preferences among Black preschool children and White preschool children. In A. K. Burlew, W. Curtis Banks, H. P. McAdoo, & D. A. ya Azibo (Eds.), *African American psychology: Theory, research and practice* (pp. 183-189). Newbury Park, CA: Sage.

Reynolds, A. L., & Pope, R. L. (1991). The complexities of diversity: Exploring multiple oppressions. *Journal of Counseling and Development, 70,* 174-180.

Rotheram, M. J., & Phinney, J. S. (1987). Definitions and perspectives in the study of children's ethnic socialization. In J. S. Phinney & M. J. Rotheram (Eds.), *Children's ethnic socialization: Pluralism and development* (pp. 10-28). Newbury Park, CA: Sage.

Russell, K., Wilson, M., & Hall, R. (1992). *The color complex: The politics of skin color among African Americans.* New York: Harcourt Brace Jovanovich.

Sanders, T. V. (1994). Socialization to race and its relationship to racial identification among African Americans. *Journal of Black Psychology, 20,* 175-188.

Sanders, T. V. (1992, August). *The multi-dimensional aspect of racial identification in everyday life.* Paper presented at Centennial Annual Convention of the American Psychological Association at Washington, DC.

Semaj, L. T. (1985). Afrikanity, cognition, and extended self-identity. In M. Spencer, G. Brookins, & W. Allen (Eds.), *Beginnings: The Social and affective development of Black children.* Hillsdale, NJ: Erlbaum.

Smith, E. J. (1991). Ethnic identity development: Toward the development of a theory within the context of majority/minority status. *Journal of Counseling and Development, 70,* 181-188.

Smith, E. J. (1989). Black racial identity development: Issues and concerns. *The Counseling Psychologist, 17,* 277-288.

Spencer, M. B. (1990). Parental values transmission: Implications for the development of African-American children. In J. B. Stewart & Cheatham (Eds.), *Interdisciplinary Perspectives on Black Families.* Atlanta: Transactions.

Spencer, M. B. (1987). Black children's ethnic identity formation: Risk and resilience of castelike minorities. In J. S. Phinney & M. J. Rotheram (Eds.), *Children's ethnic socialization: Pluralism and development* (pp. 103-116). Newbury Park, CA: Sage.

Spencer, M. B. (1984). Black children's race awareness, racial attitudes, and self-concept. A reinterpretation. *Journal of Child Psychology and Psychiatry, 25,* 433-441.

Spencer, M. B. (1983). Children's cultural values and parental child rearing strategies. *Developmental Review, 3,* 351-370.

Spencer, M. B., & Markstrom-Adams, C. (1990). Identity processes among racial and ethnic minority children in America. *Child Development, 61*, 290-310.

Spencer, M. B., Swanson, D. P., & Cunningham., M. (1991). Ethnicity, ethnic identity, and competence formation: Adolescent transition and cultural transformation. *Journal of Negro Education, 60*, 366-387.

Stevenson, H. C. (1995). Relationship of adolescent perceptions of racial socialization to racial identity. *Journal of Black Psychology, 21*.

Stevenson, H. C. (1994). Validation of the scale of racial socialization for African American adolescents: Steps toward multidimensionality. *Journal of Black Psychology, 20*, 445-468.

Stevenson, H. C. (1993a). Validation of the scale of racial socialization for African American adolescents: A preliminary analysis. *Psych Discourse, 24*, 12.

Stevenson, H. C. (1993b, August). *New theoretical considerations in assessing racial socialization attitudes in African American youth: Getting an eye's view of the "we."* Paper presented at Invited Symposium at the 101st Convention of the American Psychological Association, Toronto, Ontario, Canada.

Stevenson H. C., & Renard, G. (1993). Trusting wise ole' owls: Employing cultural strengths in psychotherapy with African American families. *Professional Psychology: Research and Practice, 24*, 433-442.

Stokes, J. E., Murray, C. B., Peacock, M. J., & Kaiser, R. T. (1994). Assessing the reliability, factor structure, and validity of the African Self-Consciousness Scale in a general population of African Americans. *Journal of Black Psychology, 20*, 62-74.

Taylor, R. D., Casten, R., & Flickinger, S. M. (1993). Influence of kinship social support on the parenting experiences and psychosocial adjustment of African-American adolescents. *Developmental Psychology, 29*, 382-388.

Thornton, M. C., Chatters, L. M., Taylor, R. J., & Allen, W. R. (1990). Sociodemographic and environmental correlates of racial socialization by Black parents. *Child Development, 61*, 401-409.

Wilson, M. N. (1986). The Black extended family: An analytical consideration. *Developmental Psychology, 22*, 246-258.

Wilson, M. N., & Tolson, T. F. J. (1990). Familial support in the Black community. *Journal of Clinical Child Psychology, 19*, 347-355.

Appendix

Scale of Racial Socialization (SORS-A) Adolescent Version

Circle the number on the line, depending on whether you 1-Disagree A Lot, 2-Disagree A Little, 3-Not Sure, 4-Agree A Little, 5-Agree A Lot with the statement. Circle only one number per question. Thank you.

(All of the following questions are of the same format as question 1. To conserve space, therefore, only the actual test questions, without the options, will be presented for questions 2-45).

1. Our society is fair toward Black people.
   1   2   3   4   5
2. Grandparents help parents to make decisions.
3. Black children will feel good about being Black in a school with mostly White children.
4. It is important for families to go to church or mosque where spiritual growth can happen.
5. Families should talk about Black slavery with their children.
6. Relatives can help Black parents raise their children.
7. Religion is an important part of a person's life.
8. Racism and discrimination are the hardest things a Black child has to face.
9. Having large families can help many Black families survive life struggles.
10. Families of Black children should teach them to be proud to be Black.
11. Children should be taught that all races are equal.
12. Children who have good times with their relatives become better people.
13. A belief in God can help a person deal with tough life struggles.
14. A mostly Black school will help Black children learn more than a mostly White school.
15. Spending good time with relatives is just as important for parents as it is for their children.
16. Black parents should teach their children about racism.

17. Black parents should talk about their roots to African culture to their children.
18. Relatives can teach children things that parents may not know.
19. Families who talk about racism to their children will lead them to doubt themselves.
20. Schools should be required to teach all children about Black history.
21. Depending on religion and God can help a person make good life decisions.
22. Families who talk openly about religion or God are helping their children grow.
23. Teachers should make it so Black children can see signs of Black culture in the classroom.
24. Only people who are blood-related to you should be called your "Family."
25. Getting a good education is still the best way for a Black child to survive racism.
26. "Don't forget who your people are because you may need them someday."
27. When children are younger than five, racism doesn't bother them.
28. Spiritual battles that people fight are more important than the physical battles.
29. Teaching children about Black history will help them to survive a hostile world.
30. "Train up a child in the way he should go, and he will not turn away from it."
31. A Black child has to work twice as hard in order to get ahead in this world.
32. Watching parents struggle to find work can make many Black children wonder if it is worth it to try and succeed in the world.

33. Parents can teach children to be proud to be Black without saying a word.
34. Black children at a mostly Black school will feel better about themselves than those who go to a mostly White school.
35. Black parents need to teach their children how to live in two worlds: one Black and one White.
36. Light skin Black persons often think they are better than darker skinned Blacks.
37. Whites do not have more opportunities than Blacks.
38. A Black child or teenager will not be harassed simply because s/he is Black.
39. More job opportunities would be open to African Americans if people were not racist.
40. Black children should be taught early that God can protect them from racial hatred.
41. Whites do not think of Black people as lazy or aggressive today like they used to believe 30 or more years ago.
42. Black parents should not teach their children to speak their mind because they could be attacked by others in society.
43. If Black parents teach their children that Blacks don't always have the same opportunities as Whites, they may help them to survive racism and be successful.
44. Black children don't have to know about Africa in order to survive life in America.
45. My family taught me very little about racism in America.

For additional information, contact:

Howard C. Stevenson, Jr., Ph.D.
Psychology in Education Division
Graduate School of Education
University of Pennsylania
3700 Walnut Street
Philadelphia, PA 19104-6216
Telephone: (215) 898-5666
Fax: (215) 573-2115/9007
E-mail: HowardS@nwfs.gse.upenn.edu

National Study of Black College Students

Walter R. Allen and Blondell M. Strong

Abstract

The National Study of Black College Students is a cross-sectional and longitudinal study that examines the patterns of Black students' adjustments, achievements, and aspirations in the context of eight predominantly White and eight historically Black state-supported universities. The study seeks to estimate the relative importance of Black students' characteristics and experiences on the adjustment, achievements, and aspirations in their specific university environment. The model underlying the study and questionnaires for graduate and undergraduated students are presented.

Background

The National Study of Black College Students (NSBCS) originated in my experience (Allen) as a young faculty member at the University of North Carolina-Chapel Hill. My duties required service on various committees concerned with so-called "minority" and "disadvantaged" students.

Time after time as the various committees deliberated and attempted to accurately assess the circumstances of Black college students, we found ourselves hampered by paucity of information. Little data of a definitive nature were available to provide information as we sought to identify and propose solutions to the problems confronting Black students. Where data could be found, it was generally of insufficient detail or breadth to be of much value.

The "data gap" on Black college students loomed in importance because many college professors and administrators seemed genuinely concerned about improving the circumstances of Black students in U.S. higher education. However, their efforts to change Black students' abysmally high drop out rates, low academic performance, general alienation, and overrepresentation in traditionally low status fields were thwarted by a lack of information. Therefore, it was decided that a study should be conducted to generate a dataset specifically targeted on Black students' characteristics, experiences and outcomes.

1. The first phase of the project, under the direction of Walter Allen,occurred during Winter, 1981, when a cross-sectional study of 2,048 Black students attending six predominantly White universities was conducted.

2. The second phase was an examination of 2,300 first year Black students at White universities during Winter, 1982, followed by the third collection of data in Spring, 1983 from 1,500 Black students studying at historically Black uni-

versities. Phases four and five provided the opportunity to follow-up longitudinally the Winter, 1982 and Spring, 1983 respondents.

Data were collected during each phase through the use of a self-administered questionnaire mailed to randomly selected undergraduates, graduate and professional students. The questionnaires took approximately one and one-half hours to two hours to complete.

Synopsis of Procedures Used to Develop Measures

The measures for the National Study of Black College Students evolved over a 15 year period (1979-1994). The originating point for these measures was a multivariate model of personal and institutional factors that combined to shape the educational experiences and educational outcomes of Black college students (See Figure 1). The model itself was developed from a careful reading and synopsis of the published literature on Black college students. From empirical and theoretical studies we were able to identify key predictors and to hypothesize the patterns of relationships linking these variables into an explanatory framework.

After the model was developed, we systematically searched the literature for measures of the key concepts. Examples of measures were compiled and evaluated. We then selected items for use in our studies. The criteria for selection were reliability, validity, previous use, and relevance to the focus of the study. In some instances several forms of the same measures were initially selected and used. Later, the best form of the item was chosen.

Our measures selection process involved compiling examples from the literature, compiling a bibliography of each measure's use, reviewing how well the measures worked empirically, whether the measures had been used with Blacks and so on. The process of selecting measures involved all members of the research team participating in the review and evaluation of measures. Where items were not available or suitable to measure concepts of interest, the team created measures. In some cases, we modified items previously used in the literature to focus more specifically on concepts of interest.

At the next stage we created draft questionnaires from these preliminary items. Draft questionnaires were then pre-tested. Results from the pre-tests were used to refine our measures and questions, ultimately resulting in the questionnaires and form of measures used in the study. With some variation to this approach, questionnaire items were revised over the six waves of the study. Empirical results from earlier waves were used to evaluate measures and to make necessary changes (e.g., modification, substitution, removal) in the instrument. Our philosophy was (and continues to be) one that views the measures and questionnaires as evolving instruments. As such, we were comfortable with an approach that allowed for some fluidity within measures and within the questionnaire. However, we also made certain to retain and repeat a core set of measures across different waves of the study.

An important part of NSBCS is the longitudinal aspect. The 1982 and 1983 respondents were followed up to determine where they were in terms of current life situations and future plans, thereby producing a dynamic picture over time to complement the static patterns at a given point in time. Thus, these individuals were reinterviewed after completing their degree programs and moving on to other activities (e.g., the workplace, armed services, or another degree program). The study also provides follow-up data on students who did not successfully complete their degree programs.

This study uses a complex model proposed by Allen (1981) to investigate relationships between family background, high school educational experiences, interpersonal relations with peers and faculty, students' feelings of anxiety and alienation, and student experiences and outcomes. Background factors consisted of mother's, father's and siblings' education, parents' occupation and income levels as well as the student's high school grade point average. Other concepts studied included student social interactions, student activities and experiences on campuses, relations with professors, involvement with Black

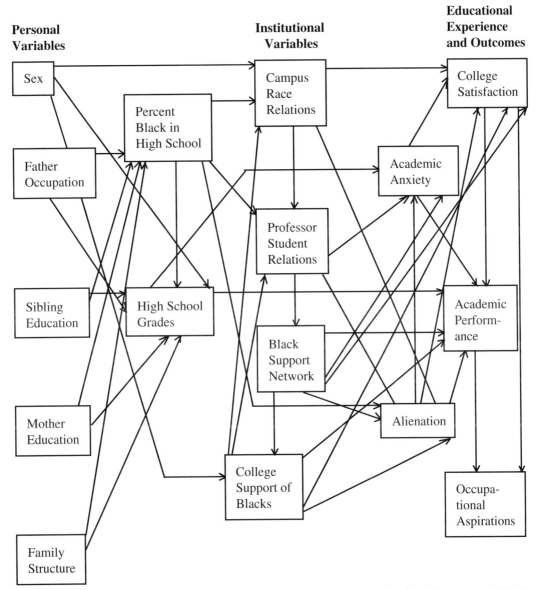

Figure 1. Interrelation of personal and institutional factors in the academic achievement of Black students in predominantly White institutions.

student support networks, university support services, and relations with other Blacks. The additional concepts included in the longitudinal instrument are experiences in present situations, i.e., position or rank held, satisfaction levels, reasons for not graduating from college.

The instrument fills the need to gather data about Black student patterns of college attendance since the early seventies, when a trend became evident that more of these students were enrolling at White campuses. Further, data was collected to estimate the rate of success of Black students in White university environments in comparison to Black university environments. A lack of understanding about what happens to Black students between the initial enrollment period and graduation or dropout made the NSBCS all the more necessary.

Conceptual Issues in the Study's Design

The National Study of Black College Students reveals a clear evolutionary sequence in its procedures and approach. The study began in 1978 as a research project focused solely on undergraduates attending the University of North Carolina at Chapel Hill. Since that time, the study has grown to encompass 16 campuses (8 Black, 8 White) and graduate/professional students as well. The participating campuses were selected to provide maximum geographic representation among the eight predominantly White and eight traditionally Black state supported universities. Attention was restricted to state supported universities because these were by far the most prolific producers of Black students with bachelors degrees. By the same token, on a volume basis, this category of institutions qualifies as the major producer of Black students with masters, professional (e.g., M.B.A., M.S.W.) and Ph.D. degrees.

We have refined the instruments and extended the design from a cross-sectional to a longitudinal data design for each campus. Analyses of the data consist of a combination of bivariate and multivariate tests. Chi-square is used to test the statistical independence and Cramers's V and Gamma are used to test the strength of association for the bivariate relationships. Multiple regression is employed to unravel complex multivariate relationships while path analysis is utilized to trace the hypothesized paths of causation.

Our conceptual plan for the dissemination of findings from the study emphasizes several different audiences. For instance, preliminary reports of a more general nature are prepared for university staff and administrators; sophisticated statistical/theoretical analyses of the data are prepared for other academia and participating students receive project newsletters which double as respondent reports and address file updates.

Although the various waves of data collection were funded generously by the Ford, Spencer, and C.S. Mott Foundations, the Project would

have floundered without a unique cooperative research design. The extraordinary cooperation of research collaborators on each of the sixteen campuses made possible the conduct of this research possible. The research collaborators consented to represent the project on their campuses, secure administration approval, to gain access to student records, to publicize the study and to generally facilitate the project. Research collaborators received compensation in the form of honoraria and access to the collected data.

The conceptual design of the study also incorporates spin-off studies. These complementary studies supplement the main datasets with additional survey ethnographic or institutional data. Spin-off studies have been undertaken by research collaborators and by graduate students. In a selected vein, the project has heavily emphasized collaborative papers and articles. Therefore, numerous jointly authored articles have been written or published. Indeed, several sources of additional funding have been secured for related, collaborative studies.

With respect to student training, we intended that this project would provide currently enrolled Black and minority (and some White) graduate students with firsthand research experience. Students were to participate as research assistants in all phases of the research from conceptualization through data collection/analyses and through the preparation of reports. Among, the specific objectives of the project, we wanted to insure that after two years each research assistant would have written at least one paper for presentation during a major professional meeting and published at least one co-authored paper. Most importantly, the student would have received by graduation a vital foundation in social science research methods-competency and leave school competent to conceive and execute a large-scale research project.

In sum, the National Study of Black College Students was conceptualized as a multi-purposed project. The functions of collaborative academic research, applied social policy research, student training and both short and long-term research objectives were structured into its design. It was viewed as an innovative collaboration among young Black Ph.D.'s and their graduate students. Above all, the project was to generate information which would help to improve Black student representation, performance and experiences in U.S. higher education. As a complementary outcome, it was hoped that the study would strengthen the academic foundations and productivity of the Black scholars (and their students) involved with the research. At this point, the major data collection activities are completed, for the next few years. Current concentrations are on data analysis and the publication of findings from the study. Sources where empirical results from the measures have been published are listed in the references (See Allen, 1981, 1984, 1985, 1986, 1987a, 1987b, 1988a, 1988b; Allen, Epps, & Haniff, 1991; Allen, Hall, & Mays, 1984; Hall & Allen, 1982, 1989; Smith & Allen, 1984).

References

Allen, W. R., Epps, E. G., & Haniff, N. Z. (Eds.). (1991). College in Black and White: African American students in Predominantly White and in Historically Black Public Universities. Albany: State University of New York Press.

Allen, W. R. (1988a). Black students in U.S. higher education: Toward improved access, adjustment and achievement. *Urban Review, 20*(3), 156-188.

Allen, W. R. (1988b). The education of Black students on White college campuses: What quality the experience? In M. Nettles & R. Thoeny (Eds.), *Toward Black undergraduate student equality in American higher education* (pp. 57-86). Westport, CT: Greenwood.

Allen, W. R. (1987a, MONTH). Black colleges vs. White colleges: The fork in the road for Black students. *Change Magazine,* pp. 28-34.

Allen, W. R. (1987b). Blacks in Michigan higher education. In J. Darden & F. Thomas (Eds.), *National Urban League: The state of Black Michigan.* East Lansing: Urban Affairs Program, Michigan State University.

Allen, W. R. (1986). *Gender and campus race differences in Black student academic performance, racial attitudes and college satisfaction.* Atlanta: The Southern Education Foundation.

Allen, W. R. (1985). Black students, White campus: Structural, interpersonal, and psychological correlates of success. *Journal of Negro Education, 54,* 134-147.

Allen, W. R. (1984). Race consciousness and collective commitments among Black students on White campuses. *Western Journal of Black Studies, 8*(3), 156-166.

Allen, W. R. (1981). Correlates of Black student adjustment, achievement and aspirations at a predominantly White southern university. In G. Thomas (Ed.), *Black Students in higher education in the 70's* (pp. 126-141). Westport, CT: Greenwood.

Allen, W. R., Hall, M., & Mays, A. (1984). Dreams deferred: Black student career goals and fields of study in graduate-professional schools. *Phylon, 45,* 271-283.

Astin, H. S., & Cross, P. H. (1981). Black students in Black and White institutions. In G. Thomas (Ed.), *Black students in higher education in the 70's* (pp. 30-45). Westport, CT: Greenwood.

Boyd, W. (1981). The forgotten side of the Black undergraduate: An assessment of academic achievements and aspirations during the 1970's. In G. Thomas (Ed.), *Black students in higher education in the 70's* (pp. 30-45). Westport, CT: Greenwood.

Braddock, J., II, & Dawkins, M. P. (1981). Prediction of Black academic achievement in higher education. *Journal of Negro Education, 50,* 319-325.

Fleming, J. (1981). Stress and satisfaction in college years of Black students. *Journal of Negro Education, 50,* 307-318.

Fleming, J. (1981a). Special needs of Blacks and other minorities. In A. Chickering (Ed.), *The modern American college* (pp. 279-295). San Francisco: Josey-Bass.

Fleming, J. (1980). *The impact of college environments on Black students.* New York: United Negro College Fund.

Hall, M., & Allen, W. R. (1989). Race consciousness among African American college students. In. B. Berry & J. Asamen (Eds.), *Psychosocial Issues and Academic Achievement* (pp. 172-197). Newbury Park, CA: Sage.

Hall, M., & Allen, W. R. (1982). Race consciousness and achievement: Two issues in the study of Black graduate/professional students. *Integrated education, 20,* 56-61.

Smith, A. W., & Allen, W. R. (1984). Modeling Black students' academic performance in higher education. *Research in Higher Education, 21,* 210-225.

Thomas, G. (1981). *Black students in higher education: Conditions and experiences in the 1970's.* Westport, CT: Greenwood.

Tinto, V. (1975). Dropout from higher education: A theoretical synthesis of recent research. *Review of Educational Research, 45,* 89-125.

Willie, C. B., & McCord, A. S. (1972). *Black students at White colleges.* New York: Praeger.

Appendix

National Study of Black College Students

Graduate and Professional Students

Section I. Personal Background Information

1. Your racial/cultural identification:
    A. Black American
    B. Black Other
    B1. West Indian (Specify nationality)
    B2. African (Specify nationality)
    B3. Hispanic (Specify nationality)
    C. Other (Specify)
2. What is your current citizenship status?
    U.S. citizen
    Permanent resident
    Temporary resident
    Other (Specify)
3. Sex: Male; Female
4. Date of birth
5. Marital status:
    Single
    Married
    Separated/divorced
    Widowed
6. Do you have children?
    Yes (Go to Q. 6A);
    No
    6A. (If Yes to Q. 6):
    How many children do you have?
7. Classification:
    Graduate school
    Professional school
    A. Name of school, department or program
    B. Degree(s) sought
    C. Degree(s) you currently hold? (Major area/s or discipline/s?)
    D. Year in present program
    E. Expected degree completion date(s)

8. Undergraduate graduating class rank:
    Upper 5%
    Upper 10%
    Upper 20%
    Upper 30%
    Upper 50%
    Lower 50%
9. Undergraduate cumulative grade point average
10. Size of your undergraduate institution:
    Fewer than 1,000 students
    1,000 - 2,500 students
    2,501 - 5,000 students
    5,001 - 10,000 students
    10,001 - 20,000 students
    20,001 - 30,000 students
    Over 30,000 students
11. Racial percentage of your undergraduate institution (i.e., percent Black):
    0 to 10%
    11% to 20%
    21% to 40%
    41% to 60%
    61% to 80%
    81% to 100%

Of all your years of education through high school graduation (grade 12), how many were spent attending integrated schools? (Please give the number.)

12. Looking back, how would you rate the overall quality of your undergraduate educational experiences?
    Excellent
    Very good
    Good
    Poor
    Very poor

13. Please circle the highest number of years of school completed by each of the following members of your family:

Years of School Completed	Brother or Sister With Most Years School	Father	Mother
1-8 years			
9-11 years			
H.S. Graduate			

Some College B.A. Degree
M.S.W., M.B.A., M.A. Degree
Ph.D., J.D., M.D.
Not Sure

14. Your parents' occupations *and* type of business or industry. (If parent/s is/are deceased, retired or unemployed, please enter previous occupation and industry.)

15. Have you spent most of your life in a rural area, small town or urban community?
   Rural area (fewer than 1,000)
   Small town (1,001 - 50,000)
   Small city (50,001 - 100,000)
   Medium-sized city (100,001 - 300,000)
   Large-sized city (Over 300,000)

16. In which state (country) did you spend most of your life to age 18?

17. With whom did you live most of the time while you were growing up (until age 18)?
   Both natural parents
   Mother and stepfather
   Father and stepmother
   Mother only
   Father only
   Grandparent(s)
   Foster parents
   Other (Please specify)

18. How many brothers and sisters do you have?
   Number of brothers
   Number of sisters
   A. What was *your* birth order (e.g., first child, third child, sixth child, last child)?

19. From the list below, circle the number indicating your parents' combined income for last year:
   Less than $8,000
   $8,001 - $10,000
   $10,001 - $12,000
   $12,0001 - $15,000
   $15,001- $18,000
   $18,001 - $21,000
   $21,001 - $25,000
   $25,001 - $28,000
   $28,001 - $30,000
   $30,001 - $40,000
   $40,001 - $50,000
   $50,001 - $60,000
   $60,001 - $75,000
   $75,001 - $100,000

20. *Work History*: (For Q. 20A-F, answer as much as is appropriate about your regular full-time jobs. *Do not* list any job that was solely for the summer.)
   A. How old were you when you got your first regular, full-time job?
   ____ Years old
   Never worked (Go to Q. 21)
   B. (If you worked) What kind of work did you do then (occupation and type of business or industry)? Job title; Major duty
   C. When you were 20 years old, what kind of job did you have? Job title; Major duty
   D. When you were 25 years old, what kind of job did you have? Job title; Major duty
   E. When you were 30 years old, what kind of job did you have? Job title; Major duty
   F. When you were 35 years old, what kind of job did you have? Job title, Major, duty

Section II. Student Status at This University

21. Where are you living during this academic year?
   A university residence hall
   A rented apartment or condominium
   A rented house
   A rented room or apartment in a private home
   My own house or condominium
   The home of my parents or other relatives or guardian
   Other (Specify)

22. Your student status this quarter/semester?
   Full-time
   Part-time

23. Graduate or professional cumulative grade point average?

24. How many schools did you *apply* to?
   A. What led you to consider *applying* to this university? [Please indicate the top three (3) reasons that influenced your decision. **Rank** these by order of importance: 1 (first); 2 (second); and 3. (third).]
   Academic reputation
   Family encouraged
   Location
   Program(s) offered

Financial considerations
College teachers/counselors encouraged
Friends encouraged
Other reason (Please specify)

25. How many schools *accepted* you?

A. Of all the schools that *accepted* you, why did you decide to attend this university? [Please indicate the top three (3) reasons that influenced your decision. **Rank** these by order of importance: 1 (first); 2 (second); and 3 (third).]
Academic reputation
Family encouraged
Location
Financial considerations
Program(s) offered
College teachers/counselors encouraged
Friends encouraged
Liked school climate/setting
Admitted here only
Other reason (Please specify)

B. Was this university your first choice?
Yes
No

26. During your graduate/professional school career, have you:

A. Read a paper or made a presentation during a professional meeting?
Yes
No (Go to Q. 26C)

B. (If Yes to Q. 26A) How many times?

C. Had a paper, article or monograph accepted for publication in your area of concentration?
Yes
No (Go to Q. 26E)

D. (If Yes to 26C) How many times?

E. Collaborated or worked closely with a faculty member on a joint research project?
Yes
No (Go to Q. 26H)

F. (If Yes to Q. 26E) Have you co-authored a publication with a faculty member?
Yes
No (Go to Q. 26H)

G. (If Yes to Q. 26F) How many times?

H. Been awarded funding to conduct a research or creative project?

Yes
No

I. (If Yes to Q. 26H) How many times?

27. What was your area of concentration when you first enrolled in this program, department or school?
General field of study
Specialization

A. Is this still your area of concentration?
Yes (Go to Q. 28)
No (Go to Q. 27B, 27C)

B. (If No to Q. 27A) What is your area of concentration currently?
General field of study
Specialization

C. (If No to Q. 27A) What factor(s) led you to change your area of concentration? [Please indicate the top three (3) reasons that influenced your decision. *Rank* these by importance: 1 (first); 2 (second); and 3 (third).]
Academic problems
Changing interests
Future employment considerations
Poor relations with faculty
Program requirements
Other reason (Please specify)

28. Have you ever seriously considered leaving this program, department or school?
Yes
No

A. (If Yes to Q. 28) What were some of the major reasons why you considered leaving this program, department or school?

29. How important is it for you to get a graduate or professional degree?
Extremely important
Very important
Somewhat important
Not at all important

30. How important is it that you graduate from this program, department or school?
Extremely important
Very important
Somewhat important
Not at all important

31. How sure are you that you made the right choice in selecting this program, department or school?

Definitely *right* choice
Probably *right* choice
Not sure
Probably *wrong* choice
Definitely *wrong* choice

32. Will you return to this program, department or school next Fall?

Will graduate before Fall 1983
Definitely *will* return
Probably *will* return
Not sure
Probably *will* not return
Definitely *will* not return

A. (If your answer to Q. 32 was "Not sure," "Probably will not return" or "Definitely will not return") What are some reasons why you might not return next Fall?

Section III. Student Experiences at this University

33. As a Black student, how much do you feel a part of your program, department or school, insofar as general activities and involvements are concerned?

Not at all
Very little
Somewhat
Considerable

34. To what extent do extracurricular activities on campus reflect your interests?

Not at all
Very little
Somewhat
Considerable

35. How often do you participate in the extracurricular activities sponsored by Black student organizations (e.g., Black Student Union, fraternities, cultural groups, etc.)?

Hardly ever
Sometimes
Often
Very often

36. We are interested in what students do in an average week. Please circle the average number of hours per week that you spend on each listed activity.

Hours per week spent on activity

None
1-5
6-10
11-15
16-20
Over 20

A. Attending class
B. Studying
C. Sleeping and resting
D. Watching television
E. Attending non-required lectures, seminars or workshops
F. Listening to music (radio, records)
G. Dating
H. Participating in club meetings or other organized activities
 I. Working a part-time job
J. Socializing with friends
K. Participating in organized athletics or intramural sports
L. Exercising (other than organized sports)
M. Interacting with family members
N. Other (Specify)

37. How intense would you say the academic competition is within your program, department or school?

Extremely intense
Intense
About average
Somewhat intense
Not at all intense

38. What are your feelings about the level of academic competition in your program, department or school?

Very positive
Positive
Neutral
Negative
Very negative

Section IV. Student Interactions at this University

39. Have you ever encountered racial discrimination in any form from anyone on this campus (i.e., symbols, gestures, words or behaviors)?

Yes
No

A. (If Yes to Q. 39) How frequently have you experienced racial discrimination on this campus?
Hardly ever
Seldom
Sometimes
Often
Very often

40. Briefly describe the most notable incident of racial discrimination experienced by you on this campus.

41. How would you rate White students at this university in regard to their relations with Black students? Do they:

A. Show high regard for Black student academic abilities?
Never
Sometimes
Often
Always

B. Avoid interacting with Black students socially?
Never
Sometimes
Often
Always

C. Treat Black students as equals?
Never
Sometimes
Often
Always

42. How would you rate your White professors in regard to their relations with Black students? Do they:

A. Have difficulty relating to Black students?
Never
Sometimes
Often
Always

B. Avoid Black student interaction outside the classroom?
Never
Sometimes
Often
Always

C. Provide encouragement to continue studies and go on for advanced degree(s)?
Never

Sometimes
Often
Always

D. Seem genuinely concerned about Black student success?
Never
Sometimes
Often
Always

E. Evaluate Black student academic performance fairly?
Never
Sometimes
Often
Always

43. How would you rate White university staff (secretaries, administrators, security police, etc.) on the following scales in regard to their relations with Black students? Do they:

A. Have difficulty relating to Black students?
Never
Sometimes
Often
Always

B. Seem genuinely concerned about the welfare of Black students?
Never
Sometimes
Often
Always

C. Treat Black students fairly and with respect?
Never
Sometimes
Often
Always

44. How would you characterize *your* relations with Whites at this university?

A. Students:
Excellent
Good
Poor
Very Poor
No Contact

B. Faculty:
Excellent
Good
Poor
Very Poor

No Contact
C. Staff:
  Excellent
  Good
  Poor
  Very Poor
  No Contact

45. How often do you interact with White students at this university in an average week?
  Several times a day
  At least once a day
  Several times a week
  At least once a week
  Less than once a week

46. How often do you interact with White faculty at this university in an average week?
  Several times a day
  At least once a day
  Several times a week
  At least once a week
  Less than once a week

47. How often do you interact with White staff at this university in an average week?
  Several times a day
  At least once a day
  Several times a week
  At least once a week
  Less than once a week

48. How would you characterize *overall* Black student relations with Whites at this university?
A. Students:
  Excellent
  Good
  Poor
  Very Poor
  No Contact
B. Faculty:
  Excellent
  Good
  Poor
  Very Poor
  No Contact
C. Staff:
  Excellent
  Good
  Poor
  Very Poor
  No Contact

49. Do you believe that there are enough Black students at this university?
  Yes
  No
A. Do you feel that there are enough Black students in your program?
  Yes
  No
B. How often do you interact with other Black students at this university in an average week?
  Several times a day
  At least once a day
  Several times a week
  At least once a week
  Less than once a week
C. How often do you interact with other Black students in your program, department or school in an average week?
  No others in the program, department or school
  Several times a day
  At least once a day
  Several times a week
  At least once a week
  Less than once a week

50. Are there any Black faculty in your program or department?
  Yes
  No (Go to Q. 51)
A. (If Yes to Q. 50) Do you believe there are enough Black faculty in your program or department?
  Yes
  No
B. Do you believe there are enough Black faculty at this *university*?
  Yes
  No
C. How often do you interact with Black faculty at this university in an average week?
  Several times a day
  At least once a day
  Several times a week
  At least once a week
  Less than once a week

51. Do you believe there are enough Black staff (secretaries, administrators, security police, etc.) at this university?

Yes

No

A. How often do you interact with Black staff at this university in an average week?

Several times a day

At least once a day

Several times a week

At least once a week

Less than once a week

52. How would you characterize *your* relations with Blacks at this university?

A. Students:

Excellent

Good

Poor

Very Poor

No Contact

B. Faculty:

Excellent

Good

Poor

Very Poor

No Contact

C. Staff:

Excellent

Good

Poor

Very Poor

No Contact

53. How satisfied or dissatisfied have you been with your social life/dating at the university?

I am already married

Very satisfied

Satisfied

Dissatisfied

Very dissatisfied

54. On the average, how often during the past year have you dated at the university?

I am already married

Less than once a month

About once a month

Two or three times a month

Once a week

Two or three times a week

More than three times a week

55. Do you receive any form of financial aid (i.e., loan, stipend, fellowship, grant, work study)?

Yes (Go to Q. 55D)

No (Go to Q. 55A)

A. (If No to Q. 55) Did you receive financial aid in the past?

Yes (Go to Q. 56)

No (Go to Q. 55B)

B. (If No to Q. 55A) Have you ever applied for financial aid?

Yes (Go to Q. 55C)

No (Go to Q. 57)

C. (If Yes to Q. 55B) Please state the reasons why you did not receive financial aid. [Then go to Q. 57.]

D. How much financial aid do you receive from university, private, state or federal funds per year?

Less than $500

$500 - $999

$1,000 - $1,999

$2,000 - $2,999

$3,000 - $3,999

$4,000 - $4,999

$5,000 - $6,000

Over $6,000

E. How much is the total amount of financial aid that you receive per category?

Grant

Loan

Academic fellowship

Teaching assistantship

Research assistantship

Work study

Outside

Non-university funding

Other (Please specify source and amount)

56. How adequate have financial aid services been to your needs?

Inadequate

Somewhat adequate

Adequate

Very adequate

57. How satisfied have you been with academic advising?

Do not receive academic advising

Very dissatisfied

Dissatisfied

Satisfied

Very satisfied

58. How helpful are campus tutorial and reme-

dial academic services to your needs?

>Do not use tutorial services
>Not helpful
>Somewhat helpful
>Helpful
>Very helpful

59. How adequate is the student health services to your needs?

>Do not use student health services
>Inadequate
>Somewhat adequate
>Adequate
>Very adequate

60. What are some of the more serious difficulties or problems (academic or personal) you have had to cope with since entering this university?

A. How do you handle your problems (academic and personal)?

B. What sources or people do you seek help from in coping with these problems?

Section VI. Student Attitudes and Opinions

61. Considering your ability, financial situation, societal attitudes, etc., how far do you actually expect to go in school?

>Some graduate/professional school
>M.A. or M.S. degree
>M.S.W.
>M.P.H. or M.B.A. degree
>M.D., D.D.S. or J.D. degree
>Ph.D. or Ed.D. degree
>Other (Specify)

A. What are some factors that might prevent you from going this far in school?

62. Considering your abilities, personal contacts, the job market, etc., what occupation do you actually expect to go into once your education is completed? (Please provide the following information on the occupation you expect to go into once your education is completed.)

>Occupation
>Specialization
>Type of business or institution

A. What are some factors that might prevent you from going into this occupation?

63. After you are in the profession which will be your life's work, when do you think you will be able to consider yourself successful enough so that you can relax and stop trying so hard to get ahead? When you are:

>"Doing well enough to stay in the profession"
>"Doing as well as the average person in the profession"
>"Doing a little better than the average person in the profession"
>"Doing much better than the average person in the profession"
>"Recognized as one of the top persons in the profession"

64. What is your religious identification?

>Christian/Protestant (Specify denomination; e.g., Methodist, Baptist)
>Christian/Catholic
>Islam/Muslim
>Other (Please specify)
>None

A. How religious are you?

>Very religious
>Religious
>Somewhat religious
>Not at all religious

65. Below is a list of statements grouped by two's about Black people. Please read the statements and check the *one* in each group you most agree with.

A. The attempt to "it in" and do what's proper hasn't paid off for Blacks. It doesn't matter how "proper" you are, you'll still meet serious discrimination if you are Black. Any Black who is educated and does what is considered "proper" will be accepted and eventually get ahead.

B. Many Blacks have only themselves to blame for not doing better in life. If they tried harder, they would do better. When two qualified people, one Black and one White, are considered for the same job, the Black won't get the job no matter how hard s/he tries.

C. The recent upsurge in conservatism shows once again that Whites are so opposed to Blacks getting their rights that is practically impossible to end discrimination in America. The recent upsurge in conservatism has been exaggerated. Certainly enough Whites support the goals of the Black cause for Americans to see consider able progress in wiping out discrimination.

D. The best way to overcome discrimination is through pressure and social action. The best way to overcome discrimination is for each individual Black to be even better trained and more qualified than the most qualified White person.

E. People who don't do well in life often work hard, but the breaks just don't come their way. Some people just don't use the breaks that come their way. If they don't do well, it is their own fault.

66. We are interested in your opinions on several topics and issues. Please read the following statements and indicate the strength of your agreement or disagreement. Do you:

Strongly agree
Agree
Disagree

A. There is a need for a national Black political party.

B. Interracial dating and marriage are equally as acceptable as within race dating and marriage.

C. Schools with majority Black student populations should have a majority of Black teachers and administrators.

D. In general, the church has helped the conditions of Black people in this country.

E. There is a great deal of unity and sharing among Black students at this university.

F. The future looks very promising for educated Black Americans.

G. Black men and women students on this campus really don't get along very well together.

H. Middle-class Blacks have more in common with middle-class Whites than they do with lower-class Blacks.

I. Participation in organized sports or athletics is usually more harmful than helpful for Black college students.

J. Black students have the same problems as White students do at this university.

67. If you were compared to most other students at this university, how would you be rated on the following points by an unbiased observer? Please indicate whether you think you would be rated among the:

Highest
Above average
Average
Below average on each point.

How would *you* be rated in terms of:

A. Your popularity with members of the opposite sex?

B. Your professors' evaluation of you?

C. Your closeness to your family?

D. Your undergraduate teachers' evaluations of you?

E. The number of friends that you have?

F. Your current physical well-being and health?

G. Your current emotional or psychological well-being and health?

H. Your self-confidence?

I. Your leadership abilities?

J. The kind of person that people in the neigh borhood or community where you grew up think you are?

K. The kind of person that you are, all things considered?

Section VII. Improving Black Student Experiences

68. What would you say are some of the most serious barriers to more Black students being accepted to attend this university?

A. What are some of the most serious barriers to more Black students **deciding to attend** this university?

69. What would you say are some of the most serious problems and difficulties that Black students who attend this university must face?

70. If you know of any Black student(s) who recently left the university for reasons other than graduation, what were some of the reasons?

71. Suppose for a moment, that you were Chancellor or President of this university. What programs or policies would you adopt in order to deal with the kinds of problems Black students experience here?

72. Please mention below any important aspects of Black student experiences at your university

that this questionnaire overlooks. How have these factors influenced you?

Undergraduates

Section I. Personal Background Information

1. Your racial/cultural identification:
   A. Black American
   B. Black Other
   B1. West Indian (Specify nationality)
   B2. African (Specify nationality)
   B3. Hispanic (Specify nationality)
   C. Other (Specify)
2. What is your current citizenship status?
   U.S. citizen
   Permanent resident
   Temporary resident (Student visa); Other (Specify)
3. Sex:
   Male
   Female
4. Date of birth
5. Classification:
   Freshman
   Sophomore
   Junior
   Senior
   Other (Please specify)
6. Marital status:
   Single
   Married
   Separated/divorced
   Widowed
7. Do you have children?
   Yes
   No
   A. (If Yes to Q. 7) How many children do you have?
8. High school senior class rank:
   Upper 5%
   Upper 10%
   Upper 20%
   Upper 30%
   Upper 50%
   Lower 50%
9. High school cumulative grade point average
10. Size of your high school (size range):

0 to 300 students
301 to 700 students
701 to 1,000 students
1,001 to 1,500 students
1,501 to 2,500 students
2,501 to 3,500 students
Over 3,500 students

11. Racial percentage of high school (i.e., percent Black):
   0 to 10%
   11% to 20%
   21% to 40%
   41% to 60%
   61% to 80%
   81% to 100%
   A. Of all your years of education through high school graduation (grade 12), how many have you spent attending integrated schools? (Please give the number.)
12. Looking back, how would you rate the overall quality of your educational experiences through elementary and high school?
   Excellent
   Very good
   Good; Poor
   Very poor
13. Please circle the highest number of years of school completed by each of the following people in your family:

Years of School Completed	Brother or Sister With Most Years School	Father	Mother
1-8 years			
9-11 years			
H.S. Graduate			
Some College B.A. Degree			
M.S.W., M.B.A., M.A. Degree			
Ph.D., J.D., M.D.			
Not Sure			

14. Your parents' occupations and type of business or industry. (If deceased, retired or unemployed, please enter previous occupation and industry.)
15. Have you spent most of your life in a rural area, small town or urban community?
   Rural area (fewer than 1,000)
   Small town (1,001 - 50,000)

Small city (50,001 - 100,000)
Medium-sized city (100,001 - 300,000)
Large-sized city (Over 300,001)

16. In which state (country) did you spend most of your life to age 18?

17. With whom did you live most of the time while you were growing up (until age 18)?
    Both natural parents
    Mother and stepfather
    Father and stepmother
    Mother only
    Father only
    Grandparent(s)
    Foster parents
    Other (Please specify)

18. How many brothers and sisters do you have?
    Number of brothers
    Number of sisters
    A. What was your birth order (e.g., first child, third child, sixth child, last child)?

19. From the list below, please circle the number indicating your parents' combined income for the last year:
    Less than $8,000
    $8,001 - $10,000
    $10,001 - $12,000
    $12,0001 - $15,000
    $15,001 - $18,000
    $18,001 - $21,000
    $21,001 - $25,000
    $25,001 - $28,000
    $28,001 - $30,000
    $30,001 - $40,000
    $40,001 - $50,000
    $50,001 - $60,000
    $60,001 - $75,000
    $75,001 - $100,000
    $100,001 - $150,000
    Over $150,000

Section II. Student Status at This University

20. Where are you living during this academic year?
    A university residence hall
    A rented apartment or condominium
    A rented house
    A rented room or apartment in a private home

My own house or condominium
The home of my parents or other relatives or
    guardian
Other (Please specify)

21. Your student status this quarter/semester?
    Full-time
    Part-time

22. Your cumulative university grade point average?

23. How many schools did you apply to?
    A. What led you to consider applying to this university? [Please indicate the top three (3) reasons that influenced your decision. *Rank* these by importance: 1 (first); 2 (second); and, 3 (third).]
    Academic reputation
    Family encouraged
    Location
    Program(s) offered
    Financial considerations
    High school teachers/counselors encouraged
    Friends encouraged
    Other reason (Please specify)

24. How many schools accepted you?
    A. Of all the schools that accepted you, why did you decide to **attend** this university? [Please indicate the top three (3) reasons that influenced your decision. **Rank** these by importance: 1 (first); 2 (second); and, 3 (third).]
    Academic reputation
    Family encouraged
    Location
    Program(s) offered
    Financial considerations
    High school teachers/counselors encouraged
    Friends encouraged
    Liked school climate/setting
    Admitted here only; Other reason (Please specify)
    B. Was this university your first choice?
    Yes
    No

25. Did you attend another college or university before enrolling here?
    Yes
    No
    A. (If Yes to Q. 25) What kind of college or university did you attend?
    Community college

Liberal arts college
University
Vocational/technical college
Other (Please specify)

26. Did you ever consider attending a historically Black college or university?
Yes
No

A. (If Yes to Q. 26) Why did you decide not to attend a Black college? [Please indicate the top three (3) reasons that influenced your decision. *Rank* these by importance: 1 (first); 2 (second); and, 3 (third).]
Academic reputation
Family members encouraged
Location; Program(s) offered
Friends encouraged
Financial considerations
Wanted integrated setting
Lacked sufficient information
High school teachers/counselors encouraged
Other reason (Please specify)

B. (If No to Q. 26) What are the reasons you did not consider attending a Black college? [Please indicate the top three (3) reasons that influenced your decision. **Rank** these by importance: 1 (first); 2 (second); and, 3 (third).]
Academic reputation
Location
Program(s) offered
Family
Friends
Financial considerations
Wanted integrated setting
Lacked sufficient information
High school teachers/counselors encouraged Other reason (Please specify)

27. What was your major when you first enrolled at this university?

A. Is this still your major?
Yes (Go to Q. 28)
No (Go to Q. 27B, 27C)

B. (If No to Q. 27A) What is your major currently?

C. (If No to Q. 27A) What factor(s) led you to change your major? [Please indicate the top three (3) reasons that influenced your decision. **Rank** these by importance: 1 (first); 2 (second); and, 3 (third).]
Academic problems
Changing interests
Future employment considerations
Poor relations with faculty
Program requirements
Other (Please specify)

28. How important is it for you to get a college degree?
Extremely important
Very important
Somewhat important
Not at all important

29. How important is it that you graduate from *this* university?
Extremely important
Very important
Somewhat important
Not at all important

30. How sure are you that you made he right choice in attending this university?
Definitely right choice
Probably right choice
Not sure
Probably wrong choice
Definitely wrong choice

31. Will you return to this university next Fall?
Will graduate before Fall 1983
Definitely will return
Probably will return
Not sure
Probably will not return
Definitely will not return

A. (If answer to Q. 31 was "Not sure," "Probably will not" or "Definitely will not return") What are some of the reasons that you might not return to this college next Fall?

32. Have you ever seriously considered leaving this university?
Yes
No

A. (If Yes to Q. 32) What were some of the reasons that caused you to consider leaving this university?

Section III. Student Experiences at This University

33. How much do you, as a Black student, feel part of the general campus life, insofar as student activities and government are concerned?

    Not at all
    Very little
    Somewhat
    Considerable

34. To what extent do extracurricular activities on campus reflect your interests?

    Not at all
    Very little
    Somewhat
    Considerable

35. How often do you participate in the extracurricular activities sponsored by Black student organizations (e.g., Black Student Union, fraternities/sororities, cultural groups, etc.)?

    Hardly ever
    Sometimes
    Often
    Very often

36. We are interested in what students do in an average week. Please circle the average number of hours per week that you spend on each listed activity.

Hours per *week* spent on activity

None 1-5 6-10 11-15   16-20   Over 20
    A. Attending class
    B. Studying
    C. Sleeping or resting
    D. Watching television
    E. Attending non-required lectures,
       seminars or workshops
    F. Listening to music (radio, records)
    G. Dating
    H. Participating in club meetings or
       other organized activities
    I. Working on a part-time job
    J. Socializing with friends
    K. Participating in organized athletics
       or intramural sports
    L. Exercising (other than organized
       sports)

M. Interacting with family members
N. Other (Specify)

37. How intense would you say the academic competition is at this university?

    Extremely intense
    Intense
    About average
    Somewhat intense
    Not at all intense

38. What are your feelings about the level of academic competition here?

    Very positive
    Positive
    Neutral
    Negative
    Very negative

Section IV. Student Interactions at This University

39. Have you ever encountered racial discrimination in any form (i.e., symbols, gestures, words or behaviors)?

    Yes
    No

 A. (If Yes to Q. 39) How frequently have you experienced race discrimination on this campus?

    Hardly ever
    Seldom
    Sometimes
    Often
    Very often

40. Briefly describe the most notable incident of racial discrimination experienced by you on this campus.

41. How would you rate white **students** at your university on the following scales in regard to their relations with Black students? Do they:

 A. Show high regard for Black student academic abilities?

    Never
    Sometimes
    Often
    Always

 B. Avoid interacting with Black students socially?

    Never

Sometimes
Often
Always
C. Treat Black students as equals?
Never
Sometimes
Often
Always

42. How would you rate your white *professors* in regard to their relations with Black students? Do they:

A. Have difficulty relating to Black students?
Never
Sometimes
Often
Always

B. Avoid Black student interaction outside the classroom?
Never
Sometimes
Often
Always

C. Provide encouragement to continue studies and go on for advanced degree(s)?
Never
Sometimes
Often
Always

D. Seem genuinely concerned about Black student success?
Never
Sometimes
Often
Always

E. Evaluate Black student academic performance fairly?
Never
Sometimes
Often
Always

43. How would you rate white university **staff** (secretaries, administrators, security police, etc.) on the following scales in regard to their relations with Black students? Do they:

A. Have difficulty relating to Black students?
Never
Sometimes
Often

Always

B. Seem genuinely concerned about the welfare of Black students?
Never
Sometimes
Often
Always

C. Treat Black students fairly and with respect?
Never
Sometimes
Often
Always

44. How would you characterize your relations with whites at this university?

A. Students:
Excellent
Good
Poor
Very Poor
No Contact

B. Faculty:
Excellent
Good
Poor
Very Poor
No Contact

C. Staff:
Excellent
Good
Poor
Very Poor
No Contact

45. How often do you interact with white **students** at this university in an average week?
Several times a day
At least once a day
Several times a week
At least once a week
Less than once a week

46. How often do you interact with white **faculty** at this university in an average week?
Several times a day
At least once a day
Several times a week
At least once a week
Less than once a week

47. How often do you interact with white **staff** at this university in an average week? Several

times a day; At least once a day; Several times a week; At least once a week; Less than once a week

48. How would you characterize overall Black student relations with whites at this university?
   A. Students: Excellent; Good; Poor; Very Poor; No Contact
   B. Faculty: Excellent; Good; Poor; Very Poor; No Contact
   C. Staff: Excellent; Good; Poor; Very Poor; No Contact

49. Do you believe that there are enough Black **students** at this university?
   Yes
   No
   A. How often do you interact with other Black **students** at this university in an average week?
   Several times a day
   At least once a day
   Several times a week
   At least once a week
   Less than once a week

50. Do you believe there are enough Black *faculty* at this university?
   Yes
   No
   A. How often do you interact with other Black **faculty** at this university in an average week?
   Several times a day
   At least once a day
   Several times a week
   At least once a week
   Less than once a week

51. Do you believe there are enough Black STAFF (secretaries, administrators, security police, etc.) at this university?
   Yes
   No
   A. How often do you interact with other Black **staff** at this university in an average week?
   Several times a day
   At least once a day
   Several times a week
   At least once a week
   Less than once a week

52. How would you characterize your relations with Blacks at this university?
   A. Students: Excellent; Good; Poor; Very Poor; No Contact
   B. Faculty: Excellent; Good; Poor; Very Poor; No Contact
   C. Staff: Excellent; Good; Poor; Very Poor; No Contact

53. How satisfied or dissatisfied have you been with your social life/dating at the university?
   Very satisfied
   Satisfied; Dissatisfied
   Very dissatisfied
   I am already married

54. On the average, how often have you dated at the university?
   I am already married
   Less than once a month
   About once a month
   Two or three times a month
   Once a week
   Two or three times a week
   More than three times a week

55. Do you receive any form of financial aid (i.e., loan, scholarship, work study)?
   Yes (Go to Q. 55D)
   No (Go to Q. 55A)
   A. (If No to Q. 55) Did you receive financial aid in the past?
   Yes (Go to Q. 56)
   No (Go to Q. 55B)
   B. (If No to Q. 55A) Have you ever applied for financial aid?
   Yes (Go to Q. 55C)
   No (Skip to Q. 57)
   C. (If Yes to Q. 55B) Please state the reasons why you did not receive financial aid (...then skip to Q. 57).
   D. How much financial aid do you receive from private, university, state or federal funds per year?
   $1- $499
   $500 - $999
   $1,000 - $1,999
   $2,000 - $2,999
   $3,000 - $3,999
   $4,000 - $4,999
   $5,000 - $6,000
   Over $6,000
   E. How much is the total amount of financial aid that you receive per category?
   Grant

Loan

Academic scholarship

Research assistantship

Teaching assistantship

Outside, non-university funding

Work study; Other (Please specify source and amount)

56. How adequate have financial aid services been to your needs?

Inadequate

Somewhat adequate

Adequate

Very adequate

Do not receive aid

57. How satisfied have you been with academic advising?

Do not receive academic advising

Very dissatisfied

Dissatisfied

Satisfied

Very satisfied

58. How helpful are campus tutorial and remedial academic services to your needs?

Do not use

Not helpful

Somewhat helpful

Helpful

Very helpful

59. How adequate is the student health services to your needs?

Do not use student health services

Inadequate

Somewhat adequate

Adequate

Very adequate

60. What are some of the more serious difficulties or problems (academic or personal) you have had to cope with since entering this university?

A. How do you handle your problems (academic and personal)?

B. What sources or people do you seek help from in coping with these problems?

Section VI. Student Attitudes and Opinions

61. Considering your ability, financial situation, societal attitudes, etc., how far do you actually expect to go in school?

Some college

B.A. or B.S. degree

M.A. or M.S. degree

M.S.W., M.P.H. or M.B.A. degree

M.D., D.D.S. or J.D. degree

Ph.D. or Ed.D. degree

Other (Specify)

A. What are some factors that might prevent you from going this far in school?

62. Considering your abilities, personal contacts, the job market, etc., what occupation do you actually expect to go into once your education is completed? Please provide the following information on the occupation you expect to go into once your education is completed.

Occupation

Specialization

Type of business or institution

A. What are some factors that might prevent you from going into this occupation?

63. After you are in the profession which will be your life's work, when do you think you will be able to consider yourself successful enough so that you can relax and stop trying so hard to get ahead? When you are:

"Doing well enough to stay in the profession"

"Doing as well as the average person in the profession"

"Doing a little better than the average person in the profession"

"Doing much better than the average person in the profession"

"Recognized as one of the top persons in the profession"

64. What is your religious identification?

Christian/Protestant (Specify denomination, e.g., Methodist, Baptist)

Christian/Catholic

Islam/Muslim

Other (Please specify)

None

A. How religious are you? Very religious; Religious; Somewhat religious; Not at all religious

65. Below is a list of statements grouped by two's about Black people. Please read the statements and check the one in each group you most agree with.

A. The attempt to "fit in" and do what's proper hasn't paid off for Blacks. It doesn't matter how "proper" you are, you'll still meet serious discrimination if you are Black.

Any Black who is educated and does what is considered "proper" will be accepted and eventually get ahead.

B. Many Blacks have only themselves to blame for not doing better in life. If they tried harder, they would do better.

When two qualified people, one Black and one white, are considered for the same job, the Black won't get the job no matter how hard s/he tries.

C. The recent upsurge in conservatism shows once again that whites are so opposed to Blacks getting their rights that is practically impossible to end discrimination in America. The recent upsurge in conservatism has been exaggerated. Certainly enough whites support the goals of the Black cause for Americans to see considerable progress in wiping out discrimination.

D. The best way to overcome discrimination is through pressure and social action.

The best way to overcome discrimination is for each individual Black to be even better trained and more qualified than the most qualified white person.

E. People who don't do well in life often work hard, but the breaks just don't come their way. Some people just don't use the breaks that come their way. If they don't do well, it is their own fault.

66. We are interested in your opinions on several topics and issues. Please read the following statements and indicate the strength of your agreement or disagreement. Do you:

Strongly agree

Agree

Disagree

Strongly disagree with the statement.

A. There is a need for a national Black political party.

B. Interracial dating and marriage are equally as acceptable as within race dating and marriage.

C. Schools with majority Black student populations should have a majority of Black teachers and administrators.

D. In general, the church has helped the conditions of Black people in this country.

E. There is a great deal of unity and sharing among Black students at this university.

F. The future looks very promising for educated Black Americans.

G. Black men and women students on this campus really don't get along very well.

H. Middle-class Blacks have more in common with middle-class whites than they do with lower-class Blacks.

I. Participation in organized sports or athletics is usually more harmful than helpful for Black college students.

J. Black students have the same problems as white students do at this university.

67. If you were compared to most other students at this university, how would you be rated on the following points by an unbiased observer? Please indicate whether you think you would be rated among the:

Highest

Above average

Average

Below average on each point.

How would you be rated in terms of:

A. Your popularity with members of the opposite sex?

B. Your professors' evaluation of you?

C. Your closeness to your family?

D. Your undergraduate teachers' evaluations of you?

E. The number of friends that you have?

F. Your current physical well-being and health?

G. Your current emotional or psychological well-being and health?

H. Your self-confidence?

I. Your leadership abilities?

J. The kind of person that people in the neighborhood or community where you grew up think you are?

K. The kind of person that you are, all things considered?

Section VII. Improving Black Student Experiences

68. What would you say are some of the most serious barriers to more Black students being *accepted* to attend this university?

   A. What are some of the most serious barriers to more Black students *deciding to attend* this university?

69. What would you say are some of the most serious problems and difficulties that Black students who attend this university must face?

70. If you know of any Black student(s) who recently left the university for reasons other than graduation, what were some of the reasons?

71. Suppose for a moment, that you were Chancellor or President of this university. What programs or policies would you adopt in order to deal with the kinds of problems Black students experience here?

72. Please mention below any important aspects of Black student experiences at your university that this questionnaire overlooks. How have these factors influenced you?

List of key terms

For additional information, contact:
Walter R. Allen
Deparment of Sociology
254 Haines Hall
University of California-Los Angeles
Los Angeles, CA 90095-1551
Telephone: (310)206-7107
Fax: (310)206-9838
Email: Allen@SOC.SSCnet.ucla.edu

Part VII

Language Assessment and Attitude Measures

African American English Tests for Students*

Mary Rhodes Hoover, Robert Politzer, Dwight Brown, Shirley A. R. Lewis, Shirley Hicks, and Faye McNair-Knox

Abstract

All people vary linguistic codes according to circumstances. African Americans often exhibit a wider range of speech varieties than Whites; thus African American children are often exposed to several very different types of language usage. They may learn African American Vernacular English (characterized by distinctive phonological, grammatical, and style features) and they may also become acquainted with standard or "network" English (exemplified by network television and radio broadcasters). The African American English Test for Students (AAETS) described in this chapter is comprised of three different tests: (1) Discrimination Test (assesses students' ability to distinguish between specific grammatical features of African American Vernacular English) (AAVE) and African American Standard English (AASE); (2) Repetition Test (assesses students' ability to repeat sentences containing specific grammatical features of AAVE and AASE); and the (3) Production Test, (assesses students' ability to produce statements in AAVE and AASE). Information on the background and use of the test and statistical data, including reliability studies, are presented.

The purpose of the African American English Tests for Students (AAETS) is to provide a more complete picture of an African American (AA) child's language proficiency, including her/his relative proficiency in the standard and vernacular forms of speech. Three different tests, which can be taken separately, comprise the battery.

1. **Discrimination Test**. This test can be administered to children in grades 2 through 6. It measures the ability to distinguish African American Vernacular English (AAVE) from African American Standard English (AASE)–an ability that has been found to correlate significantly with reading achievement and that is relevant to various standardized language and achievement tests.

2. **Repetition Test**. This test, which must be administered individually, measures the ability to reproduce African American Vernacular English and African American Standard English. It is particularly well-suited to detecting the relative knowledge of vernacular and standard varieties

---

* These tests were developed at the Center for Educational Research at Stanford's Program on Teaching and Linguistic Pluralism, directed by Robert L. Politzer

among African American children in grades 1 through 4.

3. **Production Test.** In this test, also administered individually, standard and vernacular responses are elicited with the help of spoken cues from each variety and visual stimuli. Like the Repetition Test, it gives information about relative proficiency in vernacular and standard speech. It is particularly well-suited for grades 4 through 6.

In recent years, research has increasingly focused on African American English (AAE)–its origins and characteristics; justifications for its use and acceptance in society at large, and analyses of whether, and if so how, its use affects the acquisition of reading skills. Much of the time, AAE and standard English (SE) are treated as if they were two mutually exclusive speech varieties. Yet both casual observation and formal research show that African Americans differ in the kind of language they use depending on such social and demographic variables as age, sex, education, place of origin, and socioeconomic status. In addition, any given African American (AA) person–child or adult, urban or rural, formally educated or not–may use any number of speech varieties depending on still other factors such as topic, setting, audience, and goal. Given this variability, the term African American English is most appropriately used in the generic sense to include the many speech varieties and distinctive communication patterns used by African Americans.

This paper, then, is concerned with two prevailing African American English speech varieties that should be thought of as ends of a continuum rather than discrete entities, one we shall call African American Vernacular English (AAVE), and the other, African American Standard English (AASE).

Why Study African American English?

Most tests designed for use in education are based on White middle class standards and values that consistently lead to negative evaluations of many African American students. This kind of testing bias (Hilliard, 1991) has far-reaching and long-lasting effects. Tests for language arts proficiency are a case in point. Many AA children come to school speaking African American Vernacular English, the dominant speech variety of their community. Tests based on non-African American varieties, which exclude the logic and linguistic validity of AAVE, inevitably rate such children as linguistically deprived and academically substandard, even though they have appropriately mastered the language to which they have been exposed. For example, tests have shown that many African American children indicate possession by the form *John book*. Some educators have accordingly concluded that AA children do not control the concept of possession. Other tests indicate that when some of these children are asked to repeat standard English sentences, they translate them into AAVE structures (e.g., "The two girls lost their coat" becomes "The two girl lose they coat"). This type of response has led some to label the linguistic ability of African American children deficient and inferior.

In reality, AAVE responses result from a legitimate, logical communication system through which one can express all the concepts found in other languages (Baugh, 1994; Labov, 1972). Educators concerned about effectively teaching the African American child will greatly benefit from the study of African American English, since such a study will help them recognize its legitimacy. In this way they will be better prepared to develop an academic environment for African American students that will foster mutual acceptance and respect.

The Origins of African American English

There are several theories on the origin of African American English, although most may be considered variations of one of three competing hypotheses discussed in the literature. One theory, referred to as the creolist position, asserts a fundamental relationship between the grammar of AAE and Atlantic pidgins and creoles, and hence ascribes its origins to a West African Pidgin English variety developed during the sixteenth century

(Bailey & Bernstein, 1990; Baugh, 1986; Burling, 1973; Dillard, 1972; Mufwene, 1992; Rickford, 1977, 1985). A second related explanation of AAE origins builds on Turner's (1949) seminal work on the Gullah dialect. It is the hypothesis proffered by Africanization theorists who attribute the distinctiveness of African American English to African language provenience (Mufwene, 1992; Rickford, 1977). Proponents of this view believe that enslaved Africans brought to America processed the English language through their African linguistic patterns, thereby creating vernacular, or Africanized African American English. They further contend that the resultant grammatical, lexical, phonological, and stylistic patterns of African Americans' distinctive speech varieties closely approximate those of many West African languages. The approximations represent continuities, or Africanisms, such as meaning conveyed through tone, variable usage of the copula, pronominal apposition, and a predominant view of language as verbal performance (Alleyne, 1980; Asante, 1990; Baugh, 1986; Dalby, 1972; DeFrantz, 1979; Gilman, 1993; McNair-Knox, 1988/1989; Mufwene, 1992; Morgan, 1991; Smith, 1992, 1994; Taylor, 1972; Turner, 1949; Wade-Lewis, 1988).

A third theory is the dialectologist/English-dialect or transformational position (Baugh, 1986; Mufwene, 1992), which maintains that present-day African American English displays certain features of early British provincial speech. Such features as variable presence of certain third person singular verb forms, the use of "done" preceding a regular verb, and the occurrence of invariant (durative) "be," were common in various parts of the British Isles. Since many of the overseers, foremen, and other workers who had close contact with enslaved Africans were of Scottish or Irish origin and very probably had such features in their speech, some scholars have concluded that early British provincial speech was a primary force in the development of AAVE (McDavid, 1971; Mufwene, 1992, 1993; Traugott, 1972; Williamson, 1975).

A combination of all three theories is probably correct: African American English very likely derives from African linguistic patterns, and evidences substantial influence from English and other European languages. Here in the United States it has further developed over time, and as a result of various social, historical and political conditions, into several forms. What we have termed African American Vernacular English has retained more of the African linguistic patterns. African American Standard English (Taylor, 1971) contains fewer Africanized structural features but shares several distinctive markers with AAVE.

Grammatical and Phonological Description of Varieties of African American English

African American English can most readily be recognized by distinctive grammatical and phonological features. We shall describe some of the features of AAVE and AASE so that teachers may easily identify them as they attempt to assess proficiency skills in both of these language varieties. A broader description of AAVE would include information about: vocabulary (Smitherman, 1994); tone and intonation (Cook, 1985; Davis, 1985; Pitts, 1989; Vaughn-Cook, 1972); speech events (Foster, 1989; Mitchell-Kernan, 1971; Smitherman, 1977, 1994); other more subtle markers such as discourse patterns (Asante, 1990; Baugh, 1993; Goodwin, 1993; Smitherman, 1977; Taylor & Matsuda, 1988); "counter language" (Morgan, 1991, 1993); style shifting/code switching and hypocorrection (Baugh, 1988; 1993; DeBose, 1992; Nelson, 1990); camouflaged forms/masked Africanisms and grammaticalized disapproval forms (Baugh, 1984; Rickford, 1992; Spears, 1982, 1990); nonverbal communication (Cooke, 1978; Johnson, 1971; Thompson, 1990); and in-group/out-group decisions of appropriateness (Hoover, 1978).

African American Vernacular English

Some of the most salient grammatical and phonological features of African American Vernacular English (AAVE), listed below, are reported in a large body of literature produced since the 1960's (Butters, 1987; Bailey & Bernstein,

1990; Bailey & Maynor, 1987; Bartley & Politzer, 1972; Baugh, 1983; Dillard, 1972; Edwards, 1992; Fasold & Wolfram, 1973; Labov, 1968, 1972; Labov & Harris, 1986; Rickford, 1977, 1992; Rickford & McNair-Knox, 1994; Smitherman, 1977; Spears, 1990; Williams, 1993; Wolfram, 1969; Wolfram, Williams, & Taylor, 1975). They are regularly used by AAVE speakers, but some of them are also shared by speakers of other dialects of English (for comparisons of African American English with southern English, see Bailey & Bernstein, 1990, Wolfram, 1974, and Wolfram, Williams, & Taylor, 1975; for comparisons with the speech of Latino Americans, see Bartley & Politzer, 1972, and Galindo, 1995). These features are cross-referenced to items on the Series A Discrimination, Repetition, and Production tests described in subsequent sections of this paper. Series A is the AAVE version of the tests.

AAVE Features

1. *Variable use of copula*: Henry running/ We tired/ She a doctor/ How you doing?
Discrimination items 10, 28; Repetition 1, 7; Production 1, 3, 4, 5, 9.
In AAVE, the conjugated form of the verb "to be" ("am," "are," "is") may be absent when it is followed by an -ing verb in forming the progressive tense, or by a predicate adjective, adverb, or noun in present tense constructions.

2. *Invariant "be"*: We be playing ball/ They be hitting us.
Discrimination item 26; Repetition 9; Production 5.
AAVE has an invariant use of "be" which does not vary with the subject and which expresses such aspects as habitual action, prolonged action, or a continual state of affairs.

3. *Use of "got" alone to indicate possession*: I got a ball/ I got two sisters.
Repetition item 15; Production 2, 6.
In AAVE "got" alone is often used to indicate possession.

4. *Variable use of third person singular -s verb ending*: He play baseball/ She see them.
Discrimination item 24; Production 4.
In AAVE, suffix "s" frequently does not ap-
pear on third-person singular present tense verb forms.

5. *Phonological identity of regular past and present tense forms*: He walk home yesterday/ We laugh all during Sunday school last week.
Discrimination item 17; Repetition 2; Production 14.
In AAVE, "ed" is often not used in forming the past tense. Hence the present tense and the past tense often take the same form, and tense is determined by context and/or by the use of adverbs of time.

6. *Use of "Ah mo" to indicate future tense*: Ah mo get you/ Ah mo start school tomorrow.
Discrimination 9.
In references to the future, AAVE changes the Standard English/African American Standard English (AASE) form "I'm going to" to "ah mo" by replacing the SE/AASE long "i" with the "ah" sound, and by using consonant lenition and other phonological rules to change "'m going to" to "mo."

7. *Existential "it"*: It's a man at the door/ It wasn't a bear in sight/ It wasn't anyone there.
Discrimination item 3; Production 2, 6.
In AAVE, presence is frequently indicated by the use of "it('s)" where SE/AASE uses "there is" or "there are."

8. *Multiple negation*: Don't nobody know this/ They didn't give us none/ Don't nobody want no red pencils.
Discrimination item 18; Repetition 14; Production 3.
In AAVE, double and multiple negatives are frequently used to express or emphasize negation.

9. *Possession indicated by position only*: Willie coat/ The man hat/ John book.
Discrimination item 27; Repetition 4.
AAVE may indicate possession by position only (possessor before item possessed).

10. *Possessive pronoun form variation*: They put on they new coats/ The workers got they money.
Discrimination item 19; Repetition 13; Production 11.
In AAVE, the vocalization of medial (middle) or final "r" creates a third person plural possessive form "they" where SE/AASE otherwise uses "their."

11. Use of modifier alone to indicate pluralization: Five cent/ three apple/ these book.

Discrimination item 7; Production 7.

When there are other words in the sentence indicating pluralization, AAVE may not use the "s" marker employed in SE/AASE constructions.

12. Hypercorrection of plural nouns: Lots of peoples/ two mices/ some sheeps/ those childrens.

Discrimination item 6; Production 13.

In SE/AASE usage, some nouns change form in order to indicate pluralization (e.g., man/ men; child/children; goose/geese). In AAVE, these words may be hypercorrected by adding "s" to the plural SE/AASE form.

13. Pronominal apposition: My brother he ate my apple/ My mother she told him not to come.

Repetition item 3; Production 15.

In AAVE, a subject noun is frequently followed by a corresponding subject pronoun.

14. Emphatic comparative: Things will get more better/ I'm more taller than my brother.

Discrimination item 20; Production 12.

In AAVE, comparative adjectives may be formed by placing the word "more" before either a positive ("rich") or a comparative form ("richer") of the adjective.

15. Mass noun/count noun variation: Two police/ less ideas.

Production item 8.

In SE/AASE usage, nouns are classified as either count or mass nouns. Count nouns may be preceded by cardinal numbers, indefinite articles, and other modifiers such as many, few, several (a book, an apple, two pencils, many ideas, etc.). Mass nouns frequently are not modified at all, or are preceded by the definite article or such modifiers as little, much, less (the water, much information, less information, etc.). In AAVE mass nouns sometimes function as count nouns and count nouns as mass nouns.

16. Use of "got to" to indicate obligation: I got to work/ She got to pay the bill.

Repetition item 11.

In AAVE, the use of "got to" parallels the SE/AASE use of "have to," "ought to," and/or "must" to indicate obligation.

17. Direct question word order used in indirect questions: Ask John can he come out/ He asked me did I go.

Repetition item 5.

In AAVE, the direct question word order functions parallel to the SE/AASE indirect question word order. The question is introduced by an auxiliary verb ("can," "could," "did," etc.), rather than a conjunction ("if," "whether," etc.).

18. Analogical extension of regularization: He called hisself a teacher/ I told John to open the door hisself.

Repetition item 6.

AAVE adjusts the SE/AASE reflexive pronoun "himself" to the pattern of other SE/AASE reflexive pronouns such as "myself," "herself," "yourself, which are based on the possessive. "Himself" thus becomes "hisself."

19. Variable use of "do" support: Why you want to know?/ What she say?/ You like that?

Repetition item 8.

AAVE may not use the conjugated form of the verb "to do" ("do," "does," "did") in auxiliary functions.

20. Double/multiple modal: I might could finish by tomorrow/ You might could go/ That might would work.

Repetition item 10.

In AAVE, double modals may be used if the occurrence of an event is either speculative or doubtful.

21. Use of generalized past tense form: I seen two men behind the house/ She drunk my pop/ May sung two songs/ They was hungry.

Discrimination item 11; Production 10.

In AAVE usage, the past participles of some irregular verbs may be used to indicate past tense.

African American Standard English

African American Standard English (AASE) (Taylor, 1971; see also Garner & Rubin, 1986; Hoover, 1978; Stanback, 1985; Wade-Lewis, 1988), though generally considered to be "educated" Black speech, is spoken by persons with both low and high levels of formal education. In general, AASE (Taylor, 1971) is distinguished by its similarity to Standard English grammar and its

Table 1. Relationship of African American Vernacular English to African American Standard English and Standard English

	Phonology	Grammar	Vocabulary	Tone/Intonation
AAVE	+	+	+	+
AASE	~	-	~	~
SE	-	-	-	-

Key: + Contains vernacular features. - Contains very few vernacular features. ~ Contains vernacular features in varying degrees according to the situation.

simultaneous use of varying degrees of phonological, intonational, lexical/vocabulary, and rhetorical features of AAVE. Table 1 illustrates the linguistic relationship of so-called Standard English (SE)[1] and African American Standard English to African American Vernacular English (see also Hymes, 1972, on the need to broaden language variety, topic, and key into a varied "ethnography of communication").

Students who control both varieties (AAVE and AASE) may be referred to as "bidialectal." At least one author objects to this term because it implies that the student's language is inferior and must be supported by the acquisition of a White "standard" (Sledd, 1969). Our use of this term simply means that students can understand and/or produce both varieties of their *own* language and communication system–AASE and AAVE (see Bailey, 1970, for a similar definition).

Procedures Used in Developing the Tests

The tests are based on materials developed by the Program on Teaching and Linguistic Pluralism at the Stanford Center for Research and Development in Teaching between 1970 and 1976. The research, supported by funds from the National Institute of Education, U.S. Department of Health, Education and Welfare, involved the work of the authors listed; teachers (38 in East Palo Alto, California, 11 in Dayton, Ohio, 13 in New York City); community workers (22 in East Palo Alto, California, 8 in Dayton, Ohio); three artists; three typists, and a recording technician.

Specific Information on the Tests

All of the tests can be administered, with the help of their accompanying tape recordings, by regular classroom teachers, special teachers, or possibly paraprofessionals. The tests can be given in any order. The Repetition Test and Production Test will normally serve as alternatives and will not be administered to the same children. Answers to the Discrimination Test are recorded by the pupils on a multiple-choice answer sheet. Responses on the Repetition and Discrimination Tests must be scored by the examiner on an individual pupil scoring sheet. Since the tests involve only audio-oral abilities, they can be given regardless of the pupil's proficiency in reading. The Discrimination Test is the one most easily administered and takes approximately 30 minutes of class time. The Repetition Test and the Production Test each take approximately 30 minutes for individual test administration.

General Description of the Tests

Discrimination Test

The Discrimination Test is designed to assess the student's ability to distinguish between specific grammatical features of AAVE and AASE. It contains 30 sentences, 15 in AAVE and 15 in AASE. The test is recorded on tape and the student responds by marking her or his answer sheet. It is appropriate for grades 2 through 6.

Repetition Test

The Repetition Test is designed to assess the student's ability to repeat sentences containing specific grammatical features of AAVE and AASE. The sentences to be repeated are based on two parallel tape-recorded stories (one in AAVE, the other in AASE), each of which contains 15 features which the student must repeat. The test is based on the finding by several researchers (e.g., Baratz, 1969) that in repetition tasks, children who are dominant speakers of the vernacular tend to translate standard into vernacular; whereas those who are dominant in standard tend to translate vernacular into standard. The test is appropriate for grades 2 through 6.

Production Test

The Production Test is designed to assess the student's ability to produce statements in AAVE and AASE. It consists of two parallel sets of verbal stimuli and a set of pictures (used twice) designed to induce the student to produce a specific grammatical feature in AAVE or AASE.

The verbal stimuli for both the AAVE and the AASE versions of the test are recorded on tape, and the pictorial stimuli are a set of 15 black-and-white drawings. The student is shown each drawing in numerical sequence, simultaneously listening to the accompanying verbal cue. The student then responds verbally, and the response is recorded on the answer sheet by the test administrator. The Production Test is appropriate for grades 2 through 6.

Purposes and Uses of the Tests

The tests serve as indicators of language competence by assessing the student's ability to distinguish between AAVE and AASE speech varieties; the student's ability to verbally produce, from cues, specific grammatical features in either speech variety, and the student's relative proficiency in producing the two varieties.

The tests reveal the student's "true" ability by demonstrating that s/he is competent in some variety of English, and that s/he can successfully produce the speech variety appropriate to her/his social background more successfully than another speech variety (an expected normal behavioral tendency in any group).

The tests systematically acquaint teachers with some AAVE grammatical and phonological features, thereby helping them to distinguish between children who speak AAVE and those who have speech problems. Acquainting teachers with this variety also serves to satisfy a community expectation. Hoover (1978) found that African American parents' sociolinguistic rules allow the use of AAVE in the home and community contexts, but not in school in a formal context or by non-African Americans under any condition. Parents do, however, want teachers to know the characteristics of AAVE so that its grammar is not labeled "broken" or "incorrect." [2]

The tests can also assist teachers in making educational decisions about teaching language arts. Students who are dominant in AAVE or who make low scores on the Discrimination Test, for example, should be given AASE oral practice drills using AAVE as a contrast. Such contrastive drills have been found to be effective with African American students, particularly those who have positive attitudes toward African American English (Politzer, Hoover, & Brown, 1974). The ability to discriminate between speech varieties, a skill which the drills help to develop in students, has been found to correlate positively with reading achievement (Politzer & Hoover, 1972).

Oral drills in AASE for AAVE-dominant students also appear to positively affect reading ability where used in conjunction with reading programs which incorporate discrimination elements. For example, personnel at Woodland School in Kansas City, Missouri, where bidialectal children were at grade level for ten years, used oral drill in AASE without stigmatizing AAVE, combining the instruction with an early emphasis on teaching reading through a phonic/linguistic method which focuses on discrimination between English spelling patterns, e.g., "mat" and "mate" (Thomas, 1976).

Finally, the exposure to African American language and culture provided by giving the tests

Table 2. Statistical Data/Historical Summary

Test Report	Place Administered	No. of Students*	Reliability (Cronbach α)	Main Findings
Discrimination (1): The Development of Awareness of the Black Standard/ Vernacular English Contrast among: Primary School Children: A Pilot Study. February 1972. [SCRDTMemo No. 83]	Ravenswood City School District Belle Haven School Brentwood School	38 Black 71 White	.73 .88	1. Girls achieved better than boys. 2. African American children achieved better than White. 3. Positive correlation found between test scores and reading scores for African American children.
Discrimination (2): Developmental Aspects of Pupil Performance on Bidialectal Tests. May 1975 [SCRDT Memo No. 137.]	Ravenswood City School District Brentwood School	*Grade* 11 K-1 40 3-6	-0.49 .81	1. Test was unsuccessful with grade K-1. 2. Scores improved in the upper grades.
Discrimination (3): A Black English Bidialectal Test Battery. June 1974.	Dayton, Ohio Public Schools	*Grade* 25 K-2 25 4-6	.69 .78	1. Positive correlation between test scores and reading scores at grade 4.
Discrimination (4): Teachers' and Pupils' Attitudes toward Black English Speech Varieties and Black Pupils' Achievement. June A Pilot Study. February 1972. [SCRDT Memo No. 83.]	Ravenswood City School District	372	.66	1. Test scores improved with grade level. 2. Teachers who discriminate between AASE and AAVE[a] increase their students' awareness of the difference. 3. Differential attitudes toward AASE and AAVE correlate with performance on Discrimination Test.
Repetition (1): A Test of Proficiency in Black Standard and Nonstandard Speech. February 1973. [SCRDT Memo No. 101]	Ravenswood City School District: Brentwood School	35	AAVE .49 AASE .43	1. Proficiency in AASE correlates positively with reading ability; lack of proficiency in AASE correlates negatively with reading ability.
Repetition (2): Developmental Aspects of Pupil Performance on Bidialectal Tests. May 1975. [SCRDT Memo No. 137.]	Ravenswood City School District: Brentwood School	40	AAVE .40 AASE .75	1. (See findings under Discrimination Test and Production Test in Memo No. 137.)
Repetition (3): A Black English Bidialectal Test Battery.	Dayton, Ohio Public Schools	25	AAVE .60 AASE .60	1. Positive correlation between reading scores and AASE repetition at grade 2.

(table continues)

Test Report	Place Administered	No. of Students*	Reliability (Cronbach α)	Main Findings
Production (1): A Production Test in Black Standard and Nonstandard Speech. November 1973. [SCRDT Memo No. 114.]	Ravenswood City School District Brentwood School	48 48	AAVE .25 AASE .25	1. Proficiency in AASE correlates positively with reading ability; lack of proficiency in AASE correlates negatively with reading ability.
Production (2): Developmental Aspects of Pupil Performance on Bidialectal Tests. May 1975 [SCRDT Memo No. 137.]	Ravenswood City School District Brentwood School	45 45	AAVE .48 AASE .69	1. AASE scores improve in the upper elementary grades; AAVE scores decline. 2. Dominance in AAVE correlates negatively with reading scores; for grade 6 performance in AAVE correlates positively with reading scores.
Production (3): A Black Bidialectal Test Battery. June 1974.	Dayton, Ohio Public Schools	20 15	AAVE .84 AASE .77	1. Negative correlation between AAVE production and reading scores at grade 4.
Production (4): Teachers' and Pupils' Attitudes toward Black English Speech Varieties and Black Pupils' Achievement. June 1976. [SCRDT Memo No. 145.]	Ravenswood City School District Harlem Public Schools	82 82	AAVE .75 AASE .69	1. Students' attitudinal preference for AASE over AAVE correlates positively with performance in AASE.

Note. While there is evidence of significant positive correlations of performance in AASE with reading scores (see above Repetition 1, 2, Production 1, 2), performance in AAVE does not have any "concurrent validity" in the sense of showing positive correlations with other language arts tests used currently in the schools. In other words, proficiency in AAVE constitutes an ability which has generally not been included in the school curriculum and which can thus not be shown to have concurrent validity.

*Where not otherwise indicated, all the students were African American.

[a]AASE = African American Standard English

and studying the history and characteristics of AAE has been found to increase teachers' knowledge of and improve their attitudes toward non-mainstream dialects (Hoover, Lewis, et al., 1995, this volume). Knowledge of African American language and culture and positive attitudes about them have been shown to be a valuable aid in the effective teaching of reading to African American children (Foster, 1994; Hoover, 1992; Hoover, Dabney, & Lewis, 1990; Hoover, McNair-Knox, Lewis, Politzer, 1995, this volume; Lewis, 1979; McNair-Knox, 1985; Piestrup, 1973). A summary of studies in which the tests were used is presented in Table 2.

Limitations of the Tests

The African American English Tests for Students are designed to measure student language proficiency in two speech varieties–AAVE and AASE. They are not designed to measure reading ability or any form of language disability.

Further Research and Development

The African American English Tests for Students would benefit from an adult version. The competency testing movement affects many high school and college students, often resulting in low scores for African Americans and other students of color. To avoid allegations of cognitive deficit on the part of these students, an adult version of the tests would be useful, and would establish these adults as proficient in a variety of English.

An adult version of the tests would also help to increase students' self-concept by providing them with information regarding their linguistic strengths as well as their weaknesses.

Notes

1. Fasold (1972) defines Standard English as "that form of American English which is accepted informally as standard [not...rejected as either substandard or superstandard] by those members of our society who are in a position to enforce their judgements on others i.e. school teachers and employers."

2. Lack of preference for AAVE in formal school contexts does of course not imply that parents do not approve of the study of AAVE or its background, or of the inclusion in the curriculum of aspects of African American culture such as folk tales, proverbs, and poetry, to which AAVE is obviously linked.

References

Alleyne, M. (1980). *Comparative Afro-American.* Ann Arbor, MI: Karoma.

Asante, M. (1990). African elements in African-American English. In J. Holloway (Ed.), *Africanisms in American culture* (pp. 19-33). Bloomington: Indiana University Press.

Bailey, B. (1970). Some arguments against the use of dialect readers in the teaching of initial reading. *Florida FL Reporter, 8,* 8, 46.

Bailey, G., & Bernstein, C. (1990). The idea of Black English. *The SECOL Review: Southeastern Conference on Linguistics, 14,* 1-24.

Bailey, G., & Maynor, N. (1987). Decreolization? *Language in Society, 16,* 449-473.

Baratz, J. C. (1969). A bidialectal task for determining language proficiency in economically disadvantaged Negro children. *Child Development, 40,* 889-902.

Bartley, D., & Politzer, R. L. (1972). *Practice-centered teacher training: Standard English for speakers of nonstandard dialects.* Philadelphia: Center for Curriculum Development.

Baugh, J. (1983). *Black street speech.* Austin, TX: University of Texas Press.

Baugh, J. (1984). Steady: Progressive aspect in Vernacular Black English. *American Speech, 59,* 3-12.

Baugh, J. (1986). Studies in descriptive linguistics 15: Bilingualism and bidialectalism among American minorities. In G. Nickel & J. C. Stalker (Eds.), *Problems of standardization and linguistic variation in present-day English* (pp. 84-94). Heidelberg: Julius Groos.

Baugh, J. (1988). Beyond linguistic divergence in Black American English: Competing norms of linguistic prestige and variation. In A. Thomas (Ed.), *Methods in dialectology: Proceedings of the Sixth International Conference held at the University College of North Wales, 3rd-7th August 1987* (pp. 175-186). Philadelphia: Multilingual Matters Ltd.

Baugh, J. (1993). Research trends in Black American English. In A. W. Glowka & D. M. Lance (Eds.), *Language variation in North American English. Research and teaching* (pp. 153-163). New York: Modern Language Association of America.

Baugh, J. (1994). New and prevailing misconceptions of African American English for logic and mathematics. In E. Hollins, J. King, & W. Hayman (Eds.), *Teaching diverse populations: Formulating a knowledge base* (pp. 191-206). Albany: State University of New York Press.

Bowie, R. L., & Bond, C. L. (1994). Influencing teachers' attitudes toward Black English: Are we making a difference? *Journal of Teacher Education, 45,* 112-118.

Burling, R. (1973). *English in Black and White.* New York: Holt, Rinehart and Winston.

Butters, R. (Ed.). (1987). *American Speech, 62*(1).

Cook, W. W. (1985). The Afro-American griot. In C. K. Brooks (Ed.), *Tapping potential: English and language arts for the Black learner* (pp. 260-271). Urbana: National Council of Teachers of English.

Cooke, B. G. (1978). Nonverbal communication among Afro-Americans: An initial classification. In M. A. Lourie & N. F. Conklin (Eds.), *A pluralistic nation: The language issue in the United States* (pp. 116-140). Rowley, MA: Newbury House.

Dalby, D. (1972). The African element in American English. In T. Kochman (Ed.), *Rappin' and stylin' out* (pp. 170-180). Urbana: University of Illinois Press.

Davis, G. L. (1985). *I got the word in me and I can sing it, you know: A study of the performed African-American sermon.* Philadelphia: University of Pennsylvania Press.

DeBose, C. (1992). Codeswitching: Black English and standard English in the African American linguistic repertoire. *Journal of Multilingual and Multicultural Development, 13*, 157-167.

DeFrantz, A. (1979). A critique of the literature on Ebonics. *Journal of Black Studies, 9*, 383-396.

Dillard, J. (1972). *Black English: Its history and usage in the United States.* New York: Random House.

Edwards, W. F. (1992). Sociolinguistic behavior in a Detroit inner-city black neighborhood. *Language in Society, 21*, 93-115.

Fasold, R. (1972). *Sloppy speech in standard English.* Paper presented at the Fourth Triennial Conference on Symbolic Processes. Washington, DC.

Fasold, R., & Wolfram, W. (1974). Some linguistic features of Negro dialect. In J. S. DeStefano (Ed.), *Language, society, and education: A profile of Black English* (pp. 116-148). Worthington, OH: Charles A. Jones.

Foster, M. (1989). "It's cooking now": A performance analysis of the speech events of a Black teacher in an urban community college. *Language in Society, 18*, 1-29.

Foster, M. (1992). Sociolinguistics and the African American community: Implications for literacy. *Theory into Practice, 31*, 303-311.

Foster, M. (1994). Effective Black teachers: A literature review. In E. Hollins, J. King, & W. Hayman (Eds.), *Teaching diverse populations: Formulating a knowledge base* (pp. 225-241). Albany: State University of New York Press.

Garner, T., & Rubin, D. L. (1986). Middle class Blacks' perceptions of dialect and style shifting: The case of southern attorneys. *Journal of Language and Social Psychology, 5*, 33-48.

Galindo, D. L. (1995). Language attitudes toward Spanish and English varieties: A Chicano perspective. *Hispanic Journal of the Behavioral Sciences, 17*, 77-99.

Gilman, C. (1993). Black identity, homeostasis, and survival: African and metropolitan speech varieties in the New World. In S. Mufwene (Ed.), *Africanisms in Afro-American language varieties* (pp. 388-402). Athens: University of Georgia Press.

Goodwin, M. H. (1993). Tactical use of stories: Participation frameworks within boys' and girls' disputes. In D. Tannen (Ed.), *Gender and conversational interaction* (pp. 110-143). New York: Oxford University Press.

Hilliard, A. (Ed.). (1991). *Testing African American students.* Morristown, NJ: Aaron, Press.

Hoover, M. R. (1992). The Nairobi Day School: An African American independent school, 1966-1984. *Journal of Negro Education, 61*, 201-210.

Hoover, M. R. (1978). Community attitudes toward Black English. *Language in Society, 7*, 65-87.

Hoover, M. R., Dabney, N., & Lewis, S. (1990). *Successful Black and minority schools.* San Francisco: Julian Richardson.

Hoover, M. R., Lewis, S. A. R., Politzer, R. L., Ford, J., McNair-Knox, F., Hicks, S., & Williams, D. (1996) Tests of African American English for teachers of bidialectal students. In R. L. Jones (Ed.), *Handbook of test and measurements for Black populations* (Vol. I). Hampton, VA: Cobb & Henry.

Hoover, M. R., McNair-Knox, F., Lewis, S. A. R., & Politzer, R. L. (1996). African American English Attitude Measures for Teachers. *Handbook of test and measurements for Black populations* (Vol. I). Hampton, VA: Cobb & Henry.

Hymes, D. (1972). Toward ethnographies of communication: The analysis of communicative events. In P. Giglioli (Ed.), *Language and social context* (pp. 21-44). Baltimore: Penguin.

Labov, W. (1968). *A study of the non-standard English of Negro and Puerto-Rican speakers in New York City.* Philadelphia: US Regional Survey.

Labov, W. (1972). *Language in the inner city: Studies in the Black English vernacular.* Philadelphia: University of Pennsylvania Press.

Labov, W., & Harris, W. A. (1986). De facto segregation of black and white vernaculars. In D. Sankoff (Ed.), *Diversity and diachrony* (pp. 1-25). Amsterdam: Benjamins.

Lewis, S. (1979). *Factors affecting the oral comprehension of Black elementary school children.* Unpublished doctoral dissertation, Stanford University.

McNair-Knox, F. (1985). *The effects of foreign language instruction on the reading ability of African American children.* Unpublished doctoral dissertation, Stanford University, CA.

McNair-Knox, F. (1988/89). Inter- and Intra-ethnic variation in urban vernacular English: Controversy in contemporary sociolinguistic research. *Liwuram: Journal of the Humanities, 4/5*, 223-273. Maiduguri, Nigeria: University of Maiduguri.

Mitchell-Kernan, C. (1971). *Language behavior in a Black, urban community.* Berkeley: Language Behavior Research Laboratory.

Morgan, M. (1991). Indirectness and interpretation in African American women's discourse. *Pragmatics, 1*, 421-451.

Morgan, M. (1993). The Africanness of counterlanguage among Afro-Americans. In S. Mufwene (Ed.), *Africanisms in Afro-American language varieties* (pp. 423-435). Athens: University of Georgia Press.

Mufwene, S. (1992). Ideology and facts on African American English. *Pragmatics, 2*, 141-166.

Mufwene, S. (1993). Introduction. In S. Mufwene (Ed.), *Africanisms in Afro-American language varieties* (pp. 1-31). Athens: University of Georgia Press.

Nelson, L. (1990). Code-switching in the oral life narratives of African-American women: Challenges to linguistic hegemony. *Journal of Education, 172*(3), 142-155.

Piestrup, A. (1973). *Black dialect interference and accommodation of reading instruction in the first grade.* Berkeley: University of California, Berkeley Research Laboratory.

Pitts, W. (1989). West African poetics in the Black preaching style. *American Speech, 64*, 137-149.

Politzer, R. L., & Hoover, M. R. (1972). *The development of awareness of the Black standard/ nonstandard dialect contrast among primary school children: A pilot study.* (Memorandum No. 83). Stanford Center for Research and Development in Teaching, Stanford University. (ERIC No. ED 062 464).

Politzer R. L., & Hoover, M. R. (1974). On the use of attitude variables in research in the teaching of a second dialect. *International Review of Applied Linguistics in Language Teaching, 7*, 43-51.

Politzer, R. L., Hoover, M. R., & Brown, D. (1974). A test of proficiency in Black standard and nonstandard speech. *TESOL Quarterly, 8,* 27-35.

Rickford, J. R. (1977). The question of prior creolization in Black English. In A. Valdman (Ed.), *Pidgin and creole linguistics* (pp. 190-221). Bloomington: Indiana University Press.

Rickford, J. R. (1985). Ethnicity as a sociolinguistic boundary. *American Speech, 60*, 99-125.

Rickford, J. R. (1992). Grammatical variation and divergence in Vernacular Black English. In M. Gerritsen & D. Stein (Eds.), *Internal and external factors in syntactic change* (pp. 175-200). The Hague: Mouton.

Rickford, J. R., & McNair-Knox, F. (1994). Addressee- and topic-influenced style shift: A quantitative sociolinguistic study. In D. Biber & E. Finegan (Eds.), *Sociolinguistic perspectives on register* (pp. 235-276). New York: Oxford University Press.

Sledd, J. (1969). Bidialectalism: The linguistics of White supremacy. *English Journal, 58,* 1307-1315, 1329.

Smith, E. (1978). *The retention of the phonological, phonemic and morphophonemic features of Africa in Afro-American Ebonics.* Paper presented at the Department of Linguistics Seminar Series, California State University Fullerton, Fullerton, CA.

Smith, E. (1992). African American language behavior: A world of difference. In *Yearbook/Claremont Reading Conference* (56th yearbook) (pp. 38-53). Claremont, CA: Claremont Graduate School Curriculum Laboratory.

Smith, E. (1994, April). *The historical origin of African American English: Is it English or is it African?* Paper presented at the National Black Association of Speech, Language, and Hearing Conference, Jackson, MS.

Smitherman, G. (1977). *Talkin and testifyin.* Boston: Houghton Mifflin.

Smitherman, G. (1994). *Black talk: Words and phrases from the hood to the amen corner.* Boston: Houghton Mifflin.

Spears, A. K. (1982). The Black English semi-auxiliary *come. Language, 58*, 850-872.

Spears, A. K. (1990). The grammaticalization of disapproval in Black American English. *CUNY Forum: Papers in Linguistics, 15*, 30-36.

Stanback, M. H. (1985). Language and Black woman's place: Evidence from the Black middle class. In P. A. Treichler, C. Kramarae, & B. Stafford (Eds.), *For Alma Mater: Theory and practice in feminist scholarship* (pp. 177-193). Urbana: University of Illinois Press.

Taylor, O. L. (1971). Response to social dialects and the field of speech. In R. Shuy (Ed.), *Sociolinguistics: A cross-disciplinary perspective* (pp. 13-20). Washington, DC: Center for Applied Linguistics.

Taylor, O. L. (1972). An introduction to the historical development of Black English: Some implications for American education. *Language, Speech and Hearing Services in Schools, 3*, 5-15.

Taylor, O. L. (1983). Black English: An agenda for the 1980's. In J. W. Chambers (Ed.), *Black English: Educational equity and the law* (pp. 133-143). Ann Arbor: Karoma.

Taylor, O. L., & Matsuda, M. M. (1988). Storytelling and classroom discrimination. In G. Smitherman-

Donaldson & T. A. van Dijk (Eds.), *Discourse and discrimination* (pp. 206-220). Detroit: Wayne State University Press.

Thomas, J. M. (1976). *Administration of a program where bidialectal children read at grade level.* Paper presented at International Reading Association Convention, Anaheim, CA.

Thompson, R. F. (1990). Kongo influences on African-American artistic culture. In J. Holloway (Ed.), *Africanisms in American culture* (pp. 148-184). Bloomington: Indiana University Press.

Traugott, E. (1972). *A history of English syntax.* New York: Holt, Rinehart and Winston.

Turner, L. (1949). *Africanisms in the Gullah dialect.* Chicago: University of Chicago Press.

Vaughn-Cooke, A. (1972). The Black preaching style. In W. Riley & D. Smith (Eds.), *Language and linguistics working papers* (Vol. 5, pp. 28-39). Washington, DC: Georgetown University Press.

Wade-Lewis, M. (1988). *The African substratum in American English.* Unpublished doctoral dissertation, New York University.

Williams, S. W. (1993). Substantive africanisms at the end of the African linguistic diaspora. In S. Mufwene (Ed.), *Africanisms in Afro-American language varieties* (pp. 406-422). Athens: University of Georgia Press.

Williamson, J. (1975). A look at Black English. In R. L. Williams (Ed.), *Ebonics: The true language of Black folks* (pp. 11-21). St. Louis: Missouri Institute of Black Studies.

Wolfram, W. (1969). *A sociolinguistic description of Detroit Negro Speech.* Washington, DC: Center for Applied Linguistics.

Wolfram, W. (1974). The relationship of White southern speech to Vernacular Black English. *Language, 50*, 498-527.

Wolfram, W., Williams, R., & Taylor, O. (1975). *A linguistic description of nonstandard English.* Washington, DC: Federal City College, Department of Communication Sciences.

Appendix

Key Terms

Bidialectal

Controlling two varieties of one's language, e.g., a vernacular variety and a standard variety.

Balanced Bidialectal

Having equal levels of proficiency in African American Vernacular and standard African American Standard.

African American Standard English

That variety of African American English or *Ebonics* distinguished by its similarity to standard English grammar and its simultaneous use of varying degrees of phonological, intonational and lexical features of vernacular African American English.

African American Vernacular English

That variety of African American English or "Ebonics" revealing influences from West African languages in its grammar, and phonology.

Acknowledgments

The authors wish to express their gratitude to all those whose help and cooperation made this five-year research study possible.

The following teachers were directly involved in the research: John Jacobs, Eugene King, Eph Cannon, Sal Corelli, Cynthia Cooksey, Sherry Ernst, Mary Orrison, Ruth Wilturner, Minnie Cooper, Ladessa Gardner, Margaret Williams, Pauline Breslin, Ethel Johnson, Ann Ebow, Barbara Glover, Fleta Bigsby, Shirley Carson, Annie Handy, Charles Howard, Lee Davis, Claretha Felder, Miriam Turner, Dorothy Montgomery, Eunice McGee, Shirley Hicks, Cleo Postle, Judith Triana, Anne Gage, Ann Jones, Evelyn Dansby, Vera Boyson, R. Jackson, Christine Arguillard, Neva Spillers, Rosemary Leach, Carol Prudhomme, Gary Whitfield, and Audrey McKiver of the Ravenswood City School District, East Palo Alto, California; Susan Pearch, Hermaline Rudd, Carol Smith, Theresa Petrosky, Judith Levy, Pauline Hensley, Frieda Miller, Geraldine Nooks, Mabel Retz, Lelah Niebel, and

Russel Maurice of the Dayton, Ohio, Elementary Schools; and Rosa Adamson, Carol Buschel, Paula Davis, Margaret Dickson, Beatrice Drew, Laura Heifferman, Anna Hildebrand, Lucille Hoberman, Peggy Morris, Betty Slass, Naomi Watkins, and Richard Carman of PS 100, New York. We wish to thank the typists, community assistants, artists, and recording artist for the project: typists Andrea Richardson, Maribel Quesada, and Lois Middleton; East Palo Alto community assistants Warnell Coats, Laura Saltzman, Delores Randall, Oliver Lee, Mattie Fleming, Faye Knox, Harriet McNair, James Robinson, Juanita Brockman-Croft, Carson Barnes, Alfred Butler, Marc Clemens, Debbie Sanderson, Nellie Willis, Clarence Coats, Kenneth Campbell, Louise Flythe, Ozel Griffith, Cheryl Harris, Alonzo Newbury, Gary Thompkins, and Annetter Williams; Dayton community assistants Patricia Ellis, Madella Belton, Cornell Harding, Vicki Ecton, Ruth Kilgore, Corine Tucker, Bertha Collie, and Margaret Hughes; artists Alice McNair and Moriba Abayomi (drawings for the field tests) and Bill Dallas (final drawings); and recording technician Faye Knox.

The administrators of the field-test schools, who provided great assistance, are Warren Hayman, Omowale Satterwhite, Virginia Moulden, Othene Thomas, William Rybensky, Robert Guthrie, Vince Brown, Willie Richardson, James Nichols, and Clarence Francois of the Ravenswood City School District; Edythe Ford and Paula Davis of the New York City Public Schools; and Mildred Patterson, Margaret Hughes, and Fred Stroud of the Dayton Elementary Schools. We also wish to thank Don Smothers and Mavis Knox of Nairobi College, East Palo Alto, California, for helping to arrange the administration of the tests.

For additional information, contact:

Faye McNair-Knox, Ph.D.
College of Education
Florida International University
3000 N.E. 145th Street
North Miami, FL 33187
Telephone: (305) 940-5820
Fax: (305) 956-5494

Tests of African American English for Teachers of Bidialectal Students*

Mary Rhodes Hoover, Shirley A. R. Lewis, Robert L. Politzer, James Ford, Faye McNair-Knox, Shirley Hicks, and Darlene Williams

Abstract

The battery of Tests of African American English for Teachers of Bidialectal Students (TAAETBS) consists of two parts: Test I-History and Structure of African American English, and Test II-Reading/Language Arts Pedagogy. Test I focuses on historical, cultural, structural, and stylistic aspects of African American English (AAE). Test II focuses on reading methodology, language learning theory, and cultural and language attitudes. The battery was designed to help teachers obtain an understanding of the functions and usages of AAE varieties, and to improve their attitudes toward those varieties. Reliability and validity data are presented.

Many of the nation's African American (AA) children are performing below grade level in reading, language arts, and other basic skills. The language of the African American child has been identified as one source of this problem (Bereiter & Englemann, 1966; Orr, 1987). That is, the African American Vernacular English (AAVE) of the child's home and community and the Standard English (SE) of the textbook and classroom are considered to be in conflict in some way which results in poor performance at school.

---

* These tests were developed at the Center for Educational Research at Stanford's Program on Teaching and Linguistic Pluralism, directed by Robert L. Politzer.

Research has focused on several aspects of this problem. Some scholars have been primarily concerned with describing the structural differences between AAVE and SE speech varieties (Alleyne, 1980; Bailey & Maynor, 1987; Baugh, 1983; Dillard, 1972; Fasold & Wolfram, 1974; Labov, 1968, 1972; Labov & Harris, 1986; Rickford, 1977, 1992, 1995; Rickford & McNair-Knox, 1994). Others have recommended the use of AAVE reading materials for African American children (Baratz, 1969; Simpkins, Holt, & Simpkins, 1977; Smitherman, 1977; Stewart, 1970). Still others have had teacher attitude as a major focus (Bowie & Bond, 1994; Cecil, 1988; Hoover, McNair-Knox, Lewis, & Politzer, 1996, this volume; Piestrup, 1973; Washington & Miller-Jones, 1989; Williams, Whitehead, & Miller, 1971). All of the issues have important bearings on language learning and further research on these subjects is needed.

Background

The battery of Tests of African American English for Teachers of Bidialectal Students (TAAETBS) was developed by the staff of the Program on Teaching and Linguistic Pluralism. Its content was drawn from scholarly documents in linguistics, language learning and language arts pedagogy, and works concerning dialects from studies carried out by the Program. Test reliability was obtained, and items with low or negative item reliability were eliminated. Then a national panel of educators, linguists, and community workers experienced in African American community cultural patterns met in a working conference to review the TAAETBS (see Ford et al., 1976). Members of this panel recommended the inclusion of additional items concerning AA "speech events," such as "capping" and "marking," as well as sociolinguistic and sociopolitical issues such as community expectations and values concerning schooling. Members of the panel and program staff took efforts to assure that the TAAETBS contained no deficit or exotic notions about African American language or culture.

Other items were added to the tests and revisions were made. The instruments were then administered to teachers across the nation, usually in conjunction with teacher workshops on African American English and language learning (Hoover, 1990; Politzer & Lewis, 1979).

Rationale and Uses of the Tests

It has long been recognized that teachers' language attitudes affect their relationships with pupils. African American Vernacular English speaking pupils are often the victims of negative teacher attitudes (Bowie & Bond, 1994; Foster, 1992; Hoover, McNair-Knox, Lewis, & Politzer, 1996, this volume, and Hoover, Politzer, et al., 1996, this volume). One reason many teachers view AAVE features so negatively is that they are unaware of, or do not understand, the legitimacy, logic, and function of this variety. The negative attitude toward AAVE speech is often extended to AAVE speakers–that is, the students themselves. The TAAETBS was developed to help teachers obtain a better understanding of the functions and usages of AAE varieties and to improve their attitudes toward those varieties. Use of the TAAETBS will assist teachers in a number of ways. It will:

1. measure teacher knowledge of the phonological, grammatical, lexical and stylistic features of African American English speech varieties;

2. inspire teachers to learn more about a subject with which they may be unfamiliar;

3. help teachers distinguish and identify those features and characteristics of African American English that are common to other varieties of English, and those that more specifically apply to African American and southern varieties of English;

4. help teachers distinguish among those features of African American English which are deemed academically and/or socially significant;

5. help teachers distinguish among Standard English, African American Vernacular English, and African American Standard English (AASE) speech varieties;

6. increase teachers' abilities to distinguish between speech variety differences and speech pathologies;

7. help teachers recognize their own beliefs, opinions, and knowledge about the teaching of reading and other subjects to AAVE speaking pupils;

8. provide teacher trainers, supervisors, and administrators with a body of knowledge which can be used beneficially in staff development programs about African American English and the children who use it.

The tests have been used as pre- and post-assessments for numerous teacher workshops in public schools and colleges. For example, Test I was used to measure culture-specific information growth for engineering faculty in a Minorities in Engineering program.

Table 1. Subject Categories and Item Numbers of Test Questions

Test I - History and Structure (Forms A and B)

Category	Item Number
History and Culture	1-2, 4-13, 38, 45
Structure	3, 14-37, 39
Stylistics	40-44

Test II - Reading/Language Arts Pedagogy (Forms A and B)

Category	Item Number
Language Learning	1-2, 4-5, 13
Cultural and Language Attitudes	3, 6, 15
Language Arts Methodology	7-12, 14, 16-21

Description of the Tests

The TAAETBS battery was developed to test specific knowledge and behaviors associated with the successful teaching of reading and other language arts skills to African American English speaking children. The battery consists of two tests: Test I is a test of the History and Structure of African American English, and Test II is a test of Reading/Language Arts Pedagogy.

Items in both tests are multiple choice questions with three answer alternatives. Each test is accompanied by an answer sheet containing the numbers of the test questions and the letters a, b, and c, which correspond to each possible answer alternative. Persons taking the test circle the letter of their chosen alternative on the answer sheet.

The tests of the TAAETBS battery have two versions, a pretest (Form A) and a posttest (Form B), which contain the same number of items and cover the same topics. Test I, History and Structure of African American English, contains forty-five items. It focuses on AAE historical, cultural, structural, and stylistic information. Test II, Reading/Language Arts Pedagogy, contains twenty-one items. It focuses on reading methodology, language learning theory, and cultural and language attitudes. (See Appendices for copies of tests).

Test items are classified according to subject categories and are listed according to item number in Table 1.

Test Administration

The TAAETBS is designed so that it may be administered to a group or to individuals. The test administrator should allow approximately one hour for the administration of both tests (approximately thirty minutes for Test I and approximately twenty minutes for Test II).

Reliability and Validity

These tests have been administered in a variety of sites and in slightly different versions in which the number of items varied from 44 to 45 for Test I and from 16 to 21 for Test II. In all cases, reliability (Cronbach Alpha) has been quite high. Table 2 shows the reliability scores obtained in a research project in which Forms A and B of the tests were used as pretests and posttests, respectively. The project (Politzer & Hoover, 1977) involved seventy-nine teachers in East Palo Alto, California, Miami, Florida, and Trenton, New Jersey.

Table 2. Reliability Scores of Pretests and Posttests of the TAAETBS

Test	No. of Teachers	Items	Mean Score	S.D.	Cronbach Alpha
History and Structure					
Pretest (Form A)	79	44	30.43	7.45	0.87
Posttest (Form B)	69	44	33.13	8.13	0.91
Reading/Language Arts Pedagogy					
Pretest (Form A)	79	16	11.20	3.85	0.84
Posttest (Form B)	69	16	12.11	3.66	0.85

Studies conducted at the Center for Educational Research at Stanford (Politzer & Lewis, 1978, 1979) showed that teacher scores on the African American English test correlated positively and significantly with pupil achievement, as evidenced by adjusted posttest scores measuring progress made in lessons dealing with specific topics in reading and language arts.

Limitations

The phonological features listed for identification of the patterns of AAVE, e.g., *John coat*, are rendered orthographically. They are therefore limited by alphabetical and punctuational constraints and do not completely reflect the true phonology of AAVE.

The orthographic representation (rather than the use of the International Phonetic Alphabet) also creates a problem for many community people who object to the recording of AAVE in print. Informants in a survey of African American community residents (Hoover, 1978) did not object to the oral use of AAVE in many domains; however, seeing it in print reminded them of the minstrel tradition, influencing them to reject the use of AAVE in written formats in most domains.

Further Research

Research indicates that cultural information is a key characteristic of an effective teacher of African American and other children of color (Au & Kawakami, 1994; Foster, 1994; Garcia, 1994; Hoover, Dabney, & Lewis, 1990; Ladson-Billings, 1994; Lewis, 1979; Philips, 1972). Because the AA child is often thought to be from a culture that contributed nothing or very little to the march of civilization (Toynbee, 1947; Walker, 1994), or is posited to be intellectually inferior (Herrnstein & Murray, 1994), it is important to include information on African civilization in training teachers.

The subject matter of the items included in the TAAETBS should therefore be broadened to include more on the African contribution to literacy. Recent research has revealed much information on the African contribution to literacy (Asante, 1986; Hilliard, 1986), e.g., the discovery that Africans in the Sudan developed a script which was the base of the Egyptian hieroglyphic system (Van Sertima, 1983), that Africans invented the first alphabet with vowels (Williams, 1974), and that a language/dialect of the Wolof people was the foundation for many languages of the world (Lumpkin, 1983).

Because the tests have been used with a variety of public school and college teachers, the subject matter should also be broadened to include subtests (Test II's) on pedagogy other than language arts.

References

Alleyne, M. (1980). *Comparative Afro-American.* Ann Arbor, MI: Karoma.

Asante, M. (1986). The Egyptian origin of rhetoric and oratory. In M. Karenga & J. Carruthers (Eds.), *Kemet and the African worldview* (pp. 182-188). Los Angeles: University of Sankore Press.

Au, K., & Kawakami, A. (1994). Cultural congruence in instruction. In E. Hollins, J. King, & W. Hayman (Eds.), *Teaching diverse populations: Formulating a knowledge base* (pp. 5-23). Albany, NY: State University of New York Press.

Bailey, G., & Maynor, N. (1987). Decreolization? *Language in Society, 16,* 449-473.

Baratz, J. (1969). Teaching reading in an urban school system. In J. Baratz & R. Shuy (Eds.), *Teaching Black children to read* (pp. 92-116). Washington, DC: Center for Applied Linguistics.

Baugh, J. (1983). *Black street speech.* Austin, TX: University of Texas Press.

Bereiter, C., & Englemann, S. (1966). *Teaching disadvantaged children in the preschool.* Englewood Cliffs, NJ: Prentice-Hall.

Bowie, R. L., & Bond, C. L. (1994). Influencing teachers' attitudes toward Black English: Are we making a difference? *Journal of Teacher Education, 45,* 112-118.

Cecil, N. L. (1988). Black dialect and academic success: A study of teacher expectations. *Reading Improvement, 25,* 34-38.

Dillard, J. (1972). *Black English: Its history and usage in the United States.* New York: Random House .

Fasold, R., &, Wolfram, W. (1974). *The study of social dialects in American English.* Englewood Cliffs, NJ: Prentice-Hall.

Ford, J., Lewis, S., Hicks, S., Williams, D., Hoover, M. R., & Politzer, R. L. (1976). *Report on the working conference on the SCRDT Black English Tests for Teachers* (Occasional Paper No. 15). Stanford, CA: Stanford Center for Research and Development in Teaching.

Foster, M. (1992). Sociolinguistics and the African American community: Implications for literacy. *Theory into Practice, 31,* 303-311.

Foster, M. (1994). Effective Black teachers: A literature review. In E. Hollins, J. King, & W. Hayman (Eds.), *Teaching diverse populations: Formulating a knowledge base* (pp. 225-241). Albany, NY: State University of New York Press.

Garcia, E. (1994). *Understanding and meeting the challenge of student cultural diversity.* Boston: Houghton Mifflin.

Herrnstein, R., & Murray, C. (1994). *The bell curve.* New York: The Free Press.

Hilliard, A. (1986). Pedagogy in ancient Kemet. In M. Karenga & J. Carruthers (Eds.), *Kemet and the African worldview* (pp. 131-148). Los Angeles: University of Sankore Press.

Hilliard, A. (Ed.). (1991). *Testing African American students.* Morristown, NJ: Aaron, Press.

Hoover, M. R. (1978). Community attitudes toward Black English. *Language in Society, 7,* 65-87.

Hoover, M. R. (1990). A vindicationist perspective on the role of Ebonics and other aspects of ethnic studies in the university. *American Behavioral Scientist, 34,* 251-262.

Hoover, M. R., Dabney, N., & Lewis, S. (1990). *Successful Black and minority schools.* San Francisco: Julian Richardson.

Hoover, M. R., McNair-Knox, F., Lewis, S. A. R., & Politzer, R. L. (1996). African American English attitude measures for teachers. In R. L. Jones (Ed.), *Handbook of tests and measurements for Black populations* (Vol. I). Hampton, VA: Cobb & Henry.

Hoover, M. R., Politzer, R. L., Brown, D., Lewis, S. A., Hicks, S., & McNair-Knox, F. (1996). African American English tests for students. In R. L. Jones (Ed.), *Handbook of tests and measurements for Black populations* (Vol. I). Hampton, VA: Cobb & Henry.

Labov, W. (1968). *A study of the non-standard English of Negro and Puerto-Rican speakers in New York City.* Philadelphia: US Regional Survey.

Labov, W. (1972). *Language in the inner city: Studies in the Black English vernacular.* Philadelphia: University of Pennsylvania Press.

Labov, W., & Harris, W. A. (1986). De facto segregation of black and white vernaculars. In D. Sankoff (Ed.), *Diversity and diachrony* (pp. 1-25). Amsterdam: Benjamins.

Ladson-Billings, G. (1994). Who will teach *our* children: Preparing teachers to successfully teach African American students. In E. Hollins, J. King, & W. Hayman (Eds.), *Teaching diverse populations: Formulating a knowledge base* (pp. 129-142). Albany, NY: State University of New York Press.

Lewis, S. (1979). *Factors affecting the oral comprehension of Black elementary school children.* Unpublished doctoral dissertation, Stanford University, CA.

Lumpkin, B. (1983). The Africans: Ancient showcase of African science and technology. In I. Van Sertima (Ed.), *Blacks in science: Ancient and modern* (pp. 67-83). New Brunswick, NJ: Transaction Books.

Orr, E. (1987). *Twice as less.* New York: W. W. Norton.

Piestrup, A. M. (1973). *Black dialect interference and accommodation of reading instruction in the first grade*. Berkeley, CA: Monographs of the English Behavior Research Laboratory, No. 4.

Politzer, R. L., & Hoover, M. R. (1977). *A field test of Black English tests for teachers*. (Research and Development Memorandum No. 149). Stanford, CA: Stanford University, Stanford Center for Research and Development in Teaching.

Politzer, R. L., & Lewis, S. A. (1978). *The relationship of the Black English tests for teachers and selected teaching behaviors to pupil achievement*. Stanford, CA: Stanford University, Center for Educational Research at Stanford.

Politzer, R. L., & Lewis, S. A. (1979). *Teacher workshops, Black English tests for teachers, and selected teaching behaviors and their relation to pupil achievement*. Stanford, CA: Stanford University, Center for Educational Research at Stanford.

Rickford, J. R. (1977). The question of prior creolization in Black English. In A. Valdman (Ed.), *Pidgin and creole linguistics* (pp. 190-221). Bloomington: Indiana University Press.

Rickford, J. R. (1992). Grammatical variation and divergence in Vernacular Black English. In M. Gerritsen & D. Stein (Eds.), *Internal and external factors in syntactic change* (pp. 175-200). The Hague: Mouton.

Rickford, J. R. (1995). Regional and social variation. In S. McKay & N. Hornberger (Eds.), *Sociolinguistics and language teaching* (pp. 151-194). Cambridge: Cambridge University Press.

Rickford, J. R., & McNair-Knox, F. (1994). Addressee- and topic-influenced style shift: A quantitative sociolinguistic study. In D. Biber & E. Finegan (Eds.), *Sociolinguistic perspectives on register* (pp. 235-276). New York: Oxford University Press.

Smitherman, G. (1977). *Talkin and testifyin*. Boston: Houghton Mifflin.

Simpkins, G. A., Holt, G., & Simpkins, C. (1977). *Bridge: A cross-cultural reading program*. Boston: Houghton Mifflin.

Stewart, W. A. (1970). Sociopolitical issues in the linguistic treatment of Negro dialect. In J. Alatis (Ed.), *20th Annual Roundtable* (pp. 215-223). Washington, DC: Georgetown University Press.

Toynbee, A. (1947). *A study of history*. London: Oxford University Press.

Van Sertima, I. (1983). *Blacks in science: Ancient and modern*. New Brunswick, NJ: Transaction Books.

Walker, C. (1994). The distortions of Afrocentric history. In J. Miller (Ed.), *Alternatives to Afrocentrism* (pp. 32-36). New York: Manhattan Institute.

Williams, C. (1974). *Destruction of Black civilization*. Chicago: Third World.

Williams, F., Whitehead, J. L., & Miller, L. M. (1971). *Attitudinal correlates of children's speech characteristics*. Austin, TX: University of Texas, Center for Communication Research, School of Communication.

Appendix A

Tests of African American English for Teachers of Bidialectical Students - Form A

Test I. *History and Structure*

1. African American English is most likely to have developed from:
   a) Writings prepared for minstrel shows in the 17th century.
   b) Corruptions of British Isles dialects.
   c) Influences of African and English language patterns.

2. The Gullah dialect, spoken off the coast of South Carolina and the Sea Island coast, has preserved its creole features mainly because of:
   a) Cultural and geographic isolation from mainland culture.
   b) Racial characteristics, since Gullahs are less racially mixed than other African Americans.
   c) Physiological differences in the oral cavity which affect sounds produced in the vocal tract.

3. An explanation of why many African Americans tend to reduce medial and word final consonant clusters (such as des' for desk) is probably related to:
   a) The difficulty one may have in hearing consonants as opposed to vowels in the syllable-final position.
   b) The scarcity of syllable-final consonant clusters in the relevant African languages and/or in the English they learn.
   c) The rapid movement of the tongue, lips, etc., that is required to move from one consonant to another.

4. Which of the following sets of words are culturally related to West African languages?

a) Goober, gumbo, banjo.

b) Canoe, succatosh, exotic.

c) Pinto, ranch, patio.

5. African influences on African American English come primarily from:

 a) North African languages.

 b) Swahili.

 c) West African languages.

6. African American English is likely to be most prominently spoken:

 a) Among African Americans who are least integrated with mainstream society.

 b) Wherever there are African descendants in an English environment.

 c) Among African Americans of age 10 and above who live in the Eastern United States.

7. Many of the characteristics attributed to African American English are:

 a) Found primarily in Old English.

 b) Used almost exclusively by African Americans who are recent immigrants from Africa.

 c) Shared by many other speakers of vernacular varieties of American English.

8. When African American Vernacular English speakers come in contact with standard English speakers, which of the following is least likely to occur?

 a) African American Vernacular English will disappear.

 b) Speakers will display competence in both varieties.

 c) Speakers will become hesitant in their use of language.

9. The process of change which occurs when African American Vernacular English comes into contact with standard English is called:

 a) Creolization.

 b) Pidginization.

 c) Decreolization.

10. Factors that have influenced the development of African American English in the United States are:

 a) Unlike those that have affected varieties of European languages spoken by African descendants (for example, Portuguese).

 b) Similar to those that have influenced the development of other varieties of English as spoken by African descendants (for example, Jamaican English).

 c) Explainable on the basis of the English spoken by Whites (for example, Middle English).

11. According to prevailing linguistic theory, African American English originated in:

 a) The Eastern Coastal region.

 b) The Southern Slave States.

 c) No particular geographical region.

12. Which of the following is most likely to be true of African American English?

 a) It is a dialect of English which retains its original form more than any other dialect.

 b) It has not yet had time to develop a systematic grammar.

 c) It is an evolving language variety reflecting the social experiences of its speakers.

13. As a linguistic entity African American Vernacular English is considered to be:

 a) A contemporary type of American slang.

 b) A systematic, rule-governed language having several varieties.

 c) A spontaneous form of the English language with several adaptations.

14. Which of the following sentences illustrates the use of the negative in African American Vernacular English?

 a) Didn't nobody take none of those books.

 b) He be waiting for me don't every night.

 c) Doesn't he want to go?

15. The use of the verb "to be" to signal habitual action in African American Vernacular English (such as "He always be running late") can be described as:

 a) An indication of a linguistic difference that interferes with the formulation of grammatical sentences.

 b) A form that is compatible with the habitual concept of time found in some West African languages.

 c) A conception of time which causes African American people to be time-oriented rather than place-oriented.

16. Choose the missing word or words that an African American Vernacular English speaker would be most likely to use to complete the phrase, "By the time I get back, you better _____ cleaned up this mess."

a) had
b) got to
c) be done

17. To emphasize the fact that the action of the sentence, "Willie finished that work," was completed at a much earlier point in time, an African American Vernacular English speaker would probably say:

a) Willie *been* finished that work.
b) Willie *did* finished that work.
c) Willie *really* finished that work.

18. A close paraphrase of the African American Vernacular English and Southern English phrase, "I 'mo go downtown" is:

a) I am anxious to go downtown.
b) I am going to go downtown.
c) I'm the one that's going downtown.

19. The African American Vernacular English sentence, "Didn't nobody hit John," is best interpreted as meaning:

a) Nobody wanted to hit John.
b) Somebody hit John.
c) Nobody hit John.

From the following sets, select the pair of words that may sound very much alike in the speech of African American Vernacular English speakers and some Southerners.

20. a) build   bill
    b) boy   bop
    c) blimp   bloom
21. a) tin   twin
    b) tag   tack
    c) tot   tote
22. a) make   mall
    b) messed   mess
    c) mom   mop
23 a) Bob   cob
    b) Bess   best
    c) ban   bam
24. a) roof   Ruth
    b) room   rude
    c) row   tow
25. a) help   hep
    b) who   hot
    c) hip   hop
26. a) cow   cot
    b) Carl   cart
    c) Cal   Carol

27. a) for   fur
    b) five   jive
    c) film   fill
28. a) bud   butt
    b) reckon   raccoon
    c) broom   brim
29. a) toe   tore
    b) time   tire
    c) telegraph telegram
30. a) apple   axle
    b) and   ain't
    c) asked   axed

Select the most pronounced African American Vernacular English, and sometimes Southern English, phrases in each of the following items.

31. a) John a student
    b) John dones student work
    c) John a study
32. a) readin' tests
    b) reading n' writing
    c) readin' tes'
33. a) He aimed kinda high
    b) He be going to the store
    c) Be you go?
34. a) She seem tall
    b) She be seem
    c) She talled
35. a) My mother, they
    b) My mother ised
    c) My mother, she
36. a) three coat
    b) Forthy dollars
    c) two-by-two
37. a) The money arrived
    b) Bob money
    c) Root monies

38. African American English is best described as:

a) Vernacular or informal African American speech used by Northern, urban males.
b) A way of talking proper in order to impress one's audience.
c) The range of speech behaviors used in African American communities in the U.S.

39. The identical pronunciation of "pen" and "pin" is an example of:

a) Not paying precise attention to configuration clues and the difference in the vowel sounds.

b) Poor auditory discrimination prevalent among non-mainstream speakers.

c) The overlap between some varieties of African American, Southern, and general American English.

40. An African American Vernacular English speaker who says, "John loud-talked me," is:

a) Communicating that John is hard of hearing.

b) Probably far away from John.

c) Likely to be embarrassed or amused by what John said.

41. An African American English speaker is likely to "cop a plea" when:

a) Employing a defensive strategy.

b) Quoting a policeman.

c) Imitating a lawyer.

42. You have just said, "Sit down and take this test." You immediately hear, following the statement, an African American child mimicking exactly what you said, with her hand on her hip. This is:

a) A demonstration of a different attitude toward adults found in the African American community.

b) An African American English speech event called "marking."

c) A ritualistic utterance characteristic of children who are culturally different.

43. You hear one African American child tell another, "Everybody has a cross to bear." The other child says, "What is your cross?" The first child responds, "You," and the entire group laughs. This is an example of:

a) An African American English speech event called "capping."

b) An African American English speech event called "playing the dozens."

c) An African American religious ritual.

44. "Shucking" is:

a) Removing the leaves and silk from ears of corn.

b) Running a game on someone.

c) Living with a member of the opposite sex.

45. High John the Conqueror is:

a) A religious leader in the African American church.

b) A root used for healing and religious purposes.

c) A famous slave holder.

Tests of African American English for Teachers of Bidialectal Students - Form A

Test II. *Reading/Language Arts Pedagogy*

1. In an elementary class, an African American Vernacular English speaking child is most likely:

a) To pronounce or use words that differ from Standard English but still understand Standard English.

b) Not to be able to speak aloud or understand the teacher's language.

c) To pronounce or use words in African American Vernacular English but not understand African American Vernacular English.

2. In teaching students to write Standard English compositions,

a) The first step is the correction of all vernacular English words and sentence structures.

b) One should not suggest any changes in the students' grammar as long as the composition is well-structured.

c) One may praise the organization of a composition even though it contains vernacular grammatical features.

3. Which of the following statements is true?

a) All Whites belong to the same cultural group.

b) Every person is a member of at least one ethnic or cultural group.

c) We have one American pluralistic culture which applies to us all.

4. An accent can be best interpreted in terms of:

a) The hearer's perception.

b) Poor articulation.

c) Regional grammatical patterns.

5. Many people often retain the sound patterns of their first language when speaking a second language because:

a) The second language is perceived and processed in terms of the first language.

b) The second language is phonologically more complex than the first.

c) The first language has, over time, become

adapted to characteristics of the vocal organs of its speakers.

6. Research suggests that African American parents are least likely to object to the use of African American Vernacular English in the school when their children are:
    a) Reading their textbooks.
    b) Writing class assignments.
    c) Speaking to their peers.

7. The Sullivan Programmed Reading Series is one of the few elementary reading methods that:
    a) Uses a decoding (phonic) approach.
    b) Is correctable by the child.
    c) Is written with a different alphabet.

8. Three common characteristics of predominantly African American schools where children are learning to read successfully are:
    a) A look-say approach to reading, a permissive approach to discipline, and modern facilities.
    b) A language experience approach to reading, a stimulus-response approach to discipline, and teachers under 30 years of age.
    c) A decoding approach to reading, a structured approach to discipline, and high teacher expectations.

9. The "schwa" is:
    a) One of the letters in a consonant cluster.
    b) A nonsense syllable used to teach children on Sesame Street.
    c) The 'uh' sound that occurs when a vowel is unstressed.

10. The Montessori method is:
    a) An approach to early learning through self-pacing and play-oriented equipment.
    b) A new approach to discipline utilizing biofeedback and the cognitive method.
    c) A method designed to encourage summative evaluation learning.

11. The Initial Teaching Alphabet method is:
    a) A British reading program based on highlighting and coloring certain letters in print.
    b) A British reading program that changes the alphabet to produce more predictable sound-symbol relationships.
    c) A reading program that uses only capital letters so as not to confuse the beginning reader.

12. The Whole Language Approach is a reading method in which:
    a) Children read stories written by computer analysis of regular sound-syllable correspondences.
    b) Children read stories written by linguistic experts.
    c) Children read stories written by classic authors of children's literature.

13. If an African American Vernacular English speaker pronounces "this" as "dis" and "bathtub" as "baftub," his/her pronunciation will:
    a) Not necessarily reflect his/her comprehension of these lexical items.
    b) Predict his/her verbal ability.
    c) Necessitate an intensive speech therapy component for his/her academic program.

14. The Lippincott Reading Series is one of the few decoding (phonic) reading approaches that:
    a) Is based on spelling patterns.
    b) Has a basal-reader format.
    c) Is written in syllabary format.

15. The decision to use African American Vernacular English forms in the classroom as an effective curricular strategy for African American students should be based on:
    a) A random selection of common phrases and/or idioms used by African Americans adopted for classroom use.
    b) The presence or absence of the forms in the dictionary or thesaurus.
    c) A systematic analysis of the structure of African American Vernacular English and other varieties of American English and community usage.

16. Vocabulary for sight-word reading materials is selected according to:
    a) Regularity of sound-symbol correspondence.
    b) Frequency of word usage counts.
    c) Random selection of dictionary items.

17. "Oh, look. See Spot. See Spot run" is an example of:
    a) Phonic or decoding reading approach.
    b) Sight-word reading approach.
    c) The existentialist reading approach.

18. "Spot is hot on top" is an example of:
    a) Existentialist reading approach.
    b) Sight-word reading approach.

c) Phonic or decoding reading approach.

19. Digraphs are a spelling pattern in which two consonants represent a different sound than either consonant by itself. Circle the word that contains the digraph:

    a) champ

    b) mitt

    c) blend

20. The vowel sounds in "Fat Ed is not up" are called:

    a) short vowels.

    b) long vowels.

    c) double vowels.

21. Vocabulary items for phonic or decoding reading materials are selected according to:

    a) Random selection of dictionary items.

    b) Regularity of sound-symbol correspondence.

    c) Word-usage frequency counts.

Appendix B

Tests of African American English for Teachers of Bidialectal Students - Form B

Test I. *History and Structure*

1. African American English is derived mainly from:

    a) West African and East African language dialects.

    b) West African and American Indian dialects.

    c) West African languages and certain dialects of the British Isles.

2. A dialect spoken by African Americans who live on islands off the Carolina coast and which has preserved many of its creole features is:

    a) Gullah.

    b) Taki-Taki.

    c) Gumbo.

3. The best explanation of why an African American child might pronounce the *words* "land" as "lan'" and "help" as "he'p" is that:

    a) Certain genetic qualities are inherent in African Americans.

    b) Some speech impediment is characteristic of that individual child.

    c) Certain rules are present in the sound system of the speech variety of his/her community.

4. Which of the following groups of words is derived from West African languages?

    a) Jazz, Tote, Okra

    b) Kowtow, Mango, Orange

    c) Safari, Siesta, Sheik

5. The primary African influence on African American English is:

    a) Middle Eastern dialects.

    b) West African languages.

    c) Swahili.

6. Some form of African American English is spoken by:

    a) Approximately 80% of all African Americans.

    b) Uneducated African Americans only.

    c) Primarily older African Americans.

7. Which of the following is true?

    a) African American English has no features in common with other varieties of American English.

    b) All African Americans speak African American English.

    c) Many of the characteristics of African American English are shared by many other speakers of vernacular varieties of American English.

8. The probable outcome of speakers of African American Vernacular English coming into contact with Standard English is that:

    a) African American Vernacular English will eventually become a dead language.

    b) Many of the features of African American Vernacular English will be incorporated into Standard English and vice versa.

    c) Speakers of African American Vernacular English will maintain their original speech patterns.

9. Decreolization of African American Vernacular English is a process in which;

    a) African American Vernacular English changes many of its patterns as a result of contact with speakers of Standard English.

    b) A return to a simpler pidgin language as spoken by the original Afro-American slaves.

c) Vernacular features of African American English disappear as a separate entity—a stage that African American Vernacular English is now undergoing.

10. The development of African American English in the United States was *influenced* by factors that are:
   a) Different from those that have affected other European languages spoken by African Americans.
   b) Explicable primarily on the development of English spoken by Whites.
   c) Similar to those experienced by other English-speaking African descendants in the New World.

11. The geographic region in which African American English originated is:
   a) The plantation South.
   b) The East Coast of the original thirteen colonies.
   c) The Caribbean, since most enslaved Africans came to the colonies via that region.

12. African American Vernacular English is a language that:
   a) Has not developed any systematic grammar.
   b) Is still evolving on the basis of the social experiences of its speakers.
   c) Is unlike any other American dialect in that it retains many of the archaic features of older English dialects.

13. The most accurate description of African American Vernacular English is that:
   a) It is a type of American jargon based on spontaneous rules.
   b) It is a diverse linguistic system based on precise rules.
   c) All of its grammatical features are derived from African sources.

14. The use of the negative in African American Vernacular English is best illustrated in which of the following sentences?
   a) Don't nobody know?
   b) Do nobody know don't?
   c) Does you deny it?

15. "He be going all the time," a use of the verb *to be* signaling habitual action in African American Vernacular English, is:

a) A cognitive difference denoting lack of a "g" scale.
   b) A form that is in accord with the traditional concept of time found in West African languages.
   c) A typical African American expression denoting difference in the perception of location.

16. Choose the missing word or words that an African American Vernacular English speaker would be most likely to use to complete the phrase "By the time I get home from work, you better _____ fixed up this house."
   a) worked on
   b) had
   c) be done

17. To emphasize the fact that the action of the sentence "Johnny finished that job" was completed at a much earlier point in time, an African American Vernacular English speaker would probably say:
   a) Johnny *been* finished that job.
   b) Johnny *did* finished that job.
   c) Johnny *really* finished that job.

18. "I 'mo go to the store" is an African American Vernacular English and Southern English phrase which means:
   a) I am anxious to go to the store.
   b) I am going to go to the store.
   c) I'm the one that's going to the store.

19. "Didn't nobody see Bill" is best interpreted as meaning:
   a) Nobody wanted to see Bill.
   b) Somebody saw Bill.
   c) Nobody saw Bill.

Select the most pronounced pair of words that may sound very much alike in the speech of African American Vernacular English speakers and some Southerners:

20.	a. filled	fill
	b. for	fop
	c. fall	hall
21.	a. ban	bat
	b. bag	back
	c. boy	bop
22.	a. leak	lost
	b. less	lest

c. lop lore

23. a. Bob cob
 b. guest guess
 c. bip bop
24. a. wreath reef
 b. reef ream
 c. row tow
25. a. kelp kept
 b. kettle nettle
 c. Kale Karen
26. a. Val Hal
 b. vat cat
 c. vow vowel
27. a. show sure
 b. shine fine
 c. shall shawl
28. a. cud cut
 b. call ball
 c. come cat
29. a. Poe poor
 b. pick wick
 c. pull pall
30. a. At landing Atlanta
 b. John Hall John Paul
 c. this street discrete

Select the most pronounced African American Vernacular English (and sometimes Southern) phrase in each of the following:

31. a. Martha does runs good
 b. Martha a good girl
 c. Martha goods a lot
32. a. writing desks
 b. writing 'n talking
 c. writin' des'
33. a. She be walking home
 b. She walka walka
 c. She beed walk
34. a. Henry niced
 b. Henry sing nice
 c. Henry be sing
35. a. Your brother, he
 b. Your brother, they
 c. Your brother, it
36. a. thirty twos cents
 b. thirty cent
 c. thirty centy
37. a. Annie food

b. Annie foody
c. Food for Annie

38. The range of speech behaviors of African Americans in communities throughout the U.S. is best described as:
 a) African American Vernacular English
 b) African American English
 c) Pidgin English
39. The identical pronunciation of *Ben* as *bin* is an example of:
 a) Not paying precise attention to configuration clues and unfamiliarity with vowel sounds
 b) Poor auditory discrimination prevalent among non-mainstream speakers.
 c) The overlap among some varieties of African American, Southern, and general American English.
40. "Loud talking" is a way of:
 a) Increasing the speech volume while talking.
 b) Banging objects loudly while someone else is talking.
 c) Making embarrassing or funny statements about someone.
41. "Copping a plea" is:
 a) A kind of body language.
 b) A verbal defensive strategy.
 c) A dance step.
42. In African American Vernacular English, "marking" is:
 a) A way of imitating what someone else has said.
 b) A way of emphasizing or stressing certain points that someone else has made in a speech.
 c) The act of taking mental notes or storing what someone else has said.
43. One African American person says "You're ugly." The second African American person says "I may be ugly, but you got beat with a ugly stick." This is an African American speech event called:
 a) Rapping.
 b) Capping.
 c) Slapping.
44. "Shucking and jiving" is a way of:
 a) Jerking the covers off a sleeping person.

b) Putting the iron in the fire.

c) Pulling the wool over someone's eyes.

45. High John the Conqueror is:

a) A Civil War hero.

b) A streetwise urbanite.

c) A healing substance.

Tests of African American English for Teachers of Bidialectal Students - Form B

Test II. *Reading/Language Arts Pedagogy*

1. In an elementary school class, an African American Vernacular English speaking child is most likely:

a) To understand Standard English and pronounce or use words that differ from Standard English.

b) Not to understand Standard English and pronounce or use words that differ from Standard English.

c) Not to understand African American Vernacular English and pronounce or use words that differ from African American Vernacular English.

2. When students first write Standard English compositions, the teacher's first step should be to:

a) Correct all vernacular English words and sentence structures.

b) Praise the organization of the composition even though it contains vernacular grammatical features.

c) Try to avoid Standard English verbal constructions.

3. Which of the following statements is true:

a) White Americans do not have a recognizable culture.

b) All Americans have an identifiable ethnic or cultural group.

c) All Americans belong to one pluralistic culture.

4. A description of a speaker's accent depends primarily on:

a) The speaker's inability to articulate clearly.

b) The hearer's perception of the speech.

c) A dictionary's description of correct speech.

5. People are most likely to keep the sound pattern of their first language when they speak a second language when:

a) The sound system of the second language is more complex than the first.

b) The second language is perceived and processed through the first language.

c) The sound pattern of the first language is very similar to the sound pattern of the second language.

6. Most African American parents accept their children's use of African American Vernacular English in the classroom when the children are:

a) Reading their textbooks.

b) Talking with their friends.

c) Writing compositions.

7. A widely used elementary reading method which is correctable by the child is:

a) Words in Color.

b) The Sullivan Programmed Reading Series.

c) Phonetic Keys to Reading.

8. A structured approach to discipline, a decoding reading method for word attack, and high expectations on the part of the teacher are among the characteristics of schools where African American students generally perform:

a) At grade level.

b) Below grade level.

c) Above grade level.

9. The "uh" sound that occurs when a vowel is unstressed is called a:

a) Digraph.

b) Schwa.

c) Diphthong.

10. An approach to early learning which emphasizes self-pacing and play-oriented equipment is the:

a) Montessori Method.

b) Pyramid Approach to Learning.

c) Distar Program.

11. A British reading program that changes the alphabet to produce more predictable sound-symbol relationships is called:

a) PTA.

b) TAPI.

c) ITA

12. The reading approach whereby children read stories written by authors of children's literature classics is called:

a) Whole Language.

b) Partial Phonics.

c) Language Experience.

13. If an African American Vernacular English speaker pronounces "poor" as "po" or "asked" as "axed," one can expect that her/his pronunciation will:

    a) Have nothing to do with her/his understanding of the word.

    b) Be an index to her/his language ability.

    c) Indicate the need for assistance from the speech teacher.

14. A decoding (phonic) reading approach with a basal-reader format is called:

    a) Sullivan.

    b) SRA.

    c) Lippincott.

15. African American Vernacular English words and phrases should be selected for use in the language arts curriculum based on:

    a) An analysis of the characteristics of African American Vernacular English and rules for its use prevalent in the community.

    b) The standards set by Webster's and other dictionaries.

    c) Selection of such words and phrases from slang collections.

16. Frequency of word usage count is the basis for selecting:

    a) Sight word reading material

    b) Phonic-linguistic reading material

c) English experience reading materials

17. An example of a typical sentence in a sight word method primer is:

    a) I represented the council adequately.

    b) Spot is hot on top.

    c) Oh Look. See Spot. See Spot run.

18. A digraph is:

    a) A spelling pattern made up of two consonants with each consonant representing a separate sound. (African American)

    b) A spelling pattern in which two consonants represent a different sound than either consonant by itself. (chick)

    c) A spelling pattern in which only the first consonant represents a sound. (lamb)

19. An example of a typical sentence in a phonic-linguistic method primer would be:

    a) Big pig is in bed.

    b) Please telephone the trucking company.

    c) See mother. Mother can ride.

20. Which of the following sentences contains short vowel sounds?

    a) The boot and loot are here.

    b) June plays a tune.

    c) Fat Ed is not up.

21. Regularity of sound-symbol correspondence is the basis for selecting:

    a) Sight word reading materials.

    b) Phonic-Linguistic reading material.

    c) Language experience reading materials.

For additional information, contact:

Faye McNair-Knox, Ph.D.
College of Education
Florida International University
3000 N.E. 145th Street
North Miami, FL 33187
Telephone: (305) 940-5820
Fax: (305) 956-5494

African American English Attitude Measures for Teachers*

Mary Rhodes Hoover, Faye McNair-Knox, Shirley A. R. Lewis, and Robert L. Politzer

Abstract

The battery of African American English Attitude Measures for Teachers consists of the African American English Speech Varieties Attitude Test and the African American English Teacher Attitude Scale. The speech varieties test measures attitudes toward African American Standard and Vernacular English speech varieties with reference to (1) degree of education of the speaker, (2) appropriateness, (3) educational achievement potential of the speaker, (4) preference, and (5) perceived standardness. Teachers listen to tape-recorded children's voices reading randomly ordered passages in African American Standard English and African American Vernacular English, and record their responses on an answer sheet in the test booklet. This test takes approximately 30 minutes to administer. The attitude scale measures attitudes toward African American English generally. Teachers indicate their reactions to statements printed in the test booklet by choosing one of four scaled responses. This test takes approximately 40 minutes.

Many reasons have been given for the failure of the American educational system to teach basic literacy skills to African American (AA) students, 47% of whom at 17 are functionally illiterate (Kozol, 1985). Teaching methods, income differences, home environments, and cognitive differences all have been cited as reasons for this failure; some research has focused on teacher attitudes as a major factor (Bowie & Bond, 1994; Cecil, 1988; Foster, 1992; Hoover, Lewis, Politzer, Ford, McNair-Knox, Hicks, & Williams, 1996, this volume; Johnson & Buttny, 1982; Taylor & Hayes, 1971).

The African American English Attitude Measures for Teachers (AAEAMT) are designed to measure teacher attitudes toward the language of bidialectal (see Appendix C) students, since

---

* These tests were developed at the Center for Educational Research at Stanford's Program on Teaching and Linguistic Pluralism, directed by Robert L. Politzer.

such attitudes may have a powerful impact on student achievement and self-concept. Although these tests are meant to be used primarily with teachers, they can also be used with other adults.

In developing instruments to measure attitudes, it is important to widen the scope of attitudinal categories so that teachers or parents are not labeled "racist" or "ethnocentric" on the basis of answers to questions that are incomplete or simply the wrong questions. In one example of this kind of sociolinguistic, or sociopolitical "mistake," AA parents who vetoed the use of African American Vernacular English (AAVE), i.e. dialect, readers in classrooms were labeled "bourgeois," "self-hating," and "middle-class" (Stewart, 1969). Later research disclosed that these parents, rather than hating their speech, simply had rules for its use and preferred one variety over another in certain situations (Hoover, 1978; Cazden & Dickinson, 1981). In the first instance, only the question "Does this speech belong in the classroom?" had been asked. The obvious next question, "If not, then where does it belong?," was left unasked.

Description of the Measures

African American English Speech Varieties Attitude Test

The speech varieties test is an instrument adapted from Lambert's matched-guise test (Lambert, Hodgson, Gardner, & Fillenbaum, 1960) in which judges rate the personality and/or social characteristics of a variety of speakers (heard on audio tape) unaware that they are rating the same persons more than once. The same bilingual or bidialectal speaker records two or more different speech segments, each in a different guise (i.e., language or dialect). This technique is designed to enable the test evaluator to judge a subject's reaction to the speech varieties themselves and not to the speakers.

Our speech varieties test asks teachers to rate eight speech passages. Four bidialectal African American children were recorded speaking two varieties of African American English (AAE)

each: AAVE and African American Standard English (AASE). AASE is distinguished by its "standard" grammar and varying degrees of Africanized intonation, pronunciation, and style. AAVE is characterized by divergent grammatical patterns as well as Africanized intonation, phonology, and style. Two parallel scripts of the speech varieties test were put on a single audio tape so that they could be used as pre-and post-tests in conjunction with teacher workshops (Lewis, Hoover, & Politzer, 1979). If pre-and post-testing is not involved, either version of the test–Tape Script 1 or Tape Script 2–may be used. Transcriptions of both versions are in Appendix A.

The grammatical features included in the AAVE guise are (a) the absence of specially marked forms for the third person singular verb, and (b) the use of multiple negation and inverted/preposed negatives. Examples of the former are italicized portions (2), (3), and (5) in the following paragraph, one of the guises used in the test; examples of the latter are italicized portions (1) and (4).

Wiletta *can't hardly never* (1) sit still. She say she just *have* (2) to keep busy. So she work around the house, or she *go* (3) out and shop, or else she get her girlfriend to show her the latest dance. She laugh when we tease her and say at least *nobody can't* (4) call her lazy. Cause no matter what she *do* (5) she keep busy.

The "opposite" guise, recorded by the same bidialectal child, is as follows:

Sharon King *has* (2) to cook and iron and keep house and she *almost never* (1) gets to go out and play anything. Sometimes when she gets tired, she tries to get through in a hurry or she asks her little sister to help her. And sometimes she just gets mad. But no matter what Sharon *does* (2), she still has to work and can't play. That's why Sharon *frowns* (3) so much. *Nobody wants* (4) to do all that.

Numbers in the second paragraph refer to the same features as in the first (except for feature 5, which is a duplicate of features 2 and 3), for though the story lines and vocabulary are different, the grammatical features are the same in both– albeit altered to produce different forms of the same pattern (e.g.,"can't hardly never sit still" in one guise, and "almost never gets to go" in the other).

Teachers rate the speech passages on five dimensions: education, appropriateness, achievement, personal preference, and standardness[1]. The audio tape is played to a group of teachers. The test administrator should stop the tape, if necessary, after each spoken passage to give the teachers time to rate it on all five dimensions. (The dimensions and their response scales are described in more detail in Appendix A). The teachers record their ratings by circling numbers on an answer sheet in the test booklet.

Scoring. All dimensions except appropriateness are rated on a scale of one to five–ranging, for example, from "very uneducated" to "very educated." The appropriateness dimension is rated on a scale of one to nine according to the formality associated with the setting in which the speech variety is accepted.

Ratings given to the five dimensions should not be combined, because each dimension measures a different aspect of attitude. Individual scores for each dimension are arrived at by taking the mean of the four ratings an individual gave to the vernacular guise (one rating for each vernacular passage on the audio tape) and subtracting it from the mean of the four ratings given to the standard guise (one rating for each standard passage). For example, an individual score on the appropriateness dimension would be computed as follows: if the values assigned to the four voices for the standard guise were 8, 7, 6, and 7, and the values assigned to the same voices for the vernacular guise were 4, 6, 6, and 4, the individual teacher's score for appropriateness would be

$$28/4 - 20/4 = 2 \text{ in favor of AASE.}$$

The same procedure is used to score the other four dimensions for each teacher. The possible range of scores for appropriateness is 0 to 8; for the other dimensions, the range is 0 to 4. Group scores for each dimension can be obtained, if desired, by subtracting the mean of individual scores on the vernacular guise from the mean of individual scores on the standard guise. The meaning and implications of the scores, which are of course comparisons of the two guises on a given dimension, are discussed below under "Interpretation of Results."

African American English Teacher Attitude Scale

Non-mainstream cultures can be viewed according to several models, each implying different attitudes toward these cultures. For example, there is the "deficit" model which assumes that African American culture is deficient and needs "fixing." A second perspective, the "difference" model, assumes that African American people are not deficient–ust different. The difference model, in its extreme, can lead to viewing members of non-mainstream cultures as "exotic primitives," a term coined by Sterling Brown (1933) in describing stereotyped views of African Americans in literature. The "exotic" is equated with whatever is viewed as being most different from White culture, and the most "exotic" aspects of the culture–music, art, dance–are extolled above any others. A third way of viewing African Americans and other ethnic groups is through the "excellence" or "vindicationist" perspective (Drake, 1988; DuBois, 1935; Hoover, 1990; Tribble, 1992; Turner, 1984; Van Sertima, 1983; Wilson, 1991), which sees AA culture as multifaceted, ranging from the artistic to the academic, from artists such as Aretha Franklin and Miles Davis to scholars such as W. E. B. DuBois (1935) and Paula Giddings (1984). This view assumes that African American children are capable of learning anything, and that their culture has adequate resources to facilitate such learning.

The attitude scale we have developed measures teacher attitudes toward the legitimacy and use of African American English. It is based on reactions to statements that contrast an excellence perspective with a deficit or extreme difference perspective. For example, teachers are asked to respond to statements designed to assess whether they consider AAE a rule-governed language, or whether they consider it a "broken" form of English. Other items probe whether those taking the tests believe that African American English should be preserved or eliminated; is logical or illogical; is based on historical developments, or can be explained as a physiological or psychological "problem"; is subject to the same type of sociolinguistic rules that have been observed in all speech communities, or is spoken by all African Americans at all times.

The test is a Likert-type scale consisting of 46 items. Teachers evaluate statements using a four point scale ranging from "agree strongly" to "disagree strongly." Most of the items were paraphrased from actual statements made by educators and laypersons. The test follows a model developed by Taylor and Hayes (1971) for measuring teacher attitudes.

Scoring. Test items are scored on a scale ranging from one to four. Items considered "positive" attitudinally (e.g., "African American English is a systematic, rule-governed language variety") are scored so that "agree strongly" is given the highest score of four points. Items considered "negative" attitudinally (e.g., "African American English is so broken as to be virtually no language at all") are scored in reverse fashion, with "disagree strongly" assigned the score of four points (see Appendix B). Since the test has 46 items, the range of scores can be from 46 to 184. In several test administrations, the reliability of the scale varied from Cronbach alpha 0.89 to 0.93.

Interpretation of Results

On the speech varieties test, the difference between scores assigned to African American Standard English and African American Vernacular English is of course to be interpreted as indicating the appreciation of one speech variety over the other. A large difference on the achievement dimension, in particular, may be indicative of a teacher's biases against AAVE and of a tendency to hold on to a hypothesis concerning the lower school achievement potential of the speakers.

On the attitude scale, a high score (above 160) can be interpreted as a favorable attitude toward divergent speech patterns and the achievement potential of African American students. Exceptionally low scores (below 120) tend to show significantly negative attitudes.

Low individual scores on either measure should be interpreted with caution, however; a great difference between the scores of the vernacular and standard guises on the achievement dimension of the speech varieties test, or even a low score on the attitude scale, may not necessarily indicate that the teacher has been infected by the racism still rampant in American society. Such scores, at times, simply show an acute and unfortunately accurate awareness of the fact that AAVE-speaking children are likely to end up less well educated and less achieving–not because they lack potential, but because our educational system has not yet mastered the task of educating speakers of African American Vernacular English and other non-mainstream language varieties.

Uses of the Measures

For research purposes, both of these measures have been used by administrators and researchers to assess connections between teacher attitude and pupil achievement; to measure achievement, and to measure changes in attitude brought about by the measures and by workshops (Politzer & Hoover, 1976). The measures have been especially useful in conjunction with workshops for teachers. Such workshops, usually held after both of the measures have been administered, take as their starting point concepts suggested by the measures (Lewis et al., 1979). A typical workshop reinforces the idea that African American English is a legitimate form of speech having several varieties, and gives information on community sociolinguistic rules, specific features, and successful methodologies for teaching literacy to bidialectal speakers (Hoover, 1990).

The speech varieties test especially lends itself to demonstrating to teachers that African American English is a measurable, legitimate language variety with features and sociolinguistic rules that can be codified and analyzed.

Teachers who have been involved in Center for Educational Research at Stanford (CERAS) projects, in which the tests have been given in conjunction with workshops, almost unanimously felt that the tests and workshops were highly informative. As one teacher stated, "The tests were a small education in themselves." Ninety percent of all teachers felt that the tests and workshops made them aware of the existence of African American speech as a legitimate language variety. Statements supporting this assertion included the following two: "By reading about African American English, I discovered that observed speech differences were not just 'laziness' in talking," "I never thought of African American people before as bidialectal–to me, they were just talking 'Southern.'" Several teachers also felt that their expectations of African American children's intellectual capacities increased after learning about the history and characteristics of African American English. Others felt that the information that an African American child can produce at least two speech varieties made it clear that s/he could be taught to speak a variety of "standard" English without violating community sociolinguistic rules by sounding "phony" or "talking proper" (Hoover, 1978).

Many teachers felt that the information they had received from the tests and workshops would improve their classroom teaching. As a principal involved in the research stated, "I think the tests should be used throughout the entire district as our major means of improving teachers' attitudes toward the speech and culture of African American children, thereby improving their teaching."

Comments

Teachers who show particularly low scores on the tests (for whatever reason) will benefit from information on African American English–on its rule-governed nature, its history and characteristics, and its sociolinguistic rules. Such teachers will also benefit from research on successful methods of teaching AAVE-speaking children.

We feel that most teachers genuinely want their students to learn. We also feel that when teachers are made aware that they may have absorbed some of the same biases toward non-mainstream values and cultures that the wider society holds, they may want to change. We have found in our workshops across the country that teachers are vitally interested in the issues we are addressing–issues involving research on positive attitudes leading to achievement, and on successful methods of teaching bidialectal children. In short, teachers seem to be interested in and even excited about the ideas and concepts leading to the improvement of their jobs as teachers.

Limitations

The African American English Speech Varieties Attitude Test is designed to assess teacher attitudes toward African American English as reflected in tape-recorded passages marked by two specific grammatical features e.g., multiple negation. The patterns were limited for research purposes. The test would have been exhaustive had it included more than two features, because the two features were analyzed by teachers in eight passages and have five dimensions, e.g., "Achievement." The focus on only a few patterns does constitute a limitation, however, because it does not measure the total language behavior of African American children.

Another factor which might be considered a limitation is that the tests should not be utilized without accompanying workshops or extensive reading of the sources in the reference list of this article (see also reference lists of Hoover, Lewis, et al., 1996, this volume and Hoover, Politzer, et al, 1996, this volume). Still another limitation may arise from the tape recordings, given that they only present the most unique grammatical features. As such, they could serve to plant a stereotype in teachers' minds that all African American children speak in only these patterns; for example, that all African American speech is marked by consistent deletion of word endings, as utilized by "Amos and Andy," the White comics who made the ridicule of African American speech the focus of their radio program (see Lindenmeyer, 1970). Workshops should include the inherent variability in AAVE, as exhibited in Lester's *Black Folktales* (1973) and/or as evidenced in a host of sociolinguistic studies of AAVE (for example, see Bailey & Maynor, 1987; Edwards, 1992; Labov & Harris, 1986; Rickford, 1992; Rickford & McNair-Knox, 1994); the total range of speech behavior in the African American community, and the characteristics of programs where AAVE-speaking children achieve.

A final factor that might be considered a limitation is that forcing a teacher to categorize a student's speech as "educated" or "uneducated" might serve to firmly implant a notion that may have been lying dormant in the teacher's belief system. The stereotyped notion that ignorance correlates with AAVE is particularly dangerous because it may reflect an academic reality: some students who speak AAVE in standard English speech environments may indeed perform at a lower level of achievement. This phenomenon, however, is caused by the lack of implementation of research on effective programs for AAVE-speaking students (Edmonds, 1979; Fuetsch, 1992; Hoover, Dabney, & Lewis 1990; McNair-Knox, 1985; Sizemore, 1988), rather than choice of language variety. Further demonstration that AAVE is not automatically associated with lack of achievement is seen in the research revealing that AAVE-speaking children who also speak AASE–and are therefore bidialectal–achieve as well as SE speakers (see Hoover, Politzer, et al., "African American English Tests for Students," 1996, this volume).

Further Research

In further research, the African American English Speech Varieties Attitude Test could be broadened to include features beyond the grammatical, e.g., phonological, lexical, intonational, and discourse. The African American English Teacher Attitude Scale could also be broadened

to include more than three philosophical points of view ("Excellence," "Deficit," and "Difference") regarding language and the historical background of African Americans.

Note

1. Williams, Whitehead, & Miller (1971) have isolated the dimensions education, achievement, and standardness as being especially likely to make up teachers' judgments of pupils. Ratings dealing with honesty or intelligence, which are used in many matched-guise tests, were deliberately omitted from our test.

References

Bailey, G., & Maynor, N. (1987). Decreolization? *Language in Society, 16*, 449-473.

Bowie, R. L., & Bond, C. L. (1994). Influencing teachers' attitudes toward Black English: Are we making a difference? *Journal of Teacher Education, 45*, 112-118.

Brown, S. (1933). The Negro character as seen by White authors. *Journal of Negro Education, 2*, 179-203.

Cazden, C., & Dickinson, D. (1981). Language in education: Standardization vs. cultural pluralism. In C. Ferguson & S. Heath (Eds.), *Language in the USA* (pp. 446-468). New York: Cambridge University Press.

Cecil, N. L. (1988). Black dialect and academic success: A study of teacher expectations. *Reading Improvement, 25*, 34-38.

Drake, S. C. (1988). *Black folk here and there*. Los Angeles: University of California.

DuBois, W. E. B. (1935). *Black reconstruction: An essay toward a history of the part which Black folk played in the attempt to reconstruct democracy in America.* New York: Harcourt Brace.

Edmonds, R. (1979). Effective schools for the urban poor. *Educational Leadership, 37*(1), 15-18, 20-24.

Edwards, W. F. (1992). Sociolinguistic behavior in a Detroit inner-city black neighborhood. *Language in Society, 21*, 93-115.

Foster, M. (1992). Sociolinguistics and the African American community: Implications for literacy. *Theory into Practice, 31*, 303-311.

Fuetsch, M. (1992, February 3). 2 Inglewood schools defy odds, achieve excellence. *Los Angeles Times,* p. A1.

Giddings, P. (1984). *When and where I enter: The impact of Black women on race and sex in America.* New York: Bantam Books.

Hoover, M. R. (1978). Community attitudes toward Black English. *Language in Society, 7,* 65-87.

Hoover, M. R. (1990). A vindicationist perspective on the role of Ebonics (Black English) and other aspects of ethnic studies in the university. *American Behavioral Scientist, 34,* 251-262.

Hoover, M. R., Dabney, N., & Lewis, S. (1990). *Successful Black and minority schools.* San Francisco: Julian Richardson.

Hoover, M. R., Lewis, S. A. R., Politzer, R. L., Ford, J., McNair-Knox, F., Hicks, S., & Williams, D. (1996). Tests of African American English for teachers of bidialectal students. In R. L. Jones (Ed.), *Handbook of tests and measurements for Black populations* (Vol. I). Hampton, VA: Cobb & Henry.

Hoover, M. R., Politzer, R. L., Brown, D., Lewis, S., Hicks, S., & McNair-Knox, F. (1996). African American English tests for students. In R. L. Jones (Ed.), *Handbook of tests and measurements for Black populations* (Vol. I). Hampton, VA: Cobb & Henry.

Johnson, F. L., & Buttny, R. (1982). White listeners' responses to 'sounding Black' and "sounding White": The effects of message content on judgements about language. *Communication Monographs, 49,* 33-49.

Kozol, J. (1985). *Illiterate America.* New York: New American Library.

Labov, W., & Harris, W. A. (1986). De facto segregation of Black and White vernaculars. In D. Sankoff (Ed.), *Diversity and diachrony* (pp. 1-25). Amsterdam: Benjamins.

Lambert, W. E., Hodgson, R. C., Gardner, N. C., & Fillenbaum, S. (1960). Evaluational reactions to spoken languages. *Journal of Abnormal and Social Psychology, 60,* 44-51.

Lester, J. (1973). *Black folk tales.* New York: Grove Press.

Lewis, S., Hoover, M. R., & Politzer, R. L. (1979). *SCRDT Black English workshops.* Stanford, CA: Stanford Center for Research and Development in Teaching.

Lindenmeyer, O. (1970). *Black history: Lost, stolen, or strayed?* New York: Avon.

McNair-Knox, F. (1985). *The effects of foreign language instruction on the reading ability of African American children.* Unpublished doctoral dissertation, Stanford University, CA.

Politzer, R. L., & Hoover, M. R. (1976). *Teachers' and pupils' attitudes toward Black English speech varieties and Black pupils' achievement* (R & D Memorandum No. 145). Stanford, CA: Stanford Center for Research and Development in Teaching.

Rickford, J. R. (1992). Grammatical variation and divergence in Vernacular Black English. In M. Gerritsen & D. Stein (Eds.), *Internal and external factors in syntactic change* (pp. 175-200). The Hague: Mouton.

Rickford, J. R., & McNair-Knox, F. (1994). Addressee- and topic-influenced style shift: A quantitative sociolinguistic study. In D. Biber & E. Finegan (Eds.), *Sociolinguistic perspectives on register* (pp. 235-276). New York: Oxford University Press.

Sizemore, B. (1988). The Madison Elementary School: A turnaround case. *Journal of Negro Education, 57,* 243-265.

Stewart, W. A. (1969). On the use of Negro dialect in the teaching of reading. In J. Baratz & R. W. Shuy (Eds.), *Teaching Black children to read* (pp. 156-219). Washington, DC: Center for Applied Linguistics.

Taylor, O., & Hayes, A. (1971). *Five interrelated studies to increase the effectiveness of English language instruction in schools.* Washington, DC: Center for Applied Linguistics.

Tribble, I. (1992). *Making their mark: Educating African-American children.* Silver Spring, MD: Beckham.

Turner, J. (1984). *The next decade: Theoretical and research issues in Africana studies.* Ithaca, NY: Cornell University Africana Studies and Research Center.

Van Sertima, I. (1983). *Blacks in science : Ancient and modern.* New Brunswick, NJ: Transaction Books.

Williams, F., Whitehead, J., & Miller, L. (1971). Ethnic stereotypes and judgments of children's speech. *Speech Monographs, 38,* 166-170.

Wilson, A. (1991). *Awakening the natural genius in Black children.* Bronx: African World Info Systems.

Appendix A

Transcription of the African American English Speech Varieties Attitude Test

(I = AASE guise. II = AAVE guise. Passages are presented here in the order in which they occur on the tape.)

Tape Script 1

I1. Sharon King has to cook and iron and keep house and she almost never gets to go out and play anything. Sometimes when she gets tired, she tries to get through in a hurry or she asks her little sister to help her. And sometimes she just gets mad. But no matter what Sharon does, she still has to work and can't play. That's why Sharon frowns so much. Nobody wants to do all that.

II2. Carol have a baby sister and she help take care of her. The baby play and sing and do a lot of funny things. Carol have a lot of fun taking care of the baby, and can't nobody tell her that she don't know her job.

II3. Willeta can't hardly never sit still. She say she just have to keep busy. So she work around the house or she go out and shop or else she get her girlfriend to show her the latest dance. She laugh when we tease her and say at least nobody can't call her lazy. Cause no matter what she do she keep busy.

I4. Every Saturday, John thinks he just has to go see a western movie. But none of us believes him. That's because John does his good deed thing and invites Danny. Danny does his spoiled kid act and says he can't see anything but a war movie. So they argue and neither one of them ever gets to go see a show.

II5. Do Herman have to stay inside today? I think so. Because he have the flu. What about Willie? He have to stay in too, because when Herman feel bad, Willie do all the English homework. Too bad! When one brother gets sick, neither one of them can come out.

II6. The girl down the street study a lot and do real good in school. She do her math and she do her geography and she don't never get a bad grade. And you know what else? She act real friendly and she help us if we need it. Everybody like that girl and can't nobody say nothing bad about her.

I7. Darryl has a new bike and he cleans and shines it all the time. He rides it to the playground, and then he cleans it. He parks it outside his house and then he washes it.

Sandra says Darryl just likes to show off, but Darryl doesn't care. He says at least no one can say he doesn't have a nice clean bike.

I8. My dog Rex has a dogtag. I think your dog needs one too, because he runs around outside. The teacher says if a dog doesn't stay inside, he needs a tag, in case he gets lost. You need to hurry up and get your tag because I know you don't want to lose your dog.

Tape Script II

I1. Melanie Jackson likes to sing and dance and listen to music, and she almost never gets to go too far away from a record player. Once in a while she comes out to play or she runs an errand for her mother. And of course she goes to school. But it doesn't matter what else Melanie does, she still has to hear her music and can't do without it. Nobody likes music better than Melanie.

II2. Phillip have a new baby brother at his house and he love it a lot. Phillip help his mother take care of the baby, and he play with it and sing to it too. Phillip feel real proud ;and can't nobody tell him he don't know how to take care of a baby.

II3. Josie have to go downtown tomorrow and look for an after-school job. She need to find one quick because she want to save some money so she can go to summer camp again this year. Josie do some housework but she say she do babysitting best. Josie say it don't make no difference what kind of job she gets this time, just so she get one. Cause she have to go back to camp.

I4. Every evening Mr. Green comes down our street with his truck. Mr. Green sells ice cream and sometimes he has some candy too. When Mr. Green feels good he sings for us and he does a funny dance. We all love Mr. Green, and we hope he doesn't ever stop coming down our street.

II5. Do Willie have to stay after school today? Johnny say he do because he talk out loud in class too much. Johnny talk out loud in class too, but he have a habit of getting away with it. Willie do talk a lot but Johnny do too. I feel sorry for Willie because he never get away with it when he talk.

II6. John try to come over to my house each Sunday. I say he come over because he like to eat with us . He say he come cause he want to see my brother, but neither one of us believe him. You see, John go to our same school with us and he live right down the street, and he don't never come by here no other day. So I say John come for the food.

I 7. Ella has a pretty doll and she likes to dress her and she tries to style her hair. This doll talks and crawls when you wind her up. Ella calls her doll Eileen and she tells me that the doll calls her "Mama." I'm not sure about that though, because no one else has heard that.

I 8. Anita has a big brother. He does a lot of things for her. He takes her to the park, he helps her do her homework and sometimes he teaches her to play football. Anita has a good time with her brother, and he never gets too tired to help his sister.

African American English Speech Varieties Attitude Test Directions and Dimensions

Directions: Listen to the first speaker on the tape. Then look at Dimension A (below) and choose one of the five responses. Circle the number corresponding to your choice on your answer sheet. If you can't decide, or think the child's speech has no bearing on the dimension, circle number 3. Answer each dimension in the same way (Dimension B has more choices; "No opinion" is number 5). Then listen to the second speaker, and so forth.

Dimensions on which to rate Speech Varieties

A. A person who talks like this usually is:

Very Uneduc'd	Slightly Uneduc'd	Can't Decide	Slightly Educated	Very Educated
1	2	3	4	5

B. This speech is most appropriately used in the following place:

No Place___1
Playing in the Streets___2
Playing in the Living room___3
On the Playground at School___4
No Opinion___5
Eating at Thanksgiving Dinner___6
On a Church Program___7
On a School Program___8
Any Place___9

C. A student who talks like this is most likely to be a:

Very Poor Achiever	Slightly Poor Achiever	Makes No Difference	Slightly Good Achiever	Very Good Achiever
1	2	3	4	5

D. Do you like this speech?

Dislike Strongly	Dislike Mildly	No Opinion	Like Mildly	Like Strongly
1	2	3	4	5

E. This kind of speech is:

Very Nonstan'd	Slightly Nonstan'd	Can't Decide	Slightly Stan'd	Very Stan'd
1	2	3	4	5

Appendix B

African American English Teacher Attitude Scale

Circle the response that most nearly reflects your opinion. (Questions 1-46 are of the same format as question 1. To conserve space, therefore, only the actual test question, without the options, will be presented.)

1. Most African American people's major potential is in music, art, and dance.

Agree Strongly	Agree Mildly	Disagree Mildly	Disagree Strongly
1	2	3	4

2. African Americans should try to look like everybody else in this country rather than wearing Bubas and Afros.

3. African Americans need to know both standard and African American English in the school in order to survive in America.

4. African American English is a unique speech form influenced in its structure by West African languages.

5. The reason African Americans aren't moving as fast as they could is that the system discriminates against them.
6. African American English is a systematic, rule-governed language variety.
7. African American English should be eliminated.
8. African American English should be preserved to maintain oral understanding and communication among African Americans of all ages and from all regions.
9. The African American community concept of discipline involves not letting children "do their own thing" and "hang loose."
10. African American kids have trouble learning because their parents won't help them at home.
11. It is racist to demand that African American children take reading tests because their culture is so varied that reading is an insignificant skill.
12. African American English should be promoted in the school as part of African American children's culture.
13. Standard English is needed to replace African American English to help with worldwide communication.
14. It is not necessary for African American children to learn anything other than their own dialect of African American English in school.
15. The reason African American people aren't moving as fast as they could is that they're not as industrious as they should be.
16. There is no such thing as African American English.
17. The use of African American English is a reflection of unclear thinking on the part of the speaker.
18. African American children's language is so broken as to be virtually no language at all.
19. African Americans should talk the way everybody else does in this country.
20. African American English is principally a Southern form.
21. When a child's native African American English is replaced by standard English, s/he

is introduced to concepts which will increase her/his learning capacity.
22. The home life of African American children offers such limited cultural experiences that the school must fill in the gaps.
23. African and African American hair and dress styles are very attractive.
24. African American kids would advance further in school without African American English.
25. African American English has a logic of its own, comparable to that of any other language.
26. African American children can't learn to read unless African American Vernacular English is used as the medium of instruction in the schools.
27. African American people have their own distinctive speech patterns which other people in this country should respect.
28. African American English was produced by its history in Africa and this country and not by any physical characteristics.
29. African American English can be expanded to fit any concept or idea imaginable.
30. The home life of African American people provides a rich cultural experience directly connected to African origins.
31. The reason African American children have trouble learning in school is that they are not taught properly.
32. African American English is basically talking lazy.
33. African American children can be trained to pass any test written.
34. African American children can learn to read in spite of the fact that most readers are written in standard English.
35. African American people have the same potential for achievement in math and science as any other people.
36. African American kids are advantaged through African American English; it makes them bidialectal just as Chicanos are bilingual.
37. African American English is a misuse of standard language.
38. African American children should be allowed to choose their own course of study

and behavior in school from an early age and should not be directed by the teacher.

39. Standard English is superior to nonstandard English in terms of grammatical structure.

40. African American English should be preserved because it creates a bond of solidarity among the people who speak it.

41. Acceptance of nonstandard dialects of English by teachers would lead to a lowering of standards in school.

42. African American English should be preserved because it helps African Americans feel at ease in informal situations.

43. African American English enhances the curriculum by enriching the language background of the children.

44. African American English expresses some things better than standard English.

45. Since only standard English is useful in getting jobs, it should always be preferred over African American English.

46. African American English should be abandoned because it does not provide any benefits to anybody.

Appendix C

Key Terms

Bidialectal

Controlling two varieties of one's language, e.g., a vernacular variety and a standard variety.

Balanced bidialectal

Having equal levels of proficiency in African American Vernacular English and African American Standard English

African American Standard English

That variety of African American English, or *Ebonics,* distinguished by its similarity to standard English grammar and its simultaneous use of varying degrees of phonological, intonational and lexical features of African American Vernacular English.

African American Vernacular English

That variety of African American English, or *Ebonics,* revealing influences from West African languages in its grammar, and phonology.

For additional information, contact:

Faye McNair-Knox, Ph.D.
College of Education
Florida International University
3000 N.E. 145th Street
North Miami, FL 33187
Telephone: (305) 940-5820
Fax: (305) 956-5494

Part VIII

Measures of Parental Attitudes and Values

Assessing Childrearing Practices and Attitudes of Black Parents During Infancy

Suzanne M. Randolph, Pearl L. Rosser, and Doris B. Baytop

Abstract

The "Survey of Childrearing Attitudes and Practices[1]" was developed for use with a selected sample of Black mothers to collect information about their child's development during the first year, the parents' plans for fostering growth and development, and types of child care activities in which parents engaged. Specifically, the survey was designed to complement data collected using standard child development and parent-child interaction assessments. The "Survey" consists of 12 items, many of which are open-ended and have sub-parts. Parents are asked questions about their involvement in developmental activities such as games, perceptions of good ways to teach numbers, colors, and the alphabet, plans for sending the child to preschool, child care arrangements, disciplining style and plans to change with child's age, sources of childrearing information, activities to reward children, concerns about their infant's development, infant feeding practices, and perceptions of the infant's temperament. Recommended administration is at two days after birth and nine months for all items except feeding which should be done prior to four months. The "Survey" can be administered in face-to-face or in telephone interviews; mail or self–administration is not recommended. Suggested uses include: use as a research tool to complement standard child development assessments: use in clinic or parent education center to gauge parent's responsiveness and child development knowledge related to assisting them with developing the child's potential or to correct practices with potential for child abuse and neglect, use with multiple caregivers to assess differences or consistency in practices across caregivers', and use by social service or health professionals as a screening tool to provide anticipatory guidance and determine need for family support in childrearing.

Background and Introduction

The "Survey of Childrearing Attitudes and Practices" was developed for use with a selected group of Black mothers to collect information about their child's development during the first year, the parents' plans for fostering growth and development, and types of child care activities in which parents engaged. Specifically, the "Survey" was developed as part of the Howard University Newborn Study (HUNS) (Rosser & Randolph, 1985, 1991). The HUNS was a longitudinal study of Black mothers and their infants, who were followed from 48 hours after the infant's birth through age three to establish new normative expectations for Black infants' development. Three groups of infants were followed: 1) a full term healthy group who met standard criteria for the healthy neonate (e.g., ≥ 37 weeks gestation (appropriate for gestational age), Apgar scores of ≥ 8 at 1 minute and ≥ 9 at 5 minutes, ≥ 5 and 1/2 pounds, and no medical complications; 2) a pre-term healthy group who were similar to the full term group with respect to birth characteristics and medical conditions, but different in terms of their gestational age (32-37 weeks for the pre-terms); and 3) a pre-term sick group who were 32 to 37 weeks gestation, with varying Apgar scores, and respiratory distress syndrome.

A variety of other measures were also used to collect data on these mothers and their infants from just two days after birth. These included maternal interviews about the child's temperament, confidence in caregiving, and social history; observations in the home to assess the quality of the caregiving environment and mother-infant interaction during feeding situations; infant attachment to mother; and standard infant assessments of mental and motor development. The "Survey of Childrearing Practices and Attitudes" was designed to complement these other data by providing additional information about various patterns of childrearing behavior.

Many of the survey items are open-ended, allowing for a range of responses from mothers that can be subjected to content analysis. While mothers were the specific target respondent in the

HUNS, some fathers were also interviewed, and the inspection of this small data set suggested that the "Survey" might also be useful for interviewing Black fathers about their expectations for their child's development.

Survey Contents

The "Survey" consists of 12 items, (See Appendix) many of which have subparts. The first three questions are about the parents' involvement or concern with developmental activities for their infants: playing games such as "peek-a-boo" and knowing their importance to the child's development; perceptions of good ways to teach numbers, colors, and ABC's; and plans to send their child to preschool or nursery school. The fourth question concerns the parents' child care arrangements and their perceptions of the minimal age for child care providers. Question five considers parents' disciplining style and whether they have plans to change that style as the child ages.

A subsequent question asks about the parents' sources of childrearing information, followed by whether parents liked anything in particular about raising children, and their desires for additional childrearing information. The ninth question asks what kinds of things children do to please parents and, when they do so, how the children are rewarded. Question 10 asks parents if they are having fun with their infant, things they are concerned about, and whether there is anything they would like to change about their infant. This latter series of questions is especially important for ascertaining whether parents of preterm infants who are often frail and vulnerable present particular challenges to parents.

Question 11 asks broadly about the infant's temperament using the Thomas and Chess (1977) categories ("easy," "slow to warm up," and "difficult"). Responses to this item can be used with the maternal interview about temperament to gauge how closely the mother's general perception of the infant fits with established norms for infant temperament. To date, there has been little or no work of this kind done with African American mothers and infants. The survey ends with a series of questions about infant feeding–schedule, type (breast, bottle, spoon), types of food eaten (formula, table food), and frequency.

Administration

The "Survey" was designed to be administered face-to-face at one month and nine months after birth in the interviewee's home or in a clinic setting. Because many of the questions are open ended the "Survey" can also be administered by telephone. In the HUNS, the one month administration took place in the home. The nine month interview was done by telephone. Self-administration in person or through the mail is not recommended. A subsequent version which includes closed-ended responses based on the open-ended comments gathered in the HUNS is being prepared. In face-to-face or telephone interviews, the survey can be completed in approximately 10 minutes.

Suggested Uses

In lieu of actual observations of parent-child interaction during infancy, the "Survey" provides some indication of the parent's expectations for their child's development as well as the childrearing attitudes and practices the parent expects to use in helping the child develop his or her potential. Open-ended responses allow for a number of responses that might have clinical significance–e.g., with respect to child abuse and neglect, the disciplining techniques and/or feeding practices might be revealing. The responses also permit the user to consider whether additional screening and/or assessment, including assessment of family functioning is appropriate. Researchers interested in the use of the "Survey" will find it extremely helpful in providing supplemental information which can be used to interpret or explain other findings. For example, differences in developmental outcomes between full term and pre-term infants might be explained by differential patterns of childrearing between the two groups of parents as reported in their "Surveys."

The insights gathered through use of the "Survey" also provide invaluable information about childrearing in Black families, and can be used with fathers and mothers (or mothers and grandmothers or other multiple caregivers) to examine similarities and differences in childrearing in the same family that may contribute to or hinder the child's developmental progress. The "Survey" can also be used in parent education programs as a way of estimating participants' child development knowledge and identifying key areas which should receive attention.

Pediatricians, nurses, social workers and other health professionals might also use the "Survey" to provide anticipatory guidance in the areas of child abuse and neglect if disciplining techniques or feeding practices appear extreme. Finally, social service personnel can use the information to determine whether families seem to have adequate supports to function (e.g., regular substitute caregivers of appropriate age) and to assist parents who wish to send their children to nursery school or preschool in finding affordable, quality child care settings, and where possible and appropriate, matched to the parent's childrearing style.

Researchers who use the tool are invited to contact the authors so that additional data can be gathered to generate a codeable set of responses which more adequately reflects the cultural integrity of African American families. This set of responses can then be used to refine the "Survey" and broaden its use in empirical and clinical settings.

Note

1. Development of this instrument was supported in part by Grant MCJ-110461 awarded to the second author by the Division of Maternal and Child Health, Bureau of Health Care Delivery Assistance, Health Resources and Services Administration, Public Health Service, Department of Health and Human Services; by a fellowship from the Rockefeller Foundation Research Program for Minority Group Scholars to the first author; and by the Department of Pediatrics and Child Health, College of Medicine, Howard University.

References

Rosser, P. L., & Randolph, S.M. (1991). Black American Infants: The Howard University Normative Study. In K. Nugent, B. Lester, & T. B. Brazelton (Eds.), *The cultural context of infancy*. Norwood, N J: Ablex.

Rosser, P. L., & Randolph, S. M. (1985). *Maternal perceptions, CNS organization, and cognitive development. Final Report*. Washington, DC: Maternal and Child Health and Crippled Children's Services Research Grants Program.

Thomas, A., & Chess, S., (1977). *Temperment and development*. New York: Brunner/Mazel.

Appendix

Howard University Normative Study

Survey of Childrearing Attitudes and Practices
Study I.D. __ Check One: __1 month __9 months

1. Do you plan to play any games with your baby?

____Yes ____No ____Not sure
   a. If yes, which ones? (e.g., do you play peek-a-boo?). List below.
   b. Why? (If "YES," probe to see if they know how the game is related to development) (If "No" or "Not sure," probe to see why or why not).

2. What's a good way to teach young children...:
   a. A-B-C's?
   b. Numbers?
   c. Colors?
   d. How do you plan to teach these to your child ?

3. Do you plan to send your child to preschool or nursery school?

____Yes ____No ____Not sure
   a. If yes, at what age?

4. Do you have babysitting arrangements?

____Yes ____No
   a. If yes, what are they?
   b. What ages of babysitters would you consider? (That is, how old would you want your babysitter to be, at least?)

   c. If "No," who will keep the baby if you have to go out?

5. Some parents find it necessary to punish their children in one or more of the following ways: scolding or yelling, spanking or physical punishment, sending the child to his room or to bed, taking away the child's privileges.
   a. If a one year old is doing something wrong what would you do? (Check all that apply).
   ___ (1) Scolding or yelling
   ___ (2) Physical punishment
   ___ (3) Sending the child to room
   ___ (4) Taking away privileges
   ___ (5) Talking things over
   ___ (6) Other (list): _____
   b. How about an older child? (Check all that apply).
   ___ (1) Scolding or yelling
   ___ (2) Physical punishment
   ___ (3) Sending the child to room
   ___ (4) Taking away privileges
   ___ (5) Talking things over
   ___ (6) Other (list):_____

6. Where do you get your information about raising children? Check all that apply.
   ___ (1) Mother, grandmother
   ___ (2) Other relatives (list: _____)
   ___ (3) Friends
   ___ (4) Reading
   ___ (5) Raising own brothers & sisters
   ___ (6) Raising other relatives or children
   ___ (7) Other experience with young children (list:_____)
   ___(8) Previous children of your own

7. Do you like anything in particular about raising children? (list:_____)

8. Are there things you would like more information about (or wish you knew more about)?

____Yes ____No
   a. If yes, List:

9. When parents are pleased with children, they often use methods to reward the children. What would you do to show your child you are pleased with his/her behavior? Check all that apply.
   ___ (1) Kissing and hugging
   ___ (2) Giving a gift or special privilege
   ___ (3) Praising the child

___ (4) Not making a big deal out of it
___ (5) Other (list):_____ _____)

10. Are you having fun with your baby?
    ____Yes ____No
    a. What kinds of things are you satisfied with?
    b. Is there anything you are concerned about?
    c. Is there anything about your baby you would change if you could?

11. Temperment
    Would you say your baby is:
    ____Easy
    ____Slow to Warm Up
    ____Difficult

(Use the following definitions to give mothers some sense of the kinds of baby described by these terms).

Easy. Interacts well, alert, readily available, orients well, seeks out interaction, clings, follows you, maybe smiles; has regular habits, adapts quickly to new experiences; positive expression of mood.

Slow to warm up. Expends some energy bringing him/her to alertness, but once there he/she locks on; takes a little time to get him/her to smile; a little active/fussy. Approaches new situations with hesitancy, but without strong negative reactions; adapts positively if not pressured.

Difficult. Needs a lot of stimulation; eats and sleeps all/most of the time; bothers you, you feel rejected; leaves you wondering what it is you did not do; hard to console; you find yourself following the baby. Reacts strongly and negatively to changes in situations; adapts slowly; irregular in eating and sleeping patterns.

12. Feeding: Now I would like to ask you a few questions about how you have been feeding your baby.
    a. What is your feeding-burping pattern? Probe for:
    1) Position baby is held (arms/lap/infant seat)
    2) How much taken between burps
    3) How much taken on the average
    4) How long does the feeding last
    5) Baby's schedule
    6) Burping method (pats on back on shoulder, lap soft rubs, etc.)
    7) Burping position (goes with above)
    b. Do you find it easy to burp your baby (i.e., burps quickly vs. takes some time)?
    ____Yes, quickly ____No, takes some time
    c. Can you tell when your baby still has gas?
    ____Yes ____ No ____Sometimes
    If "Yes" or "Sometimes," probe as to how?
    d. Do you think you would know when a baby has been overfed? ____Yes ____No
    If yes: How can you tell? What cues do you look for?
    e. Does your baby get hiccoughs?
    ____Yes ____No
    How often?
    What do you do to get rid of them?

For additional information, contact:

Suzanne M. Randolph, Ph.D.
University of Maryland
Family Studies
College Park, MD 20742
Telephone: (301) 405-4012
Fax: (301) 314-9161
E-mail: SR22@UMAIL.UMD.EDU

The Ecological Scale of Parental Competence

Bertha Garrett Holliday[1]

Abstract

This article describes the newly constructed Ecological Scale of Parental Competence (ESPC). A brief overview is presented of various views of the characteristics of competent parents. An ecological model of parental competence is described. This model guided the construction of the ESPC. The ESPC is described, and its limitations are noted.

What is Parental Competence?

The study of children's development and socialization fundamentally is defined by that nexus of issues related to describing and explaining: (a) those progressive physiological, cognitive, personality, and behavioral changes observed in children as they increase in age; (b) the normative sequential markers and processes of such changes; and (c) the major sources of facilitative and nonfacilitative influence on such changes. It is in regard to the latter of these issues that a significant role has been attributed to parental competence.

Historical review of the child development/ socialization literature suggests that early research on the influential role of parents on children's development focused almost exclusively on the effects of mothers' attributes and behaviors (cf. Bronfenbrenner & Crouter, 1983). Later, this dyadic (mother-child) model of parental influence was modified to include the dyadic relationship between father and child. Still later, a triadic model (mother-father-child) was proposed. This model recognized that children's development is influenced both directly by mothers and fathers, and indirectly by means of the reinforcement one spouse provides the other relative to childrearing.

Both the dyadic and triadic models assume that children's development is positively influenced when parents effectively interact with the child. Effective parent-child interactions typically are viewed by child researchers as involving such characteristics as warmth, authoritativeness, linguistic play and elaboration, reciprocity, and sensitivity to the child's changing needs and capabilities. Thus, the dyadic and triadic models of parental influence suggest that competent parents are those who frequently and effectively engage in such types of interactions with the child.

But recently, these models' major assumptions have been challenged and expanded by the family systems model. The family systems model is distinguished by its emphasis on the family as a small group with characteristic norms and roles, that is purposive, adaptive, equilibrium-seeking, and boundary-maintaining (Hill & Mattessich, 1979). Consequently, proponents of this model often describe the family and its individual mem-

403

bers through use of such concepts as networks, social support, cohesiveness/conflict, dominance, and exchange. Behavior within the family is viewed to be influenced not only by attributes of the family and its individual members, but also by family members' relationships with other systems (i.e., individuals, groups, institutions) external to the nuclear family. Because of the family systems model's concern with environmental influences on the family as a unit, it has gained ascendancy among African American family researchers (e.g., Allen, 1978; Billingsley, 1968; Staples, 1971).

The family systems model challenges and expands the dyadic and triadic models by suggesting that the developmental influence of parent-child relations is defined not only by dyadic affectional and behavioral acts, but also by the family's acquaintances, social encounters, and related joint experiencing of events. The family systems model additionally suggests that traditional concepts and measurements of parental competence[2] must be modified and expanded to include consideration of the frequency and effectiveness of parents' involvements with a diversity of persons and ecological settings.

Conceptualization of an Ecological Model of Parental Competence

According to system theorists Bates and Harvey (1975), social roles are defined by a set of normative behaviors as these are constrained by time, place, function, and the idiosyncratic characteristics of role-actor. Similarly Bates and Harvey argue that roles cluster together to define the statuses of persons in a dyadic relationship (e.g., parent-child, teacher-student). The various statuses assumed by an individual cluster together to define positions.

Through reference to such concepts, one may infer that parenthood is more than a role (i.e., normative behaviors) and it is more than a status (i.e., a set of dyadic parent-child interactions). Parenthood is a position within the family that involves multiple roles and functions. Inherent in the parent position are the dual responsibilities to interact with the child and to relate and transact

with systems outside of the family, on behalf of the child's needs and interests. As one family scholar has observed, "Children's development depends on the competence of parents to orchestrate their decisions within the family and between the family and a host of social institutions" (Dokecki, 1979, p. 1).

Of course, in operationalizing such concepts and ideas into a model of parental competence, one must grapple with issues related to specifying those categories of parents' behaviors and relations/exchanges that are most salient for and related to children's development. We addressed such issues by engaging in a three-step procedure of conceptualization: First, we identified major roles and related functions of parents; then we identified ecological domains (or systems) where those roles and functions are primarily enacted; finally we specified major classes of behavioral indicators of such roles-in-domains. Through use of this procedure, we developed the ecological model of parental competence presented in Table 1.

The Ecological Scale of Parental Competence

Description

The Ecological Scale of Parental Competence (ESPC) is a self-report interview questionnaire for use with mothers and fathers of school-age (i.e., ages 5 to 17 years) children. A copy of the ESPC is provided in Appendix A and coding instructions are provided in Appendix B. The ESPC is divided into three major sections.

Part 1. This section consists of two recognized measures of parents' psychological functioning: (a) The 25-item Personality Integration (PI) subscale of the Tennessee Self-Concept Scale[3] (Fitts, 1965); and (b) the 20-item Manifest Anxiety Scale, Short-Form[4] (Bendig, 1956). Each PI item is rated on a five-point scale and each Manifest Anxiety item is rated as "true" or "false."

Part 2. This section consists of six open-ended items. Each item solicits a parent's behavioral and verbal responses (and related rationales)

Table 1. Ecological Model of Parental Competence

Role	Function	Primary Domain for Enactment	Behavioral Indicators	ESPC Items
Model	To engage in behaviors that provide models for the child of mastery of developmental skills.	Personal	Sound mental health status as indicated by assessments of personality integration and anxiety.	IA: #1-25 IB: #1-20
			Engagement in activities involving literacy skills.	III: #1-5
			Engagement in social instrumental skills (e.g., money management, knowledge acquisition, self-reflection and articulation of feelings, and personal problem-solving).	III: #6-12
Teacher	To engage in dyadic interactions with the child in which developmental skills are demonstrated and reinforced, and behavioral limits are established, explained, and enforced.	Interpersonal	Style of parent-child interactions.	II: #1-6
			Parent-child interactions related to literacy and academic achievement.	III: #13-17
			Parent-child interactions related to knowledge acquisition and social instrumental skills.	III: #18-22
			Procedural rules and methods of punishment and reward.	III: #23-29
Allocator/ Arbitrator	To fairly allocate the family's resources (e.g., time, love, goods) among family members; to seek maintenance of family cohesion and equilibrium by arbitrating conflicts and disputes among family members.	Family	Allocation of parental responsibilities and related role satisfaction.	III: #30-39
			Allocation of family resources among children.	III: #40-43
			Style of family arbitration.	III: #44-45
Facilitator	To support child's development by (a) seeking to expand the range of the child's participation	Social Networks	Child's Participation in organized group activities.	III: #46-48

(table continues)

Role	Function	Primary Domain for Enactment	Behavioral Indicators	ESPC Items
	and networks (i.e., opportunities for role-taking) and (b) use of parent's own networks e.g., childrearing assistance from kin, friends, and neighbors).		Source, type, and frequency of childrearing assistance.	III: #49-50
Advocate/ Provider	To support child's developmental activities in institutional settings through monitoring, involvement, and advocacy, to secure resources necessary for meeting the child's basic needs.	Community/ Institutional	Type and frequency of parent's involvement with child's school.	III: #53-60
			Frequency of involvement with agencies providing social services and assistance.	III: #61-71

to a hypothetical vignette of parent-child interaction requiring sensitivity to the child's needs and developmental status. One of the vignettes is as follows:

You and the children are looking at the evening news on T.V. and (target child) angrily comments, Why are African American people always doing something wrong?

This section of the ESPC is in a preliminary stage of development. In the near future, criteria will be developed for rating parents' responses to the vignettes along multiple dimensions of parent-child interaction style.

Part 3. This section consists of 71 items[5]. These items are divided into five subsections, each of which comprises items related to one of the five roles-in-domains of the proposed model of parental competence (see Table 1). Sixty-seven of these items are multiple-choice questions with five fixed-response categories reflecting varying levels of frequency and/or intensity of specific parenting behaviors. As a precaution against response-bias, the direction of the items' response categories were randomly counterbalanced. Three items (#48, 50, 52) are open-ended requests for

information related to social networks and organizational participation. One item (#67) requests "yes/no" responses.

Administration. Although the ESPC can be group- or self-administered as a questionnaire, it is *strongly recommended* that the ESPC be *individually administered* as an *interview*. Such administration requires 15 to 30 minutes.

Uses and Limitations

The Ecological Scale of Parental Competence is in the early stages of development. However, analyses are underway of ESPC responses from a sample of African American southern mothers who were selected through use of multistage stratified area sampling methods. These analyses will provide preliminary data on the instrument's internal reliability and its ability to detect variations in parental competence (discriminant validity) associated with differences in social class, family type and constellation, and parent's psychological status.

Our experiences to date with the ESPC suggest its promise for research use in studies of African American family process and childrearing practices. Indeed, the author *strongly* encourages other investigators to use the ESPC–especially if its use results in the following types of data: (a) item-analyses and other empirical analyses related to the instrument's internal reliability and structure; (b) correlational analyses of indicators of parenting behaviors as directly observed in naturalistic or experimental settings and as self-reported on the ESPC; (c) predictive relationships between ESPC scores and indicators of children's developmental or socialization status; (d) the ESPC's test-retest reliability; (e) cross-sectional panel analyses (by age of parent or age of child), and; (f) comparative analyses of ESPC responses on multiracial samples.

Notes

1. Construction of the Ecological Scale of Parental Competence (ESPC) was supported by a Dean's Professional Development Grant (Peabody College) and by a grant from the Vanderbilt University Research Council. The author wishes to acknowledge the tireless assistance provided by Ms. Judith Davidson in conceptualizing and constructing the ESPC. Use of the ESPC is strongly encouraged. Inquiries and notification of ESPC use should be forwarded to the author.

2. Traditional measures of parental competence focus almost exclusively on attributes of dyadic parent-child interactions, parents' attitudes about childrearing along various dimensions of authoritarianism, and attributes of home environment. Examples of such measures are structured parent-child interaction tasks (e.g., Baumrind, 1971; Sigel, Flaugher, & Johnson, 1977), the Parent Attitude Research Instrument (Schaefer & Bell, 1958), the Child's Report of Parental Behavior (Schaefer, 1965), the Cornell Parent Behavior Scale (Deveraux, Bronfenbrenner, & Rodgers, 1969), and the Home Observation for Measurement of the Environment (Bradley & Caldwell, 1979).

3. The Personality Integration (PI) subscale assesses the level of an individual's adjustment or degree of personality integration as a function of identity, self-satisfaction, and behavior across five spheres of self (physical, moral-ethical, personal, family, and social). This subscale was derived through item analysis. Its items differentiate persons judged as demonstrating average or better adjustment from psychotic, personality disordered, neurotic, defensive, and norm groups. The subscale has a reported test-retest reliability of $r = 0.90$ (over a 2-week interval on 60 college students). The PI subscale has a mean of 10.42 and a *S.D.* of 3.88.

4. The short form of the Taylor Manifest Anxiety Scale consists of the 20 most consistently valid items from the full 50-item scale. Scores on the short-form have been found to correlate with the full scale scores at the level of $r = 0.93$. The internal reliability of the short-form is $r = 0.76$, which compares favorably to the full scale's reported median internal reliability of $r = 0.82$.

5. Two of these items (#45 and 46) are slight modifications of Allen's (1975) procedure for assessing (a) parent methods and frequency of punishment in childrearing, and (b) parent methods and frequency of reward in childrearing.

References

Allen, W. (1975). *The antecedents of adolescent mobility aspiration.* Unpublished doctoral dissertation, University of Chicago.

Allen, W. (1978). The search for applicable theories of Black family life. *Journal of Marriage and the Family, 40,* 117-129.

Bates, F. L., & Harvey, C. C. (1975). *The structure of social systems.* New York: Gardner Press.

Baumrind, D. (1971). Current patterns of parental authority. *Developmental Psychology Monograph, 41*(2), 1-103.

Bendig, A. W. (1956). The development of a short form of the Manifest Anxiety Scale. *Journal of Consulting Psychology, 20*(50), 384.

Billingsley, A. (1968). *Black families in Anglo-American America.* Englewood Cliffs, NJ: Wadsworth.

Bradley, R. H., & Caldwell, B. M. (1979). Home observation for measurement of the environment: A revision of the preschool scale. *American Journal of Mental Deficiency, 84*(3), 235-244.

Bronfenbrenner, U., & Crouter, A. C. (1983). The evolution of environmental models in developmental research. In P. H. Mussen (Ed.), *Handbook of child psychology: Vol. 1. History, theory, and methods* (4th ed., pp. 357-414). New York: Wiley.

Devereaux, E. C., Bronfenbrenner, U., & Rodgers, R. R. (1969). Childrearing in England and the United

States: A cross-national comparison. *Journal of Marriage and the Family, 31,* 257-270.

Dokecki, P. (1979). *A process approach to strengthening families through public policies.* Memorandum to the Carnegie Group. Nashville, TN: Vanderbilt University, Vanderbilt Institute for Public Policy Studies.

Fitts, W. H. (1965). *Tennessee Self-Concept Scale.* Nashville, TN: Counselor Recordings and Tests.

Hill, R., & Mattesich, P. (1979). Family development theory and life-span development. In P. B. Baltes & O. G. Brim, Jr. (Eds.), *Life-span development and behavior* (Vol. 2, pp. 162-204). New York: Academic Press.

Schaefer, E. S. (1965). Children's reports of parental behavior: An inventory. *Child Development, 36,* 427-424.

Schaefer, E. S., & Bell, R. Q. (1958). Development of a parental attitude research instrument. *Child Development, 29,* 339-361.

Siegel, I. E., Flaugher, J., & Johnson, J. E. (1977). *Parent-Child Interaction (PCI) Schedule.* Princeton, NJ: Educational Testing Service.

Staples, R. (1971). *The Black family: Essays and studies.* Belmont, CA: Wadsworth.

Appendix A

Ecological Scale of Parental Competence (ESPC)

I. Parent's Sense of Personal Competence

Here is a card that you should use in answering the following questions. (Review response categories and their numbers with respondent.)

1) Completely False
2) Mostly False
3) Partly False/Partly True
4) Mostly True
5) Completely True

I will read you some statements which describe various ways that people feel about themselves. For each statement, tell me which response on the card best describes how you see yourself.

____ 1. I am an attractive person.
____ 2. I am a calm and easygoing person.
____ 3. I am not interested in what other people do.
____ 4. I am a religious person.
____ 5. I have a lot of self-control.
____ 6. I am hard to be friendly with.
____ 7. I like my looks just the way they are.
____ 8. I ought to go to church more.
____ 9. I am satisfied to be just what I am.
____ 10. I understand my family as well as I should.
____ 11. I should trust my family more.
____ 12. I am as sociable as I want to be.
____ 13. I don't feel as well as I should.
____ 14. I should have more sex appeal.
____ 15. I am not the person I would like to be.
____ 16. I wish I didn't give up as easily as I do.
____ 17. I treat(ed) my parents as well as I should.
____ 18. I ought to get along better with other people.
____ 19. I often act like I am "all thumbs."
____ 20. I give (gave) in to my parents.
____ 21. I get along well with other people.
____ 22. I have trouble doing the things that are right.
____ 23. I change my mind a lot.
____ 24. I try to run away from my problems.
____ 25. I do not feel at ease with other people.

Please answer "True" or "False" to the following statements. (Questions 1-20 are of the same format as questions 1. To conserve space, therefore, only the actual test questions, without the options, will be presented for questions 2-20).

	True	False
1. I believe I am no more nervous than most others.	____	____

2. I work under a great deal of tension.
3. I cannot keep my mind on one thing.
4. I am more sensitive than most other people.
5. I frequently find myself worrying about something.
6. I am usually calm and not easily upset.
7. I feel anxiety about something or someone almost all the time.
8. I am happy most of the time.
9. I have periods of such great restlessness that I cannot sit long in a chair.

10. I have sometimes felt that difficulties were piling up so high that I could not overcome them.
11. I find it hard to keep my mind on a task or job.
12. I am not unusually self-conscious.
13. I am inclined to take things hard.
14. Life is a strain for me much of the time.
15. At times I think I am no good at all.
16. I am certainly lacking in self-confidence.
17. I certainly feel useless at times.
18. I am a high-strung person.
19. I sometimes feel that I am about to go to pieces.
20. I shrink from facing a crisis or difficulty.

II. Parental Sensitivity to Child

I am going to read some situations that parents often must deal with. For each situation, I would like you to consider the personality of your child _____, different ways that he/she responds to you, and your personal feelings about the situation. Then tell me exactly what you *most likely* would say and do. Tell me the *exact* words and actions you would use. Then tell me *why* you would use those words and actions.

OK. Here is the first situation. What would you most likely do and say–and why? (Note: A response such as "I would reassure or comfort him." is not acceptable. A response such as "I would smile at him and say in a quiet voice, 'Don't worry, I will always love you,' is acceptable. In the latter case, the respondent indicates *specific* words and actions)

1. ___(child)___ has just come home from school–silent, sad faced and dragging his/her feet. You can tell by his/her manner that something unpleasant has happened. (Record answers verbatim on Data Sheet)
2. You walk into your bedroom and find ___(child)___ putting your wallet down with a $10.00 bill in his/her hand. It is clear from his/her actions (i.e., looking shocked at your arrival, putting his/her hand with the money behind his/her back) that you have caught him/her stealing.

3. Two of ___(child)___'s friends have come over to visit with him/her. You have just noticed how quiet it has become on the porch where they have been talking. You go there and find them smoking a marijuana cigarette.
4. You are helping ___(child)___ with an arithmetic problem and she/he seems to be having difficulty. She/he suddenly exclaims: "I am so stupid! I never know the answers to any of the questions the teacher asks me. I don't want to go to school anymore."
5. You are cooking dinner and ___(child)___ comes into the kitchen and asks in a quiet, concerned voice: "Do you love me?"
6. You and the children are looking at the evening news on T.V. and ___(child)___ angrily comments, "Why are Black people always doing something wrong?"

III. Parental Behavior Competencies

I will ask you a series of questions about what you do with and for _____. When I ask a question about the things you do, pick the answer that *best* describes what you do now. Do you have any questions? (Responses should be coded *directly* onto *this* questionnaire form. Do not record responses directly onto Data Sheet. If response remains ambiguous after probing, then record response verbatim onto this questionnaire form.)

Section A (Parent as Model)

1. How many magazines do you subscribe to?
   1) None
   2) One
   3) Two
   4) Three
   5) Four or more
2. How often do you read the newspaper?
   1) Almost never
   2) Perhaps once a week
   3) Several times a week
   4) Daily
3. How often does ___(child)___ see you reading a book?
   1) Almost every day
   2) 3 to 4 times a week

3) 1 or 2 times a week

4) 2 or 3 times a month

5) Hardly ever

4. How much of your reading do you do to obtain new knowledge or information (other than for recreation only)?

    1) None

    2) Little

    3) Some

    4) Much

    5) Very much

5. How often do you listen to or attend educational lectures or discussions?

    1) Never

    2) 1 or 3 times

    3) 4-8 times

    4) About once a month

    5) More than once a month

6. How much importance do you attach to keeping up with current events?

    1) None

    2) Little

    3) Some

    4) Much

    5) Very much

7. About how much time would you say you devote to keeping up with current events (T.V. and radio news and programs, discussions, public meetings, newspapers, etc.)?

    1) Little or none

    2) 1 to 3 hours per week

    3) 1 hour per day

    4) 2 hours per day

    5) More than 2 hours per day

8. How does your knowledge of local government officials and activities compare with that of others in your community?

    5) Much more

    4) More

    3) About the same

    2) Less

    1) Much less

9. Do you think you show good money habits or good money sense?

    5) Definitely all the time

    4) Usually

    3) Sometimes

    2) Seldom

    1) Definitely do not

10. Some parents talk to their children about their own mistakes; others so not. Do you talk with _____ whenever you have made a wrong decision?

    1) Never

    2) Occasionally

    3) Sometimes

    4) Often

    5) Always

11. When you are upset or in a bad mood, how often do you find time to try to find the right words to explain to _____ how you are feeling and why?

    1) Hardly ever

    2) Sometimes I do, but most times, I don't

    3) Sometimes I do, sometimes I don't

    4) Most times I do, but sometimes I don't

    5) Almost always

12. Some parents think it is important to handle their children like others in the neighborhood; others do not. I try to be like other parents.

    1) Almost always, so we will "fit in"

    2) Often, because it's important for parents to stick together

    3) Sometimes, depending on circumstances

    4) Rarely

    5) Never, not concerned with what others do

Section B (Parent as Teacher)

13. How often does your child come to you for help on school work?

    1) Hardly ever

    2) 2 or 3 times a month

    3) 1 or 2 times a week

    4) 3 or 4 times a week

    5) Daily

14. How often do you encourage your child to go to the library?

    1) Just once in a while

    2) Once a month

    3) A couple of times a month

    4) Once a week

    5) 2 or more times a week

15. How often do you suggest that _____ watch some educational TV program such as

"Zoom" or "Electric Company" or "Kids are people too?"

    5) 2 or more times a week
    4) Once a week
    3) A couple of times a month
    2) Once a month
    1) Just once in a while

16. If _____ asks you a question you can't answer, how often do you direct him/her to a book or magazine or person that might have the answer?

    1) Never
    2) Seldom
    3) About half the time
    4) Often
    5) Almost always

17. When telling _____ how to do some new task, how often do you specifically explain what steps must come first, second, and third?

    1) Seldom
    2) Infrequently
    3) Sometimes
    4) Often
    5) Almost always

18. How often do you talk to _____ (for more than 10 minutes) about things he/she has seen on TV?

    1) Almost never
    2) 2 or 3 times a month
    3) 1 or 2 times a week
    4) 3 or 4 times a week
    5) Almost daily

19. How often does this family talk about famous Black people of the past or major events of Black history?

    5) Several times a week
    4) At least once a week
    3) 2 or 3 times a month
    2) About once a month
    1) Just once in a while

20. How often do you and _____ discuss his/her future–his/her educational plans, different kinds of jobs he/she might have?

    5) Several times a week
    4) At least once a week
    3) 2 or 3 times a month
    2) At least once a month
    1) Only once in a while

21. How often do you find the time and money to go out of your way so that _____ can experience something different from his normal routine (e.g., special site-seeing trip, going to a concert, play, or some other very special event)?

    1) Hardly ever
    2) 3 or 4 times a year
    3) At least once every other month
    4) Once a month
    5) 2 or more times a month

22. How often do you and _____ discuss the different ways that he/she might handle his/her money, or the different ways the family budget might be spent?

    5) Several times a week
    4) At least once a month
    3) 2 or 3 times a month
    2) At least once a month
    1) Only once in a while

23. When you have good reason to believe _____ has misbehaved, she/he is corrected or punished for:

    5) Both things you have seen and heard about
    4) Only things seen with your own eyes
    3) Most often for things seen by others
    2) Some of the things you see yourself, but you let a lot go by
    1) Just a few things

24. When the child does something good, he/she is praised or rewarded for

    5) Everything you see or hear about
    4) Anything which is especially good
    3) Only a very few especially good things
    2) Just a few of the things you see yourself
    1) Very few things; I expect _____ to know without being told

25. Some parents explain to children why they are being punished; others think the children should know without being told. When this child is punished, he/she is told why something is wrong or right:

    1) Very seldom
    2) Seldom
    3) Sometimes
    4) Often
    5) Very often

26. Parents often warn their children that they will be punished if they keep on doing something

wrong. When this child has been warned once, and keeps on doing something wrong, he is punished:

    1) Very seldom; I always give more than one warning
    2) Seldom
    3) Sometimes
    4) Often
    5) Almost always

27. When children are caught or punished for something wrong, they sometimes correct or try to correct their actions. Whenever this child tries to correct his ways, he is praised or rewarded:

    5) Almost always
    4) Often
    3) Sometimes
    2) Seldom
    1) Never

28. When children misbehave, parents punish them in different ways. Tell me how often you used each of the following methods of punishment with _____ during the past six months.

    Response Categories (Circle)
    1) Never or hardly ever
    2) About once a month
    3) 2 or 3 times a month
    4) At least once a week
    5) Several times a week

    A. Scolding or yelling
        1   2   3   4   5
    B. Spanking of slapping
        1   2   3   4   5
    C. Sending child to room
        1   2   3   4   5
    D. Taking away privileges
        1   2   3   4   5
    E. Talking things over
        1   2   3   4   5

29. Now, would you tell me about the methods you use to reward _____ when he/she has done something well or special. How often did you use each of the following methods of reward with _____ during the past six months?

    Response Categories (Circle)
    1) Never or hardly ever
    2) About once a month
    3) 2 or 3 times a month

    4) At least once a week
    5) Several times a week

    A. Kissing and hugging
        1   2   3   4   5
    B. Giving him/her a gift or special privilege
        1   2   3   4   5
    C. In _____'s presence, boasting about his/her accomplishments to others
        1   2   3   4   5
    D. Praising him/her
        1   2   3   4   5
    E. Not making a big deal out of it
        1   2   3   4   5

Section C (Parent as Allocator and Arbitrator)

30. How much of the daily care and supervision of your children must you do yourself?

    5) Almost all of it
    4) Most of it
    3) About half of it
    2) A little of it
    1) Very little of it

31. How do you feel about the amount of responsibility you have for the children's care?

    5) Frequently feel it is too much
    4) Often feel it is too much
    3) Occasionally feel it is too much
    2) A little of it
    1) Almost always feel good about it

32. How much of an effort is it to care for the children?

    1) Very easy
    2) Easy
    3) Somewhat easy
    4) Not too difficult
    5) Very difficult

33. How well do you think you manage to meet the needs of each child?

    1) Very well
    2) Fairly well
    3) Sometimes I do, sometimes I can't
    4) Not too well
    5) Poorly

34. Do you feel your management of the children's needs should be improved?

    1) Not at all

2) A little
3) Somewhat
4) Quite a bit
5) A great deal

35. Do you feel your efforts are appreciated by your children?
   5) Not at all
   4) A little
   3) Somewhat
   2) Quite a bit
   1) A great deal

36. How much cooperation do you get at home?
   1) A great deal
   2) Quite a bit
   3) Some
   4) A little
   5) Very little

37. In general, do you think you get as much cooperation at home as others get at theirs?
   5) Much less
   4) Somewhat less
   3) About the same
   2) Somewhat more
   1) Much more

38. How often do you feel "pulled" between the need to spend your time with the children and the need to spend your time doing something else?
   5) Almost always
   4) Quite often
   3) Sometimes
   2) Once in a while
   1) Hardly ever

39. In general, do you think your home and family life need improvement?
   1) Not at all
   2) A little
   3) Some
   4) Quite a bit
   5) A great deal

40. In general, to what extent do some of your children require more of your time and attention than other of your children?
   0) Not applicable - only one child
   1) All require about the same
   2) Some require a little more
   3) Some require somewhat more

4) Some require quite a bit more
5) Some require a great deal more

41. How often does _____ feel she/he is getting her/his "fair share" of your time and attention–all things considered?
   5) Almost always
   4) Most times
   3) Sometimes
   2) Once in a while
   1) Hardly ever

42. How much agreement is there between you and _____ about the "fairness" of his/her share of clothing and toys?
   1) Hardly any
   2) Only a little
   3) Some
   4) Quite a bit
   5) A great deal

43. Children of different ages have different privileges and responsibilities and different things they can and cannot do. In general, to what extent do your children seem to understand why there are differences in what older and younger children can and cannot do?
   1) Hardly ever
   2) Only a little
   3) Some
   4) Quite a bit
   5) A great deal

44. Children frequently argue with each other and when they do, parents often do different things at different times. Tell me how often you do each of the following:
   Response Categories (Circle)
   1) Hardly ever
   2) Once in a while
   3) Sometimes
   4) Quite often
   5) Almost always

A. Don't find out what the problem is–I just order them to stop arguing–or else.
    1   2   3   4   5

B. Find out what the problem is, and then I order them to stop arguing.
    1   2   3   4   5

C. Find out what the problem is, and then I solve the problem for them.

    1   2   3   4   5

D. Find out what the problem is, and then I suggest different ways they can solve it.

    1   2   3   4   5

E. Find out what the problem is, and then I tell them to find a solution.

    1   2   3   4   5

F. Ignore the argument.

    1   2   3   4   5

45. Children and adults also have disagreements. Tell me how often you do each of the following when _____ disagrees with some other adult.

Response Categories (Circle)

1) Hardly ever
2) Once in a while
3) Sometimes
4) Quite often
5) Almost always

A. Take aside and remind him/her that adults are to be respected and obeyed no matter what.

    1   2   3   4   5

B. Take the adult aside and get a better understanding of his/her feelings.

    1   2   3   4   5

C. Take the adult aside and give him/her a better understanding of _____'s feelings.

    1   2   3   4   5

D. Take sides with either the adult or _____ while the disagreement is going on.

    1   2   3   4   5

E. While the disagreement is going on, try to explain to one of them how the other feels –but don't take sides.

    1   2   3   4   5

F. Do nothing–let them work it out.

    1   ?   3   4   5

Section D (Parent as Facilitators)

46. In general, what do you think about people belonging to organizations?

1) Of no importance
2) Somewhat unimportant

3) Somewhat important
4) Quite important
5) Of greatest importance

47. To what extent do you encourage _____ to participate in one or more youth organizations.

1) Not at all
2) A little
3) Somewhat
4) Quite a bit
5) A great deal

48. Would you tell me the names of all the youth organizations and activities in which _____ participates (e.g., church group or choir, scouts, organized basketball team, school clubs, etc.). (List these below)

49. Sometimes parents need assistance with their children. Sometimes other people can be more helpful to children than can their parents. The next series of questions ask about ways that other adults help _____. For each question how often help is requested or given:

Response Categories (Circle)

1) Just once in a while
2) About once a month
3) 2 or 3 times a month
4) About once a week
5) 2 or more times a week

How often do you call upon family members (other than spouse)?:

A. To have a talk with _____ when he/she seems very upset about something.

    1   2   3   4   5

B. To help with his/her school work.

    1   2   3   4   5

C. To take _____ on a special outing.

    1   2   3   4   5

D. To give _____ some sense of direction (i.e., different ways _____ can use his/her time and why).

    1   2   3   4   5

E. To motivate and inspire _____; give him/her a sense of what he/she can do and achieve when grown up.

    1   2   3   4   5

F. To teach _____ some skill or task.

    1   2   3   4   5

G. To share some special knowledge or information with _____ .

    1   2   3   4   5

H. To punish or reward_____ .

    1   2   3   4   5

50. Who are these family members you call upon? Please tell me their first name, their relationship to _____, whether they are male and female, and their approximate age.

Name   Relationship   sex   age

51. How often do you call upon your friends or neighbors?:

A. To have a talk with _____ when he/she seems very upset about something

    1   2   3   4   5

B. To help with his/her schoolwork.

    1   2   3   4   5

C. To take _____ on a special outing

    1   2   3   4   5

D. To give_____ some sense of direction (i.e., different ways _____ can use his/her time and why).

    1   2   3   4   5

E. To motivate and inspire _____; give him/her a sense of what he/she can do and achieve when grown up.

    1   2   3   4   5

F To teach _____ some skill or task.

    1   2   3   4   5

G. To share some special knowledge or information with _____.

    1   2   3   4   5

H. To punish or reward _____.

    1   2   3   4   5

52. Please tell me who these friends and neighbors are. Would you tell me their first name, whether they are your friend or neighbor, how long you have known them, whether they are male or female, and their appropriate age?

Name   F or N   Yrs. Known
Sex   Age

Section E (Parent as Provider and Advocate)

53. How often do you participate in organizing or helping with the activities of those organizations your child belongs to?

0) Not applicable child belongs to no organizations
1) hardly ever
2) a few times a year
3) several times a year
4) about once a month
5) several times a year

54. How often do you participate in organizing or helping with the activities of those organizations your child belongs to?

0) Not applicable child belongs to no organizations
1) hardly ever
2) a few times a year
3) several times a year
4) about once a month
5) several times a month

55. How often do you take part in a community action or political activity which will benefit your children?

1) never or hardly ever
2) about once a year
3) several times a year
4) about once a month
5) several times a year

56. In general, how satisfied are you with the quality of teaching and education _____ is currently getting?

5) extremely satisfied
4) very satisfied
3) fairly satisfied
2) somewhat dissatisfied
1) very dissatisfied

57. Have you participated in organized discussions of school policy or planning: for example, desegregation plans, curriculum planning, discipline policy, the budget, election of board members?

1) never or hardly ever
2) a few times a year
3) several times a year
4) about once a month
5) several times a month

58. How much do you participate in the PTA or some other parent group at your child's school?

1) very active
2) active
3) somewhat active

4) somewhat inactive

5) inactive

59. How often do you visit your child's school?

1) never or hardly ever

2) 3 or 4 times a year

3) 4-6 times a year

4) about once a month

5) several times a month

60. How well, do you know your child's teacher?

1) hardly at all

2) little

3) somewhat

4) well

5) very well

61. During the past 12 months, how many times have you:

Response Categories

1) never

2) 1 or 2

3) 3 to 5

4) 6 to 8

5) 9 or more

A. Talked with _____'s teacher on the phone or at school?

    1   2   3   4   5

B. Talked with some other official at _____'s school (e.g., the principal, a social worker, a counselor, a psychologist)?

    1   2   3   4   5

C. Talked about _____ or some educational issue with a district wide school administrator?

    1   2   3   4   5

D. Attended a school board meeting?

    1   2   3   4   5

E. Talked with an elected/appointed school board member about _____ or some educational issue?

    1   2   3   4   5

Now I will ask you some questions about social service and community agencies. Such agencies include those that provide financial assistance (e.g., welfare department, veterans administration, government housing agencies and programs). Such agencies also include those that provide only services (e.g., mental health agencies, Red Cross, public health services, publicly funded health and dental clinics, YMCA, recreation centers and programs, legal aid, etc.)

62. During the past 12 months, from how many agencies have you or your family sought some kind of help in the form of *services* only?

1) none

2) 1 or 2

3) 3 or 4

4) 5 or 6

5) more than 6

63. In general, how important was it that you received the services that you and your family sought?

0) not applicable

1) unimportant

2) fairly unimportant

3) fairly important

4) very important

5) extremely important

64. During the past 12 months, how many visits did you or your family members have with the agency that services you or your family members the most?

0) not applicable

1) 1 or 2 visits

2) 3 or 4 visits

3) 5 or 6 visits

4) 7 to 12 visits

5) more than 12 visits

65. How satisfied were you with the quality of services received from that agency?

0) not applicable–did not seek such service

1) very dissatisfied

2) somewhat dissatisfied

3) fairly satisfied

4) very satisfied

5) extremely satisfied

66. In general, how do you feel about such social service agencies?

1) like very much

2) like quite a bit

3) like somewhat

4) dislike somewhat

5) dislike very much

67. During the past 12 months, from how many agencies have you or your family sought some kind of help in the form of *financial assistance*?

1) none
2) 1 or 2
3) 3 or 4
4) 5 or 6
5) more than 6

68. Does anyone in this household currently receive any of the following kinds of assistance?:

	no	yes
a. food stamps	—	—
b. social security benefits	—	—
c. veteran's benefits	—	—
d. old age pension (welfare)	—	—
e. A.D.C. (welfare)	—	—
f. disability benefits	—	—
g. unemployment compensation	—	—
h. reduce fee for babysitting	—	—

69. In general, how important to the wellbeing of the household is this assistance?

0) not applicable–don't receive such assistance
1) unimportant
2) fairly unimportant
3) fairly important
4) very important
5) extremely important

70. During the past 12 months , how many visits did you or your family members have with the agency that provides the most assistance?

0) not applicable
1) 1 or 2 visits
2) 3 or 4 visits
3) 5 or 6 visits
4) 7 or more visits

71. How satisfied were you with the service and assistance provided by that agency?

0) not applicable
1) very dissatisfied
2) somewhat dissatisfied
3) fairly satisfied
4) very satisfied
5) extremely satisfied

72. In general, how do you feel about agencies which provide such assistance?

1) dislike very much
2) dislike somewhat
3) like somewhat
4) like quite a bit
5) like very much

Appendix B

Coding Instructions

Part I

Items 1 **thru** 25 (5pt. scale)–PI of TSCS

Directions

1. Some of these items are constructed as **positive**, while others are constructed; as **negative**.

2. **Positive** items should be coded with the *original* score.

3. On **negative** items, all scores must be *reversed* before coding–i.e., scores transformed as follows:

5 _____ →1
4 _____ →2
3 _____ →3
2 _____ →4
1 _____ →5

4. Code **positive** items first, then code **negative** items.

Positive items	Negative items
1, 2, 4, 5, 7. 9, 10, 12, 17, 21	3, 6, 8, 11, 13, 14, 15, 16, 18, 19, 20, 22, 23, 24, 25

Items 1 **thru** 20 (T/F)–MAS (SF)

Directions

1. For some items, a positive (true) response is indicative of anxiety, while for other items, a negative (false) response is indicative of anxiety.

2. Responses are to be coded: 0 –not indicative of anxiety 1–indicative of anxiety

Codes

F = 1, T = 0: These are for items 1, 6, 8, 12
T = 1, F = 0: These are for items 2, 3, 4, 5, 7, 9, 10, 11, 13, 14, 15, 16, 17, 18, 19, 20

Part II
No coding categories developed to date

Part III

Items 1 thru 47
All items are precoded.

Item 48
Code **frequency** of number of activities and organizations related to
    a. church
    b. school
    c. other

Item 49a-h
Items are precoded.

Item 50
Code **frequency** of:
    a. Females < 18 years
    b. Males < 18 years
    c. Females $\geq$ 18 years
    d. Males $\geq$ 18 years

Items 51 a-h
Items are precoded.

Item 52
Code **frequency** of:
    a. (F/F) Female friends $\geq$ 18 years
    b. (F/M) Male friends $\geq$ 18 years
    c. (F/F) Female friends $\geq$ 18 years
    d. (F/M) Male friends $\geq$ 18 years
    e. (N/F) Female neighbors $\geq$ 18 years
    f. (N/M) Male neighbors $\geq$ 18 years
    g. (N/F) Female neighbors $\geq$ 18 years
    h. (N/M) Male neighbors $\geq$ 18 years

Items 53 **thru** 66
Items are precoded

Item 67
Codes
1 = No

2 = Yes

Items 68 **thru** 71
Items are precoded

(ESPC) Data sheet(1)

The following data sheets have been shortened due to space constraints. In their entirety, the sections (i.e. Parental sensitivity, parents personal competence, etc.) have all of the question numbers and corresponding answer choices.

ID# _____
Respondent _____

Part I: Parent's personal competence
    (sample of response format)
Personality Integration (25 items)
1.   1   2   3   4   5

Manifest Anxiety (20 items)
1.   0   1

Part II: Parental sensitivity
    (Record responses verbatim)
      1. Silent from school
      2. Stealing from wallet
      3. Smoking Marijuana
      4. Feeling stupid respondent
      5. Do you love me
      6. Black people doing wrong

Part III: Parental behavioral competence
(Parent as model) (12 items)
1.   1   2   3   4   5
(Parent as teacher) (17 items)
13.   1   2   3   4   5
(Parent as allocator and arbitrator) (15 items)
30.   1   2   3   4   5
(Parent as facilitator) (14 items)
46.   1   2   3   4   5
(Parent as provider and advocate) (12 items)
60a.   1   2   3   4   5

For additional information, contact:

Bertha G. Holliday, Ph.D.
1719 First St., NW
Washington, DC 20001
Telephone: (202) 336-6029
Fax: (202) 336-6040
E-mail: bgh.apa@email.apa.org

The Parental Belief Interview

Bertha Garrett Holliday and Berlinda Curbeam[1]

Abstract

This chapter describes the Parental Belief Interview (PBI), which is an instrument for assessing the manifest content of (Black) parents' beliefs (e.g., values, expectations) about childrearing and socialization. A rationale is presented for the PBI's development along with descriptions of the instrument's content and procedures. Various empirical characteristics of the PBI are presented, and related limitations and prospective uses are noted.

Rationale

Children are the objects of socialization, but parents are its subjects. For parents, socialization involves such phenomenological processes as using perceptions of their past and present experiences as a basis for projecting into the future, fashioning a vision of what life will be for their children, and determining what they as parents are both capable and able to do to best prepare their children for that future. Thus for parents, socialization is a phenomenon involving probability statement formulation, expectancies, preference identification, evaluation of resources and abilities, and strategy development. It is this constellation of processes that serves as referents for the concept of the parental beliefs.

Parents construct their socialization beliefs relative to a specific object (the child) and a specific set of circumstances (the situation). Sociologists Borhek and Curtis (1975) suggest that the definition of one's situation occurs in the context of history (that is, previous experiences of self and significant others) and is constrained by structurally imposed restrictions on alternative courses of action. Under such conditions, beliefs come to reside in groups or social organizations. Borhek and Curtis also note that when groups experience excessive restrictions and social isolation or insulation, individuals tend to be highly involved in group-centered activities. Such involvement serves to entangle and commit the individual to the group's belief system. Consequently, at the individual level, beliefs are highly pragmatic in character. Individuals may exhibit commitments to a belief, not only because of its personal utility to them, but also because of some necessity facing the group.

In a similar vein, anthropologist Ogbu (in press) observed that cultural differences exist in childrearing and socialization practices due to characteristic group differences in physical and social environments and technological and historical experiences. Such cultural differences lead different groups to prefer different cognitive and behavioral styles. According to Ogbu, when intergroup contact is characterized by dominant-subordinate relationships, the significance of such group differences is intensified and exaggerated. Consequently, the dominant group may impose restrictions on the subordinate group's social participation. In turn, the subordinate group may engage in cultural inversion, which may "lead to the emergence of an oppositional cultural frame of reference" (Ogbu, in press, p. 26). Ogbu's perspective suggests that certain child competencies and parenting strategies might be valued by a given group not only because these are deemed appropriate for their social- cultural situation, but also because these are deemed essential to the group's identity.

Such perspectives of belief are particularly provocative for issues of African American socialization. Research generally indicates that Black parents' socialization practices are non-normative and deleterious in their effects on child competence (Bartz & Levine, 1978; Hess, 1970; Kamii & Radin, 1967; McClelland, 1961). And social class variations in Black parents' childrearing attitudes are revealed as significant and systematic, but as somewhat different (i.e., less interclass variability) from those of White parents (e.g., Kohn, 1977; Tuddenham, Brooks, & Milkovich, 1974). No one has explained the racial peculiarities of these social class variations as other than a "race effect." However, the significant racial differences in socialization practices generally have been attributed to various motivation, linguistic, and cognitive deficits of individual Black parents. Such attributions reflect an individualistic-psychological perspective of belief. But a social perspective of belief (such as those of Borhek and Curtis, and Ogbu) suggests that these racial differences may be due to differences in environmental demands induced by historical racial-group differences in cultural and social participatory patterns.

The prevailing individualistic-psychological perspective of belief is associated with the assessment of parents' attitudes through use of predetermined sets of statements concerning childrearing practices, expectancies, and goals, to which parents indicate their agreement or disagreement. When used for comparative purposes across social groups and situations, this assessment approach facilitates our understanding of how belief systems differ with respect to a given set of objects and their attributes. But that is far different from determining that the attributes investigated and the differences observed are those that are phenomenologically most salient for each of the groups or situations. Nor do the results of such assessments inform us as to *how* those parents whose experiences, circumstances, and resources markedly deviate from American norms, attempt to successfully engage their childrearing and socialization tasks–and *why*.

In contrast to this normative methodological approach, the Parental Belief Interview (PBI) was developed as a procedure both for *inductively* deriving socially and culturally embedded systems of belief, and for assessing belief variations. Thus the PBI serves to advance our knowledge of both the varying content of parents' belief, and the differential functions such beliefs and related socialization practices serve in response to varying perceptions of social reality.

Conceptualization and Content

The Parental Belief Interview (PBI) consists of 22 items–9 of which are considered primary items. Fifteen of the items are open-ended, but five of these are field-coded into fixed categories. The remainder of the items have multiple-choice fixed response categories.

Conceptualization of the PBI (See Appendix A) was guided by Borhek and Curtis' (1975) theory of belief systems. Borhek and Curtis identify seven elements of a belief system. Five of those elements have been incorporated into a model of Black parental beliefs. The two other elements (criteria of validity and logic or relational rules between beliefs) were not incorporated because both are viewed as primarily theoretical in significance and frequently not explicitly known by the belief-holder. The five elements have been augmented by the element of "expectancies." According to our heuristic model, the five *dimensions* of parental belief system are:

1. **Values (VAL)**–implicit or explicit statements of what is good or bad and preferable;

2. **Substantive Beliefs and Perspective (SBP)**–statements of worldview and fact that are held with certainty and commitment; statements of where the belief system and/or the group that carries it stands in relation to other groups and worldviews;

3. **Expectancies (EXP)**–future-oriented subjective probability statements, i.e., statements of the likelihood of an occurrence;

4. **Prescriptions/Proscriptions (P/P)**–statements of action alternatives, policy recommendations, or norms; and

5. **Technology (TEC)**–statements of means to attain valued goals; (Modified from Borhek & Curtis, 1975).

Each interview item was developed in consideration of at least one of these dimensions. The PBI's nine primary items, in summary form, are:

1. Is there something different about being a Black parent instead of a White parent? (Probe.) [SBF, P/P]

2. Are there different things that Black children must learn that White children don't have to learn? (Probe.) [PSBF, P/P]

3. What are the three things most important for your child to know? [VAL, TEC]

4. What are the three things most important for your child to love? [VAL, P/P]

5. What are the three things most important for your child to do? [VAL, TEC]

6. What is the one thing you did *not* have as a child that you most want for your child? [VAL]

7. What is the one thing you *did* have as a child that you also most want for your child? [VAL]

8. What is your child's greatest weakness? [P/P, VAL]

9. What is your child's greatest strength? [P/P, VAL]

The PBI also includes items replicating the Kohn (1977) Parental Values Scale, and Radin's (1968, 1975) Future Expectations Scale (with modified response categories). The PBI additionally includes three experimental items for which coding categories have not as yet been developed.

Content Analysis Procedure

Subsequent to item construction, we developed procedures for content analysis of responses to the PBI's nine primary items. These procedures emphasized differences in the manifest content of responses, rather than differences in various inferred internal states of respondents (cf. Berelson, 1952; Gottschalk & Gleser, 1969; Marsden, 1965). Development of such procedures necessitated the administration of the PBI to a representative sample (selected through multistage stratified area sampling techniques) of 137 southern urban Black mothers of children ages 6 to 12 years. All of these mothers were screened to ensure that the target child of the interview had no physical, mental, or emotional disabilities. Interviews were individually administered in the mothers' homes by trained Black female interviewers.

After the PBI had been administered to these respondents, a 25% sample of protocols was randomly selected and used in developing a Belief Coding System (BCS). Through use of a reiterative procedure of conceptualization and classification, 45 content coding categories were defined. A summary guide to the BCS, including brief definitions of coding categories, is presented in Appendix B.

Coding procedures, PBI items, the Belief Coding System, and related information have been compiled in a 38-page code book (Holliday & Curbeam, 1983), which can be obtained from Holliday whose address is given at the end of this chapter. Use of this code book enables one to analyze citation frequencies of the BCS categories in two basic modes: One may analyze respondents' citation frequencies for any PBI item, or one may analyze respondents' citation frequencies for any BCS category across PBI items.

Empirical Characteristics

Intercoder reliability. Through use of the PBI codebook's detailed procedures, we obtained, among three coders, intercoder item reliabilities (number of agreements/total number of agreements and disagreements) that ranged from $r = 0.80$ to 0.96 with a mean of $r = 0.90$.

Content validity. This type of validity refers to the extent an instrument representatively samples its postulated content domain. Although it would be quite difficult to assess the extent to which PBI items solicit a representative sampling of the content of parental belief systems, one is able to assess the extent to which the BCS categories representatively sample that domain of concerns reflected in item responses. As previously noted, BCS categories were derived from conceptual and categorical analysis of a random 25% sample ($N = 35$) of interview protocols. When the BCS was applied to the total sample ($N = 137$), we were enabled to code responses into a total of 1,941 units of information. Only 48 (2.5%) of these units were coded in the "No Appropriate Category." Thus, 97.5% of the units of information were codable into one of the BCS categories. This indicates the high content validity of the BCS.

Factor structure. In line with social-cultural perspectives of beliefs, we sought to determine if we could derive a stable multiple factor structure of PBI responses. The frequency citations of the 20 most-cited BCS categories were submitted to a principal or common factor analysis with communalities estimated through iteration (Nie et al., 1975)[2]. These 20 categories accounted for 83% of the coded responses to the PBI's nine primary items. Both orthogonal and oblique solutions were obtained, each revealing the same stable structure[3]. The pattern matrix for the oblique rotation (simplest possible structure) is presented in Table 1. Six factors were extracted, each of which accounted for 10% to 27% of the variance in the BCS citation frequencies.

Correlations among the oblique factors ranged from $r = -0.22$ to $r = 0.14$. We previously have interpreted these factors as representing the major dimensions of Black maternal belief systems (Holliday, Henning, & Johnson, 1983).

Limitations and Uses

Although there exists some empirical evidence of the reliability and validity of the PBI and its BCS, additional confirmatory data are needed. For this reason, the authors encourage others to use this instrument. We especially encourage the PBI's use both on samples of Black mothers and fathers residing in various national regions and with multiracial and multigenerational samples. We also encourage its use in studies that include analyses of the PBI's (a) test-retest reliability, (b) its convergent and divergent validities, (c) its predictive and discriminant capacities, and (d) the stability of its factor structure. The PBI would be a most illuminating measure in studies of such substantive issues as childrearing, child development, and achievement; aspirations and expectations; family process and intervention; personality and social-class correlates.

Notes

1. Preparation of this manuscript and its research was supported by grants received by Bertha Holliday from the Peabody Professional Development Fund, the Vanderbilt University Research Council, and the Postdoctoral Fellowships for Minorities Program funded by the Ford Foundation and administered by the National Research Council.

The authors wish to acknowledge Rita Clairborne Henning's assistance with data collection and Deborah J. Johnson's assistance with data analysis.

2. In consideration of the character of the data matrix—that is, every mother did not necessarily express concern in all of the 20 belief categories—no adjustments or estimates were made for missing data. Instead, zeros were inserted in missing data cells. Rummel (1970) has indicated that this is an acceptable practice when factors are extracted from a correlation matrix rather than directly from the data matrix.

Table 1. Factor Structure of PBI Responses

| | Pattern Matrix of Common (Oblique) Factors | | | | | |
| | 1 | 2 | 3 | 4 | 5 | 6 |
	Personal Orientation	Social Orientation	Behavior (Engagement vs. Accommodation)	Developmental Locus (Self vs. Family)	Social Achievement	Value Orientation (Secular vs. Religious
Heritage	*0.74*	-0.01	0.12	0.07	-0.07	0.25
Authenticity	*0.47*	0.11	0.11	0.08	-0.03	0.06
Self-Esteem	*0.46*	-0.01	-0.08	-0.11	0.06	-0.11
Ecological Insufficiency	0.01	*0.54*	0.19	-0.08	*0.65*	-0.33
Humanism	0.11	*0.48*	-0.07	0.04	0.04	0.08
Maturity	-0.05	*0.42*	0.19	-0.16	-0.18	-0.06
Obedience/Discipline	-0.21	*0.46*	*-0.51*	0.23	-0.01	0.06
Social Competence	0.02	0.03	*0.39*	0.00	0.04	0.02
Social Interaction	-0.08	0.04	*0.38*	0.18	-0.09	0.13
Family Connectedness	0.06	-0.06	-0.08	*-0.64*	0.08	0.07
Intellectualism	0.17	-0.10	-0.16	*0.42*	0.08	-0.01
Educational Achvm't	-0.00	-0.06	-0.00	-0.00	*0.38*	0.10
Religion	-0.13	0.04	-0.06	-0.03	-0.03	*-0.36*
Occupational Success	-0.18	0.09	-0.12	-0.26	0.26	*0.51*
General Success	0.31	-0.14	-0.05	0.00	0.11	-0.27
Materialism	-0.30	-0.20	0.13	0.18	0.08	0.11
Actualization	0.28	-0.07	-0.03	0.08	0.11	-0.23
Projected Self	-0.05	0.10	-0.29	0.14	0.07	0.06
Dependence	0.05	0.13	0.34	0.07	0.19	0.03
Integrity	0.10	0.12	-0.14	-0.02	-0.10	-0.05
% of Total Variance	27.2	20.5	17.7	14.4	10.3	9.8

Note. Interpretable factor loadings of .35 or more are italicized.

3. The initial decision rule for determining the number of factors for extraction and rotation was in accordance with standard procedures: The number of factors extracted equaled that number of variables with eigenvalues greater than 1.0. Eight factors were extracted through use of this rule. However, two of these were unique factors on which one variable had a high loading and all other variables had loadings of less than .30. Rummel (1970) has noted that such factors are of little concern in a common factor analysis and can be discarded. Consequently, the analysis was repeated with a limit of six extracted factors.

References

Bartz, K. W., & Levine, E. D. (1978). Child rearing by Black parents: A description and comparison to Anglo and Chicano parents. *Journal of Marriage and the Family, 40*(4), 709-719.

Berelson, B. (1952). *Content analysis in communication research.* Glencoe, IL: Free Press.

Borhek, J. T., & Curtis, R. F. (1975). *A sociology of belief.* New York: John Wiley & Sons.

Gottschalk, L. A., & Gleser, G. C. (1969). *The measurement of psychological states through content analysis of verbal behavior.* Berkeley: University of California Press.

Hess, R. D. (1970). The transmission of cognitive strategies in poor families: The socialization of apathy and underachievement. In V. Allen (Ed.), *Psychological factors in poverty* (pp. 73-92). Chicago: Markham.

Holliday, B. G., & Curbeam, B. (1983). *Manual of instructions for coding the Parental Belief Interview.* Unpublished manuscript, Peabody College of Vanderbilt University, Nashville, TN.

Holliday, B. G., Henning, R. C., & Johnson, D. J. (1983, May). *Black maternal beliefs.* Paper presented at the Groves Conference on Marriage and the Family, Freeport, Grand Bahama Island.

Kamii, C. K., & Radin, N. L. (1967). Class differences in the socialization practices of Negro mothers. *Journal of Marriage and the Family, 29*(2), 302-310.

Kohn, M. L. (1977). *Class and conformity: A study in value* (2nd ed.). Chicago: University of Chicago Press.

Marsden, C. (1965). Content-analysis studies of therapeutic interviews: 1954-1964. *Psychological Bulletin, 68,* 298-321.

McClelland, D. (1961). *The achieving society.* Princeton, NJ: Van Nostrand.

Nie, N. H., Hull, C. H., Jenkins, J. G., Steinbreener, K., & Bent, D. H. (1975). *Statistical package for the social sciences* (2nd ed.).New York: McGraw-Hill.

Ogbu, J. U. (in press). Between phylogeny and ontogeny: Cultural diversity and human competence. In *Development and assessment of human competence.* Mediax Interactive Technologies.

Radin, N., & Epstein, A. (1975). *Final report: Observed paternal behavior with preschool children (Appendix).* Unpublished report submitted to the National Institute of Child Health and Development, Bethesda, MD.

Radin, N., & Sonquist, H. (1968). *Ypsilanti Public Schools, Gale Preschool Program: Final report.* Unpublished manuscript.

Rummel, R. J. (1970). *Applied factor analysis.* Evanston, IL: Northwestern University Press.

Tuddenham, R. D., Brooks, J., & Milkovich, L. (1974). Mothers' reports of behavior of ten-year-olds: Relationships with sex, ethnicity, and mother's education. *Developmental Psychology, 10,* 959-995.

Appendix A

The Parental Belief Interview

Q1 (Dim: SBF, P/P)
"Do you believe there is something different about being a Black parent rather than a White parent? Are there different things that Black parents must do or teach their children that White parents *don't* have to do or teach?"

This item requires *two* (2) levels of coding:

Level 1–Are Black Parents Different? Code the substantive response to the item, i.e., whether or not interviewee believes there is something distinctive about being a Black parent. The substantive response should be coded through use of *one* (1) of the following categories.

Code #	Category	Critical Criteria
1	No	The parent responds "No" and adds no qualification or restriction to that response.
2	Yes	The parent responds "Yes" and adds no qualification or restriction to that response.
3	Ambivalent	These responses generally take the form of "No, but..." A definite "Yes" or "No" answer is given, but a qualifying or restrictive statement is attached to that response.

9   "Don't Know"
       or No Response

Level 2–What is Different (or Similar) About Black Parents? What Must They Do or Teach?
Code the *verbal content* of the response:

1) Code a maximum of *six* (6) idea units.
2) Use the Belief Coding System (BCS).

Note. Most (but not all) responses will be in the domains of
—Success
—Personal Orientation
—Social Orientation
—Affective/Behavioral Attributes

Q2   (Dim: SBF, P/P)
"Do you believe there are different things that Black children must learn that White children *don't* have to learn?"

This item requires *two* (2) levels of coding:

Level 1–Do Black Children Learn Different Things? Code the substantive response to the item, i.e., whether or not Black children must learn different things, through use of *one* (1) of the categories described in Q1.

Level 2–What must Black children learn? Regardless of Level 1 responses, code the *verbal content*:

1) Code a maximum of *six* (6) idea units.
2) Use the Belief Coding System (BCS).

Note. Most (but not all) responses will be in the domains of
—Self
—Success

Q3   (Dim, Val, Tech)
"All parents believe there are certain things in life that are very important for their children....Tell me three things that you feel are most important for ___(child)___ to *know* when s/he is grown up?"

Code *verbal content*:

1) Code each of the three responses in the order it was stated by the interviewee.
2) Code through use of the Belief Coding System (BCS).

Note. Most (but not all) responses will be in the domains of
—Success
—Personal Orientation
—Social Orientation

Q4   (Dim: Val, P/P)
"Now would you tell me three things that you believe are most important for ___(child)___ to *love* when s/he is grown up?"

Code *verbal content*:

1) Code each of the three responses in the order it was stated by the interviewee.
2) Code through use of the Belief Coding System (BCS).

Note. Most (but not all) responses will be in the domains of
—Self
—Affiliation and Love
—Social Orientation

Q5   (Dim: Val, Tec)
"What are three things you believe are most important for ___(child)___ to be able to *do* when s/he is grown up?"

Code *verbal content*:

1) Code each of the three responses in the order it was stated by the interviewee.
2) Code through use of the Belief Coding System (BCS).

Note. Most (but not all) responses will be in the domains of
—Self
—Affiliation and Love
—Social Orientation

Q6   (Dim: Val)
"Many of the things parents want for their children are things that they did or did not have when they themselves were children. Would you tell me the *one* thing you did *not* have as a child which you most wish ___(child)___ to have."

Code *verbal content*:

1) Use the Belief Coding System (BCS).

Note. Most (but not all) responses will be in the domains of
—Self
—Affiliation and Love
—Social Orientation
Q7   (Dim: Val)
"What is the one thing you *did* have as a child that you most wish ___(child)___ to also have?"

Code *verbal content*:

1) Use the Belief Coding System (BCS).
Note. Most (but not all) responses will be in the domains of
—Affiliation and Love
—Social Orientation
Q8   (Dim: P/P, Val)
"All parents know their children's strengths and weaknesses in dealing with life. What is the one thing about ___(child)___ that worries you the most? That you consider to be his/her biggest weakness?"

Code *verbal content*:

1) Code "99" –if parent answers "None" or indicates child has no weaknesses; otherwise--
2) Use Belief Coding System.
Note. Most (but not all) responses will be in the domains of
Affective/Behavioral Attributes
Q9   (Dim: P/P, Val)
"What is the one thing about ___(child)___ you are most proud of? That you consider to be his/her biggest strength?"

Code *verbal content*:

Note. Most (but not all) responses will be in the domains of
—Personal Orientation
—Affective/Behavioral Attributes

Kohn (1977) Parental Values Scale

"Here is a card which lists different qualities that children have. Please read everything on the card."

01) That he/she has good manners
02) That he/she tries hard to succeed
03) That he/she is honest
04) That he/she is neat and clean
05) That he/she has good sense and sound judgement
06) That he/she has self-control
07) That he (or she) acts like a boy (or girl)
08) That he/she gets along well with other children
09) That he/she obeys his/her parents well
10) That he/she is responsible
11) That he/she is considerate of others
12) That he/she is interested in how and why things happen
13) That he/she is a good student
Q10   (Dim: Val)
"Tell me which three qualities you feel are *most* desirable for a boy/girl of ___(child)___'s age to have?"
Q11*   (Dim: Val)
"Which one of these is the *most* desirable of all?"
Q12   (Dim: Val)
"Which *three* of the qualities are *least* desirable for a boy/girl of ___(child)___'s age to have?"
Q13*   (Dim: Val)
"Which *one* of these is these is the least desirable of all?"
Q14*   (Dim: Val)
"Now would you tell me how much importance you have placed on each of the qualities in raising ___(child)___? That is, has the quality been:"
1) Not important
2) Somewhat important
3) Quite important
4) Extremely important
13 responses (1/quality)
*Item for Kohn's revised scoring procedure; not on all forms of the PBI.

Radin's (1968, 1975) Future Expectations Scale (Modified)

Q15   (Dim: Val)
"How much schooling would you like to ___(child)___ receive?"
6) Graduate or professional school
5) College graduate

4) Attend college

3) Technical/trade training

2) "Complete high school" or "High school"

1) Some high school

Q16   (Dim: P/P)

"What is the least amount of education you think ____(child)____ must have?"

6) Graduate from college

5) Attend college

4) "Complete high school" or "High school"

3) 11th grade

2) 10th grade

1) 9th grade or less

Q17   (Dim: Exp)

"Considering his/her abilities, grades, interests, and the family's financial situation, how much schooling do you actually expect ____(child)____ to receive?"

6) Graduate or professional school

5) College graduate

4) Attend college

3) Technical/trade training

2) "Complete high school" or "High school"

1) Attend high school

Q18   (Dim: Val)

"What kind of work would you like ____(child)____ to do when s/he is grown up?"

Score according to school requirements for job.

1) Less than high school completion (e.g., construction or domestic work)

2) High school education (e.g., skilled labor, office work, clerical)

3) More than high school but less than college degree (e.g., nurse, technician)

4) College education

5) Graduate or professional school

Q19   (Dim: Exp)

"Considering his/her abilities, grades, interests, and the family's financial situation, what type of work do you actually expect ____(child)____ to be doing when he/she grows up?"

[Same scoring categories as Q18]

Q20   (Dim: P/P)

"What kind of work would you not like ____(child)____ to do?"

[Same scoring categories as Q18]

Q21**   (Dim: Val, SBP)

"Why did you choose to name your child ____(child's name)____?"

Code *verbal content*:

1) Code a *maximum* of *six* (6) idea-units.

2) Use the Belief Coding System (BCS).

Q22**   (Dim: SBP, EXP)

"What did ____(child)____'s birth mean to you and the family?"

Code *verbal content*:

1) Code a *maximum* of six (6) idea-units.

2) Use the Belief Coding System.

Q23**   (Dim: Exp, P/P)

"Where is a card with different statements about success. In order of importance, with 1 as highest, 10 as lowest, list those items which will have the most positive influence on ____(child)____'s success in this society."

____A. Working and living in an integrated neighborhood.

____B. Working and living in a predominantly White neighborhood.

____C. Working and living in a predominantly Black neighborhood.

____D. Job with high status (doctor, lawyer, etc.).

____E. Job that pays good money (plumber, factory worker, construction worker).

____F. Good marriage and family life.

____G. Good ties with church and community.

____H. Good education.

____I. Strong awareness and pride in being Black.

____J. Little concern about being Black.

Item type: Fixed category.

**An experimental item; not on all forms of the PBI.

Appendix B

Summary Guide to the Belief Coding System (BCS)

Code #	Category	Critical Criteria
01	No response or "Don't know"	
05	No appropriate category	

Domain of Self

11	Self-Image & Esteem	Evaluation of self
12	Authenticity	Reflective knowledge of self; clarity of one's goals and values; acceptance of self
13	Projected Self	Presentation of self to other; personal appearance; public demeanor

Domain of Affliation and Love

21	Family Unity	Obligation and responsibility to family; value of family and its maintenance
22	Family Connectedness	Affective bonds among family members positive interchange, mutuality, reciprocity, nurturance
23	Communalism	Affiliative value (responsibility and obligation) of friends and neighbors specifically
24	Ethnic Heritage	Affiliative value of the ethnic group; knowledge and pride of one's ethnic group/community; racism
25	Affiliation-Other	Affiliative value of *other* explicit social units (e.g., country) not addressed in 21-24

Domain of Success & Achievement

31	Educational Achievement	Accomplishment (or behaviors related to) the educational sphere
32	Occupational Success	Accomplishment (or behaviors supporting) in the occupational sphere
33	Social Achievement	Accomplishment in the sphere of civic/social affairs
34	P/K/A Achievement	Accomplishment in the areas of physical and kinesthetic activities and aesthetic endeavors
35	General Success	Personal dispositions and behaviors underlying & prerequisite for achievement/success (e. g. motivation)
36	Success Impediments	Bad habits at odds with those needed for success; failure to engage in success related behaviors; precocious event that may impede success
37	Success-Other	Accomplishment of a specific kind not addressed in 31-35

Domain of Personal Orientation

4 1	Actualization	Desired values and goals that are abstract in nature; teleological statements of the goal of individual experience; state of being

(table continues)

Code #	Category	Critical Criteria
42	Intellectualism	Capacity to expand one's knowledge of people, places and things
43	Integrity	Dispositions and behaviors reflecting one's moral principles (e.g., fairness, honesty, sincerity)
44	Maturity	Adult-like behaviors involving intellectual reflection, responsibility, self-guidedness and independence
45	Personal Needs	Concern for personal needs, i.e., needs having great variation in strength among individuals (e.g., privacy)

Domain of Social Orientation

Code #	Category	Critical Criteria
51	Survival-Basic Needs	Basic survival needs, i.e., food, clothing, shelter, health
52	Survival-Social Competence	Survival in the social world; understanding and resourcefulness necessary for active coping in broad social arenas
53	Materialism	Value of material goods and possessions
54	Religiosity	Value of a supreme being and related rituals; one's relationship with same
55	Humanism	Social empathy and respect; understanding, respecting and humanely interacting with other/all groups of people
56	Ecological Insufficiency	Specific stresses and deficiencies in the social environment with emphasis on inadequate resources, insufficient social support and role overload.

Domain of Functional Skills

Code #	Category	Critical Criteria
6 I	Communication	Skill (level or quality) in modes of information exchange (e.g., talking, listening, writing)
62	Domesticity	Household tasks and skills (e.g., cooking, sewing, cleaning, childcare)
63	Financial	Behaviors and skills related to money
64	Manual/Technical	Behaviors and skills related to tools and technical knowledge
65	Social Interaction	Social interaction skills (cooperate, coordinate, participate) with others in general
66	Skills-Other	Specific functional skill not addressed in 61-65

Domain of Affective/Behavioral Attributes

Code #	Category	Critical Criteria
71	Dependence	Deficits in autonomy, self-guidedness and maturity
72	Even–Tempered	Consistency, predictability and temperance of mood
73	Habits	Characteristic, repetitive behaviors
74	Mischievous	Playfulness–often to the point of annoyance
75	Obedience & Discipline	Behavior involving the acceptance or use of authority
76	Selfishness	Inordinate concern with oneself and one's desires
77	Stubborness	Rigidly unyielding determination; defiance of authority and reason

(table continues)

Code #	Category	Critical Criteria
78	Talkativeness	Quantity or frequency of talk
79	Tenderheartedness	Disposition and behavior reflecting warmth, nurturance, affection, lovingness and sensitivity of others' feelings
81	Temperamental	Excessive sensitivity; impulsive changes of mood
82	Withdrawn	Tendency to be unspontaneous and unexpressive in affect; emotional and social detachment

For additional information, contact:

Bertha Garrett Holiday, Ph.D.
1719 First Street, NW
Washington, DC 20001
Telephone: (202) 336-6029
Fax: (202) 336-6040
E-mail: bgh.apa@email.apa.org

The Parental Questionnaire on Children's Behavioral Competence

Bertha Garrett Holliday

Abstract

The Parental Questionnaire on Children's Behavioral Competence (PQCBC) is a questionnaire interview for use in assessing, through parental report, the frequency and effectiveness of African American children's (ages 6 through 12 years) behavioral skills in the home and neighborhood settings. The conceptualization and content of the PQCBC are described. The PQCBC's empirical characteristics are noted and related data are provided. The PQCBC's past and future uses are identified.

Rationale

Until recently, most research on African American children's development was deficit-oriented. Consequently, most African American child development research is distinguished by its concern with limited numbers and types of developmental outcomes (e.g., linguistic ability or cognitive process). These outcomes typically are assessed under highly controlled laboratory-type conditions through use of either experimental tasks or brief observation. Under such conditions, African American children's behaviors frequently are compared to those of Anglican American children, and consequently are viewed as deficit and non-normative.

But increasingly, major criticisms are leveled against such procedures. In general, these criticisms relate to the procedures' predictive ability and ecological validity: are the developmental processes assessed, the procedures for assessment, and the assessment settings ones that can result in accurate predictions of the levels and types of developmental processes and skills that African American children routinely demonstrate in multiple settings, and do these procedures assess those culturally unique dimensions of African American children's development?

In contrast to such research procedures, which are concerned primarily with methods for scientific manipulation and control, an alternative research approach is emerging. This approach is concerned primarily with describing and analyzing African American children's competencies and the ecologies of their lives (cf. Ladner, 1971; Ogbu, 1981; Slaughter, 1977; Spencer, Brookins, & Allen, 1985; Wilkinson & O'Connor, 1977). This research approach is distinguished by the

433

presence of two or more of the following characteristics: (a) a substantive focus on psychological and behavioral strengths; (b) adoption of an ecological perspective as reflected by the absence of laboratory tasks, the use and investigation of multiple indicators of environment, the investigation of multiple attributes and behaviors across two or more settings, and an emphasis on interactive (rather than cause-effect) relations; and (c) abandonment of the racial comparative design. It is a developmental research approach that quite self-consciously is concerned with changes over time both in children's competencies, and in the manner in which children seek to effectively interact with, and meet the demands of different and variable social environments.

In concord with this emerging research approach, the Parental Questionnaire on Children's Behavioral Competence (PQCBC) was designed for use in assessing, through parental report, the frequency and effectiveness of African American children's behavioral skills in different settings.

Instrument Description

The Parental Questionnaire on Children's Behavioral Competence (PQCBC) is an interview questionnaire for use with mothers and fathers of children ages 6 to 12 years. A copy of the PQCBC is provided in Appendix A.

Instrument Content

The PQCBC consists of 150 items, each with fixed-response (3) categories. These response categories are indicative of latent, emergent, and mastered behavior (relative to the frequency and/or effectiveness of a child's demonstration of the item's target behavior). Responses to these items represent parents' perceptions of their children's behavioral competencies as typically demonstrated in the two settings of home and neighborhood.

Due to the broad range of behaviors assessed, items were drawn from varied sources (e.g., Gesten, 1976; Lambert, Windmiller, & Cole, 1974; Mercer & Lewis, 1979; Stott & Sykes, 1967). Other items were newly developed. In developing new items, we were careful to include

questions on various behaviors that research studies (e.g., Kochman, 1977; Young, 1970) suggest are somewhat unique to African American children (e.g., the making-up of chants and rhymes, playing the dozens, caretaking of younger siblings). Special care also was taken to ensure that the PQCBC's items not only assessed a broad domain of behavioral skills, but also that the skills assessed were of varying difficulty commensurate with the wide developmental variations expected among school-age children. In addition, all items were selected or developed to assess skill demonstration either in the home setting or in the neighborhood setting (denoted by code on the PQCBC). Also, as a means of facilitating comparisons of perceived child skills across these two settings, certain items (also denoted by code) are asked in the context of both settings. Thus, in constructing the PQCBC, we attempted to develop an instrument that incorporated behavioral, developmental, cultural, and ecological considerations.

The PQCBC items were conceptualized in terms of three major behavioral skill areas. Within each area, substantive types of behavioral skills were identified. PQCBC items are grouped by these behavioral skill areas and types. The PQCBC's major skill areas and their related behavioral skill types are as follow:

1. *Functional life skills* (84 items) are defined as the ability to effectively use and manipulate objects, technology, and social instruments encountered in day-to-day living. The major types of behavioral skills assessed are (a) mobility in space, (b) communication, (c) management and independence, (d) caretaking and supervising, and (e) consumerism.

2. *Interpersonal skills* (29 items) are defined as the ability to become a participant, to demonstrate leadership, and to cooperate and collaborate with others. The related types of behavioral skills assessed are (a) the quality and frequency of interactions with adults, and (b) the quality and frequency of interactions with siblings and peers.

3. *Problem-solving skills* (37 items) are defined as the ability to recognize, adapt to, circumvent, or change an encountered predicament. The

related types of behavioral skills assessed are (a) personal problem solving, (b) interpersonal problem solving, (c) technical problem solving, and (d) social problem solving.

Prior to the initial administration of the PQCBC, all of its items were submitted to a panel of judges for assignments to behavioral skill types and settings (home or neighborhood). The PQCBC also was pilot-tested and revised. This instrument, when individually administered as an interview questionnaire, requires 45 to 90 minutes to complete. Of course, it is expected that this time would be reduced by half when the PQCBC is individually or group administered as a questionnaire.

Empirical Characteristics

Reliability. Two major reliability studies have been conducted. On a sample of 44 African American parents of children ages 9 and 10 years, a Spearman-Brown (split-half) reliability was found of $r = 0.82$. Correlations between total PQCBC scores and scores on the 11 behavioral skill types ranged from $r = 0.11$ to $r = 0.81$. All but three (technical problem solving, interpersonal adult, and social problem solving) of these correlations were significant at the level of $p < 0.05$.

A second reliability study was conducted on the PQCBC responses of 90 representatively sampled African American parents of children ages 6, 7, 8, 11, and 12 years. On this sample, we obtained a Cronbach alpha coefficient of $r = 0.92$. A repeated measures ANOVA (respondents x items) revealed a significant effect of items controlling for the effect of respondents' individual differences ($F = 49.55$, $p < 0.001$). This suggests that response differences may not be readily attributed solely to error associated with parent's experiential differences. Correlation analyses on this sample's responses indicated that less than 10% of the items demonstrated an item-total correlation of $r < 0.05$. Over 66% of the items demonstrated an item-total correlation of $r > 0.20$.

Collectively, data from the two reliability studies suggest the PQCBC is a highly reliable instrument in terms of its conceptual-structural characteristics, the consistency of its content sampling, and the accuracy of its scores.

Discriminative capabilities. As previously noted, the PQCBC is designed to assess parents' perceptions of various child behaviors that encompass a broad range of developmental difficulty. In order to assess the extent to which individual PQCBC items are able to discriminate by age of child, a one-way ANOVA (across three child age groups) was conducted on each PQCBC item response of 65 representatively sampled African American parents. These parents had children who were either 6, 7, or 8 years of age. Significant differences ($p < 0.10$) among the child age groups were found on 31 items (21%). Two-thirds of these items were significant at the level of $p < 0.05$. It should be remembered that PQCBC items concern behaviors of children ages 6 through 12 years. Consequently, we consider the one-way ANOVA findings on 6-, 7-, and 8-year olds as indicative of the adequacy of PQCBC items to make developmental (age) discriminations.

T-test analyses also were conducted on each of the PQCBC items. These analyses involved four age groups: responses of parents of (a) 6-year olds ($N = 29$); (b) 7-year olds ($N = 19$); (c) 8-year olds ($N = 17$) and, (d) 9- and 10-year olds ($N = 44$). Within age groups, high- and low-competence subgroups were defined by median splits on total PQCBC scores. T-tests on each PQCBC item were conducted between competence subgroups for each age group. The following significant mean score differences ($p < 0.05$) were noted: Between the 6-year-old subgroups, 49 items (33%) significantly differed; among the 7-year-olds, 52 items (35%) significantly differed; 20 items (13%) differed significantly among 8-year-olds; and 40 items (27%) significantly differed among 9- and 10-year olds. In line with intended developmental thrusts of the PQCBC, *none* of the PQCBC items exhibited significant mean subgroup score differences *across* all four age groups.

Together, the ANOVA and t-test analyses suggest the great extent to which individual PQCBC items demonstrate discriminant capacity relative to both children's developmental status (age) and children's skill abilities.

Validity. During its early stages of development, the PQCBC included items analogous to those items numbered 60 through 89 on the Vineland Social Maturity Scale (Doll, 1947). These Vineland items assess skills of children ages 6 through 15 years. It was our intention to use such Vineland scores as a criterion for the PQCBC's validity. However, when we correlated the PQCBC and Vineland scores of our initial sample of 44 parents of 9- and 10-year olds, we obtained a small, negative, and nonsignificant correlation coefficient. Additional analyses revealed that the mean Vineland score for this sample of responses was 13.87 social-age years, with a standard deviation of 1.45 years. In fact, over one-third ($N = 16$) of the parents' responses received the maximum Vineland score of 15.0 years. Thus, inaccurate and nonreliable Vineland scores were obtained on over one-third of the parents' responses due to reports of children's unexpectedly advanced social maturity, the inclusion of an insufficient age range of Vineland items, and the datedness of the Vineland scale. Of course, the correlation between PQCBC and Vineland scores also must be considered as inaccurate and nonreliable.

Recently, an updated revised Vineland Adaptive Behavior Scale (Sparrow, Balla, Cicchetti, 1984) has been published. We urge its use in future studies of the PQCBC's validity.

Limitations and Uses

To date, the PQCBC has been used in research studies of (a) variations in African American children's behavior across settings (Holliday, 1985), (b) the effects of family characteristics and process on children's behaviors (Henning, 1981), and (c) the predictive relationship of maternal social support systems and child and family characteristics on children's behavioral competence (Johnson, 1985). Of course, the author welcomes continual research use of the PQCBC. In particular, the author strongly encourages studies that include investigations of the PQCBC's test-retest reliability and validity (through use of either the revised Vineland, other comparable instruments, or direct naturalistic observation). The author also encourages the use of the PQCBC on diverse populations.

References

Doll, E. A. (1947). *Vineland social maturity scale: Manual of directions.* Minneapolis, MN: Educational Test Bureau.

Gesten, E. L. (1976). A health resources inventory: The development of a measure of the personal and social competence of primary-grade children. *Journal of Consulting and Clinical Psychology, 44,* 775-786.

Henning, R. C. (1981). *The ecology of childrearing patterns of low to moderate income Black families: The development of sociobehavioral competencies in African American children. Dissertation Abstracts International, 42*(4), 1526A.

Holliday, B. G. (1985). Developmental imperatives of social ecologies: Lessons learned from Black children. In H. P. McAdoo & J. L. McAdoo (Eds.), *Black children* (pp. 53-69). Beverly Hills, CA: Sage .

Johnson, J. N. (1985). *The behavioral competence of Black children from single-parent, female-headed Black families as mediated through the family support network.* Unpublished master's thesis, Vanderbilt University, Nashville, TN.

Kochman, T. (Ed.). (1977). *Rappin' and stylin' out: Communication in Black America.* Urbana, IL: University of Illinois Press.

Ladner, J. (1971). *Tomorrow's Tomorrow. The Black woman.* Garden City, NJ: Doubleday.

Lambert, N., Windmiller, M., & Cole, L. (1974). *AAMD adaptive behavior scale, public school version, 1974 revision.* Washington, DC: American Association of Mental Deficiency.

Mercer, J. R., & Lewis, J. F. (1979). *System of multicultural pluralistic assessment (SOMPA)-adaptive behavior inventory for children.* New York: The Psychological Corporation.

Ogbu, J. U. (1981). Origins of human competence: A cultural-ecological perspective. *Child Development, 52*(2), 413- 429.

Richardson, B. B. (1981). Racism and childrearing: A study of Black mothers. *Dissertation Abstracts International, 42*(1), 125A. (University Microfilms No. 8114049).

Slaughter, D. T. (1977). Relation of early parent-teacher socialization influences to achievement orientation and self-esteem in middle childhood among low-income Black children. In J. Glidewell (Ed.), *The social context of learning and development.* New York: Gardner .

Sparrow, S. S., Balla, D. A., & Cicchetti, D. V. (1984). *Vineland adaptive behavior scales.* Circle Pines, MN: American Guidance Service.

Spencer, M. B., Brookins, G. K., & Allen, W. R. (Eds.), (1985). *Beginnings: The social and affective development of Black children.* Hillsdale, NJ: Lawrence Erlbaum.

Stott, D. H., & Sykes, E. G. (1967). *Bristol social adjustment guides.* San Diego, CA: Educational and Industrial Testing Service.

Wilkinson, C. B., & O'Connor, W. A. (1977). Growing up male in a Black single-parent family. *Psychiatric Annals, 7*(7), 356-362.

Young, V. (1970). Family and childhood in a southern Negro community. *American Anthropologist, 72,* 269-288.

Appendix A

Parental Questionnaire on Children's Behavioral Competence (PQCBC)

Children may do many different things as they grow up. Some of the questions I will ask are about activities that usually are done by children older than _____(child)_____. Other questions I will ask you are about things that are usually done by _____(child)_____. Some of the activities I ask you about may be things that you do not allow (child) to do. Other activities may be things which _____(child)_____ does not do because there is no opportunity for him/her to do them.

When I ask a question about things _____(child)_____ does, pick the answer that *best* describes what he/she does *now*. If you do not *allow* _____(child)_____ to do the activities I ask about, or if he/she *used to do* the activity, or if he/she *does not have an opportunity* to do the activity, then please tell me. Do you have any questions?

O.K. just remember to pick the answer that best describes what _____(child)_____ actually does now, or tell me if _____(child)_____ is not allowed to, or used to, or has no opportunity to do the activity asked about.

(PQCBC) responses should be recorded directly onto this questionnaire form. Do not record directly onto data sheet. If after probing, response remains ambiguous, then record response verbatim onto this questionnaire form.)

Functional/Life Skills

(Mobility)

N   1. How often does _____ walk or go on his/her bike alone or with friends to a shopping center, park, the library or places like that:
    1) never
    2) sometimes, or
    3) frequently?

N* 2. When _____ leaves home to go to school is he/she:
    1) Under the supervision of an older child,
    2) on his/her own (although perhaps with other children who are not in charge of him/her), or
    3) accompanied by an adult?

N   3. When visiting relatives or friends outside the immediate neighborhood (but in the city) does _____ usually:
    1) go with an older person,
    2) go with children his/her own age, or
    3) go alone?

N   4. When looking for a strange street, does _____ find it:
    1) By him/herself or by following directions,
    2) by going with another person, or
    3) He/she does not do this?

N   5. Does _____ go out in the evenings after dark to play with other children without an adult along?
    3) often
    2) sometimes,
    1) never?

N   6. When _____ goes to movies, ball games, or any other activities like these in the community, does he/she:
    3) go alone or with other children his/her own age,
    2) go with older children or adults, or
    1) he/she does not go to such places?

N   7. How often does _____ go about the immediate neighborhood for several blocks without you knowing exactly where he/she is:
    1) hardly ever,
    2) sometimes,

3) frequently?

N/S/ 8. Does _____ correctly read a street map of the city or a highway map of the state:
1) he/she does not read maps well,
2) with some help from an older person,
3) without any help?

N 9. When _____ takes trips to stay with friends or nonrelatives who live out of town, does he/she sometimes go:
1) Does he/she only go when his/her parents are along
2) with another person,
3) by him/herself?

N* 10. Does _____ travel alone to other parts of the city by bus or taxi:
1) rarely or never,
2) about once a month,
3) two or more times a month?

(F/L - Communication)

H/N,S/ 11. When talking to you or to brothers and sisters, does _____ speak clearly and distinctly- that is, not too low, not too fast, not stuttering:
1) rarely or never,
2) sometimes,
3) almost always?

N 12. When talking with his friends in the neighborhood, does _____ speak clearly and distinctly:
1) rarely or never,
2) sometimes, or
3) almost always?

H 13. Would you say that _____'s vocabulary is:
1) lower than normal for a child of his/her age,
2) about normal for a child of his/her age,
3) above normal for a child of his/her age?

H/S/* 14. When _____ uses a pencil, is his/her writing (not printing)
1) very difficult to read,
2) a little difficult to read,
3) very easy to read?

H/S/* 15. Without being told, does _____ read

such things such as simple instructions and comic strips,
1) never,
2) occasionally or ,
3) frequently?

N 16. Does _____ make up secret codes or talk a secret language with his/her friends:
1) never,
2) occasionally or
3) frequently?

N 17. Does _____ make up rhymes, chants, or jokes with his/her friends:
1) never,
2) occasionally or,
3) frequently?

N* 18. Occasionally does _____ write letters to friends or relatives:
1) never,
2) occasionally or,
3) without help?

H 19. Does _____ ever write stories or copy other written materials other than homework assignments:
1) rarely or never,
2) occasionally or,
3) frequently?

H/N/* 20. Does _____ make telephone calls, use the phone book, and take messages:
1) never,
2) with help, or
3) without help?

H/S/ 21. When _____ tells stories about things he/she does or imagines, are these stories:
1) he/she does not do this at all,
2) short and simple, or
3) long and involved?

N 22. Does _____ sing songs that he/she hears on the radio by him/herself or with other children:
1) rarely or never; has difficulty singing words to the songs,
2) occasionally, knows the words to some of the songs, or
3) frequently, knows the words to most of the songs.

N/S/ 23. When _____ is in a group of children, does he/she:

1) is he/she usually quiet,
2) sometimes have something to say, or
3) always have something to say?

N 24. Does_____ever speak before a crowd of people (in church, school play):
1) rarely or he/she has not done this,
2) occasionally, or
3) frequently?

H/N,S/ 25. When talking with the family, does _____ mention community news or events that he/she has read about in the newspaper or seen on the TV news:
1) never,
2) sometimes, or
3) frequently?

N 26. When talking with his her friends, does _____ mention news items that he/she has read about in the newspaper or seen on the TV news:
1) never,
2) sometimes, or
3) frequently?

N/H/ 27. Does _____ use a pay phone:
1) he/she does not ever use a pay phone,
2) with the help of another
   person, or
3) without the help of
   another person?

N* 28. Without other people's help, does_____ respond to ads by sending in coupons, requesting samples, or printed material:
1) never,
2) occasionally, or
3) frequently?

H/S/* 29. How often does _____ read the newspaper, a library book, or magazines for his/her own enjoyment or information:
1) rarely or never
2) occasionally, or
3) frequently?

(F/L - Management and Independence)

Remember to pick the answer that best describes what _____ actually does now, or tell me if _____ is not allowed to, or used to , or has no opportunity to do the activity asked about.

H* 30. When _____ uses a table knife, does he/she usually use it:

1) he/she does not use a table knife,
2) only for spreading butter and jam, or
3) for spreading and cutting up meat?

H 31. How often does _____ prepare foods by him/herself, such as hot dogs, soup, or eggs:
1) occasionally,
2) never, or
3) frequently?

H* 32. At bedtime, does _____ usually undress, put on his/her pajamas *and* go to bed:
1) with a great deal of help,
2) with a little help from someone, or
3) without help?

H/S/*33. Does _____ use a clock or watch to tell time *correctly* to the nearest quarter hour:
1) he/she does not tell time well?
2) occasionally, or
3) frequently?

H* 34. How often does _____ prepare foods by him/herself that require mixing and cooking such as scrambled eggs, pancakes, pudding, or things like that:
1) never,
2) occasionally, or
3) hardly ever?

H* 35. Does_____believe such things as Santa Claus, the Easter Bunny, and fairies really exist:
1) frequently, or
2) sometimes, or
3) hardly ever?

H 36. How much help does _____ need to use the oven to bake things like cookies, roasts, potatoes, or other foods
1) he/she doesn't use the oven,
2) a little help, or
3) no help?

H* 37. Does _____ usually comb and brush his/her hair:
1) Does someone have to do this for him/her,
2) with some help, or
3) with little help.

H* 38. When _____ takes a bath, does he/she fill the tub or turn on the shower, *and* bathe and dry him/herself:
1) with a great deal of help,
2) with a little help, or

3) without help.

H   39. Does _____ prepare food for his/her lunch, picnic, or a hike:
1) with a great deal of help,
2) with a little help, or
3) without help?

H   40. When little things need fixing around the house such as replacing a burned out lightbulb, shaking the handle on a dripping toilet, or gluing something that is broken, does _____
1) let someone else take care of it,
2) get someone to help him/her fix it, or
3) take care of it him/herself?

H* 41. Does _____ fix things by using tools such as a hammer, screw driver, bikepump:
1) never,
2) occasionally with some help, or
3) frequently without help?

H* 42. When things have to be adjusted such as mending or shortening cloth, raising or lowering bike seats, or other things like that, does _____ usually:
1) have someone do it for him/her,
2) do it him/herself with help, or
3) do it without help?

H* 43. Does _____ do simple household chores such as taking out the garbage, folding clean clothes, making up his/her bed, and setting the table:
1) he/she doesn't do such things,
2) with some help and direction,
3) without help?

Tasks Performance: _____

H* 44. At dinner time, does _____ help him/herself to food, cut-up food *and* pour catsup and salad dressing:
1) others do this for him/her,
2) with some help, or
3) without help?

H* 45. Does _____ do such household chores as dusting furniture, sweeping or mopping floors, washing dishes, or ironing flat pieces:
1) seldom or never,
2) sometimes if reminded, or
3) frequently without being reminded?

Tasks Performed: _____

H* 46. Does _____ repair broken bicycles, sew simple clothes, care for a pet, or do things like this:
1) never,
2) occasionally, or
3) frequently?

H* 47. How often does _____ completely clean any room in your home: (like the bathroom, kitchen, living room, bedroom, etc.)
1) seldom or never,
2) a few times a month, or
3) once a week or more?

H* 48. How often does _____ do large cleaning projects around the house (like washing out the inside of the refrigerator, cleaning the stove, washing a car, cleaning out the garage, or something like that:
1) never,
2) occasionally, or
3) frequently?

H/S/ 49. Does _____ use sharp knives to cut up food for cooking like stew meat, chicken, or other things like that:
1) never,
2) only when an adult is watching, or
3) frequently?

H   50. Does _____ use electric tools, a sewing machine, or other power machines:
1) seldom or never,
2) with some help, or
3) with little help from others?

H* 51. Does _____ wash and dry his/her hair:
1) someone has to do this for him/her,
2) with some help, or
3) with little help from others?

H* 52. Does _____ select appropriate clothes for the occasion and weather, *and* completely dress him/herself:
1) with a great deal of help,
2) with some help from others, or
3) with little help from others?

H* 53. How often does _____ do his/her own or the family's wash, or take the wash to and do it at the laundromat:
1) never,
2) occasionally, or
3) frequently?

H* 54. How often does _____ prepare most of the food for the family's dinner:

1) seldom or never,
2) sometimes, or
3) frequently?

(F/L - Caretaking and Supervision)

H   55. Does _____ watch out for younger children by watching for cars or moving equipment or other things that might hurt them:
    1) never,
    2) only when reminded, or
    3) frequently?

H   56. Does _____ help younger brothers and sisters learn the meaning of traffic signs (like traffic lights, stop, or crosswalk signs:
    1) never,
    2) occasionally, or
    3) frequently?
    4) Not applicable–no younger children at home

H   57. How often does _____ feed or "change" young children:
    1) not at all,
    2) sometimes, or
    3) frequently?

H/N,S/ 58. Does _____ show younger brothers and sisters how to do household tasks:
    1) never,
    2) sometimes,
    3) frequently?
    4) Not applicable - no younger children in home

N   59. Does _____ show neighborhood children how to fix toys or play games:
    1) never,
    2) sometimes, or
    3) frequently?

H/N/* 60. Does _____ babysit at home for an hour or so during the daytime:
    1) he/she does not babysit,
    2) only if there are older person nearby, or
    3) alone?

N   61. Does _____ babysit at other people's homes for an hour or so during the daytime:
    1) he/she does not babysit in other people's homes,
    2) only if there are older persons nearby, or
    3) alone?

H/N,S/ 62. How often does _____ help other children in the family with their schoolwork:
    1) never,
    2) occasionally, or
    3) frequently?

N   63. How often does _____ help his/her friends with their schoolwork:
    1) never,
    2) occasionally, or
    3) frequently?

H   64. How often does _____ take care of younger children at home during the daytime for *several* hours while adults are away:
    1) never,
    2) occasionally, or
    3) frequently?

H   65. How often does _____ help younger children in the family by feeding them and getting them off to school in the morning:
    1) never,
    2) occasionally, or
    3) frequently?
    4) Not applicable–no younger children in home

H/N/66. How often does _____ babysit at home for younger children a few hours while adults are out for the evening:
    1) never,
    2) a couple of times a month, or
    3) once a week or more?

N   67. How often does _____ babysit at other people's homes for a few hours while adults are out for the evening:
    1) never,
    2) a couple of times a month, or
    3) once a week or more?

(F/L - Consumer)

Don't forget to tell me if _____ is not allowed to, used to, or has no opportunity to do the activity asked about.

H* 68. How often do you trust _____ with small amounts of money which you give him/her to buy a few things or to make payments for you:
    1) rarely or never,
    2) sometimes, or
    3) frequently?

H/S/ 69. Does _____ make correct change for one dollar:
1) not at all,
2) only with help, or
3) without help.

N 70. When shopping for clothes, does _____:
1) Does someone else select his/her clothes for him/her,
2) select clothing with help from someone else, or
3) select his/her own clothing?

N 71. When he/she is eating at a hamburger or taco stand, does _____ order food:
1) does someone order for him/her,
2) with some help from others, or
3) with out help?

H 72. When _____ borrows money from you or others family member, does he/she:
1) usually forget to repay it (if not reminded)
2) occasionally remembers to repay it, or
3) usually remembers to repay it?

N* 73. Does _____ understand how much stamps cost for a postcard and letter, *and* is he/she able to buy them from the post office:
1) not at all,
2) only if someone helps him/her, or
3) without help.

N* 74. How often does _____ buy groceries or other things at a nearby store without a list:
1) never,
2) only with a list or when another person is along, or
3) frequently?

N* 75. Does _____ return with the correct change when sent to buy groceries or others things:
1) never,
2) sometimes, or
3) most of the time?

N* 76. Is _____ able to order merchandise from a catalogue or from a magazine ad:
1) he/she is not able to do this,
2) with help from others, or
3) without help?

N* 77. To earn money, does _____ perform chores for neighbors like washing windows, washing cars, cutting grass, or other jobs like that:
1) never,
2) occasionally, or
3) frequently?

N* 78. Does _____ often select *and* buy small items of clothing for him/herself such as ribbons, gloves, underwear, T-shirts:
1) he/she does not do this,
2) only when someone else is along to help, or
3) without other people's help?

N 79A. Is _____ given or does he/she earn at least one dollar a week:
1) rarely or never,
2) occasionally, or
3) frequently? (if response is 2) or 3), ask 79B, otherwise, ask 80.)

N 79B. Does _____ use most of his spending money for such things as:
1) buying candy, coke, or ice cream,
2) buying games, toys, going to the movies, or
3) buying school lunch, books, clothing, paying for music lessons; or does he/she save it?

N 80. Does _____ make contributions at church or to other community organizations from his/her own money:
1) never,
2) occasionally, or
3) frequently?

N 81. Does _____ have a savings account at a bank to which he/she makes deposits and withdrawals:
1) does someone else do this for him/her,
2) with the help of someone else, or
3) without help?

N 82. When _____ goes to buy some large items of clothing such as a coat, dress, or shoes, does he/she:
1) always have an adult along,
2) sometimes have an adult along, or
3) seldom has an adult along?

N* 83. Does _____ have a part-time job which he/she generally works:
1) he/she does not have such a regular part-time job,

2) 5 or less hours per week, or

3) more than 5 hours per week?

Type of Job:_____

Interpersonal Skills

(IP - Adults)

H/N,S 84. How well does _____ get along with his/her father/stepfather:

    1) not so well,

    2) fairly well,

    3) very well, or

    4) Not applicable–no father/stepfather in home?

H   85. How well do you and _____ generally get along:

    1) not so well,

    2) very well, or

    3) fairly well?

N   86. How well does _____ get along with adults in the immediate neighborhood:

    1) not so well,

    2) fairly well, or

    3) very well?

H   87. How often does _____ come to you and tell you about his/her activities during the day:

    1) never,

    2) sometimes, or

    3) frequently?

H/N,S/ 88. Does _____ ask you or some other adult in the home to help him/her with school work:

    1) never,

    2) sometimes, or

    3) frequently?

N   89. Does he/she ask other adults in the neighborhood to help him/her with school work:

    1) never,

    2) sometimes, or

    3) frequently?

N   90. Does _____ enjoy carrying on a fairly lengthy conversation (15 minutes or more) with an adult:

    1) rarely or seldom,

    2) occasionally, or

    3) frequently?

H   91. When you are doing work around the house, does _____ work along with you:

    1) seldom

    2) sometimes

    3) frequently

H   92. Without being told, does _____ call up or write adult relatives:

    1) hardly,

    2) occasionally, or

    3) often?

N   93. How often does _____ help out relatives or neighbors when they have sickness or other trouble like that:

    1) never,

    2) occasionally, or

    3) frequently?

(IP - Siblings and Peers)

H/N,S/ 94. How does _____ usually get along with his/her brothers and sisters:

    1) not so well,

    2) fairly well,

    3) very well, or

    4) not applicable- no other children in home

N   95. How does _____ get along with children in the neighborhood:

    1) not so well,

    2) fairly well, or

    3) very well?

H/N,S/ 96. When _____ accidentally gets bumped or jostled while playing with other children in the family, does he/she usually:

    1) cry or fight and stop playing,

    2) cry or fight briefly, but soon begins to play again, or

    3) get up and continues playing without making a fuss?

    4) Not applicable–no other children in home

N   97. When _____ accidentally gets bumped or jostled while playing with neighborhood children, does he/she usually:

    1) make a fuss and stop playing,

    2) make a brief fuss and then continues to play, or

    3) continue playing without making a fuss?

N   98. How often do neighborhood kids pick on

or tease _____:
1) most of the time,
2) some of the time, or
3) hardly ever?

N   99. Does _____ usually play with children who are:
1) he/she doesn't play much with other children,
2) younger than he/she is
3) about the same age or children?

H   100. Does _____ share secrets with his/her brothers and sisters:
1) seldom,
2) sometimes, or
3) frequently?
4) Not Applicable–no other children in home

H   101. Does _____ work along with brothers and sisters when doing chores:
1) seldom,
2) sometimes,
3) most of the time?
4) Not Applicable–no other children in home

N/S 102. When with a group of children his/her own age, how often does _____ act as a leader in their activities:
1) never,
2) occasionally, or
3) frequently?

N   103. When _____ meets new children his/her own age, does he/she:
1) usually hold back until they approach him/her,
2) sometimes approaches them first, or
3) usually approaches them first?

H   104. Does _____ intervene when his/her brothers or sisters argue or fight, does he/she:
1) encourage them further by teasing or does not intervene,
2) defend the appropriate sibling,
3) attempt to settle the dispute?
4) Not applicable- no other children in the home

H   105. When _____ seems to understand what mood his/her sisters and brothers are in:

1) hardly ever,
2) sometimes, or
3) most of the time?
4) Not applicable–no other children in home

N/S/* 106. (If child is male, ask the following) Does _____ usually get together with a group of neighborhood children to:
3) play sandlot ball games such as baseball,
2) ride bikes or skateboards, or
1) he does not play these types of things?

107. (If child is female, ask the following) Does _____ and his/her friends play card games (e.g., whist, spades, poker), table games (e.g., monopoly), pool or other games having strict rules and ways of scoring:
1) never,
2) occasionally, or
3) frequently?

N*   108. How often does _____ participate in organized activities such as little league football or baseball, a swimming or track team, a dance class, a marching band, a church choir, or things like that:
1) not at all,
2) occasionally, or
3) frequently?

N*   109. Does _____ attend meetings at a community center, or participate in some youth group such as boy or girl scouts:
1) never,
2) frequently, or
3) occasionally?

N/S/ 110. How often has _____ served as president or secretary or as some officer of a youth group in the community or at church:
1) never,
2) once or twice, or
3) three or more times?

N*   111. Does _____ participate in a young people's religious group
1) seldom or never,
2) a couple of times a month, or
3) once a week or more?

N   112. How many times has _____ worked in the neighborhood with other children to raise funds for the United Fund, Red Cross, March of Dimes, Sickle Cell Anemia Foundation, or some other community or church group:

1) none,
2) one or two times, or
3) three or more times?

Remember to pick the answer that best describes what _____ actually does now, or tell me if _____ is not allowed to, or used to, or has no opportunity to do the activity asked about.

Problem-Solving Skills

(PS-Personal)

H   113. When you unexpectedly have to leave _____ home alone for a short while, does he/she:

1) get very upset,
2) get a little upset, but soon calms down, or
3) he/she does not get upset at all?

H   114. When _____ is ill and has to stay in bed for a few days, does he/she:

1) whimper and complain a great deal and not want to stay in bed or take medicine,
2) whimper and complain some, but is willing to stay in bed and take medicine, or
3) whimper and complain very little and is willing to do whatever is necessary to get better?

H   115. When _____ cuts him/herself, does he/she:

1) Does he/she get upset when a cut has to be bandaged?
2) ask someone to wash and bandage it him/herself, or
3) immediately wash and bandages it him/herself?

H   116. When the family's daily routine changes because you are ill does, _____:

1) not do extra chores or complains about having to do them,

2) do extra chores without complaining if told to do so, or
3) do extra chores without being told?

N   117. When _____ is about to do something or go somewhere for the first time, is he/she usually:

1) quite hesitant and afraid,
2) a little hesitant and afraid, or
3) not at all hesitant and afraid?

N   118. When _____ is given a new household chore to do, does he/she:

1) complain,
2) say nothing, or
3) ask questions about how to do it correctly.

N/S/119. When _____ has to perform before a group (not at school), does he/she:

1) act very nervous and afraid,
2) act a little nervous and afraid, or
3) act as if he/she enjoys it.?

(PS - Interpersonal)

H/N,S/120. When _____'s brother or sister takes his/her toys or other belongings, does he/she usually:

1) cry or come to you for help,
2) get another child to help him/her get them back,
3) try to get them back him/herself?
4) not applicable- no other children in home.

N   121. When one of _____'s neighborhood friends takes his/her toys or other belongings, does he/she usually:

1) cry or come to you for help, or
2) get another child to help him/her get them back, or
3) try to get them back him/herself?

H/N 122. When a brother or sister hits _____ does he/ she usually:

1) cry,
2) get an older person to help him/her, or
3) handle it him/herself?
4) Not applicable– no other children in home.

N   123. When one of _____'s friends hits her/him, does he/she usually:

1) cry,

2) handle it him/herself, or

3) get an older person to help him/her?

H/N/124. When _____ is called a name or teased by brothers or sisters, does, he/she usually,

1) cry or run away from them,

2) defend him/herself, or

3) ignore them, but does not run away?

N　125. When _____ is called a name or teased by a group of neighborhood children, does he/she usually:

1) cry or run away from them,

2) defend him/herself, or

3) ignore them, but does not run away?

H/N,S/126. When _____ has a quarrel or fight with his/her brothers and sisters, does he/she stay angry for:

1) a couple of days,

2) a couple of hours, or

3) only a short time?

4) Not applicable–no other children in home.

N　127. When _____ has a quarrel or fight with neighborhood children, does he/she stay angry for:

1) a couple of days,

2) a couple of hours, or

3) only a short time?

H/N,S/ 128. When playing cards or table games with brothers and sisters, does _____ become angry if he/she doesn't win:

1) frequently,

2) sometimes, or

3) seldom?

4) Not applicable–no other children in home

N　129. When playing card or table games with friends, does _____ become angry if he/she doesn't win:

1) frequently,

2) sometimes, or

3) seldom?

N　130. When _____'s friends attempt to talk him/her into doing something that is wrong, does he/she usually go along with the crowd:

1) most times,

2) sometimes, or

3) hardly ever?

(P/S Technical)

H　131. How often does _____ become angry when he/she is unsuccessful at properly adjusting the T.V. picture:

1) most times,

2) sometimes, or

3) seldom?

H　132. When _____ has trouble getting all the pieces of a puzzle to fit, does he/she give up:

1) most times,

2) sometimes, or

3) hardly ever?

N　133. When a bicycle, wagon or other toy gets broken, does _____ usually:

1) let someone else take care of it,

2) get someone to help him/her fix it, or

3) try to fix it him/herself?

H/S/ 134. When _____ has trouble doing some task at home, does he/she usually:

1) give up,

2) sometimes keep trying, or

3) keep on trying until he/she succeeds?

H/N,S/135. When _____ doesn't understand some directions you have given him/her, does he/she usually ask questions:

1) seldom,

2) sometimes, or

3) always?

N　136. When _____ doesn't understand the instructions an adult neighbor or friend is giving him/her on how to fix something, does _____ usually ask questions:

1) seldom or never,

2) sometimes, or

3) always?

H/S/ 137. When _____ reads something that has a lot of words he doesn't know, does he/she usually:

1) give up and stop reading,

2) ask someone what the words mean, or

3) look up the words in a dictionary?

H　138. When all the lights go out in the house, does _____ flip the circuit breaker or put in a new fuse?

1) he/she does not know when or how to do this,

2) if someone helps him/her, or tells him/

her, or

3) without help and without being told

H   139. When the toilet gets clogged up, does _____ unclog it by using a plunger:

1) lets someone else fix it,
2) only if told to do so, or
3) without being told?

H   140. If some meat broiling in the oven catches fire, does _____ put the fire out:

1) does he/she call someone else to put it out,
2) if told what to do, or
3) without being told what to do?

(P/S Social)

H/S/ 141. When you do not allow _____ to immediately have something he/she wants, how often does he/she get angry and make a fuss:

1) almost always,
2) sometimes, or
3) almost never?

H/S/ 142. When you or some older family member criticizes _____, does he/she usually:

1) become quite angry,
2) sulk and pout, or
3) listen and consider what is being said?

N   143. Does _____ usually feel that it is unfair that he/she is not allowed to do some things that older children are allowed to do:

1) frequently,
2) sometimes, or
3) seldom?

H   144. When the family budget becomes very tight, does _____ make an effort to not ask you to buy special things for him/her (e.g., snack food, toys) when you go shopping:

1) hardly,
2) sometimes, or
3) most of the time?

N/S/ 145. When a group of children disagrees with some opinion of _____, does he/she usually continue to stick up for his/her point of view:

1) hardly ever,
2) sometimes, or
3) most of the time?

H/N,S/ 146. Does _____ question rules around the house that seem unfair or unclear to him/her:

1) never,
2) sometimes, or
3) often?

N   147. Does _____ question rules in the neighborhood or community which seem unfair or unclear to him/her:

1) never,
2) sometimes, or
3) often?

H   148. When _____ is angry or upset about something, does he/she:

1) sulk or is verbally abusive to others,
2) say nothing to anyone about the problem, or
3) confide in family or peers?

H   149. Does _____ give his/her opinions during family discussions about important decisions like major purchases, problems of other children in the family, or other things like that:

1) hardly ever,
2) sometimes, or
3) often?

Well, Mrs. _____ this is the last interview question. Let me take a moment to check that I've gotten down all of your answers. (*Make sure everything is in order. Put a checkmark* (X) *by each of the following items to indicate necessary checks have been made.*)

1) Check Data Sheet and PQCBC. Make sure all items have recorded responses. If items have been skipped, or answers have inadvertently not been recorded, tell respondent this and ask the necessary items.

2) Check that all identification information has been recorded.

3) Check that Consent Form and Request for Release of Information have been fully completed.

4) Check that voucher has been signed, and that respondent's name, address, and social security number have been recorded on an index card.

5) Check that child's first and last names have been properly spelled.

6) Give respondent Debriefing Statement.

Here is a "Debriefing Statement" which explains what I have talked about with you and your child. It also tells you who to call if you wish to get the results of the study. I personally do want to thank you Mrs. _____ for taking the time to talk with me and answer these questions. I have found your answers to be quite thoughtful and interesting. Your answers will help us in our study of Black children. As I said before, you will be receiving a check in the mail in about two weeks. Thank you again for you assistance.

Data Sheet

ID# _____

Respondent _____

1-(latent behavior), 2-(emergent behavior), 3-(mastered behavior), 4-'Used to' perform behavior frequently and successfully, 5-'No Opportunity' or 'Not Allowed' to do, but *could quickly learn* behavior, 6-'No Opportunity' or 'Not Allowed' do, and probably *would not quickly learn* behavior, 7-'Don't Know' or No Answer, 8-Not Applicable, *-Item can be scored for Vineland (Question and score carefully. Note: Codes 5&6 should be used *only* for starred (*) items. Do not use these for unstarred items)

(The following is a sample of the data sheet. In its entirety, the Section titles (Mobility, Communication, etc.) would be followed with all of the question numbers and answer choices.)

(F/L - Mobility) (Items 1-10)
1.　　1　2　3　4　5　6　7　8
(F/L-Communication) (Items 11-29)
1.　　1　2　3　4　5　6　7　8
(F/L-Management and Independence) (Items 30-54)
1.　　1　2　3　4　5　6　7　8
(F/L-Carctaking & Supervising) (Items 55-67)
1.　　1　2　3　4　5　6　7　8
(F/L-Consumer) (Items 68-83)
1.　　1　2　3　4　5　6　7　8
(I/P-Adults) (Items 84-93)
1.　　1　2　3　4　5　6　7　8
(I/P-Siblings & Peers) (Items 94-112)
1.　　1　2　3　4　5　6　7　8
(PS-Personal) (Items 113-119)
1.　　1　2　3　4　5　6　7　8
(PS-Interpersonal) (Items 120-130)
1.　　1　2　3　4　5　6　7　8
(PS-Technical) (Items 131-140)
1.　　1　2　3　4　5　6　7　8
(PS-Social) (Items 141-149)
1.　　1　2　3　4　5　6　7　8

For additional information, contact:

Bertha G. Holliday
1719 First St., N.W.
Washington, DC 20001
Telephone: (202) 336-6029
Fax: (202) 336-6040
E-mail: bgh.apa@email.apa.org

The African Based Childrearing Opinion Survey: A Research Instrument for Measuring Black Cultural Values

Wade W. Nobles and Lawford Goddard

Abstract

The African Based Childrearing Opinion Survey was developed as a means of assessing the retention of an African-based cultural orientation in Black populations in American society. The scale emerged out of an analysis of traditional African philosophy and culture. The scale consists of 35 statements that are broad in content and cover various aspects of parental attitudes about childrearing. Since socialization, or the pattern of childrearing represents the process by which new members of the society come to learn the prescribed and proscribed ways of acting and behaving (i.e., acquire a particular world-view), the practices and values imparted would reflect the intrinsic cultural value system of a people as it is mediated by the concrete conditions in which they are located. Accordingly, an analysis of attitudes towards childrearing would reveal the unique way in which a people conceptualize their reality (i.e., their conceptual universe), and reinforce their cultural orientation. The scale is organized around three general cultural domains: Ethos, World-view and Ideology. The scale consists of ten subscales which reflect the behavioral manifestations of a people's cultural orientation. As such the scale can serve as a measure of people's "cultural codification."Given that the scale was designed as a culturally specific instrument designed for African American peoples the explicit direction of the scale is Afrocentric with the higher score representing a stronger sense of Africanity or the continuation of the African cultural principles. Validity and reliability data are reported.

The understanding of Black childrearing practices and the underlying cultural spectrum of the Black population has been limited in that the imposition of ethnocentric (White) values on the analysis of Black family dynamics prevented the scientific community from clearly explicating the features of Black family life. Having accepted the "time" and "space" limitations of White social reality as well as the consistent definitions within those time and space references, American scholarship and research on the Black family has been bound only to an analysis of the existential development of Black family life in America. That is to say, the study of the Black family has been primarily a comparative analysis of Black and White family experiences.

Problems in the scientific analysis of Black family life have been further confounded by consistent transubstantive errors and an overarching methodology which is characteristic of scientific colonialism (Nobles, 1982). Stated simply, the theory of transubstantiation contends that a transubstantive error (i.e., mistake in meaning) occurs when the cultural substance of one cultural group is utilized to give meaning to and explanation of the cultural manifestations of another or different cultural group. The methodology of scientific colonialism is a process of destroying, falsifying and/or distorting information and ideas (cf:, Nobles, 1982). Through the features of unsophisticated falsification, integrated modificationism and conceptual incarceration, the methodology of scientific colonialism inhibits the process of understanding, resulting in scientific acts of omission (i.e., failure to include particular facts and/or orientations) and acts of commission (intentionally accepting certain a priori assumptions and/or denying the validity of certain orientations).

Theoretical Background

The implication of the transubstantive notion suggests that, for any given group of people, culture and history influence both their perception and awareness of events/experiences and the meaning and definitions they attribute to these events and experiences.

Since childrearing practices represent the process by which new members are inculcated into the value orientations of their community, it is one of the most important aspects of a people's reality. Socialization, or the process of socialization, influences the actual awareness of reality. It is the process whereby new members learn the prescribed and proscribed ways of acting and behaving. In so doing these new members come to acquire a particular world-view and understanding of reality. In the process of socialization it follows that the socializing agents (i.e., parents) do make some decisions about the kinds of values and attitudes they impart to their children. These values and attitudes reflect the synthesis between the aspects of culture and the concrete historical conditions in which the people are located. Thus the childrearing practices and values imparted would reflect the intrinsic cultural value system of a people as it is mediated by the historical conditions. An analysis of the childrearing practices would, in fact, reveal the unique way in which a people conceptualize their reality.

Philosophical Orientation

Nobles (1982) has suggested that the way in which a people "view the world" (i.e., their conceptual universe) is critical to all the activities they engage in, including the acceptance and/or rejection of experiences. In the experience of knowing or more particularly, in terms of science, the conceptual universe takes the form of a paradigm which in turn serves as the formalized framework which guides the assessment and evaluation of reality. Accordingly, formalized human activities are built upon and/or are consistent with a particular philosophical orientation which in turn dictates a particular epistemological paradigm.

The link between a people's culture and their conceptual universe is revealed more clearly when culture is understood as a scientific construct which has import for revealing the "meaning" human beings assign to their experiences and the events of their lives. Culture is, accordingly, the process which provides a people with a general design for living and patterns for interpreting (i.e., give meaning to) their reality. In providing a people with a particular understanding of reality (i.e., cultural factors) and a specific set of operational procedures (i.e., cultural aspects), culture influences a people's formalized framework (i.e, their paradigm or conceptual universe) which guides their assessment and evaluation of reality (Nobles, 1982). In a sense, culture could be thought of as having a deep structure and a surface layer.

The "meaning" of a people's reality is in part determined by the interplay between the deep structure, its manifestations at the surface layer and the concrete historical conditions in which the people find themselves. In terms of our model of culture, the deep structure of culture is comprised of the "factors" and "aspects" of culture.

The *factors of culture* which influence the "general design" and "patterns for interpreting reality" are those features which speak to: (1) the structure and origin of the universe; (2) the nature of being or existence; and (3) the particular character which governs/defines universal relationships. The way in which a people address these cosmological, ontological and axiological issues, in turn, combine to determine for them, a general design for living and patterns for interpreting reality. What emerges from these "factors of culture" is a people's codification of their cultural design. A people's cultural codification is found more clearly in what we call *aspects of culture*. Cultural aspects emerge directly from the cultural factors. The "aspects" of culture consist of a people's cultural ideology, ethos, and world-view. A people's *world-view* contains their most comprehensive ideas about the order of the universe and relations within it. A people's *ethos* emerges as a set of guiding principles which reflect a particular behavioral style and psychological sentiment. In effect, the ethos of a people represents their character, tone, quality or mode of being. In this triology, *ideology* emerges as the closest concept representing an instrument for determining how a people *should* see their reality. It determines in part what is considered good, valuable (desirable) and appropriate; and conversely, what is bad, dangerous (undesirable) and inappropriate in a people's social milieu. Ideology is, therefore, the map which clarifies and gives perspective to problematic aspects of a people's social reality. In so doing, it also provides the matrix for creating the collective consciousness of a people.

Black Culture

A brief explication of the culture of Black people is necessary in order to evaluate the extent to which an instrument is consistent with the conceptual universe of African (Black) people.

In terms of the philosophical answers to the cultural framework discussed above, African peoples traditionally believed that cosmologically, the universe was an interdependent structure with all things in the universe being interdependent and interconnected (Thomas, 1960; Wiredu, 1980). Ontologically, Africans traditionally viewed the nature of being as "one force or one spirit" (Temples, 1959; Thomas, 1961). In fact, all things were believed to be endowed with the same supreme force. In believing that all things were endowed with the same supreme spirit, Africans also traditionally believed that all things must be "essentially" one. This is referred to as the ontological principle of consubstantiation. Axiologically, Africans traditionally believed that universal relations were characterized by a process of interchanging syntheses (connections) and contradictions (antagonisms), and that these syntheses and contradictions were linked in participatory sets or frames which formed the whole of universal relations (Osei, 1970; Tempels, 1959; Thomas, 1961). As interchanging syntheses and contradictions, the primary characteristic of universal relations was rhythmic and harmonious.

This cultural deep structure, as a combination of factors and aspects, forms the core set of ideas and beliefs which in turn influence the traditional African conceptual universe and, subsequently, serve as the basis for an African cultural paradigm. Hence, these core answers serve to "guide" the assessment, understanding and evaluation of (as well as give meaning to) reality. The values indicative of this cultural orientation are reflected in the regard for cooperation, interpersonal connectedness, and collective responsibility. The behavioral and mental dispositions, accordingly, emphasize "commonality," "synthesis," "sameness" and "similarity," (cf:, Nobles, 1982).

We contend that so-called Black culture in the United States is the result of a special admixture of Black Americans continued African cultural orientation operating within another cultural milieu, (i.e., European American). It is that African cultural deep structure which is at the base of the African American cultural sphere. Similarly, it is the continuation of the African cultural orientation which is at the root of the special features in African American lifestyles. Though the philosophical and sometimes metaphysical elaboration relevant to these notions is beyond the scope of this paper, one can note, nevertheless, that based on an analysis of African philosophical and religious writings (in terms of cultural factors), Africans and African Americans traditionally viewed the universe as an interconnected and interdependent edifice.

Formally speaking, the African and African American world-view is reflective of and/or consistent with the formal notions of: (1) the ontological principle of consubstantiation, wherein it is believed that all beings are comprised of the same essence (spirit); and (2) the cosmological structure of interconnectedness/interdependence wherein it is believed that each and every element in the universe is connected to each and every other element in the universe. Combined, these two notions emerge in the conceptual universe of African people in such a way as to influence and determine a particular value system. In regards to particular Afrocentric values, the interpersonal dynamics of traditional African and African American lifestyles were, and are, guided by for instance, the principles of restraint, respect, responsibility and reciprocity (cf:, Sudarkasa, 1980).

Purpose of the Scale

In order to address the absence of instruments that measure the cultural orientation of the Black population, the African Based Childrearing Opinion Survey (ABCROS) was developed[1]. The instrument is designed to measure parents' values, attitudes and reported predispositions to act/believe in a particular manner indicative of the cultural attitudes and behaviors of people belonging to an African-based cultural group.

Description of the Scale

The scale is organized around three general domains–Ethos, World-View and Ideology–and

ten subscales which reflect behavioral manifestations of an African people's cultural orientation. As a cultural specific scale designed for African and African American peoples, the explicit direction of the scale is Afrocentric.

The Ethos domain pertains to a set of guiding principles which reflect rules governing human conduct. The Interpersonal Connectedness, Collective Responsibility, Adaptability and Compassion subscales are conceptualized as Ethos variables. These subscales assess the extent to which the individual's behavior is guided by an orientation that is based on the understanding and recognition that all things are "connected," that the welfare of one is dependent on the support of all, that things are flexible and changeable and that a sense of humaneness should govern interpersonal relations.

The World-View domain pertains to a people's most comprehensive ideas about order, or the way elements should relate to each other in the universe. The Cooperation and Respect subscales fall within this domain. They assess the extent to which the individual conceives of elements in an independent or cooperative framework and the nature of the dominant mode of interacting among individuals.

The final dimension of the scale is the Ideology domain. Ideology refers to the cognitive map which clarifies and gives perspective to a people's social reality. Within this domain four subscales are identified–Racial Pride, Cultural Awareness, Media Influences and Education. These scales assess the extent to which the individual emphasizes an orientation that instills a sense of pride in one's ethnicity, an awareness of past cultural traditions, a recognition of the nontraditional forms of learning and the influence or receptivity to the impact of non-African cultural information via the media.

The final revised scale consists of 35 items selected to measure the ten subscales. The items are Likert-type statements with respondents selecting one of four different options reflecting the extent of agreement or disagreement with the particular item.

Item-Pool Relevance

The scale emerged out of an in-depth analysis of African philosophy and culture. The choice and wording of the items was determined by the extent to which they reflect these philosophical principles. The items were based initially on content validity to the extent that they reflected the traditional African philosophical system as derived from an understanding of African philosophy, religion, myths and folklore. We assumed these arenas of scholarly inquiry would reflect the underlying philosophical system of African societies. From the study of African philosophy the cultural themes were selected that formed the basis for the subscales. Items that reflected these themes were then written and randomly distributed throughout the form. The items are broad in content covering various aspects of parental attitudes about childrearing.

Development of Scale

The first step in the development of the scale consisted of a compilation of a list of seventy-six (76) statements representing attitudes about childrearing. This list was then reviewed internally by a pool of Black scholars and reduced to 52 items. This scale was then submitted to a panel of national Black "experts"–psychologists, sociologists, anthropologists and philosohphers–for review and evaluation. In addition the preliminary form was administered to a pilot sample of twelve intact Black families in San Francisco. Based on the pilot data and the judgment of the panel of "experts," items which were ambiguously worded, which the respondents did not understand and which were problematic in interpretation were eliminated. Several items were rewritten. This led to the final version of 41 items that were adopted for testing in this study.

Standard procedures to safeguard against social desirability and acquiescent response sets were incorporated in the construction of the scale. The items were worded in both positive and negative directions so that the subjects could not fall into a set response mode. The wording of the items and the administration instructions were designed so that the subjects were encouraged to think before giving a response. The items of the individual subscales were scattered throughout the form itself, thereby making it difficult for the subjects to understand the real purpose of the instrument or the area being tested. The final procedure was to include items that had the same meaning but were worded differently. In this manner we could determine both the internal consistency of the responses as well as detect any acquiescence in the response mode.

Examples of subscale items are given below.

• Children should expect to be paid for doing regular household chores. (Interdependence)
• Parents should teach children to do different things around the house. (Adaptability)
• Individual gain and success is more important than sharing and showing concern for others. (Individualism)
• I learn more about child-rearing from television than from my folks. (Media-Influence).
• Children should behave openly and freely in the presence of adults. (Respect for Elders)
• Children learn as much through responsibilities at home as through school work. (Informal Education)

Administration of the Scale

The African Based Childrearing Opinion Survey is available as a four-page hand-scorable booklet or as a one page computer scorable sheet. The ABCROS can be administered either individually or as a group procedure.

In the study on which this report is based the scale was administered to subjects individually. The interview was usually conducted in the home of the respondents. The interviewers in all cases were Black, matching the race of the respondents. The African Based Childrearing Opinion Survey was administered as part of a larger data collection battery which required an average of two to three hours to complete and which was generally conducted over three different visits to the respondent's home. The African Based Childrearing Opinion Survey was generally administered on the second visit.

In an individual setting with the interviewer reading the scale items, the African Based Childrearing Opinion Survey takes 20 to 30 minutes to administer. As a self-administered instrument the African Based Childrearing Opinion Survey is completed in 10 to 15 minutes. No substantial difference is found between the self-administered and interviewer-read scales. Either method of administration is acceptable, but the researchers should be alert to the mood, interest and reading skill level of the respondent in order to determine which procedure would yield the more reliable data.

The age range of the sample of the study was 18 to 86 years. As part of our continuing development and refinement of the scale it was administered to a group of teenage parents (age 15-19) with infant children.

Scoring and Evaluation

The items were weighted so that the high score on a particular item would represent a strong sense of Africanity or the continuation of the African cultural tradition for the particular cultural feature addressed. For negatively worded items the respondent would have to disagree with the item to be considered high on Africanity. The weights for these items were reversed in the scoring and coding stage of the data manipulation. The subject's score on the individual subscale is the sum of the weighted alternatives. The subscales were comprised of different numbers of items. To take into account the fact that subjects may not respond to every item on the scale, the individual's score is determined by dividing the sum of the items by the number of items the subject responded to for that particular subscale. A similar procedure would also be followed with regards to the construction of the total score for the scale. The range of scores was 1 to 4 with the higher score reflecting a stronger sense of Africanity.

Normative Standardization and Sample Characteristics

The scale was evaluated using data from a random sample of 66 families drawn from the San Francisco Metropolitan Bay Area. This sample of 66 families yielded 85 adults ranging in ages from 18 to 86 years.

The sample population was comprised of mostly middle-aged (35-40 years of age) adults having an average of 3 to 4 children. The median family income was $11,500, slightly above the national median Black family income of $9,563 (1978). The families on the average lived mainly in two-parent households. Although the mothers were slightly better educated than the fathers, the adults in general were well educated, with the majority having completed high school and having some college education. Most rented their homes and slightly less than half owned at least one automobile. The overwhelming majority of the respondents were Protestant, mainly Baptist.

Although, the sample was relatively small, in many ways (i.e., family composition, family size, family income, and education) it approximated the features of the national Black population. In this sense the sample could be considered a normative, representative sample of the Black population.

Scale Evaluation

For the initial evaluation of the scale the total score of each individual was computed. Each item on the scale was then correlated with the total score. The logic of this analysis was that if the item is an indicator of the underlying concept which is a representation of the cultural theme then it should correlate significantly with the total score which represents the overall concept, Africanity or the African cultural orientation. Based on this initial analysis, six of the 41 items did not significantly correlate with the average score and were eliminated from further consideration. All subsequent analyses are thus based on the reconstituted scale of 35 items.

Reliability

The reliability of the scale was determined through the split-half method for assessing the consistency of items. The scale was divided into odd and even items, these were summed and the scores on the two halves were then correlated. The split–half correlation was then corrected using the Spearman-Brown formula. The reliability coefficient was 0.891

Validity

Traditionally socialization styles in African society were based on the conception of the child being already endowed with his full potential. Dynamic power is present in the child but it is shaped and given form and made willfully present, where there was only potential, by the power of human understanding in social interaction (Chernoff, 1979). This power, the essence of the child, is not revealed but directed through the sensitivity of the parent. The sensitivity in the treatment of the child represents a method of actively tolerating, interpreting and even using the multiple and fragmented aspects of everyday life to build a richer and more diversified personal experience for the child. Within the African framework a person is what others see him to be and he finds himself insofar as he is accessible to their influence. Africans expect dialogue in the socialization process, they anticipate movement in attitudes and behavior and above all they stay open to influence and change. Thus, the traditional socialization style reflects an understanding of a sense of time and presence which dictated a sense of proportion in self-awareness and an attitude of thoughtfulness in self-expression. Thus, the socialization process lays heavy emphasis on adaptability, spontaneity, alertness, persistence and interpersonal sensitivity. The implication of this process is that children learn to react to situations as they develop and parents affirm their authority over their children without destroying the child's generalized feelings of competence.

As a new instrument designed specifically for the purpose of explicating the cultural basis of African American peoples, it represents a significant departure from traditional instruments that have been developed primarily for European American populations. As such the process of establishing the validity of the instrument becomes somewhat difficult and complex.

Content validity is attributed to the instrument on the basis of the grounding of the items on the theoretical notions of Africanity. The items included in the scale were also evaluated by a national panel of Black "experts" and deemed to be valid for the purpose developed.

In addition to content validity the scale was assessed for concurrent validity using two criterion measures selected from other sections of the data collection battery.

The first measure used items from the Childrearing Preference Scale (CRPS) which was derived from items on the General Opinion Survey dealing with attitudes towards the treatment of children. The CRPS assesses the extent to which parents are positive and adaptable in their treatment of the child as shown by a willingness to engage in behavior that respects the child as a significant person. The high score represents a positive attitude towards the treatment of the child. The Black family is a child-centered system which exists for the growth and development of the child. The child is the focus of attention within the family system. Thus the treatment of the child reflects the tone and character (i.e., the ethos) of the family system.

The second criterion measure was the response to the open-ended question "how do you feel about your child teasing you?" Responses to the question were coded along the dimension of acceptance and flexibility in regards to the child's behavior. Responses such as "don't allow it" and "it is not allowed in my house" were coded as nonacceptance. Responses like "it is natural" and "it is part of growing up" were coded as acceptant. The range was 1 to 3 with 1 representing acceptant treatment of the child. It should be noted, however, that the traditional notion of "unconditional love" in Black family lifestyles results, in fact, in a childrearing approach which is accep-

Table 1. Means and Standard Deviations of ABCROS Subscales ($N = 66$)

Subscale	Mean	S.D.
Interpersonal Connectedness (interdependence)	3.00	.36
Collective Responsibility (mutual aid)	2.93	.38
Adaptability	3.12	.37
Compassion	2.96	.48
Respect	3.13	.40
Cooperation	2.77	.46
Racial Pride	3.25	.49
Cultural Awareness	3.21	.42
Media Influence	2.95	.48
Education	2.82	.41
Total	3.01	.28

tant of the child's behavior, yet not indulgent of anything a child does or wants.

The two indicators were considered to be good criterion measures in that they represent the extent to which parents are adaptable and flexible in their treatment of children.

The correlation between the Africanity Scale and The Childrearing Preference Scale was 0.572, significant at the 0.001 level, and that between the attitudes about testing and Africanity was -0.294, significant at the 0.01 level. This would indicate a high degree of concurrent validity for the scale. The scale can be validated with the World-View Scale developed by Baldwin as part of an ongoing research effort to empirically discriminate basic cultural/world-view differences (Baldwin & Hopkins, 1990). The Baldwin World-View Scale consists of 26 items tapping bipolar (Africentric and Eurocentric) dimensions of the African and European world-views. Empirical data indicate that a significant difference in world-view scores occurred between Black and White subjects regardless of age and sex. Technical assessment of the scale indicates good reliability and validity (split-half reliability corrected by Spearman-Brown Prophecy Formula .51 significant at .01 level; inter-item (internal) consistency .51 significant at .01 level). The World-View Scale shows great promise as a viable instrument for assessing world-view/cultural differences. The Magaji World-View Opinionnaire (1983) devel-

oped from the principles of African psychology explicated by Cedric X (Clark) et al. (1975) could also serve as an excellent source of further validation for our instrument. Given that both instruments are developed to measure a particular cultural orientation, we would expect a high positive correlation between them.

Technical Assessment

The means and standard deviations of the African Based Childrearing Opinion Survey subscales are listed in Table 1. All the means are generally high indicating that in general the sense of Africanity is high in the sample population.

The ten subscale scores were intercorrelated. The intercorrelations shown in Table 2 are moderately high indicating that the subscales measure distinct though somewhat related aspects of the cultural perspective of the sample. The subscale scores were also correlated with the total score. These correlations are shown in Table 3. As seen, the correlations were all high indicating that the different dimensions of the scale were all tapping different aspects of the same underlying dimension.

Additional Analysis

The average score of the reconstituted 35-item scale was rank ordered. The means were com-

Table 2. ABCROS Subscale Interrcorrelations ($N = 85$)

	Mutual Aid	Adaptability	Compassion	Respect Pride	Cooperation Pride	Racial Awareness	Cultural Influence	Media	Education
Interdependence	.26	.62	.57	.58	.43	.48	.57	.42	.40
Mutual Aid		.21	.46	.31	.34	.29	.35	.30	.39
Adaptability			.50	.48	.35	.52	.54	.42	.27
Compassion				.52	.61	.59	.52	.41	.23
Respect					.31	.42	.46	.16	.30
Cooperation						.45	.33	.45	.29
Racial Pride							.59	.59	.37
Cultural Awareness								.44	.39
Media Influences									.35

puted for the top twenty percent (20%) (the high Africanity group) and the bottom twenty percent (20%) (the low Africanity group), and a *t*-test of the difference of the means was performed to see if the scale was discriminating between respondents. The test yield a "t" of 14.01 which was significant at the 0.05 level, indicating that the sample means were different. The implication of this is that the scale does discriminate among subjects and provides us with an easily administered and readily interpreted technique for assessing the African based cultural orientation of Black parents.

Further Use of the Scale

Although devised specifically to assess attitudes about childrearing practices, the scale provides a measure of the cultural orientations of African Americans. As such it should have wide applicability in the scientific analysis of culture, social change and values transformation. We anticipate that other scholars would utilize the scale in cross-cultural studies throughout the African diaspora, as well as regional studies within American society. For example the scale could be utilized in studies in the Caribbean region and

Table 3. ABCROS Subscale–Total Score Correlations ($N = 85$)

Subscales	Subscale Total Score Correlation
Interdependence	.81
Mutual Aid	.56
Adaptability	.71
Compassion	.78
Respect	.65
Cooperation	.64
Racial pride	.73
Cultural Awareness	.72
Media influences	.65
Education	.57

Brazil to assess the nature of the continuity of African values as well as to determine the areas that have changed. Similarly, in regional analyses of American society, studies could be undertaken to document, for example, the similarities in the cultural orientations the, effects of urbanization on values transformation, and intergenerational continuities and discontinuities in cultural orientation. In our current ongoing research program we are using the scale to assess the cultural orientations of teenage parents. The scale is also being utilized in two dissertation studies in New Jersey.

Summary

The technical assessment of the African-Based Childrearing Opinion Survey indicates that the scale is both a valid and reliable instrument and that it has discriminating power. As such we believe that the scale represents a significant breakthrough in the development of measurement techniques for the scientific study of the Black experience. By revealing the underlying cultural framework of the Black population the scale could form the basis for documenting the processes of cultural change the Black population is currently undergoing. This aspect is particularly important as the scientific community looks in greater detail at the process of child development and the influence of cultural variables on this process.

Note

1. This instrument was developed as part of a Research Grant (ACYF Grant #90-C-901, Wade W. Nobles, Ph.D., Principal Investigator).

References

Baldwin, J., & Hopkins, R. (1990). African-American and European-American cultural differences as assessed by the worldviews paradigm: An empirical analysis. *The Western Journal of Black Studies, 14*, 38-52.

Chernoff, J. (1979). *African rhythm and African sensibility.* Chicago: The University of Chicago Press.

Magaji, M. (1983, August). *A comparison of African and European groups utilizing a world-view opinionnaire.* Paper presented at the 16th Annual Convention of the Association of Black Psychologists, Washington, DC.

Nobles, W. W. (1982). The reclamation of culture and the right to reconciliation: An Africentric perspective on developing and implementing programs for the mentally retarded offender. In A. R Harvey & T. L. Carr (Eds.), *The Black mentally retarded offender: A holistic approach to prevention and habilitation.* New York: The United Church of Christ Commission for Racial Justice.

Nobles, W. W. (1985). African consciousness and liberation struggles: Implications for the development and construction of scientific paradigms. *Journal of Black Studies, 1*, 34-39.

Osei, G. K. (1970). African and Afro-American family structure: A comparison. *The Black Scholar, 2*, 37-60.

Tempels, P. (1959). *Bantu philosophy.* Paris: Presence Africaine.

Thomas, L. V. (1961). Time, myth and history in West Africa. *Presence Africane, 11*, 50-92.

Thomas, L. V. (1960). A Senegalese philosophical system: The cosmology of the Jolah people. *Presence Africane, 4*, 32-33, 192-203.

Wiredu, K. (1980). *Philosophy and an African culture.* Cambridge: Cambridge University Press.

X (Clark), Cedric, McGee, D. P., Nobles, W. W., & Akbar, N. (1975). *Voodoo or IQ: An introduction to African psychology.* Chicago: Institute of Positive Education.

For additional information, contact:

Wade W. Nobles
175 Filbert St., Suite 202
Oakland, CA 94607
Telephone: (510) 836-3245

Part IX

Measures of Family Structure and Dynamics

A Typology of Household Structure in the Black Community

William W. Dressler and Susan Haworth-Hoeppner

Abstract

The nature of household and family structure in the Black community has been a continuing source of controversy, with discussions focused on the relatively high prevalence of female-headed households. This focus is problematic, however, because there has been a failure to place female-headed households within the context of the diversity of household structure within the Black community. In this chapter we propose a system for classifying Black household structures which more accurately reflects this range of diversity. This system classifies households according to marital ties, gender of household head, and types of kinship relationships among household members. The construct validity of this typology is evaluated by the between-household differences along a number of sociocultural parameters. Different ways of using the typology and implications for future research are discussed.

The study of household and family structure in African American communities has generated considerable debate and controversy over the past fifty years. The debate has revolved around a single issue: is family and household structure in the Black community indicative of "social disorganization," or are distinctive features of African American domestic groups adaptations to economic marginality and oppression? The social disorganization perspective was first proposed by Frazier (1939), who saw differences in Black household organization as deviant forms of the general American family. In Frazier's perspective, disorganization was a result of low social class and the economic marginality of males. An early opposite view was espoused by Herskovits (1941), who argued that distinctive features of Black families should not be viewed as deviant, but rather culturally different and valid in their own right. The debate has continued to the present between those who see the Black family as disorganized and contributing to poverty and pathology (Moynihan, 1965; Scanzoni, 1977), and those who see Black domestic groups as adaptations to economic marginality and oppression (Billingsley, 1968; Hill, 1972).

As Myers (1982) notes in his review of this literature, the empirical basis for this debate revolves around a single finding: there are more Black female-headed households than White. Recent estimates place Black female-headed households between 37% and 40% of the total, and White female-headed households between 11% and 15% of the total.

While the debates over Black family and household structure have been useful in clarifying a variety of issues, there are a number of shortcomings in the literature which need to be addressed in order to help further empirical work in the area. One important area in need of development is a system for classifying domestic groups or households in Black communities. Much of the debate about Black household structure has taken place in the absence of a systematic taxonomy of household types, and disputes over the implications of different types of domestic groups are fruitless if those types are not considered in relation to the overall context of community diversity.

Most often a two-category classification system is applied to Black households, distinguishing nuclear family and female-headed households. Clearly, a simple dichotomy such as this is not complete, nor is an expanded categorization based on gender of household head and presence or absence of children. Yet it is precisely these kinds of ad hoc household categories that predominate the research literature (Bianchi, 1981), especially studies based on census data. This approach is isolated from the sociocultural and developmental contexts of Black households. In a truly pioneering effort in the study of Black families, Billingsley (1968) proposed a typology consisting of three basic forms: nuclear; extended; and augmented families. These forms then varied as to the presence or absence of children and whether or not both parents were present. However, when this typology was employed in a later community study it failed to account for 40% of all households (Williams & Stockton, 1973). Finally, Shimkin, Louie, and Frate (1978) proposed a dichotomy of "strong" and "weak" families, but this refers to inter-household networks. While of clear importance (Stack, 1974), this concept does not classify domestic groups, and it suffers from a lack of operational specificity.

There is thus a need for a framework which will encompass the different types of household structures found in the Black community. Our aim in the remainder of this chapter is to address this issue, employing data collected as part of a larger study of mental health in a Black community located in the southern U.S. First, a description of the household typology and its development will be presented. Second, as a test of construct validity, the differences among household types along a variety of cultural, social, and psychological parameters will be examined. And third, systems for collecting, coding, and retrieving data on household structure will be discussed.

A Typology of Household Structure

The database from which the typology was developed is derived from research in the Black community of a small (pop. = 75,000) southern city.[1] The Black community itself has a population of approximately 20,000. In the survey research component of the larger study (Dressler, 1985; 1991) a sample of 285 households was selected from the community to gather quantitative data on mental health status, socioeconomic status, family structure, and related sociocultural factors. Sampling has been described in greater detail elsewhere (Dressler, 1985, 1991). Descriptively, two-thirds of the sample were female and one-third was male. Age quartiles were 17-34, 35-49, 50-65, and over 65. Twenty-two percent of the sample graduated from high school, and an additional 29.5% attended some college. With respect to employment, 48.4% of the respondents were employed, 10.5% were housewives, 23.9% were retired or students, and 17.2% were unemployed. About half (46.7%) of the respondents reported yearly incomes of less than $5,000.

We first experimented with Billingsley's (1968) typology, but like Williams and Stockton (1973) we found that it failed to account for about 40% of all households in the community. This failure stems primarily from the fact that the Billingsley typology requires the presence or absence of children to distinguish between households. We found (as did Williams & Stockton) that a substantial proportion of households do not

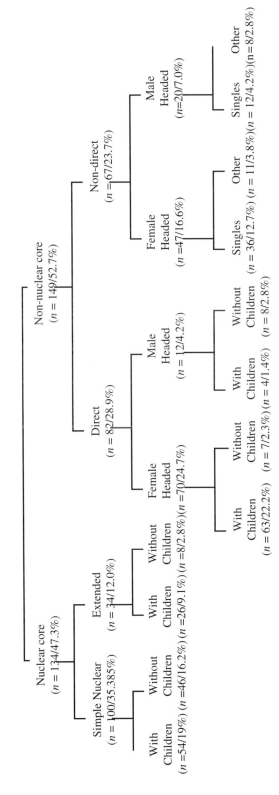

Figure 1. Differences Among Household Types on Selected Variables

contain children, but often contain other kinds of relatives and/or nonrelatives. We therefore constructed our own typology, shown in Fig. 1. The primary basis for this typology is the presence or absence of a married pair, or what we call a "nuclear core." Essentially this distinction splits the sample in half: 47.3% of the households have a nuclear family core, while 52.7% of the households contain no nuclear family.

The next step in the typology then differs for each of these groups of households. Households containing a nuclear core can be distinguished in terms of them being simple nuclear households, consisting of a single married couple with or without children (but excluding grandchildren); or extended family households, consisting of a married couple with or without children, but with the addition of other relatives. These other relatives may consist of siblings or other collateral kin, or may be grandchildren (making the household a generationally extended household). Extended family households make up 12.0% of all households, and the majority of these have children in the home.

Households with a non-nuclear family core can be distinguished primarily in terms of the nature of the relationship between the household head and other household members. We refer to these as direct and nondirect relationships. By direct relationship we mean a lineal kinship relationship, either ascending or descending (i.e., an individual living with any combination of the following relatives, but excluding any other individuals: parents, grandparents, children, or grandchildren). By nondirect relationship we mean a lateral kinship relationship (e.g., adult siblings, cousins, aunts or uncles), or nonrelatives. We recognize that this is a somewhat unorthodox categorization of kin, but it does describe well the empirical reality in the community, and it is consistent with cultural analyses of kinship in U.S. minority communities (Schneider & Smith, 1973). The distinction between direct and nondirect relationships divides the non-nuclear core households into groups of nearly equivalent size. Within direct and nondirect households, smaller subsets can be identified on the basis of gender of the household head.

The final step in the typology of non-nuclear core households distinguishes between households on the basis of other persons in the household. For households based on direct relationships this distinction is between households with children and households with other kinds of direct relationships. For households based on nondirect relationships this distinction is between persons living alone and persons living with nondirect relatives and/or nonrelatives. It is somewhat cumbersome to speak of an individual living alone as being in a "nondirect household"; however, our evidence indicates that very often living alone is a temporary affair, bridging a gap between household types (Dressler, Haworth-Hoeppner, & Pitts, 1985). Therefore, it seems appropriate to classify single persons under the category of nondirect households.

This typology conveniently classifies every household in the community. Furthermore, it helps to redirect our thinking about households. Most important in this respect is the entire concept of the female-headed household. Classifying households according to the present typology reveals different kinds of female-headed households. The one most commonly referred to in the literature and in popular conceptions of the Black family, a woman with her children and/or grandchildren, accounts for 22.2% of all households. Other types of female-headed households include women living alone (12.7%), women living with other relatives and/or nonrelatives (3.8%), and women living with parents or grandparents (2.4%). Summing up these four subtypes we find 41.1% total female-headed households. This is consistent with totals reported in the published literature, but these clearly are very different kinds of households and this should be recognized. It is also interesting that almost a quarter of all households are based on nondirect relationships. The majority of these are single persons who have been widowed; however, a portion of this subset of households is formed by the widowed person incorporating nonrelatives and/or more distant kin into his or her household.

It may seem unusual that only 12.0% of all households are extended family households, given the emphasis on extended kin in the Black community. A major function of extended kin, however, is the linkage of inter-household networks, so their importance is not necessarily in the composition of domestic groups (Dressler, 1985; Dressler et al. 1985).

Finally, it is worth noting that the "average" household, in the sense of being the modal category, is the simple nuclear family, accounting for 35.3% of all households.

Construct Validity

Construct validity refers to the assessment of validity through the determination of relationships between the factor of interest and other factors presumed to be related to it (Kerlinger, 1973: 461-464). In the present case, if the typology of household structure proposed here is a valid set of categories for the Black community, then there should be significant differences among the households on a wide variety of variables. There is no established set of variables believed to contrast among households; we therefore chose a range of variables that would provide a general sense of how households, and especially household heads, differ along a number of dimensions. Six categories of households were used to make comparisons. The level of contrast provided by direct and nondirect was felt to be too general, and it missed the female- headed household. Since a primary research interest in the literature has been to contrast that household type with other types, we chose to compare female-headed direct, male-headed direct, female-headed nondirect, male-headed nondirect, simple nuclear, and extended family households. This set of contrasts provided a sufficiently detailed breakdown of the data, while still leaving sufficient numbers of cases within categories for valid statistical analysis.

Variables chosen to contrast these household types were as follows: economic stressors, mass media use, material style of life, alcohol use, extended kin support, extended kin interaction, age of respondent, household size, and socioeconomic status.[2] Again, these are not intended to be exhaustive of differences between households, but rather to sample important theoretical domains along which households should differ. The mean differences between household types, along with the results of analysis of variance of those differences, are shown in Table 1. It should also be kept in mind that respondents were either head of household or spouse.

Differences among the households are all highly significant, and no one household type stands out as being distinct along all parameters. Differences in scores on economic stressors result primarily from the elevation of those scores in female-headed households. On use of mass media and material style of life, both types of nuclear family households are highest. Male-headed households, direct and nondirect, are highest in terms of reported alcohol use. Both types of nuclear family households are high on extended kin support, with male-headed direct reporting most extended kin interaction. Finally, women heading nondirect households tend to be older, have smaller households, and to be lowest in socioeconomic status (see Dressler et al. (1985) for a more extensive discussion of differences between households). Classifying households according to these principles yields household types that can be distinguished along theoretically relevant dimensions.

An additional bit of evidence concerning the construct validity of this typology is that when household types are broken down by age quartiles, there is strong evidence of a developmental cycle. As age of household head increases, the prevalence of female-headed direct households decreases. The prevalence of nuclear family households increases markedly up to age 64, and then declines sharply above that. The prevalence of female-headed nondirect households increases slightly up to age 64, and then sharply above that. The prevalence of male-headed households of both types shows a fluctuating pattern across age groups (see Dressler et al. [1985] for a more detailed discussion of these patterns). Thus, households are not fixed entities, but rather vary systematically over time. Since a systematic developmental cycle of household would be theoretically anticipated, this analysis provides further evidence of construct validity.

Recording, Coding, and Retrieving Household Data

Obtaining data on household structure, like any form of data collection, should be tailored to the specific needs of a research project. Here we

Table 1. Differences Among Household Types on Selected Variables

	Female headed direct (n = 70)	Male headed direct (n = 12)	Female headed nondirect (n = 47)	Male headed nondirect (n = 20)	Simple Nuclear (n = 100)	Extended (n = 34)	F	p <
Economic Stressors	2.78	2.30	2.21	2.26	2.17	2.40	7.72	0.001
Mass media use	12.47	13.66	11.42	13.00	14.08	14.18	3.14	0.008
Material style of life	9.46	9.20	9.04	8.35	11.62	11.58	9.48	0.001
Alcohol use	0.71	1.41	0.17	1.30	0.87	0.58	6.91	0.001
Extended kin support	4.15	3.91	2.11	2.35	4.80	4.88	9.84	0.001
Extended kin interaction	1.63	2.16	0.66	1.23	1.42	1.66	11.04	0.001
Age	41.6	46.0	67.0	50.15	49.0	44.6	18.20	0.001
Household size	4.3	3.6	1.4	1.4	3.3	5.0	30.71	0.001
Socioeconomic status	-0.42	-0.42	-0.76	- 0.48	0.61	0.56	28.49	0.001

will describe one way of gathering, coding, and manipulating data on household structure to generate the typology described above. Additionally, we will suggest some modifications of this procedure which might prove useful in particular kinds of research.

Table 2 shows an open-ended interview format for obtaining data on household structure. This simply involves asking the names, ages, and relationship to the respondent of every individual in the household. This information can then be coded into a data file using two 2-column fields for each household member. The first 2-column field is for the age of the household member, and the second 2-column field is for coding the relationship between that household member and the respondent. Table 3 shows a set of relationship codes we are currently using in a cross-cultural

study of household structure. This set of codes is sufficiently detailed for our present purpose, and it could be easily expandable (up to 99 different kinds of relationships) if more detailed information is deemed necessary (e.g. to distinguish father's from mother's father within grandparents).

Data on household type can then be retrieved using a series of data-modification procedures that are readily available in most standard statistical software packages, or which would be easily programmed in any of several computer languages. Table 4 shows the data-modification statements necessary to generate the six household types used in the analysis of construct validity reported above.

The data-modification statements are for the SPSS software package (SPSSX, 1986), which is

Table 2. **Open-Ended Format for Data on Household Structure**

Question: Now I would like to find out about the other people who live in this household: their names, ages, and how they are related to you.

	Name	Age	Relationship
1.	_____	_____	_____
2.	_____	_____	_____
3.	_____	_____	_____
4.	_____	_____	_____
5.	_____	_____	_____
.			
.			
.			
.			
.			
n.	_____	_____	_____

one widely available package. We use these six types as categories in our permanent data file, but one can easily move up or down in the typology with the addition of statements.

Constructing the typology begins with the definition of six new variables measuring the presence or number of the following kinds of individuals in the household: a conjugal partner of the household head; the total number of lineal kinship relationships to the household head; the total number of children (minus other lineal relatives) of the household head; the total number of lineal (excluding children) relatives; the total number of nonlineal kinship relationships to the household head; and the total number of unrelated persons in the household. By then selecting various combinations of these relationships, along with gender of the household head as shown in Table 3, the six household types can be generated.

As we noted above, the choice of procedures for collecting and coding data on household structure needs to be tailored to the specific needs of a research project. What has been just described has been a set of procedures for collecting all

possible information on the structure of a household. Where it is feasible this is the procedure that should be followed. There are other instances, however, where a more truncated procedure may be useful. For example, differences between female-headed direct households and other household types has been a focus of interest in Black community research for some time. Unfortunately, too often a sample of female-headed households is selected from case records of a social service agency, for example, which automatically introduces an uncontrolled selection factor into the research design. This selection factor may interact with other variables in unknown ways to generate unreplicable findings. An alternative to this sampling strategy would be to do a mass screening of households in the community gathering only information on household structure. In this strategy it would probably be most useful to use a set of branching questions to enable the interviewer to categorize the household during or immediately following the interview (which would take at most about 10 minutes). A sample of female-headed direct households and a compari-

Table 3. Categories for Coding Household Relationships

1 = respondent	10 = son	19 = sister's husband	28 = cousin
2 = husband	11 = daughter	20 = brother's partner	29 = male, nonrelative, friend
3 = wife	12 = stepson	21 = sister's partner	30 = female, nonrelative, friend
4 = partner/male	13 = stepdaughter	22 = brother-in-law	31 = employer
5 = partner/female	14 = grandson	23 = sister-in-law	32 = helper
6 = mother	15 = granddaughter	24 = niece	33 = household head
7 = father	16 = brother	25 = nephew	34 = father-in-law
8 = grandmother	17 = sister	26 = uncle	35 = mother-in-law
9 = grandfather	18 = brother's wife	27 = aunt	

son group could then be selected from the community.

Another, even more economical strategy, would be to use a variate of "snowball" sampling. In this approach a set of branching questions could be used to categorize the household during the initial part of the interview. Then, if the household corresponded to a type desired for inclusion in the research, the subsequent part of the interview would be conducted. This procedure could be continued until a desired number of households of each type had been obtained.

Implications for Future Research

A major task in future research will be to replicate the typology proposed here, and to determine how the distribution of household types varies across different Black communities. This typology usefully classifies every household in the sample studied here, and is therefore representative of the range of variation of households in this particular community. As we have argued elsewhere, this southern Black community is representative of only one particular type of Black community in the U.S. (Dressler, 1985, 1991; Dressler & Badger, 1985). This community is a geographically delimited, socially conservative, traditional Black community. Therefore, given that intra-cultural diversity within the Black community tends to be large (Green, 1970), it is likely that the distribution of household types within different communities will change systemically

along with the socioeconomic characteristics of those communities. One aim of future research should be to document this range of variation in the distribution of domestic groups.

A second major task of future research will be to examine theoretically relevant factors in relation to household and family structure (Dressler, 1993). For example, there have been many questions raised concerning child-rearing practices in female-headed direct versus nuclear family households (Hill, 1972). Simply comparing female-headed and nuclear family households, or worse, Black female-headed and white nuclear family households, systematically ignores a portion of the true range of variation. Minimally, a study of child-rearing practices in the Black community should compare nuclear family, extended family, and female-headed direct households, and should include the size and strength of inter-household support systems as a second factor. This is just one example. The general point is that any statement concerning the "effects of" Black household and family structure must be phrased in terms of the actual range of variation of these factors within the community.

The literature on Black household and family structure has succeeded in moving beyond inappropriate ethnic comparisons to a consideration of the adaptive potential of domestic groups and kinship systems. The typology proposed here is one attempt in the direction of placing this important focus of research on a more sound operational footing.

Table 4. SPSS Data-Modification Statements for Categorizing Households

---

Variables for categorizing households:

CS = conjugal status (1 = married/cohabiting; 0 = single)
SEX = gender of household head (1 = male; 0 = female)
CHILD = total number of children of household head in household
TLR = total number of lineal relatives in household
SUBTOT = TLR–CHILD
TNLR = total number of nonlineal relatives in household
UNREL = total number of unrelated individuals in household

Data modification statements:

IF... (CS EQ 0 AND TLR GE 1 AND SEX EQ 0) HHTYPE = Female-headed direct household
IF... (CS EQ 0 AND TLR GE 1 AND SEX EQ 1) HHTYPE = Male-headed direct household
IF... (CS EQ 0 AND TLR EQ 0 AND SEX EQ 0) HHTYPE = Female-headed nondirect household
IF... (CS EQ 0 AND TLR EQ 0 AND SEX EQ 1) HHTYPE = Male-headed nondirect household
IF... (CS EQ 1 AND CHILD EQ 0 AND TLR EQ 0 AND TNLR EQ 0 AND UNREL EQ 0) HHTYPE
= Simple nuclear
IF... (CS EQ 1 AND CHILD GE 1 AND SUBTOT EQ 0 AND TNLR EQ 0 AND UNREAL EQ 0)
HHTYPE = Simple nuclear
IF... (CS EQ 1 AND TLR GE 1 AND TNLR GE 1 AND UNREL EQ 0) HHTYPE = Extended
IF... (CS EQ 1 AND TLR GE 1 AND TNLR GE 1 AND UNREL GE 1) HHTYPE = Extended
IF... (CS EQ 1 AND CHILD EQ 0 AND SUBTOT GE 1 AND UNREL EQ 0) HHTYPE = Extended
IF... (CS EQ 1 AND TLR EQ 0 AND UNREL GE 1) HHTYPE = Extended

---

Note. These data-modification statements are set up for a data-set in which all respondents are either the head of household or spouse of head of households.

Notes

1. This research was supported by research grants 1R01MH33943 and 2R01MH33943 from the Center for the Study of Minority Group Mental Health, National Institute of Mental Health.

2. These variables were operationalized as follows. *Economic stressors* was an 8-item scale of common economic problems (score range = 1.0 - 4.0; $M(\pm$s.d.$) = 2.37$ (± 0.70); reliability = .69). *Mass media use* was a 10-item scale of frequency of watching TV, reading, etc. (score range = 0.0 - 21.0; $M(\pm$s.d.$) = 13.2$ (± 4.4); reliability = 0.75). *Material style of life* was a 12-item scale of accumulation of material culture such as TVs, stereos, cars, major appliances, etc. (score range = 0.0 - 18.0; $M(\pm = 10.3$ (± 3.2); reliability

= .78). *Alcohol use* was a single item of frequency of use (score range = 0.0 - 3.0; $M(\pm$s.d.$) = 0.73$ $(\pm (0.9)$. *Extended kin support* was an 8-item scale assessing the instrumental and emotional support provided by kin (score range = 0.0 - 14.0; $M(\pm$s.d.$)$ = 4.0 (± 2.7); reliability = .70). *Extended kin interaction* measured frequency of interaction with kin (score range = 0.0 - 4.0; $M(\pm$s.d.$) = 1.4$ (± 0.9). *Age* (score range = 17-88, $M(\pm$s.d.$) = 49.6$ (± 16.7)) and *household size* (score range = 1.0 - 11.0; $M(\pm$s.d.$) = 3.3$ (± 2.0)) are self-explanatory. *Socioeconomic status* was measured as a standardized principal components score combining occupational status, current employment status, amount of employment in past year, and income, for the household head (and spouse, if present) (score range = -1.13 - 2.89; $M(\pm$s.d.$) = 0.0$ (± 1.0)).

References

Bianchi, S. M. (1981). *Household composition and racial inequality.* New Brunswick, NJ: Rutgers University Press.

Billingsley, A. (1968). *Black families in White America.* Englewood Cliffs, NJ: Prentice-Hall.

Dressler, W. W. (1985). Extended family relationships, social support, and mental health in a southern Black community. *Journal of Health and Social Behavior, 26,* 39-45.

Dressler, W. W. (1985). *Stress and adaptation in the context of culture: Depression in a southern Black community.* Albany: State University of New York Press.

Dressler, W. W. (1991). Health in the African American community: Accounting for health inequalities. *Medical Anthropology Quarterly, 7,* 325-345.

Dressler, W. W., & Badger, L. W. (1985). Epidemiology of depressive symptoms in the Black community: A comparative analysis. *Journal of Nervous and Mental Disease, 173,* 212-220.

Dressler, W. W., Haworth-Hoeppner, S., & Pitts, B. J. (1985). Household structure in a southern Black community. *American Anthropologist, 87,* 853-862.

Green, V. (1970). The confrontation of diversity in the Black community. *Human Organization, 29,* 267-272.

Herskovits, M. J. (1941). *The myth of the Negro past.* New York: Harper.

Hill, R. (1972). *The strengths of Black families.* New York: Emerson-Hall.

Kerlinger, F. N. (1973). *Foundations of behavior research* (2nd ed.). New York: Holt, Rinehart and Winston.

Moynihan, D. P. (1965). *The Negro family: A case for national action.* Washington, DC: U.S. Government Printing Office.

Myers, H. F. (1982). Research on the Afro-American family: A critical review. In B. A. Bass, G. E. Wyatt, & G. J. Powell (Eds.). *The Afro-American family.* New York: Grune and Stratton.

Scanzoni, J. (1977). *The Black family in modern society: Patterns of stability and security.* Chicago: The University of Chicago Press.

Schneider, D., & Smith, R. T. (1973). *Class differences and sex roles in American kinship and family structure.* Englewood Cliffs, NJ: Prentice-Hall.

Shimkin, D. B., Louie, G. J., & Frate, D. A. (1978). The Black extended family: A basic rural institution and a mechanism of urban adaptation. In D. B. Shimkin, E. M. Shimkin, & D. A. Frate (Eds.), *The extended family in Black societies.* The Netherlands: The Hague: Mouton.

SPSSX. (1986) *User's Guide.* Chicago, IL: SPSS.

Stack, C. B. (1974). *All our kin.* New York: Harper and Row.

Williams, J. A., & Stockton, R. (1973). Black family structures and functions. *Journal of Marriage and the Family, 35,* 39-49.

For additional information, contact:

William W. Dressler
P. O. Box 870326
The University of Alabama
Tuscaloosa, AL 35487-0326
Telephone: (205) 348-1354   .
Fax: (205) 348-7685
E-mail: WDRESSLE@UA1VM.UA.EDU

The Development of the Black Family Process Q-Sort

M. Jean Peacock, Carolyn B. Murray, Daniel J. Ozer, and Julie E. Stokes[1]

Abstract

Recent research has challenged social scientists to examine developmental, psychological, and environmental processes that impact African American youth, particularly parenting. To address these issues a series of studies were conducted to develop and validate a Q-Sort instrument–the Black Family Process Q-Sort (BFPQ)–to investigate socialization strategies *within* African American families. The BFPQ includes the domains of race socialization, family discipline, communication, and values. Results indicated that Statements describing parents' attitudes toward their ethnic group, the dominant culture, and parenting strategies, can be sorted to identify and differentiate socialization orientations.

Introduction

Recent research has challenged social scientists to examine developmental, psychological, and environmental processes that impact African American youth, particularly parenting (see McLoyd, 1990; Tinsley, 1992). Much of the literature that pertains to African Americans employs concepts, instruments and procedures developed in Euro-American populations (see Murray & Fairchild, 1989; Murray, Smith, & West, 1989), and may be inappropriate because African American families' particular historical experience, cultural perspective, and relationship to major institutions (e.g., educational system, justice system, etc.) of society. Moreover, the role of the family has also been largely ignored in previous empirical work on personal and group identity development in African Americans (Jackson, McCullough, & Gurin, 1988). To address these issues a series of studies were conducted to develop and validate a Q-Sort instrument—the Black Family Process Q-Sort (BFPQ)—to investigate socialization strategies within African American families.

Family Research: State of the Art

Early theoretical models employed to explain the nature of the African American family developed from a deficit framework (Peters, 1988), placing responsibility for the lower status position

475

of African Americans (e.g., mental disorders, underachievement, poverty, unemployment, etc.) on the shoulders of the family (Boykin & Toms, 1985). Specifically, this cultural deprivation model suggested that past economic and social discrimination (including slavery, segregation, urbanization and residential isolation) led to *self-perpetuating* conditions (i.e., dysfunctional socialization practices and values, etc.) that resulted in the development of dysfunctional personality traits (e.g., low self-concept, an external locus of control, and aggressive or impulsive behavior) which culminated in lower status for African Americans (see Murray & Fairchild, 1989). These deficit approaches, that contrasted African American family behavior to that of Euro-Americans, offered little to aid in unraveling the essence of family life among African Americans.

After several decades of research, the validity of the assumptions of the deficit model remains dubious (Murray & Fairchild, 1989). The use of procedures, constructs, methods, and approaches developed in the majority population have yielded biased results, masked important relationships, and prevented valid interpretations of findings. Baumrind (1972) was among the first psychologists to indicate the importance of studying African American families in their own right, apart from European American families.

Baumrind found that her conceptualization of functional disciplinary practices did not easily generalize to African Americans. Baumrind conducted a separate analysis on data generated by 16 African American families who participated in a study of parental authority and preschool behavior with a predominantly Euro-American middle class sample. The sample of African American families, on the average, was of lower social class. Although the sample was small, Baumrind was impressed with the highly functional child rearing pattern (authoritarian) of African American families, whereas the optimal functional pattern among Whites was authoritative. Baumrind suggested that the authoritarian parental style was qualitatively different for African American parents. African American parents were not as emotionally rigid as were their European American counterparts; they engaged in more spontaneous expression of play and emotion; and finally, they raised exceptionally independent daughters who adapted well to the preschool setting.

The existing research on African Americans has taken a strictly "structured" or "deductive" approach. Such an approach is theory-driven, and stresses linear influences of single variables and simple interaction effects. A theory driven approach requires the use of a more or less explicit conceptual scheme to direct the choice or creation of relevant measures, and that the research results be interpreted in terms of the original assumptions. While such an approach allows for revision and improved theoretical conceptions, it cannot open entirely new theoretical possibilities. A more exploratory approach assumes a multitude of theoretical possibilities. Through successive cycles of open-ended data collection and data analysis, our initial and subsequent guesses can be brought in line with the actual facts of covariation and become increasingly informative and informed. The exploratory approach makes the ascent of the "inductive-hypothetico-deductive spiral." Unfortunately, such an approach is time-consuming and costly. Moreover, a purely exploratory approach seems unwarranted given that very recent research explicated some of the major issues on parenting within African American families in regard to race socialization (Boykin & Toms, 1985; Jackson, McCullough, & Gurin, 1988; Thornton, Chatters, Taylor, & Allen, 1990).

The development of the present socialization instrument took into consideration that for African Americans, culture as a set of adaptive processes operating independently of and interacting with social class, may play a significant role in determining socialization patterns and developmental outcomes. Thus, a combined structured/exploratory approach was employed to develop and validate an instrument to investigate the socialization practices employed in African American families. Our approach is data-driven rather than theory-driven, and focuses on within group co-variations rather than between group differences.

Q-Sort Procedure

To define the domains and to develop an assessment tool, a Q-sort was developed. The Q-sort procedure is a person-centered approach to measurement, and is noted for its heuristic and exploratory powers in terms of theory development (Kerlinger, 1972; Ozer, 1993). That is theoretical concepts can be built into the instrument, and subsequently tested using the population for which the measure is intended. This preliminary study is limited to the development of the Q-sort and defining its orientations.

Q procedures require a sampling domain consisting of concepts as opposed to people, and the sampling procedure can be random or structured, depending on the goals of the research and the sophistication of the underlying concepts (see Nunnally, 1978; Ozer, 1993 for a more detailed discussion on Q sampling). For this study, sampling was somewhat structured in that the majority of domains were identified *a priori* by extracting relevant information from the literature on African American family life and students' descriptions of their home environments. The Black Family Process Q-sort (BFPQ) includes the domains of race socialization, family discipline, communication, and values. Statements describing parents' attitudes toward their ethnic group, the dominant culture, and parenting strategies, can be sorted to identify and differentiate socialization orientations.

Racial Socialization

Racial orientations have been studied across cultures and in disciplines such as psychology and sociology (Phinney, 1990). A major problem, one that has contributed to inconclusive and contradictory findings, has been conceptual labels whose definitions varied across studies and theorists. An example is failure to distinguish labels that pertain to acculturation theory (how minority group members relate to the dominant group) and ethnic identity (how minority group members relate to their own group as an outcome of accul-

turation). A separate but related problem pertains to the dimensionality of acculturation and ethnic identity (Phinney, 1990). If acculturation and ethnic identification are opposite poles of a single dimension, movement toward acculturation denotes movement away from ethnic identity. However, if acculturation and identification are separate dimensions, what processes link the two constructs?

Phinney (1990) describes a two dimensional model that consists of four orientations used to index ethnic group behavior in response to minority status: (a) The terms biculturalism or integration have been used to indicate strong identification with both dominant and ethnic cultures; (b) assimilation or mainstream indicates strong identification with the dominant culture and weak identification with the ethnic culture; (c) separatist indicates strong identification with the ethnic culture and weak identification with the dominant culture; and, (d) marginality, indicates identification with neither culture.

Berry, Trimble and Olmedo (1986) referred to the four orientations as "acculturation attitudes," and noted that issues of how to relate to the dominant culture, and how to relate to ones own culture, when posed together, must be understood within a multidimensional framework.

Boykin and Toms (1985) presented a multidimensional conceptualization of African American parents' socialization agendas as comprising mainstream, minority, and African American cultural foci. Further, they posited that most African Americans are biculturalist, because, often, they cannot escape desires for the amenities upward mobility provides. However, ones minority focus is based on what Boykin and Toms (1985) called "adaptive orientations." Adaptive orientations are best understood within the context of various combinations of possible modes of interaction with mainstream culture: the interaction can be active or passive; it can be supportive of the status quo or supportive of system change; and the interaction can be further exemplified as system engagement or system disengagement. In short, and at risk of oversimplification, adaptive orientations may be characterized by the manner in which mainstream values, goals, and culture are embraced by minority group members. Boykin and Toms' (1985) conceptualization links socialization patterns to racial or adaptive orientations (also see Bowman & Howard, 1985; Thornton, Chatters, Taylor, & Allen, 1990) and these orientations seem to parallel an acculturation continuum.

In a study to determine the relationship between "reference-group labels" and facets of personality such as self-esteem and social competence, Rotheram-Borus (1990) identified reference labels as mainstream, bicultural, and ethnically identified. Rotheram-Borus studied 330 Black, Hispanic, Asian, and White high school students to determine the extent to which subjects identified with the dominant culture and found that reference group labels were consistently associated with differences in ethnic group values, attitudes, and behaviors.

Taken together, these studies represent conceptualizations of racial orientations or attitudes as components of acculturation and ethnic identity dimensions. Caution is necessary in generalizations across samples, due to disparate definitions and conceptual frameworks. For that reason, a measure was developed to identify and to define racial socialization in terms of ethnic identity types and acculturation strategies employed by African Americans. Below we describe the development and initial validation of a Q-sort instrument for investigating socialization strategies in African Americans. These efforts include: (1) The development of a pool of the Q-Sort items; (2) The evaluation and reduction of the item pool; (3) The construction of racial orientation prototypes; and, (4) Critical evaluation of the racial orientation prototypes.

Developing the Q-Sort Items

Items were developed by extracting relevant information from the literature on African American family life, and by soliciting students' descriptions of their families.

Subjects

The subjects were seventy-one (71) African American 10th and 11th grade students enrolled in one of three courses at a high school in Southern California. The courses were considered Black Studies courses in literature and history. Students' ages ranged from 15 to 17.

Procedure

The classroom teacher gave an essay assignment which asked each student to write on a topic relevant to Black families. The assignment was treated like any other classroom writing task; however, the instructions to students had been standardized in a meeting with the teachers. The topics to be covered were: (a) discipline; (b) freedom; (c) coping with being Black in America, (d) religion; (e) feelings and thoughts about other people who live in the same house as the students; (f) things the family did together other than school related; (g) chores at home; (h) homework; and, (i) dealing with friends and teachers.

Each teacher began the class period with "today we are going to talk about Black families; lets talk about discipline." An approximate average of 3 minutes was allowed to discuss each topic, before the topic was written on the board. At the end of the discussion, each teacher had her students write an essay about their family life to include the topics listed on the board. The students had approximately 35 minutes to complete the assignment.

Items or statements were derived in several ways. For one, statements were taken directly from students' essays. Second, items were written based on concepts representative of Baumrind's (1967) notion of authoritarian, authoritative, permissive, and indifferent parenting. Briefly stated, Baumrind determined that in terms of discipline and control, authoritarian parents were generally strict and imposing, authoritative parents were imposing but flexible and responsive, permissive parents failed to exert any control, and indifferent parents were generally uninvolved with their children.

Bowman and Howard's (1985) conceptualization of race socialization represents another basis of item generation. Bowman and Howard determined that effective race socialization strategies orient children to the realities of barriers, offering encouragement by way of useful coping devices. Bowman and Howard (1985) called these efficacious approaches "proactive," in contrast to passive approaches that downplay or overlook the existence of barriers. A further basis of item generation was Peters' (1988) summary of Black approaches to discipline, communication, and teaching styles. That is, through actions and beliefs, Black parents emphasize love and the importance of education as factors in dealing with racism.

Each item states a perception of parents' belief systems, written to capture parents' overt behaviors, and written to not specify a particular adult (e.g., mother, father), for the practical reason that the individual might be absent from the student's household. In addition, each statement began with a verb (e.g., tells, thinks, believes, instructs) to emphasize active rather than passive processes. Care was given to include an appropriate number of both positively and negatively valenced items).

Results and Discussion

One hundred fifty items were constructed from the two sources (students' essays and the literature), representing four broad domains: (a) race socialization, (e.g., tells kids in the family they must work twice as hard because of their race); (b) discipline and teaching, (e.g., allows children to stay out as late as they want); (c) family communication and interactions, (e.g., likes to see family members laugh and play around the house; and, (d) family emphasis on values such as education, religion, and life in general (e.g., thinks it is not okay for people to receive welfare).

The research team examined the 150 items and eliminated 50 items to reduce redundancy and to make a more practically useful set (see Table 1). The Q-set then consisted of 100 state-

ments (Race socialization = 44 items, discipline and teaching = 14 items, communication and interactions = 25 items, and family values = 17 items).

Evaluation and Reduction of Item Pool

The 100 Q-items were next evaluated in terms of clarity and redundancy by members of the target population and the research team.

Subjects

Two samples of subjects were used to evaluate the items. The first consisted of 122 African American students from two major Southern California universities. Their ages ranged from 17 to 57 with the mean age of 24. The subjects were all volunteers, but received experimental credit hours for their participation. Data from 25 subjects were not used in the analyses due to their failure to fully follow the item placement directions. Ninety-eight percent (98%) of the subjects self-identified as African American or Black. Two percent (2%) identified as American, or refused to respond.

The second sample consisted of 47 African American high school tenth graders. Their ages ranged from 15 to 18 (only one 18 year old student) with a mean age of 16 years. All of these students identified as African American or Black. These students participated with their parents' permission, and were paid $10.00.

Measures and Procedures

Subjects in both samples were told to use the BFPQ to describe their primary caretaker (e.g., mother, father, sister, etc.). Items were printed on cards, and subjects were first asked to begin by placing each item into one of three piles, corresponding to uncharacteristic, neutral, or characteristic of their caretaker. After three piles were made, subjects were asked to make three discriminations within each pile, and to limit the number of items per category to the fixed distribution of 8, 10, 12, 13, 14, 13, 12, 10, and 8. By

Table 1. Black Family Process 100 Sort Items by Domain

Race socialization items

1. Dislikes their racial group.
2. Happy to be a member of their racial group.
3. Tells children in family to be happy with their race.
4. Thinks being a member of his/her race is an honor and a privilege.
5. Thinks it's better to act like members of other ethnic groups than his/her own.
6. Says other races don't believe his/her racial group is intelligent.
7. Tells kids in family how to deal with being a member of their racial group.
8. Shows a strong dislike for people of other racial groups.
9. Tells kids in the family they must work twice as hard because of their race.
10. Has the power to change things at school if kids in the family are mistreated.
13. Thinks that racism is a thing of the past.
14. Tells children in family they can become anything with hard work.
16. Says people in his/her racial group have no control over their lives.
17. Talks to the kids in the family about how to achieve what they want to become.
18. Says that people make too big of a deal about race.
20. Tells the children about racial barriers.
21. Believes that for the most part, people of other races are nice.
30. Believes that people hassle people in their racial group.
31. Tells children what to do if they get stopped by the police.
34. Says race is not important.
39. Doesn't talk about Black and White relations.
40 Tells kids in the family how to act around people of other races.
41. Instructs the children in the family on how to deal with racism.
42. Talks to children about how to treat Blacks.
43. Believes that all people are created equal.
46. Tells children in family to ignore people who make nasty racial comments.
47. Tells children to get even with people who talk about their race.
50. Tells children that people will dislike them just because of their race.
51. Says that people in power (teachers, police) treat all people equally.
53. Reminds family members to remember that they are racially different.
54. Tells family members that it is best not to emphasize race.
56. Believes racial identity is very important.
69. Expects people in their ethnic group to stick together.
79. Believes character is more important than one's skin color.
81. Thinks people of their race are ignorant.
82. Thinks people of other races are ignorant.
87. Demonstrates over-sensitivity to racial issues.
88. Spends a lot of time talking about what is wrong with other racial groups.
90. Acts inferior to others from a different race.
91. Acts more ethnic than other members of their racial group.
93. Tells children that they can not necessarily expect fair play in life.
95. Dislikes authority figures.

(table continues)

Race socialization items

96. Feels very much in control of what happens in life.
97. Feels what happens in life due to others not them as an individual.

Communication items

11. Makes the children in the family feel secure.
22. Likes to see family members laugh and play around at home.
23. Respects the decisions that children make in the home.
27. Expects children to talk about their problems.
36. Likes a lot of fun things or activities in the house.
38. Uses bible verses to tell family members how to treat others.
44. Believes that children should be seem and not heard.
45. Encourages children to make their own decisions.
48. Does not ever hug or kiss kids in the family.
52. Expects children to do what adults in the family say at all times.
55. Will not allow children to question family decisions.
57. Will change decision if given good reasons.
70. Kisses and hugs children often.
71. Shows children they are liked just the way they are.
72. Shows children in family they are appreciated.
73. Uses well known sayings to teach children about the world (e.g., "What goes around comes around")
76. Goes places with kids (e.g., movies, church, plays).
77. Enjoys being part of the family members teasing one another..
78. Won't allow any teasing in the family.
84. Enjoys seeing family members having fun.
85. Says things like "you can't tell a book by its cover."
89. Seems capable of self-evaluation.
98. Demonstrates unconditional love.
99. Tries to obtain materials (e.g., typewriter, books) that children need to do well in school.
100. Acts passive in family decision-making.

Values

12. Believes that the family is responsible for elderly relatives.
15. Believes children should take care of themselves as soon as possible.
19. Believes that people should work for what they get.
24. Believes that when children get home after school, chores come first.
25. Believes that when children get home after school, homework comes first.
26. Thinks it is not okay for people to get welfare.
28. Expects children not to associate with certain kinds of people.
29. Believes that children should have chores.
32. Wants the family to eat at least one meal together.
33. Makes the children go to church.

(table continues)

Values

35. Thinks children should respect adults if adults respect children.
37. Doesn't seen interested in children's school work.
49. Believes that boys should not cry.
74. Tells children to respect their adults.
75. Helps kids with chores if they have homework to do.
80. Doesn't care if children go to church.
83. Teaches family members that family comes first.

Discipline

58. Is strict but kind.
59. Doesn't care what kids in the family do.
60. Wants to know all their children's friends.
61. Doesn't care who their children's friends are.
62. Allows children to stay out as late as they want.
63. Sets a time for children to be home.
64. Disciplines mostly by talking.
65. Disciplines mostly by hitting.
66. Disciplines mostly by taking away things (phone, car, privileges).
67. Disciplines mostly by saying "bad" things (e.g., cursing)
68. Is strict and not very kind.
86. Refuses to talk with children when disgusted or angry with them.
92. Likes to discipline through logic and reason.
94. Likes to take away children's personal things (e.g., bike, radio) when angry.

this procedure, each of the 100 Q-items receives a rating ranging from 1 (most uncharacteristic) to 9 (most characteristic). Moreover, the distribution of each subject's ratings are fixed to the same quasi-normal distribution. Block (1978) and Ozer (1993) provide more detailed discussion of this standard Q-sort procedure.

Subjects in the high school sample were told that the Q-sort was going to be used with people their age to study African American families, and for that reason, their help was needed with the wording and sentence arrangement. For each Q-sort item, these subjects: (a) rated their primary caretaker on a nine point Likert-type scale; (b) indicated on a 7–point Likert-type scale how well they understood the statement, and then circled words difficult to understand; and (c) indicated on a 7–point Likert-type scale how difficult it was to place each item. Finally, subjects were asked to write comments related to areas they thought important but not represented in the 100 items.

Results

Readability and Clarity

Analyses of the high school subjects ratings indicate that the students were able to understand each item ($M = 6.15$), and that the items were easily placed ($M = 6.3$). Eight students did not understand the word "unconditional" in number 98 ("demonstrates unconditional love"), and four students noted problems with the word "passive" in number 100 ("acts passive in family decision-making"). Responses to the question pertaining to unrepresented material were, for the most part, limited to reactions to this particular questionnaire ("too long", "interesting", "comprehensive"). However, one subject noted that the issue of "equality" was not represented. That is, she stated that her mother did not treat the children equally. A statement was added with this content to the revised Q-sort (Black Family Process Q-sort II).

Table 2. Group Means and Standard Deviations by Item

Item	High School Mean	SD (n = 47)	College Mean	SD (n = 97)
1.	2.48	1.75	2.78	1.85
2.	6.67	1.87	6.29	1.77
3.	6.70	1.68	6.21	1.76
4.	5.78	2.11	5.84	2.05
5.	2.98	1.79	3.28	2.23
6.	4.74	2.15	4.96	1.79
7.	5.38	1.87	5.19	1.84
8.	2.97	1.39	3.23	1.68
9.	5.57	2.30	5.69	2.10
10.	5.23	1.95	5.69	1.99
11.	6.76	1.65	6.91	1.90
12.	5.34	1.57	5.70	1.87
13.	3.17	1.78	2.72	1.74
14.	7.42	1.63	7.19	1.78
15.	4.76	2.16	4.36	2.05
16.	3.00	1.57	3.39	1.75
17.	6.91	1.99	6.51	1.89
18.	4.70	1.98	4.09	1.92
19.	7.12	1.63	7.00	1.63
20.	5.55	2.36	5.64	1.76
21.	5.65	2.24	5.23	1.83
22.	6.68	1.69	6.57	1.91
23	5.44	1.89	5.45	2.09
24.	4.55	2.14	4.93	1.97
25.	6.53	2.17	6.30	2.34
26.	4.59	1.82	4.52	1.82
27.	6.38	1.78	6.37	1.75
28.	5.17	2.20	5.39	2.24
29.	6.59	2.11	6.53	1.71
30.	4.95	2.14	5.37	1.78
31.	5.04	2.26	4.95	2.02
32.	5.42	2.19	5.31	2.29
33.	4.95	2.14	5.37	1.78
34.	4.17	2.50	3.64	1.95
35.	4.91	2.09	4.53	2.15
36.	5.72	2.03	5.65	1.72
37.	2.17	1.49	2.77	1.74
38.	5.10	2.44	5.10	2.37
39.	4.55	1.83	3.97	1.96
40.	4.85	2.26	4.38	1.82
41.	5.65	1.56	5.48	1.85
42.	4.95	2.07	4.70	1.63
43.	6.17	2.33	6.25	2.19
44.	3.34	1.99	3.80	2.21
45.	6.36	2.01	6.53	2.14
46.	5.19	2.28	4.93	2.26
47.	3.83	1.90	3.27	1.71
48.	3.51	2.15	2.60	1.66
49.	3.55	2.05	3.78	2.16
50.	4.22	2.20	4.96	2.21
51.	3.72	2.04	3.51	1.77
52.	5.66	2.08	5.50	2.30
53.	4.51	1.97	4.65	2.07
54.	4.12	1.43	4.34	1.73
55.	4.63	2.15	4.42	2.05
56.	6.04	1.96	6.12	1.92
57.	6.06	1.79	5.93	1.99
58.	5.23	2.39	5.89	2.04
59.	2.85	1.93	2.67	1.66
60.	5.76	2.10	6.30	2.06
61.	3.34	1.85	2.85	1.74
62.	3.29	1.93	2.89	1.75
63.	5.83	2.26	6.51	1.96
64.	6.57	1.60	6.61	2.06
65.	2.91	1.99	3.36	2.04
66.	5.57	2.50	5.17	2.37
67.	3.21	2.16	3.28	2.11
68.	3.82	1.51	2.96	1.79
69.	6.08	1.96	5.57	1.90
70.	5.93	2.10	6.56	2.14
71.	6.25	2.02	6.50	1.85
72.	6.68	1.90	6.87	1.88
73.	5.46	2.12	5.74	2.04
74.	7.12	1.84	6.82	1.81
75.	5.76	2.10	5.59	2.09
76.	6.02	1.93	6.31	1.91
77.	4.42	2.09	4.59	2.28
78.	4.95	2.02	4.45	2.06
79.	6.74	1.85	6.78	1.74
80.	3.61	2.37	3.16	1.96
81.	3.05	1.90	3.21	1.84
82.	3.38	1.84	3.31	1.73
83.	6.57	1.96	7.21	1.62
84.	7.06	1.58	6.92	1.56

Item	High School		College	
	Mean	SD	Mean	SD
	(n = 47)		(n = 97)	
85.	5.48	1.80	5.52	1.97
86.	3.97	2.33	4.09	2.07
87.	4.04	1.89	3.84	1.66
88.	3.72	1.51	3.57	1.63
89.	5.61	1.60	6.02	1.77
90.	2.87	1.34	2.82	1.87
91.	3.42	1.64	3.62	1.70
92.	5.61	2.23	5.03	2.16
93.	5.85	2.01	6.01	2.07
94.	3.74	2.35	3.61	1.91
95.	3.70	1.39	3.61	1.70
96.	5.63	1.98	5.54	2.09
97.	3.38	1.36	3.32	1.60
98.	6.46	2.24	7.08	2.18
99.	6.85	1.73	6.88	1.84
100.	4.02	2.26	3.44	2.17

Redundancy Among Items

Analyses to control for redundancy among items were accomplished in two ways. First, all items were correlated within each sample. Items highly correlated ($r > .50$) within the college sample were 2 and 3; 4 and 3; and 68 and 67. However, these correlations did not carry over into the high school sample. Items highly correlated within the high school sample were 1 and 14; 17 and 71; 26 and 36; 41 and 72; 33 and 80; and 36 and 26. Thus, no single item was redundant across samples. Second, individual item means and standard deviations were examined (see Table 2) to determine each item's capacity to discriminate among persons. Ideally one would want a number of individuals endorsing each item in each category along the continuum (1-9). Therefore, discriminating items are those with means close to 5.00, and large standard deviations.

Discussion

For the most part, members of the target population (high school students) were able to comprehend as well as use the majority of Q-sort items in their descriptions. The major accomplishment of this specific study was the verification of the readability and clarity of the Q-sort items. This outcome paved the way to search for racial group orientations.

Constructing Racial Orientation Prototypes

Seven possible racial orientations were identified that reflected, in part, information from students' essays (Study I), and theoretical concepts set forth by the research reviewed. These seven types are described below (See also Table 5).

Associationist. This family's orientation neither encourages nor discourages its members interacting with other individuals based on race, class, or culture. Members of this family would *not* take on the values or norms of other groups, but would respect group differences. Moreover, members of this family would not see the need to model other group behaviors. This family would take pride in their own group. The Associationist would not seek intergroup interaction, but would understand the necessity for such interactions in terms of convenience. In Boykin and Toms' (1985) terminology, this type would be a passive maintenance/system engagement adaptive orientation.

Biculturalist. This family's orientation would be one which accepts its own group norms as well as other group norms. The distinctive characteristic of this orientation would be the ability to adapt to various cultural norms without feeling the need to give up ones own norms. This description typifies Rotheram-Borus' type of the same name, a strong identification with both the ethnic and mainstream groups.

Assimilationist. This family's orientation would be to lose its distinctiveness and become part of the majority group. This orientation would subsequently lead to total acceptance of majority group norms and a rejection of its own ethnic

Table 3. Correlations Among the Seven Family Orientation Prototypes (Alpha Reliability Coefficients on the Diagonals)

	1	2	3	4	5	6	7
1. Associationist	(.91)						
2. Biculturalist	.93	(.94)					
3. Assimilationist	.31	.41	(.81)				
4. Separatist	.37	.30	-.19	(.93)			
5. Isolationist	.41	.36	.09	.69	(.70)		
6. Integrationist	.78	.86	.60	-.03	.14	(.85)	
7. Universalist	.77	.85	.56	-.10	.15	.91	(.95)

group norms. According to Rotheram-Borus, this type would be mainstream, and system engagement/system maintenance according to Boykin and Toms (1985).

Separatist. This family's orientation is toward maintaining distinct and separate norms, customs, values and possibly language. This orientation would discourage interactions with other groups, and such interactions would probably lead to conflict. In Rotheram-Borus terms, this view should be "strong ethnic identity" or Boykin and Toms' "openly defiant system change/system disengagement".

Isolationist. This family's orientation would be one concerned only with themselves. Such individuals would have no personal claim or stake in outside issues related to race, class, or culture unless the issues impacted their life circumstances. This orientations was derived from students' essays, and is analogous to Berry, Trimble and Olmedo's (1986) and Phinney's (1990) notion of "marginality."

Integrationist. This family's orientation would be to accept the "best" of the broader culture's norms and values. The Integrationist also maintains their racial group's values that do not conflict with the broader culture's values. Phinney (1990) indicated this orientation was often used as a synonym of biculturation.

Universalist. This label depicts a family whose orientation is one which views all people as being the same regardless of ethnicity. The Univeralist would say that he or she sees people and not race. The Universalist would not set limits on individuals with whom they associate based on race, class, or culture.

To evaluate the theoretical assumptions of these hypothetical racial orientations, and to evaluate the capacity of the Q-sort items to describe those orientations, the following study was conducted.

Subjects

Ninety-six (96) African American (i.e., 47) and Euro-American (i.e., 49) students attending a Southern California university completed 171 sorts of the seven hypothetical Black family orientations. Each subject was asked to describe two family types, but due to time constraints 21 subjects completed only one sort. Each family type was described by from 21 to 27 subjects.

These African American and Euro-American subjects were used as judges to determine differential perceptions, if any, of racial orientations. Eighty-three of the sorts were completed by African American judges, and 88 sorts were completed by Euro-American judges. The judges were all volunteers, although the majority of White judges were enrolled in introductory psychology courses and received course credit for participa-

Table 4. Extreme Means < 3.5 or >6.5 Differentiating Family Types

Item	Assoc. (1)	Bicul. (2)	Assim. (3)	Separ. (4)	Isola. (5)	Integr. (6)	Univer. (7)
1.	2.22	2.00					2.29
2.			3.21	7.33			
4.	6.80	7.04	3.13	7.22			
5.	2.33	2.99	6.96	2.48			3.00
6.							2.81
7.				7.19			
8.							2.11
9.				7.26			2.99
11.		7.30					
13.	3.33			1.74			
14.		7.55					
16.		2.85					2.59
17.	7.04	7.51					
18.				2.48			7.11
20.				7.15			
21.				3.03		6.92	
22.							6.81
28.	3.00						3.07
30.				6.88			
32.					6.66		
33.				1.92			7.11
39.		3.18		3.07			
43.				3.07		7.00	7.92
45.		7.03					
47.		2.48					2.48
50.				6.88			3.44
51.				2.37			
52.					6.71		
53.				6.88			2.63
54.			6.50	2.18			7.07
56.	6.76	6.51	3.33	7.63			
57.					3.44		
67.		2.88					2.88
68.	3.14	3.25					3.00
69.		2.45	7.88				3.44
71.	7.04	7.33					7.37
72.							7.37
76.	6.85						
79.		7.07					8.14
81.	1.95						2.00
82.			3.50				2.00

(table continues)

Item	Assoc. (1)	Bicul. (2)	Assim. (3)	Separ. (4)	Isola. (5)	Integr. (6)	Univer. (7)
83.					7.62		
85.							6.67
88.		2.96		6.66		3.04	2.77
91.			2.41	6.74			
92.							6.51
96.							6.67
98.							7.18
99.		7.33				7.04	

Procedure

Judges were told that they were participating in a study to define or operationalize Black family prototypes, and that we "needed to see if people agree with us as to what we think family types are like." Descriptions of family prototypes were ordered randomly and each description was taken from the top of the stack as subjects entered the research situation. Judges were then asked to read the description, and to think of the family as a hypothetical Black family. Judges completed their Q-sorts after receiving the standard instructions (described above) creating the same fixed nine-step quasi-normal distribution used in the item evaluation study.

Table 5. Factor Pattern Among Seven Orientation Prototypes

	Factor 1	Factor 2	Factor 3
1. Associationist	.90	.31	.06
2. Biculturalist	.93	.25	.13
3. Assimilationist	.34	.03	.92
4. Separatist	.09	.91	-.20
5. Isolationist	.14	.91	.16
6. Integrationist	.86	.01	.41
7. Universalist	.88	-.10	.34

tion. The majority of Black subjects were recruited from ethnic studies courses.

Results and Discussion

Item Analysis

Initial analyses sought to examine interjudge agreement and reliability in the Q-sort descriptions of the seven family types. Table 3 shows that the reliability coefficients are high. However, the intercorrelations among the associationist and biculturalist types and the integrationist and the universalist types clearly indicate that either these types are redundant or that the features that discriminate them are absent from the content of the Q-set.

A 7 (orientation) x 2 (race) MANOVA using the 100 items as dependent variables revealed an overall effect for family orientations, but no effect for race. Because the two races did not differ in how they sorted family orientations, the data were combined for additional analyses.

Univariate post hoc tests (ANOVAs) identified 61 items differentiating the family types. Of the 61, 37 items (60%) are categorized as race socialization descriptors. It should also be mentioned that 43 of the 61 items met the Bonferroni criterion $p < .0005$.

Univariate contrasts to ascertain specific family type differences among the 61 significant items were conducted using the Bonferroni Procedure. Comparisons among the 46 extreme means (< 3.5 or > 6.5) indicating either "most characteristic" or "least characteristic," are shown in Table 4.

The Associationist shares most of its characteristic items (see Table 4) with the Biculturalist

Table 6. Profile of the Seven Orientation Prototypes

Associationist
Most Characteristic

17. Talks to the kids in the family about how to achieve what they want to become.
56. Believes racial identity is very important.
71. Shows children they are liked just they way they are.
*76. Goes places with kids (Movies, Church, Plays).

Least Characteristic

5. Thinks it's better to act like members of other racial groups than his/her own.
13. Thinks that racism is a thing of the past.
28. Expects children not to associate with certain kinds of people.
68. Is strict and not very kind.
81. Thinks people of their race are ignorant.
88. Spends a lot of time talking about what is wrong with other racial groups.

Biculturalist
Most Characteristic

4. Thinks being a member of his/her race is an honor.
*11. Makes the children in the family feel secure.
*14. Tells children in family they can become anything with hard work.
17. Talks to the kids in the family about how to achieve what they want to become.
*45. Encourages children to make their own decisions.
56. Believes racial identity is very important.
71. Shows children they are liked just the way they are.
79. Believes character more important than ones skin color.

Least Characteristic

1. Dislikes their racial group.

13. Thinks that racism is a thing of the past.
16. Says that people in his/her racial group have no control over their lives.
28. Expects children not to associate with certain kinds of people.
39. Doesn't talk about Black and White relations.
47. Tells children to get even with people who talk about their race.
68. Is strict and not very kind.

Assimilationist
Most Characteristic

*5. Thinks it's better to act like members of other racial groups than his/her own.
54. Tells family members that it is best not to emphasize race.
99. Tries to obtain materials (e.g., typewriter, books) that children need to do well in school.

Least Characteristic

2. Happy to be a member of their racial group.
3. Tells children in family to be happy with their race.
4. Thinks being a member of his/her race is an honor and a privilege.
56. Believes racial identity is very important.
68. Is strict and not very kind.
69. Expects people in their ethnic group to stick together.
91. Acts more ethnic than most other members of their racial group.

Separatist
Most Characteristic

*2. Happy to be a member of their racial group.
4. Thinks being a member of his/her race is an honor and a privilege.
*7. Tells kids in the family how to deal with being a member of their racial group.
*9. Tell kids in the family they must work twice as hard because of their race.

(table continues)

*20. Tells the children about racial barriers.

Separatist
Most Characteristic

*30. Believes that police hassle people in their racial group.
*50. Tells children that people will dislike them just because of their race.
*53. Reminds family members to remember that they are racially different.
 56. Believes racial identity is very important.
*69. Expects people in their ethnic group to stick together.
*88. Spends a lot of time talking about what is wrong with other racial groups.
*91. Acts more ethnic than most other members of their racial group.

Least Characteristic

  5. Thinks it's better to act like members of other racial groups than his/her own.
 13. Thinks that racism is a thing of the past.
 18. Says that people make too big of a deal about race.
 21. Believes that for the most part, people of other races are nice.
 34. Says race is not important.
 39. Doesn't talk about Black and White relations.
 43. Believes that all people are created equal.
 51. Says that people in power (teachers, police) treat all people equally.
 54. Tells family members that it is best not to emphasize race.
 57. Will change decision if given good reasons.

Isolationist
Most Characteristic

 32. Wants the family to eat at least one meal together.
 52. Expects children to do what adults in the family say at all times.
 83. Teaches family members that family comes first.

Least Characteristic

 18. Says that people make too big of a deal about race.

Integrationist
Most Characteristic

 21. Believes that for the most part, people of other races are nice.
 43. Believes that all people are created equal.
 99. Tries to obtain materials (e.g., typewriter, books) that children need to do well in school.

Universalist
Most Characteristic

*18. Says that people make too big of a deal about race.
*22. Likes to see family members laugh and play around at home.
*34. Says race is not important.
 43. Believes that all people are created equal.
*54. Tells family members that it is best not to emphasize race.
 71. Shows children they are liked just the way they are.
*72. Shows children in family they are appreciated.
 79. Believes character more important than ones skin color.
*85. Says things like you can't tell a book by its cover.
*92. Likes to discipline through logic and reason.
*96. Feels very much in control of what happens in life.
*98. Demonstrates unconditional love.

Least Characteristic

  1. Dislikes their racial group.
  5. Thinks it's better to act like members of other racial groups than his/her own.
  6. Says other races don't believe his/her racial group is intelligent.

(table continues)

Least Characteristic

8. Shows a strong dislike for people of other racial groups.
9. Tells kids in the family they must work twice as hard because of their race.
16. Says that people in his/her racial group have no control over their lives.
47. Tells children to get even with people who talk about their race.
50. Tells children that people will dislike them just because of their race.
53. Reminds family members to remember that they are racially different.
68. Is strict and not very kind.
69. Expects people in their ethnic group to stick together.
81. Thinks people of their race are ignorant.
82. Thinks people of other races are ignorant.

Note. * unique items

but varies in uncharacteristic descriptors. The Separatist and the Universalist have a number of non-overlapping items, and for that reason appear distinctive. The Assimilationist shares two items with separate groups, but has a number of unique non-characteristic items. On the other hand, the Isolationist and the Integrationist have no distinctive "least characteristic" items, and only one unique "characteristic" item each.

Discussion

Perceptions of racial orientations and the characteristics that define them are similar among African American and European American judges. Judges were unable to find distinctive descriptors for the Associationist (see Table 7) orientation, as there are no unique items for that category. The Associationist prototype was strongly correlated to the Biculturalist prototype, suggesting redundancy (see Table 6). In terms of the remaining six orientations, each was defined by at least two descriptors, with the exception of the Assimilationist category. The one unique item for the Assimilationist (5, "Thinks it's better to act like

members of other racial groups than his/her own.") is consistent with the expected outcome, and for that reason, the category appears distinct. The Assimilationist category also shared item 54 ("Tells family members that it is best not to emphasize race.") with the Universalist, an orientation that de-emphasizes a racial focus.

Unique descriptors for the Biculturalist consisted of children focused items (i.e., 11, "Makes the children in the family feel secure."; and 14, "Tells children in family they can become anything with hard work."), but lacked unique descriptors pertaining to race orientations. However, a closer examination of its significant items revealed its distinctiveness derives from items shared with the Separatist and the Universalist orientations. The relationship among the items (4, 56, and 79) suggests a label perceived as representing an orientation that values ethnic identity, but takes a Universalist ("Character more important than person's skin color.") view in terms of interacting with mainstream society. Phinney (1990) intimated that the biculturalist view was the most flexible and, perhaps, the healthiest among the four orientations she highlighted. If well-being is primarily associated with general encouragement and high expectations irrespective of race, then the Biculturalist orientation suggests that agenda; but if well-being is associated with preparing minority group members to effectively cope with racism (Bowman & Howard, 1985; Thornton, et al., 1990) then the Separatist view (based on the ratings of these judges) would encompass that agenda.

The Separatist view has a number of unique items, each dealing primarily with coping mechanisms, to impart strategies on how to deal with mainstream culture. Many of the descriptors include what Bowman and Howard (1985) referred to as "proactive" racial socialization messages. Proactive messages impart practical guidelines for dealing with racial barriers before they occur, so that minority group members are not severely hampered in goal attainment. Proactive approaches are considered "healthy," especially in comparison to two additional approaches: reactive and passive. Reactive approaches often surface after perceived injustices have occurred, and they often take on defensive overtones whereas passive approaches lack well-defined strategies.

Perceptions of an Integrationist depart, somewhat, from the Biculturalist orientation for which it often serves as a synonym. It differs in that the Integrationist is not perceived as imparting racial socialization messages. Its distinctiveness also consists of one unique item and two shared items, with the Universalist and the Assimilationist views.

The Isolationist parallels its analog, marginality (Berry et al., 1986; Phinney, 1990). According to Berry et al., marginalization often occurs due to discrimination or exclusionary reasons. Because the Isolationist was described as one with little interest in mainstream or ethnic issues, it is appropriate that the three unique items pertain to one's own family.

The Universalist emerged as a very distinct orientation, with judges' perceptions of this type rejecting the importance of racial messages.

In sum, the data revealed that African American and Euro-American judges shared similar views about labels and characteristics representing dimensions of acculturation and ethnic identity. Preliminary support for six orientations was found. Four of the orientations (biculturalism, assimilation, separatism, and marginality or isolation) were consistent with the model described by Berry et al. (1986). The term "integration" was also used by Berry et al., as a synonym for biculturalism, and that relationship seems to hold for this population of judges.

Note that the Universalist was not identified by Berry et al., but judges' perceptions indicate the viability of this additional category. However, caution is necessary in interpreting these data, as additional studies are needed to empirically examine racial group orientations within target populations.

Factor Analysis. To further clarify the relations among the seven family prototypes, principal components analysis was applied to the correlation matrix reported in Table 3. Note that this is a Q, rather than R type analysis (see Ozer. 1993):

items, not persons, constitute the sample. Results of this analysis are reported in Table 6. A scree plot was generated that suggested three factors; thus, a three factor solution was extracted after varimax rotation. Table 6, shows that the Associationist, Biculturalist, Integrationist, and the Universalist loaded on Factor 1. Factor 2 consists of the separatist and the isolationist, while the assimilationist loaded on Factor 3.

The results of this factor analysis indicate that, statistically, judges' perceptions of African American families' racial orientation consist of three factors: One factor can be interpreted as an openness to both mainstream and ethnic values; a second factor seems to indicate movement away from mainstream values; and the third factor suggests a total acceptance of mainstream values. Another possibility is that the written descriptions were not clear enough to distinguish unique characterizations. Therefore, there is overlap in subjects' perceptions of the various types.

To summarize the results of judges perceptions of hypothetical African American family orientations, at least three types are clearly identifiable, and can be used as markers to discern the nature of subjects' descriptions of their own family orientations or types.

Summary and Conclusion

The purpose of this project was multifaceted. The objective was the development of the Black Family Process Q-Sort (BFPQ) to provide an avenue to examine and quantify an individual's subjective experience in terms of family dynamics. Specifically, the instrument allows the respondent to relate his or her perceptions of parents' race socialization messages and orientations, as well as relate specific disciplinary techniques, communication styles, and values.

This task was accomplished through a series of studies designed to (a) sample socialization domains, (b) verify item/domain placement, (c) reduce redundancy among items, and to (d) ascertain the usefulness of the instrument as a common language to describe family processes. Although the final product is still evolving, the Black Family Process Q-sort demonstrates a viable mechanism to accomplish the goals of the research program.

The BFPQ is timely and needed given that the way in which African American parents view their status (racial orientation)-as a subgroup of the dominant culture- influence the socialization agendas they employ (Boykin & Toms, 1985). Therefore, in the future, additional studies are planned to test the utility of the BFPQ by investigating: (1) variations in parenting processes that covary with racial orientations; and (2) racial group orientations' relationships to several personality and behavioral outcomes (e.g., self-concept, locus of control, achievement performances, etc.).

Note

1. We wish to thank Robert Kaiser whose input on data analysis was invaluable.

References

Baumrind, D. (1967). Child care practices anteceding three patterns of preschool behavior. *Genetic Psychology Monographs, 75*, 43-88.

Baumrind, D. (1972). An exploratory study of socialization effects on Black children: Some Black-White comparisons. *Child Development. 43*(1), 261-267.

Berry, J. W., Trimble, J. E., & Olmedo, E. L. (1986). Assessment of acculturation. In W. Lonner & J. W. Berry (Eds.), *Field methods in cross cultural research* (pp. 291-324). Newbury Park: Sage.

Bowman, J. P., & Howard, C. (1985). Race-related socialization, motivation, and academic achievement: A study of Black youth in three-generation families. *Journal of the American Academy of Child Psychiatry, 24*(2), 134-141.

Boykin, A. W., & Toms, F. D. (1985). Black child socialization: A conceptual framework. In H. McAdoo & J. McAdoo (Eds.), *Black children* (pp. 33-51). Beverly Hills: Sage.

Jackson, J. S., McCullough, W. R., & Gurin, G. (1988). Family socialization and identity development in Black Americans. In H. P. McAdoo (Eds), *Black families* (pp. 242-245). Newbury Park: Sage.

Kerlinger, F. N. (1972). Q methodology in behavioral research. In S. R. Brown, & D. J. Brenner (Eds.). *Science, psychology, and communication: Essays honoring William Stephenson* (pp. 3-38). New York: Teachers College Press.

McLoyd, V. C. (1990). Minority children: Introduction to the special issue. *Child Development, 61*(2), 263-267.

Murray, C. B., & Fairchild, H. H. (1989). Models of Black adolescent underachievement. In R. L. Jones (Ed.), *Black adolescents* (pp. 229-245). Berkeley: Cobb & Henry.

Murray, C. B., Smith, S. N., & West, E. H. (1989). Comparative personality development in adolescents: A critique. In R. L. Jones (Ed.), *Black adolescents* (pp. 49-62). Berkeley: Cobb & Henry.

Nunnally, J. J. (1978). *Psychometric theory.* New York: McGraw Hill.

Ozer, D. J. (1993). The Q-sort method and the study of personality development. In D. Funder, R. Parke & C. Tomlinson-Keasey (Eds.), *Studying lives through time*. Washington, DC: American Psychological Association.

Peters, M. F. (1988). Parenting in Black families with young children: A Historical perspective. In H. P. McAdoo (Ed.), *Black families* (pp. 228-241). Beverly Hills: Sage.

Phinney, J. S. (1990). Ethnic identity in adolescents and adults. *Psychological Bulletin, 108*, 499-514.

Rotheram-Borus, J. J. (1990). Adolescents' reference-group choices, self-esteem and adjustment. *Journal of Personality and Social Psychology, 59*(5), 1075-1081.

Tinsley, B. J. (1992). Multiple influences on the acquisition and socialization of children's health attitudes and behavior: An integrative review. *Child Development, 63*(5), 1043-1069.

Thornton, M. C., Chatter, L. M., Taylor, J. R., & Allen, W. R. (1990). Sociodemographic and environmental correlates of racial socialization by Black parents. *Child Development, 61*, 401-409.

For additional information, contact:
M. Jean Peacock
Department of Psychology
California State University @ San Bernadino
5500 University Parkway
San Bernadino, CA 92407-2397
Telephone: (909) 880-5570
Fax: (909) 880-7003

Measures of Marital Quality

Jerome Taylor and Janet L. McMaster-Olmes

Abstract

Cleek and Pearson (1985) found male and female divorcees rank communication problems as the leading cause of their break ups. Among clinically distressed and non-distressed couples quality of communication is a matter of priority for both partners (Chelune, Rosenfeld, & Waring, 1985). Given the centrality of communication to healthy couples and those at risk, we propose *exchange disposition, communication efficiency, receptive accuracy*, and *instrumental competence* as four measures of marital quality which affirm the importance of communication as process and outcome. The rationale, description and studies using the measures are presented.

Quality of communication process refers to depth and completeness of marital interactions. *Exchange disposition*, the relative distribution of rewards and costs associated with each partner's relation to the other, is linked theoretically to disclosive tendencies of both partners. *Communication efficiency* is the extent to which personal experiences are transmitted by one partner and received, processed, and shared by the other.

Quality of communication outcome is revealed by each partner's level of understanding of the other and by each partner's ability to manage conflicts and problems experienced by the other. Each partner's ability to judge events, people, and relations in terms similar to the partner is called *receptive accuracy*. The extent to which each spouse helps the other confront and resolve problems is referred to as *instrumental competence*.

As a set, identified measures are complementary and assess components of marital quality which may vary in configuration across couples. None is a perfect indicator of marital quality and none is necessarily implied by the others.

In this chapter we first review the theoretical basis for each indicator, followed by a section describing the development and validation of measures used to estimate each indicator. An overall summary is then provided.

Theoretical Background

Exchange Disposition

Exchange disposition is the relative distribution of rewards and costs associated with a spouse's relation to the partner. Rewards and costs are concepts derived from social exchange theory which has its basis in the belief that when one person gives something to another person, the other person will return something of equal value.

495

These exchanges should fulfill the needs of both parties and help to coordinate their interactions. People interact with others who can meet their needs and avoid those who cannot. Interaction will be judged on an analysis of the rewards and costs given and received during communication. When the apparent costs of remaining with the partner exceed the potential rewards, the relationship is at risk of dissolution. The consequence of communication is the important factor to be considered when analyzing rewards and costs which influence the disposition toward further interaction. Interpersonal exchanges are best viewed in systemic context rather than in isolation. Social exchange theory makes evident the interdependence of people and is a useful model for evaluating the level of communication between marital partners.

Thibaut and Kelley (1959) were among the first to develop a social exchange analysis of relationships which is based on elements of social learning theory and attribution theory. They assert that each person seeks a positive outcome from every interaction in such a way that "the pleasures, satisfactions, and gratifications" which are rewards outweigh the "factors that operate to inhibit or deter the performance of a sequence of behavior" which are costs (p. 12). Rewards and costs of all types are believed to be measurable on a common psychological scale. To some extent a person's needs determine what is rewarding. For each person there is a minimal level of reward relative to cost that is required for relationship maintenance. This level may vary depending on normative, cultural, legal, and religious standards as well as other opportunities available at a given time. The person who is less dependent is the one who has more power in the relationship. The more dependent person will tolerate lower rewards and higher costs. More interdependent couples are likely to desire corresponding outcomes, so they will both accommodate small differences in order to preserve harmony (Kelley, 1979).

Every person has a comparison level against which the rewards and costs of involvement in a relationship are compared with the outcomes of other similar relationships. This general comparison level is derived from beliefs about rewards and costs that are assumed to be inherent in relationships. Everyone also has a comparison level for alternatives which is derived from other opportunities for relationships available at any particular time. They are comparisons of specific alternatives. The rewards and costs of alternatives available may either enhance or decrease the perception of the general comparison level and have an influence on whether a relationship will become stronger or weaker.

Participants in a relationship do not simply react to the pattern of interaction, but each person has goals which they are able to anticipate and achieve in various combinations of behavior. Each is also able to evaluate the outcomes accruing to their partner. However, this is done only to the extent that it is believed to be in the person's long term interest to do so. This applies to both women and men and implies that differences should only result from perceived differences in long term consequences for the partners. In young couples both partners seem to be more aware of the possibilities for maximizing outcomes for each other (Kelley, 1979). It should, however, be noted that research has repeatedly shown a positive relationship between the socioeconomic status of a couple and their reported level of relational satisfaction. It is necessary to control for this factor if an evaluation of social exchange variables is to be made.

Levinger (1982) offers a social exchange perspective on the dissolution of pair relationships wherein declining attractions may be measured in terms of rewards and costs, the attractiveness of alternatives outside marriage, and declining barriers of a normative, legal, or religious sort. Similarly, Lewis and Spanier (1982) derive the following propositions from social exchange theory: 1. "the greater the dyadic rewards (costs being equal), the greater the marital quality;" 2. "the greater the dyadic costs (rewards being equal), the less the marital quality;" 3. "the greater the external rewards (outside, alternative attractions), the less the marital quality;" 4. "the greater the external costs of breaking up (normative constraints to remain married), the greater the marital quality, the greater the marital stability;" and, 5. "the greater the marital quality, the greater the marital stability:" (p. 53). Sabetelli and Pearce (1986) base their research on a parallel view of social exchange theory.

Altman and D. Taylor's (1973) theory of social penetration evaluates relationships on the basis of the exchange ratio of rewards to costs. Relatedly, Berscheid (1985) suggests that "in close relationships the personality of each is penetrated (or made known to the other person in its most complete sense, including knowledge of the individual's needs, values, and feelings)" (p. 466). The proportion of rewards to costs, or exchange ratio, will indicate a person's satisfaction with the relationship (Coleman, 1984). The larger the ratio the greater the breadth and depth of penetration. Behavioral exchanges take place on all levels of intimacy and are primarily obtained through self-disclosures. When self-disclosures are not reciprocated, mistrust is likely to result. The process of social penetration is orderly, proceeding through stages, and gradually moving from superficial to intimate self-disclosures. The decline of a relationship brings the reverse process. As the relationship progresses it is considered to be more satisfying and more likely to continue when the ratio of rewards to costs is greater. Throughout this process, evaluations of reward to cost ratios are made to determine if the relationship will continue to grow or decline. Social penetration involves interaction at multiple levels resulting in a bond between partners that "is associated with a better understanding of the meaning of transactions" (Altman & D. Taylor, 1973, p. 132).

The exchange ratio of rewards to costs has been used as the basic unit of analysis of disposition to disclose. As theorized by Altman and D. Taylor (1973), each interaction is immediately evaluated by both partners in terms of rewards and costs associated with it. From these evaluations each person forecasts the potential for rewards and costs likely to result from future interactions. If the evaluations and forecasts indicate that the relationship is more rewarding than costly, the level of disclosures is presumed to increase in scope and depth. Therefore, there is not a direct relationship between how long two people know each other and their ability to predict the other's attitudes and behavior. Intimate relations are dis-

tinguishable from non-intimate relationships by the depth and breadth of personal exchange. Walster, Walster, and Berscheid (1978) indicate that the level of self-disclosure influences the effectiveness of communication and eventually marital satisfaction. The more intimate partners become, the more information they are likely to disclose and the more disclosures they expect from their partners in return. According to Chelune, Rosenfeld, and Waring (1985) there is an increases in marital satisfaction when the amount of ambiguous communication decreases and the amount of self-disclosure increases.

A study by Hansen and Schult (1984) examined the relationship between self-disclosure and marital satisfaction. Their findings suggest that husbands' disclosures to wives are positively related to, and predictive of, husbands' marital satisfaction; wives' disclosures to husbands are a positive predictive of wives' marital satisfaction. It should be noted that they found no evidence that husbands' disclosures to wives are predictive of wives' marital satisfaction. Discrepancies between levels of self-reported disclosure output of partners is predictive of husbands' marital satisfaction but not wives' marital satisfaction. Davidson (1981) found that both husbands and wives report less satisfaction when there is a discrepancy in levels of disclosure.

The relative distribution of rewards and costs in a relation is associated with disclosure and satisfaction between people in general and intimates in particular. Consequently, *exchange disposition*, which assesses the relative distribution of rewards and costs, is a promising measure of marital quality.

Communication Efficiency

Communication is the basic element of human interaction (Watzlawick, Beavin, & Jackson, 1967). Communication quality is predictive of marital satisfaction (Noller, 1984; Snyder, 1979). Relatedly, Markman (1984) reported that communication skills are key to marital quality.

The process of one spouse communicating with the other is presumed to involve four interlocking processes: transmission, reception, submission, and corroboration (J. Taylor in preparation). Person A transmits a message to Person B, who may elect to receive the message and may then submit the message back to Person A for feedback. The final step occurs when Person A corroborates or corrects Person B's submission. The evaluation of this process is known as communication efficiency. A disturbance in any one of these processes will disturb the efficiency of communication. Inefficient communication means that the transmitter has been ineffective in making experiences of the moment known to the receiver. Closely related is the construct empathy cycle.

Barrett-Lennard (1981) proposes an empathy cycle of communication in which one person expresses an experience to the partner, the partner experiences aspects of what is communicated, the partner in some way communicates to the spouse an awareness of the person's experience, the person attends to this communication and forms a judgment of the partner's level of understanding, and finally the person provides confirming or disconfirming feedback to the partner. It is speculated that there is moderate correlation among the measures of the various phases of the cycle. This measure was developed to evaluate therapeutic relationships between therapist and client, but the components of the cycle are valuable in the evaluation of all interpersonal relationships.

Communication efficiency can be affected by individual differences in the sending or receiving of affective or cognitive messages (Dellinger & Deane, 1980). Partners may differ in the proficiency in sending or receiving verbal statements which convey affective information. Likewise, partners may vary in their ability to send or receive linear messages or metamessages (Pearlmutter & Hatfield, 1980). Linear communications are verbal or nonverbal messages received as sent, whereas metamessages are verbal or nonverbal messages whose meaning depends upon contextual nuance.

Communication efficiency can be affected by relationship patterns or redundancies as well (Scoresby, 1977). In a complementary style of communication one partner may be talkative while the other is quiet or one dominant while the other

is submissive. Symmetrical style is reflected in competitive interactions where each person tries to maximize his/her input in a discussion. When partners evaluate messages and adjust their responses accordingly, the style is said to be parallel. The mutual goal of the partners using a parallel style is to understand and be understood. Research by Markman (1981) and Metcoff and Whitaker (1982) also demonstrate that patterns of relational communication are stable between partners.

Because fullness of communicative exchanges between partners is an important indicator of how the relationship is faring, *communicative disposition* would seem to be a central component of marital quality.

Receptive Accuracy

Understanding, an outcome of the basic communication process, is the ability of a spouse to accurately predict the other partner's responses to events, people, and relations. It is complete when the intended message of the speaker is equivalent to the message received by the listener. While level of receptive accuracy between partners is one indicator of the quality of their marital relationship, relatively little research has been done on this important concept.

Laing, Phillipson, and Lee (1966) define understanding as "the conjunction between the metaperspective of one person and the direct perspective of the other" (p. 29). Comparisons of perspectives do not have anything to do with whether or not they are based in fact, but rather, whether or not they show agreement or disagreement between the partners. Couples show less understanding on issues where they do not agree, and conversely, more understanding on issues where they do agree. People seem to be more aware of when they agree than of when they disagree. As a result of their research, Laing, Phillipson, and Lee (1966) conclude that "husbands understand wives to about the same extent that wives understand husbands" (p. 82).

According to Markman (1984) "'good communication' is defined as occurring when the speaker's intended message during problem-solving discussions matches the impact on the listener" (p. 256). A positive relationship is maintained when messages are sent with positive intent and are received as being positive in impact. When good communication is defined as intent equaling impact, then it parallels the definitions of perceptual accuracy, receptive accuracy, and understanding.

Discrepancies between what the speaker intends the message to be and how it is interpreted by the receiver can lead to differing evaluations of the nature of a relationship. Bochner, Krueger, and Chmielewski (1982) report that metaperceptions of the partner are more strongly related to marital satisfaction than are accurate perceptions of the partner.

In their 1985 research, Gaelick, Bodenhausen, and Wyer define an accurate communication as "one in which the message conveyed by the communicator corresponds to the interpretations made by the recipient" (p. 1246). They found the accuracy of the recipient's perception to be significantly correlated with intent for negative communication but not for positive communication. The results of the study by Noller (1980) also indicate that subjects are more likely to perceive negative communications more accurately than they are positive communications.

Floyd and Markman (1983) found that distressed wives interpret their husbands' intent as more negative than intended, and that distressed husbands interpret their wives' intent as more positive than intended. Accurate perception of social cues is based on readiness to react to behavior and make accurate inferences about unobservable features of the behavior (Bruner, 1957). The disposition of a person's perceptual readiness affects accurate perception, partner selection, development of joint constructs, and cognitive screening of events (Markman, 1984). It must be remembered that achievement of understanding is dependent on the accuracy of attributions made about a partner's previous behavior.

To determine interpersonal metaperceptions, most people rely on their own behaviors and attitudes (Hoch, 1987). The accuracy of these metaperceptions demonstrates how well one person understands the other. Most people tend to

project their own beliefs onto the actions of others by assuming that the other person's behaviors and attitudes are similar to their own. This phenomenon is called consensus. Hoch asserts that many partners would improve their predictive accuracy by assuming that their partners' attitudes are exactly like their own and that low predictive accuracy by a spouse results from incorrectly identifying cues from the partner or incorrectly weighing these cues. Misperceptions may also be mediated by motivation or other information. Brunswik (1952) asserts that perception depends on multiple cues which are probabilistically related to the subject of interest. The attitudes, beliefs, and behaviors of the person are the most readily available information source.

In contrast, a study by Murstein and Beck (1972) supports the relationship between understanding and marital adjustment. They find perceived similarity and compatibility are more highly correlated with marital adjustment than actual similarity and compatibility. Their results suggest that it is more likely that the man will be accurately perceived than the woman and that marriage is more oriented toward the satisfaction of the man than the woman. They conclude that "perception scores would appear to be a valuable tool in assessing the viability of a marriage" (Murstein & Beck, 1972, p. 402).

"There is evidence that perceptual accuracy is related to marital happiness" (Markman, 1984, p. 265). In a study by Gottman, Notarius, Markman, Bank, Yoppi, and Rubin (1976), distressed couples rated the impact of their spouses' communication significantly less accurately than nondistressed couples. The intent of the messages sent was similar for all couples. The results of this research suggest that there is a link between intent being unequal to impact and marital distress as well as between intent being equal to impact and marital satisfaction. These conclusions have been supported in similar studies with Black (Markman & Baccus, 1982) and deaf (Ferraro & Markman, 1981) couples.

Allen and Thompson (1984) report that it is possible to "find out whether or not each partner understands how the other perceives various relational aspects by making comparisons between one partner's metaperception and the other partner's direct perception on the same relational aspect" (p. 916). To the degree that these responses conform it can be said that one partner understands the other partner. In research based on social exchange theory, the degree of social penetration leads to the level of understanding achieved which leads to the amount of relational happiness reported (Honeycutt, 1986).

Understanding, alternatively referred to as *receptive accuracy*, reflects the status of relational interaction. Therefore, it is considered a meaningful indicator of marital quality.

Instrumental Competence

The extent to which a given spouse helps the other in managing problems and conflict and in making plans reflects an important communication outcome. The resourcefulness of each spouse in addressing problems, conflicts, and plans of the other is referred to as instrumental competence. J. Taylor (in preparation) computes this competency by having spouses rate the likelihood of discussing specific problems, conflicts, and plans as well as the quality of the results associated with these discussions.

The ways people communicate in order to resolve conflicts has substantial impact on the quality of their marriages (Gottman, 1979). For relationships to survive and to be enriched it is necessary to solve problems, resolve conflicts, and make plans (J. Taylor, in preparation). Even though communication is a vehicle for managing conflicts and resolving problems, there is a distinction between communication skills and problem solving skills (Noller, 1984). Good communication will not necessarily lead to good problem solving. Skills for solving problems include: defining the problem, collecting relevant information, generating alternative solutions, evaluating the proposed solutions, choosing an appropriate solution, and defining the action that needs to be taken.

Relationships that have a cumulative history of high rewards relative to costs can better sustain conflict (Altman & D. Taylor, 1973). In a study of processes for dealing with conflict, Koren, Carlton,

and Shaw (1980) found that distressed and nondistressed couples propose solutions to problems at similar rates; however, distressed coupled are less responsive and more critical of each other. Similarly, Schaap (1984) reports that nondistressed partners tend to respond to problem solving attempts of their mates with consenting, while distressed husbands tend to respond with dissenting and distressed wives tend to respond with interrupting behaviors.

Distressed families seem to display fewer problem-solving strategies and are more ritualized in their patterns of interaction (Gottman, 1979). Positive behaviors (humor, affect, and support) are lower in distressed families who are less likely to reciprocate positive behaviors. They are less likely to reciprocate positive behaviors. In addition, distressed families demonstrate higher rates of negative communication and are more likely to reciprocate negative acts. A study of satisfying marriages by Krueger and Smith (1982) indicates that couples basically cooperate with each other during the problem-solving process even though their patterns of decision making vary. Couples who are more committed to their marriages have less difficulty with problem-solving (Swensen & Trahung, 1985).

Reiss and his associates (1981) analyzed three components of family problem-solving: 1) information gathering–generating alternative hypotheses, conceptualizing the problem in question; 2) interpretation of information–determining the conceptual style of information utilization; and, 3) communication of information–examining how each member given a unique piece of information shares and uses it to solve given problems. The family paradigm employed in this research assumes that coping strategies are related to the families' conceptions of the social world as proposed by Reiss and Oliveri (1980).

Sillars (1981) describes people as being integrative, avoidant, or distributive in their styles of communication. Bruggraf and Sillars (1987) report that husbands and wives are more avoidant than confrontative, analytic or conciliatory when it comes to discussing problems. This is consistent with results reported by Cousins and Vincent (1983). Nye and McLaughlin (1982) found that the extent to which a spouse is helpful in solving personal problems experienced by the other is more important than child care, recreation, child socialization, and housekeeper roles in predicting marital satisfaction for husbands and wives.

As couples become more committed to the relationship the use of reasoning to resolve conflicts increases (Billingham & Sack, 1987). This is consistent with the expectation that *instrumental competence* is an important correlate of marital quality.

Development and Validation

The following sections summarize approaches taken to developing and validating indicators of exchange disposition, communication efficiency, receptive accuracy, and instrumental competence.

Exchange Disposition

Development. Based on social penetration theory (Altman & D. Taylor, 1973), breadth and depth of disclosure are related intimately to perceived and forecasted rewards and costs associated with each partner's relationship to the other. While rewards and costs associated with B's relationship to A influence rewards and costs associated with A's relationship to B, we argue that the latter is a more proximal predictor of A's disposition to disclose to B than the former. Under this view, the more rewards relative to costs associated with A's relation to B, the greater the breadth and depth of disclosure from A to B. Critical in estimating disposition to disclose, then, is the operationalization of rewards and costs in interpersonal relations. J. Taylor's Affiliation Inventory is designed to accomplish this aim (cf. J. Taylor & McMillian, 1995). Eight reward and eight cost items have been written to measure the distribution of rewards and costs in A's relationship to B and B's relationship to A.

Since each item in Table 1 is rated on a 0-8 scale, the scores for reward range from 0-64 and likewise for cost. By evaluating relative magnitudes of reward and cost subtotals on A's relationship to B and B's relationship to A, it is possible to estimate the relative disposition to disclose using two procedures.

First, the theory of social penetration (SP) (Altman & D. Taylor, 1973) stresses the numerical ratio of rewards (R) over costs (C): $SP = R/C$. If $R = 40$ and $C = 20$ describes A's relation to B, then $SP = 2.0$ estimates A's disposition to disclose to B, this ratio under the theory being correlated with the ratio of rewards and costs associated with B's relation to A. The reader will notice that the ratio SP is blind to relative magnitudes of its components R and C, e.g., $R/C = 40/20 = 60/30 = 20/10 = 2.0$.

J. Taylor and his associates have proposed a second technique for partially addressing shortcomings in the SP measure (Taylor, in preparation, Taylor & Rogers, 1993; Taylor, Underwood, Thomas, & Zhang, 1990). By determining the vector length P associated with components R and C,

$$P = \sqrt{R^2 + C^2},$$
(1)

and estimating the volume of the arc subtended by angle Ø (arctan of ratio R/C) under vector P,

$$D = (P2 \times Ø \times .5)10^{-1}$$
(2)

we obtain an estimate of disposition to disclose D which partially corrects for variations in magnitudes associated with components R and C. For R = 40 and $C = 20$,

$$P = \sqrt{40^2 + 20^2}$$
$$= 44.72$$

and
$$D = (44.72^2 \times 1.11 \times .5)10^{-1}$$
$$= 110.71.$$

Using identical procedures $D = 249.11$ for the ratio 60/30 and $D = 16.09$ for the ratio 20/10. Measure D, then, provides differentiated estimates of disclosure disposition on identical R/C ratios SP. That D is a more sensitive indicator of disclosure disposition than SP is indicated in studies by McMaster-Olmes (1988) and Walsh and J. Taylor (1983). For these reasons disclosure

Table 1. Jerome Taylor's Affiliation Inventory

Instructions: Read each statement completely, carefully, and thoroughly. Indicate the frequency with which behaviors identified in the statement apply to your relation to your spouse using the following scale:

0	1	2	3	4	5	6	7	8
Never		Rarely		Sometimes		Often		Always

The higher the number, the more frequently the behavior in the statement applies to your relationship. Record this number in the blank beside the statement being considered.

Reward Items

1. I speak positively about my spouse's personality.
3. I enjoy being with my spouse.
5. I seek out ways to help my spouse.
7. I value my spouse's opinions.
9. I boast about my spouse's behavior.
11. I notice little things my spouse does well.
13. I support my spouse's goals.
15. I give assistance whenever my spouse requests it.

Cost Items

2. I turn down my spouse's requests for help.
4. I disagree with my spouse's values.
6. I complain about the least thing my spouse does.
8. I express embarrassment over my spouse's behavior.
10. I dismiss my spouse's opinions.
12. I am too busy to help my spouse.
14. I get uptight around my spouse.
16. I point out my spouse's faults.

---

disposition is recommended over social penetration as an estimate of exchange disposition.

In relation to the comparison construct introduced by Thibaut and Kelley (1959), instructions and items in Table 1 can be adjusted to estimate general comparison level. For husbands we provide the following instructions: "In relation to each item, rate the extent to which wives *should...*" *speak* positively about their husbands' personality," "point out their husbands' faults," and so on. Wives are instructed to rate the extent to which husbands *should...* " *speak* positively about their wives' personality," and so on. Under this operationalizing proposal, general comparison

level estimates are similar to a key sociological construct, role conception.

Just as D can be used to estimate exchange disposition between partners A and B, it can be utilized to estimate exchange disposition between partner A or B and outside interest C–a close relative, a best friend, or most relevantly a current or potential paramour. Where attractive alternatives exist, the measure D defined on outside interest C provides an estimate of comparison level for alternates (Thibaut & Kelley, 1959). In particular we would have A rate rewards and costs associated with B's relationship to A and then C's relationship to A. In the first instance A rates items such as "My spouse enjoys being with me" and in the second "My (outside interest *C*) enjoys being with me," both taken from item stems given in Table 1.

To the extent *D* associated with outside relation *C* is greater than *D* associated with one's mate (comparison level for alternates), or to the extent *D* associated with one's mate is less than *D* associated with expected role performance (general comparison level), the relationship is at risk to the degree legal, religious, cultural, or other normative barriers to dissolution are weak.

Validation. In their study of Japanese arranged and love-matched marriages Walsh and J. Taylor (1982) found disclosure disposition to be superior to social reinforcement, social profit, or social penetration in predicting levels of understanding of the two groups. Curlee (1986) reports that children of single mothers whose relationships with male friends reflect higher levels of disclosure disposition are less impulsive, less passive-aggressive, less repressed, less dependent, and less maladjusted generally than children of single mothers whose relationships with male friends reflect lower levels of disclosure. When comparing interpersonal profit, social penetration, and disclosure disposition in a study of mothers high and low in dysphoria, disclosure disposition was found to have a comparative advantage (J.Taylor,Underwood,Thomas, & Zhang, 1990). Research by McMaster-Olmes (1988) indicates that levels of disclosure disposition of married spouses are significantly predictive of levels of understanding they achieve. In addition, she found levels of disclosure disposition to significantly predict marital satisfaction for both husbands and wives. Details on the psychometric properties of the Affiliation Inventory can be found in Taylor and McMillian (1995).

Communication Efficiency

Development. Through successful communication one makes known to another what one currently experiences (J. Taylor, in preparation). It follows that the extent to which partner A corroborates messages sent to *B* is an important indicator of communication efficiency associ-

ated with *A*'s relation to B. Processually, four steps are implied: (a) transmission of "x" by *A*; (b) reception of "x" by *B*; (c) submission of B's interpretation of "x" to *A*; and (d) corroboration or correction of B's submission of "x" by *A*.

Since under estimating procedures recommended here *B* cannot receive more than *A* transmits, the amount transmitted initially sets an upper limit on the amount received. Correspondingly, the amount received establishes an upper limit on the amount submitted, just as the amount submitted defines the upper limit of the amount corroborated. Thus, reception is defined on transmission subspace, submission on reception subspace, and corroboration on submission subspace: $T \supseteq R \supseteq S \supseteq C$.

J. Taylor (in preparation) utilizes a Bayesian approach to estimate each component of the basic communication cycle (*TRSC*). For each component estimations are structured around *affective* and *behavioral* dispositions. For transmission affective disposition *M* is defined on "...feels like transmitting" and behavioral disposition *N* on "...actually transmits." Item 1 of Transmission evaluates the affective disposition directly: "How often do you *feel like sharing* your thoughts with your mate?" Since this and all items are rated on a 0-10 (Almost Never to Almost Always) scale, the score assigned is taken as an estimate of the probability of affective disposition *M*. Item 2 estimates the probability of behavioral disposition N: "How often do you *actually share* your thoughts with your mate?" Item 3 evaluates *congruent transmission*: "Consider those times you *feel like sharing* your thoughts. At those times, how often do you actually share them?" Formally, we estimate *p (N/M)*, the probability of transmitting given the sender feels like it. Here we evaluate congruence between affective and behavioral dispositions. Item 4 is written to estimate *reluctant transmission* defined on the *p (N/M)*: "Consider those times you do *not feel like sharing* your thoughts. At those times, how often do you *actually share* them?" The final item of transmission estimates *dissonant withholding* defined on the probability *p (M/*N): "Consider those times you *do not share* your thoughts. At those times, how often do you *feel like sharing* them?"

Table 2 gives complete item sets for each component of the communication cycle *TRSC*. The Bayesian structure of items for transmission is preserved for reception, submission, and corroboration. For reception, item 1 estimates affective disposition, item 2 behavioral disposition, item 3 congruent listening, item 4 reluctant listening, and item 5 dissonant nonlistening. Analogous interpretations apply to item sets proposed for submission and corroboration.

While J. Taylor (in preparation) describes procedures for taking full advantage of Bayesian structured item sets, only strategies for calculating adjusted component scores will be examined here. With five items per component, each rated on a 0 to 10 scale, the potential range is 0 to 50 per component. For ease of interpretation we multiply the potential range by 2, giving a transformed unadjusted range of 0 to 100 per component.

Representing transformed unadjusted component total scores as t, r, s, and c, $t = 65$ for partner A and $t = 40$ for partner B would suggest that A's transmission of experiences is perceptibly higher than B's transmission of experiences. Since we have established a range of 0 to 100, we could say A's perceived transmission is 60% of the maximum and B's is 40% of the maximum. Alternatively, we could say that A's subjective probability of transmission of experiences is .65 and B's is .40. For r, s, and c, analogous interpretation would follow that given for t.

For a complete communication cycle assume $t = 65$ for partner A, $r = 70$ for partner B, $s = 40$ for partner B, and $c = 80$ for partner A. In terms of pattern we would say that A is subjectively more inclined to corroborate (80) than transmit (65) and that B is subjectively more inclined to listen (70) than submit interpreted messages to A for corroboration (40). Further, we notice that B's unadjusted disposition to receive (70) is slightly higher than A's unadjusted disposition to transmit (65) just as A's unadjusted disposition to corroborate (80) is higher than B's unadjusted disposition to submit (40). Since J. Taylor (in preparation) argues on theoretical grounds that reception cannot exceed transmission just as corroboration cannot exceed submission, it is important to provide means for adjusting t, r, s, and c scores to

accommodate the relationship $T \supseteq R \supseteq S \supseteq C$. Following Taylor's recommendation, we let

$$T = t \tag{3}$$

from which it is possible to estimate total adjusted scores for reception, submission, and corroboration,

$$R = (T \times r)10^{-2} \tag{4}$$

$$S = (R \times s)10^{-2} \tag{5}$$

and $$C = (S \times c)10^{-2} \tag{6}$$

respectively. Under these procedures T 65, $R = 45.5$, $S = 18.2$, and $C = 14.6$. In other words we estimate that about 14.6% of messages transmitted by A to B are subsequently corroborated by A through B. We estimate, then, an unadjusted net loss of

$$
\begin{aligned}
I &= 100 - C \\
&= 85.4, \tag{7}
\end{aligned}
$$

and an adjusted net loss of

$$
\begin{aligned}
L &= T - C \\
&= 50.4, \tag{8}
\end{aligned}
$$

where unadjusted net loss is defined on the domain of transmittable experiences (100%) and adjusted net loss on the domain of transmitted experiences ($T = 65\%$). Estimate I defines loss of communication efficiency for transmittable experiences and L for transmitted experiences. Since C is critical to both, we take C as an overall indicator of communication efficiency. The larger the magnitude of C, the more A's experiences are likely to be known by B. We are quick to acknowledge, however, that there are times I and should be used to provide contextual interpretation of C.

Validation. On a sample of 100 Black inner city couples, Cronbach alpha coefficients of reliability ranged from .72 to .77 on components of the *TRSC* communication cycle for husbands,

Table 2. Jerome Taylor's Measure of Communication Efficiency

Please use the following scale to answer all questions in this inventory. Record the most appropriate number in the blank beside each statement. Do NOT write the label, only record the SCALE NUMBER in the blank.

0	1	2	3	4	5	6	7	8
Almost Never		Rarely		Sometimes		Often		Almost Always

Take a moment to reflect on the kinds of things you think about when with your spouse. Then answer questions 1 through 5. Record the appropriate SCALE NUMBER for each question, NOT the typed label.

1. How often do you *feel like sharing* your thoughts and feelings with your spouse?
2. How often do you *actually share* your thoughts with your spouse?
3. Consider those times you *feel like sharing* your thoughts. At those times, how often do you *actually share* them?
4. Consider those times you *do not feel like sharing* your thoughts. At those times, how often do you force yourself to *actually share* them with your spouse?
5. Consider those times you *do not share* your thoughts. At those times, how often do you *feel like sharing* them?

Take a moment to reflect on the kinds of things your spouse shares with you. Then answer questions 6 through 10. Record the appropriate SCALE NUMBER for each question, NOT the typed label.

6. How often do you *find your spouse's comments of significant interest* to you?
7. How often do you *actually give your undivided attention* to what your spouse has to say?
8. Reflect on those times you *find your spouse's comments of interest.* At those times, how often do you *give your undivided attention* to your spouse's comments?
9. Consider those times *you are uninterested in what your spouse has to say.* At those t i m e s , how often do you *give your spouse UNDIVIDED attention.*
10. Consider those times *your attention wanders when your spouse is talking to you.* At those times, how often are you *still interested in what your spouse has to say?*

Take a moment to reflect on how you react to your spouse's sharing thoughts and feelings with you. Then answer questions 11 through 15. Record the appropriate SCALE NUMBER for each question, NOT the typed label.

11. How often do you *feel like discussing* your understanding of your spouse's comments to ensure you know *exactly* how your spouse feels?
12. How often do you *actually discuss* your understanding of your spouse's comments to ensure you know *exactly* how your spouse feels?
13. Reflect on those times you *feel like discussing* your understanding of your spouse's comments. At those times, how often do you *actually* do so?
14. Reflect on those times you *do not feel like discussing* your understanding of your spouse's comments. At those times, how often do you *actually do so?*
15. Reflect on those times you *do not discuss* your understanding of your spouse's comments. At those times, how often do you *feel like* doing so?

Please use the following scale to answer all questions is this inventory. Record the most appropriate number in the blank beside each statement. Do NOT write the label, only record the SCALE NUMBER in the blank.

0	1	2	3	4	5	6	7	8
Almost Never		Rarely		Sometimes		Often		Almost Always

(table continues)

Take a moment to reflect on *how you deal with your spouse's misunderstanding* the way you think or feel about something . Then answer questions 16 through 20. Record the appropriate SCALE NUMBER for each question, NOT the typed label.

16. How often do *you feel like correcting* your spouse?
17. How often do you *actually correct* your spouse?
18. Reflect on those times you *feel like correcting* your spouse. At those times, how often do you *actually correct* your spouse?
19. Reflect on those times you *do not feel like correcting* your spouse. At those times, how often do you *actually correct* your spouse?
20. Reflect on those times you *do not actually* correct your spouse. At those times, how often do you *feel like correcting* your spouse?

and .80 to .86 for wives. Correlation between communication efficiency and instrumental competence was .59 for husbands and .62 for wives. For husbands the correlation between instrumental competence and the Locke-Wallace (1959) measure of marital satisfaction was .61 and for wives it was .67. Further, cross-gender correlations involving instrumental competence and communication efficiency tended to be higher than either measure and marital satisfaction. In summary there was moderate correlation among these indicators of marital quality, cross-gender correlations being more consistent for instrumental competence and communication efficiency.

Marziano (1987) studied the relationship between marital quality and child behavior in 27 Black married couples. Husbands who obtain high scores on J. Taylor's measure of communication efficiency (*TRSC*) report fewer maladaptive behaviors in their children. Husbands reporting low levels of corroboration tended to rate their children as more impulsive and overactive than husbands reporting high levels of corroboration. Husbands of wives reporting high levels of corroboration tended to perceive their children as less passive-aggressive, less repressed, less de-pendent, and less maladjusted generally than husbands of wives reporting low levels of corroboration.

Receptive Accuracy

Development. J. Taylor (in preparation) provides a systematic analysis of four levels of understanding between intimates. In research conducted thus far we have only explored the first of these levels. Accordingly, comments here are addressed to that level only. At the first level of analysis we are concerned with Partner A's perception of the relationship to Partner B and with Partner B's perception of Partner A's perception. The first of these is called a direct perception and the second a metaperception. In research to date (McMaster-Olmes, 1988) we have used the Affiliation Inventory (Table1) to estimate both forms of perception. Partner A rates items such as "I enjoy being with my mate" while partner B is instructed to "Imagine how your mate thinks about her (his) relation to you. *She (he) would say... I* enjoy being with my mate." Since Partner B rates the same 16 items of the Affiliation Inventory as Partner A, it is possible to utilize different strategies for evaluating level of understanding or misunderstanding between partners.

Correlation between Partner A's and B's ratings of individual items can be taken as one index of understanding. The sum of absolute or squared differences across items between partners are indices of misunderstanding which can be adjusted to reflect understanding. Simple difference between total affiliation scores is another possible index. We also have utilized magnitude of absolute differences associated with social profit and social penetration. However, we have found that the magnitude of correlation criterion (McMaster-Olmes, 1988) or the difference in disclosure disposition (Walsh & J. Taylor, 1983) may be the more sensitive indicators of receptive accuracy.

The difference in direct perception and metaperception is technically a measure of misunderstanding. Dividing this difference by 160, the mathematically absolute maximum likely difference between direct and metaperceptions,

$$M = (D_a - Db) / 160, \qquad (9)$$

where M represents the signed proportion of misunderstanding against the absolute maximum likely misunderstanding, 160. Where metaperception $D_b = 142.9$ and direct perception $D_a = 91.2$,

$$M = (142.9 - 91.2)/160$$
$$= +.32,$$

the positive sign indicating that partner B overestimates the amount of affiliation (rewards/costs) partner A ascribes to the relationship. The .32 magnitude further suggests that the magnitude of misunderstanding is about 32% of the maximum likely difference in misunderstanding. We estimate level of understanding, the absolute complement of misunderstanding, from

$$U = 1 - /M/ \qquad (10)$$

which in the present instance is 1 - /+.32/ = .68. Since the range on U is 0.0 to 1.0, the higher the

value U the higher the presumed level of understanding or receptive accuracy.

Whatever estimating technique is used, the reader should be mindful of problems identified by Cronbach (1958) regarding the interpretive pitfalls of indexes of perceptual matching. This article should be consulted in relation to estimates of understanding proposed here.

Validation. A study by Walsh and J. Taylor (1982) which examined levels of understanding in arranged and love-matched Japanese marriages found that couples in love-matched marriages show better understanding on the affiliative dimension (rewards and costs) than couples in arranged marriages who show better understanding on the control dimension (induction and coercion). Since love-matched marriages affirm an egalitarian ideology and arranged marriages a patriarchal ideology, the differential pattern of understanding involving these marriage types is theory consistent. In her study of 100 Black married couples McMaster-Olmes (1988) found that spouses' levels of understanding can be predicted by levels of other social exchange variables estimated from reported rewards and costs associated with spousal relations. In particular levels of social reinforcement, social profit, social penetration, disposition to disclose, consensus, and marital satisfaction significantly predict understanding of both husbands and wives.

Instrumental Competence

Development. The extent to which B is resourceful in helping A manage problems, conflicts, and plans of importance to *A* is referred to as *B*'s instrumental competence in relation to A. The first task, then, entails identification of problems, conflicts, and plans that matter to *A*. Table 3 provides items recommended by J. Taylor (in preparation) for identifying lead concerns of A.

Parts A and B of Table 3 present checklists of personal and systemic *problems* of potential urgency to partner A, and Parts C, D, and E provide checklists of personal, familial, and systemic *conflicts* of potential urgency to A. Parts F and G present checklists identifying long-range

Table 3. **Jerome Taylor's Checklist for Problems, Conflicts, and Plans**

Problems

Part A [Personal]: Check the three (3) causing you the most distress. Write the number 1 beside the statement causing the most distress, the number 2 beside the statement causing the second most distress, and the number 3 beside the statement causing the third most distress.

    __feeling critical of myself
    __feeling disappointed with myself
    __feeling angry with myself
    __feeling bored
    __feeling tense, anxious
    __feeling insecure
    __feeling down in the dumps
    __feeling frustrated

Part B [Familial]: Check the three (3) causing you the most distress. Write the number 1 beside the statement causing the most distress, the number 2 beside the statement causing the second most distress, and the number 3 beside the statement causing the third most distress.

    __feeling upset with the children
    __feeling upset with a blood relative
    __feeling upset with an in-law
    __feeling with a friend
    __feeling upset with a fellow worker
    __feeling upset over the bills
    __feeling upset with my neighborhood (or neighbors)
    __feeling upset with my job (or lack of a job)

Conflicts

Part C [Personal]: Check the two things your MATE DOES that cause you the greatest distress. Write the number 1 beside the statement causing the most distress and the number 2 beside the statement causing the second most distress.

My mate:

    __is forgetful   __has bad moods
    __nags   __is impulsive
    __acts superior   __is sloppy
    __blows up   __is irresponsible
    __is oversensitive   __is undisciplined

Part D [Familial]: Check the two things ....

My mate:

    __makes decisions without consulting me
    __is too possessive
    __fails to help with the children

                 (table continues)

Problems

    __is unfaithful
    __seems disinterested in sex
    __is too dependent
    __fails to provide emotional support
    __mismanages money
    __refuses to talk about problems
    __fails to do household chores

Part E [Systemic]: Check the two things ....

My mate:

    __criticizes my relatives
    __criticizes my friends
    __embarrasses me before others
    __fails to support my outside interests
    __refuses to go places important to me
    __interferes with my plans for the future
    __behaves inappropriately with others
    __is too dependent on her (his) parents
    __is overinvolved in outside activities
    __complains about my job (or lack of a job)

Plans

Part F [Long-range]: Check three (3) of the following statements reflecting long-range things you need to plan for. Write the number 1 beside the statement reflecting the most important planning issue, the number 2 beside the next most important planning issue, and the number 3 beside the third most important planning issue.

    __long-ranged personal goals
    __long-ranged employment goals
    __long-ranged training goals
    __long-ranged educational goals
    __long-ranged housing goals
    __long-ranged retirement goals
    __long-ranged goals for the children
    __long-ranged goals for vacation

Part G [Short-range]: Check three (3) of the following statements reflecting long-range things you need to plan for. Write the number 1 beside the statement reflecting the most important planning issue, the number 2 beside the next most important planning issue, and the number 3 beside the third most important planning issue.

    __inviting friends or relatives over
    __going out
    __arranging for babysitting

(table continues)

Problems

___setting up budget for food
___setting up budget for utilities
___setting up budget for major purchases
___setting up budget for installment purchases
___setting up budget for clothes
___setting up schedule for paying bills
___attending an activity with my spouse

---

and immediate-range *planning issues* of concern to A. All checklists were designed to sample a range of personal to systemic issues of immediate to long-term relevance to A.

Partner A is instructed to check off six of the most pressing items for problems, six for conflicts, and six for plans. In relation to each of the 12 items for problems and conflicts Partner A is then required to evaluate the extent to which Partner B is resourceful in managing each identified urgency. Table 4 provides instructions and rating procedures for estimating instrumental competence for problems and conflicts of urgency to A.

Suppose, for example, that "feeling down in the dumps" is the number one item identified in Part A of Table 3. When Partner A feels "down in the dumps", the extent to which Partner A talks it over with Partner B is estimated on the 0 to10 scale in Table 4. Next, Partner A is required to estimate the extent to which the problem is "resolved," "remains the same," or "gets worse" when the experience of "feeling down in the dumps" is shared with Partner B. This is accomplished by having Partner A apportion a total of 100 points to the three outcomes–resolves, remains, worsens. Points are assigned to outcomes such that the sum across outcomes is 100. These procedures are repeated for each of the 12 items comprising problems and plans. We note through these operationalizations that we capture the disposition of Partner A to turn to B as well as the subjective outcome of this course of action. For the six planning issues identified as pressing in Parts F and G of Table 3, the extent to which Partner A turns to Partner B is also rated on the 0 to 10 scale given in Table 4. The rating of outcomes follows a slightly different instructional procedure summarized in the last section of Table 4. As before, Partner A is required to apportion points to outcomes under the constraint that the sum comes to 100. This procedure is repeated for each of the six planning issues identified as urgent.

While J. Taylor (in preparation) details mathematical assumptions underlying the recommended approach and identifies procedures for taking full advantage of each measurement component, for purposes of discussion here attention will focus on B's overall resourcefulness in helping A manage problems, conflicts, and plans. Formally, we have two courses of action C_i– Partner A talks to Partner B (C_1) and Partner A doesn't talk to Partner B (C_2) — and three outcomes O_j–resolves or succeeds (O_1) remains or mixed (O_2), and worsens or fails (O_3). Under these definitions, then, Partner B's overall resourcefulness in helping Partner B manage problems, conflicts, and plans can be estimated from the conditional probability O_1 given C_i that is, from

$$p\,(\,O1\,/\,C1\,) = P_1 E_{11} \qquad (11)$$

where the left side of the equation defines the conditional probability, where P_i is the probability of talking, and where E_{11} is the probability that talking leads to outcome O_1 resolves or succeeds.

In estimating parameters P_1 and E_{11} we recall that 18 sets of items are rated — six for problems, six for conflicts, and six for plans. In evaluating disposition to talk each of these 18 items is rated on a 0 to 10 scale, giving a theoretical range of 0

Table 4. Procedure for Estimating Instrumental Competence in Managing Problems, Conflicts, and Plans

INSTRUCTION COMMON TO PROBLEMS, CONFLICTS, AND PLANS
Use the following scale to rate the statement you marked (#1 the statement you marked (#1, #2, or #3) in Part (A, B, C, D, E, F, G):

```
0     1     2     3     4     5     6     7     8     9     10
L___J     L___J     L___J     L___J     L___J
```

1. Using the above scale RATE THE EXTENT TO WHICH YOU TALK THINGS OVER WITH YOUR SPOUSE WHEN (# ___ of Part ___) OCCURS.

INSTUCTION COMMON TO PROBLEMS AND CONFLICTS.
For the following item, you are to assign points to each option such that the total adds to 100. The more a particular option applies, the more points you should assign. The total across the options must sum to 100.

2. WHEN YOU TALK TO YOUR SPOUSE ABOUT (# ___ of Part ___), indicate
    the extent to which:

    ___the problem is resolved
    ___the problem remains about the same
    ___the problem gets worse
Sum =   (Make sure the points assigned add up to 100)

INSTRUCTIONS UNIQUE TO PLANS:

3. WHEN YOU TALK TO YOUR SPOUSE ABOUT (# ___ of Part ___), indicate
    the extent to which the plan is implemented:

    ___with complete success
    ___with mixed success and failure
    ___with complete failure
Sum =   (Make sure the points assigned add up to 100)

to 180. We estimate the probability of talking, then, from

$$P_1 = \Sigma X1 / 180, \qquad (12)$$

where $'X_i$ is summation of ratings across $I = 18$ items rated on the 0-10 scale. If $X_i = 92$, then $P_1 = .51$. In examining the overall efficiency of the course of action talks E_{ij} we recall that 100 points are assigned to each of 18 items, generating a potential range of 1800 points apportionable to outcomes O_j. In estimating the specific efficiency that talking leads to resolution or success, then,

$$E_{11} = \Sigma S1 / 1800, \qquad (13)$$

where $'S_i$ is the summation of points apportioned to O_1 across the 18 items. If $S_1 = 750$, then $E_{11} = .42$. The instrumental competence of Partner B in relation to Partner A is then estimated which we interpret as Partner A's subjective conditional probability,

$$p\,(O_1\,/\,C_1) = .51 \times .42$$
$$= .21,$$

that is, Partner A's subjective conditional probability that outcomes are salutary when Partner B's assistance is sought for problems, conflicts, and plans of pressing significance to Partner A. We take the conditional probability $p\,(O1/C1)$ as an overall subjective estimate of Partner B's resourcefulness to Partner A. Alternately, $p\,(O1/C1)$ is an estimate of B's instrumental competence from A's perspective. Estimation of A's instrumental competence from B's perspective follows analogously.

Validation. Because of the Bayesian strategy used for estimating instrumental competence, it is not possible to calculate internal reliability, and data are not yet available for test-retest reliability. That this measure is correlated with other indicators of marital quality is summarized in the Validation section of Communication Efficiency.

J. Taylor's measure of instrumental competence was employed by Marziano (1987) to assess marital quality as related to child behaviors. Both husbands and wives who rate their spouses high in instrumental competence report fewer maladaptive behaviors in their children. Husbands rating their wives high in instrumental competence tended to view their children as less repressed and less dependent. In this context wives tended to perceive their children as less impulsive and overactive. Wives rating their husbands high in instrumental competence tended to report their children as less passive aggressive and less dependent. In this context husbands perceived their children as less impulsive and overactive, less passive-aggressive, less dependent, and less maladjusted overall. From this study it appears that perception of instrumental competence covaries with perceptions of child outcomes.

Summary

We have proposed four measures of marital quality: *exchange disposition, communication effi-ciency, receptive accuracy,* and *Instrumental com-petence.* Each is based on a communication model reflecting a systems perspective. Both process and outcome of communication can be estimated using these methods. The level and pattern of these indicators are presumed to vary across couples. None perfectly predicts marital quality and none is necessarily implied by the others.

Exchange disposition, a method of estimating communication process, seeks to improve upon social penetration (Altman & D. Taylor, 1973) as a means of evaluating disclosive properties of interaction. It refers to the relative distribution of rewards and costs associated with a spouse's relation to the partner. Levels of rewards and costs reported by marital partners have been linked to their levels of relational quality (Curlee, 1986; J. Taylor, Underwood, Thomas, & Zhang, submitted; McMaster-Olmes, 1988; Walsh & J. Taylor, 1982). As such, exchange disposition is a relatively consistent indicator of marital quality.

The process of communication can also be evaluated in terms of its efficiency. Transmission, reception, submission, and corroboration are the components of relational interaction that can be assessed using the communication efficiency measure which estimates the extent to which each spouse corrects the interpretation of messages sent by the other. Levels of communication efficiency have been associated with levels of marital quality and quality of child outcomes (Marziano, 1987).

Receptive accuracy is an indicator of communication outcome. Whether a spouse is able to gain an understanding of the inner experiences of the partner is estimated by this measure. Prediction of a partner's responses is fundamental to the assessment of receptive accuracy. Level of understanding has been found to reflect level of marital quality for both husbands and wives (McMaster-Olmes, 1988; Walsh & J. Taylor, 1982). While there are technical problems associated with the interpretation of receptive accuracy (Cronbach, 1958), it nonetheless appears to be a promising index of marital quality.

The resourcefulness of a spouse in helping the partner to manage problems, conflicts, and plans is referred to as instrumental competence, a marital communication outcome measure. The assessment of how problem situations are customarily resolved is an important aspect of marital quality which also affects quality of child outcomes (Marziano, 1987).

The measures of marital quality proposed in this chapter have relevance to investigations of relationships between intimate partners of other types, e.g., cohabiting couples, mother-daughter pairs, sibling relations, or friendship patterns. Future research will be directed toward the validation of proposed measures in relation to other measures of close relationships.

References

Allen, A., & Thompson, T. (1984). Agreement, understanding, realization, and feeling understood as predictors of communicative satisfaction in marital dyads. *Journal of Marriage and the Family, 46*, 915-921.

Altman, I., & Taylor, D. A. (1973). *Social penetration: The development of interpersonal relationships.* New York: Irvington.

Barrett-Lennard, G. T. (1981). The empathy cycle: Refinement of a nuclear concept. *Journal of Counseling Psychology, 28*, 91-100.

Berscheid, E. (1985). Interpersonal attraction. In G. Lindzey & E. Aronson (Eds.), *Handbook of social psychology* (Vol. 2, pp. 413-484). New York: Random House.

Billingham, R. E., & Sack, A. R. (1987). Conflict tactics and the level of emotional commitment among unmarrieds. *Human Relations, 40*, 59-74.

Bochner, A. P., Krueger, D. C., & Chmielewski, T. L. (1982). Interpersonal perceptions and marital adjustment. *Journal of Communication, 32*, 135-147.

Bruggraf, C. S., & Sillars, A. L. (1987). A critical examination of sex differences in marital communication. *Communications Monographs, 54*, 276-294.

Bruner, J. (1957). On perceptual readiness. *Psychological Review, 64*, 123-152.

Brunswik, E. (1952). The conceptual framework of psychology. In O. Neurath, R. Carnap, & C. Morris (Eds.), *International encyclopedia of unified science* [Vol. 1(10)]. Chicago: University of Chicago Press.

Chelune, G. J., Rosenfeld, L. B., & Waring, E. M (1985). Spouse disclosure patterns in distressed and nondistressed couples. *The American Journal of Family Therapy, 13*, 24-32.

Cleek, M. G., & Pearson, T. A. (1985). Perceived causes of divorce: An analysis of interrelationships. *Journal of Marriage and the Family, 47*, 179-183.

Coleman, J. C. (1984). *Intimate relationships, marriage, and the family.* Indianapolis: Bobbs-Merrill.

Cronbach, L. J. (1958). Proposals leading to analytic treatment of social perception scores. In R. Tagiuri & L. Petrullo (Eds.), *Person perception and interpersonal behavior* (pp. 353-379). Stanford, CA: Stanford University Press.

Curlee, J. (1986). *Effects of intimate relationships on child adjustment in a sample of Black inner city women.* Unpublished doctoral dissertation, University of Pittsburgh.

Davidson, B. (1981). The relations between partner's affective self-disclosure and marital adjustments. *Dissertation Abstracts International, 41*, 3931-3931B.

Dellinger, S., & Deane, B. (1980). *Communicating effectively.* New York: Chilton.

Ferraro, B., & Markman, H. J. (1981). *Application of the behavioral model of marriage to deaf marital relationships.* Paper presented at the annual meeting of the Midwestern Psychological Association, Detroit.

Floyd, F., & Markman, H. (1983). Observational biases in spouse interaction: Toward a cognitive/behavioral model of marriage. *Journal of Consulting and Clinical Psychology, 51*, 450-457.

Gaelick, L., Bodenhausen, G. V., & Wyer, R. S., Jr. (1985). Emotional communication in close relationships. *Journal of Personality and Social Psychology, 49*, 1246-1265.

Gottman, J. M. (1979). *Marital interaction.* New York: Academic Press.

Gottman, J. M., Notarius, C., Markman, H., Bank, S., Yoppi, B., & Rubin, M. E. (1976). Behavior exchange theory and marital decision. *Journal of Personality and Social Psychology, 34*, 14-23.

Hansen, J. E., & Schuldt, W. J. (1984). Marital self-disclosure and marital satisfaction. *Journal of Marriage and the Family, 46*, 923-926.

Hoch, S. J. (1987). Perceived consensus and predictive accuracy: The pros and cons of projection. *Journal of Personality and Social Psychology, 53*, 221-234.

Honeycutt, J. M. (1986). A model of marital functioning based on an attraction paradigm and social-penetration dimensions. *Journal of Marriage and the Family, 48*, 651-667.

Kelley, H. H. (1979). *Personal relationships: Their structure and processes.* Hillsdale, NJ: Lawrence Erlbaum.

Koren, P., Carlton, K., & Shaw, D. (1980). Marital conflict: Relations among behaviors, outcomes, and distress. *Journal of Consulting and Clinical Psychology, 48*, 460-468.

Krueger, D. L., & Smith, P. (1982). Decision making patterns of couples: A sequential analysis. *Marriage and the Family, 32*, 121-134.

Laing, R. D., Phillipson, H., & Lee, A. R. (1966). *Interpersonal perception.* New York: Springer.

Levinger, G. A. (1982). A social exchange view of the dissolution of pair relationship. In F. I. Nye (Ed.), *Family relationships: Rewards and costs* (pp. 97-121). Beverly Hills, CA: Sage.

Lewis, R., & Spanier, G. (1979). Theorizing about the quality and stability of marriage. In W. E. Burr, R. Hill, I. Nye, & I. L. Reiss (Eds.), *Contemporary theories about the family* (Vol. I, pp. 268-294). New York: Free Press.

Lewis, R., & Spanier, G. (1982). Marital quality, marital stability and social exchange. In F. I. Nye (Ed.), *Family relationships: Rewards and costs* (pp. 49-65). Beverly Hills, CA: Sage.

McMaster, Olmes, J. L. (1988). *An evaluation of seven theories of marital understanding on a sample of Black married couples.* Unpublished doctoral dissertation. University of Pittsburgh.

Markman, H. J. (1981). The prediction of marital distress: A five-year follow-up. *Journal of Consulting and Clinical Psychology, 49*, 760-762.

Markman, J. J. (1984). The longitudinal study of couples' interactions: Implications for understanding and predicting the development of marital distress. In K. Halweg & N. W. Jacobson (Eds.), *Marital interaction* (pp. 253-281). New York: Guilford Press.

Markman, H. J., & Baccus, G. (1982). *The application of a behavioral model of marriage to Black couples.* Unpublished manuscript, Bowling Green State University, Bowling Green, OH.

Marziano, D. R. (1987). *Differential utility of three constructs of marital quality in accounting for the relationship between marital quality and child behavior in Black married couples.* Unpublished doctoral dissertation, University of Pittsburgh.

Metcoff, J., & Whitaker, C. A. (1982). Family microevents: Communication patterns for problem solving. In F. Walsh (Ed.), *Normal family processes* (pp. 251-274). New York: Guilford.

Murstein, B. I., & Beck, G. D. (1972). Person perception, marriage adjustment, and social desirability. *Journal of Consulting and Clinical Psychology, 39*, 396-403.

Noller, P. (1980). Misunderstandings in marital communication of couples' nonverbal communication. *Journal of Personality and Social Psychology, 39*, 1135-1148.

Noller, P. (1984). *Nonverbal communication and marital interaction.* New York: Pergamon.

Nye, F. I., & McLaughlin, S. (1982). Role competence and marital satisfaction. In F. I. Nye (Ed.), *Family relationships: Rewards and costs* (pp. 67-79). Beverly Hills, CA: Sage.

Perlmutter, M S., & Hatfield, E. (1980). Intimacy, intentional metacommunications and second-order change. *American Journal of Family Therapy, 8*, 17-23.

Reiss, D. (1981). *The family's construction of reality.* Cambridge, MA: Harvard University Press.

Reiss, D., & Oliveri, M. E. (1980). Family paradigm and family coping: A proposal for linking the family's intrinsic adaptive capacities to its responses to stress. *Family Relations, 29*, 431-444.

Sabetelli, R. M., & Pearce, J. (1986). Exploring marital expectations. *Journal of Social and Personal Relationship, 3*, 307-321.

Schaap, C, (1984). A comparison of the interaction of distressed and nondistressed married couples in a laboratory situation: Literature survey, methodological issues, and an empirical investigation. In I. K. Halweg & N. S. Jacobson (Eds.), *Marital interaction* (pp. 133-158). New York: Guilford Press.

Scoresby, A. L. (1977). *The marriage dialogue.* Reading, MA: Addison-Wesley.

Sillars, A. (1981). Attributions and interpersonal conflict resolution. In J. H. Harvey, W. Ickes, & R. F. Kidd (Eds.), *New directions in attribution research* (pp. 279-305). Hillsdale, NJ: Lawrence Erlbaum.

Sillars, A. L. (1982). Attribution and communication: Are people "naive scientists" or just naive? In M. E. Roloff & C. R. Berger (Eds.), *Social cognition and communication* (pp. 73-106). Beverly Hills, CA: Sage.

Snyder, D. K. (1979). Multidimensional assessment of marital satisfaction. *Journal of Marriage and the Family, 41*, 813-823.

Swensen, C. H., & Trahaug, G. (1985). Commitment and the long-term marriage relationship. *Journal of Marriage and the Family, 47*, 939-945.

Taylor, J. (in press). *Communication in families.* University of Pittsburgh.

Taylor, J., & McMillian, M. (1996). Taylor's affiliation and control inventories. In R. L. Jones (Ed.), *Handbook of Tests and Measurements for Black*

Populations (Vol. 2). Hampton,VA: Cobb & Henry.

Taylor, J., Underwood, C., Thomas, L., & Zhang, X. (1990). Effects of dysphoria on maternal exchange dispositions. *Journal of Psychology, 124*, 685-697.

Thibaut, J., & Kelly, H. H. (1959). *The social psychology of groups.* New York: John Wiley & Sons.

Walsh, M., & Taylor, J. (1982). Understanding in Japanese marriages. *Journal of Social Psychology, 118*, 67-76.

Walster, E., Walster, G. W., & Berscheid, E. (1978). *Equality: Theory and research.* Boston, MA: Allyn and Bacon.

Watzlawick, P. J., Beavin, J., & Jackson, D. (1967). *Pragmatics of human communication.* New York: Norton.

Wills, T. A., Weiss, R. L., & Patterson, G. R. (1974). A behavioral analysis of the determinants of marital satisfaction. *Journal of Consulting and Clinical Psychology, 42*, 802-811.

For additional information, contact:
Jerome Taylor, Ph.D.
University of Pittsburgh
Institute for the Black Family
Dept. of Africana Studies
3T12 Forbes Quadrangle/230 South Bouquet Street
Pittsburgh, PA 15260
Telephone: (412) 648-7217
Fax: (412) 648-5656

Scales and Protocols for Assessment of Extended Family Support of Single Black Mothers

Harriette Pipes McAdoo

Abstract

Scales and protocols for developing baseline data on the impact of selected family factors on the mental health and economic stability of single Black parents are presented and substantive findings using the measures are reported.

The major overall objective of this research effort was to develop baseline data on the impact that selected family factors have in supporting the mental health and economic stability of family members in Black single-parent homes with working mothers. The American family is increasingly facing stresses that come from changes that threaten the very emotional health of individuals and family units. The stress is even more severe in minority families that have only a mother present within the home.

The specific project objectives were:

1. To obtain a profile of the stresses faced and supports needed by single mothers.

2. To examine, if single mothers are involved in the extended family network, the extent of support provided by extended family kin networks to single Black female mothers.

3. To document the patterns of interactions with kin and fictive kin.

4. To assess the positive or negative impact of reciprocity of the kin help network that may impact the stability of one-parent families.

5. To assess the coping strategies used to handle stress and role conflicts of single mothers.

6. To determine the marital status of single mothers (never married vs. previously married) on their self-esteem, coping strategies and level of satisfaction with their lives.

7. To determine the differential impact that socioeconomic status and urban vs. suburban residence has on the above five specific concerns of single Black mothers.

8. To secure detailed information on the mothers' preferred social service programs and their utilization level of existing programs.

9. To disseminate these findings to social service agencies in the subjects' area, to state and federal policy makers, and to mental health professions through:

a. Social service agency seminars in each cachment area;

b. Papers presented at professional meetings;
c. Articles published in professional journals;
d. Sharing of findings with federal agencies and Congressional leaders.

Instrument Development

The data collection instrument was compiled, and after consultants and advisors reviewed it, the complete instrument was pilot-tested on 20 families in its entirety. The principal investigator did the pretesting, along with research associates, in order to obtain a "hands on" feel of the entire procedure, its timing, and the mothers' reactions. Most questions were closed format, based on responses given during the pretests to open-ended questions. However, some questions were designed for open-ended responses in areas in which more depth was sought.

Questionnaire Items

(a) Basic background items. To increase compatibility of the study results with other earlier and ongoing studies, detailed background data on age, marital status, religion, education, employment status, occupation, income, residential character and political identification were gathered.

(b) Mobility. Mobility patterns were established using the educational and occupational ratings of subjects, both of their parents, and four grandparents. Thus, the mobility data spanned three generations, with two points of mobility available. A modification of standard Hollingshead-Redlich SES procedure was used, combining the educational and occupational data.

Coding forms, procedures, and graphing necessary to condense the cross-generational data into one of eight mobility patterns were developed by the author.

Family information on changes over the past three-generations was gathered on families of orientation, procreation and present living situation:

(1) Geographic mobility
(2) Religious affiliation
(3) Occupations
(4) Education

(c) Socio-economic status. The Hollingshead scale is most often used in research. It places greater emphasis on the occupation than on the education of the individual. This form was not felt to be satisfactory for Black adults, who often are unable to obtain jobs appropriate to their education (Scanzoni, 1977). Discrimination against Blacks has consistently meant that employment status is determined more by race than educational attainment. Therefore, we coded each parent the standard way, and then did a reverse coding as suggested by Baldwin (1973) and McAdoo (1977), giving more weight to education. Concurrently, Heiss (1971) stated that the usual methods of controlling for SES will not result in comparable groups when compared across racial groups. Heiss found that in his nationwide study that Blacks and Whites, equal in the number of years of education were not equal in earning power. He used a technique of combining education, occupation and family income to determine status. See coding manual for specific steps used to determine SES and mobility coding.

(d) Extended familism and kin-help scale. The scale was developed by McAdoo in the study of the family behavior variables antecedent to mobility (1977). It has been pretested twice, modified, and used in the field with over 300 parents. The Family Profile was used to ascertain family structure, kin help patterns, level of interaction and reciprocal obligations. It was based on the writings of Billingsley and Stack. The writings of Sussman, Litwak, Hays and Mindel, McKay and McAdoo, were also used.

(1) Extended Family Relationship/ Structure
(2) Kin Interactions
(3) Role of "Significant Other"

When a "significant other" was identified as being the person who has been the most supportive to the single parent mother, this person was interviewed. The "significant other" may or may not be kin.

Questions were developed related to the roles this person plays in the mother's life and what specific supportive tasks they perform. In addition, the Extended Familism and Kin Help Exchange questions were asked. Comparisons were made of significant other's self perceived role and mother's perception of their role.

(4) Kin Help Exchange
(5) Reciprocal Obligations and Attitudes
(6) Kin/Friend Help Exchange Network

(e) Concerns of single mothers. Additional questions were developed that related specifically to concerns of single mothers: loneliness, finances, relationship with father of child, future marital expectations, and attitudes toward nonmarital sexual activities. These questions were pilot-tested separately. We talked several hours with single mothers to obtain their concerns.

(f) Parenting issue. Questions developed in the McAdoo extended family study (1977) that were incorporated related to: child care, specific child-related concerns of Black parents, education, social activities, public media presentation of Blacks, role of religion in lives, and educational and occupational aspirations for self and children.

(g) Role conflicts and coping strategies. The questions developed by Harrison and Minor (1977), based upon the model developed by Hall (1972), were used to collect these data. Specific questions presented situations to the mother that asked her if she had conflicts in the presented situations and how she would respond to these conflicts. The roles we asked about were that of mother/worker, mother/former wife, worker/former wife. Her response to how she dealt with these conflicts was classified as one of Hall's three types of coping strategies: (1) Structural Role Redefinition; (2) Personal Role Redefinition; and (3) Reacting Role Redefinition (see coding Manual for further details). A summary code was devised so that we could see how each mother generally dealt with her conflicting roles.

(h) Motherhood. Four questions were taken from a Ladies Home Journal (1979) questionnaire that asked how mothers felt about having children. They were asked to agree or disagree that not having children would make them feel incomplete, that raising a child is a full-time commitment, that getting pregnant changed their whole lives around. They were then asked how getting pregnant changed their lives.

(i) Mental Health Variables.
(1) Anxiety. Modified versions of Depner's (1980) Acute Stress Scale and Chronic Stress Scale were used to determine approximate anxiety levels of the mothers. Mothers were asked to respond: always, sometimes, never, to how often they felt nervous, relaxed, strained or anxious to indicate their acute anxiety level. High scores represented high anxiety levels and low scores represented low anxiety levels. The Chronic Stress Scale asked how worried they were by the future, how often they have had to work too hard and how often they were able to do what they wanted to. Again, they could respond: always, sometimes, never with the higher scores representing high anxiety.

(2) General Well-Being. Mothers were asked to rate their lives during the past year on a scale of one to ten, with one meaning the best possible life and ten being the worst possible life. This question was also used in Depner's (1980) study and is useful in getting a general picture of how the mother perceived her recent life situation.

(3) Pearlin Mastery Scale. The Pearlin Mastery Scale measures the degree of control felt over one's life. Internal locus of control refers to a greater sense of self control and external locus of control refers to a greater sense of helplessness. The scale consists of seven statements representing feelings or attitudes that people often have, such as "Sometimes I feel I'm being pushed around in life," and the mothers respond that they strongly agree, agree somewhat, disagree somewhat or strongly disagree. The lower the score, the higher the mastery of the environment. The higher the score, the more the mother felt helpless in controlling her life.

(4) Self-Esteem Scale. The scale, developed by Rosenberg (1965), was used to measure attitudes about the self, including self-esteem, along a favorable-to-unfavorable dimension and was constructed for use in a large scale survey. It assesses how the individual respects herself and considers herself worthy. There are ten items on a Likert type scale, arranged in random order to reduce the error of response set. Test-retest reliability is .85. Validity of the scale has been assessed in several major studies that found significant relationships between the scale. It relates negatively to depression, depressive effort, psychosomatic symptoms, and positively to leadership and choices in a sociometric study (1971).

For this study, Depner reported three items were factored from Rosenberg's scale which were found to be predictive of self-esteem. We also narrowed the responses to two: agree or disagree. Each response was weighted so that all negative self-esteem responses were equal in weight, as were all positive self-esteem responses. High scores indicated positive self-esteem and low scores indicated negative self-esteem.

(5) Satisfaction. An assessment of the varying degrees of satisfaction with their life in general and with their family situation, provided insight on the state of the ecological system of the family. The Standard Happiness Scale used in nationwide surveys, by NORC and the University of Michigan, can offer a measure of the global degree of satisfaction with the environment. A survey made by Harris in 1976 indicated that 44 percent of the nationwide sample believed that the quality of life had decreased during the past ten years. The chief concerns were achieving a quality education for their children (89%), pollution (79%), and about strict enforcement of safe working conditions (73%). The inclusion of these scales gave an objective indication of the level of stress and overall satisfaction that could be related to the family's need for social services.

(a)   Satisfaction with Roles. A modified version of the Harrison-Minor scale was used. Mothers were asked if they were satisfied with their roles as mother, worker, and former wife, with the amount of time spent with their children, and with their relationship with the father of their children. There were three responses given to the

mothers: satisfied, workable, and dissatisfied. The higher scores indicated that the mothers were more satisfied with their roles and lower scores indicated their dissatisfaction.

(b) Satisfaction with life. The Standard Happiness Scale that had been repeatedly used in nationwide surveys was used. There may be limitations in using such a small scale for these questions, and the modification in reference to family situations are not as extensive as a longer scale, and may not be sensitive enough to measure specific, sharply defined attitudes. However, the use of this scale to measure global constructs is based on the work of Gurin et al. (1960), NORC (1964), Bradburn (1969), Hill (1971), and Harrison (1977). They have been used repeatedly to measure very global attitudes such as marital happiness and life satisfaction in general. It allowed us to compare our families with Black and non-Black in nationwide samples. Families were asked in general about their level of happiness and their satisfaction with their present family situation.

(j) Stress.

(1) Significant life Events. The Holmes and Rahe Scale of Recent Events (1967) was used to measure those events that are felt to be universal. Forty-nine events have been weighted on actual populations across the country on a scale giving a higher score for major changes (divorce, 73; death of a child, 63), and lower scores for less traumatic events (vacation, 13). Based on a clinical follow-up, Holmes had grouped the scores into three categories: Mild stress (150-199), Moderate stress (200-299), and Major stress (300+). Those in higher stress groups had greater odds on becoming physically or mentally ill within a period of time.

The Holmes scale was used two years as a guide during which change was measured. For this study a two-step time dimension was added to the scale to get an additional breakdown of significant change events that occurred within the past six months. Subjects were asked to indicate events that had happened within the past six months and those that occurred from seven months to two years previously. In addition to the overall score, the frequency of occurrence of these events was tallied, data that were unavailable from the Holmes' form. A frequency measure would provide an indication of the intensity of stress. For example, was the family subjected to one major event (e.g., personal injury, 53 pts.) over two years, or five smaller events within the past six months (with lower stress scores). The smaller stress events would have a lower Holmes score but may be even more traumatic on family members because they occurred within a shorter period of time.

An additional 16 events were added to the Holmes and Rahe Scale that were taken from Belle's (1980) study. These items deal with economic assistance, male-female relationships and female-related events. These additional events were not weighted, but the frequency of occurrence was tabulated.

(2) Frequencies, stress type. The 65 events used on the Significant Life Events Scale were put into nine categories of stress: Housing, Money, Health and Safety, Personal Habits, Work, Male-Female Relations, Personal Relations, Parenting, and Legal Areas. Each significant life event that the subject experienced was then put into one of these categories. This allowed us to ascertain which areas mothers had suffered the most stress.

(3) Perceived sources of stress. Mothers were given nine categories (Housing, Money, Health and Safety, Personal Habits, Work, Male-Female Relations, Personal Relations, Parenting and Legal Areas) and asked to rate how much stress she felt in each area on a scale of one to ten with one meaning low stress and 10 meaning high stress. This allowed us to see what the mother herself perceived to be her main sources of stress. A total stress rating was also obtained with 90 representing a high total level of stress.

Data Analysis

The planned data analysis involved the following steps:

(a) A preliminary analysis was made after the first 76 families' data were in. This was used to facilitate preparation for the final analysis to indicate any data problems and to allow for the formatting of charts and tables.

(b) On the final analysis, after all data were in, the descriptive central tendencies and cross tabulations on all variables were obtained. The first major objective was to determine the significant group differences (ANOVA) and associations (Chi square) based upon the independent variables of the design for all of the independent variables.

(c) The third objective was to test for interrelationships between the dependent quantitative variables. When appropriate, multiple regression was used to allow for a precise measurement of the amount of variance of the dependent variables that are accounted for by each independent variable.

(d) t-Tests and cross tabulations (Chi square) were computed to compare associations between perceptions of significant others' supportive roles and the independent variables.

Sample Selection and Interviewing

The sample consisted of single Black mothers over 20 years of age, employed outside of the home, with children under 18 living at home. The mothers were recruited from the Baltimore metropolitan area. This city was chosen because it is representative of Black populations in many large urban centers in the country. Based on census track information, we found that Black persons, especially single mothers, are not randomly distributed throughout the Baltimore area. Thus, we did not use a systematic sampling procedure.

Several techniques were employed in recruiting the mothers. Fliers were mailed to day care centers and Head Start programs (stratified by income), to Black churches, and to Black women's organizations throughout the Baltimore area. The mothers who participated in the project were asked to refer other mothers who were eligible candidates. An advertisement was placed in Baltimore's daily newspaper and in the major Black weekly newspaper. There was a high response rate to the newspaper advertisement, from day care centers, and from the mother referrals.

Upon locating possible candidates, research assistants explained the purpose of the project and asked a series of questions which established eligibility. If all answers met the criteria, a date and time was set for the interview. Before the interview took place, the interviewer asked the same series of questions again to ensure the mothers' eligibility. Three hundred and eighteen mothers were interviewed. A small gift of appreciation was given to all participants.

The interview lasted approximately two-and-a-half hours. Interviews were conducted by trained Black females in the mothers' homes. Half of the interviewers were themselves single Black mothers. In some instances, mothers wanted to be interviewed at our Baltimore office or at their jobs.

Training of interviewers. A corps of 10 interviewers were trained. Attempts were made to get women who were professionally trained, or who had experience on at least one previous research project. Several group sessions were held during which the following were included:

a. Purpose and value of the project
b. Research design and methodology
c. General interview technique
d. Specific approaches for the sample
e. Role-playing of interview
f. Individual and group critiques

Each interviewer was given one interview to do and then they were reviewed individually and their interview carefully edited. Each received appropriate instructions and/or additional training as needed.

Sample Description

The sample was composed of 318 single Black mothers who were raising their children alone and who were employed in the labor market in Baltimore, Maryland. All were now single, but some had been married at some point. They each had an average of 1.91 children (see Table 1).

Marital status

Fifty-six percent of the mothers were previously married, while 44 percent had never married. Of those who had been married, 29 percent were divorced, 26 percent were separated, and 2 percent were widowed. Over half of the never married mothers had been alone four years or more, and 45 percent had been alone three years or less. Only 5 percent had a live-in male partner.

Those who had never married had fewer children than the previously married ($X^2(1) = 68.27, p < .000$). More middle class mothers had been married before than the working-class mothers, half of whom had never married ($X^2(1) = 5.69, p < .02$).

Age

Their average age was 30.24 years, the youngest was 20 years old and the oldest was 50. The mothers over 30 were more likely to be married at some point ($X^2(1) = 75.57, p < .000$) and were more likely to have two or more children ($X^2(1) = 36.54, p < .000$). The older mothers also had higher educational and occupational ratings and more older ones lived alone with their children, rather than in extended or augmented family settings.

Family pregnancy; age and marital status

First pregnancy occurred on the average when our respondents were 19.75 years old, with a range from 14 to 36 years at first pregnancy. The never married mothers tended to be 19 years or older; the majority of those unmarried were under 18 years of age at that point. The younger the primipara mother, the more children she tended to bear ($X^2(1) = 19.96 p < .000$). There were no significant differences in their age at first pregnancy and their current marital status.

Seventy-three percent of the women were not married at their first pregnancy. Twenty-nine percent who were single at that time did marry later and eventually separated or divorced. More of the older mothers were married at the time of their first birth than the mothers under 30 years ($X^2(1) = 29.44, p < .000$). Those who were not married at first pregnancy had only high school educations. The highest educational levels were found among the women who were not teenage mothers and married at their first birth ($F(3, 312) = 6.22, p < .01$). Mothers who were in their teens

Table 1. Selected Background Characteristics of Single Mothers

Variable	Total %	Marital Status Ever %	Never %	Socioeconomic Status Middle %	Working %
Total	100	56	44	31	69
Marital Status:					
Separated	26	46		24	27
Divorced	29	51		40	24
Widowed	2	3		3	1
Never	44	–		34	48
Married, 1st pregnancy:					
Yes	27	46	–	41	20
No	73	55	100	59	80
Age, 1st pregnancy:					
18 and under	46	45	47	38	49
19 and over	54	55	53	62	51
Present Age:					
Under 30	54	32	82	62	39
Over 30	46	68	18	38	61
Income:					
Less than 3000	2	–	4	1	2
3,000-5,999	7	6	9	1	10
6,000-8,999	7	6	9	1	10
9,000-11,999	16	11	23	2	23
9,000-11,999	24	22	27	18	27
12,000-14,999	19	18	20	20	19
15,000-17,999	12	12	12	17	10
18,000-20,999	6	10	1	12	4
21,000-23,999	7	11	2	18	2
24,000-26,999	2	3	–	3	1
27,000-29,999	2	2	1	2	1
30,000-39,999	2	3	2	5	1
40,000+	1	2	–	2	1
Education:					
Grade School	–	–	1	1	–
Junior High School	3	4	1	2	3
High School/Trade School	37	31	44	–	53
1-2 yrs. college	20	26	32	5	39
3-4 yrs. college	19	21	17	53	4
Graduate/Professional	12	17	5	39	–

(table continues)

	Total	Marital Status		Socioeconomic Status	
		Ever	Never	Middle	Working
Variable	%	%	%	%	%
Total	100	56	44	31	69

Occupation:					
Executive/major, lesser professional	25	29	19	77	1
Administrative personnel	12	19	14	10	12
Owner of bus./clerical	47	47	48	13	63
Skilled/semi-skilled	14	12	16	–	20
Unskilled	3	2	4	–	4

Religion:					
Baptist	49	45	53	41	52
Methodist	18	20	15	20	13
Catholic	14	13	16	15	14
Other Protestants	11	13	9	4	14
Fundamentalists	4	6	2	8	2
No religion	4	3	5	2	5

Number of Children:					
One	48	27	74	54	45
Two or more	53	73	26	47	55

Note. Totals in all categories range between 99 and 101 (considering rounding errors)

and married at the first birth had more people living in the home between 3 to 5 years ($F(3, 308)$ = 3.94, $p < .05$).

Household composition

The majority of the mothers maintained households independent of their families. An average of 3.52 persons lived in the home, chiefly the mothers and their children. Eighty-three percent of the mothers indicated that they were the head of their households. The remaining 17 percent consisted of heads who were the respondents' mothers, fathers, grandparents, other relatives, and friends. The average number of adult females living in the house was 1.37 and the average number of adult males was 0.30. The mean number of people 18 years old and under was 1.85; 0.50 were preschool age, and 1.33 were school age children. The mean number of people

who were in the households between the age of: 19-25 ($M = 0.86$); 41-65 ($M = 0.31$); and over 65 years ($M = 0.04$). An average of 1.21 percent single mothers lived in the homes.

The largest number of persons ($M = 0.99$) had been living in the home between 3 to 5 years, while the next largest number ($M = 0.93$) had been at the same address for 2 years. The mean number of people living in the house more than 5 years was 0.88.

Marital status and SES were found to interact significantly on household composition for the total number of people in the house who were under 18 years and the number of school aged children. Working-class women who had been married before had more children under the age of 19 years ($F(3, 310) = 10.04$, $p < .002$) and they had more school aged children ($F(3, 310) = 4.89$, $p < .03$). However, the middle-class women who had never married had more people in the house

$(F(3, 314) = 4.58, p < .03)$. This larger household size was probably due to the fact that these middle-class women had taken in more elderly persons $(F(3, 310) = 7.15, p < .008)$, for they were probably in a better financial position to provide support to these older persons. These middle-class mothers were also significantly older than the working-class mothers. Those women who were middle-class and never married had remained in the present house significantly longer periods of time, thus allowing them to amass the resources that would enable them to be supportive to more relatives.

The household composition was viewed alone in terms of the marital status of the women. The never married women were found to be younger, and tended to have other single mothers and their children also in the home. They also had more adults in general, and they had more children of preschool ages. These residents could be interpreted as indications of those who were in greater need. These individuals would have greater supportive needs, but would be less likely in a position to provide help to the mothers in material ways.

Coping Strategies

The following are three models of coping strategies that are used by single working mothers when they are faced with conflicts between various roles (Hall, 1972).

Type 1. Structural role redefinitions. The mother can establish a new set of expectations for those sending messages about her role: her employer, her children. She can negotiate a different set of behavioral expectations. For example, she can let her employer, a role sender, know she is willing to work hard, but will be unable to work overtime because of the hours of her child's day care center. She must then negotiate with her boss on the schedule that would meet all their needs. Discussion with the child [e.g., We talked about it leading to an internal (e.g., role sender understood] or external change; redefining behavioral expectations; indication that the child does something.

Type II. Personal role redefinition. The mother can cope with conflict by redefining her own role, establishing priorities for roles or by eliminating certain tasks. As an illustration, the mother mentioned previously may decide to quit her job and take one with lower status in order to maintain family schedules. Or she may decide that she will have to temporarily remove the conflict of the mother role by sending her child to live with relatives if she is unable to negotiate with her boss or find another job. The mother removes the conflict. She will stay home with the child, or send the child away; she will separate from her husband or quit her job. She established a priority.

Type III. Reacting role behavior. The mother will continue to meet all of the conflicting demands being sent to her. She can plan ahead, organize the child's life moral center, or simply work frantically harder to get the assigned tasks completed by closing time. She simply "deals with it". She may talk to her child (e.g., I talked to her) but there is no indication of any change in the child's expectations or the employer's expectations of her. She does everything. One of these types of coping strategies is to be coded for each of the coping strategy questions.

Interjudge and intrajudge reliability are to be established. If there is disagreement between two coders, there will be consensual coding. Intercoder reliability, including non-agreements, will also be established.

Procedure for Coping Strategies' Summary

Type	Weight
I	5
II	3
III	1

Example: For four conflicts the mother used Types I, II, III and II,

Type	Weight x Frequency			
I	5	1	= 5	- fx/N
II	3	2	= 6	12/4 = 3
				(Summary Code)
III	1	1	= 1	
				12 - fx

The higher the score, the more positive the mother's coping strategies are. The lower the score, the more negative. The highest score possible is 5.

Protection of Subjects

The subjects in this study faced no detrimental effects. The design entailed having the interviewer ask the participants to share their opinions and experiences. Each participant was fully informed of the objectives and procedures that were to be used. They were told that they were free to withdraw at any point during the process.

Confidentiality was promised and the methods to do this were detailed. Each interviewer was given a list of ID numbers to use until ten interviews were completed. No names or identifying data were put on the protocol. The interviewers identified only the addresses with the ID numbers. This list was separated from the interviews and a different ID was assigned to each protocol. The list with the original numbers and addresses is kept by the principal investigator in a separate locked file. Interviewers are unable to identify specific families by this method.

References

McAdoo, H. (1988). The single mother. In B. Bryan (Ed.), *Introduction to social science*. Littleton, MA: Copley.

McAdoo, H. (1986). Strategies used by Black single mothers against stress. In M. Simms & J. Malveaux (Eds.), *Slipping through the cracks: The status of Black women* (pp. 153-166). New Brunswick, NJ: Transaction.

McAdoo, H. (1986). Societal Stress. In J. Cole (Ed.), *All American women: Line that divides, ties that bind* (pp. 187-197). New York: The Free Press.

McAdoo, H. (1984). Single Black mothers. In *Children having children: A resource notebook for Black leaders* (pp. 204-219). Washington, DC.: Children's Defense Fund.

McAdoo, H. (1983). Stress and support networks of working single Black mothers. In *Black women debunking the myths: A multidisciplinary approach*. Berkeley: University of California, Center for the Study, Education and Advancement of Women.

McAdoo, H. (1983). Societal stress: The Black family. In H. I. McCubbin & C. R. Figley (Eds.), *Stress and the family, coping with normative transitions*. Larchmont, NY: Brunner & Mazel.

McAdoo, H. (1982). Levels of stress and family support in Black families. In H. McCubbin, A. Cauble, & J. Patterson (Eds.), *Family stress, coping and social support*. Springfield, IL: C. Thomas.

McAdoo, H. (1982). Stress absorbing systems in Black families. *Family Relations, 31*(4), 479-488.

For additional information, contact:

Harriette Pipes McAdoo, Ph.D.
Department of Family and Child Ecology
Michigan State University
East Lansing, MI 48824-1030
Telephone: (517) 432-3321
Fax: (517) 432-2953

Name Index

Name Index

Subject Index

Subject Index